A COMMENTARY ON
THUCYDIDES

A COMMENTARY ON
THUCYDIDES

Simon Hornblower

Volume II
Books IV–V. 24

CLARENDON PRESS · OXFORD
1996

Oxford University Press, Walton Street, Oxford OX2 6DP

Oxford New York
Athens Auckland Bangkok Bogota Bombay
Buenos Aires Calcutta Cape Town Dar es Salaam
Delhi Florence Hong Kong Istanbul Karachi
Kuala Lumpur Madras Madrid Melbourne
Mexico City Nairobi Paris Singapore
Taipei Tokyo Toronto
and associated companies in
Berlin Ibadan

Oxford is a trade mark of Oxford University Press

Published in the United States
by Oxford University Press Inc., New York

British Library Cataloguing in Publication Data
Data available

Library of Congress Cataloging in Publication Data
A commentary on Thucydides
Simon Hornblower.
Includes bibliographical references.
1. Thucydides. History of the Peloponnesian War. 2. Greece—
History—Peloponnesian War, 431-404 B.C.—Historiography.
I. Title.
DF229, T6H65 1991 938'.007202—dc20 91-3432
ISBN 0-19-814881-X

1 3 5 7 9 10 8 6 4 2

Typeset by Joshua Associates Ltd., Oxford
Printed in Great Britain on acid-free paper by
Bookcraft (Bath) Ltd., Midsomer Norton

PREFACE AND ACKNOWLEDGEMENTS

THIS is the second volume of what will be a three-volume commentary on Thucydides. I shall produce (in the *World's Classics* series) the complete revision of Jowett's translation of Thucydides, with Introduction and notes, before moving on, probably after a gap of some years, to the third and final volume of this commentary. I repeat here the acknowledgement to the Jowett Copyright Trustees which I made in the Preface to vol. i. The chronological, textual, and other Appendices promised in the Preface to vol. i will now appear at the end of vol. iii.

The first volume contained no general Introduction; this (see further below, p. 1) was a defect, and I have tried to put it right by providing a long thematic Introduction to the present volume. This is angled throughout towards iv–v. 24, the section of Thucydides covered by the present volume, but some sections, for instance the discussion of Thucydides and Herodotus in section 2 and the accompanying Annex B, are relevant to the whole of Thucydides' work. Sometimes (though no more often than I felt to be absolutely necessary) the Introduction summarizes or actually repeats things said in the commentary itself. When considering a theme like Thucydides' presentation of Brasidas (Introduction, section 3), it was necessary to bring together items scattered over a wide area of commentary. On the other hand the reader looking for help on a particular passage has the right to find full discussion there rather than being sent back to the Introduction.

The final two-thirds of this volume of the commentary were written during the academic year 1994–5 when I was a Member of the Institute for Advanced Study, Princeton. I am grateful to the Institute for giving me this opportunity to study in a concentrated way, and for the use of its library and its computerized resources such as Thesaurus Linguae Graecae and the Pandora epigraphic data-base; I am also grateful to Glen Bowersock for his sponsorship. But I must also thank Oriel College and the University of Oxford for the sabbatical leave which allowed me to go to Princeton.

At Princeton I was greatly helped by conversation with Christian Habicht, Christopher Jones, Marcel Piérart, and especially Lisa Kallet-Marx (whose *Money, Expense and Naval Power in Thucydides' History* 1–5. 24 is the most important event in Thucydidean scholarship for many years);

v

I was also helped by correspondence with Mogens Hansen, Christopher Jones (again), Mark Munn, Philip Stadter, and Stephen Tracy. At a later stage Christopher Jones generously read and, by his acute comments, improved a version of section 4 of the Introduction, on 'Thucydides and Kinship'; but its shortcomings are mine alone. At Oxford, Robert Parker was as always a constant source of stimulus and enlightenment, and when I was at Princeton he also helped me by correspondence, particularly with the problems of iv. 121. 1 (Brasidas' reception at Skione).

In summer term 1995, immediately after my return from Princeton, I gave a course of eight graduate classes in Oxford on 'Thucydides iv–v. 24'. I express warm thanks to those who participated in this seminar and thus helped to improve the eventual book, notably Franco Basso, George Cawkwell, Katherine Clarke, Richard Fowler, David Gribble, Barbara Kowalzig, Peter O'Neill, Robin Osborne, Christopher Pelling, Philip Stadter, Tim Rood, Richard Rutherford, and Simon Swain.

I made a number of visits to Greece and Italy in connection with the present volume and I thank those institutions whose financial help made this possible, and also those individuals who accompanied me on my travels. I visited Amphipolis and other northern Greek sites in spring 1984 in the company of Hector and Elizabeth Catling and Jane Hornblower. In spring 1989 I visited Pylos, Sphakteria, Tegea, and Mantinea in the company of Victoria Harris. I enjoyed the hospitality of the British School at Rome in autumn 1990 as the base for a visit to southern Italy. In September 1992 I visited Delion and other Boiotian sites in the company of Antony Spawforth and Rosalind Thomas; I have to thank the Craven Committee of Oxford University for financial help towards this, and both it and the Faculty Board of Literae Humaniores at Oxford University for meeting the cost of a second visit to north Greece (mainly Amphipolis and Torone) in September 1995. On this occasion Professor Alexander Cambitoglou and Dr John Papadopoulos received me very hospitably and generously at Torone, and I am specially indebted to Dr Papadopoulos for kindly showing me round the site and the excavations, and for discussing the Thucydidean problems with me. I acknowledge equally warmly the hospitality and help I received at Amphipolis from Mrs Haido Koukouli-Chrysanthaki, ephor of antiquities at Kavalla, who facilitated my visit to the site and its fortifications at a very busy time for her and her team, and who discussed the fortifications and topography with me both at Kavalla and at Amphipolis. I must also thank Helen Clark, the secretary of the British School at Athens, for help with the organization of this visit.

Elaine Matthews searched unpublished files of the *Lexicon of Greek Personal Names* for me, and I thank her and Peter Fraser warmly for help in this area.

I am no palaeographer and for the most part have not studied the manuscripts of Thucydides while writing this commentary, except that in summer 1995 I examined the text of an eleventh-century manuscript in the British Library in order to settle (as I hope I have done) a curiously disputed, and purely factual, point arising at iv. 40. 2.

Annex A to the Introduction, a reprint (with typographical corrections) of my article on 'Thucydides' Use of Herodotus' in J. M. Sanders (ed.), *ΦΙΛΟΛΑΚΩΝ: Lakonian Studies in Honor of Hector Catling* (Athens, 1992), 141–54, is included by permission of the Managing Committee of the British School of Athens.

For permission to reproduce Fig. 2, the plan of Amphipolis, from D. Lazaridis' excellent posthumous book *Amphipolis* (Athens, 1994), I am grateful to Thalia and Kalliope Lazaridis; also to the Greek Archaeological Society and to the T. A. P. (Publications Office of the Greek Ministry of Culture).

This volume, like its predecessor of 1991, was expertly copy-edited by John Cordy, whose contributions have put readers and users, as well as myself, heavily in his debt. I take this opportunity of thanking him warmly for his careful and sensitive work.

Finally, my former pupil Dr. Timothy Rood read a set of proofs; his corrections and suggestions for improvement went beyond the purely typographical, and I gratefully acknowledge his help and contribution.

S.H.

Oxford
20 September 1995

CONTENTS

FIGURES

ABBREVIATIONS

Aesch.	Aeschylus	Eur.	Euripides
Ar.	Aristophanes	Hdt.	Herodotus
Arist.	Aristotle	Plut.	Plutarch
Dem.	Demosthenes	Pol.	Polybius
Diod.	Diodorus	Th.	Thucydides

AJAH	*American Journal of Ancient History*
Andrewes and Lewis, *JHS* 1957	A. Andrewes and D. M. Lewis, 'A Note on the Peace of Nikias', *JHS* 77 (1957), 177–80
APF	see Davies, *APF*
Arch. Reps.	*Archaeological Reports*
Ath. Pol.	*Athenaion Politeia* (Athenian Constitution), attributed to Aristotle
ATL	B. D. Meritt, H. T. Wade-Gery, and M. F. McGregor, *The Athenian Tribute Lists*, 4 vols. (Cambridge, Mass., 1939–53)
Babut	D. Babut, 'Interprétation historique et structure littéraire chez Thucydide: remarques sur la composition du livre iv', *Bulletin de l'association Guillaume Budé*, 40 (1981), 417–39
Badian, *From Plataea to Potidaea*	E. Badian, *From Plataea to Potidaea: Studies in the History and Historiography of the Pentecontaetia* (Baltimore, 1993)
Beloch, *Gr. Gesch.*²	K. J. Beloch, *Griechische Geschichte*, 2nd edn., 4 vols. in 8 (Strasbourg, Leipzig, Berlin, 1912–27)
Bender	G. F. Bender, *Der Begriff des Staatsmannes bei Thukydides* (Würzburg, 1934)
Bétant	E.-A. Bétant, *Lexicon Thucydideum*, 2 vols. (Geneva, 1843, repr. Hildesheim, 1969)
Bruce	I. A. F. Bruce, *An Historical Commentary on the 'Hellenica Oxyrhynchia'* (Cambridge, 1967)
CAH	*Cambridge Ancient History*
Cartledge, *Sparta and Lakonia*	P. Cartledge, *Sparta and Lakonia* (London, 1979)
CID	G. Rougemont (ed.), *Corpus des inscriptions delphiques* (Paris, 1977–)
Classen/Steup	*Thukydides*, erklärt von. J. Classen, bearbeitet von J. Steup, 3rd to 5th edns. (Berlin, 1900–22)

Connor	W. R. Connor, *Thucydides* (Princeton, 1984)
CRUX	P. Cartledge and D. Harvey (eds.), *CRUX: Essays Presented to G. E. M. de Ste. Croix on his 75th Birthday* (London, 1985)
Curty 1994	O. Curty, 'La notion de la parenté entre cités chez Thucydide', *Mus. Helv.* 51 (1994), 193–7
Curty 1995	— *Les Parentés légendaires entre cités grecques: catalogue raisonné des inscriptions contenant le terme ΣΥΓΓΕΝΕΙΑ et analyse critique* (Geneva, 1995)
Davies, *APF*	J. K. Davies, *Athenian Propertied Families 600–300 BC* (Oxford, 1971)
de Ste. Croix, *OPW*	G. E. M. de Ste. Croix, *The Origins of the Peloponnesian War* (London, 1972)
Develin, *AO*	R. Develin, *Athenian Officials 684–322 BC* (Cambridge, 1989)
*DFA*³	A. W. Pickard-Cambridge, rev. J. Gould and D. M. Lewis, *The Dramatic Festivals of Athens*³ (Oxford, 1988)
DK	H. Diels and W. Kranz (eds.), *Die Fragmente der Vorsokratiker*⁶, 3 vols. (Berlin, 1952)
Dover, *CQ* 1954	K. J. Dover, 'The Palatine Manuscript of Thucydides', *CQ* 4 (1954), 76–83
FD	*Fouilles de Delphes*
FGrHist	F. Jacoby, *Die Fragmente der griechischen Historiker*, 15 vols. (Berlin, 1923–30; Leipzig, 1940–58)
Fornara, *Generals*	C. W. Fornara, *The Athenian Board of Generals from 501 to 404* (*Historia Einzelschrift 16*: Wiesbaden, 1971)
Fornara	C. W. Fornara, *Translated Documents of Greece and Rome*, i. *Archaic Times to the End of the Peloponnesian War*² (Cambridge, 1983)
Gomme	unless qualified, refers to *HCT* iii, on books iv–v. 24
— *Greek Attitude*	A. W. Gomme, *The Greek Attitude to Poetry and History* (Berkeley, 1954)
— *More Essays*	— *More Essays in Greek History and Literature* (Oxford, 1962)
Greek Historiography	S. Hornblower (ed.), *Greek Historiography* (Oxford, 1994)
Greek World	S. Hornblower, *The Greek World 479–323 BC*² (London, 1991)
Habicht, *Gottmenschentum*²	C. Habicht, *Gottmenschentum und griechische Städte*² (Munich, 1970)
Hammond, *HM*	N. G. L. Hammond, *History of Macedonia*

	(Oxford): i (1972); ii (with G. T. Griffith, 1979); iii (with F. W. Walbank, 1988)
Hansen, *Historia* 1993	M. H. Hansen, 'The Battle Exhortation in Ancient Historiography: Fact or Fiction?', *Historia*, 42 (1993), 161–80
Hanson (ed.), *Hoplites*	V. D. Hanson (ed.), *Hoplites: The Classical Greek Battle Experience* (London, 1991)
—— *Western Way*	—— *The Western Way of War: Infantry Battle in Classical Greece* (Oxford, 1989)
Harding	P. Harding, *Translated Documents of Greece and Rome*, ii. *From the End of the Peloponnesian War to the Battle of Ipsus* (Cambridge, 1985)
HCP	F. W. Walbank, *Historical Commentary on Polybius*, 3 vols. (Oxford, 1957–79)
HCT	A. W. Gomme, A. Andrewes, and K. J. Dover, *Historical Commentary on Thucydides*, 5 vols. (Oxford, 1945–81)
Hell. Oxy.	*Hellenica Oxyrhynchia* or Oxyrhynchus Historian, ed. M. Chambers after V. Bartoletti (Stuttgart and Leipzig, 1993)
Hill²	G. F. Hill, rev. R. Meiggs and A. Andrewes, *Sources for Greek History 476–431 BC* (Oxford, 1951)
HN²	B. V. Head, *Historia Numorum²* (Oxford, 1911); a third edn. is in preparation
Hunter	V. Hunter, *Thucydides the Artful Reporter* (Toronto, 1973)
IC	M. Guarducci, *Inscriptiones Creticae*, 4 vols. (Rome, 1935–50)
IG	*Inscriptiones Graecae*
Kallet-Marx	L. Kallet-Marx, *Money, Expense and Naval Power in Thucydides' History 1–5. 24* (Berkeley, 1993)
Kirchhoff	A. Kirchhoff, *Thukydides und sein Urkundenmaterial* (Berlin, 1895)
Kl. Schr.	*Kleine Schriften*
Kraay, *ACGC*	C. M. Kraay, *Archaic and Classical Greek Coins* (London, 1976)
K/A	R. Kassel and C. F. L. Austin, *Poetae Comici Graeci* (Berlin, 1983–)
LACTOR	London Association of Classical Teachers, Original Records: a series of translations of sources for Ancient History
Lang, *Mnemosyne* 1995	M. Lang, 'Participial Motivation in Thucydides', *Mnemosyne*, 48 (1995), 48–65
Larsen, *GFS*	J. A. O. Larsen, *Greek Federal States* (Oxford, 1968)

Lauffer (ed.), *Griechenland*   S. Lauffer (ed.), *Griechenland: Lexicon der histor-ischen Stätten von den Anfängen bis zur Gegenwart* (Munich, 1989)

Lazaridis 1986   D. Lazaridis, 'Les Fortifications d'Amphipolis' in P. Lériche and H. Tréziny (eds.), *Les Forti-fications dans le monde grec* (*CNRS Colloque Inter-national 614, December 1982*: Paris, 1986), 31–8

Lazaridis 1994, or Lazaridis, *Amphipolis*   D. Lazaridis (ed. K. and T. Lazaridis) *Amphi-polis* (Athens, 1994)

Leimbach   R. Leimbach, *Militärische Musterrhetorik: Eine Untersuchung zu den Feldherrnreden des Thukyd-ides* (Stuttgart, 1985)

Lewis, *Towards a Historian's Text*   D. M. Lewis, *Towards a Historian's Text of Thu-cydides* (Princeton dissertation, 1952)

— *Sparta and Persia*   — *Sparta and Persia* (Leiden, 1977)

LGPN i   P. M. Fraser and E. Matthews (eds.), *Lexicon of Greek Personal Names,* i. *The Aegean Islands, Cyprus, Cyrenaica* (Oxford, 1987)

LGPN ii   M. Osborne and S. Byrne (eds.), *Lexicon of Greek Personal Names,* ii. *Attica* (Oxford, 1994)

LIMC   *Lexicon Iconographicum Mythologiae Classicae* (Zurich and Munich, 1981–)

LSAG[2]   L. H. Jeffery, rev. A. W. Johnston, *The Local Scripts of Archaic Greece* (Oxford, 1990)

LSJ[9]   H. G. Liddell and R. Scott, *Greek–English Lexicon,* 9th edn., rev. H. Stuart Jones (Oxford, 1940)

Luschnat, *Feldherrnreden*   O. Luschnat, *Die Feldherrnreden im Geschichts-werk des Thukydides* (*Philologus Suppl.* 34. 2: Leipzig, 1942)

Macleod   C. Macleod, *Collected Essays* (Oxford, 1983)

Malkin, *Myth and Territory*   I. Malkin, *Myth and Territory in the Spartan Mediterranean* (Cambridge, 1994)

Masson   O. Masson, 'Quelques anthroponymes rares chez Thucydide', *Miscellanea Manni,* 4 (1980), 1479–88 [= *Onomastica Graeca Selecta* (Paris, 1990), 321–30]

Maurer, *Interpolation*   K. Maurer, *Interpolation in Thucydides* (*Mnemo-syne* suppl. 150: Leiden, 1995)

Meiggs, *AE*   R. Meiggs, *The Athenian Empire* (Oxford, 1972)

Meritt, *AFD*   B. D. Meritt, *Athenian Financial Documents of the Fifth Century* (Ann Arbor, 1932)

C. Meyer, *Urkunden*   C. Meyer, *Die Urkunden im Geschichtswerk des Thukydides*[2] (Munich, 1970)

Michel   C. Michel, *Recueil d'inscriptions grecques* (Brus-sels, 1891–1927)

ML	R. Meiggs and D. Lewis, *A Selection of Greek Historical Inscriptions to the End of the Fifth Century BC*, rev. edn. (Oxford, 1988, paperback 1989)
OCD², OCD³	N. G. L. Hammond and H. H. Scullard (eds.), *The Oxford Classical Dictionary*, 2nd edn. (Oxford, 1970); S. Hornblower and A. J. S. Spawforth (eds.), 3rd edn. (Oxford, 1996)
OCT	Oxford Classical Text
OGIS	W. Dittenberger, *Orientis Graecae Inscriptiones Selectae* (Leipzig, 1903-5)
Ostwald, *Autonomia*	M. Ostwald, *Autonomia: Its Genesis and Early History* (Chico, Calif., 1982)
— *ANAΓKH*	— *ANAΓKH in Thucydides* (Atlanta, 1987)
Parker, *Miasma*	R. Parker, *Miasma: Pollution and Purification in Greek Religion* (Oxford, 1983)
— *ARH*	— *Athenian Religion: A History* (Oxford, 1996)
Poralla, *Prosopographie der Lakedaimonier*	P. Poralla, *Prosopographie der Lakedaimonier bis auf die Zeit Alexanders des Gr.* (Breslau, 1913)
Princeton Encyclopaedia	R. Stillwell, W. L. MacDonald, M. H. McAllister (eds.), *The Princeton Encyclopaedia of Classical Sites* (Princeton, 1976)
Pritchett, *EGH*	W. K. Pritchett, *Essays in Greek History* (Amsterdam, 1994)
— *GSW*	— *The Greek State at War*, 5 vols. (Berkeley, 1971-91)
— *SAGT*	— *Studies in Ancient Greek Topography*, 7 vols. (Berkeley and Amsterdam, 1965-91)
— *TPOE*	— *Thucydides' Pentekontaetia and Other Essays* (Amsterdam, 1995)
Raaflaub, *Freiheit*	K. Raaflaub, *Die Entdeckung der Freiheit* (Munich, 1985)
Rhodes, *CAAP*	P. J. Rhodes, *Commentary on the Aristotelian Athenaion Politeia* (Oxford, 1981)
RE	A. Pauly and G. Wissowa, *Real-Encyclopädie der classischen Altertumswissenschaft*, 83 vols. (Stuttgart, 1894-1980)
RFP	R. Osborne and S. Hornblower (eds.), *Ritual, Finance, Politics: Athenian Democratic Accounts Presented to David Lewis* (Oxford, 1994)
Ridley, *Hermes* 1981	R. T. Ridley, 'Exegesis and Audience in Thucydides', *Hermes*, 109 (1981), 25-46
Robert, *Études épig.*	L. Robert, *Études épigraphiques et philologiques* (Paris, 1938)
— *OMS*	— *Opera Minora Selecta* (Amsterdam, 1969-90)
Salmon, *Étude*	P. Salmon, *Étude sur la confédération béotienne* (Brussels, 1978 = *Mém. de la classe des lettres, Acad. Royale de Belgique*, vol. 63, fasc. 3

Salmon, *Wealthy Corinth* J. B. Salmon, *Wealthy Corinth* (Oxford, 1984)

Schneege G. Schneege, *De relatione historica, quae intercedat inter Thucydidem et Herodotum* (diss. Breslau, 1884)

Schneider, *Information und Absicht* C. Schneider, *Information und Absicht bei Thukydides* (Göttingen, 1974)

SEG *Supplementum Epigraphicum Graecum*

SGDI H. Collitz, F. Bechtel, and D. Hoffmann (eds.), *Sammlung der griechischen Dialekt-Inschriften* (Göttingen, 1884–1915)

Smith, *TAPA* 1900 C. F. Smith, 'Traces of Epic Usage in Thucydides', *TAPA* 31 (1900), 69–81

H.-P. Stahl, *Thukydides* H.-P. Stahl, *Thukydides: Die Stellung des Menschen im geschichtlichen Prozess* (Munich, 1966)

Stroud 1971 R. Stroud, 'Thucydides and The Battle of Solygeia', *California Studies in Classical Antiquity*, 4 (1971), 227–47

Stroud 1994 —— 'Thucydides and Corinth', *Chiron*, 44 (1994), 267–302

*Syll*³ W. Dittenberger, *Sylloge Inscriptionum Graecarum*³ 4 vols. (Leipzig, 1915–24)

Thucydides S. Hornblower, *Thucydides*² (London, 1994)

Tod M. N. Tod, *Greek Historical Inscriptions*, 2 vols. (Oxford, 1946, 1948)

TrGF *Tragicorum Graecorum Fragmenta* (Göttingen, 1971–)

Wade-Gery, *EGH* H. T. Wade-Gery, *Essays in Greek History* (Oxford, 1958)

Walbank, *HCP* see *HCP*

M. Walbank, *Proxenies* M. Walbank, *Athenian Proxenies of the Fifth Century* BC (Toronto, 1978)

Westlake, *Essays* H. D. Westlake, *Essays on the Greek Historians and Greek History* (Manchester, 1969)

—— *Studies* —— *Studies in Thucydides and Greek History* (Bristol, 1989)

Wilson J. B. Wilson, *Pylos 425 BC: A Historical and Topographical Study of Thucydides' Account of the Campaign* (Warminster, 1979)

Xen. *Hell.* Xenophon, *Hellenica*

Zahrnt M. Zahrnt, *Olynth und die Chalkidier* (Munich, 1971)

Note: Except where stated, the text of Thucydides used in this commentary is the OCT, edited by H. Stuart Jones and J. E. Powell.

In the dates given on the shoulder heads, s. refers to summer and w. to winter.

INTRODUCTION

1. *General remarks; the relation of this commentary to* HCT

THE first volume of this commentary (1991) contained no Introduction, only a brief Preface and Acknowledgements. In that Preface I expressed the hope that the commentary would be 'helpful to those students who are interested in the detail of Thucydides' thought and subject-matter but have little or no Greek'. I repeat that expression of hope here, and I return below (p. 8) to the question of accessibility. But as I have already indicated in the Preface, I must here correct my 1991 statement that the commentary would be in two volumes. I now aim to finish it in a third, which will contain the appendices promised in 1991, and some others as well. I have chosen to break the present volume at v. 24, partly because of the amount of material I have prepared; partly because v. 24 is an obvious Thucydidean break; but above all because v. 24 is the end of the section of Thucydides commented on by Gomme alone (*Historical Commentary on Thucydides*), that is, without any addition by Andrewes or Dover. *HCT* iii (which, like the present volume, covered iv–v. 24) is therefore noticeably more antiquated than the last two volumes of *HCT* (1970 and 1981).

The absence of a full-length Introduction to my vol. i was commented on by some reviewers and has given rise to misunderstanding, in particular about the relation of the present project to that of Gomme. One aim of this Introduction is to clarify that relation. Some of this Introduction, in particular this general section 1, should be taken to apply to vol. i, and indeed to my forthcoming vol. iii, as well as to the present vol. ii. But sections 2–7 are more specifically angled towards iv–v. 24, though for instance section 2 on 'Thucydides and Herodotus' (and the accompanying annexes), and section 4 on kinship (ξυγγένεια) in Thucydides, naturally have a relevance beyond iv–v. 24.

The first question must be: why write a commentary on an ancient author like Th. at all? Why write one in the 1990s on an author on whom an excellent commentary already exists, namely, Gomme, Andrewes, and Dover, *HCT*?[1] I add Andrewes and Dover, although their direct

---

[1] A. W. Gomme, A. Andrewes, K. J. Dover, *Historical Commentary on Thucydides*, 5 vols. (Oxford, 1945–1981); Gomme's vol.iii (1956) covers iv–v. 24, the subject-matter of the present volume.

contribution does not begin until v. 25, because they have much that is relevant to iv-v. 24 particularly in the long 1981 appendices to the whole work. But first the broader question, why a commentary at all? John Ma[2] has said hard things about the commentary style, which 'just plows through the text and tackles problems in an inert atomistic fashion ... the commentary [i.e. the commentary as a general phenomenon] abounds in expressions such as 'cf.', 'see', 'compare', which do not make the effort of linking gobbets of information or background into a coherent picture, but leave the responsibility of conceptualization to the reader. Under a pretence of innocent empiricism ...', and so on. Jasper Griffin in an article on commentaries in the *Times Literary Supplement* speaks similarly of 'cf.' as 'a dreaded word, so seductive in its unexamined slipperiness'; he suggests that commentaries are specially suited to the British mind, providing as they do an opportunity to 'amass illustrative material in a rather empirical way, without much theoretical comment'.[3] Again, F. W. Walbank remarked in the Preface to his Sather lectures on Polybius that 'writing a commentary is a discipline which occasionally begins to feel like a strait-jacket; and every commentator, I suspect, sooner or later feels the urge to break out and write [a more general book on his author, i.e.] something, as Polybius would say, more σωμα-τοειδής'.[4] And there we have one answer to Ma: the commentary is a useful if sometimes inevitably pedestrian exercise; but we can readily agree that the commentator owes it to readers to come clean about what he or she proposes to *do* with all those atomistic results. Walbank waited till his Sather lectures before trying to draw the 'big picture': his Introductions, even that to vol. i, do not really serve that function. Gomme, to come to him at last, wrote an introduction to vol. i of *HCT* about 'What Thucydides Takes for Granted'; this is widely and rightly well-regarded, but it was not until his Sather lectures, *The Greek Attitude to Poetry and History*,[5] that he ventured to talk about Thucydidean narrative structure at all. I return to that book in the present section. As for my own current attempt at the big picture, the object of this Introduction is precisely to try to pull together ideas scattered through my commentary on these 160 chapters.

But this has all been defensive—a way of agreeing that for a commentator as well as for the commentary's readers, a commentary is something on which to construct general propositions. What of the commentary as an end in itself? I can only reply with this possibly

[2] J. Ma, 'Black Hunter Variations', *PCPhS* 40 (1994), 49-80, at 75-6.

[3] J. Griffin, 'The Guidance We Need: Classical Commentaries', *TLS*, April 14, 1995, 13-14; for Griffin himself as commentator see his *Homer: Iliad IX* (Oxford, 1995).

[4] F. W. Walbank, *Polybius* (Berkeley, 1972), p. ix.

[5] A. W. Gomme, *The Greek Attitude to Poetry and History* (Berkeley, 1954).

reactionary view: the only way to make fully legitimate use of a particular passage of Thucydides is by means of detailed, if you like atomistic, treatment of the text, looked at (i) from as many points of view as possible (that is to say literary and religious as well as historical), (ii) with full attention to meaning and translation, and above all (iii) with an adequate comparative awareness of all the parts of Thucydides you are *not* concerned with at that moment. That is a tall order for a historian or literary scholar who merely wants to make casual use of just one passage, and that is where the commentator comes in: the student and the scholar can reasonably turn to a commentary hoping that the necessary work has been done for them. Hence another reply to the sceptic: a *genuinely* atomistic commentary on a sentence of Thucydides, i.e. a commentary not made with the thorough overall knowledge of Thucydides, and I would add of Herodotus, which would entitle the commentator to say if this or that passage is characteristic or uncharacteristic of Thucydides, would indeed be worth little. In the same way decent epigraphists, as Louis Robert always insisted, ground their interpretations on comparable texts, not just on interpretation, however clever, of the particular text in front of them, or on dissimilar texts.[6] In his 1959 British Academy memoir of Gomme, H. Kitto wrote 'his great strength as an interpreter [of Thucydides] was that any single passage was seen by him in the complete context of the whole work'.[7]

I begin with some remarks about Gomme's commentary, its strengths and weaknesses in 1995; and then I suggest how it can be improved on.

Since I shall in this Introduction and in the commentary give the appearance of being critical of Gomme, I shall start with his strengths, singling out three (each of which has, however, its less important negative aspect): first his excellent judgement of textual points, second his topographical coverage, and third his financial and other technical coverage. Then I shall discuss four weaknesses and ways in which I think he can be improved on (not the same thing: some of the scope for improvement is due not to weakness in any evaluative sense but merely to the passage of forty years since HCT iii). The four areas I shall single out in this 'drawback' section are first the lack of translation of lemmata, by which I mean the passages of Greek being commented on. Second the sheer out-of-dateness of Gomme's material; forty years is a long time, and in those years not only have archaeological and epigraphical discoveries solved some problems, but new technologies have been devised and I shall concentrate on one of those. Then I get on to two more interesting areas. The third is one on which much more should

[6] L. Robert, *Die Epigraphik der klassischen Welt* (Bonn, 1970), 47.
[7] H. Kitto, 'Arnold Wycombe Gomme', *PBA* 45 (1959), 335–44, at 340.

have been said even in Gomme's time, on any decent definition of the word 'historical' in 'historical commentary', namely religion. The fourth, literary and narratological topics, was on the face of it explicitly excluded by Gomme's title, with its restriction to historical matters. In fact, Gomme does discuss many literary points; after all, alongside Gomme, the authority on Athenian population,[8] there was Gomme, the commentator on the fourth-century Athenian comic poet Menander;[9] and I suspect his choice of the word 'historical' for the Thucydides commentary was intended to distance himself from the *linguistic* commentaries of the nineteenth century, culminating in the great but limited Classen/ Steup. For an explicit rejection of the Classen/Steup approach see now Dover's autobiography, explaining how in the 1950s he came to feel a new commentary on vi–vii was needed.[10] But at that time he could not have known that he, not Gomme, would end up writing it.

I begin with Gomme's strengths, and I start with his good textual judgement. One must remember what was available before Gomme: Classen/Steup was the most up-to-date complete commentary, and Steup was a great deleter; for instance he wildly threw out much of v. 13– 19 as interpolation (the Peace of Nikias and surrounding narrative): see below, introductory n. to v. 14–17. Gomme reacted against this tendency to delete merely difficult passages as interpolation, and usually his reasons were excellent (see e.g. v. 13. 1 n. on κωλυόντων). He was after all a professor of Greek not of history. But (and here is the negative aspect) Gomme's faultless knowledge of Greek meant that his discussions can often seem highly elliptical, because he saw no need to translate and little need to explain at any length his interpretation of the Greek. Kitto also politely criticized the way Gomme was 'sometimes influenced by literary preference rather than by palaeographic probabilities'. Examples might be iv. 117 and v. 22, where Gomme considers and approves a number of improbably drastic emendations. Gomme did not actually inspect manuscripts. An instance of this is the omission of τε at iv. 40. 2; Gomme reports a factual discrepancy between OCT (Stuart Jones–Powell) and Hude about whether ms 'M' read the word or not; but M is in the British Library! The answer (see my n. on the passage) is that Hude was right: the word is not there. I shall return to this in a moment when I talk about Gomme's untranslated lemmata.

Second, topography. Kitto's memoir speaks rightly of Gomme's 'keen eye in topography'; a section near the beginning of the *PBA* memoir explains how that eye was trained—by many visits to Greece; Gomme

---

[8] *The Population of Athens in the Fifth and Fourth Centuries* BC (Oxford, 1933).
[9] A. W. Gomme and F. H. Sandbach, *Menander: A Commentary* (Oxford, 1973).
[10] K. J. Dover, *Marginal Comment* (London, 1994), 72.

knew Greece well, spoke modern Greek fluently, and took a lively interest in Greek politics.[11] He was, in fact, a British philhellene of a familiar type for his time (he lived 1886–1959). His first work was on the topography of Boiotia and based on time spent at the BSA before the First World War;[12] he was then stationed in the Salonika theatre in the First World War where his knowledge was exploited by British military intelligence. One might note here the slightly unexpected fact that Gomme read *archaeology* in Part Two of the Cambridge classical tripos (and of course got a first). This topographical interest comes out in, for instance, his superbly detailed and strategically shrewd notes on iv. 78 (Thessalian topography). The down-side of this was the limitation to the area roughly covered by modern Greece. Again and again, the parts of the Greek world now and in Gomme's time included in modern Turkey are passed over very inadequately. I mentioned iv. 78 a few lines above. If we move back three chapters to the intriguing chapter iv. 75, we find a mention of Lamachos' visit to Herakleia Pontike on the north coast of Turkey; Gomme merely sends us to Xenophon's *Anabasis*. The lack of topographical and archaeological interest in Herakleia may help to explain why Gomme ignores the remarkable story in Justin, which Jacoby thought came from Nymphis of Herakleia, according to which Lamachos was escorted to Chalkedon in a friendly way by the people of Herakleia, dead contrary to the picture of outright failure with which Thucydides leaves us: see the commentary below. Gomme's lack of interest in Asia Minor was incidentally commented on by Louis Robert in connection with the Sandian hill near modern Söke; I discussed this in 1991 in my n. on iii. 19. 2. Gomme was also a little half-hearted in his discussions of Sicilian and S. Italian history, topography, and archaeology, e.g. he is less than adequate on the curious little war between the Epizephyrian Lokrians and their colonists from Hipponion and Medma, reported by Thucydides (our only source) at v. 5, see my n. there. But I stress that on any point of Greek mainland or island topography Gomme is excellent.

Third, finance and other technical, e.g. calendrical, problems. If the First World War is relevant to Gomme's handling of topography, the Second World War may be relevant to his interest in and handling of finance, because at that period Gomme spent four years in the Treasury in London. On Gomme and finance I part company with Kitto. For Kitto, Gomme was 'not at his best in the handling of the tribute lists. His sceptical mind instinctively suspected wide constructions but his own

[11] Kitto (above, n. 7), 341; 336.
[12] 'The Topography of Boeotia and the Theories of M. Bérard', *Essays in Greek History and Literature* (Oxford, 1937), 17–41, reprinted from *BSA* 18 (1911–1912), 159–62.

resolutions tended to be too particular and not susceptible of a wide enough extension'.[13] A brutal paraphrase of this might be that Gomme was quite rightly not taken in by the more imaginative flights of the authors of the *Athenian Tribute Lists*, and *my* criticism of Gomme in this area would be that he was not sufficiently confident of his own judgement when disagreeing with the authors of *ATL*.[14] For instance he did not go and inspect the stones but accepted the *ATL* reports, just as we saw a moment ago that it does not seem to have occurred to him to check a manuscript which was actually in the British Museum. That is, he had an exaggerated respect for supposed experts on matters surely within his own or any commentator's competence. Gomme's best methodological statement in the financial area is not found in the commentary at all but at the very end of his admirable 1953 article on Athenian resources as set out by the Thucydidean Pericles at ii. 13. He wrote: 'one may make use of a simile, of a gigantic jig-saw puzzle, or more than one puzzle, to illustrate what I think is the chief difference between us. Meritt, McGregor, and Wade Gery seem to me to be too sure of the position of the exact pieces ... whereas I think that we have far too few pieces, whether whole or broken, to be sure that many fit exactly. The most we can say is "this looks like part of a temple, but may be something else ... or may be from another picture altogether" ...'.[15] I can only applaud this. Two small examples: in Gomme's n. on iv. 120, *ATL*'s theory that the tributes of Skione and Potidaia were transposed by the stonecutter is, I now think,[16] far too easily accepted. But sometimes Gomme *was* roused to protest. Thus he refused to emend the ms. mention of Gale to Sane in v. 18. 6, on the grounds that we know too little about the history of these small north Aegean places to be confident enough to emend; and he was surely right. The emendation goes back to A. B. West's last article, published in 1937, where it was offered as a hypothesis. By the time of *ATL* iii, i.e. 1950, we were to read, with no supporting discussion at all, that Thucydides 'must be corrected'; note the illicit hardening of 1937 hypothesis into 1950 assertion. The point is small but the issue is large: should we insist that Thucydides and the epigraphic evidence, especially that of the tribute lists, be harmonized at every turn, if necessary by emending Thucydides? It is obvious even to one who was hardly born then, that part of the exhilaration of the work being done on the tribute lists in the middle of

[13] Kitto (above, n. 7) 341.
[14] B. D. Meritt, H. T. Wade-Gery, and M. F. McGregor, *The Athenian Tribute Lists*, 4 vols. (Cambridge, Mass., and Princeton, 1939–53); henceforth *ATL*.
[15] A. W. Gomme, 'Thucydides ii. 13. 3', *Historia*, 2 (1953/4), 1–21.
[16] Contrast my vol. i, p. 98.

the present century came from the excitement of the prospect of marrying epigraphy and Thucydides. But was it a shot-gun marriage? For a strong statement of the sceptical view, saying the things I wish Gomme had said more often, we had to wait until 1993 and Lisa Kallet-Marx's *Money, Expense and Naval Power in Thucydides' History 1–5.24*.[17] A good example is her discussion of the tribute of Rhoiteion in the Troad, mentioned by Thucydides at iv. 52. (This is another example of an idea propounded much more confidently in its final version in *ATL* than when it was first ventilated, this time by Meritt and West in 1934.) Noting that the 2000 Phokaian staters carried off by the Mytilenean exiles was the equivalent of 8 talents, the authors of *ATL* observed that this was 'precisely the assessment' of Rhoiteion's tribute in 425, and suggested ingeniously that the exiles 'timed their raid perfectly and made off with Rhoiteion's tribute just as it had been gathered together for transportation to Athens'. Gomme in his n. on iv. 52 mildly noted that the figure for Rhoiteion's tribute is no more than probable because all the stone has is TT i.e. two talents with a gap before it and this could be restored in several ways. For the full demolition of *ATL* see Kallet-Marx who shows that *ATL*'s words 'precisely the assessment' are completely circular. The tribute lists are in fact being supplemented to fit Thucydides who is then in turn presented as corroboration of the epigraphic record. These two examples, Gale and Rhoiteion, are minor, and deliberately so, like a number of my examples in this introductory section. I reserve until later in this Introduction (section 6) the big question, or what has traditionally been seen as the big question, raised by book iv about the relation of Thucydides to epigraphy, namely his silence about the increase of the tribute in 425. As we shall see, Andrewes in 1981 called this the most spectacular omission of all, but Kallet-Marx now argues that it was a perfectly reasonable omission by Thucydides of a measure which had no significant effect and which may not even have been an increase at all. For the moment I note only that on this issue too, Gomme expressed doubts which Kallet-Marx has taken much further. But I wish again to end positively, so I stress the continuing value of e.g. Gomme's appendix on borrowing from Athens at the end of *HCT* ii; or the calendrical material at the end of *HCT* iii, a model exposition of a fiendishly hard topic. Andrewes acknowledged as much in the next volume of *HCT*, though rejecting Gomme's conclusion that v. 20 implies Thucydides had a fixed beginning to his seasons. See Andrewes on v. 27, saying Gomme 'presents the implications [of his view] with unusual clarity and thoroughness'.[18]

---

[17] (Berkeley, 1993); Rhoiteion: 155–9.   [18] *HCT* iv. 19.

I now pass to the ways in which I think Gomme can be improved on. First the lack of translation. One reason why Oxford University Press asked me to do a new commentary was that by 1986 Gomme's high expectations in the translation department rendered *HCT* inaccessible to many students for whom it was presumably intended. So the translation of all lemmata, and of all Greek inside the notes, is one feature of my commentary which I hope makes it more appropriate than Gomme for the 1990s, however much one may regret the educational reasons which make that true. (The translations are taken from my forthcoming revision of Jowett's *Thucydides* for the *World's Classics* series.) But there is a more important point than merely the wish to be of service to students. The need to translate, i.e. to think about every single word and phrase without exception, is very salutary for a commentator. (For an example from my vol. i, see the n. on i. 140. 2, where correct translation eliminates entirely what had been seen as the most sweeping clause of the Thirty Years Peace.) If I can claim to have noticed some difficulties apparently undetected by Gomme, it is because I have had to translate *everything*. For a small example, see iv. 133. 2 n. Thucydides tells us that Chrysis the priestess of Argos set fire to the temple of Hera by setting light to—what? The Greek word is στέμματα, and Jowett, Crawley, the Penguin, and every other English translation render this by the English 'garlands'. Before I went into the problem at all deeply it struck me that this *could* not be right: 'garlands' conjure up olive leaves, laurel leaves, flowers, and so on. Not easy to set such stuff alight even if you are trying, unless you douse it with kerosene first; or unless we suppose—but why should we?—that the garlands were in dried form. So I started to chase the word στέμματα. The starting point in such a religious context ought to be epigraphy.[19] And a glance at the indexes to Sokolowski's *Lois sacrées* and the *Bulletin Épigraphique* by Jeanne and Louis Robert showed *stemmata* to be a familiar word in religious contexts. But the clinching discussion was a brilliant article by J. Servais, in *L'Antiquité Classique* 1967, actually discussing *Iliad* i. 14.[20] Servais argued conclusively that *stemmata* are usually not made of 'matière végétale' at all but are woollen fillets or strips. Such *stemmata* were used to adorn sacrificial animals but were also worn by priests round their necks. As Servais says, discussing precisely the present passage of Thucydides, 'if such *stemmata*, soaked in fat and probably also sacred oil, were hung with their ends close to a flame, it would be hard to imagine a better torch', 'on ne peut imaginer meilleur brandon'. I note in tribute to the Budé edition that it has the

[19] See Dover (above, n. 10), 73.

[20] Full references on this topic are given in my n. on the passage, and that applies to other topics in this Introductory section.

correct translation 'bandelettes', i.e. fillets. LSJ[9] briefly acknowledges the existence of this meaning, giving it as sense (2); but the same entry firmly gives Thucydides iv. 133 as an example of sense (1), 'wreath, garland, chaplet'. Gomme says nothing about *stemmata*; but had he been forced to translate it, he would surely have come up with the right answer. Incidentally and to anticipate, these Argive *stemmata* also illustrate what will be my third point in this section, Gomme's lack of attention to details of Greek religion.

But my second head in this section on drawbacks of *HCT* iii is out-of-dateness. This is the easiest of my four to demonstrate, and the only one which involves no criticism of Gomme. I need not perhaps spend too long over it.

Thucydides is a central author, and the period he covered is central in Greek history; it is therefore only to be expected that in forty years a huge bibliography should have proliferated. It would be very boring to list even the most important of such items; for instance it would be inappropriate to discuss here how Lazaridis's excavations have changed the consensus about the fortifications of Amphipolis (see nn. on iv. 102 ff.); in any case it will be seen when we move on to literary and narratological topics (below, p. 15) that some of the biggest advances in Thucydidean studies have been in that field, and so are best dealt with there. So instead of talking about particular finds and advances, I propose to single out one area only, the technological advances which have made possible certain kinds of scientifically based generalization, allowing us to move beyond Gomme. The technological revolution of the 1980s has provided us with one powerful tool above all, the computerized data-base. I refer not only to TLG (Thesaurus Linguae Graecae), the computerized thesaurus which takes just 25 minutes to print out all occurrences of a word in Greek literature, but also to the Packard epigraphic database, compiled at Ohio, Cornell, and the Institute for Advanced Study in Princeton. In section 3 below, where I discuss Brasidas and religion, I draw (p. 49) on the results of one TLG search in particular, which (I argue) helps to solve an old problem by proving, against Gomme, Classen/Steup, and the prevailing orthodoxy, that a crucial verb προσάρχομαι posited at iv. 121. 1 simply does not exist. (For another, minor but still interesting example, see v. 16. 1 n. on the meaning of the noun ἐνθυμία: does the word have a religious tinge as assumed by some translators? Here a TLG search improved on LSJ[9]— which merely gives the Thucydides passage—by showing that Cassius Dio used the word in a clearly religious sense in a context (xxxix. 11. 1) which closely imitates Thucydides; this surely makes it likelier that Thucydides v. 16 should be interpreted in a religious way.)

The example just discussed, ἐνθυμία, concerned religious scruples; it thus provides an easy transition to my third heading, Gomme's neglect of religion. I mentioned above the excellent introductory part of *HCT* i about 'what Thucydides takes for granted'. This cried out for a section on religion, a topic Gomme neglected and on which his few comments were not always happy. Take Pagondas' claim at iv. 92. 7 that 'the sacrifices are favourable to us', καὶ τοῖς ἱεροῖς ἃ ἡμῖν θυσαμένοις καλὰ φαί-νεται. Gomme did rightly note that it is unusual for Thucydides to mention battle sacrifices; contrast Xenophon. But Gomme went on in cynical first-half-of-the-twentieth-century way to remark 'Pagondas must have managed the sacrifice rapidly and cleverly'. This will not do. Jameson and others have taught us that we should distinguish between the *hiera* in the narrow sense, the leisurely sacrificing and burning of the victim, and the *sphagia* or slaughter by throat-cutting of the animal very shortly before engaging the enemy, with attention on the part of the *mantis* or seer to signs like how the blood spurted. *Sphagia* are mentioned by Thucydides just once, at vi. 69. 2. Thucydides' word in the present passage is *hiera*, a word which confusingly has a broader extension which covers both kinds of battle sacrifice, *sphagia* and *hiera* in the narrow sense. Now, to return to Pagondas, his speech was delivered at Tanagra before the army moved forward to Delion, after which Hippokrates the Athenian made a speech and Pagondas another speech. Surely then the sacrifices here referred to are the more leisurely *hiera* and Gomme's comment about rapidity and cleverness is beside the point. One might be tempted to press Pagondas' language so as to reach the same conclusion. He does after all call the sacrifices *hiera*, and as we saw Thucydides uses the distinct word *sphagia* in book vi. But this argument is not decisive because of the confusing double meaning of *hiera*, general and particular. That was an example of a throw-away and inadequate religious comment by Gomme. More often Gomme errs by straight omission. (Cf. below, p. 50 f.: important oaths, ignored by Gomme.) Here I give three examples; again, they are minor but not unimportant.

My first is from a chapter we have already looked at, iv. 133, Chrysis' burning down of the temple at Argos in winter 423/2. Gomme's notes, perfectly adequate on their own terms, are confined to two points: (i) the extra material about Chrysis to be found in Pausanias (who tells us she fled to Tegea) and (ii) the Hellanican aspect (Hellanicus chronicled the priestesses of Argos, and modern historians have been reasonably tempted to see here the key to Thucydides' uncharacteristic insertion of this female item). It could not be guessed from Gomme that the Argive Heraion was an excavated sanctuary at all, never mind the role that Thucydides iv. 133, the passage in question, had already played in modern arguments about the building history of the sanctuary at the time Gomme wrote. In 1952,[21] four years before the publication of *HCT* iii, Amandry had argued *against* the view then prevalent and often re-asserted since, namely that 423 marked an epoch in the history of the shrine, and he did so again in 1980. Amandry's view was and is that the Argives exploited the period of peace and prosperity between 450 and 420, the period of the Thirty Years Peace between Argos and Sparta, to rebuild their temple lavishly—and slowly: he thinks the work went on into the fourth century. (That is, Amandry postulated a *much* earlier starting date for the new temple, 450 not 423). Amandry's own view is, however, not without difficulties. Thucydides' word is κατεκαύθη, the regular literary and epigraphic word for complete conflagrations e.g. at Delphi: 'burnt *down*'. We must conclude either (i) that Thucydides exaggerated the extent of the fire, or (ii) that Amandry is wrong and the fire of 423 was a bigger event in the history of the sanctuary than he is prepared to acknowledge. But (iii) there is a third possibility, one which I myself favour: perhaps the old temple went on being used while a new one arose slowly nearby. However that may be, a commentary on Thucydides surely ought to mention the problem.

My second and third examples of religious omissions by Gomme also concern sanctuaries, but they are epigraphic rather than architectural, so they anticipate section 6 below, on epigraphy. They are *Syll.*[3] 78 and 79.

To take the second first, the spoils dedicated by Brasidas and the Akanthians in *Syll.*[3] 79 must have been won some time in the two years, summer 424 to 422, between Brasidas' winning over of Akanthos and his death at Amphipolis. The dedication cannot be correlated with any particular action described by Thucydides, which is itself a reminder that he did not describe everything, even in fully worked up sections of narrative. The political historian might also want to say that the text shows that though the Akanthians dithered initially they were eventually whole-hearted enough in their hostility to Athens. But the religious historian may wish to see the text from a different perspective, and here the other Delphian text comes in. *Syll.*[3] 78 (quoted below, p. 417) was associated by Pomtow with the battle between the Tegeans and Mantineans briefly reported by Thucydides at iv. 134; and in *LSAG*[2] the association is accepted. Thucydides comments that both sides erected trophies and sent spoils to Delphi. The text in *Syll.* is a curious double text. Only (*a*) survives as an epigraphic object, and is from Mantinea; this is the one dated in *LSAG*[2] to 423. Text (*b*) is a wholly restored or reconstructed inscription, reconstructed on the evidence

[21] P. Amandry, *Hesperia*, 21 (1952), 222–74, at 272; full refs. at iv. 133. 2 n. below.

of a passage of Pausanias, of the present passage of Thucydides, and of text (*a*). What is the religious interest of this double Arkadian text? And indeed of the dedication by Brasidas and the Akanthians? Alastair Jackson in Victor Hanson's collected essays, *Hoplites*,[22] says of the Tegean–Mantinean dedications that it is 'not surprising' that both sides chose to send their spoils to Delphi, rather than to Olympia which was closer; he thinks this may have something to do with Greek feelings of unease at dedicating spoils taken from other Greeks. And here I suggest we have an issue of some importance, and this is where Brasidas and the Akanthians come in. But to return to Jackson for a moment, his position is ambiguous. Two pages earlier he had said it was 'no wonder' that on the present occasion both sides sent spoils 'all the way to Delphi'. There his rather different point was that both Olympia and Delphi were simply 'famous and much-frequented shrines'. On the question of Greek spoils taken from Greeks, Jackson may be right to claim, as he does, that after 423 very few offerings of spoils taken from Greeks are reliably reported from Delphi; but there does not seem to be much sign of unease in the Ten Years War itself, compare *Syll.*[3] 79 (Brasidas and the Akanthians) and ML 74 (Messenians at Naupaktos dedicate spoils from the enemy, i.e. the Peloponnesians), and there are some other texts. It would be inappropriate to extend this discussion here, where my aim is merely to signal the existence of an intriguing problem to which literature and epigraphy can both contribute, namely possible changes at just this period in Greek attitudes to dedicating spoils taken from Greeks. Surely a commentary on Thucydides ought to present the reader with the epigraphic evidence as it bears on Thucydides. Why Gomme omitted to mention these two texts despite their obvious bearing on Thucydides is a mystery; he is after all punctilious about citing *Attic* inscriptions. There is perhaps the clue: it is entirely in keeping with Gomme's admirable mastery of finance (above, pp. 5 f.) that he should have been strong on Attic epigraphy, much of which is financial and administrative in character; but it is perhaps equally typical that he should have somewhat neglected the evidence of and about the great sanctuaries. Thus he does not indicate the religious aspect to Sparta's involvement in the First Peloponnesian War, or to the Second Sacred War, or to Sparta's founding of Herakleia. On the second of these topics I am pleased to see that Irad Malkin now describes as 'convincing' my recent attempt to see a Delphic amphiktionic aspect in the Herakleia project.[23] Gomme did not even register that on both those occasions the Spartans are described by Thucydides, in near-identical terms, as helping their

---

[22] A. Jackson, in V. D. Hanson (ed.), *Hoplites*, 246, contrast 244.
[23] I. Malkin, *Myth and Territory in the Spartan Mediterranean* (Cambridge, 1994), 233 n. 65.

metropolis, the Dorians of central Greece. But that raises a topic I shall explore, with special reference to iv–v. 24, when I talk about Thucydides and kinship, ξυγγένεια, in section 4 of this Introduction.

My fourth and final area is literary and narratological. I noted earlier that Gomme does have plenty to say about Thucydides as literature and about his relation to contemporary literature. He is, for instance, almost always alert to Aristophanic resonances; a curious exception is iv. 109, the mention of Olophyxos, a place which features in the *Birds* of 415 (line 1041, requirement to 'use the same weights and measures as the Olophyxians'). The reasonable assumption that this was a more or less topical joke always made attractive a date in the 420s or 410s (rather than the 440s) for the main coinage decree ML 45; and this has now been rendered likely on entirely different grounds, by the discovery of the fragment of the coinage decree from Hamaxitos in the Troad.[24] The argument is that Hamaxitos was not in the Athenian Empire until the 420s. It was not like Gomme to miss commenting on an Aristophanic point, but he has nothing to say on this whole aspect of Olophyxos, a place mentioned only at iv. 109 in all Thucydides. Again, Gomme's part of the commentary is full of Euripidean citations, as one notices when Andrewes and Dover take over: they have much less of that.

Gomme's title was however *historical* commentary, so complaints on the literary score are unfair. But they are tempting because Gomme does have things to say about Thucydides as literature. Thus his iv–v. 24 commentary includes references of the form 'see my Sather lectures', a purely literary work I have mentioned already.[25] As it happens that 1954 book must have been written about the time that he was working on the commentary on iv–v, after the theft from a train in 1945 of all his notes.[26] On this section it is instructive to compare the Sather lectures with the relevant bits of the commentary: the Sather lectures are much clearer and more audacious—and more vulnerable, though I would not endorse Andrewes' dismissal of an entire section of *Greek Attitude to Poetry*, that concerned with the narrative dislocation at iv. 70 (the purpose of Brasidas' northern expedition revealed only gradually). Andrewes wrote: 'the fact that the items come in order of the impact at Athens is surely a product of Thucydides' method, not his reason for adopting it'.[27] Kitto[28] did not like the book, either; he thought Gomme's 'just appraisal of detail' was not matched by a comprehensive view of the relevant works

---

[24] H. Mattingly, *Klio*, 75 (1993), 99–102.

[25] *HCT* iii. 540, 588.

[26] Kitto (above, n. 7), 340.

[27] *HCT* v. 366.

[28] Kitto (above, n. 7), speaking of Gomme's treatment of the poems and plays, but presumably referring also to Thucydides.

of literature as a whole (Homer and tragedy as well as the historians). It is certainly true that Kitto's own Sather lectures, published in 1966 as *Poiesis*,[29] are important for literary students of Thucydides in a way Gomme's lectures are not. But I hope I have said enough to show that Gomme cannot be written off as a positivist historian with no feel for Thucydides as literature.

That may not sound like much of a tribute, but it needs to be put into context, the context of neglect by historians of the literary features of Thucydides, always with the exception of the Sicilian books. To take an example: the *OCD*[2] entry on Thucydides[30] was a light 1970 revision of Wade Gery's classic 1949 entry, which includes a section on style by J. D. Denniston. The revealing feature is the bibliography: heavily skewed towards works about the composition problem, it omitted Cornford's *Thucydides Mythistoricus*,[31] and Strasburger's studies[32] which were to be so big an influence on the Thucydides material in H. Lloyd-Jones's important 1971 *The Justice of Zeus*.[33] It did include J. de Romilly's *Histoire et raison chez Thucydide*,[34] but not Gomme's Sather lectures,[35] Hans-Peter Stahl's 1966 book[36] or Kitto's *Poiesis*;[37] in fact it omitted just about every good literary study of Thucydides up to that date.

But assumptions about novelty or previous neglect in this area should be made cautiously. I give two related examples. On the last page of Averil Cameron's interesting collection of essays, *History as Text*,[38] the editor begins by conceding that Thucydides' claims to reliability have been seen as coexisting with a sense of drama and emotion; but she continues 'it is only relatively recently that Thucydides' history has attracted the kind of attention from the point of view of textuality which would not seem obvious'. A footnote directs the reader to Virginia Hunter's 1973 *Thucydides the Artful Reporter*.[39] This is, I think, a little unfair to Cornford's book of 1907. My second example concerns Hunter herself. One of Hunter's main claims concerns the relation of speeches and narrative, specifically the way ostensible prediction is fulfilled by the

---

[29] *Poiesis: Structure and Thought* (Berkeley, 1966).

[30] For the third edition of *OCD* (1996) I have myself contributed an extra section to Wade Gery's article; this ostensibly discusses work since 1970, but I have taken the opportunity to include important pre-1970 work as well, particularly that on literary aspects.

[31] (London, 1907).

[32] Collected in W. Schmitthenner and R. Zoepffel (eds.), H. Strasburger, *Studien zur alten Geschichte*, 3 vols. (Hildesheim and New York, 1982–1990); see esp. the papers in vol. ii.

[33] H. Lloyd-Jones, *The Justice of Zeus* (Berkeley, 1971; [2]1983).

[34] (Paris, 1956).

[35] Above, n. 5.

[36] *Thukydides: die Stellung des Menschen im Geschichtlichen Prozess* (Munich, 1966).

[37] Above, n. 29.

[38] (London, 1989), 207.

[39] (Toronto, 1973); 23–30 for Brasidas' speech of exhortation.

narrative itself. But take one example, her analysis at 23–30 of Brasidas' speech of exhortation at iv. 126, where she gives a parallel layout of passages to bring out the way the narrative fulfils the predictions in the speech. She nowhere cites, nor does her bibliography list, O. Luschnat's 1942 *Philologus* Supplement on the speeches by generals in Thucydides, where exactly the same point is made, with a chart giving the same parallel layout of passages.[40] Clearly, Hunter's suggestion was completely independent of Luschnat, but the duplication of effort is a warning that older works have their value, on literary as well as historical aspects of Thucydides.

All that said, I think it is true that there has been a shift in Thucydidean studies since about 1960, and that we have come to take this so much for granted that, when Momigliano's Sather lectures of the early 1960s were finally published in 1990,[41] what they said about Thucydides did not seem as exciting as perhaps it did on delivery. The shift, as Richard Rutherford shows in a forthcoming study, is towards a unitarian as opposed to an analyst approach, witness the strange look in 1995 of the 1970 *OCD* bibliography with its concentration on the composition question. As with Homer so with Thucydides, along with a unitarian approach has come a fashion for detecting patterning and minute correspondences and resonances in detail, and for studying the total and sectional architecture of the work as a whole; for book iv in particular I think of the 1981 study by D. Babut.[42] But for the whole work there is Schneider 1974,[43] Rawlings 1981,[44] and above all Connor 1984,[45] not to mention Macleod on the speeches.[46] As far as detailed patterning went, *HCT* was not satisfactory. There are some famous verbal chimes in other books, not noticed in *HCT*, but I shall take an example from book iv. Brasidas' speech at Akanthos opens (iv. 85. 1) with an arresting abstract expression 'my sending-out by the Spartans happened', ἡ μὲν ἔκπεμψίς μου γεγένηται, which seems to echo the Athenians at Sparta at i. 73. 1, 'our embassy happened', ἡ μὲν πρέσβευσις ἡμῶν ἐγένετο, and one might speculate that Brasidas is being given language reminiscent of the Athenians, those masters of forensic oratory. (Neither of the abstract nouns is found elsewhere in Thucydides.) If Gomme's refusal[47] to notice

[40] O. Luschnat, *Die Feldherrnreden im Geschichtswerk des Thukydides* (*Philologus* Suppl. 34. 2: 1942), 59–60.

[41] *The Classical Foundations of Modern Historiography* (Berkeley, 1990).

[42] D. Babut, 'Interprétation historique et structure littéraire chez Thucydide: remarques sur la composition du livre iv', *Bull. assoc. G. Budé,* 40 (1981), 417–39.

[43] C. Schneider, *Information und Absicht bei Thukydides* (Göttingen, 1974).

[44] H. R. Rawlings III, *The Structure of Thucydides' History* (Princeton, 1981).

[45] W. R. Connor, *Thucydides* (Princeton, 1984).

[46] C. Macleod, *Collected Essays* (Oxford, 1983), chs. 8–13.

[47] Contrast Classen/Steup's n. on iv. 85. 1.

such parallels seems strange to us, it may be because David Lewis was right to speak in his British Academy memoir of Antony Andrewes of the 'new generation of those who insisted on seeing the work as a completed literary whole to be read in order from beginning to end'[48] and because we belong to or have been influenced by that generation of scholars. A Babut- or Connor-style analysis of book iv, which roughly sees the Pylos episode as balanced by Brasidas in Thrace, is premissed on a unitarian approach; if you follow Andrewes in *HCT* v such an approach is excluded because in his view the narrative disintegrates after Delion (see further below, section 7). On that second view the correspondences are either coincidences or the result of over-ingenious examination. *A fortiori*, the analyst Andrewes view rules out more ambitious attempts to see Pylos as foreshadowing events at Syracuse, and the emphasis Macleod and others have placed on correspondences between books iv and vii.[49] What we *do* with these correspondences and what are the implications of the 'completed whole' view are crucial matters to which I return at the end of this Introduction. For the moment I wish to stress that, though scholars like Babut and Connor rely heavily on *HCT* for individual problems of interpretation, *HCT* gives little encouragement to the student interested in detecting patterns across widely separated sections of the work, that is, in the kind of 'deliberate cross-reference ("Fernverbindung")' which Dodds discussed in connection with Homer.[50] And the same result is produced by the way *HCT* always plunges straight into the commentary on individual *speeches* without separate introductions of the kind I myself have tried to provide, analysing them rhetorically and indicating their relation to other speeches in the work. I shall discuss speech, direct and indirect, in section 6 below.

HCT is, then, more helpful on detail than on big structural or theoretical issues. All this was no oversight on Gomme's part. He was as Kitto's memoir shows a man of sceptical cast of mind, impatient of large constructions and the literary theory which is another name for the large literary construction. (This brings with it a sort of advantage in that Gomme's literary comments, when he does make them, have not dated as they might have done if expressed in the literary theory of the time.) Literary theory tends to concern itself with texts perceived as autonomous unities more than with their authors, and is inimical to the biographical approach; by contrast an interest in Thucydides' personal biography tends to go with an analyst view and a rejection of intertextual

---

[48] D. M. Lewis, 'Antony Andrewes', *PBA* 80 (1991), 221–31, at 229.

[49] See e.g. Macleod (above, n. 46), 142. Cf. below, iv. 12. 3 n.

[50] E. R. Dodds, 'Homer and the Unitarians', in M. Platnauer (ed.), *Fifty Years of Classical Scholarship* (Oxford, 1954), 8–13, at 13. For another example see iv. 99 n. on ὁ δὲ κῆρυξ etc.

approaches. Thus as we shall see in the next section, on Thucydides and Herodotus, R. S. Stroud has recently argued that Thucydides had close personal ties with Corinth, and this leads Stroud—not altogether logically as I shall suggest—to minimize the extent to which Thucydides' text is indebted to Herodotus. Stroud appears to believe that personal inquiry and travel by Thucydides are somehow incompatible with literary borrowing and the conduct of polemic.

So far I have written as if the literary or antipositivist approach to Thucydides has had things all its own way. That would be misleading because it leaves out some formidable figures on the other 'side', above all W. K. Pritchett. The philosophy behind Pritchett's work on Thucydides, and indeed on Herodotus,[51] is that the two fifth-century historians are almost always factually right and where they appear not to be right (this is particularly true of Thucydides) we should emend so as to make them right and then go on our way as if the problem never existed in the first place. The most striking instance is at iv. 8. 6, where Thucydides appears to make his worst topographical error in the entire work; at present the emendation made by Bauslaugh in 1979 seems to hold the field, having been approved by Pritchett in 1994.[52] But it is not altogether satisfactory to hold that an emendation which had not occurred to anyone in the 1960s is now to be treated as self-evidently right. The better attitude, I suggest, is to agree to an emendation if it removes a difficulty, but never to forget that unless the text is disturbed we are carrying out the emendation in deference to and in accordance with a *hypothesis*, a hypothesis that is about the rightness and truthfulness of Thucydides, a hypothesis which is usually good and sound but which is surely not necessarily and not automatically true in every instance. That is, we should sometimes be willing to entertain the possibility that for artistic or other motives Thucydides might have bent the truth. Pritchett makes a concession in this direction at the end of his *Mnemosyne* 1973 attack on Woodhead, where he concedes that in depicting Kleon Thucydides 'departs from his usual objectivity'.[53] More usually, the views of scholars like Fehling who doubt the veracity of Herodotus, or Hunter who doubt that of Thucydides, are rejected in strong language. A gulf has thus opened up between literary and historical approaches or rather between some exponents of those approaches; and one object of this Introduction and of my commentary is to see if it is bridgeable. See esp. pp. 60 f. below.

---

[51] W. K. Pritchett, *The Liar School of Herodotus* (Amsterdam, 1993). See also Pritchett, *TPOE*.

[52] W. K. Pritchett, *EGH* 167–75.

[53] W. K. Pritchett, 'The Woodheadean Interpretation of Kleon's Amphipolitan Campaign', *Mnemosyne*, 26 (1973), 376–86, at 386.

I now move on from these rather general remarks about literary approaches to the particular area of narratology. I have suggested that there is some unfairness, given Gomme's title, in criticizing him for not writing the literary commentary he never set out to write. It would be even more unfair to castigate Gomme for not attending to narratology, because it did not yet exist—as a word. By narratology I mean the study of the rhetorical principles underlying narrative texts.[54] There is a rhetoric of narrative as well as a rhetoric of speeches, i.e. there is Longinus as well as Dionysius of Halicarnassus. Gomme, Kitto, and others back to Cornford and beyond have noticed individual features of Thucydidean narrative rhetoric, and it could be said that narratologists like Irene de Jong have merely given labels to well-known tricks of discourse. But even if there were no more to narratology than that, the existence of the labels may help by alerting us to unnoticed items. For instance de Jong has a category of 'if . . . not' episodes, what Nesselrath calls *Beinahe-episoden*, that is, vivid narrative statements of the form 'x would have happened if agent y had not intervened or action z hadn't supervened'.[55] Perhaps the best example in all Thucydides is at iv. 106. 4, where Brasidas just misses taking Eion after taking Amphipolis: 'if the ships commanded by Thucydides himself had not arrived at top speed, the place would have fallen'. It is nice that the most explicit use of this Homeric story-telling device should relate to an event in which Thucydides himself was involved. The very same ch. 106 contains (para. 2) an instance of another narratological technique well studied by de Jong, that of significant attributive discourse or denomination:[56] Westlake[57] once noted that by referring in that chapter to his colleague Eukles not as Eukles but as the Athenian general in the city, Thucydides may be underlining Eukles' responsibility for safeguarding Athenian interests at Amphipolis, and this would have had a bearing on Thucydides' own responsibility. This simple example shows that a narratological insight can be arrived at without the language of narratology. We discussed another example above, the argument between Gomme and Andrewes about how Brasidas' northern expedition is described before the thinking behind it is revealed. Chapters iv. 70 and 79–81 are not just a piece of delay or narrative anachrony (deviation): we are told about this

[54] See I. de Jong, *Narrators and Focalizers: the Presentation of the Story in the Iliad* (Amsterdam, 1987), p. x, for this definition; see my 'Narratology and Narrative Techniques in Thucydides' in S. Hornblower (ed.), *Greek Historiography* (Oxford, 1994), 131–66, at 131.

[55] De Jong (above, n. 54), 68–81; H.-G. Nesselrath, *Ungeschehenes Geschehen: 'Beinahe-Episoden' im griechischen und römischen Epos von Homer bis zum Spätantike* (Stuttgart, 1992).

[56] I. de Jong, *Narrative in Drama: the Art of the Euripidean Messenger-Speech* (Leiden, 1991), 94, and 'Studies in Homeric Denomination', *Mnemosyne*, 46 (1993), 289–306.

[57] H. D. Westlake, *Essays on the Greek Historians and Greek History* (Manchester, 1969), 132.

important strategic development only casually and in the context of events unfolding at Megara. And Gomme and his continuators were always alert to Thucydides' related habit of introducing material where it is most relevant rather than at the first and most obvious place. But I am convinced that the categories and vocabulary of de Jong are valuable in helping with the *systematic* identification of such subtleties. Thus the power of the description of Brasidas' blitzkrieg march on Amphipolis at iv. 103 ff., in the evening with the snow coming on, is partly due to the adroit management of narrative pace or rhythm; that urgent and unusually detailed description is placed right after a very different and episodic sort of chapter, 102, which covers the whole history of Amphipolis from 500 BC and Aristagoras. I shall return to narratology, and in particular to the concept of focalization, in section 3 when we shall see that Thucydides' judgements on Brasidas are rarely direct but usually focalized through one of those on whom he makes an impression for good or bad.

The central question, which has already begun to crystallize during the above discussion, is this: should iv–v. 24 be regarded as a finished and experimental work of art as the currently fashionable unitarian view has it (Babut, Connor)? If so, such exceptional features as the verbatim inclusion of treaties at iv. 118 and v. 18 and 23, or the oratio obliqua at iv. 96–97, need an artistic explanation. Or should we stick with Andrewes' 1981 analyst view that the whole is a fragment needing further work from Thucydides which it never got? Or can we disregard compositional questions and treat the text narratologically as a unit, accepting that the man Thucydides might have left it incomplete but regarding biographical fact as simply irrelevant to its status as an autonomous text? In the final section (7) of this Introduction I shall discuss the structure and peculiar features of iv–v. 24 and try to offer an answer.

2. *Thucydides and Herodotus (with special attention to iv–v. 24)*

I begin this section with Thucydides' only paragraph of explicit discussion of his predecessors, and I am not now thinking of the famous sentence about Hellanicus at i. 97. 2, but of the immediately preceding sentence. It runs as follows: '*all* my precedessors', οἱ πρὸ ἐμοῦ ἅπαντες,[58] 'have composed narratives about either Greek history before the Persian Wars or about the Persian Wars themselves', ἢ τὰ πρὸ τῶν Μηδικῶν Ἑλληνικὰ ξυνετίθεσαν ἢ αὐτὰ τὰ Μηδικά. The translation I have here adopted for

---

[58] These four words are in the dative in the Greek, which contains an extra thought irrelevant here so I have suppressed it: τοῖς πρὸ ἐμοῦ ἅπασιν ἐκλιπὲς τοῦτο ἦν τὸ χωρίον καὶ ἢ τὰ πρὸ τῶν Μηδικῶν, etc., i.e. the period between the Persian and Peloponnesian Wars was neglected *by* them and they have composed narratives, etc.

ξυνετίθεσαν, 'composed', differs slightly but significantly from that offered by LSJ⁹ who give this (with an instruction to 'cf.' Th. i. 21. 2, see below) as the only example of the sense 'narrate in writing'; it also differs from Bétant who has *conscribere*; but there seems no justification for introducing 'writing' which begs what we shall see is a crucial question. In the first place, Plato, Aristophanes, and others use the word ξυντίθημι about Homer and Hesiod composing *mythoi*.⁵⁹ In the second place, Thucydides could have used his favourite word ξυνέγραψαν⁶⁰ to describe the activity of his precedessors but does not, and I would say it is significant that he does not. Why it is significant is a matter to which I shall return shortly. Let us return to the sentence as a whole. It implies three things. First, that Thucydides had predecessors, plural, note ἅπαντες, '*all* those before me'; second, that they treated not just the Persian Wars but Greek history (or however we translate *Hellenika*, literally 'Greek affairs') before the Persian Wars; and third, that he was familiar with their work. In the scholarly literature the sentence I have here concentrated on has tended to be overshadowed by the better-known remark about Hellanicus and his inadequate account of the Pentekontaetia.

There is another relevant general passage in Thucydides. It is at i. 21. People, Thucydides says, who relied on the kind of evidence I have just alluded to would not go astray, because it is better than that of the poets on the one hand, who exaggerate in what they hymn about, ὑμνήκασι, and of the *logographoi* or prose-writers on the other hand, who have composed ξυνέθεσαν (same verb as at i. 97. 2), with the object of giving pleasure to the ear, ἐπὶ τὸ προσαγωγότερον τῇ ἀκροάσει ... These are the only occurrences in Thucydides of the verb ξυντίθημι in the sense of literary activity, and I suggest that we should take them in the same way both times, as meaning 'compose', without prejudice to the question whether the composition was oral or written. Indeed Thucydides' word ἀκροάσει suggests (despite Gomme *HCT* i, p. 139) that he had recitation in mind for both poets and logographers, whether or not there was a formal written text. Thucydides' distinction poets/logographoi is thus not between oral and written, but between poetic and prose composition, which you might or might not hear read or recited aloud. Again, Thucydides shows awareness of prose predecessors in the plural.

With these two statements by Thucydides, contrast two recent statements by Stroud: 'Thucydides was not a "book-historian" ...'; and again 'most modern research on Herodotus, Thucydides, and Polybius is conducted by scholars reading books in a library, whereas these

---

⁵⁹ Plato, *Rep.* 377d; Ar. *Frogs* 1052.

⁶⁰ For ξυγγράφειν, 'collect and write down', see *Thucydides* (London, 1987; 2nd, corrected impression 1994), 8 n. 2.

historians spent most of their time in travel, examining monuments, and talking to hundreds of informants'.[61]

Some of what Stroud says here about travel and informants I can only applaud. It seems to me, for instance, a better picture of Herodotus' methods than that offered by Detlev Fehling. But I do not feel quite as confident as Stroud about how exactly the three named historians spent '*most* of their time'; and though I agree that Polybius travelled, examined monuments, talked to informants, I am unhappy about lumping him in like this with the two fifth-century historians. Polybius lived and wrote in the second century BC, and in between those centuries, the fifth and the second centuries, fall the golden ages of Athenian, Alexandrian, and Pergamene scholarship. Polybius' books xii and xxxiv, on history-writing and geography respectively, have led Peter Derow in a recent essay on historical explanation, to remark that Polybius was 'a pro'.[62] He glosses this as meaning that Polybius was 'a historian writing for people who were accustomed to read histories ... his bibliography, as it were, lists some dozens of authors, which is pretty good for the ancient world'. But let me leave Polybius to the Polybians, noting only that I do believe that Polybius was aware not just of Timaeus but of at least the methodological sections of Thucydides, despite a famous piece of apparent ignorance about the Congress of Gela.[63] But Polybius in the preserved part of his work mentions Thucydides only once, and that only to say that Theopompus began where Thucydides left off, i.e. this is not a proper citation (viii. 11). This virtual silence produces a problem which cannot detain us now. The problem is, however, similar in some ways to Thucydides' silence about Herodotus. There can be no strict proof of influence, polemic, or use without an explicit mention by name, and Thucydides' text contains no such mention—which brings me to the theme of the present section. What was Thucydides' relation to Herodotus, whom he never mentions?

Stroud's article is about Corinth, and makes valuable points about Thucydides' excellent detailed knowledge of Corinthian affairs. Stroud is interested in Thucydides' biography in a way which modern literary theorists would find unfashionable, but he makes a good case for thinking that Thucydides visited Corinth during his exile and found out about Corinth in that way rather than out of books. Whether we can go further and say with Stroud that Thucydides was actually 'resident' there[64] is not

[61] R. S. Stroud, 'Thucydides and Corinth', *Chiron*, 24 (1994), 267–302, at 301 and 275 n. 10.

[62] P. Derow, 'Historical Explanation: Polybius and his Predecessors', in *Greek Historiography* (above, n. 54), 73–90, at 84.

[63] See *Greek Historiography*, 60–1; *JHS* 115 (1995), 59.

[64] Stroud (above, n. 61), 302.

so obvious. It seems to me that *visits* to Corinth (and Sparta—and Argos—and Mantinea—and so on) would answer as well: exiles regularly moved around a good deal. But Stroud is particularly concerned to demolish what he calls the 'tale' that Thucydides spent his exile in Thrace, writing his history under a plane-tree, a tale handed down by Marcellinus and Plutarch. Stroud misrepresents my own views on this point, in two distinct respects. First, he cites[65] my 1987 book on Thucydides and speaks of 'Hornblower's acceptance of the tale of literary exile in Thrace', a reference to the Marcellinus story which two pages earlier he rightly calls a tale. The statement here contained is simply untrue. So far from accepting the tale at that point in my 1987 book on Thucydides I do not mention it there, or at any other point in that book, or in anything else that I have written. Had I mentioned it I would have dismissed it for exactly Stroud's reasons. Second, Stroud speaks of the virtual neglect by three scholars (of whom I am one) of Thucydides' own autobiographical statement at v. 26 that he spent his exile not least among the Peloponnesians. So far from neglecting this on the page cited by Stroud I quoted it in full and in pride of place, making the additional comment that Thucydides' personal wealth was surely relevant to his ability to make these travels[66]—a point now made by Stroud at length, with comparisons of Corinth to Las Vegas and so forth. But the idea that Thucydides spent time in Thrace, which I certainly do believe probable without for a moment subscribing to tales about plane-trees and the like, was of course based on something, in fact on Thucydides' own text. Stroud is in fact doing in a twentieth-century scholarly idiom what Marcellinus did in *his* scholarly idiom, namely making a conjecture about Thucydides' life based on Thucydides' writings, an ancient habit which Mary Lefkowitz has taught us to look out for.[67] The difference between Stroud and Marcellinus is that if Stroud had been living at the time of Marcellinus and had his good idea about Thucydides and Corinth, he would have made it a factual item in his biography of Thucydides. In 1994 one is expected to call it a hypothesis, add footnotes, and send it to a learned journal. To stay with Thrace for a moment, I should like to focus on Amphipolis. Thucydides' knowledge of Thrace is obviously good, and it is a common scholarly move to attribute it to his Thracian background. We shall see below that this is a sceptical reply, and a plausible one, to claims that Thucydides' Thracian material has a

[65] Stroud, 301, see also 299 where he sets out the ancient authorities for the 'tale'.
[66] See my *Thucydides* (above, n. 60), 3, 'He says at v. 26 that the leisure he now enjoyed (he does not add anything about his private financial means, though these were also surely relevant) enabled him to spend time with the other combatant side in the war, the Peloponnesians'. For Las Vegas see Stroud, 303. For rejection of anecdotes about Th., see my *Thucydides*, 136.
[67] M. Lefkowitz, *The Lives of the Greek Poets* (London, 1981).

relation to the Thracian material in Herodotus. But if we are to play the 'where-did-Thucydides-spend-his-exile?' game, two Amphipolitan passages need highlighting. At iv. 103. 5, speaking of 424 BC, he says that at that time the walls did not go down to the river crossing *as they do now*. And at v. 11. 1, again talking about Amphipolis but this time in a part of the narrative dealing with 422 BC, he mentions the *present* agora, πρὸ τῆς νῦν ἀγορᾶς οὔσης; that is, he is contrasting the state of affairs as it was in 422 with some later state known to himself. The significance of these passages is surely that he not only knew Amphipolis and Thrace (which is obvious from his statement about his mining interests, iv. 105), but that he spent time in Amphipolis *after* his exile.

So much for Corinth and Thrace; I have no difficulty in supposing that the hoteliers of Amphipolis got some of Thucydides' custom as well as those of Corinth, though no doubt Thucydides had his guest-friends in both places so that his wealth would have enabled him to bring gifts rather than pay hotel bills. What has any of this got to do with Thucydides and Herodotus, and how do Corinthian (or Amphipolitan) visits, long or short, refute the idea that Thucydides had predecessors of whose work he was aware? The answer is: I have no idea. They do not. But Stroud, as we saw, appears to think there is a mysterious incompatibility between being a book-historian on the one hand and travelling and interrogating people on the other. There is, surely, not the smallest obstacle to believing both things about Thucydides. What I do not share is Stroud's certainty about how Thucydides spent '*most* of his time'.

Stroud's aim is, however, more precise than merely to establish that Thucydides was not a book-historian: he wants to postulate Corinthian informants where previous inquirers like myself have suggested written or other literary traditions. Let us look at some examples given by Stroud.[68] At i. 13, Thucydides discusses Corinth, the tyranny, early ship-building, and so on. Stroud does not like suggestions like Forrest's about thalassocracy lists as a source here, or Jacoby's about shadowy figures like Euagon of Samos.[69] All this Stroud thinks was picked up by

---

[68] Stroud, 271–7. In this volume I cannot systematically go over parts of Th. covered in my vol. i, but Stroud's treatment of the First Peloponnesian War leaves some unease. At 279–80 Stroud rightly notes the wealth of what a literary theorist might call Corinthian-focalized detail at i. 105–6. He also (n. 18) rightly praises Lewis's 'perceptive and valuable' account of Corinth's aspirations and tactics in the war (as set out in G. Shrimpton and D. J. McCargar (eds.), *Classical Contributions: Studies in Honor of M. F. McGregor* (Locust Valley NY, 1981), 71–8; cp. more briefly *CAH* v². 106–7). But Lewis's main thesis (about Corinthian/Argive rivalry over the Nemean Games) is certainly not derived from Th. It would therefore appear that Th.'s Corinthian informants about this war were generous but not very penetrating. Or perhaps Th. was told the truth, but did not have ears to hear, i.e. he failed to understand or elucidate a topic of what to him was an uncongenial sort, for the reasons suggested at *HSCP* 94 (1992), 169–97 (esp. 179 for the Nemean Games).

[69] Thalassocracy lists: Stroud, 274 f., arguing against W. G. Forrest, 'Two Chronographic Notes:

Thucydides by 'actually visiting Corinth and by interrogating there οἱ τὰ σαφέστατα Πελοποννησίων μνήμῃ παρὰ τῶν πρότερον δεδεγμένοι (i. 9. 2), "those of the Peloponnesians who have received the clearest traditional accounts from men of former times" . . .'. So far so good; my trouble with this is that it is so one-sidedly Corinthian, not surprising in a paper called 'Thucydides and Corinth'; but a dangerous platform for generalizations about Thucydides' methods in general. Was the whole *Archaeology* picked up in this way? For instance—to stay with i. 9—what about the complicated mythology later in that chapter, Eurystheus' mother exiled because of the death of Chrysippus and so on? Thucydides was extraordinarily lucky to come across Corinthian sailors who were such polished spare-time mythographers. (Compare Stroud, 303, on Thucydides interrogating Corinthian generals and sailors and 'peering at warships'.) Or what about i. 12 and the material about the occupation of Boiotia sixty years after the fall of Troy? That is normally thought to be an attempt to reconcile some awkward discrepancies between the Homeric *Catalogue of Ships* and the rest of the tradition;[70] it was clever of those same Corinthian sailors to point Thucydides in the direction of so elegant a solution. Even if we substitute 'Boiotian boiotarchs and farmers' (or some other helpful and hospitable group) for 'Corinthian generals and sailors', it seems perverse to deny that Thucydides might have been working within a literary tradition, even when the context shouts out for such an explanation. Let us return to the Greek words at i. 9. 2 quoted by Stroud (see above for οἱ τὰ σαφέστατα . . ., 'those of the Peloponnesians', etc.). These words are introduced by λέγουσι δέ, 'those of the Peloponnesians . . . say'. Does this imply interrogation of well-informed Corinthian individuals, whether sailors or scholars or both? Surely Thucydides is thinking rather of literary accounts, in poetry or prose; λέγουσι, 'they say', is entirely appropriate for literary accounts, which might, even in Thucydides' day, have been performed orally. (See further below, pp. 26 f.)

My second example brings me at last to Thucydides and Herodotus. It is the mention by the Corinthians in Thucydides of the loan by Corinth to Athens of 20 ships for use against Aigina, i. 41. 2, compare Hdt. vi. 89. Stroud rejects the idea (hardly *my* idea) that Thucydides got this from Herodotus. According to Stroud, the story 'belonged to the large store of facts that he laboriously checked by cross-questioning . . . His informants

---

I. The Tenth Thalassocracy list in Eusebius', *CQ* 19 (1969), 95–106. Euagon: Stroud, 275 n. 10, arguing against F. Jacoby, *Atthis* (Oxford, 1949), 361 n. 56.

[70] See my 'Thucydides and Boiotia' in *2nd International Congress of Boiotian Studies, Levadhia 1992* (forthcoming).

must have included Corinthians'.[71] As Annex A to the present Introduction, I reprint, with purely typographic corrections, my 1992 article, which is Stroud's target here. The article was called 'Thucydides' use of Herodotus'[72] and was devoted to the issue of factual dependence by Thucydides on Herodotus. In the first part I argued that there is a certain amount in Thucydides generally which presupposes Herodotus. In the second part I put a more ambitious challenge, which had to with Thucydides' speeches. Do they, I asked, contain any major item of information about earlier history, i.e. about the periods covered by Herodotus, which is not also known to us from Herodotus? Note the careful formulation. If not—and neither Stroud nor J. J. Kennelly in his recent study of Thucydides' knowledge of Herodotus,[73] has even mentioned, let alone taken up, my challenge—then there is surely a *prima facie* case for supposing that in speeches Thucydides was to an unusual degree dependent on Herodotus for his material about the past. I added that, if true, this had interesting consequences for the old question of the authenticity of the speeches. However, I postpone that aspect until section 5 on speeches and indirect discourse in iv–v. 24. The two main exceptions to my speeches thesis both, oddly, concern Plataia, and both seem to deal with events of 479, i.e. the end of the period which Herodotus covered. They are ii. 71, Archidamos on the promise of inviolability to Plataia,[74] and the problematic iii. 55, where the Plataians say they share citizenship with Athens (see my note on that passage).

Before I get on to the texts, and I shall angle my discussion to texts in iv–v. 24, I must dispose of some more general methodological objections to my general approach. Stroud's objection, as we have seen, appears to be basically grounded on the *a priori* assertion that because ancient historians spent 'most of their time' looking at places and talking to people other than historians, it follows that they never read or heard or were influenced by or tried to correct each other or earlier literary figures. The illogicality of this is obvious. Obviously, I wish to say they did both.

Kennelly's objection of principle, as opposed to his handling of

---

[71] Stroud, 277. 'Hardly my idea': as will be seen from the relevant entry in Annex B, which (see below, p. 140) lists passages where Th. may be dependent on Hdt., the idea that Th. got these twenty ships from Hdt. goes back at least to Köhler in 1891.

[72] Not, as Stroud, 270 n. 6, has it, 'Thucydides and Herodotus'.

[73] J. J. Kennelly, *Thucydides' Knowledge of Herodotus* (diss. Brown, 1994; version printed from microfilm, Ann Arbor, 1995). I owe my original awareness of this dissertation to comments, about it and its relation to my own work, made by W. F. Wyatt Jr. to an electronic discussion group on Thucydides in March 1995; these comments were shown to me by a friend at Princeton during my stay there.

[74] On which see E. Badian, *From Plataea to Potidaea: Studies in the History and Historiography of the Pentecontaetia* (Baltimore, 1993), 109–23.

particular texts, to which I shall soon turn, is that Herodotus' date of publication was late, i.e. 414, or at any rate well down into the Ten Years War; and this he thinks rules out borrowing by Thucydides from Herodotus. Like C. W. Fornara,[75] Kennelly relies heavily on Hdt. vi. 98, apparently implied knowledge of the death of Artaxerxes I in 424, and, for the very late 414 date, ix. 73 on Decelea. Kennelly needs to get rid of the obvious objection that even if those passages carry the implication Fornara thinks, Herodotus might have given recitations or otherwise given his material to the world informally and in advance of publication, whatever we mean by that word. He therefore rejects the recitation hypothesis. But to get rid of the recitation hypothesis it is not enough to ridicule the particular story in Diyllos (*FGrHist* 73 F3) about Herodotus' enormous fee for reciting at Athens. And here I must confess that I do believe in the recitation hypothesis, and that for me this belief makes it unnecessary to spend very long on this objection of principle, but I must say something. The issue goes much wider than silly (or not silly) stories in Diyllos, and has to do with the wholesale reinterpretation, which has taken place in recent years, of the relation between orality and literacy; on this general topic Kennelly denounces 'the pervasive over-emphasis which has been placed on the oral nature of classical literature';[76] I could not disagree more. On the contrary, the essential is said elegantly by Rosalind Thomas in her 1992 book *Literacy and Orality*, not cited by Kennelly. She goes further than merely arguing that Herodotus gave readings, though she certainly says that, referring with approval to J. A. S. Evans's 1991 book and Oswyn Murray's 1987 article, both of which assume or argue for extensive pre-publication of the Histories.[77] Thomas actually suggests, and I find the suggestion very plausible, that there are 'oral features' not just to Herodotus but to Thucydides as well.[78] That is, parts of Thucydides' work may have been written with recitation in mind. In the first volume of my commentary (i. 22. 4 n. on ἐς μὲν ἀκρόασιν) I had already suggested that some parts of the work in high finish, like the Corcyraean *stasis* section, might have been read and tried out at symposia. At i. 22 Thucydides says he wants his work to be a possession for ever *rather* than a temporary *agonisma* or prize recitation,[79] and this does not

---

[75] C. W. Fornara, 'Evidence for the Date of Herodotus' Publication', *JHS* 91 (1971), 25–34. See also his book *Herodotus: an Interpretative Essay* (Oxford, 1971).

[76] Kennelly (above, n. 73), 37.

[77] R. Thomas, *Literacy and Orality in Ancient Greece* (London, 1992), 125, citing J. A. S. Evans, *Herodotus, Explorer of the Past: Three Essays* (Princeton, 1991), 90, and O. Murray, 'Herodotus and Oral History' in H. Sancisi-Weerdenburg and A. Kuhrt (eds.), *Achaemenid History*, ii. *The Greek Sources* (Leiden, 1987), 93–115.

[78] Thomas, 103–4.

[79] On the notion of *agonisma* or competition here implied, see R. Thomas, 'Performance and Written Publication in Herodotus and the Sophistic Generation', in W. Kullmann and J. Althoff

quite exclude such recitation.[80] Note in particular the word ἀκρόασιν, used again, as in the preceding chapter (21) which we discussed earlier, but this time (ch. 22) used about Thucydides' own work. The Penguin elides what on the traditional view is a difficulty, by translating 'easier to *read*'; but Jowett was right to say 'disappointing to the *ear*'.

It will now, I hope, be clear why I began as I did with that curiously neglected sentence from Thucydides i. 97 about those who ξυνετίθεσαν Greek history before Thucydides, and why I insisted that there is no necessary implication about writing; or rather, about writing a formal text written all at once. In the next section, when dealing with the epic background to Brasidas, I shall be mentioning the so-called New Simonides. This is a poetic text which treats the Persian Wars, a historical event, but does so a generation before Herodotus. The implications of this for fifth-century historiography have still to be evaluated. Boedeker has suggested interestingly that a recitation of a historical poem like that of Simonides could have been one of the things Thucydides had in mind by *agonisma* at i. 22 and by *mythodes* at i. 21. 1.[81]

It will be seen that I regard objections framed in terms of Herodotus' publication-date as very unrewarding and old-fashioned. But even if we accept the premiss, it is not enough to assert a 'publication date' of 414 for Herodotus. What about the date at which Thucydides made *his* work on the Ten Years War available? (We shall see that for Kennelly books v–viii of Thucydides hardly exist.) At one point Kennelly[82] proposes that Thucydides' Pisistratid digression in book vi was available before 424 and that Herodotus was reacting to it, not the other way round. This is startling and strained, but in 1992 I recognized the possibility that the two men were 'in a real sense contemporaries and rivals' (see below, p. 123) and the intertextual implications of this particular suggestion about Th. vi. 54 ff. do not bother me unduly.[83] But it is hardly logical to propose wildly early pre-publication by Thucydides of this isolated bit of *his* work, while refusing to countenance the surely easier hypothesis of

(eds.), *Vermittlung und Tradierung von Wissen in der griechischen Kultur* (Tübingen, 1993), 225-44, at 244, arguing that Th.'s 'contest to be heard for the moment', ἀγώνισμα ἐς τὸ παράχρημα ἀκούειν, 'must bring strongly to mind the rhetorical and epideictic performances of the sophistic generation'. See also Boedeker (below, n. 81).

[80] For Th.'s different ways of negating propositions see below iv. 62. 3 n. on τοὺς δ᾿ ἀντὶ τοῦ πλέον ἔχειν etc.

[81] D. Boedeker, 'Simonides on Plataea: Narrative Elegy, Mythodic History', *ZPE* 107 (1995), 217-29, a paper I first heard and admired at the APA convention at Atlanta, Ga., in December 1994.

[82] Kennelly (above, n. 73), 144.

[83] See also *Greek Historiography*, 22 n. 41, where I discuss the possibility that on certain issues 'Th. may be in a way prior to Hdt.'. I was there thinking of the relation between e.g. Hdt. vi. 108 and Th. iii. 68 (interest of both historians in Plataia, a topical subject in the early 420s). We can add that Hdt. viii. 126 ff. spreads himself on Potidaia—because it was in the news at the beginning of the Peloponnesian War? Cp. Th. i. 56 ff. See also below, iv. 104. 4 n. on ἐπὶ τὸν ἕτερον etc.

pre-publication, in the form of recitation, by Herodotus. In any case the most extreme simultaneous proponent of a late view of Herodotus and an early view of Thucydides has still to reckon with book v, and above all with the Sicilian books of Thucydides, which on any view are later than 414; not to mention book viii. And if we are realistic about the Archidamian War books, which include e.g. material (ii. 99 ff.) about Archelaos of Macedon who only began his reign in 413, and which as we shall see in the next section explicitly compare Brasidas to developments later than the Sicilian expedition (iv. 81), we shall not see a problem, in terms of composition dates, about a Thucydides who is aware of Herodotus. See also below, Conclusion, pp. 120 ff.

To summarize so far. I stress the significance of i. 97. 2 and i. 21 as showing that Thucydides had predecessors, and that he was aware of them. If in both places we take the crucial verb to mean 'compose' without begging the question of writing, we shall be willing to imagine Thucydides reacting not merely to written narratives but to recited ones, like Simonides—or Herodotus. I agree with those who say that Thucydides did not have Herodotus only in mind here and elsewhere—v. 20 on dating by eponyms is surely aimed at Hellanicus (see my nn. on the ch.); but I do think Herodotus was one of the more obvious people he had in mind and on my rendering of ξυνετίθεσαν we can bypass the pseudo-problem of Herodotus' publication dates. Finally, nothing I have said or believe about predecessors prevents me from agreeing that Thucydides was an assiduous researcher out in the field.

That is all I think we can get from Thucydides' general methodological remarks, and from his remarks on his predecessors; and since he does not name Herodotus, we must now turn to those particular Thucydidean texts which have been thought to show dependence. I stress that the case for dependence is cumulative, as I have already indicated when discussing Stroud. That is, it is not enough to object to (for instance) my line about the 20 Corinthian ships, you must take on my thesis as a whole. Hence the extended list, covering all of Thucydides, which I have given as Annex B. At the beginning of his third chapter Kennelly[84] announces a 'systematic investigation of the actual degree of familiarity with the work of Herodotus which is evinced by Thucydides'. He is right that for a refutation of my position a systematic investigation was called for, but his own thesis in its present form does not provide it. The first step ought to be to collect and list all those passages of Thucydides which have been claimed to show familiarity with Herodotus. Obviously I could not provide anything so rebarbative in a Festschrift

---

[84] Kennelly (above, n. 73), 81.

article, but Annex B, with its 138 items, is an attempt which may be of use in future investigations. (A few are discrepancies, not parallels.)

Modern works (none of them cited by Kennelly) which argue for particular intertexts between Thucydides and Herodotus are cited below, in the course of Annex B. They include: G. Schneege's 60-page 1884 Breslau dissertation in Latin, on the historical relationship between Thucydides and Herodotus (good on particular passages, though slanted towards the Ten Years War); Schmid-Stählin's history of Greek literature, which has a useful list of passages in a footnote; Connor's 1984 book on *Thucydides* which discusses a number of parallels, easily pursued by chasing the index under 'Herodotus'; the entire output of Colin Macleod, for whom Herodotus, 'another tragic historian', was 'the most direct influence on Thucydides';[85] Immerwahr's *Form and Thought*; and H. Strasburger's famous and twice-reprinted article in *Hermes* 1958. The argument of the relevant part of Strasburger was developed in 1978 by Nanno Marinatos Kopff and Hunter Rawlings III. The parallel in question is an intriguing one, and is itself nowhere mentioned by Kennelly. It is the apparent echo of Herodotus' word for 'utter destruction', πανωλεθρία (see Hdt. ii. 120. 5) at Th. vii. 87. 6, at the end of the Sicilian expedition, where it appears in the form πανωλεθρίᾳ δὴ τὸ λεγόμενον. See Annex B under Th. vii. 87. 6. In between Strasburger and Marinatos–Rawlings, the alleged Herodotean resonance here had been denied by Dover in *HCT* for oddly unconvincing reasons to do with the religious outlook of the two men; but Strasburger's case was reasserted strongly by Connor in 1984, and I mentioned it in my 1987 book and discussed it in my 1992 article. Kennelly, then, has ignored one of the most discussed and most interesting candidates for a Herodotean allusion in Thucydides. Incidentally, Thucydides at vii. 87. 6 describes an event of 413; this is problematic even on the latest seriously held assumption about Herodotean 'publication dates', i.e. 414. Or rather it would be problematic for Kennelly if he showed awareness of the passage at all. Kennelly has, in fact, omitted the many significant Herodotean parallels in Th. v–viii altogether, except to make three points: (i) he asserts the non-Herodotean origin of the Zankle material, Th. vi. 4. 5 f.; (ii) he mentions the battle of the Champions at Th. v. 41; and (iii) he offers (see above) an unusual view of the Pisistratid excursus in book vi. (For references see Annex B under the relevant Thucydidean passages.) And yet, as we have seen, Kennelly claims to offer a systematic investigation of his topic, with no announcement of or apology for any restriction to the Ten Years War narrative. It is only to *that* narrative, i.e. to Th. i–v. 24,

---

[85] Macleod (above, n. 46), 157.

that theories about Herodotus' 414 publication date can possibly be relevant, even on Kennelly's own assumptions. The phrase 'systematic investigation' recalls exactly, but in view of Kennelly's non-citation of Macleod coincidentally, Colin Macleod's remark that 'the relation between Thucydides and Herodotus, so important and so obvious, has never been adequately or systematically investigated'.[86]

There are two basic strategies available for opposing my suggested parallels. Both are adumbrated in my 1992 article (Annex A below), which is by no means dogmatic about particular instances. First, if a parallel is simple and obvious, then the move will be to cry 'common knowledge' i.e. to admit the similarity but say there is no need to posit a debt. If the parallel is more lengthy and complex, the move will be to point up the discrepancies, and there will be some, and to say 'look at these discrepancies, they show Thucydides wasn't following Herodotus faithfully, therefore he wasn't following him or criticizing him at all'. As to the first strategy, I myself in 1992 listed a number of passages which though offering parallels did not, I argued, require us to suppose Herodotus was in Thucydides' mind; I added that sometimes other people such as Hellanicus may have been the objects of his remarks. We have already seen that one of Stroud's concerns was to deny that Thucydides got the twenty Corinthian ships from Herodotus, and Kennelly independently rejects my suggestion as well. Proof can hardly be had. But it is no disproof to urge against me, as Kennelly does,[87] that Thucydides might have cited other examples of Corinthian *euergesiai* listed in Herodotus such as their arbitration in Athens' favour against Thebes (Hdt. vi. 108), and that it is arbitrary to suppose that he went to Herodotus for just this one. In the context of the argument between the Corcyraeans and Corinthians, in which naval power features so prominently, an earlier naval *euergesia* was obviously a suitable reminder.

The other strategy, again borrowing from my own arguments against myself, is to point up discrepancies. Thus in what I still regard as one of the clearest bits of indebtedness in a speech, the allusion at Th. iii. 55 to the sixth-century Athenian rebuff of the Plataians and their approach to Kleomenes as described as Hdt. vi. 108, Kennelly simply repeats the list of small discrepancies from Hdt. which I noticed in 1992 and which I accounted for there. The point of principle is important. It was not to be expected that Thucydides should feel himself obliged to show a Talmudic respect for Herodotus' text. The historical events may be Herodotean but the rhetorical use made of them is new and we should expect variations or changes of emphasis. See, for instance, Annex A,

---

[86] See above, n. 85.   [87] Kennelly, 78.

p. 131, for the non-Herodotean Theban claim that their government in 427 was different in type from the medizing government of 480—an obvious rhetorical ploy. Finally, Kennelly notes that Thucydides did not get from Herodotus the statement that Plataia fell in the 93rd year after its alliance with Athens. Indeed he did not, but that statement is not part of the speech, it is in the narrative

But all this is to operate in far too narrow a framework of argument. My 1992 challenge was and is to find past events mentioned in Thucydidean speeches which are wholly unknown to us from the Herodotean tradition. I think I have not so far emphasized strongly enough how remarkable it is that the available pool of *topoi* about pre-479 history should apparently be so small. Did nothing happen in the seventh, sixth, and early fifth centuries BC, not to mention earlier periods, which Herodotus did not mention but which Thucydidean speakers might have done? Surely those centuries were teeming with incident, and yet (as Robin Osborne pointed out in the *BSA* for 1989[88]) virtually the only known Athenian event from the seventh century BC is the conspiracy of Kylon. Osborne's point was, not that nothing really happened, but that our evidence is very bad. How odd then that precisely this event, the Kylon affair, should feature in both Herodotus and Thucydides—odd, that is, on premises which deny the possibility of dependence. Incidentally my 1992 article was careful (see below, p. 128) to set out how much of Thucydides on the Kylon affair is *not* in Herodotus. But that weakens my thesis about speeches not at all, because the Kylon affair, like the 93-year date which I mentioned above, is not in a speech; and I have always said that in narrative and in digressions Thucydides cites alternative traditions, e.g. Hecataeus, more freely. Hence the non-Herodotean material in Thucydides' *Sikelika* is also irrelevant because Dover long ago suggested Antiochus as a source for that (see Dover cited at iv. 133. 3 n. on ἔτη δέ etc.). I shall return to the significance of the point about speeches versus narrative in section 5 (below, p. 84).

So much in defence of my general method and conclusions. I now move on to books iv–v. 24 which are after all the subject of this volume.

As it happens, the speeches in this section of Thucydides do not have many references to past history from the period covered by Herodotus; they do, in the form of *paradeigmata* used by e.g. Pagondas and Hippokrates, contain interesting references to pentekontaetia history, i.e. past history from the period covered by Thucydides himself; and I shall discuss those in section 5 (below, p. 84 ff.). But Herodotean allusions do not seem to occur in the iv–v. 24 speeches. That is not because such

---

[88] R. Osborne, 'A Crisis in Archaeological History? The Seventh Century BC in Attica', *BSA* 84 (1989), 297–322 at 296, compare 321.

references dry up after book iii; on the contrary I believe (see below, p. 84) that Alcibiades' claim that his family were hostile to tyranny presupposes Herodotus vi. 123 on the *misoturannoi* Alkmaionids. And Connor has detected a Herodotean similarity in the Melian Dialogue where v. 105. 2 on the law of the stronger resembles Xerxes at vii. 8; but that is a rather different sort of case, a similarity of sophistic argument, not an example of knowledge of the past taken from Herodotus. (See Annex B, entries under the relevant Thucydides passages.) So all my examples in what follows are taken from narrative, that is, they do not have a bearing on my stronger thesis and challenge, which had to with the speeches in Thucydides. Nevertheless they raise plenty of Herodotean issues; but I hope it will be remembered that I have never denied that in narrative and digressions Thucydides draws more freely on non-Herodotean tradition. I now take the iv–v. 24 passages in order.

That means I must first discuss and defend my 1992 suggestion that ἀτραπός or 'path' at iv. 36. 3, in a context explicitly discussing Thermopylai, presupposes Hdt. vii. 175, τὴν δὲ ἀτραπόν, δι' ἥν ἥλωσαν οἱ ἀλόντες Ἑλλήνων ἐν Θερμοπύλῃσι. The Greek in Thucydides is τῇ ἀτραπῷ περιελθόντων τῶν Περσῶν, 'when the Persians got round them by *the path*', the well-known path, I suggested. I grant that the story was not invented or first put into circulation by Herodotus. But Thucydides' language is brief and allusive—though not obscure; I conceded in 1992 that the word ἀτραπός was not quite unique in Thucydides, being used at iv. 129. 4. Kennelly,[89] however, offers the following argument against me: there were just two words the Greeks could choose from for path or track, ἀτραπός and τρίβος. Kennelly rules out τρίβος, as being less concrete and specific. Therefore, he says, for a specific path leading from one place to another there is no other word than ἀτραπός, i.e. Thucydides could not have expressed himself in any other way even if he had wanted to. This sounds neat, but it overlooks the most obvious word of all, namely ὁδός. For ὁδός used by Thucydides in precisely the sense 'mountain path' see v. 10. 10, the aftermath of the battle of Amphipolis: the Athenians fled πολλὰς ὁδοὺς τραπόμενοι κατὰ ὄρη. (For the first accusative here compare, with Classen/Steup, v. 58. 4.) Jowett translates v. 10. 10 as follows: 'by various mountain paths' and the Penguin has 'by various tracks over the mountains' For another use of ὁδός in this sense see Arr. *Anab.* iv. 29. 2, a 'rough and difficult path' (Brunt translates 'track') up Aornos, ὁδὸν τραχεῖαν καὶ δύσπορον. Returning to iv. 36, if Thucydides, working in complete independence of Herodotus and assuming ignorance of Herodotus on the part of his readers, had nevertheless wanted to allude to the Thermopylai incident, he could have

---

[89] Kennelly, 71 f.

spelt things out rather more, something on the lines of 'when the Persians came round by a ὁδός which a traitor called Ephialtes had showed them'. For Thucydides at iv. 36, the only point of the Pylos–Thermopylai comparison is the encirclement; the path is irrelevant and he could even have dispensed with the noun and rephrased things altogether. But a formulation with ὁδός would in light of v. 10. 10 have been perfectly good Greek. We should avoid the dictionary-fixated outlook which sees a path as a path, and a road as a ὁδός, as if the two notions were as distinct in ancient Greece as they are in modern America or Britain.

All that said, I happily admit that since 1992 the New Simonides (below, p. 40) has changed things for me as far as the Persian Wars go, by introducing a whole potential stage of narrative treatment earlier than Herodotus. (We should not overdo the novelty of Simonides; I suppose Solon's statement[90] that he freed the black earth is a kind of narrative poem about a recent historical event; but it is not exactly an epic handling.) Anyway, I might now wish to say that Herodotus in his turn may conceivably have been echoing Simonides or similar poetic treatments. (This is all conjectural because what we have of the New Simonides can be firmly associated only with the battle of Plataia, though we know that Simonides commemorated Thermopylai in epigram.) But it is surely very plausible to suppose that '*the* path' had embedded itself in the tradition, and I stand by my suggestion that it was the diction of Herodotus which was immediately influential on Thucydides. In any case the Persian Wars themselves feature in only a small percentage of the Thucydidean texts which bear on Herodotus. But before I leave iv. 36 and Thermopylai, let me mention a text in Th. vii which bears on the problem, the occurrence of the rare and epic word περισταδόν, found only at vii. 81. 4, about the surrounding of the Athenians in their Sicilian withdrawal. It occurs at *Iliad* xiii. 551, but also at Hdt. vii. 225. 3, about Thermopylai. Connor[91] adduced the parallel in favour of his general comparison of that Sicilian episode to Thermopylai. (Connor cited C. F. Smith's 1900 study of epic usage in Thucydides, for which see below, p. 46 n. 112). If this is right, it surely increases the chances that ἀτραπός is also some kind of intertext, given that at iv. 36 Thermopylai is actually mentioned, contrast vii. 81. A final point: Thucydides introduces the Thermopylai comparison at iv. 36 by saying 'to compare small with great', ὡς μικρὸν μεγάλῳ εἰκάσαι. This is a different attitude from that at i. 23. 1 where he was polemically concerned to minimize the Persian Wars by comparison with his own war; the attitude

---

[90] F 34 West, lines 5-7. [91] *Thucydides* (above, n. 45), 199.

at iv. 36 is in fact Herodotean. Is this perhaps a further indication that he here follows Herodotus, whereas at i. 23. 1 he rejected him? But both texts, I would say, indicate *awareness*. Note also that the apologetic 'to compare small with great' is itself Herodotean, see Hdt. iv. 99. 5, where he compares Attica to the Scythian coast and says λέγω δὲ ὡς εἶναι ταῦτα σμικρὰ μεγάλοισι συμβαλεῖν. Finally, if we accept that there is a Herodotean allusion here in Thucydides' choice of vocabulary, we need to ask *why* it is here? Connor,[92] without specifically discussing ἀτραπός, connects the Thermopylai parallel with the Spartan surrender a few chapters later (iv. 40. 1): 'an expectation that Spartans would resist as they had at Thermopylae underlines the surprise at their surrender on Sphacteria.' Our conclusion about ἀτραπός enhances Connor's already attractive suggestion.

I pass now to iv. 102, the chapter about the background to the fall of Amphipolis. This begins with a statement about location: this, he says, is the site which Aristagoras the Milesian tried to colonize when fleeing from King Darius, but he was expelled by the Hedonians. This is one of only two allusions in Thucydides to the Ionian Revolt (the other is vi. 4. 5). One might have thought the Revolt would feature in the *Archaeology*, but it does not. Anyway, the story of Aristagoras' Thracian failure is also told by Herodotus, v. 124–6, cp. v. 11. In particular, I think Thucydides' word φεύγων is pejorative and shows that Th. followed or at least agreed with Herodotus' view (v. 124. 1) that Aristagoras was a poor-spirited creature who fled for that reason. But as I said in 1992 the verbal similarities are not close, and the historical facts could (especially in view of Thucydides' Thracian connections) be put down to common knowledge, or to awareness of authors other than Herodotus, and in 1992 I therefore classed this among passages for which no relationship with Herodotus need be posited. However, Macan, in his commentary on Hdt. v. 126, thought that Thucydides was here correcting or amplifying Herodotus' version, which was less full; and Lisa Kallet-Marx has pointed out to me a point I missed in 1992, namely that for Thucydides' purposes in this chapter, which is about *Athenian* attempts to take over the place, the actions of the *Milesian* Aristagoras were strictly irrelevant. Note the methodological point where Thucydides basically agrees with Herodotus but differs from him in detail, the sceptical move is to say that the discrepancies prove independence. But the same discrepancies may be evidence of silent correction.

I move on seven chapters now to iv. 109. This is about the Athos peninsula. One can readily admit that Xerxes' canal does not by itself

---

[92] Connor, 118 n. 19.

require us to remember our Hdt. vii. 122, but with Thucydides' ἔσω προύχουσα Gomme compared Hdt. vii. 22. 3 αἱ δὲ ἐκτὸς Σάνης, ἔσω δὲ τοῦ Ἄθω οἰκημέναι. More important is the list of five minor Thracian places which follows. Thucydides' order is Thyssos, Kleonai, Akrothooi, Olophyxos, and Dion. Herodotus' order is almost but not quite the reverse (vii. 22. 3): Dion, Olophyxos, Akrothoon, Thyssos, Kleonai. Kennelly remarks that the order is not the same and leaves it at that, i.e. he is using the discrepancy to prove Thucydides' independence. Kennelly, whose discussion is evidently reliant on Gomme, has not dug deep enough. In particular he has not asked which order is the correct one. The crucial point is the order Thyssos then Kleonai; on this it looks as if Thucydides was silently correcting Herodotus, whether or not Thucydides was right to do so. But was he? Care is needed here because Thucydides' order has itself been evidently influential on the speculative archaeological identifications offered by, for example, Michael Zahrnt,[93] e.g. those of Thyssos at Zographou and Kleonai at Xiropotamu. But the argument is not circular because the periplograph Ps.-Skylax (66) has Thucydides' order, and, as the authors of *ATL* remark, he was writing an account of a coasting voyage and must have known what he was talking about, i.e. he did not just transcribe Thucydides. Lest it be thought an eccentricity of my own to see a Herodotean aspect here, I note that Gomme says that Herodotus' description 'looks like Thucydides' authority', while adding 'though he repeats the information doubtless because he knew the country himself'. Gomme does not, however, discuss the small discrepancy which is my reason for arguing not merely dependence on but correction of Herodotus. To return briefly to Stroud, it will be seen that I am here supposing that Thucydides used his personal travels and knowledge to correct an error in a literary source. If Thucydides were nothing more than the book-historian which I am supposed to believe him to be, he would have lacked the means to correct Herodotus, because Skylax's periplous was a fourth-century production. I invoke Skylax merely to establish the correct relative ancient location of the five sites. I should say finally that the surviving parts of Hecataeus' *periodos* do not deal with this area, though if they did we might want to feed them into the equation somehow. From Herodotus' error, though, I feel that Hecataeus did not cover this bit of coastline in detail. Note finally the point of principle. It is not enough to direct attention to discrepancies between Thucydides and Herodotus because they may prove, not independence from, but correction of the original.

There is a further small but telling item in this chapter. Thucydides

[93] Zahrnt, 184, 182, 191, 194; see Annex B below under Th. iv. 109. 3, where other references are given.

concludes about these wild and woolly Athos places 'they are inhabited by a mixed population of barbarians, speaking Greek as well as their own language', οἰκοῦνται ξυμμείκτοις ἔθνεσι βαρβάρων διγλώσσων. With this compare Hdt. vii. 22. 2, also about Athos, οἰκήμενον ὑπὸ ἀνθρώπων, 'is inhabited by men', where Macan suggested adding βαρβάρων or διγλώσσων, precisely on the basis of Th. iv. 109. This suggestion appears in the apparatus to the 1926 issue of Hude's OCT of Herodotus, having appeared too late for the first printing. Either emendation, but especially the more striking διγλώσσων, would increase the similarities between Herodotus and Thucydides, though obviously it would be circular to invoke the emended text as further 'proof' of Thucydides' dependence on Herodotus. Macan's note is amusing: the transmitted text of Herodotus, he says, is almost impossible: 'it is inhabited by men [not by wild beasts, as you might expect from my description]'. However, Powell's lexicon to Herodotus finds no difficulty in taking ἄνθρωποι in the sense 'inhabitants', i.e. human beings. But the emendation remains attractive.

Before I leave ch. 109, I may mention a further intriguing amplification of the information provided by Herodotus, on the topic of the occupants of Lemnos. Thucydides, still talking about the ethnic make-up of the Athos peoples, mentions Pelasgians descended from the Tyrrhenians, i.e. Etruscans, who once inhabited Lemnos. Now Pelasgians are said at Hdt. v. 26 to occupy Lemnos, but the Etruscan presence on Lemnos is Thucydides' own contribution; at i. 57. 1 Herodotus does connect Pelasgians and Tyrrhenians and Krestonians, but that is not the same thing (the same chapter also puts the Pelasgians in Attica). Modern philology provides unexpected support for Thucydides over the Etruscan–Lemnian connection, by detecting Etruscan features in a fifth-century stele from Lemnos; see Rix, Heurgon, and Penney cited in Annex B under Th. iv. 109. Did Thucydides know something that Herodotus did not, and was he keen to tell us about it? In general we may say that when talking about these northern places, Thucydides insists, as Herodotus did not to anything like the same extent, on their colonial relationships. But I wish to reserve that whole splendid topic until section 4, Thucydides and ξυγγένεια.

It will be seen that I stand by my 1992 thesis, and that the small qualifications I now feel inclined to make are the result of the publication of the New Simonides, not of the criticisms of Stroud and Kennelly, neither of whom have raised any category of objection that I had not myself allowed for, both of whom have attended to a mere fraction of the evidence, and both of whose individual objections can be easily dealt with. I confess that while agreeing that we are dealing with probabilities, not provable certainties, and that there is always going to be room for argument about individual items, I find it hard to see why anybody approaching the problem with detachment should want to maintain so perverse a general position as that Thucydides 'worked largely, if not entirely, in independence [or even 'ignorance'] of Herodotus'.[94] One motive is the desire to vindicate a late publication date for Herodotus; but I suggest that such a rigid approach in terms of publication dates is itself old-fashioned and should be abandoned.

What finally of Stroud? Most of his essentially Corinthian case I have discussed by now, but I wish to end as I began with those Thucydidean 'predecessors' of i. 97. 2. That passage was concerned with the period of and up to the Persian Wars, it was not about predecessors who had covered the Peloponnesian War. Stroud objects to my suggestion that Thucydides kept up with the literature on his subject; 'there were', he says,[95] 'not too many books yet written that could tell him about the Peloponnesian War'. Again this sounds neat at first, but is directed against a straw person, somebody who thinks that Thucydides was engaging intertextually with authors of works devoted to the Peloponnesian War. Rephrased a little, that yields what I mean, namely that Thucydides was engaging intertextually with one author in particular whose work contained forward allusions to the Peloponnesian War. I refer of course to Herodotus, and to the striking fact that where we find Peloponnesian War items both in Thucydides and in Herodotus, Thucydides can each time be plausibly supposed to be correcting Herodotus. I give four well-known examples, all taken from Annex B: (i) with Th. ii. 8. 3 on the earthquake on Delos contrast Hdt. vi. 98; (ii) Th. ii. 2. 1 on the Theban attack on Plataia seems to correct Hdt. vii. 233; (iii) with Th. ii. 27. 1 on the Aeginetans compare Hdt. vi. 91, where however there is an additional curse motif; and (iv) Th. ii. 67, on the killing of Aristeus, eliminates the religious element from an episode at Hdt. vii. 137. How odd that on all these points Thucydides should differ from Herodotus. Of course we could take the topsy-turvy publication theory and say that Herodotus was correcting Thucydides, but I have perhaps said enough about such theories already. And I do not want to go here into all the passages outside iv–v. 24 which I discussed in 1991–2, including the one normally, though not by any means always, thought to be anti-Herodotean, namely the Spartan paragraph at i. 20; see below, pp. 126, 139. Nor have I talked, as I did in my 1987 book, about general thematic differences between Thucydides and Herodotus, for instance their different attitudes to women, religion (see v. 16. 2 n.), causation, and so on.

---

[94] Kennelly, 1, cf. 3.   [95] Stroud, 301, citing my *Thucydides*, 3.

That is not because these issues are not important or relevant, but because the sceptic can always say that Thucydides' different outlook reflects independence and ignorance, not a desire to distance himself from or improve on Herodotus. The first thing, as it seems to me now and as it seemed to me in 1992, is to establish, at the level of detail, Thucydides' knowledge of what Herodotus had said, and to try to refute the position that Thucydides wrote in ignorance of Herodotus. It is depressing to recall that, before World War One, Jacoby wrote in his Pauly article on Herodotus:[96] 'of course Dahlmann's idea that Thucydides didn't know Herodotus' work at all, or that he wasn't engaged in polemic against him at all, is something that scarcely anybody believes any longer.'

3. *Thucydides' presentation of Brasidas: iv. 11–v. 11 as the* aristeia *of Brasidas?*

Plato, towards the end of the *Symposium*[97] (221c), makes Alcibiades praise the uniqueness of Socrates in a priamel or paratactic comparison. You may, he says, compare Brasidas and others to Achilles, or you may compare Pericles to Nestor or Antenor, but you will never be able to find a likeness to Socrates. This comparison of Brasidas to Achilles makes a good starting-point for this section. I propose to see how far this comparison can be pushed; it reads to me as if it was expected to be familiar, perhaps even a sympotic *topos*. Any student of Thucydides' debt to epic must be interested in any Homeric colouring which Thucydides gives to the man who out-generalled him in 424. If that man was a super-man then it might follow that Thucydides' own performance was excusable: as Wade-Gery put it in the *OCD* entry under Thucydides,[98] 'not to have been a match for Brasidas does not prove him a bad general'. Actually the question of Thucydides' own responsibility for Amphipolis seems to me one of those intriguing but essentially unanswerable questions: unanswerable because virtually all the evidence is Thucydidean. So my interest in the Homeric aspect of Brasidas is simply part of a wider

[96] *RE* suppl. ii. 505.

[97] 221c: οἷος γὰρ Ἀχιλλεὺς ἐγένετο, ἀπεικάσειεν ἄν τις καὶ Βρασίδαν καὶ ἄλλους, καὶ οἷος αὖ Περικλῆς, καὶ Νέστορα καὶ Ἀντήνορα—εἰσὶ δὲ καὶ ἕτεροι—καὶ τοὺς ἄλλους κατὰ ταῦτ' ἄν τις ἀπεικάζοι· οἷος δὲ οὑτοσὶ γέγονε τὴν ἀτοπίαν ἄνθρωπος, καὶ αὐτὸς καὶ οἱ λόγοι αὐτοῦ, οὐδ' ἐγγὺς ἂν εὕροι τις ζητῶν, οὔτε τῶν νῦν οὔτε τῶν παλαιῶν . . . 'If you are looking for a parallel for Achilles, you can find it in Brasidas and others; if Pericles is your subject you can compare him to Nestor and Antenor (and they do not exhaust the possibilities); and you can make similar comparisons in other cases. But our friend here is so extraordinary, both in his person and in his conversation, that you will never be able to find anyone remotely resembling him either in antiquity or in the present generation . . .' (tr. W. Hamilton, Penguin). The passage is adduced by Howie, *Parnassus* 1992 (see n. 99 below), 445.

[98] *OCD*³ 1517, col. 1.

conviction that Thucydides owed a debt to epic, and in particular that he may—as J. G. Howie has plausibly suggested[99]—have seen in Brasidas, who was one of the war's few outstanding military heroes, an opportunity to write a heroic *aristeia* (for which word see below). As a historian I do have an interest in Thucydides' emphasis or over-emphasis on the heroic individuality of Brasidas, but that interest has little to do with whether Thucydides was unjustly exiled. It is rather that the heroic emphasis leads me to wonder if the exaggeration, which such a handling inevitably implies, has led to historical distortions; for instance, did it lead Thucydides to depict Brasidas as more of an independent operator than he really was or even can have been at this period of Spartan history? So in the first half of the present section I shall try to make the case that Thucydides handled Brasidas in a distinctive and heroic way; in the second half I shall ask what historical distortions this handling may have produced.

The general issue of the relation between fifth-century historiography and epic is an excitingly topical subject, with the recent publication of

---

[99] J. G. Howie, "*Η ΑΡΙΣΤΕΙΑ ΑΠΟ ΤΟΝ ΟΜΗΡΟ ΕΩΣ ΤΟΝ ΞΕΝΟΦΩΝΤΑ*", *Parnassos*, 34 (1992), 425–88, in Greek, with English summary at 447–8. Drawing on T. Krischer, *Formale Konventionen in der homerischen Epik* (Munich, 1971), Howie sets out the elements of the major *aristeia* in Homer, 'a pattern of propitious beginnings, achievement, mishap, recovery, and triumph passed through by certain heroes of the *Iliad*, including Achilles and Hector'; the mishaps include the wounding and fainting of Brasidas, which I discuss below. As regards Th. and Brasidas, Howie argues as follows (I quote his summary in full because the publication is out-of-the way):

'By subtly echoing the Homeric scheme Thucydides makes Brasidas resemble a Homeric hero, so that his courageous conduct and serious wounds at Pylos and the number of lucky breaks enjoyed by the Athenians (particularly the fire that swept Sphacteria before Cleon arrived) cast a negative light on the Athenian victor at Pylos and on Sphacteria, like that shed on Hector and the Trojans as assisted by Zeus, and palliates the Spartan defeats, as if Brasidas were a Homeric hero who could look forward to renewed success after recovering from his wounds. Brasidas' successes against the Athenians at Megara and in the Thraceward region are then the hero's recovery, and the victory over Cleon the triumph over a prominent adversary compromised and compelled to fight by the hero's renewed success. Cleon, on the other hand, is made to look at best like Hector, forced after disproportionate success to fight a superior adversary and killed while fleeing before the walls of Amphipolis. Brasidas, too, is killed, fighting courageously, and is buried splendidly and honoured with a heroic cult. Thus, the lucky fulfilment of Cleon's mad promise to take Sphacteria is like the luck of the man who acts wickedly and is saved by good luck from the charge of madness in Solon's *Prayer to the Muses* (F13W. 69 f.). Any version, known or conceivable, more creditable to Cleon is eliminated by the motif of chance in the manner of Pindaric myth-revision or Herodotean apologia. In Brasidas Thucydides presents an exemplary figure comparable in instructive value with Homer's heroes, and here, too he emulates the poet after already claiming, in his *Prooemium*, to recount a conflict on a larger scale and with more suffering than the Trojan War (see *Klio* 66 (1984), 502–34). Knowledge of his readers' culture enables Thucydides to cast Brasidas and Cleon in these instructive roles, with an effort as partisan as it is timeless'.

It will be seen that I agree with and applaud much of this; in what follows I offer some additional literary points before proceeding, in the second half of this section, to consider the historical problems created by Th.'s presentation of Brasidas, particularly in his relation to the Spartan home government. Howie's fine article does not discuss this problem, or the Akanthos speech.

An English translation of Howie's paper is projected and would be very desirable.

what is being called 'the New Simonides'.[100] The interest of the new text for our purposes is twofold: first, it seems to describe, in elegiac verse, the battle of Plataia in 479 and thus provides a literary account of the Persian Wars at least a generation earlier than Herodotus; second, it draws an explicit parallel between the Persian Wars and the Trojan. The new text provides a bridge between epic and historiography. The New Simonides is a missing link, a more obviously epic handling than Herodotus of what were none the less events in living and recent memory. We saw in section 2 (above, p. 29) that Thucydides' Sicilian narrative ends with a Herodotean allusion which itself suggests Homer; the New Simonides gives extra point to such intertexts. We recall for instance that one theme of Thucydides' *Archaeology* is to assert the superiority of the Peloponnesian War to the Trojan as well as to the Persian war.

But though I have just been rolling Thucydides and Herodotus together as people who both had the Trojan War in mind, there are big differences. Thucydides' Homeric allusions tend to be less obvious than those in Herodotus, who lets his characters talk at solemn moments in fragments of Homeric hexameters, 'on the razor's edge', 'Agamemnon would groan aloud', and so on. That sort of thing is much rarer in Thucydides,[101] though we shall be noticing an unobtrusive hexameter in Brasidas' speech at Akanthos.

With all that as preface, I turn to the section of the Peloponnesian War with which we are concerned, and to Plato's analogy between Brasidas and Achilles. What kind of things is Plato's Alcibiades likely to have had in mind? First and most obvious, both Brasidas and Achilles died παναώριος, 'cut off before their time', 'doomed to an untimely end', as LSJ translates the word (*Iliad* xxiv. 540, where Richardson[102] suggests there is a hint that Achilles did not live to look after Peleus). Second, both are forceful and individual speakers, see further below and section 6 (on speeches). Third, both are men of ἀρετὴ καὶ ξύνεσις (iv. 81. 2). Or, as the Budé edition of the *Symposium*[103] puts it, Brasidas left behind the memory of 'un beau chef et d'un beau charactère'. But we shall need to investigate whether Brasidas merely *seemed* to have these qualities, being really an artful deceiver—and we know what the Homeric Achilles thought of such people: he hated them like the gates of Hades.[104] Fourth and finally, I suggest that the solitariness of Brasidas, ostensibly alienated

---

[100] The 'New Simonides': P. Oxy 3965 with Parsons' commentary, and M. L. West, 'Simonides Redivivus', *ZPE* 98 (1993), 1–14; D. Boedeker (above, n. 81).

[101] See *Greek Historiography* (above, n. 54), 67.

[102] N. J. Richardson, *The Iliad: A Commentary*, vi. *Books 21–24*, general editor G. S. Kirk (Cambridge, 1993).

[103] (1966), 88 n. 3.

[104] *Iliad* ix. 312–13 with J. Griffin, *Homer: Iliad IX* (Oxford, 1995), n. on the passage.

from the jealous *protoi* or 'first men' back home (iv. 108. 7), has something Achillean about it. But again, one of my tasks will be to investigate whether this alienation was real, or a literary device by Thucydides, or a political convenience adopted or acquiesced in by a cynical Sparta which wanted to capitalize on Brasidas' successes.

Let us look more closely at Thucydides' handling of Brasidas. He does not feature for the first time in book iv, but in book ii; he is first mentioned for his action at Peloponnesian Methone (ii. 25) where Thucydides uses the characteristic verbs διαδραμών and ἐσπίπτει for his dash to save the place; and then later in books ii and iii he is found as adviser, ξύμβουλος, to Knemos and Alkidas in turn (ii. 85. 1; iii. 69. 1). Already at Methone the specification of Brasidas by reference to his speed is, as Connor puts it, 'all the more striking when the reader remembers the repeated criticism of the Spartans for their slowness',[105] e.g. i. 71. 4. But despite these early appearances of Brasidas, there is no doubt that his time of glory is in iv–v. 24 which can thus be called his *aristeia* (fem. sing., contrast the neuter pl. sense, below, p. 355). This is a term which has been used since antiquity for those books of the *Iliad* in which a single hero dominates the narrative for a period, like Diomedes, Agamemnon, and Menelaos in books v, xi, and xvii respectively (the *aristeia* of Diomedes was called just that as early as Herodotus: ii. 116. 3). From the *Iliad* we are familiar with heroes like Poulydamas who play a minor role before their major one,[106] so there is nothing unHomeric about an episode like Methone coming before the main *aristeia*.

Brasidas enters book iv at Pylos, urging on his troops as trierarch until he is wounded and swoons away. Thereafter he disappears for fifty-five chapters, until he is abruptly dropped into the Megarian narrative at iv. 70. We discussed the peculiarities of this passage above (p. 13), where we saw that it is a striking instance of narrative displacement. Thucydides tells us that Brasidas was in the region of Megara because he was preparing an expedition to the Thraceward region—a remarkably casual way of telling us about a plan which must have been formulated some time earlier, and which was to be decisive in ending the whole Ten Years War. Moreover, the motive for the Brasidan expedition is delayed still further, until 78–9. This is an example of what Oliver Taplin, in connection with Homer, calls the 'technique of increasing precision'.[107] What is the point of this? One effect is to increase the impact of Brasidas' thunderclap appearance at Megara. It cannot be said that we have been waiting for his reappearance in the way that we wait for Achilles to

---

[105] Connor, 128 n. 45.
[106] *Greek Historiography*, 162 n. 79, citing *Iliad* xiv. 449, xviii. 249 ff. and xxii. 100.
[107] O. Taplin, *Homeric Soundings* (Oxford, 1992), 198.

re-enter the fray; but we have been told enough about him to realize that he is indeed, as Thucydides says at 81, δραστήριος, a supremely energetic man. In a distinction offered by Gill,[108] Brasidas is defined in terms of character rather than personality, an initiative-taking agent rather than as psychologically passive. Brasidas' reappearance is a surprise, but once he has appeared, it is *not* a surprise that Megara eludes the Athenians, as a direct result of Brasidas' intervention. At 78 Brasidas runs through Thessaly, where we are told he has his friends, ἐπιτήδειοι, in this, the homeland of Achilles. This chapter recalls our first meeting with Brasidas at ii. 25, because it is full of words indicative of speed, running, and so on. Only when Brasidas has arrived in Perdikkas' territory does Thucydides pause to tell us why the expedition happened at all and to describe, in ch. 80, the atmosphere in Sparta, including worries about helots, at the time when Brasidas left. We learn (79) that Brasidas had been brought there by the Thracians and by Perdikkas. But there is some complexity here to which we shall have to return, because it is important for the understanding of Brasidas' position: in ch. 81 Brasidas is sent out by the Spartans in response to northern requests; but is also said to be positively eager to go. That is, Thucydides sees Spartan policy as being on the one hand suggested by northern friends and putative allies, and on the other hand as being pushed along by Brasidas' personal initiative. Lewis[109] is well aware of the double aspect to Brasidas' northern mission: he writes 'Brasidas jumped at the idea; events would show that he was capable of improving it beyond anything dreamed of or thought desirable in Sparta'. That is suitably circumspect but we shall have to return to it. I take Lewis's point to be that the Spartans did not think it desirable that Brasidas should implement a genuine liberation programme. But we still need to decide, first, what kind of understanding Brasidas had reached with the home authorities before he set out, an important topic on which there is neglected Thucydidean evidence; and second, whether Brasidas' plans for liberation were genuine in any sense which need have alarmed the Spartans. In fact our question is, was Brasidas ever an independent operator?

But for the moment I want to pass in review the other main sections in which Brasidas features. His first big success is at Akanthos, and I shall suggest in a moment that his oratory is highly distinctive (85–7). Then the Delion fiasco interrupts the Brasidas narrative, which resumes at 101 after which Brasidas is never really off-stage; and indeed (see the chart at Fig. 1) he is dominant for the next 45 chapters until his death at v. 10,

---

[108] C. Gill, 'The Character-Personality Distinction in Greek Literature', in C. Pelling (ed.), *Characterization and Individuality in Greek Literature* (Oxford, 1991), 1–31.
[109] D. M. Lewis, *CAH* v² (1992), 426.

with the exception of a couple of chapters at the end of book iv. There is nothing like this successful centrality of one individual anywhere else in Thucydides. One can even say that ch. 11 which describes his funeral represents a kind of *Iliad* xxiii or Funeral Games; it is unusual for Thucydides to dwell on the burial and funerary rites of *any* of his individual characters (there is of course ii. 34 which gives very full coverage to the *collective* burial of the Athenian war dead). The closest parallel to the material about Brasidas is the material about Pausanias at i. 134. 4; but there is also Themistokles at i. 138. 4, and Lichas at viii. 84. 5. Contrast the fullness of Xenophon on Agesipolis (*Hell.* v. 3. 19) or Ephorus on Agesilaos (Diod. xv. 93. 6). That would seem to be the end of the *aristeia*, but let me speculatively recall that for Achilles one aspect of being *panaorios* was being unable to care for his father in his old age. Now Brasidas' father was called Tellis, a patronymic with which Thucydides regularly provides him; Tellis in person makes just two closely connected appearances in Thucydides, at v. 19 and 24, where he is one of the swearers to the peace and alliance with Athens of 421. Both these appearances are immediately after the death of his famous son. Thucydides is hardly the man to emphasize the poignancy of this replacement of son by bereft father, but I offer Tellis as Peleus.

That is all rather general and I now look at the micro-picture. Is there any evidence that Thucydides had a distinctive vocabulary for Brasidas, a 'language of Brasidas' like the 'language of Achilles' which has been so vigorously debated since Adam Parry first propounded the idea?[110] But perhaps an equally helpful analogy, given that Thucydides is a prose historian, would be Syme's theory[111] that Tacitus gives Tiberius a special vocabulary. And, vocabulary apart, is there evidence that Thucydides handled Brasidas in any other unusual way? First vocabulary used of and by Brasidas. The first mention of Brasidas in book iv repays analysis in Homeric terms. As we saw, he is a trierarch at Pylos, chs. 11–12, where he distinguishes himself in the fighting from the ships. He urges on the

---

[110] A. Parry, 'The Language of Achilles', in *The Language of Achilles and Other Papers* (Oxford, 1989), ch. 1; M. Reeve, 'The Language of Achilles', *CQ* 23 (1973), 193–5; J. Griffin, 'Words and Speakers in Homer', *JHS* 106 (1986), 36–57, at 50–6, and in *Iliad IX* (above, n. 103), 110, n. on lines 307–429; R. Martin, *The Language of Heroes* (Princeton, 1993), 146–205, 220–2 for Achilles' special use of repetition. Brasidas represented in a distinctive way? See A. Boegehold, 'Thucydides' Representation of Brasidas Before Amphipolis', *CP* 74 (1979), 148–52; E. F. Francis, 'Brachylogia Laconica: Spartan Speeches in Thucydides', *BICS* 38 (1991–3), 198–212, esp. 211 for Brasidas' fondness for abstract nouns in -σις.

[111] R. Syme, *Tacitus* (Oxford, 1958); but on such 'idiolects' see A. N. Sherwin-White's review, *JRS* 49 (1959), 143: '... the changes in vocabulary may be less obvious to the ordinary reader than to the counting-machine of the Professor ... Would a reader be aware that Tacitus had only once used *diligere* when he applied it to the relationship between Sejanus and Tiberius, or does he experience a special shudder when Tiberius is described by the rare noun *tristitia*?'

44

FIG. 1. Thucydides iv–v. 24: chart showing the distribution of attention

(● almost always = a complete chapter, very occasionally a part chapter)

Book iv:

1–2, Sicily	●●	summer 425
3–6, Pylos	●●●●	summer 425
7, Thrace	●	summer 425
8–23, Pylos	●●●●●●●●●●●●●●●●	summer 425
24–5, Sicily	●●	summer 425
26–41, Pylos	●●●●●●●●●●●●●●●●	summer 425
42–5, Solygeia and Corinthian operations	●●●●	summer 425
46–8, Corcyra	●●●	summer 425
49, Anaktorion	●	summer 425
50, Artaphernes	●	winter 425/4
51, Chios	●	winter 425–4
52, Athenian operations on Mytilenean *peraia*	●	summer 424
53–7, Kythera	●●●●●	summer 424
58–65, Sicily, conference of Gela	●●●●●●●●	summer 424
66–74, Megara	●●●●●●●●●	summer 424

45

troops, and the verb used for this at 12. 1, ἐπέσπερχε, is most unusual in prose: it is in fact epic and poetic in flavour;[112] cp. *Iliad* xxiii. 430, Aesch. *Sept.* 689. To continue the Brasidas narrative, he is wounded, faints, and falls into the outrigger. The word for 'faints' is found here only in Thucydides. The word is ἐλιποψύχησε, and this is a Homeric expression and notion for swooning,[113] though more normally if your *psyche* leaves you you are dead. But it is certainly the expression for a Homeric swoon. So at *Iliad* v. 696 Pelagon pulled a spear from the thigh of Sarpedon, and his *psyche* left him, τὸν δὲ λίπε ψυχή, though he soon regains consciousness; similar is *Iliad* xxii. 467: when Andromache sees the dead Hector, she faints or rather temporarily breathes out her *psyche*, ἀπὸ δὲ ψυχὴν ἐκάπυσσε. It would be wrong to claim that the verb was *outré* in prose: Xenophon (*Hell.* v. 4. 58) uses it for Agesilaus' swoon; but I do think there is a Homeric resonance in the Thucydides passage, and in any case, the most remarkable thing is that he should record such a detail at all.

I move now to the main part of the *aristeia*. I have noticed already that in the first and most important Thucydidean passage about Brasidas' character, to which I shall return later, we are told he was though energetic, a doer, 81. 1 where the Greek word is δραστήριος. This is found at only one other place in Thucydides, at ii. 63. 3 in the mouth of Pericles. But for the full picture of Brasidas, or Brasidas as he seemed to be, we need to add 84. 2, where he is favourably assessed as a *speaker*, οὐδὲ ἀδύνατος, ὡς Λακεδαιμόνιος, εἰπεῖν. That is, Brasidas the effective doer is matched by Brasidas the effective speaker, and we think of *Iliad* ix. 443 and Phoinix's characterization of a leader as a speaker of word and a doer of deeds; this double requirement is also fulfilled by Pericles who was said (i. 139. 4) to be λέγειν τε καὶ πράσσειν δυνατώτατος.

Brasidas finally confronts us directly at 85–7 with his speech at Akanthos. Is the style distinctive? We have already noticed (p. 15) the opening abstract noun ἔκπεμψις, and the speech has other unusual abstract expressions, for instance 85. 3, 'I am surprised that you close your gates against me', where the Greek means literally 'I am surprised at your gate-shutting-out of me', θαυμάζω δὲ τῇ ἀποκλήσει μου τῶν πυλῶν. The strangest is at 87. 1, the quasi-Homeric word περιωπή; 'quasi-Homeric', because in Homer it means a 'vantage-point', as at *Iliad* xiv. 8, but in Thucydides, who uses it here only, it apparently means 'carefulness'. Brasidas' whole expression is οὕτω πολλὴν περιωπήν . . . ποιούμεθα, 'so much carefulness do we show'. I cannot here list all

---

[112] C. F. Smith, 'Traces of Epic Usage in Thucydides', *TAPA* 31 (1900), 69–81.

[113] J. Bremmer, *The Early Greek Concept of the Soul* (Princeton, 1983), 4. As Howie (above, n. 99), 438, cp. 427, observes, the wounding itself is a typical part of the *aristeia* pattern.

oddities of detail, but I must make good a promise to mention the hexameter in the speech, at 85. 5, ἐλευθερίᾳ, καὶ τῶν ἄλλων Ἑλλήνων, δεινὸν ἂν εἴη. Not an obvious or intrusive one but there all the same. More generally the speech is urgent and has a lot of repetition, a feature which Martin has recently shown[114] to be very much a feature of the Homeric Achilles; thus Brasidas uses the word ἐλευθερία ('freedom') and cognates eight times in the speech, and there is repetition of ἐπι-φέρειν and of τιμωρὸς ἀδύνατος. (See detailed nn. on 85–7.) The insistence of Spartan liberation is understandable because it is some time since we have heard anything about it (nothing since bk. iii), indeed Brasidas starts with an apology for being so long coming.

So far I have written as if I think the speech is entirely a literary concoction, but as it happens this is almost unique among Thucydides' speeches in that it contains material which we can be absolutely sure was delivered. There are two relevant sentences in particular. The first is 85. 7, where Brasidas says that at Nisaia (the port of Megara) the Athenians refused to fight despite superior numbers. But at 108. 5 Thucydides says categorically and in his own person that this very statement by Brasidas was false. The statement at 108 is therefore hard evidence that Brasidas really did make this claim about Nisaia which was thus ἀληθῶς λεχθέν, 'actually said', in the formulation at i. 22. As Lewis put it,[115] 'this is the only Thucydidean speech which is demonstrably not free composition'. There is another statement in the speech which tends in the same direction, and this is of great interest for its bearing on another question also, that of Brasidas' relations with the Spartans at home. At 86. 1 he claims 'I have made the authorities at Sparta swear the most solemn oaths to respect the autonomy of any allies I bring over to their side'. Without corroboration from the narrative, this would be hard to believe, coming as it does straight on top of an identifiable lie (that about Nisaia), quite apart from the extraordinary prestige it implies Brasidas enjoyed at Sparta. But as it happens, narrative corroboration exists, at 88. 1, where we are told that the Akanthians 'made Brasidas give pledges to stand by the oaths which the authorities at Sparta had sworn before they sent him out, to respect the autonomy of the allies'. These oaths have not detained previous commentators (see above, p. 10, for Gomme), but they are important for the same reason that 108. 5 is important, as showing that that part of the speech was really delivered. The material about the oaths is important for another reason too, a historical one: if Brasidas really did extort these oaths from the home government we cannot assume quite as readily as modern scholars sometimes do, that his

---

[114] Above, n. 110.   [115] *CAH* v². 436 n. 142.

liberation propaganda and policies were at variance with the wishes of the home government. (See further below.) A final comment on 88: the verb for 'made him give pledges' is the unusual and Homeric πιστόω.[116]

The Akanthos speech is, I conclude, a cocktail of things actually spoken and things invented by Thucydides, and the speech has more in this second, that is, invented, category than I propose to list here. So we need to be cautious about using it for the reconstruction of a special and peculiarly Thucydidean 'language of Brasidas'. It would for instance be perverse to deny that Brasidas really did say a good deal about liberation. After Akanthos there is the Delion interlude; we then meet Brasidas rapidly moving against Amphipolis, a marvellously realized episode, as we noticed in section 1 above, when discussing narrative pace or rhythm. When Amphipolis is securely in Brasidas' hands, Thucydides pauses for another assessment of Brasidas, 108. 2: he showed himself 'generally moderate', ἑαυτὸν παρεῖχε, an expression I shall return to because it is crucial, and impressed the Athenian subject cities with his mildness, πραότητα. The word is used here only in all Thucydides, and the simple adjective πρᾶος never. The same is true of Thucydides' word for 'attract-ive' two paragraphs later, 108. 5: Brasidas told the allies things ἐφολκὰ καὶ οὐ τὰ ὄντα 'attractive but untrue'. (This is where Thucydides says that Brasidas' claim about Nisaia was a lie.) The whole important chapter ends with the statement that the leading men of Sparta were jealous of Brasidas. It has often been noticed that the judgements in this paragraph are less flattering to Brasidas than those in 81, and because 81 contains a specific reference to the war after the Sicilian expedition, scholars have argued that 108 was written first and that Thucydides changed his mind in a favourable direction about Brasidas. In my com-mentary I argue against this; and see below section 7, p. 121.

Brasidas' next speech is at 126 before the fighting with the Illyrians. There are further instances of unusual language here, such as para. 5 ἐπανάσεισις for the brandishing of weapons, or the boldly metaphorical use of αὐτοκράτωρ as an adjective for 'battle', 'the style of battle in which every man is his own commanding officer'. The narrative here-abouts has a good deal about what Brasidas was thinking or intending, and this is a good point to mention Mabel Lang's recent statistical study of participially expressed motivation in Thucydides, that is to say places where an agent's actions are prefaced by a word like 'knowing','wanting', 'perceiving'.[117] There are six top scorers in Thucydides: Brasidas, Nikias, Kleon, Demosthenes, Alcibiades, and (the one which surprised me at any rate) Perdikkas. Anyway Brasidas is no. 1. Nikias is a close second, but

---

[116] See C. F. Smith (above, n. 112), 80.

[117] M. Lang, 'Participially Expressed Motivation in Thucydides', *Mnemosyne* 48 (1995), 48–65.

nearly all his participles come from the Sicilian books. This seems further justification for arguing that Brasidas has a special status in Thucydides' narrative.

Brasidas' final full speech is at v. 9, and contains a Tyrtaean appeal to his second-in-command Klearidas to be a brave man, ἀνὴρ ἀγαθὸς γίγνου. But that is not quite Brasidas' last speech of all, which is at v. 10. 5: 'these men don't intend to fight, look how their spears and heads are waving', a contemptuous and confident cry, moments before Brasidas' own death, the shock of which is thus heightened. That then is Brasidas' *aristeia* in detail.

I have not discussed all Brasidas' speeches; but I anticipate section 5 by noting a further peculiarity of his speeches, specifically of his political speeches in the north. We shall see that Thucydides takes the trouble to indicate the respects in which Brasidas' post-Akanthos speeches departed from the Akanthos blueprint; I call this the periodically adjusted manifesto. This is, as we shall see, an innovation, and one not used again for any character other than and after Brasidas. (Nikias at vii. 69 improves on a slightly earlier speech, but one delivered to the same constituency and on the same occasion.) There are good reasons why this is appropriate treatment (no other character is represented on the 'campaign trail' in the same way); but in the context of the present section we should note the simple point that Thucydides bothers to do for Brasidas what he does for no other character.

Finally in this sub-section, we must reckon with the possibility that one method by which Thucydides underlines the extraordinariness of Brasidas is by giving him religious or quasi-religious coverage in ways which are not characteristically Thucydidean. This possibility depends on the detailed elucidation of three difficult texts; but because of the complexity of the second and third of them I deal with these in the commentary, merely referring forward to them briefly here. First there is the 'epiphany' or divine manifestation at Torone, iv. 116 (Brasidas offers a reward for the capture of the Torone fort but gives it to Athena because he judges that there had been divine intervention). The second is iv. 121. 1, a crux of great importance. The people of Skione came out to greet (προσήρχοντο) Brasidas 'like an athlete'. In the commentary I argue that Thucydides wrote some form of the imperfect of the verb προσέρχομαι, 'I come up to', rather than a form of the (actually non-existent) verb προσάρχομαι, which is supposed to mean 'offered first-fruits to'. (But it is possible that the imperfect which Thucydides actually wrote was the more normal form προσῇσαν, which is how Pollux—I argue—remembered iv. 121. 1.) The 'first-fruits' interpretation is the orthodoxy, and would be obviously and excitingly religious in its implications both for

Brasidas in particular and for the athletes generally to whom he is compared. But the idea of 'going up to greet' Brasidas, which on my view is implied by the verb προσέρχομαι, is itself remarkable enough, suggesting as it does the *adventus* or 'going-out-to-greet' a homecoming victorious athlete. Such extravagant welcomes, by which living individuals were given star treatment for a brief moment, had a religious tinge. No other person in Thucydides is described with this sort of detail. The battle of Amphipolis, with Kleon fleeing before the walls of the city, is Homeric in ways explored by Howie (above, n. 99). Finally there is the cult of the dead Brasidas at Amphipolis (v. 11. 1), a counterpart to his treatment at Skione when living. All this adds up to powerful and unique religious treatment.

I now pass from the first or more literary part of this section to the second and more historical part. If Brasidas is given this special literary handling, we need to ask what follows, and what Thucydides wanted us to *do* with these epic resonances. I now return to the historical circumstances of Brasidas' original mission. His sending out, his ἔκπεμψις as he himself would call it, is, as we saw, vaguely described at 81, where a double initiative is implied. On the one hand the Chalkidians and Perdikkas had asked for an army, on the other hand he himself is eager to go.

What was Brasidas' standing at this time? The starting-point must be the astonishing oaths (86. 1, the Akanthos speech), by which he claims to have bound the Spartans, a claim corroborated by the narrative at 88. 1. The language of 88 is crucial. The construction is indicative and categorical in its reference to the oaths which the Spartan authorities had sworn when they sent him out, τοῖς ὅρκοις οὓς τὰ τέλη τῶν Λακεδαιμονίων ὀμόσαντα αὐτὸν ἐξέπεμψαν. If he had wanted to, Thucydides could have included a distancing verb like 'which he had *said* the authorities had sworn', i.e. he could have left it open whether he thought Brasidas' claim was a lie. It seems that Thucydides believed that Brasidas made the claim, and unless we believe that Brasidas could perjure himself over a matter of oaths, or that the oaths *were* sworn but not through Brasidas' agency, we should accept that Brasidas' prestige was indeed great enough to allow him to force the Spartan authorities to swear them. This, if Thucydides was correctly informed, has the further interesting consequence that the later Spartan breaches of autonomy were instances not just of aggression but of actual impiety. Incidentally these oaths help to explain the Spartan insistence in the Peace of Nikias on the autonomous but tribute-paying status of Akanthos and other places; see my n. on v. 18. 5—a much discussed passage, but the oaths of 86 and 88 have never so far as I know been mentioned in connection with it. I do not suggest that the Spartans kept their oaths in any serious way. On the contrary they violated autonomy by installing proto-harmosts at iv. 132; and their betrayal in 421 of Brasidas' northern acquisitions was total and shameful.[118] What I am suggesting is that the insertion of the word 'autonomous' in this clause of the Peace of Nikias allowed the Spartans not just to feel politically better about their betrayals (this motive has often been noted) but that the word 'autonomy' also helped silence any religious qualms they may have felt about those oaths of 424.

So Brasidas made the Spartans swear these oaths. Let us turn from Brasidas to these Spartans. Thucydides tells us they wanted to get rid of some helots (80. 2); and it has also been more positively suggested, e.g. by Raaflaub,[119] that they wanted conquests to bargain with. This is, however, not stated by Thucydides as their original motive. It is a modern inference from the retrospective statement at 81. 2 that as a result of what Brasidas achieved the Spartans as a matter of actual fact had places to give in return for what they wanted to recover (he adds that they also enjoyed some lightening of the war on the Peloponnese). Raaflaub's suggestion may be right, but it is a nice example of a modern historian reasoning like Thucydides and inferring motivation from results. Lewis[120] is the only modern scholar to see the difference between intending a result and capitalizing on it: 'bargaining counters' may merely be what Brasidas' gains turned out to be, and here we should remember those oaths about autonomy. Brasidas' claim about the oaths implies not just that the authorities had reservations, but that these reservations had been discussed and overcome. This surely implies both that Brasidas had enormous prestige and that he was to some extent carrying out a policy which had been agreed and understood before he left. Contrast with this some statements by modern scholars. Brunt[121] writes 'it is evident that the home government and Brasidas were not of one mind on the purpose of the expedition'. Kallet-Marx[122] says trenchantly that Brasidas does not represent official policy, and that the Spartan leadership as a whole may still not have grasped the necessity of striking at Athens' financial power (a reference to 87. 3, from Brasidas' Akanthos speech; this is, as Kallet-Marx 172 rightly insists, an interesting reference in a Thucydidean speech to the importance of Athenian

[118] K. Raaflaub, *Die Entdeckung der Freiheit* (Munich, 1985), 252–3; A. B. Bosworth, 'The Humanitarian Aspect to the Melian Dialogue', *JHS* 113 (1993), 37.

[119] Raaflaub (above, n. 118), 252 n. 172.

[120] D. M. Lewis, *Sparta and Persia* (Leiden, 1977), 69 n. 121.

[121] P. A. Brunt, 'Spartan Strategy in the Archidamian War', *Phoenix*, 19 (1965), 255–80, at 275 = *Studies in Greek History and Thought* (Oxford, 1993), 107. A footnote directs the reader to the Appendix on Spartan factions, but this, though valuable, does not address the particular problem of Brasidas. (But I agree with Brunt's comment in his text a few lines later, that Brasidas 'was probably, like Lysander after him, a powerful and ambitious political figure, and not just a romantic war-hero'.)

[122] L. Kallet-Marx (above, p. 7 and n. 17), 171.

tribute). Again, Lewis judged that Brasidas' 'ambitious plans found no welcome at Sparta', and Westlake that he was 'pursuing policy divergent from the Spartan government'.[123] It is surely reasonable and correct to suppose that Brasidas favoured the sending of the expedition, but strictly the Greek just means he was personally keen to go ('jumped at it' as Lewis says); and we should not forget that the *initiative* came from the Chalkidians and Perdikkas, not from anyone at Sparta at all.

So which is the better view, that Brasidas' successes reflected, or that they were in opposition to, what Sparta wanted? The Thucydidean Brasidas is an unusual type of Spartan, raising expectations which later Spartans did not satisfy. For a firm statement of this view see iv. 81. 3, where however Thucydides might have added that Brasidas' own behaviour as liberator was not impeccable; thus, as Bosworth notes,[124] the Athenians were able to recapture Mende largely because Brasidas, off in Macedonia in pursuit of *la gloire*, left the place far too weakly defended (see iv. 123 and 130 ff.). But Kallet-Marx may well be right that in 424 other Spartans did not see the importance of removing revenue-producing cities from Athens.

On the one hand, the view of Brunt, Kallet-Marx, and Lewis is certainly well grounded in the text. The most explicit statement of tension is at 108. 7, the remark about the jealousy felt for Brasidas among the *protoi*. And the mission of Ischagoras at 132, who brings out young men (proto-harmosts, perhaps) to govern the newly taken Thracian cities, has often been seen as evidence of a Spartan wish to curb Brasidas. On the other hand there is full co-operation between him and the Spartan commissioners over Skione at 122. 4. Skione went over to Brasidas two days after the 423 armistice which basically froze territorial assets on a footing of *uti possidetis*; the date was disputed between the angry Athenians and the Spartans, though Thucydides for once adjudicates and tells us that the Athenians were in the right. At 122. 4 some Spartan commissioners go out and 'lay claim to Skione, relying on the evidence of Brasidas'. One might cynically say they would be unlikely to do anything else, but the passage does show that the Spartans were happy to take their cue from Brasidas when territorial gains were in

---

[123] D. M. Lewis, *CAH* v². 428; Westlake, 'Thucydides, Brasidas and Clearidas', *Studies* 78–83 (repr. from *GRBS* 21 (1980), 333–9) 81; see also Westlake, *Individuals in Thucydides* (Cambridge, 1968), 148, for Brasidas and 'the opponents of his policy at home'. Against this, note Plut. *Mor.* 219d (letter by Brasidas to the ephors). In his review of Connor (*JHS* 105 (1985), 185) Westlake claimed that Th. 'seems to have considered deception in war to be commendable (cf. vii. 73. 3), except perhaps in breach of oaths'. This shows an interest in oaths, and might have been a cue to bring on the oaths mentioned by Brasidas at Akanthos; but Westlake does not explain which oaths he has in mind. (Incidentally I see no commendation by Th. at vii. 73. 3.)

[124] Bosworth (above, n. 118), 37 n. 39.

question. Ch. 117 also has an evident bearing on the question, but the relevant sentence is desperately corrupt and cannot here be invoked without circularity. There is some more explicit evidence at v. 12–13: Rhamphias and some other leading Spartans are on their way to Brasidas with reinforcements; they turn back only when they hear he is dead, and Thucydides makes this interesting comment: 'they felt that they were not competent to carry out the plans of Brasidas, and in any case the Athenians had been defeated and had left the country.' The Greek is difficult, οὐκ ἀξιόχρεων αὐτῶν ὄντων δρᾶν τι ὧν κἀκεῖνος ἐπενόει. I have here changed Jowett's tendentious translation 'the great designs of Brasidas' as being too favourable or too sarcastic. The Greek just means 'what he intended' or 'had in mind'. Incidentally it seems clear, despite possible corruption of the kind suspected by Steup, that both parts of the explanation, Brasidas' plans and the Athenian defeat, represent the thinking of Rhamphias and his colleagues, and are not factual statements by Thucydides. Even on the neutral translation 'the plans of Brasidas', the implication is surely that Rhamphias thought, or reckoned the Spartans at home would think, that Brasidas' plans were merely impracticable now, not that there was anything wrong with them in principle. This, then, is the final piece of evidence that Brasidas and the Spartan decision-makers back home were pulling in the same direction, always assuming that Thucydides had any evidence for what Rhamphias thought, i.e.this is not just inferred motivation. On the other hand, we should not neglect the implication of the masculine singular verb ἐπενόει, 'what Brasidas intended'. The realities of Spartan decision-making are arcane to us. The best approaches are those which allow for tensions and indecision.[125]

At this stage I suggest we briefly broaden the argument and look at Sparta's way of doing things more generally. In the fourth century the Spartans sometimes found it convenient to disapprove of or distance themselves from policies or actions of their nationals while profiting from those actions or policies; one thinks of Phoibidas' seizure of the Theban Cadmea in the 380s, when the Spartans 'punished the offender but condoned the offence', as Plutarch put it, *Pelopidas* 6. The same may have been true in the fifth century. Thucydides iv. 117 on just about any reading of the corrupt Greek seems to say the Spartans were happy to go on benefiting from Brasidas' achievements. But we may readily imagine that if Brasidas had been less successful things would have been different. Literary considerations are also relevant, if I am right that part of Thucydides' aim is to present Brasidas as a man apart, a romantic

---

[125] Such as the excellent study by S. Hodkinson, 'Social Order and the Conflict of Values in Classical Sparta', *Chiron*, 13 (1983), 239–81. On the difficult v. 13. 2 see n. there.

53

loner; but he was never as cut off from home as, say, Hannibal in Italy, or the Roman commanders in Spain who caused J. S. Richardson to develop the concept of peripheral imperialism, i.e. policy made by the men on the spot because of the distances from, and slowness of communications with, the Roman senate.[126] Brasidas was not quite a free agent in this sense—witness what we said above about Ischagoras and Rhamphias. It is true that Thessaly was always difficult to get through, see Th. iv. 78 for precisely this point; but Ischagoras made it past the hostile Thessalians, and Rhamphas might have done so but for the turn of events. I must digress briefly on this. Gomme was right to insist that the Greek of v. 13. 1 means that the Thessalians 'were for preventing' the passage of Rhamphias, present participle κωλυόντων. It does not mean, as Steup thought, that the Thessalians actually stopped Rhamphias, in which case the motive about Brasidas' plans and the Athenian defeat would indeed be superfluous. So we need not and should not follow Steup who urged the deletion of the entire chapter on grounds of illogicality. I conclude that Brasidas' relations with the Spartans were more ambiguous, i.e. less bad, than is sometimes allowed. But we are ignorant about what really went on at Sparta, and like Thucydides himself at v. 68 we should be willing to admit as much. 'Sparta' and 'the Spartans' are abstractions, and there were no doubt divisions; Thucydides lets us glimpse them at v. 16 discussing Pleistoanax's recall from exile. Moreover, it is only to be expected that relations might deteriorate or improve over time. What for instance did Spartans at home think when they heard of Brasidas' rapturous reception at Skione (iv. 121. 1)?

From Brasidas' original mission and his relations with the Spartans back home I pass to his actual conduct. Let us return briefly to iv. 81. We saw that there was a double aspect to his mission: the northern powers asked for a Spartan army, and Brasidas wanted to go. That is not the only ambiguity in that chapter. At para. 2 he shows himself a man of justice and moderation and causes some places to revolt, while 'others he took by treachery', τὰ δὲ προδοσίᾳ εἷλε τῶν χωρίων. Jowett's translation is 'while others were betrayed to him', which smooths over the difficulty that the verb is active, 'he *took* places by treachery', and this does not look much like justice or moderation. But the point is, I suppose, that his perceived justice and moderation were what gave rise to pro-Spartan factions.

Here I think we come to the heart of the matter. Our feeling that Brasidas was an upright man, by contrast with the crooks back home in Sparta, is based very largely on the language of the important chapter iv. 81. We have seen that iv. 81. 2 says Brasidas 'showed himself just and

[126] J. S. Richardson, *Hispaniae: Spain and the Development of Roman Imperialism 218–82 BC* (Cambridge, 1986), 177.

moderate to the cities', ἑαυτὸν παρασχὼν δίκαιον καὶ μέτριον ἐς τὰς πόλεις. The nuance of translation here is crucial, and I must pause over it. I have changed Jowett's 'he gave an impression of justice and moderation in his behaviour towards the cities', partly because 'impression' is too openly cynical, partly because we do not want anything as concrete as 'behaviour', partly because the same expression is used at 108 of Brasidas and there Jowett has 'he showed himself'; one should surely be consistent over so close a parallel. The Penguin has 'conduct towards the cities', but this resembles behaviour in being a shade too concrete. Connor[127] has 'he presented himself as moderate and just to the cities', and this is better in that it avoids emphasis on actual conduct or behaviour, but 'presented himself' is a touch too cynical. The neutral 'showed himself just and moderate to the cities' is best. Thucydides does seem to be affirming Brasidas' justice and moderation, though it is true that there is in παρασχών a subtle emphasis on the perception of others. The closest Thucydidean parallel is the statement (i. 130. 2) that Pausanias 'made himself inaccessible', δυσπρόσοδόν τε αὐτὸν παρεῖχε.[128] This does not mean that Pausanias 'showed himself inaccessible but wasn't really'.

In his interpretation of this crucial passage, Connor reacts against the tendency of, for instance, Brunt and Gomme to assume that Thucydides himself shared the favourable evaluations of Brasidas there reported. Brunt had spoken of 'Thucydides' eulogy on Brasidas' justice'[129] and Gomme says Thucydides may have drawn 'perhaps too roseate a picture of Brasidas'.[130] Connor by contrast suggests here, as throughout his very clever discussion of Brasidas, that Thucydides was primarily concerned to report impressions, though Connor is rightly too cautious and scrupulous to deny that any of iv. 81 is authorial; his formulation is 'there is relatively little in the passage that indicates the author's own view and a great deal concerning contemporary reaction to him'.[131] That is, the focalizers are (in the main) people other than Thucydides. As a general comment on ch. 81 that is sound, but against Connor there is still the obstinate ἑαυτὸν παρασχὼν δίκαιον καὶ μέτριον, which was surely what Brunt and Gomme had in mind and which, as we have seen, should not be translated in a way which implies 'showed himself but wasn't'. Much the same is true of 108. 2 and the almost identical phrase μέτριον ἑαυτὸν παρεῖχε. Here Connor[132] thinks the focus is 'only secondarily on

---

[127] Connor, *Thucydides* (above, n. 45), 130–2.

[128] Bétant, 294, under παρέχειν, giving iv. 81 and i. 130 as instances of 'se gerere'; this seems better than LSJ⁹ under παρέχειν A. II. 3, 'with reflex. Pron. and a predicative, *show*, *exhibit* oneself so and so'.

[129] Brunt (above, n. 121), 276 = 107 of the 1993 reprint.

[130] Gomme, *Greek Attitude* (above, n. 5), 158.

[131] Connor, 131.

[132] Connor, 134.

Brasidas', the main theme is the rashness of the northern allies who trusted him. Again Thucydides seems to accept that Brasidas *showed* a moderation which he really did possess, i.e. Thucydides is the primary focalizer, a crucial point. This then is favourable. But at 108. 5 Thucydides says explicitly that Brasidas was a plausible liar, ἐφολκὰ καὶ οὐ τὰ ὄντα λέγοντος. No actual contradiction such as need make us embrace theories about late insertions and the like; but bluntly unfavourable and calling for an explanation.

Let us return for the moment to 81, in particular the sentence further down where Brasidas' ἀρετὴ καὶ ξύνεσις works favourably on the allies. The passage begins as if categorically and authorially attributing *arete* and *xynesis* (intellectual ability) to Brasidas, and this attribution is not cancelled; but Thucydides immediately slides to an emphasis on what people heard about it and their experience of it.

What does *arete* mean here? This is one of the hardest Thucydidean uses of the word to translate, and illustrates my point in section 1 above (p. 8) about the discipline of translating every word; Gomme only got away with ignoring the problem of interpretation by ignoring that of translation, indeed by ignoring the word altogether. The use of *arete* here also illustrates another of my points, about progress since 1955. Much has been written since 1955 about *arete*, beginning with Adkins's book of 1960, after which there were important contributions by Lloyd-Jones and Dover.[133] The problem with iv. 81 as with many other occurrences of *arete* is to know how far there is an ethical content. My own translation will be 'honourable conduct', which indicates that Brasidas' behaviour was thought to conform to the highest values to be looked for in a male military leader, while allowing that those values allotted esteem to an amalgam of soldierly, ethical and functional qualities.

So much for the evaluations of Brasidas in these two chapters, 81 and 108; there is much for which Thucydides is not the focalizer; but an important residuum for which he is. We need to ask the further question whether what Brasidas actually *does* proves him moderate, just, sincere, a man of *arete* and so on.

First, moderation. Two narrative passages come into question here. In the first, 105. 2, Brasidas offered moderate terms to the inhabitants of Amphipolis, τὴν ξύμβασιν μετρίαν ἐποιεῖτο. This was effective. The second concerns Torone, iv. 114. 1-2. The Athenians ask for a truce of one day; Brasidas grants them two days. The word 'moderate' is not used, but Babut[134] is right to see this as another example of Brasidas'

---

[133] A. W. H. Adkins, *Merit and Responsibility* (Chicago, 1960); H. Lloyd-Jones, *The Justice of Zeus* (above, n. 33), 2, 136-7, 158; K. J. Dover, *Greek Popular Morality in the Time of Plato and Aristotle* (Oxford, 1974), 60-1, 67-8, 165-6.   [134] D. Babut (above, n. 42), 432.

moderation. We need feel no difficulty about accepting that 'moderate' was Thucydides' authorial judgement on him; moderation is a weapon which can be wielded effectively by the most cynical of operators. Thus I have stressed Brasidas' rhetoric at Akanthos (iv. 85–7), but the same speech notoriously contained threats which weighed with the Akanthians as much as did the fine words (iv. 88. 1). If there was moderation here it was a matter of style and tact. The threat was real enough.

But what of the bigger claims, justice, *arete*, i.e. honourable conduct, and so forth? In particular, how reliable and sincere a liberator was Brasidas? Skione joined Brasidas of its own accord. The anger of the Athenians against the Skionaians was chiefly caused by the line Brasidas took over the dates. And when the Athenians settle down in front of Skione the place is, like Mende (on which see below), seriously denuded of defenders. Skione's punishment by Athens was terrible: v. 32. In the fourth century the fate of Skione was bracketed with that of Melos as the two great Athenian outrages (Isoc. iv. 100). But Skione was a Spartan outrage too because of the cool way Sparta betrayed it.[135] Indeed the elaborate and moving description of Skione's welcome to Brasidas (iv. 121) gains poignancy from the juxtaposition with the report of Kleon's proposal to put the male population to death (iv. 122. 6).

Then there is Mende. We saw that the loss of Mende was at least partly due to undermanning as a culpable result of the way Brasidas denuded the Pallene promontory of troops. The other reason is to be found at iv. 130, the behaviour of Polydamidas, a revealing incident. Polydamidas had been left in command of Mende by Brasidas; so much incidentally for autonomy. There was more than one faction at Mende and though the Athenians were known to be nearby, things inside Mende might have gone either way; but the issue was decided in two (for Sparta) disastrous seconds. One of the democratic group yelled 'we don't want to go out and fight'. Polydamidas now made a capital blunder: he seized the man and handled him roughly. All hell broke loose, the democrats grabbed their weapons, and Mende was back in Athenian hands. We are surely meant to reflect that Brasidas would have been rather better at crowd control than this. But if we are allotting blame, Brasidas deserves some, because Polydamidas was not one of the *archontes* brought out from Sparta; these do not arrive till ch. 134. He was Brasidas' own appointment. It is unfair to criticize the appointment without knowing the talent-pool available; but there is no doubt that things were coming apart for Sparta in the north even before clumsy Spartan home authorities began to assert themselves.

[135] Bosworth (above, n. 118), 37.

We are also surely meant to reflect that this is harsh Spartan liberation in action; the incident recalls the reasons given at iii. 93 for the failure of Herakleia in Trachis, the severe and unjust behaviour of the governors sent out by Sparta, and the phrase for 'unjust', οὐ καλῶς, is reiterated constantly by Thucydides to describe Spartan liberation, first about Alkidas in book iii (32. 2) and then again and again to describe the mess Sparta made of Herakleia (see *JHS* 1995, 67). With Polydamidas' physical violence, very much a feature of Spartan upbringing[136](Xen. *Lak. Pol.* ii. 3) compare Herodotus' description (vi. 75) of the way Kleomenes I goes round hitting in the face with his staff any Spartiate he meets. So there is certainly a contrast between Brasidas and Polydamidas, but it is one of style; and anyway we should not forget that Polydamidas was Brasidas' man.

During the vital period when Mende was returning to Athenian control, and Skione was being invested, Brasidas was away campaigning against the Illyrians. And here I must touch briefly on an aspect I have so far wholly neglected, the purely military. Whatever Thucydides' reservations about Brasidas as liberator, there is genuine admiration, which the reader cannot help but share, for Brasidas' extrication of his troops from Illyria at 125 ff., a first-class piece of professional soldiering. After a speech magnificently scornful of barbarian fighting methods, Brasidas forms a hollow square and leads an orderly retreat over a huge distance and under hostile pressure and after abandonment by Perdikkas' Macedonians; Brasidas himself brought up the rear with 300 picked men. It was a very tight spot indeed, out there in the middle of nowhere, and vastly outnumbered. Thucydides was a soldier too, and his admiration shines through.[137] And we can add Brasidas' behaviour minutes before his death at Amphipolis. He tells his men (v. 9. 10) I will show you I can not only give advice but fight too, and fight he does.

Before I leave Brasidas in policy and action, let me pause over the comparison to and contrast with the man who briefly succeeds him, Klearidas. Westlake devoted one of his last articles[138] to an interesting study of Klearidas, where he argued that Thucydides treats Klearidas much as he treats Brasidas himself, i.e. he acts like Brasidas, pursues policies divergent from the Spartan government, uses deceit, and is contrasted with conventional Spartans. Some of this I have already quarrelled with, for instance the remark about policies divergent from the Spartan government; as for the contrast with conventional Spartans,

---

[136] W. G. Forrest, *A History of Sparta 90–192 BC*² (London, 1980), 91; and see my n. on iv. 130, citing Redfield.

[137] Everything said by Hammond, *HM* ii. 108 and n. 1, seems to me absolutely right.

[138] Above, n. 123.

we cannot keep reduplicating Brasidas-types indefinitely or we will end up with *Brasidas* as the conventional Spartan. But let us look more closely at Klearidas' most important contribution to history. At v. 21, straight after the Peace of Nikias, he refuses to hand over Amphipolis, then makes a quick visit to Sparta to see if the relevant clause of the Peace of Nikias is renegotiable, finds it is not, and returns to Amphipolis. He takes with him instructions to give up Amphipolis, or if that was impossible to pull out all the Peloponnesian forces there. Westlake makes the sound point, a point which to some extent tells against his own argument, that Klearidas' disobedience in not handing over Amphipolis in the first place cannot have been condemned because he is allowed to return there. As for the Spartans, their instructions to Klearidas are as Gomme says 'in direct violation of the treaty'. So what is their game? And who is the deceiver, Klearidas, the Spartans back home, or both? What *is* certain is that Klearidas gets no specially heroic treatment in the manner of Brasidas.

We must now ask, where does all this leave the Achillean figure of Brasidas? At the purely military level, the comparison was, as I have just indicated, well deserved. Plato's conception may even derive from this aspect of Thucydides' picture. Plato took care over historical details in the *Symposium*.[139] But to return to Thucydides, what of the perceived justice and moderation of Brasidas? Was it all irony? Or are we right to have a lingering sense that in Thucydides' view Brasidas was let down by unimaginative and brutal policies at home? Was he a radiant Siegfried, struck down by a stab in the back, a *Dolchstoss im Rücken*? The assessments at iv. 81 and 108 are certainly intended to bring out the impression Brasidas made on other people; but they cannot be written off in their entirety as mere reports of how gullible people were imposed on, because there is an irreducible quantum of Thucydidean approval. But on the evidence of Thucydides' own narrative, the strongest case for Brasidas as a sincere liberator resides in those oaths of 424 which have been so neglected by modern scholars; though if we accept them as relevant to Brasidas' attitudes, we must also recall that the odious

[139] See R. B. Rutherford, *The Art of Plato* (London, 1995), 66–8, on the relation between Plato and Th.; cp. (for the *Symposium* in particular) ch. 7. Historical details in *Smp.*: in addition to the Delion φυγή of *Smp.* 220e (with φυγῇ ἀνεχώρει τὸ στρατόπεδον cp. Th. iv. 96. 6 φυγὴ καθείστηκει παντὸς τοῦ στρατοῦ) and the Potidaia siege (with the food-shortages of *Smp.* 219e–220a cp. the cannibalism at Th. ii. 70. 1), note *Smp.* 193a, Arkadians dioikized by the Spartans. If this is a reference to Xen. *Hell.* v. 2 and the events of 385 BC, it is a gross anachronism; see, however, H. B. Mattingly, *Phronesis*, 3 (1958), 31–9, referring it to Th. v. 29. 1; *contra*, Dover, *Phronesis*, 10 (1965), 2–20, and Andrewes in *HCT*. (But Gomme's ms. comment, apparently approved by Andrewes, that Plato was 'about 11 in 418'—and thus presumably would not have known about events of that time—is surely wrong. You might as well say that Cicero was disqualified from getting details of the 90s BC right, a period for which he is our best source, cp. E. S. Gruen, *Roman Politics and the Criminal Courts* (Berkeley, 1968)).

Spartans swore them. Thereafter Brasidas has some glorious speeches, but for the people who were seduced by his rhetoric the results were soon catastrophic. At 108. 5 Thucydides explicitly says the rhetoric was lies. There are instances of genuinely moderate behaviour by Brasidas, but this was sound politics, ξύνεσις perhaps.

But then we need to ask, why the Homeric presentation? My answer is that Thucydides was indeed infatuated, up to a point, by the literary Brasidas he had created. One might speculate psychologically about real-life infatuation with the man who had bested him at the military level, and make Thucydides Salieri to Brasidas' Mozart; but that does not work because if the military genius was Brasidas, the artistic genius was Thucydides. Instead I should like to offer, not for the first time in this section, the parallel of Tacitus, this time for his picture of Germanicus. There was Tacitus the realist, the 'consular historian' as Syme put it, the man who approved Tiberius' policy 'consiliis et astu res externas moliri' and who surely approved of Tiberius' recall of Germanicus and the reasons for it: 'satis iam eventuum, satis cladium' (*Annals* ii. 26). But there was also Tacitus the romantic, who compared Germanicus to Alexander (ii. 73, where admittedly Tacitus is not himself the focalizer), and who in more general vein (*Annals* iv. 33) regretted or pretended to regret that he was not a. military historian, recording the deaths of famous generals which he says refresh the reader's mind. The qualification 'or pretended to regret' is important: there is surely some subversive intention in the Germanicus portrait and a good deal of literary posturing involved in Tacitus pretending that he wished he were Livy. He wished nothing of the sort. But Germanicus did enable him to spread his artistic wings. In the same way Brasidas enabled Thucydides to spread his artistic wings and soar over the whole epic sky. But that is a different matter from Thucydides' judgement of Brasidas and the appalling human costs of the liberation he brought.[140]

In conclusion, my aim has been to show that the problem of Thucydides' presentation of Brasidas is soluble only by the simultaneous application of literary and historical methods. I have argued that the historical problem is that of an apparently but implausibly alienated and isolated Brasidas; and that the solution seems to lie at least in part with literature, that is, with the way part of Thucydides was seduced by his own romantic picture of Brasidas as a sort of loner or outcast, a Spartan

---

[140] Westlake, *Individuals in Thucydides* (above, n. 123), 153 remarks that Th. 'does not at the same time consider whether Brasidas himself may have been unwise in exploiting his success too eagerly. The revolts of very small towns probably proved a liability. Their military resources were slender . . .' and so on. This, by looking at the matter entirely from Brasidas' own point of view, is surely too kind to him and the Spartans. For a better view see iv. 123. 2 n. on καὶ ἅμα etc. (Connor on Mende). Germanicus: Pelling in T. Luce and A. Woodman, *Tacitus and the Tacitean Tradition* (Princeton, 1993), 59–85.

not made like other Spartans. It is part of this picture that Thucydides occasionally represents Brasidas as morally better than other Spartans who were in reality much of his way of thinking. Conversely, Brasidas cannot just be savoured as a literary concoction like Achilles, without some evaluation of hard historical items like the oaths of 424 and the Polydamidas episode.

4. *Thucydides and ξυγγένεια (kinship)*

I begin this section with an introduction about ideas of racial kinship among the Greeks and about the reasons why the topic can be considered an aspect of religious inquiry. The second part of this section will be about the kinship terminology used by Thucydides. I shall discuss the terms οἰκεῖος and ξυγγενής (old Attic form of συγγενής), which feature prominently in the modern literature: as it happens, two key texts come from book iv. But I shall also suggest that Thucydides' language for kinship relations is more varied than is sometimes allowed; I shall argue this point by reference to a third key text in particular, which again and happily for a commentary on Thucydides iv–v. 24, comes from book iv. The third part will discuss other particular passages and groups of passages. I shall try to explain why Thucydides routinely 'flags' colonial ties more often and more scrupulously in book iv than in other parts of his work. It is this fact (for fact it seems to be) which makes a discussion of kinship specially appropriate in a commentary on iv–v. 24, though as pointed out above, it is also relevant that iv–v. 24 happens to contain several key texts other than this routine sort of 'flagging' but bearing on the general issue of ξὺγγένεια. In general, I shall seek to show that kinship is more prominent in Thucydides than is sometimes realized, partly because scholars have restricted themselves to an excessively narrow range of terms (cp. above) and partly because exciting Hellenistic inscriptions have skewed debate towards that, later, period of Greek history. I shall conclude by discussing the most exciting recently published epigraphic text of all, the long Kytinion inscription from Xanthos, and shall suggest that despite its third-century date it sheds brilliant light on two passages of Thucydides, the account of the Spartans' motives for the Tanagra campaign, an account in which the metropolitan Dorians in general and Kytinion in particular feature prominently; and of their motive for the founding of Herakleia, again in terms of the Dorians of the metropolis—both sets of motives framed by Thucydides in terms of kinship, though without using the word ξυγγένεια.

My ultimate conclusion will be that on this as on other religious topics Thucydides provides important evidence. I have been criticized by the authors of a recent source-book on Greek history for saying 'incorrectly' that Thucydides neglects religion; they go on to say that in fact Thucydides provides important evidence for Greek religion, as if this somehow refuted my position.[141] My actual position was and is that Thucydides in his narrative tends to confine religion to people's conscious or announced motives, but does not think that, in the language of i. 23, it provides the 'truest cause' or ἀληθεστάτη πρόφασις for their actions; to that extent he neglects the *importance* of the religious factor which he nevertheless documents for us so valuably. In the article in question I sought in particular to dig a bit deeper than Gomme had done into the religious background to two episodes: the Spartan foundation of Herakleia Trachinia (on which I shall say more, but from a different angle, later in the present section) and the Athenian purification of Delos. But for much of the time I was operating with Thucydidean materials and details which Gomme and other commentators had simply disregarded because they were not highlighted or foregrounded by Thucydides himself. Similarly the historian of religion ought to be grateful to Thucydides for the religious items I have discussed already in this Introduction—the Argive Heraion chapter and the three Brasidas passages (above, pp. 10 and 49). The truth, as I suggested in section 1 (above, p. 10), is that Thucydides takes for granted a lot of knowledge of Greek religion and its rituals.[142]

But this section is about kinship in particular. I begin as promised with some reflections of a general sort. The idea of racial kinship (ξυγγένεια) was connected in ancient Greek minds with myth and religion. There were two reasons for this. First, the peoples who were thought to be connected by kinship traced their origins to common mythical, or sometimes heroic, ancestors. And second, they had cults in common. Thus the Ionians thought that their eponymous ancestor was Ion, son of Apollo (or, according to an alternative tradition, son of Xuthus the son of Hellen); and Ionians shared in the ritual of the Apaturia. A metropolis, or founding city of a colony, often passed on its cults to that colony or daughter city; see, for instance, Tod 195 for Miletos and Olbia. This 'mother–daughter' relationship was a common type of kinship or ξυγγένεια between cities. It involved religious and other kinds of reciprocity. Relationships, as in any family, might go wrong, like that between Corinth and Corcyra;[143] indeed I suggest that the Corcyraeans' stress on

---

[141] M. Dillon, *Ancient Greece: Social and Historical Documents from Archaic Times to the Death of Socrates* (London, 1994), 42, 233, referring to S. Hornblower, 'The Religious Dimension to the Peloponnesian War, Or, What Thucydides Does Not Tell Us', *HSCP* 94 (1992), 169–96.

[142] For a position resembling (and specifically approving) my own, see J. Bremmer, *Greek Religion* (*Greece and Rome New Surveys in the Classics*: Oxford, 1994), 90 and n. 41.

[143] M. W. Frederiksen, *Campania*, ed. N. Purcell (London, 1984), 197 and n. 160.

their links with the Homeric Alkinoos and Scherie is subtly anti-Corinthian (see Th. i. 25. 4 and iii. 70. 4 for the temenos to Alkinoos). That is, the Corcyraeans are claiming an older connexion than anything which could be conferred by Corinthian oikists. In any case there was no single or simple model for colonial relationships. Sometimes, a colonial relationship gone sour produced more than ordinary bitterness; thus in the late fifth-century Athenian honours to Neapolis[144] there is a deliberate erasure deleting the statement that the Neapolitans were colonists of the Thasians. (Cf. Th. v. 11. 1: Amphipolis.) And Thucydides, listing the allies who fought in the final sea-battle at Syracuse (vii. 57), carefully notes some surprises, daughter cities fighting against their *metropoleis*. Nevertheless, it is a reasonable starting position to assume that initial closeness often meant subsequent friendliness and reciprocity.

Naturally, ξυγγένεια of this inter-city kind is prominent in Herodotus, for whom reciprocity was so important,[145] and to whose outlook religion was central. Examples are the references to the Dorian invasion (ix. 26), to the connection between Argos and the Persians *via* their common ancestor Perseus (vii. 150), and to the racial factor at the point near the end of the work (ix. 106) where the Athenians are said to object to the Spartans making decisions about their own (the Athenians') colonists. Above all, there is the early reference to the Bones of Orestes (i. 65), a piece of propaganda by which the Spartans asserted a claim to the inheritance of Agamemnon. This recurs six books later (vii. 159) in the mouth of Syagros the Spartan, who says in fine Homeric manner that Agamemnon the son of Pelops would groan aloud if he knew that Gelon had taken the leadership of the Greek cause from Sparta. The claims made by Spartans on these two occasions, and by other Herodotean Spartans such as Kleomenes (v. 72. 3), look superficially anti-Dorian or rather pre-Dorian. But there is no real inconsistency between such passages and others in Herodotus (and indeed Thucydides) which *stress* the Dorianism of Sparta, e.g. Th. iii. 92. 5, the aggressively Dorian advertisement for Herakleia. As Richard Buxton has recently shown, Greeks were able, without discomfort, to use a myth at one time, repudiate or ignore it at another, and re-use it at another time again.[146] He

---

[144] ML 89 = Fornara 156. See further below, p. 73.

[145] J. Gould, *Herodotus* (London, 1989), and 'Give and Take in Herodotus', *Fifteenth Myres Memorial Lecture* (Oxford, 1991).

[146] R. Buxton, *Imaginary Greece* (Cambridge, 1994), 196. Christopher Jones points out to me that later sources, at least, show that cities did indeed have multiple myths, which they could use at different times or in different places; Cyrene is a fine example with its complicated ancestry (including both Minyans and Dorians: L. Malten, *Kyrene* (Berlin, 1911), 162, 170; F. Chamoux, *Cyrène sous la monarchie des Battiades* (Paris, 1953), 169–91). Later, Dionysius, *Ant. Rom.* i. 9 ff. on Rome, or Libanius' Antiochene Oration, are further examples.

specifically discusses the Spartan exploitation of Orestes and Agamemnon, a myth which still had some life in it when Agesilaos in the early fourth century sacrificed at Aulis where Agamemnon had sacrificed (Xen. *Hell.* iii. 4. 3).[147]

But Xenophon, as has often been noted, has in some ways more in common with Herodotus than with Thucydides. What of Thucydides? We might perhaps expect ξυγγένεια to feature and matter less in Thucydides, with his more pragmatic outlook. But in fact Thucydides is even more assiduous than Herodotus in registering colonial relationships, witness the *Sikelika* (vi. 2–5) with its high density of colonial relationships (see also below, p. 74, for book iv as specially rich in routine information of this sort); and it will be my contention that kinship, sometimes assumed to be specially important only in the Hellenistic period,[148] plays a bigger role in Thucydides' History than at first appears. In particular I shall discuss some interesting passages in which ξυγγένεια and words like ξυγγένεια are not actually used (though Thucydides does use that noun seven times) but which make complete sense only if we interpret them in the light of Greek ideas about ξυγγένεια.

This brings us to the second part of this section, which is about the Greek vocabulary for kinship relations, especially that used by Thucydides.

O. Curty has recently argued[149] that Thucydides distinguishes between οἰκειότης and ξυγγένεια as between different strengths of blood-relationship, and that ξυγγένεια is specially apt for kinship between Dorian or between Ionian cities. οἰκειότης, by contrast, is (he thinks) a weaker term, and is reserved by Thucydides for occasions like the Spartan appeal to Athens in 425, when the kinship connection being

---

[147] Syagros: A. Griffiths, *LCM* i (1976) 23 f., but see *Greek Historiography* 66.

[148] A. Giovannini, 'Greek Cities and Greek Commonwealth', in A. Bulloch, E. S. Gruen, and others (eds.), *Images and Ideologies: Self-Definition in the Hellenistic World* (Berkeley, 1994), 265–95, at 278 f. On the idea of kinship as evidenced by Hellenistic inscriptions see also D. Musti, 'Sull' idea di συγγένεια in iscrizioni greche', *ASNP* 32 (1963), 225–39, and above all O. Curty, *Les Parentés légendaires entre cités grecques: Catalogue raisonné des inscriptions contenant le terme ΣΥΓΓΕΝΕΙΑ et analyse critique* (Geneva, 1995). This important work, as the subtitle indicates, collects the συγγένεια inscriptions (sometimes in full, sometimes in part). It also provides French translations, critical notes, and commentaries. The second section (pp. 215–67) offers discussion of terminology and other general issues. I shall refer to inscriptions in this book as e.g. Curty (1995), no. 1.

[149] O. Curty, 'La Notion de la parenté entre cités chez Thucydide', *Mus. Helv.* 51 (1994), 193–7 (= Curty 1994). Curty 1994 discusses earlier work, such as M. Casevitz, *Le Vocabulaire de la colonisation en grec ancien* (Paris, 1985), but not Eernstman (below, n. 152), and the same is true of Curty 1995. Although Curty 1995 is far longer and more substantial than Curty 1994 I shall naturally have more to say about the shorter and earlier study because of its specifically Thucydidean subject-matter. On the distinction between συγγένεια and οἰκειότης Curty 1995, 224 (cp. 226), where his statement that συγγένεια indicates 'la parenté par le sang tandis qu' οἰκειότης défint un lien sans consanguinité', is preferable to Curty 1994, not just as a general proposition but as a proposition about Thucydides. I have not seen G. Crane, *The Blinded Eye* (1996).

appealed to is merely factitious, a pretext. This does not in fact work because at vi. 6. 1 kinship is a pretext, but the word used is ξυγγενέσι. But let us look more closely at that Spartan speech at Athens in 425, iv. 19. 1; properly examined it is, as C. P. Jones points out to me, an even more serious obstacle for Curty than is vi. 6.[150] The Greek of iv. 19 is: διδόντες μὲν εἰρήνην καὶ ξυμμαχίαν καὶ ἄλλην φιλίαν πολλὴν καὶ οἰκειότητα ἐς ἀλλήλους ὑπάρχειν: 'They [i.e. the Spartans] offer peace, alliance, and generally friendly and close relations.'

Before we deal with the precise force of οἰκειότητα we must ask what kind of closeness might be envisaged here. For the understanding of this it is necessary to look at the Spartan offer contained in the sentence as a whole. The offer is not very attractive (nothing is said about territorial concessions); but there were always Athenians who could be expected to respond to such appeals for 'dual hegemony'. De Romilly compares a fourth-century speech of the Athenian Kallistratos reported by Xenophon (*Hell.* vi. 3. 17), an appeal to power politics comparable to the Spartans' final sentence in Thucydides (iv. 20. 4). But the Thucydidean reference to οἰκειότητα, a word for close friendship sometimes implying kinship or religious closeness (see my nn. on i. 60. 1 and iii. 86. 4) may imply something warmer and more sentimental, with which we might compare the Athenian Kallias' speech on the same fourth-century occasion (Xen. *Hell.* vi. 3. 3): Kallias recalls the showing by Triptolemos of the secrets of Demeter and Kore to Herakles the founder of Sparta, and to the Dioskouroi, the Spartans' 'fellow-citizens' (for whom see iv. 110. 1 n.). This is not quite an obvious way of arguing for Athenian–Spartan co-operation because (as Tuplin has shown) the theme seems better suited to an assertion of Athenian primacy. Nevertheless Kallias shows the *kind* of thing which could be done with myth. Perhaps οἰκειότητα in the present passage of Thucydides is a hint that the speech actually delivered by the Spartans contained a sentimental appeal of this general type (albeit one less rooted in specifically Athenian self-esteem, unless the Spartans were really setting out to flatter their listeners); but if so it is not surprising that the tough-minded Thucydides does not let them develop it. I conclude that the word οἰκειότητα may look backwards as well as forwards, that is, that the Spartans may have included Kallias-type appeals to mythical closeness.[151]

---

[150] I am indebted to illuminating conversations and correspondence at Princeton (1995) about this passage, and about the whole subject-matter of the present section, with Professor C. P. Jones of Harvard University, who is preparing a book on the topic.

[151] For Kallistratos see de Romilly, *Thucydides and Athenian Imperialism*, trans. P. Thody (Oxford, 1963), 178. For Kallias see C. J. Tuplin, *The Failings of Empire: A Reading of Xenophon Hellenica 2. 3. 11–7. 5. 27* (*Historia Einzelschrift* 76: 1993), 105–8. See also now Parker, *ARH* 99 and n. 133, cf. 143 f. Note also his p. 174 and n. 76 on Th. ii. 29 (Tereus; Thrace/Athens 'kinship').

But closeness of the Kallias sort is still not the same thing as kinship, and here things get very difficult for Curty, because there was no actual kinship between Athens and Sparta at all, only vague religious or mythical ties of the sort just discussed. On the meaning of the word οἰκεῖος, the essential discussion is in a Dutch dissertation by J. P. A. Eernstman of 1932, which contains an English summary of conclusions.[152] The truth is that οἰκεῖος and ξυγγενής do not, as Curty appears to think, indicate different degrees of blood-relationship ('une parenté moindre').[153] On the contrary, ξυγγενής refers to the sharing of γένος i.e. is 'objective, almost clinical'.[154] οἰκεῖος, though originally referring to the οἶκος, has long since acquired an emotive colouring, 'familiar', 'intimate', which may cover relatives but also close friends. The word οἰκεῖος is thus sometimes used when the speaker would like to be able to say ξυγγένεια but cannot. There is a good example (pointed out to me by C. P. Jones) in Speusippos' *Letter to Philip*:[155] καίτοι χρῆν πρῶτον μὲν τὴν ὑπάρχουσαν οἰκειότητα πρὸς τὴν ἡμετέραν πόλιν αὐτὸν μὴ λαθεῖν . . . Ἡρακλῆς γάρ, . . . ὄντος νόμου τὸ παλαιὸν ἡμῖν μηδένα ξένον μυεῖσθαι, βουληθεὶς μυεῖσθαι γίνεται Πυλίου θετὸς υἱός,' 'he should not forget his existing οἰκειότης towards our city; for when Herakles wanted to be initiated, despite the existence of a law prohibiting the initiation of foreigners, he became the adoptive son of Pylios'.[156] We shall see (below) that in Thucydides οἰκειότης or κατὰ τὸ οἰκεῖον can sometimes be used by extension to mean 'kinship' or 'in virtue of kinship', as at iii. 86. 4 and i. 9. 2, where those expressions are mere variants for ξυγγένεια and κατὰ τὸ ξυγγενές. At i. 9. 2 κατὰ τὸ οἰκεῖον, 'in virtue of close relationship', is used of Eurystheus entrusting power to his kinsman Atreus. But strictly speaking, οἰκεῖος and οἰκειότης are subjective words supervenient on a relationship of ξυγγένεια, not inherent in it. That is the implication of Hellenistic inscriptions which use the adjectives οἰκεῖος and συγγενής (or the nouns οἰκειότης and συγγένεια).[157] Expressions like οἰκείως ἔχειν, διακείμενος, and so on, are of course very common to describe the

---

[152] J. P. A. Eernstman, *ΟΙΚΕΙΟΣ, ΕΤΑΙΡΟΣ, ΦΙΛΟΣ, ΕΠΙΤΗΔΕΙΟΣ: Bijdrage tot de Kennis van de Termiinologie der Vriendschap bij de Grieken* (diss. Utrecht, 1932).

[153] Curty (above, n. 149), 196; contrast the better view expressed in Curty 1995, and cited above, n. 149.

[154] The phrase is taken from a letter sent me by Professor Jones (above, n. 150).

[155] In R. Hercher (ed.), *Epistolographi Graeci* (Paris, 1873, repr. Amsterdam, 1965), 630. On the use of mythological argument in this letter see M. M. Markle, 'Support of Athenian Intellectuals for Philip: a Study of Isocrates' *Philippus* and Speusippus' *Letter to Philip*', *JHS* 96 (1976), 80–909, at 97 f.

[156] On all this see J. Boardman, 'Herakles, Peisistratos and Eleusis', *JHS* 95 (1975), 1–12, at 6.

[157] See R. Herzog and G. Klaffenbach, *Asylieurkunden aus Kos* (*Abh. Akad. Berl.* i, 1952), no. 12 (Curty 1995, no. 24a) of c240 BC, lines 10–12: ὑπαρχόντων τε αὐτοῖς παρ' ἁμεῖν τῶν μεγίστων καὶ ἀναγκαιοτάτων, συγγενείας τε καὶ οἰκειότατος καὶ ἰσοπολιτείας, and again lines 16–17, ἐμφανίζοντας τὰν οἰκειότατα καὶ εὔνοιαν. Similarly *SEG* xii. 511, line 22 (Curty 1995, no. 83), ἡ τοῦ δήμου πρὸς τοὺς συγγενεῖς ἀληθινὴ καὶ οἰκεία διάθεσις.

attitude of kings, say, towards a city with which they are on good terms. Returning to Thucydides iv. 19, we see that the Spartans use οἰκεῖος because, like Speusippos, they would like to be able to say ξυγγένεια but cannot because no actual blood-relationship exists.

The second book iv passage relevant to this problem is 64. 3 from Hermokrates' speech at Gela in 424. οὐδὲν γὰρ αἰσχρὸν οἰκείους οἰκείων ἡσσᾶσθαι, ἢ Δωριᾶ τινα Δωριῶς ἢ Χαλκιδέα τῶν ξυγγενῶν, 'There is no disgrace in people giving way to other people who are close to them, whether Dorians to Dorians, or Chalkidians to the others of their race'. That is, to other Ionians. Curty,[158] as part of his argument that οἰκειότης is always in Thucydides the weaker, ξυγγένεια the stronger term, and that ξυγγένεια is confined to Ionian links with Ionians and Dorian links with Dorians, says that in the present passage Thucydides begins with a 'generalizing formula', a 'proverbial expression' ('constation proverbiale') including the οἰκ- concept; then he uses the more precise ξυγγενῶν at the end of the sentence when he really is talking about Dorians and Ionians in a precise way. This is ingenious; but though we may concede that οἰκεῖος here means, as often, 'familiars', 'intimates', whereas Dorians and Ionians are not just familiar but actual kin, nevertheless οἰκεῖος in the first part of this carefully balanced sentence surely corresponds to, and differs only very slightly from, ξυγγενής in the second part. Similarly at iii. 86, both οἰκειότης and κατὰ τὸ ξυγγενές ('in virtue of kinship') are used indistinguishably and in the same chapter, both times to describe Ionian kinship. I must justify 'indistinguishably' as applied to iii. 86. It is true that iii. 86 uses οἰκειότης for the motive described as a pretext, but we have seen already that vi. 6. 1 undermines Curty's attempt to argue that Thucydides reserves the word οἰκειότης for such fictitious motives or pretexts.

So much for the two main words considered by Curty. I conclude that, though Thucydides might sometimes use οἰκεῖος as a virtual loose synonym for ξυγγενής on occasions when ξυγγένεια relations undoubtedly existed, nevertheless he does not forget that ξυγγενής has a precise and technical meaning which makes it inappropriate for merely close relations like those offered by Sparta to Athens in 425. It is misguided to see both terms as indicating blood-relationships of different strengths; they are different but overlapping sorts of word.

That is my first objection to Curty. My second is that he does not consider a wide enough range of terms. I pass now to some passages where Thucydides is in my view talking about a relationship of kinship even though he does not use the usual language. I examine the third of the

---

[158] Curty 1994 (above, n. 149), 196–7.

key book iv passages, namely iv. 72. 1, where Thucydides describes the Boiotian decision to help Megara, threatened by Brasidas: ἅμα δὲ τῇ ἕῳ οἱ Βοιωτοὶ παρῆσαν, διανενοημένοι μὲν καὶ πρὶν Βρασίδαν πέμψαι βοηθεῖν ἐπὶ τὰ Μέγαρα, ὡς οὐκ ἀλλοτρίου ὄντος τοῦ κινδύνου, 'At dawn the Boiotians appeared. Even before they were summoned by Brasidas, they had intended to relieve Megara; for the danger was close to home [lit. 'not foreign to them']'. Gomme saw the present passage in purely military terms—the threat to Boiotia if Megara was in hostile hands, so that in the event of invasion help could not get through from the Peloponnese—and that is undeniably present in the words οὐκ ἀλλοτρίου, 'close to home'. (Similarly Lewis cited the present passage in support of the proposition that Megara was 'essential for communications between the Peloponnese and Boeotia'.[159]) With this we might compare iv. 6. 1: the Spartans thought that the trouble at Pylos affected them nearly; it was οἰκεῖον σφίσι. But at iv. 72. 1 (the Megara passage) there is, I suggest, another aspect to οὐκ ἀλλοτρίου as well. There was an old sentimental connection between Boiotia and Megara, based on the story that Megara was founded by Boiotia; thus Hellanicus makes Megareus, the eponymous founder of Megara, come from Boiotian Onchestos.[160] So Thucydides' expression here is comparable to οἰκήια κακά, 'troubles close to home', at Hdt. vi. 21. 2 (said of Athenian feelings about the fall of their daughter city Miletos). In other words, Thucydides is alluding to a kinship tie. (Cf. iv. 75. 1 n. on δέκα etc.: Herakleia Pontike.)

Curty has nothing on the present passage in his study of relationships between cities in Thucydides; he confines himself to too restricted a set of Greek terms.

If I am right that the religious or sentimental aspect is relevant, Thucydides' point about Megara and Boiotia would be comparable to his reports in earlier books (i. 107. 2 and iii. 92. 3) that Sparta sent military help to Doris because Doris was Sparta's metropolis or mother-city, on which I shall have more to say at the end of the present section. (Note that the mother metaphor seems to have been the automatic one. 'Patropolis' exists in Greek but is exceedingly rare. The comic poet Antiphanes uses it precisely to make the point that 'we talk about a *metropolis* not a *patropolis*'.[161])

The focalization in iv. 72 is interesting: Thucydides is saying that the Boiotians *felt* the danger was their own. He does not commit himself on

---

[159] *CAH* v². 387.

[160] K. Hanell, *Megarische Studien* (Lund, 1934), 24–35, citing e.g. *FGrHist* 4 F 78 (Megareus from Onchestos).

[161] Antiphanes F219 in Kassel/Austin *PCG* ii (1991): μητρόπολίς ἐστιν, οὐχὶ πατρόπολις ⟨πόλις⟩.

the question whether Boiotians or Athenians[162] were really the founders of Megara. As it happens there is also evidence, very indirect but nevertheless real evidence, of the *Athenian* claim in book iv. It is the mention of the temple of Nisus in the text of the 423 truce; Nisus, via Pandion, is part of the Athenian propaganda claim to have founded Megara.[163] To elucidate: Nisus, one of the four sons of Pandion, was given the Megarid at the time of the mythical division of Attica, when Lykos got NE Attica, Pallas the Paralia, and Aigeus the Pedias or plain-region and the city of Athens. Nisus was probably a Megarian hero originally, but was later grafted onto the family of Pandion so as to support Athenian claims to the Megarid. This is clearly provocative, as Kearns says; the alternative version made Megara a Boiotian foundation; that is a reference to the myth I have discussed already in connection with 72. 1 n. (Note again the very obliquely stated kinship connection. If we wish to trawl Thucydides for kinship connections, we cannot just mechanically go through Bétant or TLG looking up ξυγγενής or οἰκεῖος though we have to do that as well.) No doubt Athenian claims to be Megara's 'metropolis' were relevant, in some circles, to Athenian interest in Megara at all times.

It would be possible to see οὐκ ἀλλοτρίου at iv. 72. 1 as a piece of 'presentation through negation': the Boiotians did *not* in the end take the view which some of them had advocated (or which you might have expected them to take, given their habitually introverted outlook), namely that Megara was really no concern of theirs; for this sort of argument compare 95. 2, the speech of Hippokrates before the battle of Delion. But I prefer to see the iv. 72 negative as a strengthened positive, 'Megara was very close to home'.

Thucydides is not the only author to avoid the word συγγένεια while expressing the thought. In the *Third Philippic* Demosthenes (ix. 30) speaks of the wrongs committed by the Spartans and the Athenians in the time of their hegemony, and exculpates the offenders by saying in effect 'at least those wrongs were committed in the family, by true-born Greeks'; it is (he says) like a son wasting his own inheritance.[164]

---

[162] Hanell (above, n. 160), 35–48, for the ancient view which made the Athenians the founders.

[163] Th. iv. 118. 4, with E. Kearns, *Heroes of Attica* (*BICS Supp.* 57, 1989), 115–17 and 188, citing Soph. *TrGF* F 24; *FGrHist* 329 F 2; G. Berger-Doer, *LIMC* vi. 1 (1992), 302–5, under 'Lykos II'.

[164] Dem. ix (*Phil.* iii), 30: καὶ μὴν κἀκεινό γ᾽ ἴστε, ὅτι ὅσα μὲν ὑπὸ Λακεδαιμονίων ἢ ὑφ᾽ ἡμῶν ἔπασχον οἱ Ἕλληνες, ἀλλ᾽ οὖν ὑπὸ γνησίων γ᾽ ὄντων τῆς Ἑλλάδος ἠδικοῦντο, καὶ τὸν αὐτὸν τρόπον ἄν τις ὑπέλαβεν τοῦτο, ὥσπερ ἂν εἰ υἱὸς ἐν οὐσίᾳ πολλῇ γεγονὼς γνήσιος διῴκει τι μὴ καλῶς καὶ ὀρθῶς, κατ᾽ αὐτὸ μὲν τοῦτ᾽ ἄξιον μέμψεως εἶναι καὶ κατηγορίας, ὡς δ᾽ οὐ προσῆκων ἢ ὡς οὐ κληρονόμος τούτων ὢν ταῦτ᾽ ἐποίει, οὐκ ἐνεῖναι λέγειν. 'Any troubles inflicted on the Greek states by Sparta or ourselves were at least injuries inflicted by genuine inhabitants of Greece, and one would look upon them in the same way as on a true-born son, who had come into considerable property, but made some mistake or committed some injustice in the administration of it' (slightly adapted from the trans. of A. N. W. Saunders in the Penguin *Greek Political Oratory*).

Before we move away from questions of vocabulary, let us note the way Thucydides uses the words he uses, both obvious and less obvious words. As we saw, the long form of the noun ξυγγένεια occurs seven times, but Thucydides is particularly fond of the form κατὰ τὸ ξυγγενές, 'in virtue of kinship'. See for instance vi. 88. 7, where the Syracusans make appeal to Corinth κατὰ τὸ ξυγγενές. Like many of his leading words and phrases, κατὰ τὸ ξυγγενές features in the *Archaeology*: see i. 6. 3, where it refers to the borrowing by the Ionians of an Athenian style of dress. We have already noticed that three chapters later, at i. 9. 2, we find the similar phrase κατὰ τὸ οἰκεῖον, 'in virtue of close relationship', used of Eurystheus entrusting power to his kinsman Atreus. This passage reminds us of the point argued for above (p. 68), that Thucydides' vocabulary for kinship is not confined to the obvious words ξυγγενές, ξυγγένεια.

I now turn to my third main section, the evidence, other than that already considered, for the importance to Thucydides of kinship ties. Curty can again act as a foil because he seems to believe that de Romilly and Édouard Will in the 1950s finally demonstrated the spuriousness for Thucydides of the Dorian/Ionian opposition.[165] He does not seem to know J. Alty's good article on 'Dorians and Ionians' of 1982, which used iii. 86. 2 and viii. 25 in particular to argue that, on the contrary, Thucydides was well aware of the real importance of that kinship opposition.[166] The evidence, however, goes much wider than Dorian kinship with Dorians and Ionian with Ionians. We shall be concerned with Aiolian relationships as well, i.e. Boiotian; and more generally with the relationships between colonies and mother-cities. But I shall begin with a sub-division of Dorianism, the Argives and their kinship with the royal house of Macedon. Then I talk briefly about the Ionians. Then the Aiolians. Finally, I shall talk about colonial relationships generally.

First, a caution is needed. Some Thucydidean passages in which racial kinship is prominent are really taken from Herodotus, like so much else in Thucydides, or so I argued in section 2 above. And that is true of my first example, which concerns the Argives and the Macedonian kings. Thus Thucydides on the Argive origin of the Macedonian kings (v. 80 and ii. 99) is surely indebted to Herodotus (v. 22 and viii. 137, see Annex B under the two Thucydidean passages). But in the later passage (v. 80) we are told that in 418 BC Perdikkas king of Macedon was considering leaving his Athenian alliance because Argos had recently done so,

---

[165] Curty 1994, 195, citing E. Will, *Doriens et Ioniens* (Strasbourg, 1956), and J. de Romilly, *Thucydide et l'impérialisme athénien*² (Paris, 1951), 76 = *Thucydides and Athenian Imperialism* (above, n. 151), 82.

[166] J. Alty, 'Dorians and Ionians', *JHS* 102 (1982), 1–14.

and he himself was of Argive descent, ἦν δὲ καὶ αὐτὸς τὸ ἀρχαῖον ἐξ Ἄργους. The language recalls that of Th. ii. 99, part of a Macedonian section (ii. 99–100) which draws heavily on Herodotus; compare the reference at i. 100 to the eight Macedonian kings before Archelaus, which echoes Herodotus (viii. 137). But at v. 80, Thucydides makes an extra point. He is saying, not only that the Macedonian kings were originally Temenids from Argos, but that Perdikkas was actually motivated by thoughts of this Argive connection (in fact by what would now be called considerations of ethnicity). There is a problem of focalization here: was it Perdikkas who adduced the consideration about Argive descent, or is this Thucydides' gloss on Perdikkas' actions? Andrewes comments about the v. 80 passage 'considerations of race and origin are often advanced by ancient writers as motives for political action, and they may have been more effective than we are inclined to imagine'. The new Kytinion text, with which I shall be ending this section, reinforces Andrewes' point; and for Argos see Livy xxxii. 22. 11 (198 BC).

Much interesting work has been done recently on the importance of Argive descent, real or fictitious. Scholars like J. Strubbe have sifted the evidence for the Hellenistic period, some of it usually dismissed as invented tradition.[167] It is true that the Hellenistic world was a Macedonian-dominated world, and that in some quarters it became expedient to assert a link with Argos because that is where the kings of Macedon came from. So for instance an inscription published by Stroud in 1984 shows that late fourth-century Aspendos in Pamphylia claimed to have been founded from Argos (*SEG* xxxiv. 82; Curty 1995, no. 3). Similarly the late fourth-century Argive honours to Nikokreon of Cyprus (Tod 194) begin with a claim by Nikokreon that Pelasgian Argos is his motherland. But we cannot write off all this sort of thing as flattery from after the time of Philip II and Alexander the Great.[168] There is, after all, the evidence of Herodotus and Thucydides that the Macedonian kings were claiming Greek pedigree, via Argos, as early as the fifth century. Neat corroboration of the Herodotean and Thucydidean picture was

---

[167] J. Strubbe, 'Gründer kleinasiatische Städter: Fiktion und Realität', *Anc. Soc.* 15–17 (1984–6), 253–304.

[168] Though the two great fourth-century rulers of Macedon surely affected the way earlier periods were viewed. Is Aristotle's description of the archaic Argive Pheidon as a king who became a tyrant (*Pol.* 1310b27) influenced by the contemporary career of Philip II, whom that description fits so well?

For Aspendos, which is not straightforward, see further *CAH* vi², 232 n. 147 citing on the one hand Lewis, *Sparta and Persia*, 144 n. 55 (Aspendos not Greek at all on the evidence of the coins), but on the other hand *FGrHist* 4 Hellanicus F 15 (fifth-century Greek interest in Aspendos' origins). Christopher Jones points out to me that Aspendos' dialect was Doric; see also C. Habicht in C. Habicht and C. P. Jones, 'A Hellenistic Inscription from Arsinoe', *Phoenix*, 43 (1989), 317–46, at 338.

published by M. Andronikos in 1979, a mid fifth-century tripod originally won at the Argive Heraia and found in the most famous and splendid Macedonian tomb at Vergina: *SEG* xxix. 652 (cp. xi. 330): παρ' ἥρας Ἀργείας ἐμὶ τὸν ἀϝάθλον. This is evidently an heirloom, and suggests that the kings competed not just at Olympia, as Herodotus (v. 22) told us Alexander I did, but at Argos itself. I return at the end of this section to Argead descent, when I discuss the Kytinion text.

Argos was not the only Dorian place which post-classical Greeks were proud to claim as their metropolis. Another is Sparta. Both cities were members of Hadrian's panhellenion,[169] an institutionalized manipulation of ancient myth and history; so until recently it was assumed that as the Spartans were hardly great colonizers apart from their eighth-century BC foundation of Tarentum, most of the places which in Hellenistic and Roman times claimed to be colonies of Sparta were inventing their own pedigrees. That sceptical picture has now been put in question by Irad Malkin[170] in his brilliant *Myth and Territory in the Spartan Mediterranean*. He seeks to defend the validity of many of the relevant claims, some at the level of hard historical fact, some at the level of a perception so early as to amount to a kind of historical fact. And this is where Thucydides comes in, because he is our main evidence (see iii. 92–3) for the historical colony of Herakleia in Trachis to which Malkin devotes a chapter;[171] and Thucydides also attests, in the mouth of the Melians in book v, the Spartan foundation of Melos seven hundred years before the Peloponnesian War, v. 112. 2. Malkin also reminds us that Thucydides (at iv. 53) is really evidence for a colonial relation between Sparta and *Kythera*.

There is, then, no doubt that Dorian ξυγγένεια is important not just in the Hellenistic and Roman periods but also in Thucydides.

I pass on to the Ionians, and this relationship matters a good deal less in post-classical times; no doubt this is a function of the greater Dorian conservatism which P. M. Fraser brought out so well in his discussion of Callimachus' Cyrene.[172] As for Ionianism, we have looked at several Thucydidean passages already: iii. 86 on Leontini and Rhegion; Hermocrates at iv. 64; and vi. 6 on the excuse for the Sicilian expedition. But perhaps the most important Thucydidean use of the kinship motif

---

[169] A. J. S. Spawforth and S. Walker, 'The World of the Panhellenion', *JRS* 75 (1985), 78–104, and 76 (1986), 88–105.

In addition to Argos and Sparta, there is (as Christopher Jones reminds me) Arkadia: L. Robert, *A travers l'Asie Mineure* (Paris, 1980), 135, and *Documents d'Asie Mineure* (Paris, 1987), 265 n. 61; P. Weiss, 'Mythen, Dichter und Münzen von Lykaonien', *Chiron*, 20 (1990), 221–37.

[170] I. Malkin, *Myth and Territory in the Spartan Mediterranean* (above, n. 23); see also his 'Colonisation spartiate dans le mer égée: tradition et archéologie', *REA* 95 (1993), 365–81, at 379–80 (Kythera).

[171] Malkin, *Myth and Territory*, ch. 8.

[172] P. M. Fraser, *Ptolemaic Alexandria*, i (Oxford, 1972), 787–8.

anywhere is at i. 95. 1; it contains the canonical phrase κατὰ τὸ ξυγγενές. Thucydides there tells us that the Ionians were particularly prominent among those Greeks who appealed to Athens to take up the leadership of Greece after the Persian Wars. First, they asked them to lead 'in virtue of kinship'. This applies to the Ionians only. Second, they (and here the implied subject is wider, not the Ionians only but all the Greeks on the deputation) asked Athens not to hand them over to the violence of Pausanias. So we have a double motive, positive and negative: a sense of kinship, and fear of Pausanias. On the whole, Thucydides' History gives coverage to motives of the second, rather than the first, more sentimental, type. But there was certainly a religious and sentimental dimension to the Peloponnesian War, a dimension we can glimpse from time to time thanks to Thucydides' own coverage—valuable but muted—of such matters. The reference to Ionian kinship at i. 95 is a brief allusion to a major element in fifth-century Athenian propaganda,[173] the projection of Athens as mother-city of the whole empire, irrespective of the colonial realities. To put that another way, the concept of ξυγγένεια was stretched until jt had become almost a metaphor for a relationship of obedience and control. The metaphorical or fictional superseded the actual kinship ties. Such is the apparent implication of the Athenian honours to Neapolis (ML 89) already mentioned. Near the beginning of the inscription we read 'the Neapolitans near Thasos are to be praised because, although colonists of the Thasians, they were nevertheless not prepared to revolt from Athens although under siege by the Thasians and the Peloponnesians'. The interesting point is that the words 'although colonists of the Thasians' have been deliberately erased. The Athenian alignment was paramount at Neapolis, which seeks to erase the historical fact that the city was really a Thasian *apoikia*. Thucydides himself notes such inversions of the colonial norm, e.g. at vii. 57, a passage which I have also mentioned above (p. 63). It describes the line-up before Syracuse, and remarks (para. 5) that the Aiolians fought against their fellow-Aiolians and founders the Boiotians, and that the Dorian Kytherians fought against the Dorian Spartans whose colonists they were. (Thucydides underlines the paradox by the device known as *polyptoton*, the emphatic repetition of a word in different cases: Αἰολῆς Αἰολεῦσι.) See also iv. 7 n. on Ἠιόνα . . .

The mention of Aiolians at vii. 57 enables me to pass to the Boiotians. It is an intriguing fact that the Boiotians seem, at least in Thucydides, to be particularly ξυγγένεια-conscious. I have already examined one

---

[173] See J. Heinrichs, *Ionien nach Salamis: die kleinasiatischen Griechen in der Politik und politischen Reflexion des Mutterlands* (Bonn, 1989); B. Smarczyk, *Untersuchungen zur Religionspolitik und politischen Propaganda Athens im Delisch-Attischen Seebund* (Cologne, 1990).

concealed example, the Boiotian kinship connection with Megara at iv. 72. But Boiotian consciousness of kinship explains some other small puzzles. In my commentary on iii. 64 I suggested that the reason why the Thebans single out Aigina as a victim of Athenian atrocities is because the nymphs Thebe and Aigina are sisters: Hdt. v. 79 ff. (Incidentally this is also relevant to section 2; see Annex B under Th. iii. 64 for this as an item possibly elaborated from Herodotus.) The third kinship tie affecting the Boiotians is that with the people of Lesbos. It is explicitly insisted on at viii. 100: exiles from Lesbos are said to have been commanded by Anaxandros the Theban κατὰ τὸ ξυγγενές, 'in virtue of kinship'; but there are two other passages which the same connection helps to explain. First, iii. 5. 2, Hermaiondas the Theban is sent to Mytilene, which Cawkwell[174] found puzzling. Surely the kinship tie is at least part of the explanation; compare the explicit allusion to Lesbian/Boiotian kinship just above at iii. 2. 3: καὶ Βοιωτῶν ξυγγενῶν ὄντων. The second is from book viii. The Spartan king Agis at viii. 5 plans to move against Euboia, but mysteriously gets diverted to Lesbos instead by the Boiotians. Surely the kinship factor explains this decision. The reason why the Boiotians are so kinship-conscious is perhaps that they had so rich a mythology.

I now move away from Dorians, Ionians (including the extended colonial duties claimed by Athens) and Aiolians, to Thucydides' mention of colonial ties generally. It is a noticeable feature of book iv (and early v) that it contains so many descriptions of the casual type 'x, colonists of y'. Ridley's useful list[175] gives 23 instances in the whole work (including repetitions like Galepsos, which is twice said to be a Thasian colony (iv. 107. 3; v. 6. 1), and Stagiros, which is twice said to be an Andrian one (iv. 88. 2; v. 6. 1). Of these no less than 15 come from iv–v. 24. Andrewes, discussing the only case in book viii, comments[176] that Thucydides 'often mentions colonial connections, some relevant (e.g. through the whole story of Corinth, Kerkyra, and Epidamnos), some not (e.g. the Parian origin of Thasos at iv. 104. 4), and the latter are frequent enough to show that he found the matter interesting in itself, which squares with the attitude shown in vii. 57'. This is sound comment in itself: I suggest that

---

[174] G. L. Cawkwell, 'Thucydides' Judgment of Periclean Strategy', *YCS* 24 (1975), 53–70, at 56 n. 10; see my comm. on iii. 5. 2.

[175] R. T. Ridley, 'Exegesis and Audience in Thucydides', *Hermes*, 109 (1981), 25–46, at 39–40, using the list to prove 'Thucydides' interest in colonisation'. Note that the list does not include passages of the viii. 100. 3 type, i.e. those expressed by a formula of the κατὰ τὸ ξυγγενές type, where 'in virtue of kinship' presupposes but does not baldly state that community *x* was an *apoikia* or colony of community *y*.

[176] The comment is to be found in Andrewes's n. on viii. 62. 1, but the discussion is of the 'flagging' at viii. 61. 1 of Abydos as a Milesian colony.

there is a hierarchy of the relevant Thucydidean passages. At the top are those where he mentions a colonial or kinship factor and insists explicitly on its relevance (e.g. the passages which use κατὰ τὸ ξυγγενές, 'in virtue of kinship', or the account of Perdikkas' motives at v. 80); a little below that level is the full note of the i. 107. 2 type, where we are told that Doris was 'the metropolis of the Spartans' and we are surely meant to reflect on the implications of this; next, there are passages where the colonial connection is not explicitly mentioned but is surely taken for granted, for instance the borrowing, by the Syracusans from the Corinthians, of a technical improvement in trireme construction, vii. 36. 2, cp. 34 (with this we may contrast vi. 88. 7 where the Corinth/ Syracuse kinship point is made explicit, cp. above, 70); near the bottom end are the notes, without obvious significance, of the type mentioned by Andrewes (Parian origin of Thasos, iv. 104), but these can sometimes be promoted to the 'significant' category (Andrewes himself considers whether viii. 61–2, on Miletos and Abydos, might have significance in its context). Further towards the bottom are inconsequential repetitions of material already given (Stagiros; Galepsos). In addition and strictly below even the Paros/Thasos or Stagiros categories are such semi-concealed and therefore not provable instances as iv. 72. 1 (Boiotia and Megara: see above). But if I am right about iv. 72 it really belongs in the middle and rewarding (because arguable) category of passages whose significance is real but is not insisted on by Thucydides unequivocally; I call it 'semi-concealed' because οὐκ ἀλλοτρίου, 'not foreign' or 'close to home', is an important signal. Altogether concealed are passages where Thucydides leaves us to conjecture that a colonial factor might be relevant but gives no immediate hint of this by his language, e.g. viii. 5. 2, where Agis is persuaded by Boiotians to act against Lesbos; for the understanding of this we need to invoke passages (such as iii. 2. 3 or viii. 100) where the Lesbian–Boiotian link is explicitly mentioned. Occasionally we find passages whose significance is enhanced by a colonial relationship which is nowhere even hinted at by Thucydides himself.[177] To return to Andrewes's general point, is the 'irrelevant' Paros/Thasos category to be explained merely by reference to Thucydides' 'interest' in such relationships? Perhaps so, but this does not explain the concentration in book iv. On this, Ridley (n. 175 above) remarks of his list as a whole: 'as one might expect from the geography of Greek colonisation, these towns are mostly from the N. Aegean or western Greece and Italy'; this is a valid observation: the book iv concentration of colonial 'flagging' will then be merely a function of the intensive northern campaigning. An

---

[177] See iv. 75. 1 n. on δέκα etc.: Herakleia Pontike/Megara link.

75

alternative explanation might be that iv–v. 24 is to a peculiar degree unfinished. (On this aspect of book iv—unfinished or innovative—see further section 7 below.) This explanation would account for such clumsiness as the repetition of the Thasian origin of Galepsos but is hardly adequate for book iv as a whole; after all, book viii is often thought to lack the final polish but has only one colonial 'flag' (viii. 61), to which should be added the two Boiotian/Lesbian allusions (viii. 5 and 100). I conclude that Thucydides did indeed have a fondness for noticing colonial relationships, but that Ridley is right that he indulged this taste with particular frequency when speaking of the two traditional areas of thick Greek settlement. It is true that Ionia was in a sense colonial territory, over which Athens asserted 'metropolis' status; but Thucydides in book viii could hardly be expected to say 'a colony of the Athenians' every time he mentioned an Ionian city. (Amphipolis at iv. 102. 1 *is* so described, but see n. there: that ch. is elaborated for special reasons.)

Gomme treats this whole topic sketchily and arbitrarily. He allows iv. 84, 88, and 103 to pass without commenting on this feature of the narrative at all, although Thucydides there notes that Akanthos (ch. 84) Stagiros (88), and Argilos (103) were all colonies of Andros. The first passage, at any rate, is surely of particular interest because of Plutarch's *Greek Question* 30, which describes the race for Akanthos at the time of its foundation. Gomme waits until iv. 104. 4 (Thasos described as a colony of Paros) before remarking dismissively that this is 'a detail not relevant here', but he admits that it 'corresponds' to the information given at 84, 88, and 103, and he adds refs. to some other nearby passages (including his own note on 75. 2, where he comments that Thucydides says that Chalkedon was a Megarian colony, but that Thucydides oddly fails to add that Herakleia Pontike was one too). In fact Gomme's list at 104. 4 n. leaves out 109. 3, where Thucydides says that Sane was a colony of Andros; the omission is regrettable because it is at 109. 3 that Gomme's best, though still inadequate, note on the whole subject is to be found. At 109. 3 he observes that 'as usual, Thucydides records the colonizing state', and he gives another (incomplete) list of book iv passages (104. 4 is omitted). Finally, at 120. 1 (Skione) Gomme tells us to 'note the usual interest taken in the origin of the Greek colonial states', and refers back to 109. 3 n. but to nothing else. It seems he woke up rather late to the need for a note on the issue, and then spread his references around somewhat unhelpfully, above all providing no direct cross-reference between his two chief notes on the issue, at 104. 4 and 109. 3.

Gomme's Skione comment is particularly inadequate. What Thucydides tells us at iv. 120. 1 is that φασὶ δὲ οἱ Σκιωναῖοι Πελληνῆς μὲν εἶναι ἐκ Πελοποννήσου, πλέοντας δ' ἀπὸ Τροίας σφῶν τοὺς πρώτους κατενεχθῆναι ἐς τὸ χωρίον τοῦτο τῷ χειμῶνι ᾧ ἐχρήσαντο Ἀχαιοί, καὶ αὐτοῦ οἰκῆσαι, 'the Skionaians, according to their own account, came originally from Pellene in the Peloponnese, but on their return from Troy their ancestors were blown off course to Skione by the storm which hit the Achaian fleet; and they settled there'. This is an intriguing and uncharacteristic mention by Thucydides[178] of one of the *nostoi* (returns from Troy) of which Odysseus' was the most famous.[179] In Thucydides, the only other mention of foundations by people wandering after the fall of Troy is at vi. 2. 3, though the founders there are not returning 'Achaians' (Greeks) like Odysseus or Diomedes but displaced Trojans like Aeneas.

The particular oikist or founder of Skione is known from an unexpected source, a *coin* of c480 depicting the 'Achaian', i.e. Greek, hero Protesila(o)s. This is confirmed, more or less, by Konon (*FGrHist* 26 F 1 (xiii)), who says that Protesilaos returned from the Trojan War with Priam's sister Aithilla as his prisoner, and landed between Skione and Mende. But there is a difficulty: Protesilaos, famously, was the first Greek to be killed in the Trojan War, and therefore did not return home, let alone found Skione *en route*. The best solution, to the Konon problem at any rate, is that Protesilaos founded Skione after the *first* expedition against Troy, under Herakles and Telamon.[180]

Gomme (whose only comment on any of the above was, as we saw, to tell the reader to 'note the usual interest taken' in the colonial aspect) was troubled by φασὶ δέ, 'the Skionaians say', which Jowett renders 'according to their own account'. After all (Gomme points out), the male Skionaians were put to death in 421: v. 32. 1. I cannot feel that the difficulty is enormous (Gomme worried about whether Thucydides wrote the words in question before 421, and if after, whether he simply did not bother to change them; or whether Steup was right that Thucydides meant that he interrogated the surviving but enslaved Skionaian women and children). Surely the present tense is timeless; Thucydides, who describes Skione's enthusiasm in these chapters so well, never touching on the menace round the corner from Kleon, could hardly write: 'the Skionaians say (or they used to before they were wiped out by Athens) ...'

Finally, what is all this detail about Skione doing? I suggest that it is a

---

[178] His contemporaries, like Ion of Chios who wrote a *Foundation of Chios*, saw things differently; for the influence exerted by Ion's work on so relatively late a writer as Callimachus see Fraser (above, n. 172), 746. In Th., ii. 68. 3 is loosely comparable.

[179] For the traditions about the Italian foundations of Diomedes (the hero of *Iliad* v) see P. M. Fraser at *Greek Historiography* (above, n. 54), 183.

[180] For all the above see refs. at iv. 120. 1 n.

focusing device, like the athletic reception of Brasidas at iv. 121. 1 (above, p. 49 f.). Skione's fall was in its way as dreadful as that of Melos. The Melian Dialogue was one highlighting technique, the Skione material represents another. The Skione treatment was appropriate where Thucydides did not wish to spoil the suspense by anticipating Skione's eventual destruction.

I return to Thucydides' references to the Andrian origins of Akanthos, Stagiros, and Argilos. They may after all have been relevant even by Gomme's (presumably military and political) criteria. Meiggs[181] observed that Athens may not have been too popular with Andros after the mid-century cleruchy, and he suggests that by joining Brasidas these northern places were striking a blow for their injured metropolis. This is ingenious, but note two qualifications. First, Sane is an Andrian colony but resists Brasidas (iv. 109. 5; Meiggs omits Sane altogether). Second, Andrians are found fighting alongside other Athenian allies at about this period (iv. 42. 1), so the metropolitan Andrians were not so disaffected after all.

But it is (it may be said) easy to find fault with a commentator's distribution of attention. It is more important to ascertain the commentator's views. Gomme seems to have two. First, colonial details like the Parian origin of Thasos are somehow not 'relevant', but are provided by Thucydides for the sake of uniformity; that is, because they 'correspond' to other similar details. The implication of this seems to be that there is something *more* relevant about those other similar details, but this is not obviously true. Why is the Andrian origin of (for instance) Akanthos more relevant than the Parian origin of Thasos? Neither Andros nor Paros features directly in the narrative hereabouts. It is surely more plausible to suppose, with Andrewes (above), that Thucydides thought these details were important for some reason other than *direct* relevance to military narrative. That brings us to Gomme's second and surely correct point, that these passages display the 'usual interest taken' in colonial origins (120. 1 n.). But is the interest taken by Thucydides? Or by Greeks generally? The passive leaves it unclear. In any case the reader surely needs to be told explicitly that such colonial relationships were important because they sometimes did give rise to action at the political and military level.

I have dwelt on this aspect of Gomme's commentary because the above analysis of the second half of book iv enables us, I hope, to see more clearly that there is something wrong with a commentary which ignores the colonial or metropolitan factor even when Thucydides

---

[181] R. Meiggs, *The Athenian Empire* (Oxford, 1972), 335, 525.

insists on it and its 'relevance' in the most clear and explicit language. I refer to i. 107. 2 and iii. 92. 3. On both occasions the Spartans take action in Central Greece because they wish to defend their 'metropolis', the tiny region of Doris which was a staging post in the Dorian Invasion. On the first Thucydidean occasion this involves them in the Tanagra campaign,[182] on the second it is one of the causes of the foundation of Herakleia in Trachis. I have argued elsewhere[183] that on both occasions there is an amphiktionic aspect to Sparta's behaviour; in 457 the Spartans were defending what was at that time their only point of leverage in the amphiktiony; in 426 they were, I believe, trying to acquire a new vote in that organization. But now I wish to stress a different aspect. The importance of the Dorians of the Metropolis is beautifully illustrated by a long, recently published text (*SEG* xxxviii. 1476; Curty 1995, no. 75: 206 BC) concerning an appeal to the Xanthians, of Lycia in Asia Minor, by the people of Dorian Kytinion, a town about 15 miles north of Delphi. The background[184] is that some twenty years earlier Kytinion in Doris had suffered first from earthquakes, then from an invasion by Antigonos Doson in the 220s at a time when the younger men were away defending Delphi. The Aitolians, who controlled Delphi at this time, feature as fellow-Dorians and fellow-sufferers. The appeal to kinship, συγγένεια, is as strongly put as it could be:[185] the Xanthian birth of Leto's children Apollo and Artemis is put in first place,[186] with a

---

[182] On which see now J. Roisman, 'The Background of the Battle of Tanagra and Some Related Issues', *L'Ant. Class.* 72 (1993), 69–85.

[183] Above, n. 141.

[184] For which see lines 93 ff. (part of document D, recapitulated at lines 30 ff. from Document A), 'King Antigonos [Doson] invaded Phokis at a time when earthquakes had destroyed parts of the walls of our cities and our young men were away defending the sanctuary of Apollo at Delphi; he entered Doris and razed parts of the walls of all our cities and burned down the houses; so we beg you to remember the existing ties of kinship between us and you: do not let Kytenion (*sic*), the greatest of the cities of the Metropolis, be wiped out, but help us (ἀξιάζομες οὖν ὑμὲ μνασθέντας τᾶς συγγενείας τᾶς ὑπαρχούσας ἁμὶν ποθ' ὑμὲ μὴ περιιδεῖν τὰμ μεγίσταν τᾶν ἐν τᾶι Ματροπόλ[ι πό]λιν Κυτένιον ἐξαλειφθεῖσαν, ἀλλὰ βοαθοῆσαι ἁμίν). With this compare Th. i. 107. 2, 'the Phokians made an expedition against the Dorians, who inhabit Boion, Kytinion, and Erineion, and are the mother people of the Spartans, they took one of these towns . . .' (καὶ Φωκέων στρατευσάντων ἐς Δωριᾶς τὴν Λακεδαιμονίων μητρόπολιν, Βοιὸν καὶ Κυτίνιον καὶ Ἐρινεόν, καὶ ἑλόντων ἐν τῶν πολισμάτων τούτων . . .). Cf. Parker, *ARH* 224 and n. 27.

[185] See line 32 (from Document A), εὔνοιαν διὰ τὴν συγγένειαν, 'goodwill because of kinship', and again 46–9, διά τε τὴν ἀπὸ τῶν θεῶν συγγένειαν καὶ τῶν ἡρώων καὶ διὰ τὸ τὸν βασιλέα Πτολεμαῖον ἀπόγονον ὄντα Ἡρακλέους ἀναφέρειν τὴν συγγένειαν ἐπὶ τοὺς βασιλεῖς τοὺς ἀφ' Ἡρακλέους, 'both because of their kinship from [i.e. because of their shared descent from] the gods and heroes, and because king Ptolemy is a descendant of Herakles and traces his descent to the kings who are descended from Herakles'.

[186] Lines 17–18 for Leto as τὴν τῆς πόλεως ἀρχηγέτιν τῆς ἡμετέρας. On the meaning of the word *archegetis* I am indebted to comments by Christopher Jones, who hopes to deal with the matter in print; see meanwhile O. Jessen, *RE* 2 (1895), 441–4, and W. Leschhorn, *Gründer der Stadt* (*Palingenesia* 20: Stuttgart, 1984), 109–15; also I. Malkin, *OCD*[3] entry on *archegetes.*.

reference to Leto as *archegetis*, founder (lit. 'author', 'initiator') of Xanthos (for this word cp. Th. vi. 3. 1, the altar of Apollo Archegetes at Sicilian Naxos). Asklepios is then said to have been born in Doris, and there are elaborate mythological references to Chrysaor, Aletes, and so on; the genealogy is via Homer's Bellerophon. At lines 40 ff., the Argead descent of Ptolemy V is invoked because it makes him too a Dorian.[187] The text thus unites a number of themes we have looked at in the present section. With all this compare Thucydides' account at i. 107 of the Spartan reprisals for the Phokian invasion of Doris of the Metropolis, including Kytinion which is specifically mentioned. The kinship motif is similarly stressed at iii. 92. 3 as part of the appeal of the Dorians. We can, I think, imagine that the Dorian speech on this occasion, which is part of the background to the founding of Herakleia in Trachis, would have looked as flowery as Thucydides' is bald, and that the Kytinion text, and Xenophon on Triptolemos (above, p. 65), give an idea of the kind of thing Thucydides preferred not to expand on. The enormous religious value of the Dorians of the Metropolis shines through the Kytinion inscription, and is surely present in Thucydides i. 107, though Gomme passed the passage by with no comment whatsoever. Gomme did not know about the Kytinion text, but he should surely have commented on the word metropolis. My conclusion, which I assert even more strongly than in 1992, is that Thucydides' outline and oblique reportage of these crucial themes should not mislead us into ignoring them as Gomme and others have regularly done. There is more of this sort of thing in Thucydides than is usually thought; and it is more important than is usually thought.

But I end this sub-section with an expression of doubt. I have argued that Thucydides' inclusion of colonial relationships is not normallly pointless or mechanical. But we have noticed v. 6. 1, where we are told that Kleon attacked Stagiros, a colony of Andros, and Galepsos, a colony of Thasos. But we have already been told these two colonial facts at iv. 88 and iv. 107 respectively. The most recalcitrant unitarian is going to find it hard to come up with a motive for so pointless a repetition,[188] and with this minor curiosity I finish the present section. It looks forward to section 7 where we shall ask whether iv–v. 24 is innovative or merely lacks the final revision which would, we are assured by the analysts, have eliminated such repetitions.

[187] καὶ μάλιστα τῶι βασιλεῖ Πτ[ο]λεμαίωι ὄντι συγγενεῖ Δωριέων κατὰ τοὺς βασιλεῖς τοὺς ἀφ' Ἡρακλέους Ἀργεάδας.

[188] Unless (as my pupil Mariam Rosser-Owen suggests to me) they can be seen as operating almost like Homeric epithets of the 'windy Pylos' variety. In fairness to Th., he does repeat the information that Doris was the metropolis of Sparta, i. 107. 2 and iii. 92. 3; that is, the repetitions in iv and v are not without parallel. But in both i. 107 and iii. 92 the information about Doris is needed to explain Sparta's actions.

5. *Speeches, direct and indirect, in iv–v. 24*

In the first part of the present section I shall look at the speeches in iv–v. 24 to see what help new work on this section of Thucydides gives us on an old problem, that of authenticity. In this section I shall first consider speeches before battles, because the very first speech in iv–v. 24, namely Demosthenes' at iv. 10, purports to be such a speech. The historicity of such pre-battle speeches is at the time of writing a controversial topic. Then I shall look at one aspect of the Spartan speech at Athens, iv. 17–20, namely the disputed topic of Thucydides' relation to the rhetorical handbooks. Third, I shall return to one aspect of section 2 above (Thucydides and Herodotus), and look at Thucydides' treatment of the past in speeches. I noted above that Herodotean *paradeigmata* do not, as it happens, occur in the speeches in iv–v. 24; but Thucydides does make Pagondas and Hippokrates use *paradeigmata* taken from the pentekontaetia, and this will give me an opportunity to re-open my 'Herodotus' thesis to the extent that it bears on the old problem of the authenticity of the speeches. Fourth and last in this 'authenticity' section, I shall return briefly to the insufficiently exploited technique I mentioned, with acknowledgement to David Lewis, when discussing Brasidas at Akanthos in section 2. That is, I shall examine those interesting pairs of passages in book iv which provide narrative corroboration of things said in the speeches. One of them was detected by Lewis, the other to my knowledge not.

In the second, distinct but related, part of the section I turn from iv–v. 24 as a provider of new ways of looking at old problems, and look at novelty itself. That is, I shall discuss two innovative features of the speeches in that section. The first is what I shall call the 'periodically adjusted manifesto', by which I mean the way Brasidas' original Akanthos speech is used as an assumed basis for what he says subsequently. This enables Thucydides to report only departures from or additions to the original version—a new technique which I shall suggest has much in common with the method of a modern candidate for political office, or (depending on one's view of the authenticity question) with the methods of the journalists who accompany the candidate on the campaign bus or aeroplane. But despite that carefully agnostic qualification about just whose methods are in question, I do in fact suggest that this innovative technique does after all take us back to the first part of the present section because the technique surely presupposes in a strong sense that Brasidas really did say what Thucydides represents him as saying. The second innovation will be the use of extended indirect discourse for the argument between the Athenians and the Thebans over the dead at Delion, iv. 97–9.

But I begin as I promised with battle exhortations, and Thucydides iv. 10. Until 1993[189] nobody, I think, regarded the battle speeches as *more* problematic than other speeches in Thucydides (except to note that responsions between for instance Phormio and the Peloponnesian commanders at ii. 87–9 are specially implausible because delivered in different places at almost the same time; contrast the Corinthians and Pericles at i. 120 ff. and 140 ff., where there was a time-lag which could have allowed reports to get back to Athens). Thus Luschnat in the 1940s and Leimbach in the 1980s wrote entire books about the military speeches in Thucydides, without apparently feeling special qualms about what they were studying. Hansen's article, which takes in the medieval and early modern periods as well as the ancient, seeks to throw doubt on the historical reality of all, not just Thucydidean, battlefield speeches by commanders. He argues that in real life speeches by generals took the form of 'a few apophthegms that could be shouted by the general as he traversed the line or of a speech made to the officers only who passed it on to the soldiers'. In favour of Hansen, note that the Duke of Wellington thought it a waste of time addressing troops, because only a handful could hear him.[190] As for the ancient Greek world, one Thucydidean passage, not considered by Hansen, weakens his case. It is v. 69. 2, just before the battle of Mantinea in 418. After giving a précis (in 69. 1[191]) of the *paraineseis* or speeches of encouragement given by the Mantinean, Argive, and Athenian commanders, Thucydides goes on to deal, admiringly, with the Spartans. He says that they merely sang war-songs to each other and reminded each other of what they knew already, *namely that long previous training is more to be relied on than eloquent exhortations uttered just before going into action.*[192] The italicized words here seem to indicate that the 'eloquent exhortations' despised by the Spartans *were*, to a greater extent than Hansen acknowledges, a recognized rhetorical genre in real life. Pritchett disagrees with Hansen, but does not use v. 69. 2.[193] I deal with some of the detailed evidence in my commentary (see esp. introductory nn. to iv. 92, 95, 126, v. 9 and 69). It will be seen that I am not always persuaded by Hansen. Ehrhardt[194] also disagrees with

---

[189] M. H. Hansen, 'The Battle Exhortation in Ancient Historiography. Fact or Fiction?', *Historia*, 42 (1993), 161–80.

[190] J. Keegan, *The Mask of Command* (London, 1987), 143. Hansen, 176 n. 96, deplores the absence of any treatment by Keegan, in *The Face of Battle* (Harmondsworth, 1978), of Henry V's exhortation before Agincourt, but it is Keegan's later book which treats this general topic.

[191] With Hansen, 168.

[192] Λακεδαιμόνιοι δὲ καθ' ἑκάστους τε καὶ μετὰ τῶν πολεμικῶν νόμων ἐν σφίσιν αὐτοῖς ὧν ἠπίσταντο τὴν παρακέλευσιν τῆς μνήμης ἀγαθοῖς οὖσιν ἐποιοῦντο, εἰδότες ἔργων ἐκ πολλοῦ μελέτην πλείω σῳζουσαν ἢ λόγων δι' ὀλίγου καλῶς ῥηθεῖσαν παραίνεσιν.

[193] See generally Pritchett, *EGH*, ch. 2. On Th. iv. 10 in particular see Pritchett, 56.

[194] C. Ehrhardt, 'Speeches Before Battle', *Historia*, 44 (1995), 120–1.

Hansen. He is more concerned with Roman history than with Greek, but his method resembles my argument above from v. 69. 2, that is, he has found two passages (Plut. *Ti. Gracch.* 9, Caes. *BG* ii. 20) which indirectly imply that giving pre-battle speeches was normal military practice.

The second topic in this part of my paper is the nature and extent of Thucydides' debt to the rhetorical handbooks. This has a bearing on the authenticity question because the more Thucydides' speakers, especially people like Spartans, can be shown to be operating in an academic tradition, the greater Thucydides' own input is likely to have been. Colin Macleod in particular was fond of and good at detecting parallels between Thucydides and the so-called *Rhetoric to Alexander*.[195] I take it that his point was that Thucydides was conforming to rules, though Macleod was also concerned to show that, though Thucydides' speakers use the tools of forensic oratory, his method 'contrasts significantly with what is usual in such contexts'.[196] In 1987, however, I suggested that the influence might have been two-way; could the speeches in Thucydides not have exerted an influence on the kind of thing we find in the fourth-century handbooks?[197] In particular I noted that the Spartan arguments at Athens in 425 (Th. iv. 17–20) resemble those at *Rhet. Alex.* 1425a36 ff.: Thucydides' Spartans say 'it is not reasonable for you to think that because of your recent strength and your recent acquisitions, fortune also will always be on your side. True wisdom is shown by those who make careful use of their advantages in the knowledge that things will change . . . they will make peace while they are doing well.' The *Rhet. Alex.* says 'if those whom we are advising are getting the upper hand, the first thing to say is that sensible people should not wait till they have a fall but should make peace while they have the upper hand', and so on. If I was right this slightly increases the probability that the speeches represent what was really said, or at least removes one argument for inauthenticity, by making Thucydides' speeches less boringly academic. I have argued elsewhere[198] against objections which have been or could be made against my thesis, and in particular against the view that in the fourth century BC Thucydides was a forgotten figure who could have influenced nobody.

I hope to have established (see the work cited in n. 198) that Thucydides was known in the relevant fourth-century circles. I do also believe he was known to the author of *Rhet. Alex.* in particular, and the case for

---

[195] Most easily accessible in vol. xiv of the Loeb Aristotle. For Macleod's use of this work see esp. his *Collected Essays*, 64–78 (ch. 10), on the Mytilenean speeches in book iii.

[196] Macleod, 103, discussing the Plataian debate.

[197] *Thucydides*, 47–9.

[198] S. Hornblower, 'The Fourth-century and Hellenistic Reception of Thucydides', *JHS* 115 (1995), 48–68.

thinking so goes beyond the rhetorical tricks and turns advocated by the treatise. Note the recommendation at 1424a35: a public burial ground in a beautiful situation outside the city ἐν καλῷ πρὸ τῆς πόλεως, should be set aside for war-dead; with this compare the beautiful suburb in which Thucydides' Pericles delivers his funeral oration, ἐπὶ τοῦ καλλίστου προαστείου τῆς πόλεως (ii. 34. 5). I conclude that Thucydides could have influenced the handbooks, though it is certainly true that there was probably some fairly well developed theory before Thucydides.[199] But we should hesitate before using the handbooks to argue that Thucydides' speeches are artificial and thus inauthentic.

I now turn to my third head in this authenticity section, the treatment of the past in speeches in iv–v. 24. I noted in section 2 (above, p. 31) that the speeches in iv–v. 24 lack obvious Herodotean allusions and *para-deigmata* (historical examples). I suggested, however, that this was chance (rather than evidence that Herodotean allusions dry up after book iii), because for instance Alcibiades in Thucydides book vi (89. 4) claims his family are traditionally tyrant-haters, and this is, I believe, a reference to the Alkmaionids and the word μισοτύραννοι which Herodotus (vi. 121. 1, 123. 1) uses about them. If I am right that there is particularly indebtedness to Herodotus in Thucydidean speeches as opposed to narrative, this is a peculiarity which is more easily and economically explained by the hypothesis that such indebtedness represents Thucydides' own contribution, than by the hypothesis that the real-life speakers all raided Herodotus for their *paradeigmata*. To that extent my views about Herodotus in Thucydides' speeches tend to favour the idea that the speeches contain invented material. This may perhaps be seen as a special case of a more general principle, namely that if we can isolate *any* special feature common to most or all of the speeches, that feature will tend to favour the hypothesis that we are dealing with a single mind, i.e. that of Thucydides.

But the few *paradeigmata* in book iv are, as I have noted, not Herodotean. Two in particular call for discussion. The first is iv. 92. 6, Pagondas' invocation of the Boiotian defeat of Athens at Koroneia in 446. The second is iv. 95. 3, Hippokrates' matching or nearly-matching invocation of Oinophyta in 457, an Athenian victory which gave Athens control of Boiotia for ten years. Is this pair of allusions authentic or inauthentic? Let us for the moment assume that Pritchett is right against Hansen, and that such speeches *could* have been made. We still need to ask if there are other signs of Thucydidean interference. To the sceptic

---

[199] See R. B. Rutherford, 'Learning from History: Categories and Case-histories', in R. Osborne and S. Hornblower (eds.), *Ritual, Finance, Politics: Athenian Democratic Accounts Presented to David Lewis* (Oxford, 1994), 53–68, at 59 n. 26.

who says that Hippokrates answers Pagondas in an implausible way, given that he can have had no way of knowing what Pagondas had said, we can surely answer that such references to well-known defeats or victories are exactly the kind of thing to raise morale, and that Pagondas and Hippokrates are deploying very much the expected *paradeigmata*. But let us look more closely at Hippokrates in particular. οἳ τούσδε μάχῃ κρατοῦντες μετὰ Μυρωνίδου ἐν Οἰνοφύτοις τὴν Βοιωτίαν ποτὲ ἔσχον, 'who in times gone by were led by Myronides to victory over these Boiotians at Oinophyta, and then occupied Boiotia'. See i. 108. 3 for the battle of Oinophyta in 457; the *Pentekontaetia* narrative is here echoed with verbal closeness (ἐστράτευσαν ἐς τοὺς Βοιωτοὺς <u>Μυρωνίδου</u> στρατηγοῦντος, καὶ <u>μάχῃ ἐν Οἰνοφύτοις</u> τοὺς Βοιωτοὺς νικήσαντες τῆς τε χώρας ἐκράτησαν τῆς Βοιωτίας). Such echoes by Thucydidean speakers of Thucydides' own narrative surely do tell against the authenticity of the relevant section of a speech.

The corresponding sentence of Pagondas similarly but less strikingly picks up from i. 107 the reference to Athenian occupation of Boiotia. But Pagondas' immediately preceding words tend at first sight in exactly the opposite direction; that is, they seem to be that rare thing, a statement about the past, contained in a Thucydidean speech and derived neither from Herodotus nor from Thucydides' own narrative elsewhere. The words in question are ὅτε τὴν γῆν ἡμῶν στασιαζόντων κατέσχον, 'once, owing to our internal dissensions, the Athenians took over Boiotia'. Dissensions between Boiotian cities, or inside Boiotian cities? Lewis[200] takes the reference here and at iii. 62. 5 (where the Greek is κατὰ στάσιν) to be to inter-city *stasis*. Gehrke,[201] by contrast, appears to take it to refer to struggles inside the cities. The closest Thucydidean parallel to Lewis's sense of στασιάζειν or στάσις is Hermokrates at iv. 61. 1, as Dr. T. Rood points out to me. Alternatively, one would have to say that Pagondas was for rhetorical purposes treating federal Boiotia as a unit so that struggles between its members were a kind of *stasis*. This is just possible, though I incline to Gehrke's view. On either interpretation, both iv. 92. 6 and the parallel passage at iii. 62. 5 are remarkable as references, in a speech, to a factual detail *not* given in the relevant piece of narrative. But Pagondas is perhaps inventing the fact for a rhetorical purpose, namely to extenuate the military implications of the Athenian takeover ('a convenient fiction for any defeated state': Gomme); in which case the present passage would be like the Theban claim about 'isonomous oligarchy' at iii. 62. 3,

---

[200] D. M. Lewis, *CAH* v². 116, citing Ar. *Rhet.* 1407a2, a quotation from Pericles on conflict *between* Boiotian cities.

[201] H.-J. Gehrke, *Stasis* (Munich, 1985), 166 n. 16, who, however, also cites Ar. *Rhet.* as in n. 200 above.

which is not from Herodotus, but is suspect[202] because it suits the Thebans' case so neatly.

Hippokrates (95. 3) makes a near-matching appeal to the battle of Oinophyta:[203] unlike Pagondas in his reference to Koroneia (92. 7), Hippokrates does not say that there were veterans of Oinophyta actually present in the Athenian army, and he does not say 'we' but 'our fathers': either this is accurate reporting by Thucydides or (more likely) it is careful composition: Oinophyta was eleven years earlier than Koroneia and the chances of Oinophyta veterans being present in 424 were surely that much less than the chances of Koroneia veterans being present.[204]

In conclusion I accept that the *paradeigmata* in iv. 92 and 95 are on the one hand historically commonplace and could well have been used by the real life Pagondas and Hippokrates; but on the other hand they are distinctively Thucydidean in their elaboration. In particular the speech of Hippokrates echoes the book i narrative very closely.

The fourth and last category I wish briefly to discuss in this section is narrative corroboration of items in speeches. We saw (above, p. 47) that Brasidas' speech at Akanthos was (as Lewis noted) one speech we can be sure was not free composition (quite apart from its main 'liberation' theme, cf. p. 277 below), because at iv. 108. 5 Thucydides explicitly says that Brasidas' claim at iv. 85. 7 about the Athenian refusal to fight at Nisaia was a seductive lie. To Lewis's example I added the oaths which Brasidas at iv. 86. 1 tells the Akanthians he made the Spartans swear before he set out. These oaths are then specifically stated in the narrative at 88. 1 to have affected the decision of the Akanthians to go over to Brasidas; Thucydides adds that they made Brasidas give pledges to stand by these oaths. In section 3 I was primarily concerned to explore the implications of these oaths for Brasidas' position *vis-à-vis* the Spartan authorities back in Sparta. Here I repeat the simpler point that iv. 88 is narrative confirmation that Brasidas' speech did indeed contain something about the oaths. That the speech contained identifiable lies is irrelevant to this point; to put the matter in Thucydidean language, ἀληθές is not the same as ἀληθῶς λεχθέν.

I now turn to the second half of this section. So far I have looked at iv–v. 24 for its bearing on the old problem of authenticity. I now pass to actual novelties, but these also have implications for authenticity.

First, what I call Brasidas' periodically adjusted manifesto, an expression which needs explaining. Thucydides reports Brasidas' speech in

---

[202] See my comm.

[203] Rutherford (above, n. 199), 60.

[204] Leimbach, 76, rightly notes that Hippokrates passed over the Athenian defeat at the battle of Tanagra, which immediately preceded Oinophyta.

85-7, but after the Delion narrative, which occupies 89-101, the whole narrative becomes 'markedly selective', as Andrewes put it.[205] Now at 120. 3 (Skione) Thucydides tells us that Brasidas repeated what he had said at Akanthos and Torone, and at 114. 3 that at Torone he more or less repeated what he had said at Akanthos. This surely means that the Akanthos speech is specially important for Thucydides' purposes. This does not quite prove authenticity, but it strengthens the idea that Brasidas really made those Akanthos pledges.

Thucydides does not, however, confine himself to reporting that at Torone and Skione Brasidas repeated his Akanthos message; this would not be too different from reporting, for instance, that Pericles added other things of the sort he was accustomed to say in order to cheer the Athenians up (ii. 13. 9).[206] What he does at Torone and Skione is more interesting than that. Let us examine the report of Brasidas at Torone (iv. 114). Akanthos is certainly the blueprint, but 114. 3-5 is not a précis of 85-7, but adds the arguments particularly appropriate to the new situation. For instance, at Torone, where the citizens were split, he needs to include a section (114. 3) urging no reprisals. And the proclamation of 114. 1, that anyone who wanted could come out and go home, exercising their citizen rights without fear, calls for a special section (114. 4). But there are parallels to Akanthos even in what Thucydides does report: the claim to have come to Akanthos in a spirit of impartiality (86. 4) has some resemblance to 114. 3; and *eunoia*, goodwill towards Sparta, features at both 87. 2-3 and 114. 4. Most important, Akanthos-style 'Zwangsbefreiung', 'freeing by force' (as Raaflaub calls it[207]) recurs at Torone: para. 5, the Toronaians must expect to be punished for acts of disloyalty.

This is a new Thucydidean technique for handling speeches: he gives in full the basic Brasidan patter (Akanthos) and thereafter adds the variants. (It is true that at the end of ii.13. 9, after the detailed financial exposé which fills much of the chapter, we were told[208] that Pericles added his more usual optimistic arguments designed to show that the Athenians would win through; this is not, however, an explicit reference to i. 140-4, optimistic though some of that speech was. Contrast the explicit references to Akanthos here and in iv. 120.) With this new technique one might compare modern campaign speeches:[209] the candidate has a basic speech which he or she adapts to the particular place of

---

[205] *HCT* v. 364.
[206] On which see L. Kallet-Marx, 'Money Talks: Rhetor, Demos and the Resources of the Athenian Empire', in *RFP* 227-51.
[207] K. Raaflaub (above, n. 118), 252.
[208] See above for this passage.
[209] T. H. White, *The Making of the President 1960* (New York, 1961), 291; 367.

delivery or to topical events or statements by the opponent. Brasidas, *unlike* other Thucydidean speakers but like a modern political candidate with a programme, travels around a good deal within a short space of narrative. Hence the new technique for reporting him. In the language of the analysis of Corcyraean *stasis* (iii. 82. 2), the essential phenomenon varies in form, τοῖς εἴδεσι διηλλαγμένα, according to circumstances.

Let us move on to the Skione address. Thucydides begins (iv. 120. 3): 'he succeeded in crossing, and summoned a meeting of the Skionaians. He repeated what he had said at Akanthos and Torone', περαιωθεὶς δὲ καὶ ξύλλογον ποιήσας τῶν Σκιωναίων ἔλεγεν ἅ τε ἐν τῇ Ἀκάνθῳ καὶ Τορώνῃ. Thucydides refers us to the Akanthos speech when covering Brasidas at Torone, and to the Akanthos and Torone speeches when covering Brasidas at Skione. In the present passage the cross-reference does not mean 'what Brasidas said at Skione was the basic Akanthos speech plus the extra Torone material at 114' (which was appropriate to Torone only); it surely means that the basic Akanthos message was repeated *both* at Torone *and* again at Skione, with appropriately different new material each time. Skione differs from both Akanthos (where he needed to win over the populace as a whole) and from Torone (where the place was already his when he made his speech, but where there had been a sharp political division); Skione by contrast had already come over of its own accord. The Skionaians therefore get congratulated. There is (as we noted above, p. 57) strong irony in what follows, given the casual way Skione was abandoned by Sparta after the Peace of Nikias; as Bosworth says, the 'fine words' at Skione 'meant little'.[210]

There are a number of noteworthy passages which are peculiar to the Skione material. (i) At 120. 3 Brasidas says the Skionaians 'deserved the highest praise', καὶ προσέτι φάσκων ἀξιωτάτους αὐτοὺς εἶναι ἐπαίνου. Here we are perhaps meant to recall the praise, ἔπαινος, awarded to Brasidas on his first appearance: ii. 25. 2. (ii) Skione is implied (incorrectly, see my note) to be an island, 'so that although . . . cut off from the mainland and as exposed as if it were an island, it had nevertheless chosen freedom without prompting' [lit. 'being nothing other than islanders'], καὶ ὄντες οὐδὲν ἄλλο ἢ νησιῶται αὐτεπάγγελτοι ἐχώρησαν πρὸς τὴν ἐλευθερίαν. (iii) Brasidas flatters the Skionaians by saying 'they were not such cowards as to wait until they were forced to do what was obviously in their own interests', καὶ οὐκ ἀνέμειναν ἀτολμίᾳ ἀνάγκην σφίσι προσγένεσθαι περὶ τοῦ φανερῶς οἰκείου ἀγαθοῦ. As Gomme, says, this is not very polite about Akanthos or Torone. (iv) Brasidas

[210] A. B. Bosworth (above, n. 118), 37.

specifically mentions that the Athenians currently hold Potidaia: ὑπὸ Ἀθηναίων Ποτείδαιαν ἐχόντων. Potidaia has not featured since ii. 79, if we leave the problematic iii. 17 out of account. (v) Finally, the speech ends resonantly but surely ironically with a reference to honour, 'and pay them the highest honour', καὶ τἆλλα τιμήσειν. The final word τιμήσειν also closed (in the form τιμήσει) the Spartan speech exactly one hundred chapters earlier, at 20. 4. At 20. 4 the word was used for a proposed deal by which Sparta would betray its allies ('the rest of Greece will pay both of us the greatest honour'). We are perhaps meant to reflect that neither of these Spartan rhetorical invocations of 'honour' is, in the end, honourable. Such a striking pair of parallel closures look like Thucydides' own contribution.

I suggest that in these Brasidan speeches to northern towns we have a novelty, namely the combination of on the one hand an instruction to the reader or hearer to bear in mind a given speech, which is explicitly cross-referred to, plus on the other hand extra material intended to be specific to the places addressed. Not only is this a novelty, it is not repeated subsequently, in bks. v. 25-viii. Now it might be said that no other speaker in Thucydides performed anything like the Brasidas role, a role which made it appropriate to represent him as moving from place to place with a basic speech module to which extra components could be fitted. Maybe so, but if so we still have the interesting conclusion that Thucydides develops a new technique for a new situation. Above all, it is important that Thucydides bothers to do things this way; he does so, surely, because he wishes (above, p. 49) to accord special treatment to Brasidas. The alternative view would be that the speeches lack the final polish and that the references back to Akanthos are Thucydides' instructions to himself to produce a blend of Akanthan material and new material. This would, however, have been more repetitive and dull, and I prefer to think that Thucydides is here innovating.

My second novelty and my final topic in the present section is the extended *oratio obliqua* [indirect speech] at 97-9, the Boiotian–Athenian exchange about the Delion dead. The manner of this section represents a departure for Thucydides: as Andrewes remarks,[211] 'it is a far longer piece of *oratio obliqua* than is to be found elsewhere, even in viii'. I would add that it differs from Pericles' speech of encouragement at the beginning of the war (ii. 13, see above) in that that earlier speech was not part of an argument between two speakers. Andrewes's remark is found in a section on 'indications of incompleteness' in Thucydides' account of

---

[211] *HCT* v. 365. For the notion that direct speech belongs to the final stage of composition see H. D. Westlake, 'The Settings of Thucydidean Speeches', in P. Stadter (ed.), *The Speeches in Thucydides* (Chapel Hill, 1973), 90-108, at 103.

the Ten Years War; he believes that the narrative quality drops in the latter part of the Ten Years War (but see below, introductory note to 102–8), and connects this with Thucydides' exile. Andrewes apparently regards an innovation like the present piece of indirect speech as part, or an anticipation, of the post-Delion deterioration in quality. And yet he himself notes that Brasidas still has two speeches of normal type (i.e. in direct speech) to deliver, at iv. 126 and v. 9. Following this hint, we should consider whether the present section is (not a clumsy aberration to be rectified later, but) a deliberate experiment, just as the Melian Dialogue at the end of book v is an experiment. As we shall note shortly, Orwin[212] has compared the content of iv. 97–9 to that of the Melian Dialogue; perhaps there is a parallel to be made at the level of presentation also. Thucydides, that is, was feeling towards an impersonal and dialectical mode of argument, more suitable than formal speeches to what he wanted to do. (But see iv. 97. 4 n. for a peculiarly Boiotian word.)

If this was Thucydides' intention, was the experiment a success or a failure? In some ways the exchange, especially the Athenian view presented at 98, is a speech of normal type, and a very sophistical effort too. The speech (let us call it that) is usefully discussed by Orwin,[213] who calls it a 'neglected passage' and sees in it a foreshadowing of the Athenian attitudes expressed in the Melian Dialogue. Most recent critics (see 98. 1 n.) have protested against the special pleading involved in Gomme's view that Thucydides spread himself over the aftermath of Delion because he deplored the Boiotian refusal to allow the Athenians to collect their dead and regarded this refusal as 'another evil resulting from war'—as if the Athenians were blameless.

The Athenians begin by denying that they have caused or intend to cause intentional damage to the sanctuary; they take their stand on their right of possession, asserting what for the classical period is an unusually brash claim, that of 'spear-won territory' (see para. 2 and, more explicitly, 8). This is a Homeric concept which revives in the Hellenistic period, but is not much heard of in prose historians of the classical period in between. Any offences we have committed (the Athenians say, para. 6) have been done under necessity and will therefore be pardoned by the gods; after all (they say) if you do wrong involuntarily you are allowed to take refuge at an altar. Modern critics have fastened on the speciousness of this argument: the Athenians are not in fact in Boiotia as a result of some involuntary lapse; they are invaders.

So far so good; the speech puts the sophistical Athenian position very well. The main difficulty with this whole debate is a simple historical

---

[212] See below, n. 213, and iv. 98. 1 n.
[213] C. Orwin, *The Humanity of Thucydides* (Princeton, 1994), 91–6, at 96.

one: did the battle take place in Boiotia or Attica or neither, i.e. on the borders? Different speakers, and Thucydides himself, give or imply different answers to this question, which the speakers seem to feel makes a difference to the moral issue because the dead lay on the battle site (it makes no difference to the actual issue because the Boiotians are in control of the site and the dead). The difficulty is compounded by the ambiguous focalization of Thucydides' handling, with its alternations between indirect speech and authorial comment. These alternations leave one occasionally in genuine uncertainty whether a statement is a gloss on something reported to have been said, or part of the report. This is true above all of ch. 99, 'the battle had taken place on the borders, and the Boiotians knew that the territory of Oropos, in which the dead lay, was actually subject to Athens'. There is some unclarity here but it perhaps reflects the lack of clarity about border areas in general, and perhaps also the marginality of Oropos in particular, currently subject to Athens but not an integral part of Attica with deme status and so on. But to be strict: if the battle was on the borders, the dead (one would have thought) must have been on the borders too, rather on territory definitely subject to Athens. iv. 99 is the most explicit indication that the battle site was positively in Attica; the negative statement that as a border area it was 'not in Boiotia' (91; 92. 1) is easier to understand than the positive.

In his note on iv. 99, Gomme discussed the Boiotian reply, namely that if the disputed territory was spear-won by Athens, there was nothing to stop the Athenians coming to get their dead back. He commented on this that its dishonesty 'lay simply in the fact that the field of battle was not Delion. They admit in fact that the field of battle is Athenian territory.' Here it is not clear how much the Boiotians *do* admit out loud, beyond the simple fact that the Athenians can have the bodies back if they quit Boiotia. That is, the whole section about what the Boiotians 'knew' or 'thought' may include a good deal of interpretation by Thucydides rather than just being his account of what was said. This differs from the usual authenticity problem because with conventional speeches we are usually clear where the speech ends and Thucydidean comment or narrative begins again. In iv. 99, the words 'and they pretended to be unwilling to make a truce about territory which did not belong to them' are probably Thucydides' comment, as Classen/Steup and Gomme rightly say. But even here the focalization is strictly unclear.

What though of the historical issue: where was the battle fought? Delion, the site and sanctuary fortified by the Athenians, is in Boiotia (see iv. 76. 4, Delion is 'in the territory of Tanagra', a Boiotian city), but is not where the battle was actually fought. The expression 'battle of

Delion' is thus inaccurate although, as we shall see, it has some Thucydidean authority. The following passages are relevant to the actual battle site. At 91 line 24 of the OCT, we are told that the Athenians are no longer in Boiotia, but they, or most of them, were on the borders of the territory of Oropos, the Oropia. At this time (see ii. 23. 3 and my note), the border district of Oropos was in Athenian hands. Anyway, the Athenians not in Boiotia. It is true that the focalizers are the boiotarchs who opposed giving battle, but the sentence gives an expansion and explanation of the reasoning of those Boiotarchs, i.e. Thucydides seems to accept the factual point that the Athenians are now out of Boiotia. Pagondas, evidently replying to those same Boiotarchs, says that 'no one among us ought ever to have allowed the thought to enter his head that we should not fight them unless we catch them on Boiotian soil' (92. 1). Here too the clear implication is that the Athenians are no longer in Boiotia, indeed μὴ ἐν τῇ Βοιωτίᾳ here picks up οὐκ ἐν τῇ Βοιωτίᾳ at 91 line 24. The startling text is in Hippokrates' speech at 95, where he says 'it is true that we are in foreign, i.e. Boiotian territory, ἐν τῇ ἀλλοτρίᾳ, but we shall be fighting for our own'. Lazenby has recently discussed the motives which impelled hoplites to fight; he stresses the need to feel you were in effect about to 'defend your home and loved ones', even if you were actually in somebody else's territory as an aggressor, and he then cites the present passage.[214] But the curious thing is that in the present instance there was a much easier rhetorical move open to Hippokrates, which he oddly does not choose to avail himself of, namely to assert that the Athenians *were* inside, and thus defending, Athenian territory. The battle was in fact on the borders, ἐν μεθορίοις, ch. 91 line 25, and 99 line 10, but all parties except Hippokrates (that is, the boiotarchs, Pagondas, and Thucydides himself with the exception of some retrospective references about to be noted) appear to accept that the fighting was in Athenian or at least not in Boiotian territory. (That is, Gomme was incautious in taking the location of the battlefield to be uncontroversially in Attica.) If I had to explain the anomaly of Hippokrates at 95, I would suggest that Hippokrates and his troops are uneasily aware that Delion, which they had fortified, *was* in Boiotian territory, hence the rhetorical need to face that issue boldly. Alternatively, the speech could originally have been written for delivery *at Delion*. There is incidentally no doubt at all that Hippokrates has definitely left Delion by now to join the rest of his army (93. 2 αὐτὸς οὐ πολλῷ ὕστερον ἐπῆλθε), leaving only 300 horse to guard Delion. The point has not had the attention it deserves, though in his note on the problematic phrase in Hippokrates' speech at 95

---

[214] J. F. Lazenby, in V. D. Hanson (ed.), *Hoplites*, 105.

Gomme briefly but correctly says 'contrast 91, οὐκ ἐν τῇ Βοιωτίᾳ ἔτι εἰσί'. We are not yet quite out of the wood, because in a retrospective reference at 108. 5 Thucydides refers to 'the defeat in Boiotia' (actually 'among the Boiotians', ἐν τοῖς Βοιωτοῖς). This is compatible with his other retrospective references (namely v. 14. 1 and 15. 2, where the battle is 'at Delion'); but it is loose.

Gomme's comment on 95 (i.e. his instruction to 'contrast 91') shows that he saw the difficulty; but he did not try to explain why the odd one out among the various passages, namely Hippokrates' statement, is the one which runs counter to rhetorical expectation. All would be explicable if Hippokrates were exploiting the border nature of the conflict to make things rhetorically easier for himself, but actually he makes them harder. But my subject in this section is the indirect speech which results from the battle, and which is concerned with the return of the dead and has so much to say about conquered territory and about the locations of this or that element in the argument. I suggest that the use of *oratio obliqua* makes a hard issue harder. That is, Thucydides' experiment here, if that is what it is, has, particularly at 99, resulted in some loss of clarity about the issues in dispute between the Athenians and Boiotians. The fall-back or Andrewes position is that this indirect speech is provisional; but that raises issues which I postpone until section 7.

6. *Thucydides and epigraphy; personal names in iv–v. 24*

In section 1, we looked at some inscriptions ignored by Gomme, notably *Syll.*³ 78 and 79; and discussed the relation of Thucydides to the financial evidence of the tribute lists and of the reassessment decree of 425 (*IG* i³. 71; ML 69; Fornara 136). A little more still needs to be said about the financial documents. The evidence of the tribute lists is not new; what is new here is a thesis, that of Kallet-Marx:[215] she argues that Thucydides' omission in book iv of the 425 reassessment is not as startling as earlier scholars had thought, and that Athens' financial position throughout the Archidamian War was, contrary to most modern opinion and *some* Thucydidean indicators, healthy. That issue, then, concerns new views about old texts. In section 4, by contrast, I used a very new inscription— the Kytinion inscription from Xanthos, with its rich material about ξυγγένεια—for the elucidation of Thucydides i. 107 and iii. 92 in particular, and Thucydides' ideas about kinship in general.

I must briefly return to the financial problem and to the use and abuse of the tribute lists and related evidence. The most ambitious claims in

---

[215] *Money, Expense and Naval Power in Thucydides' History 1–5. 24* (above, p. 7 and n. 17).

this department were made by Woodhead in 1960 in an article whose main new claim was that Thucydides, for reasons of personal malice, suppressed some northern conquests of Kleon, which can be returned to history by the study of the epigraphic assessment after that of 425 (*IG* i³. 77).[216] Thirteen years later Woodhead's conclusions were rejected by Pritchett,[217] who pointed out the precariousness of the dating of the text, and observed (his p. 379) that the tributes of two of the places, Singos and Mekyberna, were a mere 10 drachmae, so that Thucydides' omission of the notional recapture of such one-donkey villages is trivial. On the main points Pritchett was surely right, but it is worth noting against him that his point about the 10 drachmae is downright misleading. The normal tribute of Singos was 2 talents. The 10 drachmai assessment was abnormal, and must be due to factors outside our knowledge.[218]

Kallet-Marx's study of the relation of Thucydides to epigraphy is more serious. From epigraphic evidence (*IG* i³. 71, see above), but not from Thucydides, we know that assessed levels of tribute were increased in 425/4. This reassessment is prosopographically linked to Kleon via its proposer Thoudippos, probably Kleon's son-in-law: Thoudippos is an exceedingly rare name at Athens.[219] Gomme[220] described this as 'the strangest of all omissions in Thucydides', Andrewes[221] called it 'the most spectacular omission of all', and M. I. Finley[222] listed it among the 'astonishing gaps and silences' in Thucydides, 'whole chunks of history that are left out altogether'. How true is all this? Kallet-Marx's acute and important recent discussion[223] has reopened the question.

She begins by rightly insisting that the sharpness of the 425 increase must remain uncertain because of the loss of the grand total (960–1000 or 1460–1500 talents?) and because we do not know the figures for the two previous reassessments—normally dated to 430 and 428, though Kallet-Marx again doubts these dates, on the grounds that Thucydides' mention of *argurologoi* ships has exerted a pull on the dating of these assessments (see below iv. 50. 1 n.). But, she rightly points out, the adjective only means 'money-collecting' not 'tribute-collecting', and we have no automatic right to connect them with tribute at all, let alone

---

[216] A. G. Woodhead, 'Thucydides' Portrait of Kleon', *Mnemosyne*, 13 (1960), 289–317.

[217] W. K. Pritchett, *Mnemosyne* 1973 (above, n. 53). On I. Spence, 'Thucydides, Woodhead and Kleon', *Mnemosyne*, 48 (1995), 411–37, see introductory n. to v. 2–3.

[218] Singos' normal tribute was 1–4 talents, usually 2; Mekyberna usually pays 1 talent, but two thirds of that sum (i.e. 4000 drachmai) in 447/6–438/7: see Zahrnt 228 f.; 203 f.

[219] M. Osborne and S. Byrne (eds.), *Lexicon of Greek Personal Names*, ii (Oxford, 1994), entry under Θούδιππος (three entries only; nos. 1 and 2 related).

[220] *HCT* iii. 500.   [221] *HCT* v. 363.

[222] Introduction to Penguin *Thucydides: The Peloponnesian War* (rev. edn., Harmondsworth, 1972), 26.

[223] Kallet-Marx 164–70.

tribute reassessment. Lewis[224] came close to this position when he said in his introductory discussion of Thucydidean selectivity: 'we are left to wonder, for example, whether there were indeed only three tribute-collecting expeditions during the Archidamian War (ii. 69, iii. 19, iv. 50) or whether it is not rather the case that these were regular annual events (cf. Arist. *Ath. Pol.* 24. 3) which Thucydides only reports when something of interest occurred.' Kallet-Marx has convinced me (contrast my note on ii. 69. 1) that the *argurologoi* ships are not to be connected with re-assessments of tribute.

But then Kallet-Marx[225] accepts for the sake of argument that the increase in 425 was to 1460 talents and that it was sudden, and asks, 'would we expect Thucydides to have mentioned it?' Her answer, essentially, is in the negative, because (she argues) of the probability that the reassessment was largely ineffective, and because Thucydides is not interested in assessments *per se*—indeed 'he mentions no reassessments at all' [after 478]—but in results. Had the decrees of 425 been a great success *as a financial measure*, he would have mentioned it. She concedes[226] that the decree may have been psychologically and symbol-ically important, not least as a physically imposing document; this aspect of the epigraphy of imperial Athens (the aim to 'intimidate rather than simply to convey information') has been cogently argued for by Thomas.[227] This emphasis on the symbolic or visual side of inscriptions is a striking feature of recent work on Greek epigraphy, and it has a bear-ing on the tribute lists. As Davies has put it, 'how many people before the twentieth century AD do we suppose ever brought a step-ladder in order to consult the top lines of the First Stele of the Tribute Quota lists?'[228]

I return to the detail of Kallet-Marx's argument. Her claim that Thucydides mentions no reassessments at all is strictly true, but what of vii. 28. 4? There he tells us that in 413 the Athenians substituted a five-per-cent tax on shipping instead of the allied tribute, thinking that it would bring in more revenue. As it happens, we think that they got their sums wrong, because tribute was soon reimposed. That is, we have here a measure which (*a*) is a kind of reassessment and which (*b*) seems to have been a financial failure, i.e. it did not deserve inclusion in the narrative, judged strictly by financial results. I suppose one reply might

---

[224] D. M. Lewis, *CAH* v². 5.

[225] Kallet-Marx, 167.

[226] Kallet-Marx, 170.

[227] R. Thomas, 'Literacy and the City-State in Archaic and Classical Greece', in A. K. Bowman and G. D. Woolf (eds.), *Literacy and Power in the Ancient World* (Cambridge, 1994), 33–50, at 44 (also, on the 425 reassessment decree in particular, 47 n. 38, pointing out that it was to go on two stelai, one of the acropolis, i.e. for maximum publicity, one in the *bouleuterion*.

[228] J. K. Davies, 'Accounts and Accountability in Classical Athens', in *RFP* 201–12 at 212.

be that Thucydides' aim in vii. 28 was to stress financial poverty, but equally one might say that the 425 reassessment could have been used to stress the 'grasping for more' of iv. 21. 2, cp. 65. 4.

As for the effectiveness of the measure, it is true that the next assessment was less ambitious, and this might mean that the tributes assessed in 425 simply could not be collected. The usual view (see ii. 65 5 n.) links the 425 assessment to the aggressive and confident mood described at iv. 65. 4 and elsewhere, and to Kleon in particular (though Gomme[229] was not convinced; he also doubted whether there was any connection between the hypothetical extra revenues brought in by the assessment, and a supposed increase in jury pay at this time.[230] If that connection could be proved, that would be evidence for the decree's financial effectiveness). That confident mood did not survive Delion, and (more relevant to the problem of Thucydides' silence about the reassessment) it perhaps did not survive the allied discontent and pro-Spartan feeling mentioned at iv. 108. 3. As Lewis puts this argument,[231] 'it is more than surprising that this assessment does not appear as a factor when Thucydides has to discuss allied attitudes to Athens in the next year' (and we can add that even apart from the financial implications of the decree, the symbolic or intimidating aspects need to be remembered, see above). We should not complain that Thucydides does not mention the assessment without also asking *in what context* we should have expected him to mention it. In general it is remarkable that after i. 99 tribute grievances feature so little in the story of Athens' relations with the allies; for instance, there is nothing at vi. 76 (Hermokrates at Kamarina, contrast 85. 2, Euphemos) or viii. 2 or in the Melian Dialogue, despite ML 69 col. 1. 65; see below p. 99 and v. 111. 4 n. Brasidas does make an interesting mention of tribute in a speech, at iv. 87. 3, but his point there is that he cannot allow the Akanthians to injure Sparta by continuing to pay tribute to Athens. As Kallet-Marx notes,[232] this implies that tribute is a source of Athenian strength. So by keeping the 425 assessment out of sight in book iv Thucydides is at least being consistent.

Another possible context in which Thucydides might have mentioned the assessment would have been in connection with Kleon. Thucydides was surely not going to give credit to Kleon for the measure even if he thought it was financially called-for; but he could have made it part of an anti-demagogic indictment, as Theopompus did (see Plut. *Arist.* 24).

There is (cf. above, p. 7) a risk of overvaluing both tribute and the evidence of the tribute lists just because we have it. First tribute. One of Kallet-Marx's points is that Athens had sources of wealth other than

---

[229] *HCT* iii. 502.   [230] For this argument see D. M. Lewis, *CAH* v². 421.
[231] Lewis (above, n. 230), 420.   [232] Kallet-Marx (above, n. 17), 172.

tribute,[233] so that even if Athenians did increase the tribute this affected part of their income only. I list the evidence for non-tributary income:

(i) After about 465 Athens acquired the rich mineral holdings of Thasos, i. 101. 3. In about 446 the Thasians' tribute is raised from 3 to 30 talents, and this is sometimes taken to be evidence that between 465 and 446 Athens had been extracting revenue from the area in other ways, presumably by exploiting their silver-mines on the Thasian *peraia* or mainland opposite. On this view Thasos got back rights over its *peraia* in 446. But other explanations for the tribute record are possible; for instance Thasos may have finished paying an indemnity in the 440s, after which Thasian tribute went up again.[234] In fact we simply do not know: all such arguments are hypothetical and run a danger of circularity, as we shall see below. But there can be little doubt that Athens exploited the silver of the region (not to mention that of Attica itself: Laurion).

(ii) Economically valuable Amphipolis pays revenue but not tribute, iv. 108. 1.

(iii) The *argurologoi* ships need not (see above) be collecting tribute as such.

(iv) The liturgy system is played down for obvious rhetorical reasons at ii. 13, but Karkinos' trierarchic dedication[235] shows that it is as old as the mid-fifth century. (For the *eisphora* see iii. 19. 1 n. on καὶ αὐτοί etc.)

(v) Aristophanes in the *Wasps* (lines 658 ff.) lists other types of revenue, including taxes and court-fees.[236]

(vi) Sacred rents are attested by Thucydides and inscriptions.[237]

(vii) The Athenians, as we saw, went over to a five-per-cent tax on shipping in 413 (Th. vii. 28, cp. Tod 114 = Harding 26, line 8).

(viii) The first Kallias decree (ML 58 A7) mentions a *dekate* or tithe.

I conclude that Kallet-Marx has a good case against those who find Thucydides' omission of the 425 reassessment surprising. On Athenian finances generally I continue[238] to be unhappy about the heavy borrowing from the sacred treasuries (ML 72), borrowing which she argues is

---

[233] Kallet-Marx, 141–9; 167; 176; 199.

[234] Return of mainland possessions: *ATL* iii. 259. Ending of indemnity: R. Meiggs, *The Athenian Empire* (above, n. 181), 84 f.; D. M. Lewis, *CAH* v². 138.

[235] Hill² B 42; cp. *Old Oligarch* iii. 4.

[236] For which see also Th. vi. 91. 7, ὅσα ἀπὸ γῆς καὶ δικαστηρίων ὠφελοῦνται, 'the profits which they make by the land or by the law-courts', which some have emended to ἐργαστηρίων, 'from the mining workshops'.

[237] Th. iii. 50. 2, with I. Malkin, 'What Were the Sacred Precincts of Brea? (*IG* i³. 46)', *Chiron*, 14 (1984), 43–8. Note the fishing rights and sacred land on the island of Rheneia next to Delos, rented out on the evidence of ML 62. See now Parker, *ARH* 145.

[238] *CR* 44 (1994), 333–6.

normal financing. But she is right[239] that there is a lot we do not know about the background to this.

Second, the tribute lists. Again and again the authors of *ATL* and even Gomme himself (despite the admirable 'jig-saw puzzle' reservations I mentioned above, p. 6) sought to correlate changes of tribute with the behaviour of a place as attested in the literary sources. But the truth is often that no such correlations really exist. It is not just (see above) that Thucydides does not report, and his anti-Athenian speakers do not make, complaints about tribute in a general way. There is the additional and alarming point that particular cities do not fit the schemes laid down for them, at least not without circularity. I discussed the relatively trivial instance of Rhoiteion in section 1 (above, p. 7). Now I take a more serious case, Argilos near Amphipolis. Thucydides (iv. 103. 4) implies longstanding bad feeling between Argilos and Athens.

The tribute record of Argilos[240] is in any case problematic: it paid ten and a half talents in 454/3, one talent in 446/5 to 438/7, and 1000 drachmas in 433/2. *ATL* iii. 5-6 and 62, following a suggestion of Perdrizet, thought that the 454/3 total of ten and a half was impossible (absolutely too large, and also out of line with the rest of Argilos' record) and emended it to one and a half; Zahrnt approves the change. Gomme and Meiggs, with whom I agree, rejected the emendation. Meiggs pointed out that the mistake is not a natural one for the cutter to make, and conjectured that 'if Brea [for this topographically mysterious Thracian colony see ML 49] was carved out of the territory of Argilos', the 'sharp reduction' between 454/3 and 446/5 is intelligible. This argument is also used by the emenders to explain the hypothetical drop from one and a half to one. All parties agree that the final drop to 1000 drachmas was compensation for the founding of Amphipolis (see above on Thasos). It will be seen that the tribute record of Argilos can hardly be used, without circularity, for the elucidation of Thucydides. Gomme, for instance, writes that 'successive reductions of the tribute payable by Argilos did not appease her jealousy of Amphipolis', but without knowing the scale of the reductions we cannot say whether they were relevant at all. Gomme's remarks about failing to 'appease the jealousy' of Argilos are an ingenious but strained way of acknowledging that the political behaviour of Argilos is not obviously a function of its tribute record. Kallet-Marx does not discuss Argilos, but it reinforces her general position.

[239] See L. Kallet-Marx, 'The Kallias Decree, Thucydides, and the Outbreak of the Peloponnesian War', *CQ* 39 (1989), 94-113, at 102.

[240] For Argilos and its tribute see *ATL* iii. 5-6, 62; Gomme, *HCT* iii. 576 n. 1; Zahrnt 159; Meiggs, *AE* 159 n. 3.

Argilos, then, is a good if extreme example of a worrying mid-twentieth-century tendency to force Thucydides and imperial epigraphic data into agreement. I hope none of the above will be misunderstood as facile or philistine depreciation of the historical interpretation and exploitation of the tribute quota lists themselves; an example is Lewis's masterly, posthumously published, study of the epigraphic record for 453–450.[241]

I now turn to some other types of inscription. I leave out of account those inscriptions whose dates are too uncertain to illustrate Thucydides without circularity. Thus we now have new fragments of the Spartan war fund (ML 67), and these may bear on the material about Chios in Thucydides' narrative of winter 425/4 (iv. 51); but it now seems possible that the inscription belongs early in the Ionian War.[242] Equally, I am absolved from discussing, in the present context, the proposed redating to 418 of Athens' alliance with Egesta:[243] the inscription bears most obviously on Thucydides' account of the preliminaries to the main Sicilian Expedition (see esp. vi. 6. 2). Equally I am strictly absolved from discussing the relation between the epigraphically preserved Athenian alliance with Argos, Mantinea, and Elis (*IG* i³. 83) and the text of Thucydides (v. 47), because this is outside the period covered by the present volume (though see below, p. 117, discussing the role of documents in the history). Finally, I shall not say anything about the relation between the inscriptions (ML 67, 69) and Athens' treatment of Melos, because the two Melian episodes (iii. 91; v. 84 ff.) fall before and after iv–v. 24.

Inscriptions on stone are not the only documents which have a bearing on the text of Thucydides. For instance, Habicht has noted the Thucydidean interest of the bronze shield found in a cistern in the Athenian agora, bearing the inscription *ΑΘΗΝΑΙΟΙ ΑΠΟ ΛΑΚΕΔΑΙΜΟΝΙΩΝ ΕΚ ΠΥΛΟ*, 'the Athenians [dedicated this] from the Spartans taken at Pylos'.[244] Choice item though this is, it hardly tells us anything we did not already know. The discovery of a potsherd at Torone inscribed with the name of Athena (*SEG* xxxviii. 589) similarly corroborates book iv, this time on a minor point of N. Greek topography: the existence of a temple to Athena on the Lekythos peninsula at Torone (iv. 116. 2, see n.

---

[241] D. M. Lewis, 'The Athenian Tribute-Quota Lists, 453–450 BC', *BSA* 98 (1994), 285–301; this built on generations of patient and often extremely ingenious work by earlier scholars.

[242] ML 67 with p. 312 of 1988 reprint; W. T. Loomis, *The Spartan War Fund. IG v.1.1 and a New Fragment* (*Historia Einzelschrift* 74, 1992); B. Bleckmann, 'Sparta und seine Freunde im Dekeleischen Krieg: zur Datierung von *IG* v.1.1', *ZPE* 96 (1993), 297–308; M. Piérart, *BCH* 119 (1995), 253–82.

[243] ML 37 with *SEG* xxxix. 1.

[244] *IG* i³. 522. See J. Camp, *The Athenian Agora* (London, 1986), 71 f., with photograph and drawing. Pausanias was shown, in the Painted Stoa (*Stoa Poikile*), shields said to have been taken from the Spartans who were captured at Sphakteria (Th. iv. 38), see Paus. i. 15. 4, with C. Habicht, 'Pausanias and the Evidence of Inscriptions', *CA* 3 (1984), 40–56, at 47. See the dust-jacket of this book.

there). Slightly more informative are the sling-bullets found at Corinth and now in the Ashmolean Museum in Oxford; they are inscribed with the name of the Corinthian commander Lykophron, mentioned by Thucydides in the context of the Solygeia campaign.[245] If the name is really that of Thucydides' man, the most the bullets show is that slingers not mentioned by Thucydides were present at the battle. However we should not be too worried at the thought that things happened in the years 431–411 which Thucydides does not explicitly mention. In any case neither shield nor sling-bullets contradict or appear to contradict Thucydides, as does my next category of documentary evidence.

This category is not Greek at all, nor is it inscribed in the usual sense. But the Babylonian evidence relating to Th. iv. 50 is documentary evidence, so it belongs in the present section. The problem was set out by Lewis in 1977, and its implications for Thucydidean narrative technique were noted by Andrewes in 1981.[246] But the problem was not really solved until 1983 by the Chicago orientalist Matthew Stolper.[247]

Thucydides (iv. 50, under winter 425/4) tells us that the Athenians captured the Persian Artaphernes. Afterwards (ὕστερον, para. 3) they sent him back to Ephesos with some ambassadors. But these ambassadors 'found that Artaxerxes the son of Xerxes had recently died; for he died about then', οἱ πυθόμενοι αὐτόθι βασιλέα Ἀρταξέρξην τὸν Ξέρξου νεωστὶ τεθνηκότα (κατὰ γὰρ τοῦτον τὸν χρόνον ἐτελεύτησεν), so they returned home, ἐπ' οἴκου ἀνεχώρησαν. About *when* did he die? Lewis discussed in detail the evidence of dated oriental documents; his discussion stimulated, but has been superseded by, that of Stolper, who shows that Babylonian documents attest quite certainly that Artaxerxes I died in his forty-first regnal year, in fact between December 424 and February 423. There are even some dated by anticipatory use of the 42nd regnal year. But Thucydides himself, by his mention of the eclipse of 52. 1 (21 March 424) *after* his mention of Artaxerxes' death, had been thought to provide hard evidence for the king's death-date: the king must have died before 21 March 424. What then of the documents? Does Thucydides undermine them? Or do they undermine him? Or what? The whole period was one of dynastic convulsion, and Lewis's preferred suggestion was Ed. Meyer's old idea that that 'Artaxerxes' 41st year is in part or whole a chronological device protracted after his death to cover uncertainties about the succession'. That is, the oriental evidence could

---

[245] C. Foss, *Arch. Reps.* (1974–5), 41, nos. 3 and 4. For Lykophron see Th. iv. 43. 1 and following narrative.

[246] D. M. Lewis, *Sparta and Persia* (Leiden, 1977), 71 n. 140; Andrewes, *HCT* v. 366.

[247] M. Stolper, 'The Death of Artaxerxes I', *Arch. Mitt. aus Iran*, 16 (1983), 223–46, and at *CAH* vi². 237; see also Lewis, *CAH* v². 422 nn. 131–2.

(Lewis thought) be forced into agreement with the assumed implications of Thucydides, so as to produce a death-date earlier than 21 March 424. But from other Babylonian evidence Stolper[248] refutes this idea that year 41 of Artaxerxes was a fictional device; the better view[249] is that Artaxerxes did indeed die in his 41st year and that the supposed argument from Thucydides is unsound: Thucydides is capable of giving material 'far beyond its chronological context'. The king did indeed survive many months after 22 April 424 and thus into his 41st regnal year as conventionally computed. But there is no contradiction with Thucydides. There are, it is true, historical difficulties about the new view.[250] In particular, it is a consequence of Stolper's dating that the Athenians must be supposed to have waited nearly a year before sending their ambassadors to Ephesos with Artaphernes. Why should they have waited so long? We could follow up and adapt a suggestion of Lewis[251] and argue that the Athenians felt newly vulnerable after Delion (autumn 424), and so decided to approach Persia once again. That is probably as good an explanation as we can get. But Thucydides has reported the whole episode in so meagre a way that we need not feel ashamed to admit ignorance about the motives for Athens' actions. The alternative is to suppose that Thucydides made a mistake of a whole year, and now that Stolper, building on a suggestion of Lewis, has offered a solution which avoids that alternative, we should accept the offer; and at the same time accept that there are aspects of the episode which we do not fully understand.

The issue of Artaxerxes' death is a pretty if unusual example of a problem solved by the combined application of narratological insight and familiarity with oriental material. The documentary evidence at first blush appears to contradict Thucydides, but ceases to do so when his narrative technique (here, 'prolepsis') has been properly understood.

In the second part of this section, I turn to personal names in iv–v. 24. This is an issue with a large epigraphic content, as can be seen by a glance at either of the published volumes of the *Lexicon of Greek Personal Names* (*LGPN*). In terms of bulk, most of our evidence for Greek personal names is epigraphic; and despite the fallibility of stone-cutters, such epigraphic evidence can sometimes serve as a control on the literary record with its risks of scribal corruption.[252] In a more simple sense,

---

[248] Stolper 1983 (above, n. 247), 229–30.

[249] Stolper 1983, 230, taking his cue from the alternative offered by Lewis himself at *Sparta and Persia*, 71 n. 140.

[250] I am grateful here to George Cawkwell for his sceptical comments.

[251] D. M. Lewis, *Sparta and Persia*, 77: after Delion 'it might have seemed urgent to mend their diplomatic fences'.

[252] Cf. iv. 8. 9 n. (Jameson on the Spartan name ?Molokros) or 78. 1 n. on Τορύμβας.

inscriptions may show that a name recorded by a historian in a particular ethnic context is indeed frequent in or even peculiar to the area in question. This may help with historical problems. Thus, to take an example from later Greek history, Derow showed that the rare name Kleemporos, mentioned by Appian in connection with the outbreak of the First Illyrian War, is found in an Illyrian epigraphic context.[253] This does not quite prove the correctness of the non-Polybian tradition[254] but it shows that, if it was invented, whoever invented it was remarkably well-informed. That is, the detail is authentic even if false.

Turning to Thucydides, if we can show that the names he records are authentically and distinctively Thessalian, Boiotian, or whatever, the commonsense conclusion is that the bearer of the name existed. That is, personal names are not just a fascinating topic in themselves (at least I find them so) but they are a *means by which the accuracy of Thucydides can be checked*. There are various sceptical moves one could make in reply to this (e.g. 'local colour'), but none is plausible. Personal names seem to have interested Gomme not at all, and I shall hardly be mentioning him. True, onomastic aids as scientific as *LGPN* did not then exist, but much had been done by Wilamowitz and Robert and it was available.

Where a region is epigraphically rich, like Attica, one can make more progress still, by risking identifications with other known individuals. Athenians are not only epigraphically numerous, they also have demotics, though not Thucydides' Athenians, and these demotics can be an aid to precise identification; an example is Hagnon of Steiria.[255] The most impressive application of prosopography of this sort was by Andrewes and Lewis in their 1957 study of the Peace of Nikias;[256] this built on Lewis's brilliant observation that the middle ten of the seventeen names of Athenian swearers given by Thucydides (v. 19. 2) were in official Athenian tribal order. The timing of this article was, I suspect, not fortuitous. It appeared a year or so after the relevant vol. of *HCT*; Lewis was presumably working through his copy of Gomme and wanted to see whether Gomme had spotted the point. So much for Athenians. But something can be done with Corinthians too, and I shall be looking at the names at iv. 119, which include Peloponnesians as well as Athenians.

I start with a simple instance where an unusual name in Thucydides can be exploited to enhance the probability that he knew what he was talking about. It is from iv. 78. 1, Στρόφακος πρόξενος ὢν Χαλκιδέων,

---

[253] P. S. Derow, 'Kleemporos', *Phoenix*, 27 (1973), 118–34. The inscription is R. K. Sherk, *Roman Documents from the Greek East* (Baltimore, 1969), no. 24. Add now *SEG* xxxi. 594, 596.

[254] See W. V. Harris, *War and Imperialism in Republican Rome 327–70 BC* (Oxford, 1979), 195 n. 4.

[255] See v. 11. 1 n. on καταβαλόντες for the evidence of Cratinus and of an ostrakon published in 1991.

[256] A. Andrewes and D. M. Lewis, 'A Note on the Peace of Nikias', *JHS* 77 (1957), 177–80.

'Strophakos who was the proxenos of the Chalkidians'. The importance of the Chalkidian connection becomes properly clear only at 79. 2 where we learn that the Chalkidians (and Perdikkas) had already summoned Brasidas. 'Strophakos' is a good Thessalian name, see *IG* ii². 2406 line 7, Μένων Στρωφάκο[υ, 'Menon son of Strophakos'. Christian Habicht has recognized this Attic inscription as a list of Thessalians: see iv. 78. 1 n. Clearly, Strophakos is an authentic Thessalian, and we can surely conclude that Thucydides' information about Brasidas' central Greek friendships was good. Similarly Nikonidas of Larisa (Th. iv. 78. 2) turns out to have a very rare name indeed; but it is well attested in precisely Thessaly.[257] This kind of specific onomastic evidence could have been used by Herman to strengthen his study of ritualized friendship.[258] Gomme's only comment on all these Thessalian names was on Panairos. He asked, 'where did Thucydides get these names from, and what was his purpose in recording them?' This was rather feeble. The answers to the two questions are: (i) from reliable sources; (ii) in order to emphasize, by means of informed specificity, the excellence of Brasidas' contacts.

Next a trickier individual, this time a Boiotian, Ptoiodoros (iv. 76. 2). Thucydides is talking about the pro-Athenian plot inside Boiotia which culminated in the Delion fiasco. It was engineered he says 'mainly at the instigation of Ptoiodoros, a Thespian exile', καὶ Πτοιοδώρου μάλιστ' ἀνδρὸς φυγάδος ἐκ Θεσπιῶν ἐσηγουμένου. I have changed the Oxford text ἐκ Θηβῶν ('a Theban exile'); the variant 'Thespian' is not recorded in the apparatus to the OCT, but in two manuscripts it is given in the margin as a variant, and Gomme was surely right to prefer it. Pro-Athenians are well attested at Thespiai.[259] Ptoiodoros is a good Boiotian name (see iv. 76. 2 n.) and there is no justification whatever for emending it[260] to Potamodoros, merely because we happen to know from an inscription that a Boiotian (actually from Orchomenos) called Potamodoros was honoured at Athens as a benefactor: *IG* i³. 73.

Thucydides is generally well-informed on Boiotian names; Pagondas (iv. 91) may be a historical character attested elsewhere, a kinsman of Pindar whose patronymic was supposed to have been Pagondas. A partheneion of Pindar (F94b Snell/Maehler, line 10), written for members of Pindar's own family, mentions an Agasikles son of Pagondas who may be

[257] For Nikonidas (spelt Νικονίδας, omicron at the second syllable) cp. Plut. *Luc.* 10 (Νικωνίδης, a Thessalian siege-engineer) and *IG* ix. 2. 211 (Melitea in Phthiotic Achaia). See further iv. 78. 2 n.

[258] G. Herman, *Ritualized Friendship and the Greek City* (Cambridge, 1987).

[259] See the Athenian inscription *IG* i³. 23 (Thespian proxenoi, one called Athenaios, line 7), with Lewis, *CAH* v². 116 n. 74; Th. iv. 133. 1, vi. 95. 2; and *IG* i³. 72 (about whose date Lewis, the editor of *IG*, changed his mind: the positioning in *IG* implies 424, but he eventually preferred 414, the date of Th. vi. 95).

[260] With M. Walbank, *Athenian Proxenies of the Fifth Century* BC (Toronto and Sarasota, 1978), 252-3.

Thucydides' Pagondas.[261] Pagondas' colleague as boiotarch at Delion, Arianthidas son of Lysimachidas, is probably the Boiotian admiral on Lysander's victory monument at Delphi for Aegospotami (ML 95d) [. . .]θιος [Λυσι]μαχίδαο. Gomme's n. on him is better ('another small detail learnt and recorded').

I turn now to the names appended to the truce of 423 (iv. 119. 2); particularly interesting because they are not just Athenian or Spartan. The first-mentioned Spartans are Tauros son of Echetimidas and Athenaios son of Perikleidas. The patronymics here and throughout the list of names, are notable; Gomme was surely right to think that they featured in the original list, i.e. are not Thucydides' own carefully researched insertion. But in any case they conform to one of his categories for inclusion of patronymics, namely that they all (one assumes) held importance offices of state.[262] The name Echetima (feminine name) occurs at Sparta's colonies Melos and Thera, and the phil-Athenian family of Athenaios son of Perikleidas is well-known from literary sources.[263]

Now for the Corinthians. Valuable recent work has been done here by Stroud,[264] who supported his thesis about Thucydides' specially good knowledge of Corinth by pointing to the high total of Corinthians with patronymics in Thucydides. He shows that 52% of all Thucydides' Corinthians have patronymics, which is higher even than the total for all Athenians, 50%, and much higher than that for Sparta, barely 25%. And the total of Corinthians named once only but given patronymics is again the highest of any ethnic group. I have already (above, p. 21f.) discussed the implications of Thucydides' good knowledge of Corinth, and suggested that it does not impose the conclusion that Thucydides actually resided there as Stroud supposes, though we can surely agree that Corinth was one of the main places Thucydides has in mind when he says (v. 26) that he visited the Peloponnese in his exile.

Stroud can, however, be supplemented at the level of detail about individuals (no sling-bullets in Stroud, for instance). Thucydides tells us the delegates included the Corinthians, Aineas son of Okytos and Euphamidas son of Aristonymos, Κορινθίων δὲ Αἰνέας Ὠκύτου, Εὐφαμίδας Ἀριστωνύμου. The 'influential and anti-Athenian' Corinthian family of Aineas was elucidated by Wilamowitz:[265] Aineas may be

---

[261] U. v. Wilamowitz-Moellendorff, *Pindaros* (Berlin, 1922), 436; C. M. Bowra, *Pindar* (Oxford, 1964), 99 f. Note the Pagondas at *SEG* xxxii. 436 (Theban victor at the Mouseia); see further my n. on iv. 91.

[262] G. T. Griffith, 'Some Habits of Thucydides When Introducing Persons', *PCPhS* 187 (1961), 21–33, at 21.

[263] Full references for these and the following items are given in my commentary on the chapter.

[264] R. S. Stroud, 'Thucydides and Corinth' (above, n. 61), esp. 269 f., for the Corinthian patronymics.

[265] *Kleine Schriften*, iii. 371.

a grandson of Adeimantos son of Okytos, the Corinthian leader mentioned by Herodotus (viii. 5, 59, etc.); this Adeimantos was father of the well-known Aristeus whose activities are described by Thucydides himself (i. 60. 2; ii. 67) as well as by Herodotus (vii. 137). I suppose Wilamowitz assumes an Okytos II, son of Adeimantos, brother of Aristeus and father of Aineas.

'Aineas', Αἰνέας, is not a rare name, if we assume it is some form of the Homeric Αἰνείας (some manuscripts of Thucydides spell the name Ἐν–). A general point: the orthography of Thucydidean names should probably *not* be altered to conform to epigraphic usage, see iv. 76. 2 n. on καὶ Πτοιοδώρου . . . and 78. 1 n. on Στρόφακος . . .; also v. 18. 6 n.

For Euphamidas see ii. 33. 1, where he and other Corinthians restore the tyrant Euarchos to Astakos; he also attends and makes an intervention at a conference held at Mantinea, v. 55. 1 (probably the same person, though he is not there given his patronymic). There is a possible later epigraphic occurrence of the name Euphamidas at Roman Corinth.

For the names of the other individuals (Sikyonians, Megarians, Epidaurians) see my commentary below.

'The Athenians were the generals Nikostratos son of Diitrephes, Nikias son of Nikeratos, Autokles son of Tolmaios', Ἀθηναίων δὲ οἱ στρατηγοὶ Νικόστρατος Διτρέφους, Νικίας Νικηράτου, Αὐτοκλῆς Τολομαίου. For all three men see 53. 1 (they served together against Kythera). Wilamowitz[266] said that the names were in the official Athenian tribal order, Nikostratos probably from I (Erechtheis, 'Nikostratos wird aus der Erechtheis gewesen sein'), Nikias from II (Aigeis), Autokles from X (Antiochis). But this is not right, because Nikostratos is now believed to be from the deme Skambonidai which is in Leontis (tribe IV).[267] For Wilamowitz's point about tribal order to be right we would have to suppose that the order of the first two names has been transposed. In favour of this (it might be said) is the order at 53. 1: Nikias, Nikostratos, Autokles. That is, as things stand, Thucydides' narrative preserves the correct tribal order, the truce text not! But the order at 53. 1 is more likely to be the result of putting the famous man (Nikias) first; I cannot believe Thucydides in his *narrative* bothered about the tribal order, which he disregards at e.g. ii. 23. 2 (V, VII, II). The official list of names of swearers to the Peace of Nikias, to which I now turn, is a different matter; as we have seen (above) Andrewes and Lewis showed that the sixth to fifteenth Athenian names at v. 19. 2 are in tribal order.

It is an odd fact that Wilamowitz's two essays on the truce of 423 and

[266] *Kleine Schriften*, iii. 370–1.
[267] See iii. 75. 1 n., and *LGPN* ii, entry under Νικόστρατος no. 146.

on the Peace of Nikias have virtually disappeared from the scholarly literature. This seems to be due to the great scholarly authority of Gomme, who I suspect merely overlooked them. But Wilamowitz's essays have good things to say generally, and in particular he was fascinated by names for their own sake, though some of his own suggestions were wild; he did moreover, as we have just seen, anticipate Lewis and Andrewes, who do not cite him, by looking for a tribal order in a sequence of Thucydidean Athenians. Though as it happens he looked in the wrong place.

Andrewes and Lewis suggest that the first two names are religious experts (Lampon, Isthmionikos), then follow three probable generals (Nikias, Laches, Euthydemos), then the ten-man board (see v. 19. 1 n. on ὤμνυον etc.), then Lamachos and Demosthenes, who are separated from the generals and are therefore perhaps not generals themselves this year (though this cannot be ruled out); they were perhaps added when 'the presiding officer called for two more names' and someone suggested this well-known pair. This convincing analysis is accepted in *LGPN* ii and in Develin's standard reference work on Athenian officials,[268] and post-1957 work generally has only served to reinforce the Andrewes/Lewis thesis (though their thesis has influenced some of the identifications accepted in the reference books). For instance, it now seems certain from an ostrakon, if not from Cratinus, that Hagnon was from the deme Steiria and is thus from Tribe III Pandionis, where on the Andrewes/Lewis view he ought to be (see v. 11. 1 n. on καταβαλόντες).

Of the ten-man board as a whole Andrewes and Lewis (180) say, 'it seems to be composed of sound and trustworthy men, not specially committed to war or peace, and not the leading politicians of the time. The active work was no doubt done elsewhere, and mainly by Nikias and Laches (Thuc. v. 43. 2)'; they note in particular that Pythodoros, Hagnon, and Aristokrates were men of property (for *APF* refs. see below under the individual names). It is curious that Wilamowitz, who, as we have seen, (wrongly) believed the three Athenians at iv. 119. 1 (see note there) were in tribal order, should apparently not have looked for tribal order at v. 19. 2.

I shall not here discuss the individual Athenian names in detail, reserving such discussion for the commentary.

Andrewes and Lewis made the further suggestion, basing themselves on Diodorus' mention of a ten-man commission (xii. 75. 4), that Athens and Sparta had each appointed a ten-man board to conduct preliminary negotiations, a stage Thucydides must on this hypothesis have omitted

---

[268] R. Develin, *Athenian Officials 684–321 BC* (Cambridge, 1989).

to describe in detail—if true, a nice instance of Thucydidean selectivity. Sparta asked for parity, which explains why the (normally Athenian) number ten features in a Spartan context; as Andrewes and Lewis say,[269] boards of *three* are more common at Sparta, though ten advisers were appointed to supervise Agis (Th. v. 63. 4). It seems from Diodorus' account that Sparta's allies complained that they were not represented on this board (see their later complaints at 29. 2). The suggestion of Andrewes and Lewis is extremely neat, and very probably right. But Diodorus' ten-man commission as it stands looks suspiciously like the Roman diplomatic use of *decem legati* (cp. xxix. 11 for the Peace of Apamea), and one might wonder whether Diodorus has not creatively reworked what he found in Ephorus. (By 'as it stands' I mean that Diodorus actually says the ten-man boards were appointed *after* the peace, and Andrewes and Lewis have to suppose that this is a confusion by Diodorus or his source with events *before* the peace.) See below, p. 116.

Would Thucydides have kept all the names in a hypothetical final version? And even if we think he would, can we accept that he would virtually repeat two lists of seventeen names at ch. 24? I return to this in the next and final section.

7. *Conclusion: iv–v. 24 as a work of art*

In this final section I consider Thucydides iv–v. 24 as a work of art— innovative or merely incomplete? Those recent studies[270] which examine the internal structure of book iv, and detect a deliberate architecture, tend to go with a unitarian approach. I put that vaguely, rather than saying that they 'assume' or that they 'presuppose' a unitarian approach, because one might perfectly well say that Thucydides intended the architectural plan, but did not, for whatever reason, complete the details. However, all argument about Thucydides soon becomes, precisely, an argument about details. Thus Connor and Babut press details very hard and ingeniously, finding significance in apparent loose ends. As it happens, our section of Thucydides contains episodes which have seemed to many investigators to be undigested and indigestible, most obviously the treaties at iv. 118 and v. 18 and 23; but there is also the indirect speech we discussed in section 5 (above, p. 89; 93).

The latter part of book iv and the beginning of book v cover the first period during which Thucydides was in exile, and many a scholar, before, after, and including Wilamowitz, has sought a biographical explanation for the state of the sixty-odd chapters after the fall of

---

[269] *JHS* 77 (1957), 177 n. 4. For the *ten* Athenian tribes see above, p. 102.
[270] Above all Babut and Connor (above, nn. 42 and 45); see further below.

Amphipolis.' In the present section I shall pay particular attention to iv. 108–v. 24, without wishing to imply that Pylos and Demosthenes were less important. Nor should we forget the western material whose full function, if that is not too question-beggingly teleological, does not become clear until books vi–vii. For instance, the fact given at v. 5, that Phaiax persuaded the usually pro-Syracusan Lokri to agree to make a treaty with Athens, is of great interest, and it is tantalizing that we are never told how relations broke down again, as they had obviously done by the time of the hostility recorded as a matter of course in vi. 44.

I begin with some remarks on structure in the light of recent work; then I discuss the episodes which have generated suspicions that iv–v. 24 is a fragment. In this category I start with the last three chapters of iv and the first of v, with their untypically varied content; then I consider the documents, iv. 118, v. 18, and v. 23. I end with my conclusions about date of composition.

On the structure of book iv as a whole see, as well as Connor (invaluable here as always), the illuminating study, taking ingenuity to its limits, by D. Babut. Babut, who inevitably takes in the early part of book v as well, argues[271] that the chopped-up ('morcelé') composition of book iv is more than just the price Thucydides paid for strict chronological method. (Not always strict, as we saw above, p. 101, when discussing iv. 50. 3, the death of Artaxerxes). It enables Thucydides to balance episodes and themes against each other. The Pylos narrative in the first part of the book is balanced, symmetrically and inversely, by Brasidas in Thrace and Chalkidike at the end of the book. (The Athenians at Pylos, and Brasidas in Thrace, exploit the other side's negligence; and both seek successfully to provoke disaffection: with chs. 41 and 55 compare 108, the result of the taking of Amphipolis.) The Chalkidic section also mirrors Kythera at 53–5[272] (I think he means that Nikias at Kythera capitalizes on Pylos as Brasidas capitalizes on Amphipolis). In the first half of the book Athens had been amazingly successful. After Kythera, everything starts to seesaw the other way.[273] Megara (66–74), a semi-success for Athens (see esp. 73. 4 ἐπειδὴ καὶ τὰ πλείω . . .), is the structural hinge.[274] Boiotian (the Delion campaign) and Thracian affairs are interwoven by Thucydides, not out of chronological clumsiness or 'maladresse'[275] but to make the point, insistently, that the Athenians should not have been seduced by the Delion sideshow: they woke up too

[271] Babut, 417.
[272] Babut, 420.
[273] Babut, 426, 'la situation commence à basculer'.
[274] Babut, 427, 'la charnière structurale'.
[275] Babut, 436.

late to Brasidas. That is the basic Babut picture, by which Connor in particular has been influenced.[276]

Babut's theory involves some implausibility and strain at the level of detail. Thus the wintry weather at Amphipolis (iv. 103) is supposed[277] to correspond to the bad weather at Pylos, iv. 3; I do not find this specially illuminating. And the same is true of the suggestion[278] that Brasidas' wound and lost shield (iv. 12) correspond to the trophy after the battle of Amphipolis (v. 10) and the death of Kleon at the hand of a peltast. But we shall see that one Pylos/northern parallel in particular, to be mentioned below (p. 114), helps with the problem of the digestibility of the documents in our section of narrative.

There is a further reason, not discussed by Connor or Babut, for seeing the whole of iv-v. 24 as regulated by a plan, namely the pause points with their cross-references of language. This feature cannot easily be paralleled in other sections of Thucydides.

At intervals, in six places, Thucydides pauses to comment on the morale of one or both sides: iv. 41; 55; 80-1; 108; 117; v. 14-16. (To make the point more clearly: if we take the whole of iv-v. 24 as a unit of 159 chapters, the pauses occur at 41, 55, 80, 108, 117, 150.) There is a notable degree of interrelation of language between the six excurses. Note for instance the reiterated words for fearing (ἐδέδισαν, iv. 55. 3; 117. 1, cp. δέος at iv. 108. 1; v. 14. 2; or φοβούμενοι and other φοβ- words, iv. 41. 3; 55. 1; 80. 3; 108. 1; 117. 1). Of the two, δέος is said (see LSJ⁹) to be more long-lasting than φόβος, and this certainly suits the Athenian preoccupation with Amphipolis (which continued well into the fourth century), see iv. 108. 1. Let me take one in particular, iv. 55, the second of the six excurses on morale. It most obviously resumes iv. 41 and anticipates iv. 80 and v. 14. 3, but there is also a clear relation to the fourth excursus, iv. 108: with iv. 55. 1 Πύλου δὲ ἐχομένης καὶ Κυθήρων, 'Pylos and Kythera were in the hands of the enemy', compare 108. 1 ἐχομένης δὲ τῆς Ἀμφιπόλεως, 'now that Amphipolis was in enemy hands'. Classen/Steup discussing 108 rightly noted that it is a sort of Athenian counterpart, 'eine Art Gegenstück', to the account of low Spartan morale in 55.

I ought also to discuss ch. 117, which introduces the truce of 423; it is the fifth and penultimate of the six excurses on morale which punctuate iv-v. 24. Like the sixth and last (v. 14 ff.), which prepares us for the Peace of Nikias, it pays attention to both sides. But 117 is textually the

---

[276] See also H.-P. Stahl, *Thukydides* (above, n. 36), 140-57, for the fluctuations of fortune in iv-v. 24.

[277] Babut, 423.

[278] Babut, 420-1.

most problematic of the six. I fear I agree with those who think para. 2 is corrupt beyond retrieval; see my commentary. In any case the word ηὐτύχει looks forward to the final excursus about morale, namely v. 16. 1, where ὁ μὲν διὰ τὸ εὐτυχεῖν is also used about Brasidas. And note that both passages have ἐδέδισαν ('they were afraid'), iv. 117. 1 and v. 14. 2.

On any grand scheme of Thucydides' work, such as that of Rawlings,[279] the first half of book iv is central. (I shall not discuss Rawlings' case because in his scheme book iv corresponds to an unwritten book ix about which he has ingenious conjectures to make but they *are* just conjectures.)

I now deal with that opening section in particular before going on to the end of iv. In chs. 1–19, the Athenians occupy Pylos and cut off a Spartan force on Sphakteria. This episode is in Thucydides' presentation the turning-point of the Archidamian War. Westlake, however, has argued[280] that Thucydides, partly through topographic misunderstandings, exaggerated the importance of the Pylos affair and the extent of the Spartan reverse, and minimized the general mood of dissatisfaction at Sparta with the progress of the war. The latter, Westlake argues, was the real reason why the Spartans sued for peace at chs. 17 ff. I think Westlake unduly minimizes Spartan anxiety about their prisoners, but there is some force in the 'general dissatisfaction' argument; it is also relevant to the 425 proposal that Pleistoanax who favoured peace (v. 16–17) had been back in Sparta since 427/6 (see v. 16. 3 n. on ἔτει etc.). But in all this we are, as so often, correcting Thucydides out of Thucydides.

I now turn to the chapters which do not easily fit into this grand Babut-Connor scheme according to which the halves of iv–v. 24 are the two flanges of a huge door, and the door itself is central to the whole work. The awkward chapters I refer to are iv. 133–5, to which should perhaps be added v. 1 (the book-divisions can be disregarded). Can they be explained as anything other than scraps or leftovers?

Chs. 133–5 cover events at Thespiai, Argos, Skione; the battle between Mantinea and Tegea; Brasidas' attempt on Potidaia. Wilamowitz[281] thought that the bittiness of chs. 133 and 134, and Thucydides' failure to make clear the significance of the Thespiai and Tegea/Mantinea incidents in particular, was evidence that Thucydides' information about Greek affairs was beginning (now that he 'had retreated to the fastness of his Thracian possessions') to be patchy; Wilamowitz thought the section lacked the final authorial elaboration. (This was all part of

---

[279] H. R. Rawlings III, *The Structure of Thucydides' History* (above, n. 44).

[280] H. D. Westlake, 'The Naval Battle at Pylos and its Consequences', *CQ* 24 (1974), 211–26 = *Studies in Thucydides and Greek History* (Bristol, 1989), ch. 5.

[281] *Kl. Schr.* iii. 376 and n. 1.

Wilamowitz's argument that the truce at 118 was an insertion; I come to this later.) In similar vein, Andrewes[282] remarked that these chapters illustrated the 'sporadic and mostly scrappy' quality of the references to non-northern events in the post-Delion narrative (Andrewes was discussing 'indications of incompleteness' in Thucydides' narrative of the Ten Years War). But this is not the only place where Thucydides, in a manner foreshadowing Tacitus in the *Annals*, lumps together a number of disparate items at the end of a campaigning year, or becomes more expansive; the motive may partly be to vary the handling after a long narrative of uniform texture.[283] In such sections (this is conspicuously true of ii. 102 with its mythical content, and iii. 116 on the eruption of Etna), he allows himself to relax his customary austerity. This may be relevant to the Chrysis story below. Finally, we should not forget that after the truce military activity was meagre, so that he allows in material which might not normally qualify for inclusion. (But 'padding' is not habitual with Thucydides: v. 82–3, a whole year covered in two chapters, shows that if he had little to say he was happy to be suitably brief.)

First 133, Chrysis' burning down of the Argive Heraion. Syme's statement[284] that she is the only female agent in Thucydides is a slight exaggeration. Wiedemann[285] says that it is tempting to see the explanation for her disappearance as 'due to a subconscious feeling on the historian's part that this is the kind of chance calamity for which women are to blame'. Perhaps, but to make this point Thucydides did not need to give us, in addition, the name of her successor Phaeinis. For another suggested motive for allowing the admittedly untypical Chrysis incident into the history see below. See also introductory n. to 133–4.

Since Hellanicus wrote a 'Priestesses of Argos', and since Thucydides criticizes Hellanicus by name (i. 97), scholars have reasonably felt that Hellanicus is somehow the key to the inclusion of the whole of the present uncharacteristic passage. Smart,[286] as part of his argument that Thucydides had a strong desire to improve on Hellanican chronology, thinks that part of Thucydides' motive in this paragraph is 'to indicate that the relationship between such eponymous schemes [as Th. rejects at v. 20. 2–3] and the events they encompassed was contingent not natural'. Smart suggests that the present passage about Chrysis makes

---

[282] *HCT* v. 364.

[283] See ii. 102 (Acheloos); iii. 115–16 (Sicily; Etna); vi. 7; vii. 18.

[284] R. Syme, 'Thucydides', *PBA* 48 (1962), 39–56 (= *Roman Papers*, vi (Oxford, 1991), 72–87), at 41. This article will be referred to by the original pagination.

[285] T. E. J. Wiedemann, 'ἐλάχιστον . . . ἐν τοῖς ἄρσεσι κλέος: Thucydides, Women and the Limits of Rational Analysis', *G & R* 30 (1983), 163–70, at 168.

[286] J. D. Smart, 'Thucydides and Hellanicus', in I. S. Moxon, J. D. Smart, and A. J. Woodman (eds.), *Past Perspectives* (Cambridge, 1986), 19–35, at 24, cp. 32.

this 'beautifully clear': the 'chance event of her leaving a burning lamp occurred in the middle of a natural seasonal unit [here he quotes the present passage] and resulted in a ludicrous division of a naturally connected series of events, i.e. the ten-year war, between two priestesses and so between two chronological eras.' The clumsiness of the formula here used about Chrysis is certainly effective preparation for the methodological polemic at v. 20, though 'ludicrous' is perhaps too strong. Dover[287] wondered if Thucydides was prompted to include the Chrysis story because Hellanicus' account of the priestesses of Argos had only recently been published and it stopped before 423, i.e. Thucydides was continuing Hellanicus' work rather than criticizing his methodology. To which Gomme[288] replied that Thucydides may have inserted the present passage later. This bears on 'recently published', but it might still be true that Thucydides was giving an item not covered by Hellanicus.

Another motive for including the present passage may be to prepare us for the importance of Argos in book v, starting with v. 14. 4.

As for the function of 134 in particular (the battle between Tegea and Mantinea), it is true that it is isolated from its immediate context, but it too prepares us for the Peloponnesian events which take up so much of book v. Even Wilamowitz[289] conceded this much: the Mantinea–Tegea battle 'is connected with the break-up of the Peloponnesian League, about which book v has so much to say'. Lewis calls this battle 'an extreme case of return to local priorities' after the truce; he notes that it is evidence of the common tendency of Mantinea and Tegea to expand into western Arkadia; elsewhere he conjectures that the battle at iv. 134 was not the first attempt either city had made to extend its influence in that direction.[290]

Finally there is Brasidas' attempt at Potidaia at iv. 135 and v. 1. iv. 135 reminds us that we are still basically in the middle of Brasidas' *aristeia* (see above, p. 41), while v. 1 with its material about Pharnakes is the merest hint of the Persian theme so seriously understated in book v and so important in book viii. In this chapter the dog that does not bark is Amorges.[291]

To conclude: one can, I think, find plausible explanations for all the individual items at iv. 133–v. 1; and together they have a preparatory function. In any case it is a Thucydidean habit to collect loose ends at the end of a year and this is just a conspicuous example. As for book iv as a

[287] K. J. Dover, 'La colonizzazione della Sicilia in Tucidide', *Maia*, 6 (1953), 39–56, at 41, repr. in H. Herter (ed.), *Thukydides* (Darmstadt, 1968), 344–68.

[288] *HCT* iii. 625.

[289] *Kl. Schr.* iii.376 and n. 1.

[290] *CAH* v². 429; 104.

[291] A. Andrewes, 'Thucydides and the Persians', *Historia*, 10 (1961), 1–18.

unit, the Babut/Connor theory is attractive but involves some straining of detail. As for the centrality of book iv in the whole work, there is I think much to be said for the view that Thucydides exaggerated the significance of Pylos in the war. One can take Westlake's theory a little further and say that what really lost the Spartans the Ten Years War was the failure to win the battle of the hearts and minds. They started out with the *eunoia* insisted on so strongly at ii. 9, but then it evaporated as successive commanders behaved badly, οὐ καλῶς, Alkidas in Asia Minor, and the various Spartans, including Alkidas, who ruined the Herakleia Trachinia project (above, p. 58). On this view the Spartan failure in the Ten Years War was a gradual affair, a loss of confidence which even Brasidas, or especially Brasidas, was unable to arrest. So there was no real 'charnière', no hinge, outside the tidy mind of the historian.

I turn now to the documents: the truce of 423 (iv. 118–19), the Peace of Nikias (v. 18–19), and the Alliance (v. 23–4). A fundamental distinction needs to be made at the outset between two related but distinct issues, not always kept clearly enough apart. First, would Thucydides have retained raw-looking material like the treaties in a finished version? Second, do the documents sit comfortably in their particular narrative contexts? (If not, that might mean they were inserted later.) One could perfectly well answer Yes to the first question but No to the second.

To an unusual degree the arguments about the documents depend on details of interpretation: it is above all the sheer quantity and minuteness of detail which marks off these chapters (iv. 118; v. 18 and 23) from even the most photographically complete sections of Thucydidean narrative. I must therefore refer the reader to the commentary, and introductory discussions, for the full treatment and for my conclusions, which I summarize here.

Kirchhoff's classic study[292] argued that the narrative seemed ignorant of the detailed stipulations and clauses of the truce and of the Peace of Nikias, and that Thucydides therefore visited the Metroon and saw the archival text of the peace only after 404. (Kirchhoff's position about the Peace of Nikias was different from his position over the 423 truce because he thought that the narrative before *and after* iv. 118–19 was written earlier than the truce treaty, but by contrast he thought that chs. v. 21 onwards—not just 25 onwards—were written after 404 and in knowledge of the detail of the treaty.) But Thucydides died, Kirchhoff thought, before he had time to adjust his narrative to the newly incorporated material. Gomme was surely right to reject this. Kirchhoff's position

[292] A. Kirchhoff, *Thukydides und sein Urkundenmaterial* (Berlin, 1895).

demanded too high a level of consistency and uniformity of texture from Thucydides. We can add one or two particular arguments against Kirchhoff (and Wilamowitz, who agreed with his general position). I should like in particular to draw attention to what I believe to be an unnoticed feature of 118. 4, τοὺς μὲν ἐν τῷ Κορυφασίῳ 'the Athenians at Koryphasion'. That means 'at Pylos'. Now at iv.3. 2, near the very beginning of our section, Thucydides adds an unusual though (see n. there) not wholly uncharacteristic explanatory comment about a place name, namely that Koryphasion is the Spartan name for Pylos. I suggest that this in itself gratuitous remark prepares us for the use, both at iv. 118 and in the equally documentary v. 18. 7 (Peace of Nikias) of Koryphasion in documentary contexts. This is a small piece of evidence tending against Kirchhoff's view that the documents were later insertions. Again, iv. 119. 3—and here I claim no originality—speaks of negotiations about a more lasting peace, περὶ τῶν μειζόνων σπονδῶν. This is one of the passages in Thucydides' own narrative which are consistent with the detail of the truce treaty, see 118. 6 and 13–14, also v. 15. 2. But 119. 3 does not quite require knowledge of the treaty, because the negotiations about a more lasting peace were an independently ascertainable fact.

For Babut, the truce near the end of book iv corresponds to that at ch. 16, near the beginning of the book: both register the marked superiority of one side (Athens at 16, Sparta now), while saving the face of the other [in ch. 16 the face-saving is not very prominent to my eye, though 118. 4 did leave Athens in possession of Pylos, Kythera, and Minoa]; after both treaties expire, a more decisive victory follows: Sphakteria; the defeat of the Athenians before Amphipolis.

There is an important point here, and this is the Pylos/northern parallel I promised to return to. The truce at ch. 16 anticipates in a small but interesting and portentous way the most striking innovation of 118–19 (and, we must add, v. 18–19 and 23, the Peace of Nikias and the consequent alliance), namely the inclusion of near-documentary material in the narrative. As we have just seen, Babut, as part of his structural parallel between the Pylos and Chalkidic narratives, compares iv. 16 and iv. 118. Similarly, but from a very different starting-point, Andrewes[293] remarks that ch. 16, with its free use of documentary language and the full detail about the rations, two Attic choinikes of barley, two kotylai of wine, and so on, might be thought to anticipate 118 (the truce of 423). But he immediately goes on to concede that the narrative at 26–7 and 39 explains the detail about the rations, and that generally the great difference is that 16 (unlike 118) contains no detail calling for explanation that

[293] Babut, 424–5; Andrewes, *HCT* v. 365.

has not been given in the narrative; 'and it is this, with the full verbatim transcription, that constitutes the real innovation at iv. 118–19.' (Andrewes was discussing 'indications of incompleteness' in Thucydides' narrative of the Ten Years War.)

Andrewes instances 118. 2, the reference to 'those present', implying absentees, 118. 3, the issue of Delphic funds, and 118. 4, Troizen. I believe we should reject the Kirchhoff theory of wholesale interpolation, and the associated dogma that there was a stylistic law prohibiting ancient historians from including such documents (Andrewes[294] has good remarks on this, and gives modern references, to which add the 'stop-gap' theory of R. Syme, who hankered after such a law). But when we have rejected all this, we are still left with the problem, *why* did Thucydides include these documents? Andrewes's general view was that the quality of the narrative had begun to deteriorate towards the end of the Ten Years War, partly because Thucydides was now in exile. Andrewes's discussion of the truce treaty in the context of incompleteness leads one to suppose that he thought the documents (and under this head we must include v. 18–19 and 23) would eventually have disappeared when Thucydides gave the narrative the final polish; and eventually he made this belief explicit.[295] The choice (he wrote) is between belief that Thucydides was deliberately adopting a new method, and belief that 'the full verbatim documents might in the final version have been replaced by shorter summaries'. He added that 'the latter appears to me very much more likely'. (On this view the documents were left where they are *either* by Thucydides himself *or* by an editor who found two versions, the full text and a brief summary, and opted for the text. That is, there are three possibilities in all, the 'new method' thesis, and two versions of the 'eventual replacement' thesis.) Perhaps the 'incompleteness' theory is right. But despite the occasional difficulties of reconciling treaty texts and narrative, it seems to me (and here at last I come clean about the main theme of this Introduction) that the 'innovation' view is in the end

---

[294] *HCT* v. 374 f. For the 'stop-gap' theory see Syme (n. 284), 46: 'In book v certain documents are quoted verbatim. For example, the Peace between Athens in 421; also the Alliance (v. 18 f.; 23 f.). We cannot say that the documents are objectionable in themselves. It is not for us to lay down laws for a writer of the fierce idiosyncrasy of Thucydides. But one conceives a doubt when one sees that in each of these documents seventeen names of Spartans occur and seventeen of Athenians, who are witnesses. There are historians who like to sprinkle their narration with personal names for various reasons: zeal for authenticity or the parade of erudition. Thucydides is an economical writer. These names have no meaning whatsoever. Further, he even inserts two documents of armistice and alliance between the Spartans and the Argives in the Dorian dialect (v. 77; 79). These pacts, concluded in the winter of 418/17, were ephemeral, quickly broken by a revolution at Argos, with open war ensuing. Surely the plain answer is that the texts are stop-gaps.' Note that this ignores iv. 118–19 completely.
[295] *HCT* v. 383.

preferable to the 'incompleteness' view. The issue goes wider than the treaty documents. (i) Not only is the Melian Dialogue at the end of book v an innovation; there is also (ii) the long exchange in indirect speech as early as iv. 97. 2–99, which we discussed in section 5 (above, p. 89 ff.); we can if we wish make a virtue out of the slippery focalization of e.g. iv. 99. And (iii) iv. 16 with the 425 truce terms is, while not an actual document, undoubtedly innovative as we have seen, though we may concede that its inclusion is explicable in a way that 118 is not. (iv) See also iv. 76. 1 n.

Why then are the documents (to come back to them) there at all?

First, it may have attracted Thucydides that there was an almost literal concreteness about a truce, treaty, or alliance text about to be recorded on stone. By the late 420s both sides were reaching near-exhaustion; but what stood in the way was a reluctance to be cheated territorially or in other ways. The discussions must have been extremely concrete. In the run-up to the Peace of Nikias, the language of v. 17. 2 (as I hinted in the preceding section, see above, p. 106, citing the 1957 study by Andrewes and Lewis) may mask the preliminary work of two ten-man commissions whose existence is almost totally concealed by Thucydides. The Greek is τόν τε χειμῶνα τοῦτον ἦσαν ἐς λόγους, 'discussions went on through the winter'. Both in 423 and 421, the treaties gave the hard nuggets of diplomacy in a form which could certainly have been more elegantly and more briefly paraphrased. But some concreteness and immediacy would have been forfeited—and some clarity too. By clarity I do not mean that the texts make everything instantly clear; on the contrary they raise (as will be seen from the commentary) abundant problems of their own. But Thucydides may have decided that, for instance, by not giving the terms of the Thirty Years Peace in book i, he had left some big issues obscure (as they certainly are).

Second, another reason for including the 421 treaty and alliance (but not the 423 truce) is their emphasis on oaths.[296] Certainly there was a connection between oath-taking and the act of inscription. At v. 56. 3 we are told that Alcibiades persuaded the Athenians to write under their inscribed copy that 'the Spartans have not kept their oaths'. Thucydides wishes to rub in the inefficacy of these oaths.

Third, structural considerations. The inclusion of documents can be or has been justified in the following sort of way: for Connor,[297] 'they help mark out the stages in an otherwise complex and amorphous diplomatic

---

[296] D. T. Steiner, *The Tyrant's Writ: Myths and Images of Writing in Ancient Greece* (Princeton, 1994), 66–7, for a good discussion of the importance, from the ritual aspect, of the oaths in Thucydidean and other treaties, and of the connection between oath-taking and the act of inscription; Connor, *Thucydides*, 147.

[297] Connor, *Thucydides*, 146.

narrative. Their placement emphasizes the major stages in the rapidly changing patterns of Greek diplomacy ... The armistice in 4. 118–19 follows swiftly after the setbacks at Delium and Amphipolis. As a sequel to the battle of Amphipolis two documents, the treaty and the alliance between Athens and Sparta, proclaim co-operation between the two rivals.' Here the 'major stages' suggestion works much less well for the truce at iv. 118 than for the peace and alliance at v. 18 and 23 (see above on the oaths); as for the peace and alliance, the co-operation so elaborately proclaimed soon turned to acrimony, and I suppose the next move might be to say the documents are ironically included, i.e. Thucydides is not stressing co-operation so much as preparing us for the acrimony. One may start at this point to feel the documents are cards that can take any trick. But Connor is right to stress[298] that Thucydides' narrative is not homogeneous: it allows him for instance to include the Homeric Hymn at iii. 104 and the language of the Delphic oracle at v. 16, about Pleistoanax.

Fourth, there is the possibility, as Philip Stadter has suggested to me,[299] that Thucydides 'feels that [treaty texts] tell us as much as any speech about the thinking of the two parties'. This is a good point, but what do we learn about the parties' thinking from the detail that Phainippos was the Athenian *grammateus* or secretary (iv. 118. 11)?

Fifth and last, I can perhaps make a suggestion of my own, which is in terms of Thucydides' anxiety to demonstrate, boldly and assertively, his own microscopic precision. This is not quite the same as what Syme (above, n. 294) disparagingly called zeal for authenticity or parade of erudition. Syme was in any case talking of the personal names, not the treaties. I am thinking of the attitude of mind which at v. 20 rejects eponymous dates because you could not be sure what part of the year events fall in. The documents are an extreme case of Thucydides' desire to get small things right, and to emphasize that he had done so. A comparison of the epigraphically preserved Quadruple alliance (Athens, Argos, Mantinea, Elis, *IG* i³. 83) and Thucydides' version (v. 47) shows the proud emphasis was justified. I conclude that Thucydides could have intended to include the documents as an innovation, although the peace and truce (v. 18; 23) present fewer difficulties than the truce (iv. 118).

I mentioned above the Athenian decree at 118. 11 ff. This leads me to note one oddity. Syme and Andrewes both use the word 'verbatim', and I have used the word 'raw'. Is there any evidence the other way, i.e. of tinkering by Thucydides? The oddity is iv. 118. 11 again, ἔδοξε τῷ δήμῳ, without mention of the *boule*. Gomme thought we should simply emend

---

[298] Connor, *Thucydides*, 145, an excellent discussion.
[299] In a letter dated 8 March 1995.

by adding τῇ βουλῇ καί, and he was surely right to reject Kirchhoff's constitutional explanation that the involvement of the *boule* was purely formal. But though Gomme may be right it is remarkable that the manuscripts are unanimous in omitting the *boule*, and one cannot help recalling how little the *boule* features in Thucydides' narrative even where we should expect it. Thus Badian has pointed out that i. 139[300] implies that the Spartan proposals up to that point had been dealt with by the *boule* who finally decide to let them go before the *ekklesia* to be dealt with once for all. Did Thucydides consciously or subconsciously repress the *boule* in the iv. 118 document? Another omission in this decree is the archon-date, but that does not become a regular feature until about 421, though it is found in inscriptions of the 430s (e.g. ML 63-4, Rhegion and Leontini). Thucydides hardly took his aversion to eponymous dating so far as to drop it if it was there in the original.

I reserve full discussion of the Peace and Alliance (v. 18-19 and 23-4) to the commentary. But I must say something about 20. 1. 'The treaty was concluded at the end of winter, just at the beginning of spring, immediately after the City Dionysia.' That is (probably) 13 Elephebolion. But at 19. 1 Thucydides said that the treaty was to begin on 25 Elephebolion. Perhaps, as Gomme suggested, some time was allowed for communication. The actual dates, then, can be reconciled; but the form in which they are given is different. The dating in 20. 1 conforms to Thucydides' normal method of dating by summers and winters. Gomme and Kirchhoff were very troubled by this, and Gomme this time agreed with Kirchhoff to the extent of supposing that Thucydides did not see a verbatim copy of the text until later. But surely Thucydides could, from the outset, have juxtaposed two kinds of dating, given that one is in a document, the other in his own narrative. Robin Osborne has suggested to me that Thucydides is preparing us for the chronological discussion at v. 20.

The personal names attached to the truce of 423, and to the treaty and the alliance of 421, have been felt peculiarly problematic (Andrewes held strongly that Thucydides' hypothetical final version would not have repeated them,[301] and Syme as we have seen (n. 294) asserts that 'these names have no meaning whatsoever', a surprising remark from that eminent prosopographer). The problem needs to be broken up smaller. I have no difficulty accepting that Thucydides would have included the names at iv. 119 and v. 19—again the proud precision—but I cannot see the point of repeating the 34 names of v. 19 just four chapters later, after

---

[300] See my n. there, citing the treatment which is now to be found as Badian, *From Plataea to Potidaea*, 157.

[301] *HCT* v. 374.

the alliance at v. 23. It is true that Homer had often repeated material wholesale, and one can often think of reasons, e.g. in terms of narrative pause, why such repetition is effective (compare the epic lists in Milton[302]); but I can think of no precedent in Herodotus. (See also above, p. 80: Stagiros, Galepsos repetition; and iv. 56. 2 n.: Thyrea.)

I have already prepared the way for my conclusion on these difficult issues, which needs (see above) to be put in two parts, one an answer to the presence of raw diplomatic material at all, the other an answer to the problem of the compatibility of the documents and their surrounding narrative. On question (i) I believe the documentary material could have stood in a final version, though I find the repeated list of proper names hard to swallow. On the other issue (ii) I agree with Gomme against Kirchhoff on the truce and the Peace of Nikias and have offered some additional points (Koryphasion; and the suggestion that two kinds of dating formula could exist side by side). I have not here discussed the difficulties about the alliance and the movements of the delegates, for which see 22. 1 n.; these difficulties, in particular the problems of reconciliation with 27. 1, are very intractable even after we have accepted Lloyd-Jones's inspired emendation αὖθις for αὐτοί at 22. 1.

I end this section and this Introduction by saying something about date of composition, a traditional but unavoidable problem. My conclusions have already been implied in much of the above, particularly in section 2 when I differed from Fornara and from Kennelly, for whom the Ten Years War narrative was actually issued so early that Herodotus replied to it, not *vice versa*. That is, I reject those fantastically early assumptions about the date at which Thucydides gave his History to the world. At the same time, however, I argued on the basis of expressions like ἀκρόασιν at i. 22. 4 that parts of Thucydides' work could have been presented provisionally and orally in sympotic contexts. I would include the Melian Dialogue in this category and (more relevant to the theme of this volume) perhaps 97–9. I do not have a problem with a Thucydides who took written notes of names like Strophakos and Ptoiodoros. Nevertheless, I would (cf. p. 26) take literally Thucydides' formulation at i. 22 which does not quite exclude parts of the work being originally display pieces for oral recitation, μᾶλλον ἢ ἀγώνισμα ἐς τὸ παράχρημα ἀκούειν. For this sort of reason one might want to avoid talk of publication date for Thucydides, just as I certainly would prefer, following Thomas and Murray, to avoid it for Herodotus. But one cannot altogether avoid the composition question, in view of those passages which specifically allude to events later than their context or which must

---

[302] *Greek Historiography*, 11, citing Barbara Everett.

have been written later than their context. In the present section I have discussed all the most obvious sections claimed by scholars for this category, namely the treaties which Kirchhoff thought could only have come to Thucydides' attention after 404, whereas the surrounding narrative was, he argued, written up straight away. I do not think we are forced to this conclusion, though I accept that v. 22 and 27 are not compatible and that the narrative would have needed more work. So too for speeches like Hippokrates at iv. 95, which (cf. p. 92) may originally have been written to be delivered at Delion, not at the battle site. All this, I believe, implies a rather late date for the whole iv–v. 24 narrative, and that is borne out by the use of 'the first war', ὁ πρῶτος πόλεμος, at v. 20. 3 and 24. 2. On the other hand there is a notorious book iv passage which has been thought definitely early. At iv. 48. 5, Thucydides says that the *stasis* at Corcyra ended 'as far as this war was concerned', ὅσα γε κατὰ τὸν πόλεμον τόνδε. But Diodorus, drawing on Ephorus drawing on some unknown source, mentions great *stasis* at precisely Corcyra in 410/9: xiii. 48. Many, including Dover,[303] have taken this to show that the sentence was written before and probably well before 410; but the imitation of Thucydides in this whole section of Diodorus is patent, as Dover himself conceded, and it is surely possible *either* that the 410 episode is straight fiction *or* (less drastically) that *something* happened in 410 but it was not in reality such as to impress Thucydides with the need to change his book iv formulation. An alternative hypothesis might be that the two *stasis* sections, the thematic one in book iii and the less famous but actually more horrible narrative one in iv. 46–8, were composed (ξυντίθημι not ξυγγράφω) early and provisionally as a unit for sympotic recitation. I mentioned this general possibility in section 2. On this view Thucydides might simply not have got round to updating a closing rhetorical flourish. One thinks of Oscar Wilde's remark when attention was drawn to an error in one of his works: 'who am I to tamper with a masterpiece?' What other hard indicators do we have? The remark at iv. 74. 4 about the Megara counter-revolution, that no such revolution carried out by so few ever lasted so long, is said by Dover to 'impose itself as a late passage'. Though this fits my general view, I am unhappy at pressing a superlative which may (compare above on Corcyra) be little more than a rhetorical flourish, a characteristic Thucydidean closure. Dover and others take Hermokrates at iv. 60. 2, with his talk of larger Athenian expeditions, πλέονί ποτε στολῷ, to be an anachronism—that is, to indicate knowledge of the later expedition of book vi;[304] and Dover

---

[303] *HCT* v. 411. But see below, iv. 48. 5 n.: perhaps by 'this war' Th. meant the Ten Years War.

[304] See also below, Introductory n. to v. 4–5: those chh. may presuppose bks. vi–vii, as may v. 16. 1 (καταλιπεῖν ...; ὁπότε ...); and the Pylos/Sicily parallels (p. 16) may be *pre*-echoes: iv. 12. 3 n.

thought a few ships, ὀλίγαις ναυσί, could be so described only by comparison with 415.[305] However, as Gomme noted, Hermokrates' word τετρυχωμένους, 'exhausted', is not a specially good description of Sicily in 415, and the passage is less than a definite forward allusion to 415. More certainty attaches to iv. 81. 2 with its explicit allusion to the war after Sicily, in the context of the appraisal of Brasidas—even if we decline to see the final sentence as an explicit contrast with Lysander.[306] That sentence says Brasidas left behind a hope that others would be like him. Ch. 81 has often been thought to be at odds with the ostensibly more critical appraisal of Brasidas at 108, a topic we discussed in section 3. We there saw that, though much of both 81 and 108 is focalized through other people, there is in both chapters a residue of Thucydidean judgement, some favourable, some not. This allows us, if we wish, to follow Connor, who concludes[307] that by 108 'the reader is now [after hearing Brasidas and seeing him in action] prepared for a more explicit and critical analysis of Brasidas' claims'; thus the differences between 81 and 108 will be differences of emphasis.[308] The alternative is Andrewes's view that the two chapters are 'not fully co-ordinated' and that this is an indication of incompleteness. In this connection I need to address another use of ὕστερον (cp. above, p. 100, on Artaxerxes). In 108 Thucydides says the Athenian allies thought they were in no danger, but in fact Athenian power was afterwards proved to be as great as their own mistake in underestimating it, ἐψευσμένοι μὲν τῆς Ἀθηναίων δυνάμεως ἐπὶ τοσοῦτον ὅση ὕστερον διεφάνη. The most historically insouciant literary critic must be prepared to give a meaning to ὕστερον here. Westlake[309] argued against Gomme that the subject of the sentence is the Chalkidic cities, not the whole empire, and that 'afterwards' refers to the period 423–421, as being the only period for which the remark is true of those cities; it does not refer to the Ionian War after the Sicilian Disaster. If that is so (Westlake argued) 108 was written or thought before 81 and Thucydides changed his mind in a favourable direction about Brasidas. This is all too strict. Even if Westlake is right against Gomme (and incidentally Dover) about 'afterwards', Gomme could still be right that the sentence was an insertion (Gomme thought a post-404 insertion). In any case there is a fallacy in Westlake's reasoning. Even if the passage *refers* to 423–421, it could nevertheless have been written, or thought, at a much later date (including the composition date of 81. 2, whatever we take that to have been). So nothing follows about the compositional

---

[305] On all this (and on 81. 2) see *HCT* v. 411–12.   [306] See 81. 3 n.

[307] Connor, *Thucydides*, 134.

[308] Compare a forthcoming study by D. Gribble on Thucydides' handling of Alcibiades.

[309] H. D. Westlake, 'Thucydides 4.108.4', *Essays*, 138–44.

relation to ch. 81. Moving away from 81 and 108, we may complain that on a post-404 perspective, v. 1 ought to have been amplified by mention of Pissouthnes/Amorges; on the other hand that same chapter, with its explicit cross-reference to the Delos purification, not only resumes i. 8 and iii. 104 but anticipates viii. 108. 4, the penultimate chapter of the whole work and the fourth and last reference to the purification. Thus i. 8 and viii. 108 enclose the entire history in a handsome ring in which v. 1 is a deliberate and centrally placed precious stone. This is an argument against any incoherence theory of iv–v. 24.

In conclusion there is little or nothing that absolutely forces us to suppose that iv–v. 24 'dates', in any sense of that word, from a point very soon after the events it describes, though I have three qualifications to that: (i) I am sure Thucydides took a written note of e.g. the name Strophakos and perhaps lost no time doing so; (ii) I think there are awkward fits between the narrative before and after v. 24 and that these imply incomplete revision; and (iii) I would not exclude some kind of preliminary recitation of e.g. 46–8 (Corcyra) and 97–9 (the post-Delion argument between the Athenians and Thebans). On the other hand there are passages that probably or (in the case of 81) certainly allude to very much later events. The way is thus open for a view of iv–v. 24 as innovatory and exciting and late, though never wholly revised and at some points less than wholly satisfactory. That is not feeble and evasive compromise, because I put the weight firmly on innovative as opposed to incomplete.

ANNEX A
*Thucydides' use of Herodotus**

In another Festschrift due to appear at about the same time as this one, Christopher Pelling, in a paper on Thucydides' Archidamos and Herodotus' Artabanos, examines an aspect of Thucydides' relation to Herodotus.[1] I wish to

---

* A reprint (with typographical corrections) of my article in J. M. Sanders (ed.), *ΦΙΛΟΛΑΚΩΝ: Lakonian Studies in Honor of Hector Catling* (Athens, 1992), 141–54.

[1] In M. Flower and M. Toher (eds.), *Georgica: Greek Studies in Honour of George Cawkwell* (London, 1991). More directly relevant to the theme of the present paper is an as yet unpublished short paper by David Lewis. I did not know of the existence of this until I showed him mine (see n. 36), and there is some overlap, though the scope and conclusions of his article are different. I have left mine essentially as it stood when I showed it to him, incorporating only his specific suggestions for improvement. In particular his article deals in some detail with the similarities and differences between Th. i. 89–95 and the relevant passages in Herodotus (for all this see also my commentary); note for instance the important difference, discussed in my *Greek World 479–323 BC* (London, 1983), 22–3, between Hdt. viii. 3. 2 and Th. i. 95. 7 on whether Sparta acquiesced happily in Athenian leadershp after 479. Here Herodotus is the more cynical of the two.

look at another, more strictly factual, aspect of that relationship. Many texts I shall be considering have a Spartan aspect, and this, I hope, makes it appropriate to explore the topic in a collection of Lakonian studies in honour of Hector Catling.[2]

It is not in dispute that Thucydides in some sense reacted against Herodotus (whom however he never names; it is Hellanicus who enjoys the doubtful privilege of being the only prose writer whom he names, in the partly polemical i. 97; the poets Homer and Hesiod are also named, the latter not as an authority, but merely for the manner of his death). Indeed it is usually thought that the first lengthy piece of polemic in Thucydides—which, appropriately enough [in a collection of *Lakonian Studies*], concerns Sparta—is directed against Herodotus. I refer to the well-known loss of temper in i. 20 about the Pitanate lochos and the votes of the Spartan kings. I have no space to go into the composition question—how big an interval of time separated the 'publication' of Herodotus' *Histories* from Thucydides' own literary activity. It is even possible that the two men were in a real sense contemporaries and rivals. I do think, however, that Thucydides' *Pentekontaetia* took its present form pretty late, as a riposte to the appearance of Hellanicus' work in or soon after 404.

I do not however wish to re-examine here such chestnuts as the Pitanate lochos. (See vol. i of this commentary.) Instead, I wish to offer and test three working hypotheses about Thucydides.

(i) Thucydides assumes knowledge of Herodotus. There are occasions, in narrative and speeches, when Thucydides would be barely intelligible, or actually unintelligible, to a reader who did not know Herodotus very well. A corollary is that Thucydides knew Herodotus' text very well, or even had Herodotus' book 'open in front of him'. (The inverted commas are intended to signal awareness of, but refusal to discuss, the problem of the exact form in which Herodotus was available to Thucydides.) If the present hypothesis is accepted, one would have to suppose that Herodotus was indeed available, either 'published' in quotable form, or committed to memory in Thucydides' head.

(ii) The second and related hypothesis is that Thucydides' speeches follow Herodotus when dealing with the past; virtually no factual historical detail in a Thucydidean speech is not already known to us from Herodotus. Elsewhere, i.e. in the wartime narrative and in digressions, Thucydides, when he has occasion to mention past events, uses alternative traditions much more freely.

(iii) Finally I shall turn to Thucydides' treatment of the proper names of some individuals, including the principles—if any—according to which he mentions or omits to mention the name of an individual. Herodotus is relevant here too. One (but only one) explanation of Thucydides' refusal to stress the religious or other significance of some proper names is his rejection of Herodotus' approach. Herodotus, in common with many early Greek writers, saw significance in names for themselves.

[2] My friendship with Hector goes back to 1978, when he involved me in the planning for the first of the BSA/DES courses for teachers. I participated as a lecturer in four of these courses, and one of the things I most value is the affectionate working relationship with Hector thus built up. This paper is an inadequate expression of that affection, and of gratitude.

I

My first hypothesis is not concerned with each and every Herodotean reminiscence in the pages of Thucydides. After all, some, like the phrase κακῶν ἄρξει (Melesippos at ii. 12) which at one level is an echo of Herodotus, are best seen as shared echoes of Homer (see also Ar. *Pax* 435-6, which Sommerstein now sees as a reminiscence in its turn of the real-life Melesippos);[3] we must reckon with the possibility that the historical Melesippos really said something of the sort. It is a question how far the 'adviser' or 'warner' characteristics of Archidamos in Thucydides and Artabanos in Herodotus are indebted to Homeric prototypes like Pouludamas or Nestor. It is hard to say how far Thucydides' Archidamus presupposes a knowledge of Herodotus' Artabanus. Other apparently close parallels, which are discussed in my commentary, are perhaps best seen as reflections of contemporary discussions; for instance Th. iii. 104. 1/Hdt. i. 64. 2 (Pisistratus' purification of Delos, which is likely to have been recalled in the Athens of 426) or Th. v. 41. 2/Hdt. i. 82 (the battle of the Champions between Sparta and Argos). Note, in any case, one Delian detail at Th. iii. 104. 2, repeated from his own i. 13. 6 (Polykrates dedicted Rheneia to Apollo) that is not in Herodotus. The reference to Aristagoras and northern affairs at Th. iv. 102. 2 presupposes the facts at Hdt. v. 126. 2 and ix. 75, but the similarities are not striking. Finally, ii. 102, on the River Acheloos, may be an attempt to improve on Hdt. ii. 10, but if so the allusion is hardly obvious or aggressive.

So too when we find a passage in Thucydides which looks like polemic against somebody, we should not too easily assume that the target is Herodotus. A famous instance is Thucydides' recording of the end of the Pisistratid tyranny, the traditions about which have recently been examined by Rosalind Thomas in her interesting book about Athenian oral tradition: whoever Thucydides was getting at, it was not Herodotus.[4] Even on minor issues the same caution is needed. Thus at ii. 8. 3, Thucydides says that the first ever earthquake on Delos was in 432; contrast Hdt. vi. 98 for an earthquake in 490: 'the first and last up to my time'. A number of solutions have been propounded; the simplest is that Herodotus believed in a 490 earthquake while Thucydides, as David Lewis writes, 'for some reason did not and says so with customary indirectness'. Lewis goes on to suggest in a footnote, 'He need not be correcting Herodotus, but must, I think, be correcting somebody'.[5]

---

[3] A. H. Sommerstein (ed.), *Aristophanes Peace* (Warminster, 1985) ad loc. See also Pol. xi. 5. 9 with commentary in F. W. Walbank, *A Historical Commentary on Polybius*, vol. ii (Oxford, 1967). In this same general category we might place the words used at Th. vii. 87. 6 about the failure of the Sicilian expedition, 'utter destruction, as the saying goes', πανωλεθρίᾳ δὴ τὸ λεγόμενον. This recalls Hdt. ii. 120. 5, where πανωλεθρίη is used about the fall of Troy. Thucydides' whole phrase perhaps suggests a common source, maybe even an epic poem. Note also that the idea found in Hdt. iii. 84. 2/Th. ii. 65. 9, about demagogy turning into monarchy, may be as old as Solon; see S. Hornblower, *Thucydides* (London, 1987), 70 n. 97, citing Stroheker.

[4] *Oral Tradition and Written Record in Classical Athens* (Cambridge, 1989).

[5] 'Apollo Delios', *BSA* 55 (1960), 194, and n. 15, but Lewis now tells me that he no longer thinks that Th. ii. 8. 5 must be correcting something.

It is certainly true that in reading Thucydides we need to be on our guard against Herodotean resonances all the time, and from the word go. Take for instance the passage very early in Thucydides about Minos' thalassocracy: he was, we learn, 'the first of whom we know by hearsay', ὧν ἀκοῇ ἴσμεν, to have ruled the waves (i. 4. 1). On the face of it, this is a valuable acknowledgement by Thucydides of oral tradition, and one might be tempted to speculate about early epic poems, orally transmitted thalassocracy lists, and so forth (which may indeed ultimately lie behind what we have here). Look, however, at Hdt. iii. 122; 'Polykrates is the first Greek thalassocrat of whom we know, τῶν ἡμεῖς ἴδμεν, apart from Minos' and other possible earlier, non-human candidates. Given that Thucydides mentions the naval power of Polykrates in its place (i. 13. 6), it seems likely that he has simply rearranged Herodotus' material (though we cannot exclude the possibility that Hecataeus of Miletos had already used some such phrase). Incidentally, Herodotus emerges as the more sceptical of the two ('apart from Minos' is dismissive, as is the implication in 'human' that Minos is mythical) on the historicity of the 'Minoan Thalassocracy'.[6] On the other hand Thucydides adds the word 'hearsay' which is not in Herodotus. We might be tempted to conclude that Thucydides is posing as more sceptical than Herodotus, when in fact, the Greek word, ἀκοή, does not have the pejorative sense of 'hearsay' (see also Th. vi. 55). Perhaps the point of ἀκοή is to stress, more precisely than Herodotus had done, the legitimacy of using 'hearsay' evidence when dealing with such ancient events. In any case 'hearsay' should, I am suggesting, be seen as part of an argument with Herodotus, not as a direct statement about Thucydides' own route of access to the tradition. This, then, is an example of a passage, the proper elucidation of which is impossible without reference to Herodotus, although its meaning is perfectly clear; Thucydides expected his readers to recall or turn up the relevant bit of Herodotus.

What I am interested in identifying is the kind of Thucydidean text which positively assumes knowledge of Herodotus, and reads awkwardly or even mystifyingly without such knowledge. Arguably there is one very early indeed: the reference to the 'war between the Peloponnesians and the Athenians, how they fought against each other' (i. 1. 1) seems to me clumsier in its context than the equivalent phrase at the very beginning of Herodotus, a phrase which is thus presupposed.

This echo of Herodotus on war raises an interesting issue, a silence in Thucydides which is a kind of 'echo' of a silence in Herodotus. Scholars have been struck by Thucydides' silence in the *Archaeology* about the First Sacred War: should he not have mentioned it at i. 15? (For the debate about the historicity of the war see my commentary on i. 112. 5). The problem, in its Thucydidean aspect, largely disappears if we grasp that Thucydides' target was Herodotus, who had discussed the Trojan, Lelantine, and Persian Wars, but not the First

---

[6] The latter is a topic to which an entire Swedish symposium has recently been devoted: R. Hägg and N. Marinatos (eds.), *The Minoan Thalassocracy: Myth and Reality* (Stockholm, 1984). Some of the contributions show an alarming deference to Thucydides' authority in this murky area.

Sacred War. So Thucydides followed suit, arguing for the relative insignificance of the three wars Herodotus had discussed, but not bothering even to mention a war which Herodotus had not mentioned.

We have noted the Pitanate lochos and the Spartan kings; these passages have been rightly pounced on by commentators interested in the surprisingly difficult question whether Thucydides' strictures were justified.[7] We should not lose sight of a more simple feature; the way in which knowledge of Herodotus' text is assumed. It surely is right to say that Thucydides' meaning would be unintelligible to us without Herodotus' text. Still staying with Sparta, and still in the *Archaeology*, the reference to the stated privileges, $\dot{\rho}\eta\tau o\hat{\iota}s$ $\gamma\acute{\epsilon}\rho a\sigma\iota$, of the early 'kings'[8] at i. 13. 1 may well be just a severely telescoped account of the long section on the privileges of the Spartan kings at Hdt. vi. 51 ff. It is more certain that the passage about Spartan *eunomia* at i. 18. 1 is derivative from Hdt. i. 65 ($\eta\dot{\upsilon}\nu o\mu\acute{\eta}\theta\eta = \epsilon\dot{\upsilon}\nu o\mu\iota\acute{\eta}\nu$), even allowing for the possibility that Tyrtaeus in the seventh century had already applied the word to Sparta. This derivation has the important historical consequence that we should be very careful about treating Thucydides as 'corroborating' Herodotus on the relevant and much disputed points of early Spartan history (especially the chronological ones: Thucydides' calculations, 400 years and so forth, may be independent in a sense, but may have been done on the basis of Spartan king lists preserved elsewhere in Herodotus).[9] Thucydides 'improves' on Herodotus not only by introducing the concept of *stasis* (see below) but also by what he says at i. 19 about the different methods of control used by Athens and Sparta.

Naturally, Thucydides has his own structural reasons for including this Spartan material, in particular the theme of Sparta as 'liberator from (real-life Archaic) tyrants.'[10] This theme first appears in i. 18 and derives from passages like Hdt. v. 92—a passage which itself presupposes that the liberation motif is generally familiar—and is intended to prepare us for its own extension, the idea of Sparta in 431 as liberator from the metaphorical tyranny of Athens. That is an idea first heard of in the Corinthian speech at i. 124. 3 and stated most emphatically in the important and authorial ii. 8. 4. (It also underlies the parallelism at i. 75-6 between Persia at the beginning and Athens at the end of the *Pentekontaetia*.) And the idea (also i. 18) of Sparta as free from *stasis*, an idea not explicitly expressed at Hdt. i. 65, will be needed at, for instance Th. viii. 24. 4, where the reference to Spartan political moderation and happiness has a special point, embedded as it is in a book largely about *stasis* at Athens in 411. That is, it is surely intended to make the contrast with Athens. (Not that Thucydides' Book viii shows Spartan institutions coping all that well with the strains of war, but at least Sparta avoided revolution.)

---

[7] D. H. Kelly, 'Thucydides and Herodotus on the Pitanate Lochos', *GRBS* 22 (1981), 31-8.

[8] Inverted commas in deference to R. Drews, *Basileus* (New Haven, 1983).

[9] See my commentary.

[10] R. Bernhardt, 'Die Entstehung der Legende von der tyrannenfeindlichen Aussenpolitik Spartas im 6 und 5 Jhdt. v. Chr.', *Historia*, 36 (1987), 257-89. It might be objected that Th. did not need Hdt. to tell him that the Spartans were anti-tyrant, but in fact, Bernhardt suggests that this 'legend' was relatively late to develop.

Again, the section about the material insignificance of Sparta compared to Athens (i. 10) has a double function: it redefines what Thucydides, perhaps a little unfairly, took to be Herodotus' method; the right ἔργα to judge a city by are not physical but human (perhaps an allusion to Hdt. iii. 60 on Polykrates' Samos). The whole argument certainly takes for granted Herodotus' point about the transience of cities' power, i. 5. 4. At the same time, this section polarizes Athens and Sparta for us. It was the human toughness of Sparta which would prove too strong for glittering Athens in the end (a polarity familiar from Herodotus, who had presented Greek toughness in opposition to Persian glitter). However, Herodotus had himself used his introductory book to bring out the polarity between Athens and Sparta, by having Croesus discover that Athens was the strongest Ionian state—an excuse to tell us about the Pisistratids—and Sparta the strongest Dorian—so we get the story of Lycurgus. (I am not overlooking Herodotus' other likely motives for including these excursuses, such as the desire to structure the pre-499 material around eastern history: Greek history had to be fitted in somewhere.)

The sheer amount of this Spartan material so early in Thucydides prompts a tentative interim conclusion: he assumes Herodotus' material, but seeks in small ways to correct (Pitanate lochos, etc.) and in large ways to better it. We are left with Thucydides' distinctive picture of a Sparta different from Athens (i. 10, i. 18), unwalled and unadorned (he actually says 'inhabited by villages', but I think the implication is that Sparta lacks walls, cp. iii. 94. 4). Sparta is nevertheless powerful out of proportion to appearances (i. 10), free from tyrants at home and hostile to them elsewhere, also free from *stasis* (all this at i. 18); and Sparta controls its allies not by tribute but by installing oligarchies congenial to itself (i. 19). Some of this is in Herodotus, for instance the general balancing of Sparta and Athens (Hdt. i. 59 juxtaposed with i. 65); the opposition to tyrants is assumed at Hdt. v. 92 and freedom from *stasis* is implied in εὐνομίην at i. 65, just as earlier stasis (Th. i. 18) is implied by κακονομώτατοι at Hdt. i. 65. But Thucydides not only picks up the word εὐνομία but is specific about *stasis*, which is a preoccupation of his. And he will (not at i. 18 but later) extend Spartan opposition to tyrants to cover not just individuals but states. Walls, which Thucydides implies Sparta does not have, are another preoccupation peculiar to him; here his desire to part methodological company with Herodotus has led him to underrate a physical feature which elsewhere he stresses as a sign of strength (though Thucydides may also be implying that Sparta's unwalled condition was a function of its unassailable geographical position and was thus a sign of strength.) Finally, the chapter (i. 19) about methods of control is his alone.

It is in his references to the Persian Wars that Thucydides most conspicuously assumes knowledge of Herodotus in his readers. That was perhaps to be expected, and in any case neither he nor his speakers share all Herodotus' judgements. More revealing are those references at points where Thucydides' guard is down. I am thinking of the narrative of the escape from Plataia (book iii), where I shall suggest that topographical knowledge is assumed in a way which makes some passages hard to understand without knowledge of Herodotus ix, the narrative of the battle of Plataia in 479.

But first the Persian War allusions. I leave aside the *Archaeology*, noting only, and not for the first time,[11] Lewis's point that Thucydides does not seek to minimize the Persian Wars by attacking Herodotus' numbers (as modern scholars do) but by saying that the whole thing was settled very quickly in two land and sea battles (i. 23. 1). That is, he accepts the basic Herodotean framework, though drawing different conclusions about the importance of the Persian Wars. (Note, however, that at iv. 36. 3 he returns to Herodotus' priorities, when he apologizes for comparing small—Sphakteria—with great—Thermopylai. The book iv passage may derive from Herodotus: it uses Herodotus' word ἀτραπός for the path at Thermopylai, a word found once only in the rest of Thucydides.) Let us move on to i. 73 ff., the Athenians' speech at Sparta. It was Themistokles, they say, who was most responsible for the sea battle taking place ἐν τῷ στενῷ, 'in the narrows'. This is a very brief and allusive phrase; it surely presupposes Herodotus viii. 60, ἐν στεινῷ. But the passage is, it may be said, just about intelligible as it stands: the story was after all a famous one. What follows is less clear: 'you honoured Themistokles more than you did any other foreigner'. Surely very cryptic indeed without knowledge of Herodotus viii. 124. 3, where we are told that the Spartans gave Themistokles a magnificent reception after Salamis, voting him a wreath, a carriage and an escort as far as Tegea. Of course (it may be argued) the real-life Spartans might be expected to know what their real-life ancestors had done. To pursue that would take us too far into debates about the authenticity of Thucydides' speeches; in any case I shall return below (at II) to the status of such 'ancient history' (ancient, that is, from Thucydides' point of view) as he preserves in speeches. Before we leave this speech, note that the words 'a city which no longer existed' (ἀπό τε τῆς οὐκ οὔσης) recall Herodotus viii. 61. 1, the Corinthian Adeimantos' sneers at Themistokles.

Moving on in book i, the words ἐκλιπόντων τῶν βαρβάρων at i. 89. 2 (the Persians abandon Sestos) are scarcely intelligible without the detailed story at Herodotus ix. 114–8; and the account at Th. i. 137. 4 of the contents of Themistokles' letter to the Great King, with its repeated definite articles ('the warning he had given to Xerxes of the withdrawal ... the bridge') surely assumes Herodotus viii. 75, 110. 3. While we are in this generally 'Herodotean' and chatty section of Thucydides, note that the Kylon chapter (126) is tricky. A good deal is taken for granted factually: true, we are given the information, hardly necessary in the context, that he was an Athenian and an Olympic victor (both apparently taken from Herodotus v. 71), but notoriously we get no direct indications of his date from either author, except that Thucydides says he was son-in-law of Theagenes of Megara, a detail not in Herodotus. Note that this is narrative, not a speech (see II below for the significance of this). The Kylon chapter as a whole is very different from Herodotus in its factual detail and its general handling. Finally, Th. i. 138. 6 surely echoes Hdt.

---

[11] Hornblower, *Thucydides* (n. 3), 202.

ix. 64. 1: Thucydides expected his readers to know what made Themistokles and Pausanias λαμπροί.

Let us move on to the narrative at Th. iii. 20 ff., the penultimate phase of the siege of Plataia. At 24. 1, we are told the escapers 'kept on their right hand the heroon of Androkrates'. Again the definite article: Thucydides surely intends his readers to remember that this landmark (which has not yet been securely identified) featured in the narrative of Herodotus (ix. 25). The same is to a lesser extent true of Dryoskephalai immediately afterwards (cp. Hdt. ix. 39), and to a lesser extent of Erythrai and Hysiai. Agreed, a narrowly Athenian or Boiotian readership might have been expected to know what he was talking about in the last three cases (we might wish to protest that Thucydides was writing a 'possession for ever' but in fact he makes other equally parochial assumptions elsewhere). The heroon of Androkrates, on the other hand, does seem to me an extreme instance of an assumption of literary knowledge of the text of Herodotus. (Contrast Thucydides' often more helpful normal manner when dealing with topography, for instance ii. 18. 2 or iv. 8. 6.)

The selection of material so far considered does suggest that Thucydides expected his readers to be thoroughly *au fait* with Herodotus. We can go further and suggest that 'the heroon of Androkrates', 'the narrows', the Spartan honours to Themistokles, and his message to the King, as well as the 'Pitanate lochos', are not intelligible without reference to Herodotus, though if one is allowed degrees of unintelligibility one might wish to rank them somehow: such a ranking would have to take into account the likelihood that a given item would have been familiar from general oral knowledge. (I am not here over-looking the bare and desperate possibility that some or all of these items feature in authors other than Herodotus and known to Thucydides but not to us. But let us confine ourselves to what is probable and plausible.) Other expressions, like 'hearsay' said of Minos, have small point except from a Herodotean angle.

II

My second hypothesis could most briefly be put in terms of a challenge: how many references are there to ancient (i.e., essentially pre-479) events which are both contained in Thucydides' speeches rather than his narrative and are not already known to us from Herodotus? My answer is: extremely few. (I shall consider separately the intriguing case of *pentekontaetia* events known only from Thucydides' speeches; it is not a long list.)

A preliminary point however must be got out of the way. It needs, I hope, no elaborate proof that in sections other than the speeches Thucydides draws on sources other than Herodotus; for instance, at some points of the *Archaeology* (the material about the House of Atreus in i.9 being an example), in much of the Kylon/Pausanias/Themistokles digressions, in the antiquarian material about Athens at ii. 15-16, in the detailed material about Sicily at the beginning of book vi (the *Sikelika*), and in the Pisistratid digression in the same book. (But is the reference at vi. 54. 6 to the Pisistratids governing by the existing laws a reminiscence of Hdt. i. 59. 6?) It has also been suggested that some of the information about Epirus, scattered through books i and ii, derives from Hecataeus of Miletos.[12]

Let us turn to the use of Herodotus in speeches. It may be objected that, except for the Persian Wars, allusions in speeches to early events are bound to be few, so I am making a trivial claim. I hope that on the contrary it will emerge that there are more such allusions than one might think.

If we proceed in chronological order of event mentioned, pride of place goes to an indirectly Spartan item contained in an exchange of speeches not normally thought of as rich in 'ancient history': the Melian Dialogue. At v. 112. 2, the Melians say that their city was founded by Sparta 700 years ago. This is not directly from Herodotus. The chronological question has wide ramifications to do with the return of the Herakleidai, and I attempt no summary here, but confine myself to quoting Andrewes, who in his note on the present passage concludes that it implies that Thucydides 'had a relatively high date for the fall of Troy, something like the date implied in Hdt. ii. 145. 4'.[13] So Thucydides may not here be entirely independent of Herodotus after all.

We now jump to the sixth century (leaving aside references to Athenian autochthony, which is a commonplace,[14] and anyway features in Thucydides' own *Archaeology*). Next in time, perhaps, is the claim of Alcibiades at vi. 89. 4 that his family has always been hostile to tyranny; on the face of it, an important item, and one independent of Herodotus. Dover does not discuss the possible relation to Herodotus, noting only that the theme is developed in Isocrates 16; but the latter is a derivative concoction, itself indebted to Thucydides. Classen/ Steup however calmly and briefly assume that the reference is to the Alk- maionids, from whom Alcibiades was descended on his mother Deinomache's side.[15] If this is right, we surely have here (though Classen/Steup do not say so) no more than a reference to a famous passage of Herodotus about Alkmaionid hostility to tyranny, vi. 123. 1, and the value of the Thucydidean allusion is much reduced. But a doubt persists: it is perfectly true that Alcibiades was as much an Alkmaionid as Pericles was, but Thucydides himself never makes the connection, either when treating Alcibiades, or when treating the Alkmaionids (as he does at i. 126; vi. 59. 4).

[12] N. G. L. Hammond, *Epirus* (Oxford, 1967), 446–58, drawing on L. Pearson.

[13] A. W. Gomme, A. Andrewes, and K. J. Dover, *Historical Commentary on Thucydides*, iv (Oxford, 1970).

[14] V. Rosivach, 'Autochthony and the Athenians', *CQ* 37 (1987), 294–306.

[15] If however the reference is to Alcibiades' paternal descent, what genos is referred to, the Salaminioi/Eurysakids or the Eupatrids? J. K. Davies, *Athenian Propertied Families* (Oxford, 1971), 10–12, accepted Wade-Gery's arguments against the existence of a separate genos called the Eupatridai, but Davies curiously failed to take account of the protest voiced against Wade-Gery by C. Hignett, *History of the Athenian Constitution* (Oxford, 1953), 315–16. (The evidence for a Eupatrid genos goes wider than Isoc. 16.) In any case we must now reckon with the French scholars Bourriot and Roussel who do not think that gene were an institution of any antiquity at all. But even the revi- sionists can hardly deny that Alcibiades had sixth-century paternal ancestors of some description. Note in any case the parallel claims of Andocides i. 106 and ii. 26.

The most striking example of exploitation of Herodotus in a Thucydidean speech is, however, to be found in the exchange of speeches between the Plataians and the Thebans in book iii. The résumé of early Theban–Plataian relations at 54-5 (the Plataians), picked up by the Thebans at 61-4, follows Herodotus with unmistakable closeness. Th. iii.55. 1 can only be called a close paraphrase of Hdt. vi. 108. 1-3, the Plataian appeal to Kleomenes in 519 BC, and the language in which he rejects their appeal, and advises them to approach Athens instead. So too the mention of Plataian participation in the battle of Artemisium is taken from Hdt. viii. 1. 1, down to the reference to Plataian naval inexperience. There are differences of detail: in a rhetorical effort it is not surprising that at 54. 3 the Plataians claim to have been the 'only' Boiotians on the right side in the Persian Wars; this overlooks e.g. the Thespians at Hdt. viii. 222 (Thermopylai. Thucydides' omission is incidentally taken over by the author of Dem. lix).

There is, however, an important new item in this speech: the statement at 55. 3 (not contradicted by the Thebans at 63. 2) that Athens had already, at the time of the speech and perhaps long before, granted the Plataians citizenship. I cannot go into this vexed question here, but must refer to the long note in my commentary. For the moment I wish to note that Michael Osborne in his recent work on naturalization calls the Plataians' claim an 'obvious untruth'.[16] This is strong language, and I wonder if Thucydides is not being disposed of too easily; it is certainly disquieting that here, for once, on an issue where Thucydides and the fourth-century orators disagree (the latter make the citizenship grant the result of the events of 427), the weight of modern historical authority is in favour of the orators not Thucydides.[17]

The Thebans begin with some very ancient history (61. 2), the expulsion by the Thebans, long ago, of the 'mixed population' of Boiotia. This is new; but the Thebans, for the most part, are merely referring to facts expected to be familiar from Thucydides' own *Archaeology*, see i. 12. 3. They then claim that if Plataia did not side with the Persians, that was only because Athens did not. This suggests Hdt. viii. 30 on why the Phokians did not medize (hatred of Thessaly). There follows the second interesting and important claim in these speeches which is not in Herodotus (or anywhere else): Thebes in the Persian Wars was 'not governed by an isonomous oligarchy'. The respectful treatment given in modern textbooks about Theban history to this forensic claim is surprising, and a function of our lack of other information about Thebes' constitution c480. I wonder if it is not a fiction, conditioned by the rhetorical need of the Theban speaker to say 'non sum qualis eram'. Indeed one could argue that the material about Theban medism at Hdt. ix. 86-7 (where 'the Thebans' surrender their arch-medizers) might already have suggested to an attentive reader of Herodotus that the Theban claims as reported by Thucydides (in effect, we were 'dynastically governed and had no say in our city's policy') were completely phoney.

---

[16] *Naturalization in Athens*, vol. 2 (Brussels, 1982), 11.
[17] W. Gawantka in *Isopolitie* (Munich, 1975), 174-8, anticipated Osborne.

The final item before we get to the Persian Wars proper is the loan of ships by Corinth to Athens for use against Aigina. The reminder to this effect at i. 41. 2, the Corinthian speech, is surely taken straight from Hdt. vi. 89 (I shall have more to say about this Corinthian speech in a moment).

References to the Persian Wars in speeches are frequent and often rather vague; we have however already noted some close echoes of Herodotus in the Athenian speech at i. 74. The claim there made about the size of Athens' naval contribution is dependent in a rough way on Herodotus, though there are problems about the figures.[18] The general claim recurs in Euphemos' speech at Kamarina (vi. 83. 1), but here, as elsewhere, we must reckon with internal inter-relatedness between Thucydidean speeches—not a topic which can occupy us here. Speakers who, like Hermokrates at vi. 33. 6, imply that the Persians failed through their own fault, are perhaps merely echoing each other (see e.g. i. 69. 5), and making points which suit their (usually anti-Athenian) argument. We should not scour Herodotus, the admirer of Athens' achievement in 480, for relevant passages. In any case, Xerxes did, in Herodotus, make frequent mistakes (often after warnings or specific advice from people like Artemisia or Demaratos); that is inherent in Herodotus' whole picture of the hybristic nature of the expedition. In any case, there is, in Thucydides, an extra point to this talk of Persian mistakes, because Athens too would fail through its own mistakes.

The best candidates for Thucydidean pre-479 speech material not in Herodotus are thus the statements about Plataian citizenship and about the Theban constitution in 480. But the date and even historicity of the grant of citizenship are uncertain; it is not sure that it fell in the period covered by Herodotus. As for Thebes' constitution, this was very relevant to Herodotus, but we have suggested that this claim may not deserve much credence. As possible extra candidates, we may add the foundation of Melos and the political attitudes of Alcibiades' family in the sixth century.

For the sake of completeness, let us note (before we pass to the period after 479) an event from 479 itself, after the Persian Wars but before the *pentekontaetia*. Archidamos refers at ii. 71. 2 to a guarantee by Sparta of Plataian autonomy. This item complicates the already complicated story of early Plataian history, and cannot be fully discussed here. It does however qualify as an event known only from a Thucydidean speech.

Herodotus did not, of course, systematically cover the *pentekontaetia*, i.e. 480–430. Factual references to this period in Thucydidean speeches are rare, sometimes surprisingly so (in particular, the paucity of allusions to the First Peloponnesian War is, as the late Sir Ronald Syme observed, 'not a little strange').[19] Of the references which we do find, some merely assume knowledge of events in Thucydides' own *Pentekontaetia*; in this category are the references to the battle of Koroneia at iii. 62. 5 and 67. 3 (the Plataian and Theban speeches) and at iv. 92. 6 (Pagondas); also to Oinophyta at iv. 95. 3 (Hippokrates, an obvious reply to Pagondas on Koroneia). Note that none of this

---

[18] K. R. Walters, '400 Athenian ships at Salamis', *RhM* 124 (1981), 199–203.
[19] *Proceedings of the British Academy* 48 (1962), 49. [See above, p. 111 n. 284.]

carries implications for the date of the composition of the *Pentekontaetia*: there was never a time when Thucydides did not know—or expect his readers to know—that there was a battle of Koroneia. In the same category, in a way, belongs the Plataian claim at iii. 54. 5 to have helped the Spartans at Ithome. This is strictly a new fact, but in book i we had already been told that Spartan allies other than the Athenians were there: i. 102. 1. We could even say that ii. 27. 2 is exactly comparable: the Aiginetans are given land by Sparta because they too had helped at Ithome. This is a new fact, and since it comes in a statement of Spartan motives it could be called a mini-speech.

Material about Athens' relations with the allies in the years 480–430, and her foreign policy generally, is sparingly given in speeches, and such material as we are given often merely picks up narrative or authorial statements. Thus the list of excuses for Athenian attacks on allies (vi. 76: Hermokrates) mostly amplifies the authorial i. 99 (though the reference at vi. 76 to allies making wars on each other, τοὺς δὲ ἐπ᾽ ἀλλήλους στρατεύειν, is new—it was not mentioned even in the run-up to the Samian revolt where it would have been relevant). So too with the mention by the Mytileneans at iii. 13. 1 (their speech at Olympia) that they tried to revolt even before the beginning of the war, but the Spartans would not give them the help they asked for. This merely picks up the narrative iii. 2. 1 (the verbal correspondence could hardly be closer). Some scholars have seen significance in the non-mention of the Peace of Kallias at iii. 10. 4 and have used this silence as evidence against a formal pact.[20] This seems to me an illegitimate use of an argument from silence. If anything, I would say that the phrase 'dropping hostility against the Mede' is as close as we could expect a Thucydidean speaker to get to a mention of the Peace.

The only important new *pentekontaetia* fact known only from a speech is at i. 40. 5 and 41. 2: the Corinthians remind Athens not just of the ships for use against Aigina, but of a major incident otherwise not known from Thucydides or any other source (but just possibly corroborated by the broken opening to ML 56), a Peloponnesian League vote on whether to fight Athens over Samos in 440. The Corinthians voted against war.

Athenian domestic politics is not the kind of topic we can expect to feature in Thucydidean speeches, but note the renunciation in the 460s, by an ancestor of Alcibiades, of his Spartan proxeny (vi. 89. 2, Alcibiades' speech at Sparta), an event with domestic implications—it is surely somehow connected with his ostracism.[21] But the fact has already been given in the narrative v. 43. 2 in a more satisfactory version (there we were told that the ancestor was, in fact, a grandfather).

I have included this material for comparison. My concluding suggestion is that, in speeches, where Thucydides was making a huge creative effort of a special sort, he was content to take his facts on trust from Herodotus, or to let his 'audience' do so, to an exceptional extent. For the years 479 onwards, where Herodotus was not available, Thucydides, in speeches, gives (with one major

---

[20] A. J. Holladay, 'The *détente* of Kallias?', *Historia*, 35 (1986), 503–7.
[21] Davies (n. 15), 15.

exception) no facts which are both important and new, in the sense of not being derived from his own narrative, especially that in i. 89–118. I have argued elsewhere that his vocabulary is less technical and precise in speeches than in narrative.[22] It is perhaps a corollary of this that the speeches should on the whole 'recycle' familiar factual material, and should on occasion give it in less specific form than it took in the corresponding section of narrative (thus Alcibiades' grandfather becomes just an ancestor). I suspect that my conclusions, if right, weaken further the claim of the speeches to the kind of authenticity claimed in i. 22. We should also consider the possibility that already, in Thucydides' time, the conventions of the genre demanded that historical allusions in political speeches should not be too startling or recondite. But we know too little about fifth-century political oratory apart from Thucydides to be sure about this.

III

Finally, I turn to proper names, and to some individuals. I have (again) argued elsewhere that Thucydides was unlike Herodotus in his lack of interest in names as names.[23] Puns on proper names do not occur in Thucydides, although the opposite was implausibly claimed, in the case of three individuals, by Enoch Powell half a century ago.[24] However, it is arguable that in this area the attitudes of the people whom Thucydides was writing about were closer to Herodotus' attitude than to Thucydides' own, and that Thucydides has thus occasionally omitted a dimension. One area where names might be thought to have significance is religion, not an area where Thucydides' coverage is always adequate. (We should expect this to be particularly true of the Spartans, for whose religiosity, see vii. 18. 2.) I might add, without disrespect to Gomme's great work, that Thucydides' main English commentator shared some of his subject's blindness in this department. But in fairness it must be added that some important work on Greek religion has appeared only since Gomme's time.

I offer an example, taken from volume i of my commentary and justified more fully there. The account at iii. 92–3 of the Spartan foundation of Herakleia Trachinia, partly in response to an appeal from the Trachinians and from their own 'mother city' Doris, is a rich digression: the religious formalities are observed, the invitation to participants is sent out on a racial basis (that is to say [see above, p. 62], there is a religious aspect here too). One item which has caused scholarly surprise is the news that one of the 'oikists', or founders, was Alkidas, not a man whose performance in East Aegean waters in the earlier part of the book was so brilliant as to prepare us for his further employment in this way[25] (we cannot say for sure that it was actually a promotion). Gomme says

[22] *Thucydides*, 96–100.
[23] *Thucydides*, 93–4.
[24] 'Puns in Herodotus', *CR* 51 (1937), 103–5, but see Hornblower (n. 3), 94 n. 88.
[25] J. Roisman, 'Alkidas in Thucydides', *Historia*, 36 (1987), 385–421, attempts a rehabilitation of Alkidas, but is not interested in his name.

contemptuously 'the discredited nauarchos ... rewarded with an easy post in the aristocratic manner'. Is that all there is to the choice of Alkidas?

I suggest it is not quite all, but to explain why I must first look at Diodorus' account of the founding of Herakleia (xii. 59). Diodorus has the motif of 'kin-ship', συγγένειαν (compare Thucydides on Doris, specific mention of which has slipped out of Diodorus), but there is in Diodorus an additional ground for Sparta's acceptance: their ancestor Herakles had lived in Trachis in ancient times (and, we can add, had allegedly died there: see Sophocles' *Trachiniai*). Now, one of Herakles' names was Alkidas (the Doric form);[26] what was more appropriate than for the Spartans to send a real-life Alkidas to bring the Dorian colony luck? (Note that Diodorus is not strictly necessary for my suggestion; the place was, after all, being called Herakleia—but the specific mention of Herakles is nice corroboration.) We might compare the selection in the late fourth century of the talismanically-named Miltiades to lead an Athenian colony to the Adriatic.[27] If I am right (and note that another of the Herakleia oikists was called Damagon: 'leader-out-of-the-people') this would be an instance of Thucydides neglecting to explain the religious significance of a fact he never-theless records faithfully. (There is, I suggest, another example in the same chapter: the name of the Trachinian ambassador is Tisamenos, 92. 2. In myth, this was the name of Orestes' son, an Achaian who fought against the Herakleidai, thus an anti-Dorian figure: the Achaians were specifically excluded from the Herakleia invitation, 92. 5. But in the sixth century Tisamenos' bones, like Orestes', were taken back to Sparta, in what may have been a political gesture:[28] Tisamenos was an excellent choice of ambassador).

A good parallel is the religiously significant 'monosandalism' of the escapers from Plataia (iii. 22. 2), for which Thucydides gives a prosaically practical explanation. But we must be glad that he preserved the fact at all. All this has been well elucidated by Vidal-Naquet and Edmunds.[29]

Herodotus might have made something more of Alkidas: at ix. 91 the Spartan Leotychidas, told of the name of the Samian Hegesistratos ('leader of the army'), said, 'I accept the omen'. It may be that Thucydides wished to distance himself from his predecessor's methods.

Alkidas raises the more general question of Thucydides' inclusion or omission of the names of individuals in his work, and of his coverage of those he does mention. One principle of inclusion or exclusion very relevant to the subject of this paper is Herodotean: does the name of the person, or an ancestor, feature in Herodotus? Some years ago, H. D. Westlake suggested that the full and favourable coverage of Aristeus the Corinthian in book i, where he is active at Potidaia, is to be explained by a desire to redress an injustice done by Herodotus to Aristeus' father Adeimantos.[30] (We noted this man earlier for his

---

[26] U. Wilamowitz, *Herakles* (Berlin, 1909), 49, citing Pi. *Ol.* 6. 68. [27] Tod no. 200.

[28] Paus. vii. 1. 8 with D. Leahy, 'The Bones of Tisamenus', *Historia*, 4 (1955), 26–38. [See now A. Wright, 'Tisamenus—A Relevant Name in Thucydides', *LCM* 19 (1994), 66 f.]

[29] P. Vidal-Naquet, *The Black Hunter* (Baltimore, 1986), 61–5, at 64; L. Edmunds, 'Thucydides on Monosandalism', *GRBS Monograph* 10 (1984) = Sterling Dow Studies, 71–5.

[30] *Essays on the Greek Historians and Greek History* (Manchester, 1969), 74–83.

gibes at Themistokles.) Westlake added that Aristeus may have been one of Thucydides' informants; we shall return to this as a possible reason for the mention of a proper name. Incidentally, Aristeus himself is the subject of one of Herodotus' forward references (for another, see below): his summary execution is mentioned at Hdt. vii. 137 as the final stage in the working out of a sequence of divine displeasure. Thucydides, who also mentions the episode (ii. 67), shows more indignation but eliminates the religious element: correction of Herodotus again.

Another example, hinted at already above, is Eurymachos, son of Leontiades (ii. 2. 3), one of what Gomme memorably called a 'long-lived and mischievous family'. Here, Thucydides is careful to make clear that the attack on Plataia was led not by Eurymachos, but by two named boiotarchs, Pythangelos, son of Phyleides, and Diemporos, son of Onetorides. Herodotus, as it happens, had mentioned the incident in another of his rare forward references, but said that Eurymachos himself was in command (vii. 233); he also gave a different total for the force. Thucydides is evidently correcting Herodotus; but this is not a correction like the Pitanate lochos: one could read the passage without being aware that there was a concealed polemic here. All three names, the boiotarchs and Eurymachos, are needed for the correction; hence the prosopographic fullness.

Not all names with a Herodotean resonance are there for any obvious polemical reason. Lakon, son of Aeimnestos, is the Spartan proxenos at Plataia (iii. 52. 5). The man's own name ('the Lakonian') is easily explained, compare Lakedaimonios as the name of the son of the Lakonophile Kimon, or the implications of the information about the name Alcibiades given at viii. 6. 3. But this is not all, because there is a Herodotean connection here too: one manuscript of Hdt. ix. 72. 2 has Aeimnestos (rather than the Arimnestos printed in modern editions) as the name of the Plataian who witnesses the death from wounds of a beautiful Spartan called Kallikratidas.[31] Stein, in his note on the passage, suggested long ago that the first Aeimnestos called his son Lakon to commemorate the death scene. The proxeny fits neatly into this picture.

There are other reasons for Thucydides' naming of individuals. One may be that this is a conscious or unconscious way of signalling an informant. Occasionally, when the man or his family are otherwise known, we can make a conjecture about the route by which Thucydides got his material. An example is at iii. 20. 2: Eupompidas, son of Daimachos, is named as one of the leaders of the break-out from Plataia, under vividly described siege at the time. Daimachos is a rare name, but a Daimachos of Plataia wrote about India in the Hellenistic period (*FGrHist* 716) and this, together with Th. iii. 20, makes it likely that the fourth-century historian Daimachos (*FGrHist* 65) was a Plataian and related to Thucydides' Eupompidas. This Daimachos is known to have written a treatise on siegecraft (*FGrHist* 3 and 4) so perhaps the family was Thucydides' source for the account of the 'state-of-the-art' siege tactics in books ii and iii.

In a recent article, Gabriel Herman has fastened on the other Plataian named

---

[31] This was pointed out to me by David Lewis in 1988, and has now been noticed independently by Herman (below, n. 32), 93 n. 35.

at iii. 20. 2, the *mantis* Tolmides, son of Theainetos. He points out acutely that the famous Athenian general Tolmides had a diviner called Theainetos; perhaps the onomastic coincidence is due to a proxeny relationship of some sort.[32] So far, so good, but I am less happy with Herman's general suggestion that one reason for 'name-suppression' in Thucydides is the historian's feeling of solidarity with upper-class proxenoi who might be compromised with the demos if his own writings supplied the right kind of 'incriminating evidence'.[33]

There are, in any case, more baffling instances, like the Syracusan general who is given a speech at vi. 41, but left anonymous. The Spartan commander at iii. 5. 2 (Plataia) is not named, despite the importance of the events in which he is involved, nor are the five Spartan judges who arrive later in the same chapter to 'try' the Plataians. We might think that Thucydides feels reprobation for the ruthless behaviour of all six, but if so, naming would surely be a worse punishment for a historian to inflict than non-naming. In any case, there are instances where a man who behaves heroically is not named, for instance, the commander of the Athenian ship which performed the brilliant periplous at ii. 91.[34] As far as Sparta goes, we should never forget Thucydides' complaint at v. 68 about the difficulties of finding out about Sparta; that is, 'name-suppression' may, especially in a Spartan context, be a tendentious modern expression for unavoidable ignorance on Thucydides' part. To return to the five judges, perhaps keeping them anonymous was a literary device to make them more chilling, like a hooded figure at an *auto-da-fe* or a Ku Klux Klan executioner. But that does not account for the military commander.[35]

We must conclude that the reasons for the naming or non-naming of individuals by Thucydides are varied, and that some oddities should be left in the oddity category. But I hope I have shown that in this area too, the Herodotean dimension can be crucially important.[36]

ANNEX B

Thucydides and Herodotus: list of parallel passages suggested, discussed, accepted, or rejected by modern scholars (including some discrepancies)

Abbreviations (other than those in the main list at p. xi)

C/S   Classen/Steup
H 1   S. Hornblower, *Thucydides* (London, 1987, reissued with corrections, 1994)

---

[32] 'Nikias, Epimenides and the Question of Omissions in Thucydides', *CQ* 39 (1989), 83–93.

[33] Ibid. 93. But see my commentary on ii. 29. 1 for proxeny in Thucydides, who mentions eleven instances—not a large total, but not evidence of systematic suppression either.

[34] I. Whitehead, 'The Periplous', *G&R* 34 (1987), 178–85, at 180–1.

[35] Pelling suggests to me that these anonymous Spartans 'speak for Sparta', just as the anonymous general reflects a common-sense Syracusan opinion against which the primadonnas Athenagoras and Hermokrates can play out their quarrel.

[36] This paper has been kindly read and improved by David Lewis and Christopher Pelling. It has also been indirectly improved by Lewis's comments on my Thucydides commentary. See also n. 1.

H 2	S. Hornblower, *A Commentary on Thucydides*, i. *Books i–iii* (Oxford, 1991)
H 3	— in J. Sanders (ed.), *ΦΙΛΟΛΑΚΩΝ: Studies ... Catling* = Annex A above, by whose page nos. I cite.
H 4	— in S. Hornblower (ed.), *Greek Historiography* (Oxford, 1994)
H 5	— *A Commentary on Thucydides*, ii. *Books iv–v. 24* (Oxford, 1996)
How and Wells	W. W. How and J. Wells, *A Commentary on Herodotus* (Oxford, 1912)
Immerwahr	H. Immerwahr, *Form and Thought in Herodotus* (Cleveland, 1966)
Jac.	F. Jacoby, *RE* suppl. ii, 'Herodotus', 205–520, at 505–6
Kennelly	J. J. Kennelly, *Thucydides' Knowledge of Herodotus* (diss. Brown, 1994; microfilm facsimile, Ann Arbor, 1995)
Macan	R. W. Macan, *Herodotus, Histories Books iv–vi and vii–ix* (London, 1895–1908)
Schm.-St.	W. Schmid and O. Stählin, *Geschichte der griechischen Literatur* (Munich, 1920–48), ii. 663–4 n. 7
Stein	H. Stein, *Herodotus* [commentary] (Berlin, 1881–96)

[*Note*: Commentaries, i.e. C/S, H 2, H 5, *HCT*, How and Wells, Macan, Stein, are not cited by page; the ref. is, unless stated, to the relevant section of the commentary]

Th. i. 1, opening, size of wars/Hdt. i. 1, vii. 19–21:
   Jac. 505; Schm.-St.; Connor, 248; H 2; H 3, 125
Th. i. 2. 5, early Athenians sedentary or not?/Hdt. i. 56 ff.:
   Schneege, 23–4; Immerwahr, 199
Th. i. 3. 2–3, name for Greeks/Hdt. i. 56:
   Schneege, 20
Th. i. 3. 2, extent of Pelasgian occupation of Greece (all or most?)/Hdt. viii. 44:
   Schneege, 22
Th. i. 4, thalassocracies of Minos and Polykrates/Hdt. iii. 122:
   Schneege, 26–7; H 2; H 3, 125; Kennelly, 114–19
Th. i. 6, Greek dress/Hdt. v. 87. 3:
   Schneege, 25; H 2
Th. i. 9, Trojan war undertaken by the Atreidai in particular/Hdt. vii. 20. 2:
   Schneege, 26
Th. i. 10. 1–2, *erga* or building works as criteria for greatness/contrast Hdt. iii. 60. 1:
   H 3, 127
Th. i. 10. 1–2, greatness of cities transitory/Hdt. i. 5. 4:
   J. de Romilly, *Histoire et raison chez Thucydide*² (Paris, 1967), 295
Th. i. 11, Trojan War/Hdt. ii. 112:
   Schneege, 26

Th. i. 12, Cadmeans/Hdt. v. 57–61:
Immerwahr, 117 n. 119

Th. i. 13. 1, hereditary *basileiai* and their *gerea*/Hdt. vi. 56 ff.:
H 2

Th. i. 13. 6 (cf. iii. 104. 2), Polykrates and Rheneia/not in Hdt.:
see H 3, 124

Th. i. 13. 6, Massalia/Hdt. i. 166 ff.:
H 2; Kennelly, 107

Th. i. 14. 2–3, Athens and Aigina/Hdt. vii. 144. 2, cp. vi. 49–50, 85–93:
Jac. 505; *HCT*; H 2

Th. i. 15, *non*-mention of First Sacred War/absent from Hdt. also:
N. Robertson, *CQ* 28 (1978), 50–1; H 3, 125; Kennelly, 68–70

Th. i. 15. 3/Hdt. v. 99 Lelantine War:
C/S; Stein; *HCT*; H 2; Kennelly, 69–70

Th. i. 17, Pisistratid lack of achievement/Hdt. i. 64. 1–2 and v. 78:
Schneege, 28; Immerwahr, 200 n. 28; H 2

Th. i. 18. 1, Spartan deposition of tyrants/Hdt. v. 65 and v. 92:
Schneege, 28–9; H 2; H 3, 127

Th. i. 18. 1, Spartan *eunomia*/Hdt. i. 65:
Immerwahr, 199 n. 27; H 3, 126; Kennelly, 123 ff.

Th. i. 20. 2, fall of Pisistratids/Hdt. v. 55 (Th. and Hdt. agree on the essentials
and Th. is probably contradicting some third party):
Schneege, 9; U. v. Wilamowitz-Moellendorff, *Aristoteles und Athens*, ii (Berlin,
1893), 108–20; J. K. Davies, *APF* 446 ff.; R. Thomas, *Oral Tradition and Written
Record in Classical Athens* (Cambridge, 1989), ch. 5; D. M. Lewis, *CAH* iv²
(1988), 287–300; H 2; Kennelly, 138 ff. [see also on Th. vi. 54 ff.]

Th. i. 20. 3 Pitanate *lochos*/Hdt. ix. 53. 2:
Bibliography extensive. See esp. Schneege, 9; C/S; Macan; Jac. 505; Schm.-
St.; *HCT*; H. T. Wade-Gery, *EGH* 76 f.; D. H. Kelly, 'Thucydides and Herod-
otus on the Pitanate Lochos', *GRBS* 22 (1981), 31 ff.; N. Jones, *Political
Organization in Ancient Greece* (Philadelphia, 1987), 11; H 2; Kennelly, 128 ff.

Th. i. 20. 3, votes of Spartan kings/Hdt. vi. 57. 5:
Schneege, 8; C/S; Macan; How and Wells; Jac. 505; Schm.-St.; *HCT*; H 2;
Kennelly, 130 ff.

Th. i. 21. 2, marvelling/Hdt. preface:
J. Cobet, in I. Moxon, J. Smart, and A. Woodman (eds.), *Past Perspectives* (Cambridge, 1986), 8; T. Scanlon, *Historia*, 43 (1994), 165

Th. i. 22. 4 *agonisma*/Hdt. *passim*:
H 2

Th. i. 23. 1–3 Persian Wars/Hdt. vii. 19–21 and *passim*:
Schneege, 37 n. 3; Jac. 506; H 2; D. M. Lewis, *ap.* H 1, 108, 202

Th. i. 23. 6 cause of Peloponnesian War/Hdt. vi. 98. 2:
Schneege, 53

Th. i. 32. 1 and 4, Corcyraean isolationism/Hdt. vii.168, cp. 145:
Schneege, 47

Th. i. 41. 2, Corinthian loan of 20 ships/Hdt. vi. 89:
  C/S; U. Köhler, *Rh. Mus.* 46 (1891), 5 n. 1; Macan; L. H. Jeffery, *AJP* 83 (1962), 49 n. 10; H 2; H 3, 132; Stroud, 277 and n. 12; Kennelly, 77-9

Th. i. 60. 2, etc., Aristeus son of Adeimantos/Hdt. vii. 137, etc.:
  Westlake, *Essays* (1969),74-83; H 3, 135 f., and see below under Th. ii. 67

Th.i. 69. 5 Xerxes' army from all Asia/Hdt. vii. 157. 1:
  Schneege, 38

Th. i. 73. 4, Marathon/Hdt. vi:
  Schneege, 37-8; H 2; K. R. Walters, *Rh. Mus.* 124 (1981), 204

Th. i. 74. 1, number of Ath. ships at Salamis/Hdt. viii. 44, 48 and 61:
  C/S; K. R. Walters, *Rh. Mus.* 124 (1981), 199; H 2; Kennelly, 85-7

Th. i. 74. 1, Salamis fought 'in the narrows'/Hdt. viii. 60β:
  H 2; H 3, 128

Th. i. 74. 1, Themistokles saved Peloponnese/Hdt. vii. 139. 3-4 and 144. 2:
  Schneege, 38; Immerwahr, 139 n. 177

Th. i. 74. 3, Athens 'a city which didn't exist'/Hdt. viii. 61. 1:
  C/S; H 3, 128

Th. i. 75. 2, beginning of Delian League/Hdt. viii. 3:
  Schneege, 49-50; and see under Th. i. 95. 1 and vi.76. 3

Th. i. 80-5, Archidamus as warner/Hdt. vii. 10-12 (Artabanus):
  H. Bischoff, in W. Marg (ed.), *Herodot* (1962), 302 ff.; C. Pelling, in *Georgica: Greek Studies... Cawkwell* (1991), 120 ff.; Kennelly, 99 n. 160

Th. i. 89-118, the *Pentekontaetia*/Hdt.'s terminal date?:
  Jac. 506; Gomme *HCT*, i, p. 1; T. S. Brown, *AHR* 59 (1954), 840; Immerwahr, 9; Kennelly, 54-60; on i. 97. 2 (Th.'s predecessors) see above, pp. 19 f.

Th. i. 89. 2, siege of Sestos/Hdt. ix. 114. 2-118:
  Schneege, 18; C/S; Jac. 505; *HCT*; H 2; H 3, 128

Th. i. 89. 3, Ἀθηναίων τὸ κοινόν/Hdt. ix. 117:
  Schneege, 16-17

Th. i. 89. 3, walls of Athens/Hdt. ix. 13:
  C/S; Jac. 505; *HCT*

Th. i. 93. 3, Themistokles' archonship/Hdt. vii. 143. 1:
  HCT; H 2

Th. i. 95. 1, beginning of Delian league:
  see above under Th. i. 75. 2

Th. i. 95. 1 and 7, deterioration of Pausanias/Hdt. ix. 78, cp. v. 32:
  Schneege, 45-6

Th. i. 100, Amphipolis/Hdt. ix. 75:
  Schm.-St.; see also below under Th. iv. 102. 2

Th. i. 122. 2, appeal to Sparta against Athens the tyrant city:
  cp. above on Th. i. 18. 1

Th. i. 126, Kylon/Hdt. v. 71 (but note discrepancies):
  all commentators; Schneege, 10-12; Jacoby, *Atthis*, 186-8; Andrewes, *CAH* iv². 387; S. D. Lambert, *Historia*, 35 (1986), 105 ff.; R. Thomas, *Oral Tradition & Written Record* (1989), 227 ff.; H 3, 128; Kennelly 108-14

Th. i. 127–38, Pausanias-Themistokles excursus/Hdt. v. 32, vii. 143, etc.:
C. Patterson, '"Here the Lion Smiled": A Note on Thucydides 1. 127–138', in
R. M. Rosen and J. Farrell (eds.), *Nomodeiktes: Greek Studies in Honor of Martin Ostwald* (Ann Arbor, 1993), 145–52

Th. i. 128. 7, Pausanias' marriage offer/Hdt. v. 32:
Schneege, 47; H 2; Patterson (above), 148, where for '5. 43' read '5. 32'

Th. i. 132. 1, Pausanias' relationship to Pleistarchos/Hdt. ix. 10. 2:
Schneege, 46–7

Th. i. 137. 4, Themistokles' letter/Hdt. viii. 75 and 110. 3:
Schneege, 42–3; H 3, 128; Kennelly, 66 n. 118

Th. i. 138. 3, Themistokles' independence from Mnesiphilos/Hdt. viii. 57–8:
Schneege, 44; Jac. 505; Schm.-St.

Th. i. 138. 6, greatness of Pausanias and Themistokles/Hdt. ix. 64. 1
(Pausanias), vii. 143–144. 1 (Themistokles):
Schneege, 40; H 3, 128 f.; Kennelly, 65

Th. ii. 2. 1 and 3, details of Theban attack on Plataia/Hdt. vii. 233:
Schneege, 18–19; C/S; Macan; *HCT*; C. Reid Rubincam, *LCM* 6 (1981), 47–9; H 2; H 3, 136; Kennelly, 93 n. 151

Th. ii. 8. 3, Delos earthquake/Hdt. vi. 98. 1:
Schneege, 14–15; Stein; C/S; Macan; *HCT*; D. M. Lewis, *BSA* 55 (1960), 194 and n. 15; H 2; H 3, 124 and n. 5; Kennelly, 94–9

Th. ii. 12. 3, ἀρχὴ κακῶν/Hdt. v. 30. 1 and 97. 3, vi. 67:
Walbank, *HCP* ii, on Pol. xi. 5. 9; Sommerstein on Ar. *Peace* 435–6; H 2; H 3, 124

Th. ii. 15, no Athenian synoikism pre-Theseus/Hdt. ix. 73:
Schneege, 29

Th. ii. 23, ravaging of Attica, also iii. 26/Hdt. ix. 73:
Jac. 505

Th. ii. 27. 1, treatment of Aiginetans/Hdt. vi. 91. 1:
Stein; Macan; H2

Th. ii. 34. 5, burial of Athenian dead in battles/Hdt. ix. 85:
Schneege, 19; Stein, C/S; Macan; Jacoby, *JHS* 64 (1944), 37–66; *HCT*;
M. Ostwald, *Nomos and the Beginnings of Athenian Democracy* (Oxford, 1969), 175; N. Loraux, *Invention of Athens* (1986); H 2; Kennelly, 88–93

Th. ii. 39. 4, law/Hdt. vii. 104:
Macleod, 145; T. Scanlon, *Historia*, 43 (1994), 271

Th. ii. 41. 1, self-sufficiency/Hdt. i. 32. 8:
K. Gaiser, *Das Staatsmodell des Thukydides: Zur Rede des Perikles für die Gefallenen* (Heidelberg, 1975), 65–72; C. Macleod, *Collected Essays*, 151–2; K. Raaflaub, *Arethusa*, 20 (1987), 236 n. 40; T. Scanlon, *Historia*, 43 (1994), 143–76

Th. ii. 41. 4, marvelling/Hdt. preface:
T. Scanlon, *Historia*, 43 (1994), 165, and see above on Th. i. 21. 2

Th. ii. 62. 1 f., imperialism/Hdt. vii. 49:
Connor, 70 and n. 46

Th. ii. 65. 9, demagogy becomes monarchy/Hdt. iii. 82. 4:
H 2; H 3, 124 n. 3

Th. ii. 67 death of Aristeus/Hdt. vii. 137:
C/S; Jac. 505; H 2; H 3, 136

Th. ii. 71. 2, promise about Plataia/not in Hdt.:
H 2; H 3, 149; E. Badian, *From Plataea to Potidaea* (Baltimore, 1993), 109–23; Kennelly, 93

Th. ii. 97. 1, 'a man travelling light' (εὔζωνος)/Hdt. i. 72. 3, etc.:
H 2

Th. ii. 97. 4, Persian gift-giving/Hdt. iii. 140, ix. 109. 3, and other passages in H. discussed by H. Sancisi-Weerdenburg, *Historia*, 37 (1988), 372–4:
Kennelly 105 (denying that Persian kings give gifts in Hdt.!)

Th. ii. 97. 6, Scythians/Hdt. iv. 46 and v. 3:
Schneege, 13; C/S; Schm.-St.; Kennelly, 121–2

Th. ii. 99, expansion of Macedon/Hdt. viii. 138:
Schneege, 51–2

Th. ii. 99. 3, Argive origins of Macedonian kings/Hdt. v. 22, viii. 137 ff.:
C/S; Hammond, *HM* ii. 3 ff.; H 2; *SEG* xxix (1979), 652, and see below on Th. v. 80

Th. ii. 100. 2, eight kings of Macedon before Archelaos/Hdt. viii. 137. 1 and 139:
Schneege, 50–1; C/S; Hammond, *HM* ii. 44; H 2

Th. ii. 102. 2, Acheloos/Hdt. ii. 10. 2:
C/S; F. Sieveking, *Klio*, 42 (1964), 170; H 2

Th. iii. 24. 1, *heroon* of Androkrates/Hdt. ix. 25:
C/S; H 2; H 3, 129; Kennelly, 67

Th. iii. 24. 1, Dryoskephalai/Hdt. ix. 39:
C/S; H 2; H 3, 129

Th. iii. 54. 3, Thespians omitted/contrast Hdt. viii. 222:
H 3, 131; Kennelly, 75

Th. iii. 54. 4, Plataian naval inexperience/Hdt. viii. 1. 1:
Schneege, 48; H 2; H 3, 131; Kennelly, 73–4

Th. iii. 55.1, Plataian rejection by Kleomenes, etc., in 519/Hdt. vi. 108:
Schneege, 48; C/S; *HCT*; H 2; H 3, 131; Kennelly, 73–7

Th. iii. 55. 3, Plataians as Ath. citizens/date and historicity disputed; not in Hdt.:
H 2; H 3, 131; Kennelly, 74

Th. iii. 58. 5, Plataian gods invoked in 479/Hdt. ix. 61. 3:
Schneege, 48–9

Th. iii. 62. 2, Theban medism/Hdt. ix. 86–7:
Schneege, 49; H 2; H 3, 131; Kennelly, 75–6

Th. iii. 62. 3, 'a form of government than which nothing . . .'/Hdt. v. 92 α 1:
H 2

Th. iii. 64. 3, Thebes–Aigina link/Hdt. v. 79 ff.:
H 2

Th. iii. 82. 6–8, sophistry of the *stasiotes*; effect of *stasis*/Hdt. iii. 72, 82:
Macleod, 138 n. 34; 129

Th. iii. 92. 2, Oitaians/Hdt. vii. 217. 1:
H 2

Th. iii. 104. 1 (cf. i. 8, viii. 108), purification of Delos by Pisistratus/Hdt. i. 64. 2:
C/S; H 2; H 3, 124; see also below on Th. v. 1

Th. iii. 104. 4-5, Homeric Hymn/Hdt. iv. 35 (Olen of Lycia):
H 2, p. 524, citing Allen and Halliday

Th. iv. 36. 3, the ἀτραπός at Thermopylai/Hdt. vii. 175, 213 ff.:
C/S; H 3, 128; Kennelly, 71-2; H 5

Th. iv. 61. 5, rule of stronger/Hdt. vii. 8a:
Connor, 152, 156, and cp. below on Th. v. 105

Th. iv. 62. 4 προμηθία/Hdt. iii. 36. 1:
Connor, 125 n. 37

Th. iv. 102. 2, Aristagoras and the Amphipolis site/Hdt. v. 11 and 126; ix. 75:
Schneege, 52; C/S; Macan; Schm.-St.; *HCT*; H 3, 124; Kennelly, 100; H 5

Th. iv. 102. 2, Drabeskos disaster/Hdt. ix. 75:
Schneege, 53; H 5; see also above on Th. i. 100

Th. iv. 109. 2, Xerxes' canal/Hdt. vii. 22:
C/S; *HCT*; H 5; Kennelly, 101; R. Jones, *et al.*, *BSA* 89 (1994), 277-84

Th. iv. 109. 3, Mt. Athos Places/Hdt. vii. 22. 3:
C/S; *ATL* i. 464; *HCT*; M. Zahrnt, *Olynth und die Chalkidier* (Munich, 1971),
184, 182, 191, 194; Kennelly, 101 n. 163

Th. iv. 109. 4, 'bilingual barbarians'/Hdt. vii. 22. 2 with Hude's 1926 apparatus:
Macan; H 5

Th. iv. 109. 4, Pelasgians, Etruscans on Lemnos/Hdt. v. 26, cp. iv. 145, vi. 136-7:
Schneege, 23 (Pelasgians); H. Rix, *Gedenkschrift . . . Brandenstein* (Innsbruck,
1968), 213-22; J. Heurgon, *CRAI* 1980, 578-600; J. Penney, *CAH* iv² (1988),
725; H 5 (Etruscans)

Th. v. 1 (also vi. 94. 1) cross-referencing formula/Hdt. vii. 108. 1:
HCT; H 5; see above on Th. iii. 104. 1

Th. v. 31. 2, Elis and Lepreon war/Hdt. iv. 148. 4:
HCT; for this and following items see vol. iii of this commentary

Th. v. 41, 'Battle of the Champions'/Hdt. i. 82:
C/S; *HCT*; Immerwahr, 37 n. 66; H 3, 124; Kennelly, 132 n. 212

Th. v. 65. 2, κακὸν κακῷ ἰᾶσθαι/Hdt. iii. 53. 4 (and proverbial):
C/S; *HCT*

Th. v. 75. 1, only a single Spartan king goes on campaign/Hdt. v. 75. 2:
C/S; *HCT*

Th. v. 80: see above on ii. 99. 3

Th. v. 89 ff., Melian Dialogue/Hdt. viii. 111:
Immerwahr, 322 n. 40

Th. v. 104, Melian trust in gods/Hdt. viii. 13 and 143:
Schneege, 58 (for Hdt. viii. 13); Connor, 157 and n. 42 (for Hdt. viii. 143)

Th. v. 105. 2, rule of stronger/Hdt. vii. 8a:
C/S; F. Heinimann, *Nomos und Phusis* (Basle, 1945), 167 n. 7; Immerwahr, 322
n. 40; Connor, 156, and see above on Th. iv. 61. 5

Th. v. 112. 2, date of foundation of Melos/Hdt. ii. 145. 2:
HCT; H 3, 130

Th. vi. 4. 2, Gelon depopulates Megara Hyblaia/Hdt. vii. 156. 2:
Schneege, 31; *HCT*; see also below on Th. vi. 94. 1

Th. vi. 4. 3, foundation of Gela (Lindians, Antiphemos)/Hdt. vii. 153:
Schneege, 31

Th. vi. 4. 4, Akragas, Kamikos/Hdt. vii. 170. 1:
Schneege, 1–32

Th. vi. 4. 5–6, Zankle occupied by Samians, renamed Messina/Hdt. vi. 22 ff., vii. 164:
C/S; *HCT*; Macan (and at VII–IX, vol. 2, 19 n. 3); Kennelly 4–8

Th. vi. 5. 3, Kamarina/Hdt. vii. 154. 3:
Schneege, 32

Th. vi. 9–18, Sicily debate/Hdt. vii. 8–18:
K. v. Fritz, *Die Griechische Geschichtschreibung*, i (Berlin, 1967), 727; V. Hunter, *Thucydides the Artful Reporter* (Toronto, 1973), 181 n. 7; N. Marinatos Kopff and H. R. Rawlings III, *PdelP* 33 (1978), 333 n. 4

Th. vi. 18. 7, expansion/Hdt. vii. 8a:
Macleod, 150

Th. vi. 18. 7, my opponent doesn't respect laws/Hdt. iii. 82, end:
Macleod, 87–8

Th. vi. 32. 2, ἅμιλλα of ships setting out for Sicily/Hdt. vii. 44:
Connor, 175 n. 43

Th. vi. 33. 5, preventing withdrawal of invader/Hdt. viii. 108–10:
Connor 175 n. 44, 198 (where for 9. 108–10 read 8. 108–10)

Th. vi. 46, Egestan trick/Hdt. iii. 123:
J. Hart, *Herodotus and Greek History* (London, 1982), 60; H 1, 23

Th. vi. 50. 1 and 61. 6, Alcibiades' own trireme/Hdt. viii. 17, Kleinias the great-grandfather of Alcibiades:
HCT; E. F. Poppo and J. M. Stahl, *Thucydidis libri octo* (Leipzig, 1882–8), n. on vi. 61. 6.

Th. vi. 53. 3, Pisistratids harsher towards end/Hdt. 62. 2:
Schneege, 35

Th. vi. 54 ff., fall of Pisistratids/Hdt. v. 55–65:
all commentators, and Schneege, 32–4; Jac. 505; Kennelly, 138 ff.; see also on i. 20. 2; and cf. Wade-Gery, *OCD*³ 1518 col. 2: those who think books 6 and 7 early 'may suspect ... (a very slippery question) in 6. 54. 1 ignorance of Herodotus' history—but cannot prove their suspicions'.

Th. vi. 54. 5–6, nature of Pisistratid rule (good)/Hdt. i. 59:
Schneege, 35; Schm.-St.; H 3, 130

Th. vi. 59. 3, Hippoklos/Hdt. iv. 138. 1:
Lewis, *CAH* iv² (1988), 300

Th. vi. 76. 3–77, slavery theme/Hdt. i. 169. 1, vi. 32:
Schneege, 49–50

Th. vi. 76. 3, beginning of Delian League:
see above under Th. i. 75. 2

Th. vi. 82. 4, Ionians betrayed Athens in 480/Hdt. viii. 85. 1:
Immerwahr, 232 n. 128

Th. vi. 89, Alcibiades' family (Alkmaionid side) as tyrant-haters/Hdt. vi. 123:
C/S; H 3, 130

Th. vi. 94. 1 (cross-referencing formula):
see above under Th. v. 1 and vi. 4. 2

Th. vi. 100, Syracusans retire from the sun/Hdt. vi. 11–13:
Immerwahr, 247 n. 29

Th. vi (end) and vii (beginning)/Hdt. viii (end) and ix (beginning):
J. de Romilly, *Histoire et raison chez Thucydide*² (Paris, 1967), 73 and n. 1;
Immerwahr, 79 n. 2

Th. vii. 57. 4, Styra Dryopian?/Hdt. viii. 46. 4:
C/S; *HCT*

Th. vii. 73. 3, Syracusan trick/Hdt. viii. 75 f.:
Connor, 198 (where for '7. 72. 2' read '7. 73. 3')

Th. vii. 81. 4, περισταδόν/Hdt. vii. 225. 3:
C. F. Smith, *TAPA* 31 (1900), 74; Connor, 199 n. 38 (Arr. *Anab.* v. 17. 3 uses
the word, and Bosworth's commentary (1995) notes the Thucydidean allusion; but on the same page he notes Herodotean resonances as well. Arrian
may have had both authors in mind when he used περισταδόν)

Th. vii. 85. 4, πλεῖστος φόνος/Hdt. vii. 170. 3:
C/S; Jac. 505; Schm.-St.

Th. vii. 87. 6, πανωλεθρία/Hdt. ii. 120. 5:
H. Strasburger, *Hermes*, 86 (1958), 39 n. 3 = H. Herter (ed.), *Thukydides*
(Darmstadt, 1968), 529 n. 83 = W. Schmitthenner and R. Zoepffel (eds.),
H. Strasburger, *Studien zur alten Geschichte*, ii (Berlin and New York, 1982),
707; *HCT*; N. Marinatos Kopff and H. R. Rawlings III, *PdelP* 33 (1978), 331–7;
Connor, 125 n. 37; H 1, 148 n. 50; H 3, 124 n. 3. (C/S compare Hdt. vi. 37. 2);
N. Dunbar, *Aristophanes Birds* (Oxford, 1995), n. on 1239–40

Th. viii. 89. 3, splits in oligarchies/Hdt. iii. 82. 3:
How and Wells; Newman, *Ar. Pol. Comm.* iv. 350

Th. viii. 102. 3, Protesilaos/Hdt. ix. 116. 2, cp. 120. 4:
C/S; D. Boedeker, *CA* 7 (1988), 35 n. 18; H. 4, 65 n. 160

[Note: the above list does not include some pairs of Hdt. and Th. passages
which are often discussed together, and which bear on Hdt.'s supposed date of
composition or publication, but whose relation to each other is not exactly
intertextual. See Th. iv. 53–7, Kythera/Hdt. vii. 235; Th. iv. 57. 3, Aiginetans/
Hdt. vi. 91. 1; Th. vii. 27–8, Decelea/Hdt. ix. 73 (cf. above on Th. ii. 23). See my
nn. on the Th. iv passages. Finally, Hdt. viii. 126 ff. may (see above, p. 27 n. 83)
show that Hdt. was interested in Potidaia for topical reasons, cf. Th. i. 56 ff.; cf.
also, for Corinth/Corcyra tension, Hdt. iii. 49. 1 with Th. i. 13. 4, 38. 1.]

BOOK IV

On the structure of book iv as a whole see Introduction above, pp. 108 ff. citing and discussing W. R. Connor, *Thucydides*, and D. Babut, 'Interprétation historique et structure littéraire chez Thucydide: remarques sur la composition du livre iv', *Bulletin de l'association Guillaume Budé*, 40 (1981), 417–39, abbrev. Babut.

At intervals, in six places, Th. will pause to comment on the morale of one or both sides: see above, p. 109.

1–41. THE PYLOS EPISODE

1–6. *The Athenians occupy Pylos*

This episode is in Th.'s presentation the turning-point of the Archidamian War. Westlake, however, has argued that Th. exaggerated the importance of the Pylos affair and the extent of the Spartan reverse, and minimized the general mood of dissatisfaction at Sparta with the progress of the war: see 'The Naval Battle at Pylos and its Consequences', *CQ* 24 (1974), 211–26 = *Studies*, ch. 5. For discussion of this see Introduction above, pp. 110; 113.

The book opens with Sicilian material, but this is soon (chs. 2 and 3) blended in with events at Corcyra and Pylos; these initial chapters should not, therefore, be chopped up too finely as by Gomme in his arrangement. See my introductory n. to iii. 86: some of the threads kept separate in book 3 are now drawn together.

Th.'s treatment of the Pylos/Sphakteria episode is, as individual nn. below will show, remarkable for its (undue) stress on the elements of chance. See J. de Romilly, *Thucydide et l'impérialisme Athénien* (Paris, 1951), 151 = *Thucydides and Athenian Imperialism*, tr. P. Thody (Oxford, 1963), 174; Stahl, *Thukydides*, 140 ff.; Hunter, 61 ff. (against which see D. Babut, 'Épisode de Pylos-Sphactérie', *Revue de Philologie*, 60 (1986), 59–79); Schneider, *Information und Absicht*, 95–9; L. Edmunds, *Chance and Intelligence in Thucydides* (Cambridge, Mass., 1975), 176 ff.; H. Erbse, *Thukydidesinterpretationen* (Berlin and New York, 1989), 163–6. See also Howie (Introduction, p. 39, n. 99) for an ingenious suggestion—part of his *aristeia* theory—that Th. stresses chance in the Pylos episode order to 'throw a negative light' on Kleon, who thus becomes the over-fortunate Hector to Brasidas' Achilles.

Th.'s account of Pylos 425 BC, and its topographical difficulties, real and supposed, have generated a great deal of modern writing. W. K. Pritchett, 'Pylos and Sphakteria', *SAGT* i (1965), ch. 1, is basic. On the whole section iv. 2–41 (with the omission of chs. 7, 24–5) see J. B. Wilson, *Pylos 425 BC: A Historical and Topographical Study of Thucydides' Account of the Campaign* (Warminster, 1979): gives Oxford text, facing translation, and historical notes at end; very factual; shows no awareness of Westlake, *CQ* 1974. An earlier version by Wilson and T. Beardsworth appeared in article form in 1970, see below, 13. 4 n. There is also a good military account of the Sphakteria campaign in J. F. Lazenby, *The Spartan Army* (Warminster, 1985), 113–25, and an annotated filmstrip by W. Ball, *Pylos 425* (Old Vicarage Publications, Congleton, Cheshire, 1990). In 1994 W. K. Pritchett returned to the problems of Pylos, defending Th. with some impatience against modern critics: 'Thucydides and Pylos', *EGH* 145–77 (ch. 4), esp. 146 n. 1; no mention of Wilson at any point. For Pylos itself see S. Grunauer von Hoerschelmann, in Lauffer (ed.), *Griechenland*, 577–8.

1. 1. τοῦ δ᾽ ἐπιγιγνομένου θέρους περὶ σίτου ἐκβολήν: 'In the following summer, about the time when the corn comes into ear'. That is, about April 425. For Th.'s indications of time see ii. 1 introductory n. Συρακοσίων δέκα νῆες πλεύσασαι καὶ Λοκρίδες ἴσαι: 'ten Syracusan and ten Lokrian ships'. For Lokri in S. Italy ('Epizephyrian Lokri') and its close connections with Syracuse see iii. 86. 2 n., and add F. Parise Badoni, *Princeton Encyclopaedia*, 523–4; K. Lomas, *OCD*[3], entry on 'Locri Epizephyrii'; and *Locri Epizefirii: Atti del Sedecesimo Convegno di Studi sulla Magna Grecia*, 2 vols. (Naples, 1977). See further below, v. 5 nn. Μεσσήνην: 'Messina'. See iii. 90. 2 n. for the spelling, and iii. 90. 4 for the Athenian takeover of Messina. For Messina see G. Vallet, *Rhégion et Zancle* (Paris, 1958) and B. S. Ridgway, entry under Zankle in *Princeton Encyclopaedia*, 998–9. On the change of name see vi. 4. 6 and n. On the present episode see D. Musti, in *Locri Epizefirii* (preceding n.), 87–8, noting that it implies a less drastic takeover of Messina by Lokri than that in 422, see v. 5. 1 n. on ἐγένετο etc.

αὐτῶν ἐπαγαγομένων: 'by the invitation of the inhabitants'. Steup wanted to read αὐτῶν ⟨ἀνδρῶν⟩ ἐπαγαγομένων, i.e. to make the invitation come from 'some men' of the Messinians, i.e. a sub-group only; but see J. de Romilly, 'Thucydides and the Cities of the Athenian Empire',

BICS 13 (1966), 1–12, at 8, calling this 'obviously wrong: although it is only part of the city, the responsibility is felt as being common'.

2. ὁρῶντες προσβολὴν ἔχον τὸ χωρίον τῆς Σικελίας: 'they saw that Messina was the key to [lit., 'means of entering', LSJ⁹] Sicily'. This obvious strategic truth hardly needs modern illustration, but see M. Howard, *Grand Strategy IV: August 1942–September 1943* (London, 1972), 504. Cp. vi. 48, and for the importance of Messina to Dionysius I for control of the straits see Lewis, *CAH* vi². 141, 144.

μείζονι παρασκευῇ ἐπέλθωσιν: 'would come and attack them with a larger force'. This need not betray knowledge of the great expedition of 415. See 60. 2 n. on πλέονί ποτε στόλῳ.

οἱ δὲ Λοκροὶ κατὰ ἔχθος τὸ Ῥηγίνων: 'The Lokrians took part because they hated the Rhegians'. See iii. 86 (though this passage goes further than that one); also iv. 24. 2, echoing the present passage closely.

2. 1. Ἆγις ὁ Ἀρχιδάμου: 'Agis son of Archidamos'. See iii. 1. 1 and 89. 1 and nn. (Agis) and 95. 2 n. on καὶ ἢν νικήσωμεν etc. (invasions).

2. τάς τε τεσσαράκοντα ναῦς: 'the forty ships'. See iii. 115. 4.

Εὐρυμέδοντα καὶ Σοφοκλέα· Πυθόδωρος γὰρ ὁ τρίτος αὐτῶν: 'Eurymedon and Sophokles. The third general, Pythodoros'. For Eurymedon see iii. 80. 2 n. and for Pythodoros and Sophokles iii. 115. 5 n. See generally Develin, *AO* 126 f. For the expression here used (not quite the same as τρίτος αὐτός) see Fornara, *Generals*, 32: the difference from the more usual type of expression, for which see 42. 1 n., is not to be explained by the assumption that τρίτος αὐτός was a technical or legal term and so avoided by Th. when, as here, it was inappropriate for some undisclosed reason. Instead, the difference here is to be explained by 'the manifest inapplicability of the other term when all the generals are not together'. That is, Th. could not say of Pythodoros that he was 'himself the third' when he was somewhere else.

3. εἶπον: 'They were given instructions' [lit. 'they' i.e. the Athenians of para. 2 'told them to . . .']. The usual vagueness about just which Athenians did the telling; we must assume the Assembly is meant, but see e.g. i. 50. 5 n. at end; i. 139. 3 n.; iii. 3. 5 n.; iii. 36. 5 n.: there were other bodies at Athens with diplomatic and military functions, but their activities tend to be invisible in Th.

οἳ ἐληστεύοντο ὑπὸ τῶν ἐν τῷ ὄρει φυγάδων: 'who were being harassed by the exiles in the mountain'. See iii. 85. I have kept Jowett's 'exiles', although as often in Greek history this is misleading if it suggests a formal decree was necessarily passed; but the English 'refugees' suggests poverty, homelessness, etc., which may also be misleading about expatriate groups in Greece. See *OCD*³ under 'exile, Greek'.

4. Δημοσθένει δὲ ὄντι ἰδιώτῃ: 'Demosthenes ... had no command' [lit. 'being a private citizen']. But he was general-elect, see iii. 102. 3 n. and Develin, *AO* 127. This helps to explain the very considerable latitude he is now given, surprising that that is in any case, see next n.

αὐτῷ δεηθέντι εἶπον χρῆσθαι ταῖς ναυσὶ ταύταις, ἢν βούληται, περὶ τὴν Πελοπόννησον: 'but now at this own request the Athenians allowed him to make use of the fleet round the Peloponnese in whatever way he chose'. In book iii (see e.g. 94. 3, 109. 2, and nn.) we have noted some striking examples of freedom of action permitted to Athenian generals by the Assembly; now we have an even more startling case, a man who is not even a general (though he is a general-elect, see preceding n.) is given a free hand with an Athenian fleet.

3. 1. καὶ ὡς ἐγένοντο πλέοντες κατὰ τὴν Λακωνικήν: 'When they arrived off the coast of Lakonia'. Lakonia here includes Messenia, see Wilson, 47 and n. 1: a storm (see below) off *Lakonia* would not force the Athenians to put in as far away as *Pylos*.

κατὰ τύχην χειμὼν ἐπιγενόμενος: 'it so happened that a storm came on'. So begins a chain of events and actions which Th. represents as accidental or spontaneous even when (it is reasonable to suppose) they were not. F. M. Cornford, *Thucydides Mythistoricus* (London, 1907), 88 n. 2 (cp. 90) notes that in the present passage we have κατὰ τύχην, 'by chance' rather than the weaker verbal form ἔτυχε, 'it happened that', which can just be a way of saying that an event occurred. Thus, says Cornford, 'the note of accident is clearly sounded'. Maybe, but unlike some of what follows, the storm was a genuinely fortuitous event. See also next n. J. Roisman, *The General Demosthenes and his Use of Military Surprise* (*Historia Einzelschrift* 78: Stuttgart, 1993), ch. 3, 'Pylos and its lessons', argues (see esp. 35 f., cp. 38) that Demosthenes' planning and intelligence, in the technical military sense, were good, but that his predictions came true 'to a large part because of luck' and Spartan mismanagement.

Babut, 423, as part of his Pylos/Chalkidike equation (see Introduction pp. 108 f.), compares 103. 2 and 5, the wintry weather at Amphipolis.

2. καὶ ὁ Δημοσθένης εὐθὺς ἠξίου τειχίζεσθαι τὸ χωρίον (ἐπὶ τοῦτο γὰρ ξυνεκπλεῦσαι): 'Demosthenes immediately urged them to fortify the place; this (he said) was why he had accompanied the fleet'. The words 'he said' have to be supplied because of the infinitive, which shows that what we have here is indirect speech. If, however, we read ξυνέπλευσε, with some manuscripts and editors (including Jowett), the meaning will be 'this was why he had accompanied the fleet'; that is, the aside is an authorial comment by Th. about what Th. believed to be

Demosthenes' real motive, not a report of a statement by Demosthenes. But there is no difficulty about supposing that Demosthenes made this comment to his colleagues: Classen/Steup thought it improbable that he would not have divulged his intentions to them earlier, but perhaps he did (the Greek would then mean something like 'that (he reminded them) was why', etc.). I follow the reading of Gomme and of de Romilly in the Budé.

It is certainly remarkable that the occupation of Pylos should have depended on a chance storm (see 1 n. above); it is possible, as Gomme, 439, seems to have thought (but contrast 488 n. 2, where he allows for local knowledge and advice by Messenians) that Demosthenes' idea was formed on earlier cruises past this coastline (but it would be too strong to speak of a fixed intention on his part: otherwise he would surely have made some effort to provide the soldiers in advance with the proper tools for the job he envisaged). But against Gomme on this point see H. Erbse, *Thukydides-Interpretationen* (Berlin, 1989), 164. Erbse (165) remarks that the accident of the storm was responsible, not for Pylos being occupied at all, but for its occupation as early as 425.

As von Fritz notes (*Die Griechische Geschichtsschreibung*, ii (Berlin, 1967), 303 n. 104, the ulterior motive—desire to establish a base to which helots would desert—is not given till 41 below. See n. there for the puzzle why Athens did not make more use of this class weapon.

Not only it is likely that Demosthenes had marked down this particular spot previously: fortification of the general kind here envisaged was an issue ventilated already, under the name *epiteichismos* or *epiteichisis*, in the pre-war discussions of book i, see i. 122. 1 n. and 142. 2. See 3 n. below.

καὶ ἀπέφαινε πολλὴν εὐπορίαν ξυλῶν τε καὶ λίθων: 'he pointed out to them that there was plenty of timber and stone'. On the material about Pylos and Sphakteria, in this ch. and in ch. 8, see R. T. Ridley, 'Exegesis and Audience in Thucydides', *Hermes*, 109 (1981), 25–46, esp. 40 and n. 58: he notes (evidently with the present passage in mind) that 'many matters are introduced in the form of arguments by Demosthenes'; that is, to put it narratologically, the material about Pylos is offered as a piece of embedded or secondary focalization, the secondary focalizer being Demosthenes, but at the same time we hear the voice of the primary narrator-focalizer Thucydides. But then, from ἀπέχει γάρ to Κορυφάσιον, Th. as primary narrator-focalizer 'drops' the secondary focalizer altogether, and offers explanatory material about Pylos which is needed for the military narrative about to be offered by himself (see Ridley, 40). The first sentence of para. 3 then gives the dismissive view of Demosthenes' colleagues, and this enables Th. elegantly to return to giving primary narrator-focalizer material—e.g. about the language of the ὁμόφωνοι Messenians—in the form of embedded focalization, i.e. through the mouth of Demosthenes. (See 3 n. below on ὁμοφώνους, a very rare word in Th.; its authorial use at 41. 2 guarantees that in the present passage, also, the primary narrator–focalizer Th. is present.)

καὶ ἐρῆμον: 'uninhabited'. On this as one of Pylos' advantages see Wilson 48 ff.

ἀπέχει γὰρ σταδίους μάλιστα ἡ Πύλος τῆς Σπάρτης τετρα-κοσίους: 'Pylos is about forty-six miles away [73 km.] from Sparta'. Lit. '400 stades'; Jowett reckons 185 m. to a stade. For stades see i. 63. 2 n. with Bauslaugh, *JHS* 1979 (8. 6 n. on ἡ γὰρ νῆσος etc.), there cited (who in the present instance reckons the distance at 70 km. and suggests a 'Thucydidean stade' of 175 m. (To the references at i. 63. 2 n. add now S. Pothecary, 'Strabo, Polybius and the Stade', *Phoenix*, 49 (1995), 49–67, arguing that the geographical writers *did* have a fixed stade, of 185 m., and that the correct conversion ratio of Roman miles into stades is 8:1. She does not however discuss the problem of Thucydides' stades). The route implied here by Th. must, like the present-day Langadha pass, go across Mt. Taygetos, thence to Pylos via Pharai, the modern Kalamata: Telemachus' route in *Odyssey* iii. 488. For Cartledge, *Sparta and Lakonia*, 240 f., Th.'s '400 stades' is just 'wrong': 'by the easiest route via Oresthasion in south-west Arcadia it is some 600 stades or 90 kilometres' (so too Dover, *HCT* iv. 468); but see Pritchett, *SAGT* i (1965), 18: there was an ancient road across Taygetos running south of the Langadha, which 'would accord with the figures in Thucydides'.

For Pylos see Wilson, 145, map C. An excellent impression of the whole Pylos/Sphakteria complex is given by R. V. Schoder, *Ancient Greece from the Air* (London, 1974), 194 f.: plates and plans.

καλοῦσι δὲ αὐτὴν οἱ Λακεδαιμόνιοι Κορυφάσιον: 'The Spartans call it Koryphasion'. This is not exactly a pointless thing to tell us, nor wholly uncharacteristic (cp. iv. 76. 3, 102. 3, and vi. 2. 2 for the old and new names or epithets for Orchomenos, Amphipolis, and Sicily, though that is not the same as the giving of alternative names in use at the same time). But the information gains point considerably in view of the appearance of the Spartan name Koryphasion in the truce document at 118. 4 and in the Peace of Nikias at v. 18. 7. The present passage may well therefore have been written with those passages already in mind; if that is right it tells against Kirchhoff's view that the documents were late insertions into the narrative. See 118. 4 n. and introductory n. to 117–19.

Why did the Spartans not call Pylos 'Pylos'? It is possible (as Robin Osborne suggests to me) that they wanted to 'deny the Messenians a

part in the heroic Greece of Nestor' (who ruled Pylos). For strong
Messenian feelings about Pylos see 41. 2 n. on καὶ οἱ ἐκ τῆς Ναυπάκτου
Μεσσήνιοι ὡς ἐς πατρίδα: the Messenians at Naupaktos send help to
Pylos because it was their fatherland.

Pritchett, *EGH* 161 n. 28, notes that Xen. *Hell.* i. 2. 18 uses the form
'Koryphasion', which 'indicates how much he wrote from Lakedaimonian informants'.

**3. οἱ δὲ πολλὰς ἔφασαν εἶναι ἄκρας ἐρήμους τῆς Πελοπον-
νήσου, ἢν βούληται καταλαμβάνων τὴν πόλιν δαπανᾶν:** 'The
other generals said that there were plenty of desolate promontories on
the Peloponnese which he could occupy if he wanted to waste public
money'. [On the text see Maurer, *Interpolation*, 55 f. There is no need to
emend: the Greek of the last three words means literally 'if he wanted
the city to waste money'. Maurer sees irony here: capturing deserted
headlands will be the decision of Demosthenes alone, but it will be the
city that will be spending its resources. 'The grammatical contradiction, I
fancy, points to the fact that, unlike the speakers, Demosthenes is a
person not in office'.] One of the few approximations to a joke in Th.,
and a rather dry one. See, for another joke in this section, 40. 2 and n.,
and for Th.'s work as an altogether 'drier biscuit' than Hdt.'s see Jasper
Griffin, *New York Review of Books*, 9 April 1987, 11.

For de Ste. Croix, *OPW* 209, the present passage is evidence that
epiteichisis (for which 3. 2 n. above) had been discussed at Athens but
rejected on grounds of cost; see also Cawkwell, *YCS* 24 (1975), 67.

καὶ ὁμοφώνους τοῖς Λακεδαιμονίοις: 'and spoke the same dialect
as the Spartans'. See 112. 4 and n. The adjective is found only here and at
41. 2 in Th., perhaps a mild piece of 'clustering' (see *Greek Historiography*,
17 n. 30). The focalizer here is certainly Th. as well as (perhaps more
than) Demosthenes, see above, 2 n. on καὶ ἀπέφαινε etc. For the
awkward repetition at 41. 2 see n. there.

**4. 1. ὡς δὲ οὐκ ἔπειθεν οὔτε τοὺς στρατηγοὺς οὔτε τοὺς
στρατιώτας, ὕστερον καὶ τοῖς ταξιάρχοις κοινώσας, ἡσύχαζεν
ὑπὸ ἀπλοίας:** 'He had been unable to persuade either the generals or
the soldiers (for he had subsequently disclosed his plans to the taxiarchs
as well). So because the weather was still unfit for sailing he was forced
to remain doing nothing'. The point of the parenthesis about the
taxiarchs or divisional commanders is that they relayed Demosthenes'
proposals to the men. The text has been suspected, but is ably defended
by R. Weil, 'Stratèges, soldats, taxiarques (Thucydide, IV, 4, 1)', *Revue de
Philologie*, 62 (1988), 129-33. The usual alteration has been to delete the
reference to the soldiers altogether (by deleting τοὺς στρατιώτας); so

Steup, Gomme (who makes other suggestions), T. J. Quinn, *Hermes*, 95 (1967), 378–9, followed by Westlake, *Individuals in Thucydides* (Cambridge, 1968), 108. But Weil shows that this is unnecessary and undesirable: it is perfectly plausible that Demosthenes, who was 'a bit of a demagogue' (Weil, 130), should have wanted to involve the ordinary soldiers in his plans: 'the soldiers were citizens, who tomorrow would be electors and perhaps judges as well.' It is important for Weil (132 f.) that the verbs should be translated as pluperfects: he *had* been unable to persuade anybody, but then there was a change of heart due to inactivity: 'that is how he [Th.] thinks crowds behave.'

The last three words of the Greek have also caused difficulty; the manuscripts have ἡσύχαζεν, '*he* remained inactive'; this has been emended, again unnecessarily, to the plural ἡσύχαζον, '*they* remained inactive'.

ὁρμὴ ἐνέπεσε: 'were seized with an impulse' [lit. 'an impulse fell on, seized them']. Most commentators have been struck by this extraordinary 'impulse', which fitted so well with Demosthenes' plans; see e.g. Edmunds (above, introductory n.), 179, and add J. de Romilly, *Histoire et raison chez Thucydide* (Paris, 1956, 2nd impression, 1967), 167. For the verb see ii. 48. 2 n.; the mss. here have ἐσέπεσε.

2. σιδήρια μὲν λιθουργὰ οὐκ ἔχοντες: 'since they had no iron tools'. See 3. 2 n. on καὶ ὁ Δημοσθένης etc.

ἐπὶ τοῦ νώτου ἔφερον ἐγκεκυφότες: 'they carried it on their backs, stooping down'. As Weil (1 n.), 132, says, such picturesque detail is more in Hdt.'s manner than Th.'s; see, however, ii. 4. 4 n. and Connor, 'Narrative Discourse in Thucydides', in M. Jameson (ed.), *The Greek Historians: Literature and History. Papers pres. A. E. Raubitschek* (Saratoga, 1985), 1–17.

τὸ γὰρ πλέον τοῦ χωρίου αὐτὸ καρτερὸν ὑπῆρχε καὶ οὐδὲν ἔδει τείχους: 'the position was in most places so naturally strong as to have no need of a wall'. Th. is probably thinking primarily of the precipitate east face of the Pylos promontory, facing the modern lagoon.

5. 1. οἱ δὲ ἑορτήν τινα ἔτυχον ἄγοντες: 'The Spartans, who were just then celebrating a [lit. 'a certain'] festival'. See Popp, *Die Einwirkung von Vorzeichen, Opfern und Festen auf die Kriegführung der Griechen im 5. und 4. Jahrhundert v. Chr.* (Diss. Erlangen, 1957), 118 ff.: the festival cannot be identified but it must have been a minor and short affair or the invasion of Attica could not have gone on at the same time (2. 1; this presumably applies in other years in which there was an invasion at about now). Popp thinks that by 'a certain' Th. seeks to bring out the discrepancy between the attitude of the Spartans [frivolous] and the requirements of the situation. R. B. Strassler, 'The Opening of the Pylos Campaign', *JHS*

110 (1990), 110–25, esp. 119, suggests that the Spartans delayed because of fears of helot revolt; but it is hard to believe that Th. would not have known about this, or that he would not have brought it out into the open if he did know about it.

ῥᾳδίως: 'easily'. An ominous word: people in Th. who think things can be done 'easily' tend to be deluding themselves, see ii. 3. 2 n. on ἐπιθέμε-νοι etc.

2. ταῖς δὲ πλείοσι ναυσὶ τὸν ἐς τὴν Κέρκυραν πλοῦν καὶ Σικελίαν ἠπείγοντο: 'with most of the ships hastened on their way to Corcyra and Sicily'. But for the possibility that they left some men with Demosthenes see Wilson, 65.

6. 1. οἱ δ' ἐν τῇ Ἀττικῇ ὄντες Πελοποννήσιοι ὡς ἐπύθοντο: 'The Peloponnesian army in Attica, when they heard . . .'. For estimates about how long all this took see Wilson, 72, suggesting about 18 days between the first Athenian fortification and the seafight on ch. 14, and allowing *c.*9–19 days for messages to go to Sparta and Attica, and for the first Spartan troops to arrive.

νομίζοντες μὲν οἱ Λακεδαιμόνιοι καὶ Ἆγις ὁ βασιλεὺς οἰκεῖον σφίσι τὸ περὶ τὴν Πύλον: 'King Agis and the Spartans thought that what was happening at Pylos affected them very closely'. For the thought, cp. 72. 1 and n., though there I argue that there is an extra, religious, dimension.

7. *Athenian capture and loss of Eion*

On this chapter see (in addition to *HCT*) Gomme, *The Greek Attitude to Poetry and History* (Berkeley, 1954), 136: its function is partly preparatory, to remind us that Athens' position in this area is weak—very relevant to the events of chs. 78 ff. Nevertheless the news of Brasidas' Thracian expedition is very abruptly broken at 70. 1, see n. there.

Σιμωνίδης Ἀθηναίων στρατηγός: 'Simonides, an Athenian general'. Otherwise unknown; we are now very close in time to Th.'s own command in this area (though he was involved with a different Eion, see next n.). Perhaps we are meant to reflect that Simonides, though no more successful than was Th., was more personally fortunate (no action was taken against him).

Ἠιόνα τὴν ἐπὶ Θρᾴκης Μενδαίων ἀποικίαν, πολεμίαν δὲ οὖσαν: 'Eion in the Thraceward region, a colony of Mende, but now hostile to Athens'. Not the Eion of i. 98. 1, iv. 50 and 102 ('Eion on the Strymon'). This Eion, also in the Chalkidic region, is not securely identified, see

Zahrnt, 58 and 187, suggesting a position on the west of the Chalkidic peninsula.

For the punctuation (no comma after Θράκης) see F. Sieveking, 'Die Funktion geographischer Mitteilungen im Geschichtswerk des Thukydides', *Klio*, 42 (1964), 73–179, at 147.

For Mende, near Skione on the Pallene peninsula of Chalkidike, see 123. 1 n. on ἐν τούτῳ δὲ Μένδη ...

For the 'flagging' of a colonial tie see i. 30. 2 n. and Ridley, *Hermes* 1981, 39. Commentators see in 'but' (δέ) a contrast with still loyal Mende, in which case this is another example, though not a very strong one, of a significant mention of a colonial attachment; significant, because it points to a departure from colonial norms (the colony goes one way, the metropolis another). Another function of the label here may be to make clear the distinction between this Eion and the other more famous Eion. See Introduction, p. 73.

καὶ Βοττιαίων: 'and Bottiaians'. See i. 57. 5 n. on καὶ Βοττιαίοις, where they are again linked to the Chalkidians.

ἐξεκρούσθη: 'he was driven out'. For the 'clustering' of this verb in the latter part of book iv see 102. 2 n. on τὸ δὲ χωρίον etc.

8–16. *The Spartans are cut off on Sphakteria and surrender their ships*

8. 1. καὶ οἱ ἐγγύτατα τῶν περιοίκων: 'and the Perioikoi in the neighbourhood of Pylos'. Jowett in his text gives 'in the neighbourhood of the city', i.e. Sparta, and puts the alternative trans. in a footnote, but Classen/Steup and Cartledge, *Sparta and Lakonia*, 241, are right to prefer Pylos. Cartledge conjectures that the *perioikoi* in question were those of Methone and Kyparissia. For *perioikoi* see i. 101. 2 n. and add G. Shipley, in J. M. Sanders (ed.), *ΦΙΛΟΛΑΚΩΝ: Lakonian Studies presented in H. Catling* (Athens, 1992), 211–26. Ridley, *Hermes* 1981, 34, cp. 44, notes that whereas Th. recognizes the special need for information about Sparta and Spartan institutions, esp. the kings, the army, helots, and to a lesser extent the assembly and the ephors, he does *not* define either the *perioikoi* or the *neodamodeis*, for whom see v. 34. 1 n.

2. τὸν Λευκαδίων ἰσθμόν: 'the Leukadian isthmus'. See iii. 81. 1 n.

4. ἐλπίζοντες ῥᾳδίως αἱρήσειν: 'they thought they could easily take it'. See above, 5. 1 n.

5. καὶ τοὺς ἔσπλους τοῦ λιμένος ἐμφάρξαι: 'to block up the mouths of the harbour'. The obvious way of taking this is as a reference to the openings at the north and south ends of the island of Sphakteria, but because there are difficulties about Th.'s measurements (see 6 nn.), scholars have tried other possibilities (some of which require that we give unusual senses to λιμήν, but against this on the purely linguistic level see Pritchett, *EGH* 149–51). Thus Wilson, 73 ff., thinks the two 'mouths' were (*a*) the north end of Sphakteria (the Sikia channel) and (*b*) the entrance to the small bay known as Voidokilia. On this view the Spartans did not intend to block off the southern opening to the Bay of Navarino at all. (But as Cawkwell noted in a review of Wilson, *CR* 31 (1981), 132, this is itself an objection to the theory: why should the Athenians not have responded by coming round via the southern opening?).

Earlier views (e.g. Classen/Steup), which sought to make some explanatory use of the 'Osmyn-Aga' Lagoon, may be disregarded in the light of the demonstration by Pritchett, *SAGT* i (1965), trenchantly reasserted in *EGH* (1994), 154–61, that the lagoon area was the site of a Hellenistic settlement, and is therefore (it is argued) likely to have been dry land in 425 as well; see also R. Baladié, *Le Péloponnèse de Strabon* (Paris, 1980), 244.

We should take Th.'s phrase the obvious way (see beginning of this n.) and face the consequences.

6. ἡ γὰρ νῆσος ἡ Σφακτηρία καλουμένη τόν τε λιμένα, παρατείνουσα καὶ ἐγγὺς ἐπικειμένη, ἐχυρὸν ποιεῖ καὶ τοὺς ἔσπλους στενούς, τῇ μὲν δυοῖν νεοῖν διάπλουν κατὰ τὸ τείχισμα τῶν Ἀθηναίων καὶ τὴν Πύλον, τῇ δὲ πρὸς τὴν ἄλλην ἤπειρον ὀκτὼ ἢ ἐννέα: 'The island which is called Sphakteria stretches along the land and is quite close to it, making the harbour safe and the entrances narrow. There is a passage for two ships at the one end, which was opposite Pylos and the Athenian fort, while at the other the gap between the island and the mainland is wide enough for eight or nine' [read: 'is eight or nine stades wide']. Both these distances, as given, are too short, though the second is more seriously out than the first. The distance between the south end of Sphakteria and the *modern* town of Pylos, on the mainland (not to be confused with the ancient promontory north of the island) is about 1400 yards or 1280 m. This would allow a passage for much more than 8 or 9 triremes. Wilson, 75, further notes that the *northern* or Sikia channel is also somewhat wider than Th. implies. The gap is 150 yards or 137 m., wider than Th.'s 'passage for two ships'.

R. A. Bauslaugh, 'Thucydides IV 8.6 and the South Channel at Pylos', *JHS* 99 (1979), 1–6 (see for this article i. 63. 2 n.), offers an ingenious solution which would save Th.'s credit: he suggests that the text is at fault and the word ⟨σταδίων⟩ has dropped out after ὀκτὼ ἢ ἐννέα. That is, what Th. meant was that the distance across the south channel was 'eight or nine *stades*'. Bauslaugh's theory was endorsed by Pritchett in 1994, *EGH* 167–75, and I accept it as the best way out. Note that Bauslaugh's view requires a stade which is definitely on the short side

(130–150 m.), even allowing for the fluctuations which he establishes in his list at 5 f. On this list see *Greek Historiography*, 26 f.: the implication of Bauslaugh's tables is to establish that Thucydides was less precise over his indicators of distance than we would expect, given his general pre-occupation with, and (largely justified) reputation for, factual precision; cp. i. 63. 2 n. In fairness to Th., it is an imprecision he shares with all his fellow Greeks, but it is one which did not bother him; contrast his pre-occupation with chronology. See now Pritchett, *TPOE* 131 n. 8.

See Ridley, *Hermes* 1981, 40 and n. 58, for this section, which provides 'the most detailed geography on any campaign in the History'.

For Sphakteria itself see R. Scheer, in Lauffer (ed.), *Griechenland*, 636.

καὶ μέγεθος περὶ πέντε καὶ δέκα σταδίους μάλιστα: 'The island is about fifteen stades long' [i.e. 2775 m., assuming a 185 m. stade; Jowett has 'a mile and three quarters']. But the true distance would be more like two and three-quarters of a mile or 4440 m. So perhaps we should read 24 or (on a 175 m. stade) 25 stades. Th.'s mistake would be even worse if by μέγεθος he meant 'circumference', the sense the word seems to have at vi. 1. 1, applied to the island of Sicily.

7. τοὺς μὲν οὖν ἔσπλους ταῖς ναυσὶν ἀντιπρῴροις βύζην κλῄζειν ἔμελλον: '[The Spartans] intended to block up the mouth of the harbour by ships placed close together with their prows outwards'. This is the natural (and correct) way of taking this sentence. See Pritchett, *EGH* 147–9, and Wilson, 73 f., on Gomme's strange theories (the word βύζην supposed to refer to taking the plug out of the ships so as to sink them; and ἀντιπρῴροις supposed to mean 'the two triremes [i.e. those in the northern exit] facing each other').

8. ἐκπολιορκήσειν τὸ χωρίον κατὰ τὸ εἰκός: 'and would probably be able to take the fort'. There is much free ascription of motive to the Spartans hereabouts, see Hunter, 65, and below, 13. 4 n.

9. ἦρχε δ᾽ αὐτῶν Ἐπιτάδας ὁ Μολόβρου: 'they were under the command of Epitadas son of Molobros'. There was a famous Spartan ephor called Epitadeus who passed an amendment to Lycurgus' arrangements; this amendment made possible the alienation of land (Plut. *Agis* 5. 3). The importance and even historicity of this Epitadeus is disputed, but the Epitadas of the present passage has played a part in arguments about dating: was the reformer (it has been asked) perhaps the grandson of Th.'s similarly-named man? See A. J. Toynbee, *Some Problems of Greek History* (Oxford, 1969), 337 ff., and D. MacDowell, *Spartan Law* (Edinburgh, 1987), 105.

The name Molobros has been read (by an emendation of A. Böckh) in ML 67 = Fornara 132, lines 8–9 of the inscription on the side; but W. T. Loomis, *The Spartan War Fund: IG V 1, 1 and a New Fragment* (*Historia*

Einzelschrift 74: 1992), 53 f., returns to Molokros. M. H. Jameson, ap. Loomis, suggests that the name of Epitadas' father was Molokros and that the name has been wrongly transmitted as Molobros by all manuscripts of Th.

9. 1. Δημοσθένης δὲ ὁρῶν: 'When Demosthenes saw'. Mabel Lang, in an interesting study, 'Participial Motivation in Thucydides', *Mnemosyne*, 48 (1995), 48–65, discusses the way Th. uses participles, as here, for the attribution of motive. It is worth summarizing her results. She takes the six individuals with 'the greatest number of actions participially motivated' (50), namely Brasidas with 20 (see Introduction p. 48), Nikias with 19, Kleon and Demosthenes with 11 each, Alcibiades with 9, and Perdikkas with 6. She gives (52) the particular participles used, which recur strikingly from agent to agent: all 6 characters have βουλόμενος ('wishing'), 5 have νομίζων ('thinking' or 'realizing'), 4 have αἰσθόμενος, γνούς, ὁρῶν ('perceiving' or 'realizing'; 'knowing'; 'seeing' or 'realizing' or 'perceiving'; the last is the participle used in the present passage). This 'sameness of expression', she continues (53), suggests strongly 'that what we are dealing with here is neither a historian's intimate knowledge of individuals' mind-sets and motives nor a closely reasoned interpretation of actions taken, but rather a narrative technique which links actions and actors chainwise'. [Note that strictly this theory, according to which Th.'s handling is uniformly artificial, ought to render redundant such discussion, of degrees of 'possible intimacy' between Th. and the agents in question, as Lang has herself just offered at 50–1.] She suggests (54) that in all this, Th. 'seems to have been strongly (and unconsciously?) influenced by Herodotus' and gives some Herodotean comparative material in her second appendix. As for the particular case of Demosthenes, she suggests that Th. was 'particularly enthusiastic' about him and reports his campaigns so vividly that 'many have thought that he was a personal source'. She claims that all but one of Nikias' motivated actions come from books vi and vii; v. 16. 1 is the only exception she admits (see n. there). But see iv. 28. 1 n.

Lang's study is valuable, though it should not be forgotten that she restricts herself to motivation, belief, or knowledge expressed by *participles*; cp. 70. 1 n. on καὶ ὡς ᾔσθετο etc. Take e.g. iii. 51. 2, 'Nikias wanted ...', ἐβούλετο δὲ Νικίας. Had Th. expressed this by the participle βουλόμενος, 'wanting', as he might well have done, Lang's statistics on Nikias (above) would be affected. Cf. 70. 1 n. on καὶ ὡς ...

ἐκ λῃστρικῆς Μεσσηνίων τριακοντόρου καὶ κέλητος ἔλαβον, οἳ ἔτυχον παραγενόμενοι: 'a thirty-oared privateer and a light boat belonging to some Messenians who had just arrived'. Again, the word ἔτυχον has a slight nuance of fortuitousness (lit. 'they happened to have arrived'); but this is so weak that Jowett's trans. (with which Gomme and Westlake, *Individuals in Thucydides* (1968), 109 n. 1, concur) is justified in eliminating it altogether: see 3. 1 n. on κατὰ τύχην etc. Hunter, 66, exaggerates, when she ridicules Th.'s talk of 'some passing Messenians'; 'did the traditional enemies of Lakedaimon', she asks, 'always float around off her shores this way?' Th.'s Greek is compatible with an earlier summons by Demosthenes to the Messenians at Naupaktos. At the most it was chance that their arrival occurred just now.

A *triakontor* or 'thirty-oar' was a fast ship, to judge from Hdt. viii. 21. 1 where one is used for dispatches, see Morrison and Williams, *Greek Oared Ships* (Cambridge, 1968), 131; see also ibid. 245 for a *keles* or *keletion*: as one could guess from the present passage, it is a 'small boat used by pirates' (and by Brasidas: 120. 2).

2. τοὺς μὲν οὖν πολλοὺς τῶν τε ἀόπλων καὶ ὡπλισμένων: 'the greater part of his forces, armed and unarmed'. On the numbers see Wilson, 65: Th.'s language in this ch. suggests that he had greater forces than are specifically enumerated; that is, he had been left some by the other two generals (5. 2 n.).

ἢν προσβάλῃ: 'if they were attacked'. As they duly were, see 11. 2 n. on προσέβαλλε etc., citing Hunter.

10. *Speech by Demosthenes*

This short and structurally simple speech begins with some general considerations about courage versus rational calculation—do not weigh up the dangers too carefully—and then goes on to weigh up the dangers with reference to the particular circumstances, and the skills of each side. Cp. Westlake, *Individuals*, 109 n. 3: the rest of the speech 'virtually contradicts' the initial anti-intellectual sentiment, by 'analysing Athenian prospects with typically Thucydidean penetration'; see also Leimbach, 63 and n. 22. As for the general considerations, Th. sometimes allows different speakers to veer in different directions: at ii. 40. 3 Pericles stressed the need for calculation (ἐκλογίζεσθαι, λογισμός, see below, 1 nn.) plus courage; at ii. 87. 4 the Peloponnesian commander accused the Athenians of possessing skill without courage. Despite Demosthenes' echoes of Pericles in the present ch., it would be excessively subtle to read as much into them as into, say, Kleon's or Alcibiades' echoes of Pericles. Demosthenes' point (courage, not calculation) is appropriate to the situation envisaged: his men are about to be faced with intimidating relays of triremes thrashing towards the shore.

The subsequent narrative picks up Demosthenes' words at a number of points; see detailed nn. below, and compare ii. 83–92, introductory n.

The speech is discussed by Luschnat, *Feldherrnreden*, 32–43, and Leimbach 56–63; see also Westlake, *Individuals*, 109 and n. 3, calling the speech a 'largely conventional' exercise in encouragement. For the argument between Hansen and Pritchett about whether ancient generals really did deliver speeches before battles, see Introduction, above pp. 82 f.

1. ἐκλογιζόμενος ... λογισμόν: 'making calculations ... reflection'. Cp. ii. 40. 3 and n., and see above, introductory n.

2–3. ἢν ἐθέλωμέν τε μεῖναι καὶ μὴ τῷ πλήθει αὐτῶν καταπλαγέντες τὰ ὑπάρχοντα ἡμῖν κρείσσω καταπροδοῦναι ... μενόντων μὲν ἡμῶν ... ὑποχωρήσασι δὲ καίπερ χαλεπὸν ὄν: 'if we will only stand firm and do not throw away our advantages ... if we stand firm; when we have once retreated, the ground, though difficult in itself', etc. The key words here, μενόντων and ὑποχωρήσασι ('stand firm', 'retreat') are used at 12. 2 to describe what actually happens: the Athenians *do* stand firm; they *don't* retreat. See Hunter, 67: as elsewhere, Th. (she says) supplies 'purposes in the *logoi* which [the purposes, presumably] anticipate the *erga*'.

On the construction of the sentence 'stand firm and do not ...' see Boegehold (v. 8. 3 n.), 149.

μὴ ῥᾳδίας αὐτῷ πάλιν οὔσης τῆς ἀναχωρήσεως: 'for it will be hard for him to retreat'. On this reading μὴ ῥᾳδίας, 'hard' [lit. 'not easy'] is adjectival, but W. Morel, 'Zu den griechischen Romanschriftstellern I: klassischer Sprachgebrauch bei Chariton und Heliodor', *Mnemosyne*, 9 (1941), 281–2, argued for the retention of the manuscript reading ῥᾳδίως (adverb, i.e. 'not easily'), comparing Heliodoros viii. 11. The meaning is not affected.

4. κατ' ὀλίγον γὰρ μαχεῖται: 'only a few of them can fight at a time'. Picked up by 11. 3 and 4; see Hunter (as above) and Luschnat, 41. See also v. 9. 2 n.

καὶ οὐκ ἐν γῇ στρατός ἐστιν ἐκ τοῦ ὁμοίου μείζων, ἀλλ' ἀπὸ νεῶν: 'we are up against an army which may be superior in numbers, but is not equal to ours in other respects: for they are not on land but on board ship'. On οὐκ ἐκ τοῦ ὁμοίου, 'not equal' [lit. 'not from a footing of equality'] here see E. Fraenkel, *Aeschylus: Agamemnon* (Oxford, 1950), 669, comm. on line 1423. Fraenkel paraphrases the present passage as follows: 'the Spartans cannot use their numerical superiority on land under the same conditions, in the same way, and in the same strength (as we use our troops), but must rely on the fleet (and perhaps successive landings of smaller units)'.

5. εἴ τις ὑπομένοι καὶ μὴ φόβῳ ῥοθίου καὶ νεῶν δεινότητος

κατάπλου ὑποχωροίη: 'if a man is not frightened out of his wits at the splashing of oars and the threatening look of a ship bearing down upon him, but is determined to hold his ground . . .'. For the noise of a sea-battle as frightening see vii. 70. 6. There are a number of parallels between the present section and the final part of the Syracuse narrative, see below, 12. 3 n.

11. 2. Θρασυμηλίδας ὁ Κρατησικλέους: 'Thrasymelidas son of Kratesikles'. Diodorus' version of the name is Thrasymedes (xii. 61. 3), and Lewis, *Towards a Historian's Text of Thucydides*, 39 f., finds this, or some similar form (e.g. Thrasymedidas), 'considerably more attractive'.

προσέβαλλε δὲ ᾗπερ Δημοσθένης προσεδέχετο: 'he made his attack just where Demosthenes expected'. See Hunter, 67, for the way this fulfils the expectation at 9. 2.

3. οἱ δὲ κατ' ὀλίγας ναῦς διελόμενοι, διότι οὐκ ἦν πλέοσι προσσχεῖν: 'The Peloponnesians had divided their fleet into relays of a few ships, because there was no space for more'. Cp. 10. 4 n.

4. πάντων δὲ φανερώτατος Βρασίδας ἐγένετο: 'Brasidas distinguished himself above all others'. The fourth appearance of the 'man of energy' (δραστήριος, 81. 1); for the first, an equally vigorous effort, see ii. 25. 2 and n. (The second and third were as adviser to Knemos, then Alkidas, ii. 85 ff.; iii. 69, 76, and 79). But note here the rapid introduction, suited to the narrative: no patronymic or designation as Spartan or Spartiate, by contrast with the beginning of all the other Brasidas episodes; see esp. iv. 70. 1 and n. for the very different way he is introduced at the beginning of his main ἀριστεία (for this notion see Introduction, p. 41 and iv. 66–135, introductory n.).

τριηραρχῶν γάρ: 'he was a trierarch'. In the sense that he was commander of a trireme; in a Spartan context the word does not have the financial implications which it sometimes has in Athens, see ii. 24. 2 n. (Gomme's n. on the present passage is misleading.)

καὶ ὁρῶν: 'whenever he saw'. For the participially expressed motivation see 9. 1 n. on Δημοσθένης δὲ ὁρῶν. Brasidas, who dominates so much of books iv–v. 10, heads Mabel Lang's list (*Mnemosyne* 1995) of Thucydidean agents whose motives are confidently expressed with such participles. See Lang, 50, though her remarks about Th.'s ability to read Brasidas' mind are unfair: 'he seems', she says, 'to have done so with significantly little effect in the two cases involving his [Th.'s] own generalship (4. 103. 2, 105. 1)'.

ξύλων φειδομένους: 'Don't spare the timber'. For 'timber' used idiomatically (and disparagingly) to mean specifically expendable ship-timber, i.e. ships, Gomme cites Hdt. viii. 100. 2 and Xen. *Hell.* i. 1. 24. We

might also compare the tragic use of δόρυ, 'plank', to stand for the whole
ship, as at Euripides, *Andromache* 793, with P. T. Stevens's n. (Oxford,
1971). See further 26. 7 n. for the reason for normal Spartan caution.

ἀντὶ μεγάλων εὐεργεσιῶν: 'who had done so much for them' [lit. 'in
return for great benefits']. For 'euergetism' in a Spartan-allied context
see ii. 27. 2 = iv. 56. 2 (Aiginetan help to Sparta at Ithome). The theme
also runs through the Plataian/Theban exchange at iii. 53 ff., where the
Plataians—not of course Spartan allies, but nevertheless in some sense
under Spartan protection, see ii. 71. 2 and nn.—adduce their benefits to
Greece in general and Sparta in particular (see iii. 58. 3 n.). Now a
Spartan speaker stresses the other side of the relationship. Exactly what
benefits Sparta *did* confer on her allies and friends is unclear; presumably
they were supposed to be grateful for the protection of the Spartan
military machine, or for having Sparta prop up their oligarchic govern-
ments, see i. 19.

ὀκείλαντας: 'they must run aground'. Bow first, see J. S. Morrison and
R. T. Williams, *Greek Oared Ships* (Cambridge, 1968), 311. The Homeric
word is (not ὀκέλλω, as Morrison and Williams say, but always) κέλλω,
as at *Odyssey* ix. 149, 546 etc.

12. 1. ἐπέσπερχε: 'he urged on'. See Smith, *TAPA* 1900, 69–81, at 72:
this word is epic (*Iliad* xxiii. 430) and Aeschylean (*Seven against Thebes*
689), but 'foreign to good Attic prose' (Krüger); for the significance of
this in connection with the heroically-presented Brasidas see Introduction, p. 46, cf. 41.

τὴν ἀποβάθραν: 'the landing ladder'. A gangplank which was run out
from the shop to the shore. The technical English word is 'brow', according to Morrison and Coates, *The Athenian Trireme* (Cambridge, 1986),
237 ('a gangway or ladder on which a man can face the shore while
descending from a ship'), cp. 243 under *apobathra*. For discussion of the
whole of the present passage see Morrison and Coates, 163 f.: 'this picture of a trieres [trireme] in action is unique even if the action itself is
untypical'.

τραυματισθεὶς πολλὰ ἐλιποψύχησέ τε: 'after receiving many
wounds, he fainted'. Literally, his soul left him, see J. Bremmer, *The Early
Greek Concept of the Soul* (Princeton, 1983), 15, for this Homeric expression and notion (*Iliad* v. 696, cp. xxii. 467 with nn. by Kirk and Richardson); and see below end of n. on ἡ ἀσπίς, etc. and Introduction p. 46.

καὶ πεσόντος αὐτοῦ ἐς τὴν παρεξειρεσίαν: 'and fell into the outrigger'. Not 'the fore part of the ship' (Jowett, which I have changed) or
'the bows of the ship' (Warner, Penguin). The outrigger, for which see
Morrison and Coates, 163 ff. and glossary at 246, was 'a structure built

out from the side of the trieres [trireme] to accommodate the tholes [rowlocks] of the uppermost file of oarsmen'. The present passage, which implies that the *parexeiresia* was something which Brasidas could somehow fall into without falling further, whereas his shield fell right through it and went into the sea, is one of the most important 'hints for the reconstructor' (Morrison and Coates, 164).

ἡ ἀσπὶς περερρύη ἐς τὴν θάλασσαν, καὶ ἐξενεχθείσης αὐτῆς ἐς τὴν γῆν οἱ Ἀθηναῖοι ἀνελόμενοι ὕστερον πρὸς τὸ τροπαῖον ἐχρήσαντο ὃ ἔστησαν: 'His shield slipped off his arm into the sea, and was washed ashore; the Athenians retrieved it and used it for the trophy which they raised'. This trophy was erected on the spot; but a bronze shield has been found in the Athenian agora, with an inscription showing that it was dedicated 'from the Spartans at Pylos': see 38. 5 n. on τούτων ζῶντες etc.

'So great was the effort needed to hold their equipment that when hoplites became worn out or lost concentration they instinctively dropped their shields': Hanson, *Western Way*, 67, citing the present passage among others.

The description is unusually detailed and lively, but this was not the shield of an ordinary soldier, cp. ii. 25. 2 n.: where Brasidas is concerned, Th. enjoys using the whole paint-box. Gomme cites Plato, *Symposium* 221c, the comparison between Brasidas and Achilles, and there is (cf. pp. 43-6) something Homeric about the hero rushing forward, then fainting from his wounds, while the enemy get his armour, with Brasidas' swoon cp. perhaps Hector's at *Iliad* xi. 356 ff. and see above n. on τραυματισθείς etc. See above, p. 46, and introductory n. to 66-135.

Babut, 420-1, as part of his thesis that Pylos at the beginning of the book is mirrored by Chalkidike at the end, notes that Brasidas and Kleon change roles. Brasidas is wounded and loses his shield in a narrative in which Kleon is dominant [but not quite *yet*]; to this correspond the trophy, v. 10. 12, and the death of Kleon at the hand of a peltast, v. 12. 9.

2. τῶν Ἀθηναίων μενόντων καὶ οὐδὲν ὑποχωρούντων: 'the tenacity with which the Athenians held their position'. The words closely recall Demosthenes' exhortation at 10. 2-3, see n. there.

3. ἐς τοῦτό τε περιέστη ἡ τύχη ὥστε Ἀθηναίους μὲν ἐκ γῆς τε καὶ ταύτης Λακωνικῆς ἀμύνεσθαι ἐκείνους ἐπιπλέοντας: 'It was a strange turn of fortune: the Athenians were preventing the Spartans, who were attacking them by sea, from landing on the Lakonian coast'. On the 'heavy emphasis' here see Macleod, *Collected Essays*, 142, comparing vii. 75. 7, an important para., full of antitheses and strongly underlined reversals. (See below iv. 62. 3 n. on τοὺς δ᾽ ἀντί etc.). In particular the remnants of the Athenian fleet after the Sicilian disaster are there

described as reduced to operating on land only, no longer sailors but out of their element. Macleod suggests that Th., in the present section, already has the events at Syracuse in mind. Such Pylos/Syracuse correspondences (see esp. vii. 71. 7) have been much remarked in recent years; see Rawlings, *Structure*, 174; S. Flory, 'The Death of Thucydides and the Motif of "Land on Sea"', in R. Rosen and J. Farrell (eds.), *Nomodeiktes: Greek Studies in Honor of M. Ostwald* (Ann Arbor, 1993), 113–23, at 119–20. See above, Introduction, pp. 16 and 120 n. 304.

13. 1. ξύλα ἐς μηχανάς: 'timber with which to make siege machines'. Since catapults had not yet been invented (ii. 71–78, introductory n.), this can only refer to such crude implements as battering-rams and scaling-ladders.

ἐς Ἀσίνην: 'to Asine'. There were three Peloponnesian places called Asine, one in Lakonia, one SE of Argos, and this one, in Messenia, a perioikic foundation resettled from Argive Asine. It is modern Korone (Venetian Coron), and is on the east side of the prong of land which forms southern Messenia, complementing Pylos and Methone (Modon, the other Venetian fort of the area) on the west.

2. τεσσεράκοντα: 'forty'. The text is at fault here; we need a number larger than 40 in view of 2. 2, 5. 2, and 8. 3: there were 40 to start with, a figure first reduced by 5, then raised by 2, making 37. If 4 Chian and an unspecified number of Naupaktan ships now 'raised' the total to some figure, that figure must be greater than 40. Read perhaps 50, or 44, with Lewis, *Towards a Historian's Text*, 113 f.

3. ἐς Πρωτὴν τὴν νῆσον: 'the island of Prote'. North-west of Pylos; see Cartledge, *Sparta and Lakonia*, 193 (graffiti).

4. οὔτε ἃ διενοήθησαν, φάρξαι τοὺς ἔσπλους, ἔτυχον ποιήσαντες: 'had somehow neglected to close the mouths as they had intended'. J. Wilson and T. Beardsworth, 'Pylos 425 B.C.: the Spartan Plan to Block the Entrances', *CQ* 20 (1970), 42–52, at 50 (approved by Westlake, *CQ* 1974, 216) conjecture that the Spartans may have thought the Athenians had gone away for good, not just to nearby Prote. But we should not forget that the alleged intention may itself be something of a conjecture—on the part of Th., see 8. 8 n.

τῷ λιμένι ὄντι οὐ σμικρῷ: 'the enormous harbour' [lit. 'the harbour, which was not small']. Th. is sometimes criticized for failure to grasp just how big the harbour was, and even the present passage is said to be a 'palpable understatement' if Th. intended to suggest 'only that it was large enough for a sea battle to be fought in it': Westlake, *CQ* 1974, 215. This is reasonable criticism, but note that the Greek words used ('not small') should be translated positively, i.e. Th. is stressing the harbour's size.

14. 2. κεκωλῦσθαι ἐδόκει ἕκαστος ᾧ μή τινι καὶ αὐτὸς ἔργῳ παρῆν: 'everyone thought that the action was at a standstill where he himself was not involved'. The thought and the expression are strikingly like ii. 8. 4; but they read more naturally here, in a concrete situation, than there, where the context is very general and political.

3. οἵ τε γὰρ Λακεδαιμόνιοι . . . ὡς εἰπεῖν ἄλλο οὐδὲν ἢ ἐκ γῆς ἐναυμάχουν . . .: 'the Spartans were so to speak fighting a sea-battle from the land . . .'. For Th.'s stress on this inversion of the normal state of affairs see 12. 3 n.

5. καταστάντες δὲ ἑκάτεροι ἐς τὸ στρατόπεδον: 'Both sides retired to their encampments'. Given that 8. 7–8 implied that it would be difficult for the Athenians to find a base from which to operate, we should perhaps have expected some indication 'what sort of base the Athenians now had, or where': Andrewes, *HCT* v. 364, listing this as one of the 'indications of incompleteness' in Th.'s narrative of the Ten Years War.

15. 1. ὡς ἐπὶ ξυμφορᾷ μεγάλῃ: 'it was regarded as a complete disaster'. Westlake, *CQ* 1974, 218, considers this a grossly exaggerated reaction: 'any reader of this passage who had not paid attention to the preceding narrative (14) might infer that the fleet had been virtually annihilated . . .'.

2. καὶ ὡς εἶδον ἀδύνατον ὂν τιμωρεῖν τοῖς ἀνδράσι: 'they realized that nothing could be done for the men' [lit. that it was impossible to protect, help, relieve . . .]. On the verb see Westlake, 218 f., who takes it to mean ' "assist" or "relieve" in the widest sense'. As Westlake notes, Th. repeats at vii. 71. 7 his assessment of the Pylos situation. Were the Spartan officials on the spot right to be so pessimistic? Westlake, 220 f., thinks their conclusion was 'indefensible' (221); S. Hodkinson, 'Social Order and the Conflict of Values in Classical Sparta', *Chiron*, 13 (1983), 239–81, for the institutional background to such Spartan losses of nerve, and his 270 for the present phase of Spartan history. On the other hand, J. Wilson and T. Beardsworth, 'Bad Weather and the Blockade at Pylos', *Phoenix*, 24 (1970), 112 ff., at 116 ff., examine the chances of a Spartan breakout succeeding and rate them low; we should not, therefore, (they suggest) blame the Spartans for excessive inactivity. Westlake's view, that the Spartan despair was too absolute, is preferable: even if a break-out was unlikely to succeed, it seems feeble not to have attempted *some* military action to relieve the stranded men.

σπονδὰς ποιησαμένους τὰ περὶ Πύλον: 'make a truce at Pylos'.
That is, the truce is local; but see 16. 1 n.: there is one concession which
goes well beyond Pylos. With this truce Babut, 424–5, as part of his
structural parallel between the Pylos and Chalkidic narratives, compares
that at 118. Similarly, but starting from a very different starting point,
Andrewes, *HCT* v. 365, remarks that ch. 16, with its free use of documentary language and the full detail about the rations, might be thought
to anticipate 118 (the truce of 423). But he immediately goes on to concede that the narrative at 26–7 and 39 explains the detail about the
rations, and that generally the great difference is that 16 (unlike 118)
contains no detail calling for explanation that has not been given in the
narrative; 'and it is this, with the full verbatim transcription, that constitutes the real innovation at iv. 118–119'. (Andrewes is discussing
'indications of incompleteness' in Th.'s narrative of the Ten Years War).
See Introduction, pp. 114 f.

**16. 1. καὶ τὰς ἐν τῇ Λακωνικῇ πάσας, ὅσαι ἦσαν μακραί, παρα-
δοῦναι κομίσαντας ἐς Πύλον:** 'and shall bring to Pylos any other
war-ships which are in Lakonia, and surrender them also'. This is a
surprising concession by Sparta, even if the number of ships in Lakonia
was small (perhaps as few as ten, see Wilson, 92 f.: if the Spartans started
out with sixty ships, see 8. 2, and we allow about ten for ships lost or dis-
abled, then—since sixty were handed over, 16. 3—ten will also be the
total of the ships elsewhere in Lakonia). But the surrender of such ships
was a very public humiliation, and extended the scope of the truce in
such a way that it went beyond Pylos, see 15. 2 n. on τὰ περὶ Πύλον.
Cartledge, *Sparta and Lakonia*, 242, suggests that 'Lakonia' means Asine
and perhaps Gytheion.

For the documentary language, and the historiographical status of the
truce, see previous n.

σῖτον ... τακτὸν καὶ μεμαγμένον, δύο χοίνικας ἑκάστῳ Ἀττι-
κὰς ἀλφίτων καὶ δύο κοτύλας οἴνου καὶ κρέας, θεράποντι δὲ
τούτων ἡμίσεα: 'a fixed quantity of kneaded flour, amounting to two
Attic *choinikes* of barley-meal for each man, and two cupfuls of wine, and
also a piece of meat; for an attendant, half these quantities'. It is useless
(cp. i. 63. 2 n. on stades) to try to render these quantities in modern
metric terms, though a cup is usually reckoned at about a quarter of a
litre and a *choinix* at about a litre, see entry on 'measures' in *OCD*[2] and
OCD[3]. Comparative figures are more helpful: a single *choinix*—here, the
helot ration—is the (less generous) daily ration of corn assumed by Hdt.
at vii. 187. 2; Spartan *kings* get two (or four) *choinikes*, Hdt. vi. 57. 3. For
status differentiation by amounts of food allotted (kings get more

than ordinary Spartiates, who get more than helots) cf. J. Griffin, *Homer on Life and Death* (Oxford, 1980), 14, with references. See also below, vii. 87. 2 n.

καὶ ὅπλα μὴ ἐπιφέρειν τῷ Πελοποννησίων στρατῷ: 'and [the Athenians] shall not attack the Peloponnesian forces'. The only restriction on Athens in the whole of this very unequal truce, see Cartledge, 241.

17–20. *Spartan speech at Athens*

A striking feature of this speech—as I have noted before, see *Thucydides*, p. 56—is that it stands alone: there is no reply. That is, the speech is unsuccessful, but Kleon's successful reply is not reported; Th. merely gives, in a couple of sentences at 20. 2, what were surely only his final recommendations, and then at 22 there is a brief summary of some abuse by Kleon of the ambassadors' behaviour. It is not uncommon for Th. to give a losing speech, but it is strange to give the losing speech but not the winning one, while making clear that a winning one was nevertheless made. (For a mention of unreported losing speeches see i. 139. 4, introducing the winning speech of Pericles). If we ask why Th. did this, the answer has something to do with his attitude to Kleon: he was unwilling to dwell on Kleon's victory in the debate. This explanation does not quite dispose of the problem: after all, in the Mytilenean debate Th. allows Kleon plenty of effective points with which the reader sympathizes. But at least Th. there had the satisfaction of knowing that in the end Kleon would lose the debate. Again, Th. could have made Kleon victorious in the argument with the Spartans but still given him a repellent speech illustrating that dangerous Athenian 'desire for more' (to use the language of 21. 2) which Th. felt characterized this phase of the war. The best we can say is that, where Kleon is concerned, Th.'s handling is more than usually irrational.

The distortions do not end there: H. Flower, 'Thucydides and the Pylos Debate', *Historia*, 41 (1992), 40–57, argues ingeniously that Th. suppressed entirely an earlier debate of the Athenian assembly at which Nikias had been formally voted the command; she thinks Th. wished to direct exclusive attention onto Kleon and to play down the responsibility of Nikias, whose resignation of the command would have seemed more obviously frivolous if Th. had told the full story. There is nothing implausible about the suggestion that Th. suppressed an entire debate, see i. 50. 5 n., and *Greek Historiography*, 140–3.

To return to chs. 17–20, the Greek is difficult and (a related point) the text is often problematic: copyists, like us, had difficulty understanding it.

Tortuous argumentation is used for the presentation of often simple or even threadbare thoughts; this is a good way for Th. to underline the impossibility of the Spartan speakers' diplomatic position: they are offering little or nothing, but asking much. The wrapping-paper needed to be fancy because there was not much inside.

The speech conforms to the rules laid down in the *Rhetoric to Alexander* (see i. 32–43, introductory n.) 1425a36 ff. for the appropriate way to ask for a peace when a war is not going your way. Particular parallels will be noted below as they occur; and see generally *Thucydides*, 48 f., J. H. Finley, *Three Essays on Thucydides* (Cambridge, Mass., 1967), 36 and n. 53. See above, p. 83: such parallels may indicate awareness of Th.'s speeches, as I suggested at *Thucydides*, 47, and in this commentary (introductory n. to i. 32–43; see, however, Rutherford, *RFP* 59 n. 26); for awareness of Th. in the fourth century in general and among Aristotelians in particular see S. Hornblower, 'The Fourth-Century and Hellenistic Reception of Thucydides', *JHS* 115 (1995), 48–68.

This speech has not been much discussed by scholars, but see Westlake, *CQ* 1974, 221 f. (calling it 'among the most puzzling of Thucydidean speeches' because the speaker is being less than frank). Westlake, as part of his general thesis (see introductory n. to 1–6), thinks the Spartans are made to express greater than necessary despair about the immediate situation, in order to avoid making the more damaging admission that the war was going generally badly for Sparta. See also de Romilly, *Thucydides and Athenian Imperialism* (introductory n. to 1–6), 172–9, though she does not seem to me right to think (172, 173) that in this speech Th. is giving his own judgement of the situation; also Hunter, 74 ff. and E. D. Francis, 'Brachylogia Laconica: Spartan Speeches in Thucydides', *BICS* 38 (1991–3), 198–212, at 205–6. Francis (296) notes the frequency in the speech of abstract nouns in -σις (I take these to be 17. 3 ὑπόμνησιν, 18. 5 δόκησιν and ξυνέσεως, 19. 1 διάλυσιν, 20. 2 ἀνάπαυσιν and καταλύσεως); for this feature cp. below introductory n. to 85 (Brasidas at Akanthos). For Francis's views see further 17. 2 n.

There are no very convincing grounds for dating this speech late, see 19. 4 n.

The Spartans begin (17. 1–2) with an apology for their un-Spartan eloquence, then (up to the end of ch. 18) they elaborate the theme that fortune is capricious and that it is wise to be moderate in good fortune; only at 18. 1–2 do they glance at the immediate situation: at 18. 1 the speakers pick up, from the preceding narrative, the theme of role-reversal, and insist that their own recent setback is due to a non-recurrent error of judgement. After this long preamble comes a concrete offer (19. 1), but it turns out not to be very concrete at all, and the speech rapidly returns to generalities, this time rather more implausible and paradoxical than those in 17–18: the line now taken is that it is better policy not to use an advantage when you have it, and that it is easier to bury big differences than small ones. The final ch. 20 comes back to the immediate position, but this time notice is taken of the rest of the Greeks. But the concern for them voiced at 20. 2 turns out to be hypocritical because the speech ends (20. 4) with a remarkable and cynical 'dual hegemony' proposal in which the rest of Greece will have to acquiesce. The structure is thus, roughly: general, particular, general, particular.

17. 1. ὅτι ἂν ὑμῖν τε ὠφέλιμον ὂν τὸ αὐτὸ πείθωμεν καὶ ἡμῖν ἐς τὴν ξυμφορὰν ὡς ἐκ τῶν παρόντων κόσμον μάλιστα μέλλῃ οἴσειν: 'in the hope that you will grant us terms which will be advantageous to you and as honourable as possible to us in our present misfortune'. The usual balancing of honour against expediency, as in the opening sections of the Corcyraeans' speech at i. 32–3 and of the Mytileneans' at iii. 9–10.

2. τοὺς δὲ λόγους μακροτέρους οὐ παρὰ τὸ εἰωθὸς μηκυνοῦμεν: 'If we speak at some length, this will be no departure from the custom of our country' [lit. 'will not be contrary to what is usual' with us Spartans, the point being that we Spartans can be free with words when necessary; see the rest of the passage]. De Romilly, 175, says that by the words 'contrary to what is usual' Th. 'himself recognizes that there is something unusual about the speech'; but as with the genuinely 'laconic' Sthenelaidas at i. 86, it is impossible to say whether this is artificial, i.e. an attempt to depict a speaker as self-consciously un-laconic, or whether, as is just possible, it was remembered at Athens that the Spartans really did make such a disclaimer. Francis (above, introductory n.), 205, notes the 'sustained syntactic complexity' of the argument and conjectures that by making the Spartan ambassadors speak like Athenians (cp. 85. 1 n.), Th. may be wittily suggesting that they had to acknowledge publicly at Athens the efficacy of intelligent debate and rhetorical persuasion. Francis (212) calls this speech 'the one national attempt at rhetorical sophistry'; he clearly regards it as Th.'s attempt at representing Sparta and its leaders i.e. as a literary depiction.

In the above I have avoided the word 'characterization', which is not straightforward. See C. Gill, in C. Pelling (ed.), *Characterization and Individuality in Greek Literature* (Oxford, 1990), 2, who starts from a distinction between characterization, where the stress is on the individual as moral agent and involves moral judgement by the author, and the portrayal of personality, where the individual is passively presented. I suppose the Spartans here are given personality, rather than being characterized.

For Spartan speech-habits see further 84. 2 n. (Brasidas).

πλέοσι δὲ ἐν ᾧ ἂν καιρὸς ᾖ διδάσκοντάς τι τῶν προύργου λόγοις τὸ δέον πράσσειν: 'but to be rather more free with words when speeches are needed to achieve results, by showing what the situation demands'. Francis (above, introductory n.), 205, aptly compares Hdt. iii. 46, where the Samians at Sparta make a long speech, 'as was natural with people in great need of help'.

4. αἰεὶ γὰρ τοῦ πλέονος ἐλπίδι ὀρέγονται διὰ τὸ καὶ τὰ παρόντα ἀδοκήτως εὐτυχῆσαι: 'because they have already succeeded beyond all expectation, they become over-confident and grasp for more'. Th.'s own view was that the Athenians were indeed 'grasping for more': 21. 2. (The noun used to describe this is *pleonexia*, the regular word for 'exorbitant ambition', see iii. 82. 6 and 8, with n. on 82. 6.) But this does not mean he accepts the Spartans' general evaluation of the position, as de Romilly thinks; see introductory n.

The words here translated 'already' are τὰ παρόντα, lit. 'in respect of present circumstances', cp. Jebb on Soph., *Electra* 214.

18. 1. οἵτινες ἀξίωμα μέγιστον τῶν Ἑλλήνων ἔχοντες ἥκομεν παρ' ὑμᾶς: 'we have the greatest reputation in Greece, but are now reduced to coming here'. I have inserted 'reduced to' to make the sentence run better; the Greek just means 'we have come'; Jowett's 'who formerly enjoyed the greatest prestige of any Hellenic state' is a little too free: the Spartans are not saying that they have actually lost their high reputation. But the idea of reversal is certainly present in this para., see next n.

πρότερον αὐτοὶ κυριώτεροι νομίζοντες εἶναι δοῦναι: 'the favour which at one time we should have expected to be able to give'. The Spartans take over from the narrative (see 12. 3 and n.) the theme of role-reversal.

2. δυνάμεως ἐνδείᾳ ... ὑβρίσαντες ... γνώμῃ σφαλέντες: 'decline in our power ... pride ... we made an error of judgement'. What error exactly is referred to? Perhaps the failure to block off both ends of the harbour, 13. 4. But the language of the whole sentence is portentous and is more appropriate to a large-scale enterprise like the Sicilian expedition; see 12. 3 n. for the parallel, by which Th. may in the present passage have been seduced into exaggeration.

3-4. ὥστε οὐκ εἰκὸς ὑμᾶς διὰ τὴν παροῦσαν νῦν ῥώμην πόλεώς τε καὶ τῶν προσγεγενημένων καὶ τὸ τῆς τύχης οἴεσθαι αἰεὶ μεθ' ὑμῶν ἔσεσθαι. σωφρόνων δὲ ἀνδρῶν ...: 'So you should not suppose that, because your city and your empire are powerful at this moment, you will always have fortune on your side. Sensible men ...'. The word here translated 'empire' is almost a euphemism, the Greek literally means 'your city and the things added to it'.

With this admonition compare *Rhetoric to Alexander* 1426a36 ff.: 'when we are trying to stop a war that has already begun, if those whom we are advising are getting the upper hand, the first thing to say is that sensible people (τοὺς νοῦν ἔχοντας) should not wait till they have a fall, and next that it is of the nature of war to ruin many even of those who are successful in it ... and we must point out how many and how incalculable are the changes of fortune that occur in war.' See above, p. 83.

4. σωφρόνων δὲ ἀνδρῶν οἵτινες τἀγαθὰ ἐς ἀμφίβολον ἀσφαλῶς ἔθεντο (καὶ ταῖς ξυμφοραῖς οἱ αὐτοὶ εὐξυνετώτερον ἂν προσφέροιντο), τόν τε πόλεμον νομίσωσι μὴ καθ᾽ ὅσον ἄν τις αὐτοῦ μέρος βούληται μεταχειρίζειν, τούτῳ ξυνεῖναι, ἀλλ᾽ ὡς ἂν αἱ τύχαι αὐτῶν ἡγήσωνται: 'Sensible men make sure of their gains by guarding against the uncertainties of the future, and when disasters come they can meet them more intelligently; they know that the chances of war dictate its general course, and that they cannot interfere with that one theatre which happens to suit them'. Not an easy sentence. The words ἐς ἀμφίβολον, 'against the uncertainties of the future', lit. 'towards the doubtful', may be corrupt; LSJ⁹ translate the whole first clause 'prudently count their good fortune as doubtful'.

R. C. Seaton, *CR* 14 (1900), 223–4, thinks that μέρος, 'part', here translated 'theatre', may also be corrupt, having entered the text as part of a marginal gloss.

With the general sense of the passage Seaton compares vi. 78. 2 and iv. 64. 1; and add vi. 18. 3. See Schneider, *Information and Absicht*, 98, for the stress on fortune, chance.

5. δόκησιν: 'a reputation'. For the Greek word see ii. 35. 2 n., and for the sense of 'glory', 'reputation' see Eur. *Andromache* 696, ἀλλ᾽ ὁ στρατηγὸς τὴν δόκησιν ἄρνυται, 'the general gets the glory', a line from a famous passage, on which see A. Aymard, 'Sur quelques vers d'Euripide qui poussèrent Alexandre au meurtre', *Études d'histoire ancienne* (Paris, 1967), 51–82. See also introductory n.: this is one of the six -σις words in the speech.

19.1. Λακεδαιμόνιοι δὲ ὑμᾶς προκαλοῦνται ἐς σπονδάς: 'The Spartans invite you to make peace with them'. Suddenly the speaker swoops to the particular, see introductory n.

διδόντες μὲν εἰρήνην καὶ ξυμμαχίαν καὶ ἄλλην φιλίαν πολλὴν

καὶ οἰκειότητα ἐς ἀλλήλους ὑπάρχειν: 'They offer peace, alliance, and generally friendly and close relations'. This is not very attractive (nothing is said about territorial concessions); but there were always Athenians who could be expected to respond to such appeals for 'dual hegemony'. De Romilly, *Thucydides and Athenian Imperialism* (introductory n. to 1–6), 178, compares the Athenian Kallistratos at Xen. *Hell.* vi. 3. 17, an appeal to power politics comparable to the Spartans' final sentence at 20. 4 below, see n. But the ref. here to οἰκειότητα, a word for close friendship sometimes implying kinship or religious closeness (see i. 60. 1 n.; iii. 86. 4) implies (though see below) something warmer and more sentimental, with which cp. the Athenian Kallias' speech on the same fourth-century occasion, *Hell.* vi. 3. 3: Kallias recalls the gift of grain by Demeter and Kore to Herakles the founder of Sparta, and to the Dioskouroi, the Spartans' 'fellow-citizens'. Maybe οἰκειότητα in the present passage is a hint that the speech actually delivered by the Spartans contained some such sentimental appeal, but if so it is not surprising that the tough-minded Th. does not let them develop it.

Curty 1994, 196, argues that Th. distinguishes between οἰκειότης and ξυγγένεια and that ξυγγένεια is specially apt for kinship between Dorian or between Ionian cities; οἰκειότης by contrast is a weaker term, and is reserved by Th. for occasions like the present Spartan appeal, when the kinship connection being appealed to is merely factitious, a pretext. But (as C. P. Jones points out to me) the present passage is a serious obstacle for Curty, because there was no kinship between Athens and Sparta at all, only vague religious ties of the sort discussed above. See 64. 3 n. and above, Introduction, p. 65 ff.

In view of the insubstantial character of the Spartan offer, it is hard to think that Th. means us to conclude *either* that Athens was simply wrong to refuse it *or* that the Spartans give his own, Th.'s, view of the situation, as de Romilly thinks, see above.

The reference here to 'alliance', ξυμμαχία, invalidates the view of Schwartz (67. 3 n. on ὅπως τοῖς etc.) that the alliance of v. 22–3 (421) was an impossibility (and was interpolated by an editor); see Dover, *HCT* v (1981), 429–30. As Dover says of the present passage, 'this is, after all, a very public utterance, and even if we choose to believe that no Spartan envoy said any such thing, it remains an element in Thucydides' own picture of Spartan–Athenian relations'. See further below, introductory n. to v. 22–23.

2. οὐκ ἦν ἀνταμυνόμενός τις καὶ ἐπικρατήσας τὰ πλείω τοῦ πολεμίου κατ' ἀνάγκην ὅρκοις ἐγκαταλαμβάνων μὴ ἀπὸ τοῦ ἴσου ξυμβῆ: 'not for one side to take its revenge on the enemy, using its advantage to force the swearing of unequal oaths'. For the phrase μὴ ἀπὸ τοῦ ἴσου 'unequal' [lit. 'from a position of equality'] see i. 99. 2, iii. 10. 4 and nn. The word for 'on the enemy', πολεμίου, is an emendation for πολέμου, 'in war', and is surely right: a specific subject is needed for ἃ προσεδέχετο, see next n. Here I have departed from OCT.

παρὰ ἃ προσέδεχετο: 'to surprise your enemy' [lit. 'contrary to what he expected']. See previous n.

3. ἀνταποδοῦναι ἀρετήν: 'to return benefit for benefit'. For this sense of ἀρετή see iii. 58. 1 n. Contrast ii. 40. 4: Pericles had said that the recipient of a favour might indeed return it, but would feel coldly towards his benefactor and act correctly only out of a sense of obligation.

The Spartans are arguing against one main assumption of Greek popular ethics, see generally M. Whitlock Blundell, *Helping Friends and Harming Enemies* (Cambridge, 1989), ch. 2.

4. καὶ μᾶλλον πρὸς τοὺς μειζόνως ἐχθροὺς τοῦτο δρῶσιν οἱ ἄνθρωποι ἢ πρὸς τοὺς τὰ μέτρια διενεχθέντας: 'Men are more ready to make such concessions to their greatest enemies than to those with whom they have only a small quarrel'. With the thought Jowett rightly compares v. 91. 1, see n. there. Neither passage shows definite awareness of the end of the whole war, when Sparta treated Athens more leniently than some of Sparta's allies wanted.

20. 2. καὶ τοῖς ἄλλοις Ἕλλησιν ἀνάπαυσιν κακῶν: 'and relieve the sufferings of the rest of Greece'. Before applauding this solicitude on Sparta's part for the smaller states, we should note that their 'relief' is to be granted at the price of the political subordination referred to at para. 4 below. For the -σις word ἀνάπαυσις see introductory n.

πολεμοῦνται μὲν γὰρ ἀσαφῶς ὁποτέρων ἀρξάντων· 'They are not sure whether it was we or you who drove them into war'. The diffidence seems to go beyond the requirements of diplomacy: Sparta is represented as creeping towards the position described at vii. 18. 2, where they are said to have decided that they themselves started the war.

σκοπεῖτε: 'Consider'. Francis (206) notes that no other Spartan in Th. uses this verb.

4. ἡμῶν γὰρ καὶ ὑμῶν ταὐτὰ λεγόντων τό γε ἄλλο Ἑλληνικὸν ἴστε ὅτι ὑποδεέστερον ὂν τὰ μέγιστα τιμήσει: 'If you and we unite [lit. 'say the same things'] you can be certain that the rest of Greece, from its position of inferiority, will pay both of us the greatest honour'. In other words, the Spartans are made to propose a sell-out of their own allies: the contrast with the liberation propaganda of ii. 8. 4 is complete. For an equally blunt expression of the same idea see Ar. *Peace* 1082, produced in 421 but perhaps looking back to just this moment.

But Th. may have inserted the present passage, so damaging to Sparta in its implications, as part of his general blackening of Spartan acts and motives. See Badian, *From Plataea to Potidaea*, ch. 4. (This possibility is not excluded by Th.'s account of the Spartans' private calculations—desire not to cut a poor figure with their allies—as given in the following narrative, at 22. 3: this may well be no more than his own conjecture. That is, it does not provide factual corroboration of this part of the speech.) Gomme's witty comment, that the Spartans no doubt went back to their allies loudly proclaiming that of course Sparta had looked after their interests, assumes too readily that the Spartans spoke exactly as Th. reports. In favour of thinking they did so speak, see v. 18. 11 with the (slightly inaccurate) back-reference at 29. 2-3: Sparta's allies are outraged at the clause, γράμμα, in the peace of Nikias which reserves to Athens and Sparta (rather than Sparta and her allies) the right to make later changes. But that was perhaps thoughtless drafting.

For τιμήσει, 'will pay us honour', see also 120. 3 n. on καὶ τἆλλα τιμή- σειν: Brasidas uses the same emphatic word of closure in his indirectly reported speech at Skione. Brasidas tells the Skionaians that in view of their revolt from Athens he would pay them the highest *honour*—a heavily ironic use of the word in view of Skione's fate. Both times, 'honour' leaves a nasty taste.

21-23. *The Athenians refuse the Spartan offer*

21. 1. νομίζοντες τοὺς Ἀθηναίους ἐν τῷ πρὶν χρόνῳ σπονδῶν μὲν ἐπιθυμεῖν, σφῶν δὲ ἐναντιουμένων κωλύεσθαι: 'They remembered that Athens had wanted a truce some time earlier, but had failed because Sparta had refused'. See ii. 59. 2 (430 BC). Dionysius of Halicarnassus, *On Thucydides*, ch. 14, noted the difference in Th.'s handling of the two episodes: the earlier was recorded very baldly, with no speeches on either side.

2. τοῦ δὲ πλέονος ὠρέγοντο: 'they were grasping for more'. See 17. 4 n. Th.'s comment on Athenian behaviour is too sweeping and severe; he gives the impression of unanimity among 'the Athenians', but from *FGrHist* 328 Philochorus F128 (the details of which are unfortunately confused, see Jacoby's comm.) we learn that opinions were sharply divided and that one vote had to be taken three times; see Lewis, *CAH* v². 416.

3. Κλέων ὁ Κλεαινέτου, ἀνὴρ δημαγωγὸς κατ' ἐκεῖνον τὸν χρόνον ὢν καὶ τῷ πλήθει πιθανώτατος: 'Kleon son of Kleainetos, a popular leader of the day who had the greatest influence over the people' [lit. 'a man who was a popular' etc.; see 81. 1 n. on ἄνδρα etc.]. Kleon has already, at iii. 36. 6, been given a full introduction, complete with patronymic as here, and in very similar though as we shall see not quite identical language. Griffith, *PCPhS* 187 (1961), 28, thinks Th. wrote the present passage first, and then made it slightly stronger (which it is) in book iii. Thus βιαιότατος, 'violent/forceful', is used of Kleon at iii. 36. 6 but not repeated here, for some reason or none. (On the trans. of this word see J. A. Andrews, 'Cleon's Ethopoietics', *CQ* 44 (1994), 26–39, at 26 n. 5. Andrews may well be right to insist that at iii. 36. 6 both meanings—'violent' as well as 'forceful'—are present. At iii. 36, T. Rood prefers 'violent' because of ἐς τὰ ἄλλα, 'in other respects', which Rood thinks picks up the decree of execution just mentioned—unless Th. means Kleon was forceful *on other occasions too*. Note that Cic. *Brut.* 28, surely from Th., has 'turbulentum', which conveys more than violence.) There is another difference, though one which hardly helps with the composition problem: in the present passage, the word δημαγωγός, 'demagogue', is used for the first and only time in Th. (See, however, viii. 65. 2 for the abstract noun δημαγωγία, 'demagogy'.) For the not very common Greek word *demagogos* see M. I. Finley, 'Athenian Demagogues', *Studies in Ancient Society*, ed. Finley (London, 1974; repr. from *Past and Present*, 21 (1962)), 3; K. J. Dover (ed.), *Aristophanes: Frogs* (Oxford, 1993), 69 n. 1 (but against Dover's view that the word was not derogatory see Xen. *Hell.* v. 2. 7).

Nevertheless it must be accepted that the resemblances between the two passages are close. For Andrewes, *HCT* v. 364, this near-repetition of iii. 36 is one of the 'indications of incompleteness' in Th.'s narrative of the Ten Years War; see also Dover on vi. 72. 2, concluding that at the time of his death Th. had not decided which of Kleon's introductions to delete (it cannot automatically be assumed that the second would be the one to disappear, because Th. is perfectly capable of delayed introductions). But Dover does allow that Th. might have been willing to 'introduce the same character twice in different connections', and the small differences noted above may suggest that Th. had his reasons for keeping both introductions. 'Violent', if we accept that crude trans. (see above), is more appropriate for Mytilene, whereas demagogic skills were specially necessary to dispose of the specious Spartan appeal.

τοὺς ἐν τῇ νήσῳ παραδόντας: 'the men in the island must first of all surrender'. From the Spartan point of view this was unthinkable at this stage, as Gomme notes; to that extent the territorial demands which follow are hardly important.

ἐλθόντων δὲ ἀποδόντας Λακεδαιμονίους Νίσαιαν καὶ Πηγὰς καὶ Τροιζῆνα καὶ Ἀχαιῖαν, ἃ οὐ πολέμῳ ἔλαβον, ἀλλ' ἀπὸ τῆς προτέρας ξυμβάσεως Ἀθηναίων ξυγχωρησάντων: 'the Spartans were then to restore Nisaia, Pegai, Troizen and Achaia—places which had not been taken in war, but had been surrendered by Athens under a previous treaty', lit. 'when they [the Spartans on the island] arrived [at Athens] the Spartans were to restore', etc.

The reference ('the previous treaty') is to the Thirty Years Peace of 446, see i. 115. 1 and n.

As Lewis says, *CAH* v². 387, 'if Cleon is asking for Nisaea and Pegae as part of a permanent settlement, that is a demand for Megara as a whole'. For the bearing of this demand, and the Spartan reaction to it, on events at Megara soon after see 66. 3 n. on οὐ δυνατόν, etc.

Later in the summer the Athenians devastated Troizenian territory (45. 2 n. on ἐλῄστευον etc.) and made a separate agreement with Troizen, attested only by 118. 4, see n. there on καθ᾽ ἃ ξυνέθεντο.

κατὰ ξυμφορὰς καὶ ἐν τῷ τότε δεομένων τι μᾶλλον σπονδῶν: 'in a time of reverse, when the Athenians were more anxious to make peace than they now were'. See i. 115. 1 n.: this is relevant to the question whether the 446 peace was (or was perceived at Athens to be) a victory for Athens.

22. 1. ξυνέδρους: 'commissioners'. This word just means 'people who sit with/together' and has no technical sense in Th.; it is used of the Melian representatives at v. 86. In the fourth century it was used for the members of the Second Athenian Confederacy, and came to be used more or less technically, Tod 123 lines 43–4, cp. Tod 175. Presumably the Spartans wanted the *boule* or Council of 500 to take a hand, in what they surely knew was the usual way, cp. v. 45. 1, where a preliminary diplomatic audience before the Council is treated as normal. (Had the Spartans, now as at v. 45, already been seen by the Council? Th. does not say so, but in this area that does not prove it did not happen, cp. iii. 36. 5 n. for his neglect of this kind of technical point. But perhaps the present occasion was so dramatic, and the subject of so much excited talk in Athens, that the Spartans were heard by the Assembly straight away.)

κατὰ ἡσυχίαν: 'quietly'. See previous n.: this language is perhaps more appropriate to a conference organized by, or with its Athenian members drawn from, the Council; at any rate the *Spartans* may have assumed so, coming as they did from a city with very different decision-making traditions. (See further nn. on v. 45 ff.)

2. τῷ μὲν πλήθει οὐδὲν ἐθέλουσιν εἰπεῖν: 'they were unwilling to speak openly before the people'. This mention of the 'people', i.e. the assembly, tells against Ostwald's suggestion (*From Popular Sovereignty to the Sovereignty of Law* (Berkeley, 1986), 206–7) that Kleon's activity in chs. 21–2 took place in the Council, and that he was a Councillor for the second time in 425 BC (he had been one in 428/7). See Lewis, *CR* 39 (1989), 280–1.

3. μὴ ἐς τοὺς ξυμμάχους διαβληθῶσιν εἰπόντες καὶ οὐ τυχόν-τες: 'if they spoke and did not succeed, the terms they offered might damage them in the eyes of their allies'. See 20. 4 n.

23. 1. ἄλλα οὐκ ἀξιόλογα δοκοῦντα εἶναι: 'other petty breaches of the treaty which hardly seemed worth mentioning'. Th. does not quite condemn the Athenians openly ('seemed' could mean 'seemed to the Spartans'); but the implication is surely disapproving. See also next n.
ἀδίκημα ἐπικαλέσαντες: 'protesting against the injustice'. Again, see previous n., this is formally ambiguous: the injustice might be only in the minds or mouths of the Spartans. But in this part of the narrative, so critical of the Kleon-led Athenians, words like 'injustice' are surely meant to lodge in our memories and leave a cumulatively bad impression of Athens or Kleon: see, for this point and generally for the focalization issue hereabouts, *Greek Historiography*, 159 and n. 73. If this is right, i.e. there is authorial condemnation of Athenian sharp practice, it is worth recalling the famously bitter remarks about *Spartan* duplicity at *Andormache* 445 f., a play which some would date about 425, though there is no certainty, see the introduction to P. T. Stevens's edn. (Oxford, 1971), 15–21. Stevens cautiously favours c.425. See further below, v. 15. 2 n. on ἀλλ' οἱ Ἀθηναῖοι.

24–25. *Sicilian campaigning*

24. 1. ἐν τούτῳ δέ ... ἐν τῇ Σικελίᾳ: 'Meanwhile ... in Sicily'. See chs. 1 and 2.
2. τῶν Ῥηγίνων κατὰ ἔχθραν: 'who hated the Rhegians'. See 1. 2 and n.
4. ῥᾳδίως χειρώσεσθαι: 'they would easily get control of the place'. See iii. 94. 3 n. As usual when Th. uses this kind of expression, things were not destined to be as easy as that.
5. καὶ ἔστιν ἡ Χάρυβδις κληθεῖσα τοῦτο, ᾗ Ὀδυσσεὺς λέγεται διαπλεῦσαι: 'it is the so-called Charybdis by which Odysseus is said to have passed'. An interesting aside, surely inserted to spice the narrative, rather than because it was intended to be geographically helpful (not reader was going to say 'Oh, Charybdis: now I know where he means'). Compare iii. 104, with its Homeric quotations: one purpose of that digression was to enliven an austere slab of military writing. But the aside is uncharacteristic of Th., being more in the manner of Herodotus or Hecataeus of Miletos, see below.

There is no doubt that Th. wrote these words. It might just have been possible to doubt it (such chatty asides are after all not common in Th.) and regard them as a 'learned' intrusion by a commentator—especially since the scholia on Thucydides show no awareness of the Homeric allusion, a circumstance which might tempt one to regard the sentence as an intrusion made after the scholiasts' time, whenever that was. But there is fortunate and decisive evidence in favour of authenticity. It is provided by a reference to this passage, as coming from Th.'s 4th book, in a scholiast to another author, Aelius Aristides, at vol. iii Dindorf, p. 640 line 34 (commenting on *Or.* xlvi in Dindorf's numbering, iii in Behr's, treatise entitled 'On the Four', ch. 309).

With the present passage cp. Xen. *Anab.* vi. 2. 2 on the Acherusian Chersonese, where Herakles is said to have descended in pursuit of Cerberus. The manner is Herodotean or even Hecataean, cp. Hdt. vii. 26. 3 on Kelainai where a Phrygian story says (λόγος ἔχει) Apollo hung up the skin of Marsyas, or *FGrHist* 1 Hecataeus F 239 about Herakleia on Latmos in Caria, referring to *Iliad* ii. 868. (So the Xenophontic passage is not necessarily an example of reception of Thucydides in the *Anabasis*, on which topic see *JHS* 1995, 50–1).

For the Charybdis episode see *Odyssey* xii. 101–10 (Circe's description of the whirlpool), 237–43 (Odysseus' men watch it), 426–46 (Odysseus gets past it). For the location problem see Heubeck's n. on xii. 73–126 in A. Heubeck and A. Hoekstra, *Commentary on Homer's Odyssey* vol. ii, books ix–xvi (Oxford, 1989), citing *FGrHist* 1 Hecataeus F 82 and the present passage of Th. as evidence that 'in antiquity the passage between Skylla and Charybdis was at an early date localized at the Straits of Messina'. But there is a risk of circularity here: the Hecataeus passage is merely a brief quotation from Stephanus of Byzantium, saying that Hecataeus put Skylla in Europe. Jacoby assigned this to a Sicilian book of Hecataeus, presumably under the influence of Th. iv. 24, though Eur., *Medea* 1342–3, 'Tyrrhenian Skylla', may also be supporting fifth-century evidence (and the tradition may be even older: for Eratosthenes' belief that Hesiod put Odysseus' wanderings in Italy and Sicily see Strabo 23 = frag. 150. 25–6 M–W). By Polybius' time, see xxxiv. 2–4 with Walbank's commentary (again from Strabo 23–5), the western location of Skylla and Charybdis was well established. See now C. Mackie, *CQ* 46 (1996) 110.

In any case, Th. (or the tradition he drew on) was the kind of target Eratosthenes had in mind when he said (Strabo 24) that you would find the scene of Odysseus' wanderings when you found the cobbler who sewed up the bag of the winds.

What is the force of Th.'s λέγεται, 'is said'? H. D. Westlake, 'ΛΕΓΕΤΑΙ in Thucydides', *Mnemosyne*, 30 (1977), 345–63, at 359, takes it to imply misgivings about the (post-Homeric) scholarly tradition which sought to locate Charybdis; cp. vi. 2. 1 n. on the Laestrygonians. But in the present passage the word could just refer more loosely to what Homer said: 'this place is *called* (κληθεῖσα) Charybdis; it is where Homer says Odysseus passed through'. Actually, Homer notoriously distances himself from the Charybdis story and the other adventures of books ix–xii, by having Odysseus recount his own adventures to the Phaiakians. Th. is therefore a very long way from guaranteeing the story. He says, in effect, that Homer says that Odysseus says, etc.; λέγεται is thus doing a kind of double duty. On this view it is the word κληθεῖσα, 'is called', which contains the allusion to modern traditions (modern for Th., that is); perhaps local traditions rather than scholarly ones.

Sieveking (7 n. on 'Ηιόνα etc.), 131, discusses this passage, unconvincingly: consistently with his view that geographical material in Th. always serves directly to make the narrative intelligible, he thinks that by mentioning Charybdis Th. is offering a proof of the narrowness of the straits. Better is Ridley, *Hermes* 1981, 37 n. 47, 'the allusion to Ulysses [!] is surely for literary dressing and because of Thucydides' respect for Homer'.

25. 2. ἐς τὰ οἰκεῖα στρατόπεδα: 'to their own berths'. The Greek word is that normally used for 'camps', but that does not sound right in English in a nautical context, and Jowett's 'stations' is unfamiliar in this sense except as part of the expression 'battle-stations'. But the words may in any case be intrusive, see next n. (unless ἐς just means 'in the direction of', without any implication that they actually got there).
τό τε ἐν τῆ Μεσσήνῃ καὶ ἐν τῷ 'Ρηγίῳ: 'at Messina and near Rhegium'. Perhaps this and the previous words should be deleted. The fleet which disperses with the loss of one ship is the Syracusan only, and it does not yet reach Messina; but the mention of *two* 'camps' or berths suggests that the movements of both the Athenian and the Syracusan ships are being described.
καὶ νὺξ ἐπεγένετο τῷ ἔργῳ: 'Night ended the battle'. For similarly terse language cp. i. 51. 2 and 5, and nn.
3. ἐπὶ δὲ τὴν Πελωρίδα τῆς Μεσσήνης: 'at the promontory of Peloros near Messina'. Cape Peloro or Faro, the easternmost tip of Sicily; not the northernmost, as the scholiast wrongly says: see K. Ziegler, *RE* xix. 397–400, noting that the present passage is the earliest attestation anywhere. See also D. Asheri, *CAH* iv². 761.
4. χειρὶ σιδηρᾷ: 'an iron grapnel' [lit., an 'iron hand']. See L. Casson, *Ships and Seamanship in the Ancient World* (Princeton, 1971), 121 n. 87, curiously not mentioning the present passage.

5. **ἀποσιμωσάντων:** 'making a sudden twist outwards'. An extremely rare verb in surviving Greek prose (the noun ἀποσίμωσις occurs at Appian, *BC* iv. 71, in a naval context); its cool occurrence in this piece of plain narrative shows that the language of naval manœuvres must have been an everyday thing to most Athenians. Its meaning is not quite clear. Jowett's trans. is based on the scholiast's comment; but H. T. Wallinga, *The Boarding-Bridge of the Romans: Its Construction and Function in the Naval Tactics of the First Punic War* (Groningen, 1956), 40, n. 3 to his p. 39, suggests that Th.'s verb may mean either 'backing water', or alternatively, since the literal meaning of the word seems to be 'to make snubnosed', that it may mean to attack and break off a ship's ram. (The trans. 'backing water' would be wrong if Gomme were right to say that the following word προεμβαλόντων meant this, but see next n.) More recent books on ancient Greek triremes and naval warfare do not help. In view of the uncertainty I have retained the traditional translation.

Marcellinus 52 oddly gives the noun ἀποσίμωσις among Thucydidean coinages, but actually (see above) Th. uses the verb.

καὶ προεμβαλόντων: 'struck the first blow'. See previous n.

7. **Καμαρίνης ἀγγελθείσης προδίδοσθαι Συρακοσίοις ὑπ' Ἀρχίου καὶ τῶν μετ' αὐτοῦ:** 'the Athenians had heard that Kamarina was to be betrayed to the Syracusans by a certain Archias and his associates'. For Kamarina cp. iii. 86. 2 n. on ξύμμαχοι δέ etc. and see now the excellent discussion by D. Asheri, *CAH* v². 158–9: it was restored by the mid-fifth century, after its depopulation in the 480s (Hdt. vii. 154–6, cp. Dover *HCT* on vi. 5. 3), starts minting silver coins called *litrae*, and has an Olympic victor, Psaumis, in *c.*450 (Pindar, *Ol.* iv and v). An important recent find from Kamarina is a set of fourth-century inscriptions, *SEG* xxxiv (1984), nos. 940–1, connected with sales of land, and listing proper names, all of which are purely Greek: see R. J. A. Wilson, *Arch. Reps.* 1987–8, 116, describing other work on the site. See also *SEG* xli. 778–95, fifth-century allotment plates attesting a 'rational creation' of phratries, perhaps after the democratic refoundation of 461 BC.

Jowett's 'a certain' masks the abruptness of the mention of Archias, who has not been mentioned before; the Greek just means 'by Archias'.

ἐστράτευσαν ἐπὶ Νάξον τὴν Χαλκιδικὴν ὅμορον οὖσαν: 'they made war upon Naxos, a Chalkidian city which was their neighbour'. For Sicilian Naxos see P. Pelagatti, *Princeton Encyclopaedia*, 612–13. This mention of Naxos by Th. is evidence that Naxos, whose population (together with that of Katana) had been transferred to Leontini in 476, had now been resettled, the original population returning from Leontini: D. Asheri, *CAH* v². 150, 158. For 'Chalkidian' see 61. 4 n.

9. καὶ παρακελευόμενοι ἐν ἑαυτοῖς ὡς οἱ Λεοντῖνοι σφίσι καὶ οἱ ἄλλοι Ἕλληνες ξύμμαχοι ἐς τιμωρίαν ἐπέρχονται: 'and shouted to each other that the Leontines and their other Greek allies were coming to help them'. This oblique (and factually mistaken) reference, focalized through the Naxians themselves, is the first we have heard of Leontini in the present piece of narrative (they were said at iii. 86. 2–3 to be allies of the Rhegines and Athenians). At para. 10 we will learn that the Leontines are indeed involved in the present episode of fighting: they capitalize on Messinian weakness by marching against Messina where they suffer heavy losses. Leontini will be important as part of the background to the great Sicilian expedition of 415, and Th. keeps us in mind of the place, see v. 4. 2 n. on Λεοντῖνοι γάρ etc.

11. μετὰ τοῦ Δημοτέλους: 'Demoteles'. Gomme remarks on the definite article, which is certainly unusual. Perhaps a patronymic (father's name) has dropped out ('Demo—— the son of Demoteles').

12. ἄνευ τῶν Ἀθηναίων: 'the Athenians took no part'. So the first Athenian involvement in Sicily fizzles out (though see the puzzling 48. 6 and n.). The next main involvement was in 422, see v. 4, though Th. gives some domestic Sicilian material at iv. 48. 6 and 58–65 over which fear of Athens throws a shadow. Diplomatic contacts no doubt continued; M. Walbank, *Proxenies*, no. 40 (*IG* i³. 160) may date from the 420s and refer to the first Athenian involvement, though a reference to the 415 expedition is also possible: it is heavily restored but seems to confer proxeny (for which status see ii. 29. 1 n.) on some (?four) Sicilians in recognition of help with a Sicilian expedition (Walbank) or help to Athenian visitors to Sicily (*IG*). See also Walbank, no. 66, fourth-century reinscribing of a grant of proxeny to Archonides, probably the Sikel king mentioned at Th. vii. 1. 4 n., see n. there. The original grant may date to the 420s, though the late 430s or the years 420–415 are also possible.

26–41. *The Pylos episode concluded*

26. 2. ἔπινον οἷον εἰκὸς ὕδωρ: 'and drinking such water as they could get'. Here the meaning of οἷον εἰκός is 'as was natural', rather than 'as was probable', and the reference, as T. Rood convinces me, is to the quality (not the quantity) of water to be expected. For ?another view (no trans. offered) see Westlake, *Essays*, 159 f. and n. 23.

3. στενοχωρία: 'a narrow space'. The word is rare in Th. outside the Sicilian book vii, where it is used five times (36. 4; 44. 2; 49. 2; 70. 6; 87. 2). Otherwise it is found only here and at iv. 30. 2 below, also at ii. 89. 8). For the general parallelism between Pylos and Sicily see 12. 3 n.

4. ὕδατι ἀλμυρῷ χρωμένους: 'had only brackish water to drink'. See

Pritchett, *SAGT* i (1965), 25 ff., for this: modern difficulties in identifying a brackish water-supply may be explained, not by imputing error to Th. or his informants, but by reference to the 'normal hydrogeological phenomenon' that normally fresh water from such a source becomes brackish with constant use.

5. καὶ τῶν Εἱλώτων τῷ ἐσαγαγόντι ἐλευθερίαν ὑπισχνούμενοι: 'offering ... freedom in the case of helots who would get bread to the island'. See next n.

6. καὶ μάλιστα οἱ Εἵλωτες: 'especially the helots'. It follows, from the combination of paras. 5 and 6, that some helots got their freedom in this way, if we assume that the Spartans kept their promise despite the failure of the whole Pylos operation. We should like to know how many were freed and how exceptional such an offer was. After the battle of Leuktra in 371, we are told that 6000 helots were enrolled in the army with an offer of freedom: Xen. *Hell.* vi. 5. 28 f. Cawkwell, *CQ* 33 (1983), 392, thinks it possible that such promises were made even earlier than 425. (The incident described at 80. 3–4 below is ambiguous evidence: the promise of freedom was made but the helots disappeared in sinister circumstances.)

7. τετιμημένα χρημάτων: 'they had been financially valued in advance' [I have inserted the words 'in advance' to make the sense clearer]. The meaning is that the destruction of the ships was done with the prior agreement of the Spartan authorities. Why does Th. go out of his way to give this information? Perhaps in order to bring out the point that Sparta was not a sea-power and Spartans were normally cautious about risking ships which were precious because rare, see 11. 4 n. on 'sparing the timber' (Brasidas urges them to put caution aside).

27. 1. ἐν δὲ ταῖς Ἀθήναις πυνθανόμενοι: 'When news reached Athens ... they'. A subject (in fact, 'the Athenians') has to be supplied in the Greek, as also in my trans. As usual, we should like to know just which Athenians Th. has in mind: general worries might be generally felt, but the para. goes on to give some detailed military thinking. This could simply represent Th.'s own assessment; or it could reflect discussions between the generals, or in the Council.

The following account of events in the Assembly is one of Th.'s least objective sections: in particular, states of mind are regularly attributed to Kleon, although Th. is not likely to have had evidence for what was going on inside the head of a man normally thought by modern scholars to have been a personal enemy of his. Examples are noted where they occur, and see *Thucydides*, 78 and n. 22; 166.

3. Κλέων δὲ γνούς: 'Kleon knew'. See previous n., and for the general

point (Th.'s attribution, without evidence, of knowledge or emotion), see
i. 5. 1 n. on ἡγουμένων, and add I. J. F. de Jong, 'Between Word and
Deed: Hidden Thoughts in the *Odyssey*', in I. de Jong and J. P. Sullivan
(eds.), *Modern Critical Theory and Classical Literature* (Leiden, 1994),27–50.
But the treatment of Kleon is particularly glaring, with its repeated use
of γνούς, 'knowing'. For the participially expressed motivation see 9. 1 n.
on Δημοσθένης δὲ ὁρῶν, citing Mabel Lang. See esp. her remarks at 50:
'the idea of Cleon confiding his thoughts and plans to Thucydides seems
absurd'.

Θεογένους: 'Theogenes'. The OCT reading is Θεαγένους, 'Theagenes';
but it is the reading of only one, and not the best, manuscript: the
others have The*o*genes, and this spelling is preferred by Andrewes and
Lewis, *JHS* 77 (1957), 178 f. (followed by Develin, *AO* 131, and
M. Osborne and S. Byrne, *LGPN* ii, Θεογένης, no. 15), who think this
man is the Theogenes of v. 19. 2, etc., a swearer to the Peace of Nikias
(see n. on that passage where again the spelling is not quite certain).
See also D. M. MacDowell's n. on Ar. *Wasps* 1183, and N. Dunbar's on
Birds 822–3.

4. καὶ γνούς: 'He knew'. See 3 n.

**παρῄνει τοῖς Ἀθηναίοις … ὡς χρὴ κατασκόπους μὲν μὴ
πέμπειν μηδὲ διαμέλλειν καιρὸν παριέντας:** 'he advised the Athenians … not to send a mission, which would only be a loss of valuable
time'. This may well have been sensible advice, if we disregard the discreditable motive with which Th. introduces it (Kleon's reluctance *either*
or deny them and be shown up as a liar).

5. Νικίαν τὸν Νικηράτου: 'Nikias son of Nikeratos'. But this, the
famous, Nikias (contrast ii. 85. 5, see n. there) has already been introduced formally, with patronymic, at iii. 51. 1. If a special explanation is
needed, perhaps we should imagine that this is an echo of Kleon's actual
words, which may have included his enemy's name given in full for contemptuous emphasis. But for 'Griffith's law' (important officers of state
given patronymics) see 119. 2 and n.; Nikias gets his patronymic not only
here but at 53, 119, and 129.

ἐχθρὸς ὤν: 'and an enemy of his'. Lewis, *CAH* v². 5, notes that
occasional brief statements like this on political developments exemplified by hostility between individuals (he compares vi. 15. 2) represent
Thucydidean selectivity. Th. describes political developments very
partially: Athens must have been full of such political enmities as that
between Kleon and Nikias. To Lewis's examples we can add such
non-Athenian examples as 132. 2 on Perdikkas' generally good relations
with leading Thessalians, a selective comment about what must have
been an enormous and complicated web of such friendships and guest-

friendships, many of them known to Th. in much greater detail than he allows us to perceive.

εἰ ἄνδρες εἶεν οἱ στρατηγοί: 'if the generals were men'. See G. Großmann, *Politische Schlagwörter aus der Zeit des Peloponnesischen Krieges* (Zurich, 1950), 111-15, for such 'manliness', i.e. courage, as a slogan of the democracy.

28. 1. ὑποθορυβησάντων ἐς τὸν Κλέωνα: 'were in a state of near uproar against Kleon'. The word θόρυβος is the regular word for disturbance in the lawcourts, see V. Bers, 'Dikastic *Thorubos*', *CRUX*, 1 ff., at 4, calling the present passage 'a sort of duel between the speaker and the crowd', i.e. an extension of law-court manners to the Assembly. (The prefix ὑπο- weakens the verb, hence my word 'near'.)

καὶ ἅμα ὁρῶν αὐτὸν ἐπιτιμῶντα: 'and when Nikias heard Kleon's criticisms'. Lit. 'when he saw', an odd choice of verb, even if, with Jowett, we dilute it to 'perceived'. Note in any case that where Nikias is concerned Th. avoids tendentious words like 'knowing', which in the present section are reserved for Kleon (or Kleon and Demosthenes jointly, as at 37. 1). See generally 27. 3 n. The effect is to confer on Nikias an aloofness which Kleon is denied. (See also introductory n. to 17-20 for H. Flower's suggestion that Th. further exculpated Nikias by omitting an Assembly debate altogether.) But Dr. T. Rood rightly points out that ὁρῶν here should be added to Lang's statistics about Nikias, see 9. 1 n. on Δημοσθένης etc. (cf. her p. 63).

2. γνοὺς δὲ: 'but when he realized'. See 27. 3 n.

3. οἷον ὄχλος φιλεῖ ποιεῖν: 'typical crowd behaviour'. See V. Hunter, 'Thucydides and the Sociology of the Crowd', *CJ* 84 (1988/9), 17-30, esp. 22 f. on the present passage. She argues that Th. does not have a 'sociology' of the crowd, only a 'psychology', i.e. he does not think that the behaviour of the crowds differs qualitatively from that of individuals.

4. Λημνίους δὲ καὶ Ἰμβρίους: 'the Lemnian and Imbrian forces'. For conjectures about the totals which Kleon asked for (and got: 30. 4) see Wilson, 104 f., concluding that he brought with him 1500-2000 troops, not counting ships' crews. On the Lemnians and Imbrians see Dover, *HCT* on vii. 57. 2. Lemnos and Imbros were close together in the northeast Aegean, although nowadays Lemnos is Greek and Imbros Turkish. Lemnos was captured by Athens in about 500 BC, see Hdt. vi. 136. 2 and 137-40, with R. Parker, in *RFP* 343 n. 21 (although Miltiades colonized Lemnos direct from the Chersonese, the early casualty list *IG* i³. 1477 seems to list Lemnians by Attic tribes). Imbros, as Parker and Dover note, shared Lemnos' history, but we do not know exactly when it became Athenian. Kleon's excellent force at Amphipolis also included Lemnians and Imbrians, see v. 8. 2.

καὶ πελταστάς: 'and peltasts'. For peltasts (light-armed troops, named from their shields) see ii. 29. 5 n. on καὶ πελταστῶν.

ἔκ τε Αἴνου: 'from Ainos'. A rich city in Thrace, 11 miles from Drabeskos; it paid 12 talents tribute in 454. Ainians are found as Athenian allies in 415, see vii. 57. 5.

καὶ ἄλλοθεν τοξότας τετρακοσίους: 'and four hundred archers from other places'. It is possible that the text originally mentioned another place or places, which has/have dropped out (the words for 'and'—τε and καὶ—are not in the positions we should expect).

5. τοῖς δὲ Ἀθηναίοις ἐνέπεσε μέν τι καὶ γέλωτος τῇ κουφο-λογίᾳ αὐτοῦ: 'The Athenians laughed at his boast'. For laughter in Th. (rare, and always unpleasant) see iii. 83. 1 n. on καὶ τὸ εὔηθες. See further 29. 1 n.

τοῖς σώφροσι: 'the wiser of them'. For the group of words in σωφρ- see nn. on i. 32. 4 and 79. 2. Here the word does seem to be used in a favourable sense and without irony (or oligarchic overtones), although the attitude of these 'wise' Athenians does not strike us as admirable: if Kleon failed and was killed, his would surely not be the only Athenian life lost: A. G. Woodhead, 'Thucydides' Portrait of Cleon', *Mnemosyne*, 13 (1960), at 314.

29. 1. καὶ ψηφισαμένων Ἀθηναίων αὐτῷ τὸν πλοῦν: 'and the Athenians had passed the vote for his expedition'. Develin, *AO* 130, believes, against earlier views, that Kleon was not a *strategos*, but that we should 'view this as an extraordinary appointment' (he goes on rather oddly 'although we may include it among the generals').

2. πυνθανόμενος τὴν ἀπόβασιν αὐτὸν ἐς τὴν νῆσον διανοεῖ-σθαι: 'because he had heard that he was already intending to make an attack on the island'. This, unlike some of Th.'s other conjectures about Kleon's motives, may be soundly based, if Th. interrogated Demosthenes at some point. If Kleon was in touch with Demosthenes (and 30. 4 seems to support the idea that he was, see n. there) it makes his 'boasting' (28. 5) less reckless.

ἡ νῆσος ἐμπρηθεῖσα: 'a fire which had broken out in the island'. For this fire, one of the most striking 'accidents' of the whole campaign, see 30. 2 n.

30. 1. ἀπὸ δὲ τοῦ Αἰτωλικοῦ πάθους: 'by his experience in Aitolia'. See iii. 98. 2 n. Demosthenes is one of the few men in Th. who is said to profit from previous mistakes (his own or other people's) or experience, see *Thucydides*, 158, also citing vii. 42. 3; Schneider, *Information and Absicht*, 70-4. On the fire generally see Wilson, 100 ff.: it enabled

Demosthenes to get an idea not just of Spartan numbers but of their tactical dispositions.

2. τῶν δὲ στρατιωτῶν ἀναγκασθέντων: 'they had been forced'. See 40. 1 n. on οὔτ᾽ ἀνάγκῃ οὐδεμιᾷ.

ἄκοντος: 'unintentionally' [lit. 'unwilling']. This accidental act deserves emphasis, unlike some of the 'chance' occurrences which have been detected or magnified by modern scholars in the Pylos/Sphakteria narrative (see e.g. 9. 1 n.).

4. καὶ ἔχων στρατιὰν ἣν ᾐτήσατο: 'he brought with him the army which he had asked for'. Who is the subject of the second 'he'? Strictly it could be Kleon (so Gomme), in which case 'asked for' would refer to the request made in the Assembly at 28. 4. But it is more likely, as seen by Grote, *History of Greece*, v. 251, that 'he asked for' refers to Demosthenes, in which case this is valuable further evidence that Kleon and Demosthenes had already been in communication, see 29. 2 and n.

31. 1. τοὺς ὁπλίτας πάντας: 'all their hoplites'. But Wilson (104) suggests that some must have been left guarding Pylos.

νυκτὸς . . . ἐπιβιβάσαντες: 'whom they had embarked . . . by night'. For this translation see Wilson, 110; the alternative and usual tr. is to take νυκτός, 'by night', with ἀνηγάγοντο, 'they set off'.

2. ὧδε γὰρ διετετάχατο . . . οὕτω μὲν τεταγμένοι ἦσαν: 'The enemy's dispositions were as follows . . . That was how the Spartan troops were distributed'. For this kind of ring formula see e.g. Hdt. vii. 89. 1 and 100. 1. Wilson (106 ff.) conjectures a total Spartan force of about 1000 men (420 Spartiates plus an unstated number of helots).

32. 1. ἔν τε ταῖς εὐναῖς ἔτι καὶ ἀναλαμβάνοντας τὰ ὅπλα: 'still in their beds and trying to grab their weapons'. Compare iii. 112. 3 and n. for a very similar Athenian attack, also organized by Demosthenes. Babut, 422, noting the exploitation of surprise and negligence, compares Brasidas at Amphipolis, see 103. 5 and n. on καὶ οὐ etc.

2. πάντες πλὴν θαλαμιῶν: 'all but the lowest tier of rowers'. For the 'thalamioi' see Morrison and Coates, *Athenian Trireme*, 133, 137 n. 8, 247: this is the only time the word occurs in Th., and is quite uninformative, a good example of his tendency to take technical naval terminology for granted. The key text is Aristophanes, *Frogs* 1074, where the reference to 'farting into the face of the *thalamax*' (a variant for 'thalamioi') shows where the thalamioi were positioned.

On Athenian numbers see, again, Wilson, 104 ff.: perhaps 11,000 in all.

3. πανταχόθεν κεκυκλωμένους: 'completely surrounded'. With this whole section Babut (422) compares iii. 2 (Torone), κατὰ νώτου καὶ ἀμφοτέρωθεν.

33. 1. βουλόμενοι ἐς χεῖρας ἐλθεῖν: 'wanting to come to close quarters'. These four words of Greek say it all: Th. assumes (it can only be an assumption, the usual easy attribution of motive) that the Spartans want a traditional hoplite battle, but the Athenians break the 'rules' and deny it them. See Lazenby, *Spartan Army* (1-6, introductory n.), 117, and in Hanson (ed.), *Hoplites*, 105.

34. 1. τῇ γνώμῃ δεδουλωμένοι ὡς ἐπὶ Λακεδαιμονίους: 'over-awed by the thought that they would be facing Spartans'. On the respect generally felt in Greece for Spartans as soldiers, see Lazenby, in Hanson (ed.), *Hoplites*, 105, and Hanson, *Western Way*, 98-9, with references, e.g. Lys. xvi. 17, 'thinking that it is a terrible thing to fight the Spartans'. In Th., cp. v. 75. 3, the 'misfortune in Sphakteria' [lit. the 'disaster in the island'] lowered Sparta's military reputation until the outcome of the battle of Mantinea (418) restored it; see also iv. 40. 1 below.

2. γενομένης δὲ τῆς βοῆς ἅμα τῇ ἐπιδρομῇ ἔκπληξίς τε ἐνέπεσεν: 'The shout with which they accompanied the attack dismayed the Spartans'. For such battle yells see Hanson, *Western Way*, 150 (where for 32. 3 read 34. 2, i.e. the present passage).

καὶ ὁ κονιορτὸς τῆς ὕλης νεωστὶ κεκαυμένης ἐχώρει πολὺς ἄνω: 'Clouds of ashes arose from the newly-burnt wood'. Babut (423) compares the accidental collapse of the tower at Lekythos, 115. 3. He does not dispute that the incidents occurred but thinks it significant that Th. chose to include them.

3. οὔτε γὰρ οἱ πῖλοι ἔστεγον τὰ τοξεύματα: 'their felt caps did not protect them against the arrows'. Caps or jackets? The scholiast gives both possibilities, and Jowett prefers 'jackets' or rather 'cuirasses'. But see J. K. Anderson, *Military Theory and Practice in the Age of Xenophon* (Berkeley, 1970), 30 ff. (quite possible that 'the Spartans at Sphacteria had no better protection than a strong felt cap'), Lazenby (1-6, intro-ductory n.), 46, and Hanson, *Western Way*, 83. But I doubt if Anderson is right (32) when he supposes that 'the conservative [Th.]' means to imply criticism of the inadequate 'new-fangled headgear'. For the kind of felt cap Anderson assumes see N. Sekunda, in J. Boardman (ed.), *Plates to CAH v and vi* (1994), 176, no. 192 (and perhaps 177, no. 194).

δοράτιά τε ἐναπεκέκλαστο βαλλομένων: 'and the points of the javelins broke off where they struck them'. See Hanson, *Western Way*, 83: at least their breastplates had provided some protection, so as to allow them to go on resisting.

ὑπὸ δὲ τῆς μείζονος βοῆς τῶν πολεμίων τὰ ἐν αὐτοῖς παρα-
γγελλόμενα οὐκ ἐσακούοντες: 'they were unable even to hear the
word of command, which was drowned by the shouting of the enemy'.
See 2 n. above, and for the general difficulty of hearing anything in a battle, see Hanson, *Western Way*, 71-2 (who is, however, there partly concerned with the problems caused by metal 'Corinthian' helmets, which
these Spartans were not wearing).

35. 1. ἐχώρησαν ἐς τὸ ἔσχατον ἔρυμα τῆς νήσου: 'fell back on the
fortification at the end of the island'. On Mt. Elias; see Wilson, Map B.
**4. καὶ χρόνον μὲν πολὺν καὶ τῆς ἡμέρας τὸ πλεῖστον ταλαιπω-
ρούμενοι ἀμφότεροι ὑπό τε τῆς μάχης καὶ δίψης καὶ ἡλίου
ἀντεῖχον:** 'For a long time, and indeed for most of the day, both armies
held their own, although they were suffering from the exertion of the
battle and thirst and the heat of the sun'. See Hanson, *Western Way*, 79,
citing the present passage, for the heat and dehydration which must
often have resulted from wearing unventilated hoplite armour in
summer conditions. (But the Spartans, at least, were not wearing metal
helmets, if *piloi* at 34. 3 means felt caps, see n. there; alternatively, they
were not wearing metal breastplates.)

36. 1. ὁ τῶν Μεσσηνίων στρατηγός: 'the commander of the Messenian contingent'. His name was Komon, according to Paus. iv. 26. 2, an
unusual instance of a name omitted by or not known to Th., but known
to us from other evidence.
2. τοὺς μὲν τῷ ἀδοκήτῳ ἐξέπληξε: 'their surprise appearance caused
panic on the Spartan side'. For ἀδόκητος used of surprise attacks see
Pritchett, *GSW* 2 (1974), 156, and cp. below, v. 10. 7.
**3. καὶ γιγνόμενοι ἐν τῷ αὐτῷ ξυμπτώματι, ὡς μικρὸν μεγάλῳ
εἰκάσαι, τῷ ἐν Θερμοπύλαις:** 'and to compare small with great, they
were in the same position as their countrymen at Thermopylai'. For
Thermopylai, where the Spartans made a famous suicidal stand against
the Persians in 480, see *CAH* iv² (1988), 555-9 (Hammond), and J. F.
Lazenby, *The Defence of Greece* (Warminster, 1993), ch. 6. The present
reference implies an interestingly different attitude from that at i. 23. 1,
where Th. was polemically concerned to minimize the Persian Wars by
comparison with his own war. See next n.
τῇ ἀτραπῷ: 'the path'. The well-known path, mentioned at Hdt. vii.
175 and 212? That is, is Th. here recalling Hdt.? This word for path is
found on only one other occasion in Th., at iv. 129. 4, where there is
admittedly no Herodotean resonance or Persian War angle. See Annex
A, p. 128. But in the light of criticism by Kennelly (Introduction,

p. 32) I must defend my 1992 suggestion that ἀτραπός or 'path' at iv. 36. 3, in a context explicitly discussing Thermopylai, presupposes Hdt. vii. 175, τὴν δὲ ἀτραπόν, δι᾽ ἣν ἥλωσαν οἱ ἁλόντες Ἑλλήνων ἐν Θερμο-πύλῃσι. The Greek in Th. is τῇ ἀτραπῷ περιελθόντων τῶν Περσῶν, 'when the Persians got round them by *the path*', the well-known path, I suggested. I grant that the story was not invented or first put into circulation by Hdt. But Th.'s language is brief and allusive—though not obscure; I conceded in 1992 that the word ἀτραπός was not quite unique in Th., being used at iv. 129. 4. Kennelly, however, (71–2) has the follow-ing argument against me: there were just two words the Greeks could choose from for path or track, ἀτραπός and τρίβος. Kennelly rules out τρίβος, as being less concrete and specific. Therefore, he says, for a specific path leading from one place to another there is no other word than ἀτραπός, i.e. Th. could not have expressed himself in any other way even if he had wanted to. This sounds neat, but it overlooks the most obvious word of all, namely ὁδός. For ὁδός used by Th. in precisely the sense 'mountain path', see v. 10. 10, the aftermath of the battle of Amphipolis: the Athenians fled πολλὰς ὁδοὺς τραπόμενοι κατὰ ὄρη. (For the first accusative here cp. with Classen/Steup v. 58. 4.) Jowett translates v. 10. 10 as follows: 'by various mountain paths', and the Penguin has 'by various tracks over the mountains'. For fuller discussion see above, Introduction, pp. 32 ff.

Finally, what was the point of the Thermopylai comparison? See Connor, 118 n. 19, noting that 'an expectation that Spartans would resist as they had at Thermopylai underlies the surprise at their surrender on Sphacteria' (for which see 40. 1).

37. 1. γνοὺς δὲ ὁ Κλέων καὶ ὁ Δημοσθένης: 'Kleon and Demos-thenes realized'. See 28. 1 n. on καὶ ἅμα etc. (But Th. may subsequently have talked to Demosthenes, so the present passage is not quite like the simple instances of 'Kleon knew'.)

τοῦ κηρύγματος ἀκούσαντες: 'when they heard the proclamation offering terms' [I have added 'offering terms' to make the meaning clearer; the reference is to the proclamation whose content is not revealed until para. 2. Classen/Steup jib at this and emend to του κηρύγματος, 'if they heard a proclamation']. For 'proclamation', κήρυγμα, see 105. 2 n. on the word.

38. 1. Στύφων ὁ Φάρακος: 'Styphon son of Pharax'. Possibly a relative of the Pharax who is active in Sicily at the end of the century, see Poralla, *Prosopographie der Lakedaimonier*. As Cawkwell, *CQ* 33 (1983), 389, says, it is impressive that Th. can (cf. next n.) give the order of seniority of these Spartan commanders.

τῶν πρότερον ἀρχόντων τοῦ μὲν πρώτου τεθνηκότος Ἐπιτάδου, τοῦ δὲ μετ' αὐτὸν Ἱππαγρέτου ἐφῃρημένου ἐν τοῖς νεκροῖς ἔτι ζῶντος κειμένου ὡς τεθνεῶτος: 'Epitadas, who was in command, had been killed already; Hippagretas, who was next in line, was actually alive but was thought dead and was among the dead bodies'. For the high mortality rate of generals in hoplite battles see Hanson, *Western Way*, 112–15, and Pritchett, 'Deaths of Generals on Battlefield', *EGH* 130–8.

κατὰ νόμον: 'as the law required'. But the Greek could just as well mean 'according to custom'; see v. 66 for an account of the Spartan chain of command, something Th. reports almost with surprise, though we should regard it as a natural way of running an army. Similarly he may just be saying that the arrangement described in the present passage was typically Spartan and orderly.

3. Λακεδαιμόνιοι κελεύουσιν ὑμᾶς αὐτοὺς περὶ ὑμῶν αὐτῶν βουλεύεσθαι μηδὲν αἰσχρὸν ποιοῦντας: '"The Spartans tell you to act as you think best, but you are to do nothing dishonourable"'. A marvellously unhelpful reply, nicely summing up the conflict in Spartan values between taking an initiative yourself and looking to others for direction. See Hodkinson (15. 2 n. on καὶ ὡς εἶδον etc.), esp. his 267 on the Spartan inability to cope psychologically with the new situation which Sphakteria presented; but see also Lazenby, *Spartan Army*, 121, for a high estimate of the Spartan achievement: he suggests that Th. means us to think that if the Spartans *had* been able to come to close quarters (33. 1 n.) they would have won despite numerical inferiority.

5. εἴκοσι μὲν ὁπλῖται διέβησαν καὶ τετρακόσιοι οἱ πάντες: 'Four hundred and twenty men in all crossed over to the island'. Perhaps this figure represents 35 age-groups of units (*enomotiai*) of 12 men, see Toynbee (8. 9 n.), 396, and Lazenby, 46, 116.

τούτων ζῶντες ἐκομίσθησαν ὀκτὼ ἀποδέοντες τριακόσιοι, οἱ δὲ ἄλλοι ἀπέθανον: 'of these, two hundred and ninety-two were brought to Athens alive, the rest had been killed'. A bronze shield has been found in a cistern in the Athenian agora, bearing the inscription *ΑΘΗΝΑΙΟΙ ΑΠΟ ΛΑΚΕΔΑΙΜΟΝΙΩΝ ΕΚ ΠΥΓΟ*, 'The Athenians (dedicated this) from the Spartans taken at [lit. 'out of'] Pylos': *IG* i³. 522. See J. Camp, *The Athenian Agora* (London, 1986), 71 f., with photograph and drawing. Pausanias was shown, in the Painted Stoa (Stoa Poikile), shields said to have been taken from the Spartans who were captured at Sphakteria, see Paus. i. 15. 4, with C. Habicht, 'Pausanias and the Evidence of Inscriptions', *CA* 3 (1984), 40–56, at 47. Presumably 'Pylos' on the inscribed shield refers to the whole area, including Sphakteria.

καὶ Σπαρτιᾶται τούτων ἦσαν τῶν ζώντων περὶ εἴκοσι καὶ ἑκατόν: 'There were about a hundred and twenty surviving Spartiates'. That is, full Spartan citizens. Sparta's subsequent diplomatic efforts, 'moving heaven and earth' (Lewis, *Sparta and Persia*, 31) to recover this relatively small number of Spartiates, may indicate that Sparta was already beginning to feel the manpower pinch which became acute in the fourth century. See further v. 68. 1 n.

ἡ γὰρ μάχη οὐ σταδαία ἦν: 'for there was no regular battle'. For this kind of explanation of low casualties cp. v. 11. 2 διὰ τὸ μὴ ἐκ παρατάξεως, which means much the same as the expression used here; see P. Krentz, 'Casualties in Hoplite Battles', *GRBS* 26 (1985), 13–20, at 19–20.

39. 2. ὁ γὰρ ἄρχων Ἐπιτάδας ἐνδεεστέρως ἑκάστῳ παρεῖχεν ἢ πρὸς τὴν ἐξουσίαν: 'the commander Epitadas had not served out full rations'. This is impressive, in view of what we have been told at ch. 26 about the difficulties the Spartans had getting food. But Th. makes no comment.

3. καίπερ μανιώδης οὖσα ἡ ὑπόσχεσις: 'the mad promise' [lit. 'the promise, though mad']. It would have been fairer of Th. to say that the promise *seemed* mad, and it is possible that with the suffix -ωδης the word has this nuance ('like madness'): Schneider, *Information und Absicht*, 21 n. 29. See further Howie (Introduction, p. 39 n. 99), 440 and 448, citing Solon F 13 W 69 f.

40. 1. παρὰ γνώμην τε δὴ μάλιστα τῶν κατὰ τὸν πόλεμον τοῦτο τοῖς Ἕλλησιν ἐγένετο: 'Nothing which happened during the war caused greater amazement in Greece'. A typical rhetorical superlative; for the content see 34. 1 n. See also 36. 3 n. on τῇ ἀτραπῷ, at end of n., and Connor there cited; Connor remarks that the present passage implicitly reintroduces the Thermopylai theme explicitly mentioned at 36. 4.

οὔτ' ἀνάγκῃ οὐδεμιᾷ: 'or in any other extremity' [lit. 'necessity']. On 'necessity' here see Schneider, *Information und Absicht*, 106, and M. Ostwald, *ANAΓKH*, 9 and 47, detecting here irony and a contrapuntal use of 'necessity', because, as he puts it, 'the precondition of the surrender had been created by the ἀνάγκη of the Athenian troops of finding a more convenient place for their meals' (a ref. to 30. 2).

2. ἀπιστοῦντές τε μὴ εἶναι τοὺς παραδόντας τοῖς τεθνεῶσιν ὁμοίους: 'And no one believed that those who surrendered were men of the same quality as those who had been killed'. Schwartz (67. 3 n. on ὅπως τοῖς etc.), 298, approved by Wankel (see next n.), 38 n. 3, wished to bracket τοῖς τεθνεῶσιν, 'those who had been killed', and to take ὅμοιοι in the technical Spartan sense 'peers', 'Spartiates'. But there is no certain use of the word in this sense in Th.; see v. 15. 1 n.

Something may, however, have gone wrong with the sentence elsewhere, because the connection with what precedes is awkward linguistically. Steup wanted to insert a finite verb like 'they despised', κατεφρόνουν, after ὁμοίους, referring to those who surrendered; Hude deleted τε, for which deletion he claimed some manuscript authority, the eleventh-century British Library ms. Add. 11727 ('M'); I examined the relevant page myself on 11 July 1995 and confirm that τε is quite certainly not there, as G. Alberti's 1992 ed. also confirms. This I hope settles the factual point which Gomme left open (see above, Introduction, p. 4) by saying that the reading without τε was 'according to him [Hude] but not according to Stuart Jones-Powell, the reading of M'. Gomme suggested ἀπιστούντων, a genitive absolute instead of a nominative participle. None of these suggestions affects the meaning much.

εἰ οἱ τεθνεῶτες αὐτῶν καλοὶ κἀγαθοί: 'where were the brave men—all killed?' [lit. he asked 'if the dead ones were the "fair and brave" ones']. On the meaning of καλοὶ κἀγαθοί see Gomme, 'The Interpretation of ΚΑΛΟΙ ΚΑΓΑΘΟΙ in Thucydides 4. 40. 2', *CQ* 3 (1953), 65–8, as well as his n. in *HCT* and the addendum at 731–2; H. Wankel, *Kalos Kai Agathos* (diss. Würzburg, 1961); de Ste. Croix, *OPW* 371–6, esp. 372–3 on the present passage; Dover, *GPM* 41–5; Andrewes, *HCT* on viii. 48. 6; Sommerstein on *Knights* 185. The expression is hard to translate (and I have simply kept Jowett's trans. unaltered) because it combines the idea of physical, aesthetic, and moral excellence or beauty on the one hand, with a political/social/economic sense on the other: in the fifth century, but apparently not in the fourth, it can sometimes refer to a definite class. But though de Ste. Croix strongly stresses the social side, the phrase is not just a 'class label', as Dover (43) points out: 'the use of *kalos kagathos* to denote or imply "belonging to a high social class" by Greek writers whose views and sentiments are anti-democratic tells us nothing of interest or importance, no matter how numerous the examples.' But in Th., who is evidently one of the 'anti-democratic' writers Dover has in mind, the class sense is undoubtedly present on the two occasions he uses it (see Gomme 1953, 66: in both Thucydidean places it is 'political'). The other place is viii. 48. 6, where it is combined with 'the so-called', ὀνομαζομένους. This, see Andrewes's n., is Th.'s way of expressing scepticism about whether the people in question really possessed the qualities of excellence implied. But Andrewes's own use of 'upper class', just before, shows that he accepts that a particular social or economic group is meant. (See now F. Bourriot, *Historia* 45 (1996), 129 ff.)

In the present passage, the play on the two senses of ἀγαθός (see the

Spartan reply below) is taken by Wankel (45) to show that the social
sense ('Standesbezeichnung') of the whole expression καλὸς κἀγαθός
was not generally recognized. But this goes too far. Wankel is right that
in the Spartan reply the idea of simple bravery is strongly present, but it
is not the only idea present: de Ste. Croix (372–3) has a point: 'the
Spartan hoplites had been overcome by archers and the like, men of no
consequence, who would not be brave in the right way'. See next n.

πολλοῦ ἂν ἄξιον εἶναι τὸν ἄτρακτον, λέγων τὸν οἰστόν, εἰ τοὺς
ἀγαθοὺς διεγίγνωσκε: '"the spindle (meaning the arrow) would be a
valuable weapon, if it picked out the brave"'. One of the few jokes in Th.,
and a very bleak one; see *Thucydides*, 191 and n. 1. I suppose part of the
point of 'spindle' is that it is a female instrument. For the full understanding of the remark one must remember the prejudice against the archer
as a low-grade warrior, as at Homer, *Iliad* xi. 385, where τοξότα, 'archer',
is hardly more than a word of abuse; see also Plut. *Mor.* 234e, cited by
Gomme. See Hanson, *Western Way*, 15. The prejudice in its fullest sense
extended to all infantry fighters except hoplites, cp. v. 10. 9, Kleon killed
by a Myrkinian peltast.

The attitude to weapons here implied is (facetiously) 'animistic'; on
this topic see M. W. Edwards. *The Iliad: A Commentary*, v. *Books 17–20*
(Cambridge, 1991), 51.

41. *Spartan morale and Athenian greed*

This is the first of the six occasions in iv–v. 24 on which Th. stands back
to comment on morale; see Introduction p. 109.

2. οἱ ἐκ τῆς Ναυπάκτου Μεσσήνιοι ὡς ἐς πατρίδα: 'the Messenians of Naupaktos regarded the place as their fatherland'. See 3. 2 n. on
καλοῦσι δέ etc. The motive is in effect a kinship motive of the kind discussed in the Introduction, section 4.

πλεῖστα ἔβλαπτον ὁμόφωνοι ὄντες: 'did great harm, because they
spoke the same language as the inhabitants'. For Andrewes, *HCT* v. 364,
this repetition of 3. 3, see n. there on καὶ ὁμοφώνους etc., is one of the
'indications of incompleteness' in Th.'s narrative of the Ten Years War.

**3. τῶν τε Εἱλώτων αὐτομολούντων καὶ φοβούμενοι μὴ καὶ ἐπὶ
μακρότερον σφίσι τι νεωτερισθῇ τῶν κατὰ τὴν χώραν, οὐ
ῥᾳδίως ἔφερον:** 'they were extremely worried because the helots were
deserting, and they were afraid that revolution would extend over the
whole country'. Babut (420) compares 108. 1 and 3, the disaffection of
Athens' allies after Amphipolis: 'the fall of Amphipolis is the strategic
and psychological replica of the Spartan defeat at Pylos.' Babut (422) also
compares 80. 2. For the helot problem see next n.

ἀλλὰ καίπερ οὐ βουλόμενοι ἔνδηλοι εἶναι τοῖς Ἀθηναίοις: 'although reluctant to reveal their situation to the Athenians'. A surprising remark, if applied narrowly to helot worries, and if true (and it may just be Th.'s conjecture about the Spartans' thinking); see Lewis, *Sparta and Persia*, 28. It is hard to believe that the Athenians were really unaware of the scale of the helot problem; though it is certainly remarkable that they did so little actively to promote helot unrest, see my *Greek World*, 133. On the helot threat (real or exaggerated?) see 80. 2–3 n.

4. οἱ δὲ μειζόνων τε ὠρέγοντο: 'were keen to get more' [lit. 'stretched out for more']. For this theme see 21. 2 and n. (very similar language), also 65. 4, where the thought is the same, but is more elaborately expressed.

On the peace overtures here described see Ar. *Knights* 794–6 with Sommerstein's n., and Boegehold (v. 16. 1 n. on πόνων . . .), 154.

42–45. ATHENIAN OPERATIONS AGAINST CORINTHIAN TERRITORY

For this section within the structure of book iv see Babut, 426 (an Athenian success, insufficiently exploited: the balance of the book is soon to turn against Athens). On the campaign in its general strategic context see Salmon, *Wealthy Corinth*, 318 ff., stressing the Corinthian weakness it attests. The battle of Solygeia is very fully studied by Stroud 1971; see also Stroud 1994, at 285–7. The topographical conclusions of Stroud 1971 are accepted by J. Wiseman, *The Land of the Ancient Corinthians* (Göteborg, 1978), 56 ff., and by Salmon. The purpose of the campaign is disputed: Andrewes, *HCT* v. 363, discussing 'indications of incompleteness' in Th.'s account of the Ten Years War, remarks 'we should be grateful for a clearer exposition of the Solygeia campaign'. Stroud 1971, 245 ff., and Salmon, 320 n. 34, are probably right to reject the old suggestion that Nikias' (unsuccessful) aim was to establish a permanent fort at Solygeia: the probable site of Solygeia is too far inland for this to be convincing. Instead (Stroud), the raid was intended to cause the maximum damage before moving on to the main objective, the establishment of the fort at Methana, 45. 2. For the ulterior thinking behind Methana see 45. 2 n.

The brief Solygeia campaign features, or may feature, in a surprisingly wide range of ancient sources. Th.'s account is so vivid and detailed that it has often been thought (e.g. by Gomme, iii. 494) that he himself participated; but see 43. 3 n. on ἦν γάρ . . . and Stroud 1994, 286, who (without ruling out the participation hypothesis) prefers, as part of his thesis that Th. in exile spent a lot of time at Corinth, to believe that he talked extensively to Corinthian informants. He notes the accuracy and specificity of Th.'s topographical indicators, and that Th. is 'remarkably well informed about Corinthian defence plans prior to the Athenian landing'. (By contrast, Stroud notes, Th. never tells us the purpose of the Athenian landing in the eastern Corinthia). This is an interesting and valuable point, but the Solygeia narrative is not the only place where Th. is 'remarkably well informed' about people's plans; the word 'informed' may mislead if it is meant to imply that all such information was necessarily based on knowledge or inquiry rather than on intelligent conjecture. That is, there is much inferred motivation in Th., throughout the narrative.

In addition to Th.'s account we have:

(i) A virtually certain mention of it in the *Knights* of Aristophanes (produced at the Lenaia—February—of 424) at lines 595–610; see Sommerstein's comm. (Warminster, 1981) on 604, and see further below 44.1 n.

(ii) A possible allusion at ML 69 = Fornara 136 (the 'Thoudippos decree' reassessing the tribute of the allies, see ii. 65. 5 n.), line 34, where 'the expedition', [hε] στρα[τιά], is taken by Meiggs and Lewis, p. 196, to refer to Nikias' Corinthian expedition, described in the present section of Th., rather than to Kleon's success at Sphakteria. The 'Nikias' possibility is allowed even by B. D. Meritt, in G. Shrimpton and D. McCargar (eds.), *Classical Contributions: Studies in Honour of M. F. McGregor* (New York, 1981), 92, who however insists on the closeness in time to Kleon's success, and thus on Kleon's connection with the reassessment.

(iii) Two sling-bullets found 'at Corinth' and inscribed with the name of the Corinthian commander Lykophron (for whom see 43. 1, etc.): C. Foss, *Arch. Reps.* (1974–5), 41, nos. 3 and 4. The bullets are in the Ashmolean Museum at Oxford. If this identification is right it would be evidence that slingers were present, though not mentioned by Th.; but the identification is not certain (Salmon, 319 n. 33), and Th.'s silence about slingers is an argument against it.

(iv) It has been thought that a scene from the battle was depicted on a dedicatory relief from Eleusis, see G. Bugh, *The Horsemen of Athens* (Princeton, 1988), 91 ff. (and fig. 10), giving references. But as Bugh says, Th. (44. 1) is categorical that the Corinthians had no cavalry, whereas the relief seems to give cavalry to both sides. Even allowing for artistic licence, this is surely an argument against the identification.

We can, however, confidently say, despite these uncertainties, that the battle, esp. in its cavalry aspect, was a fillip to Athenian morale, hence Aristophanes' confident lines.

42. 1. καὶ Ἄνδριοι: 'and the Andrians'. An inscription (*LSCG* 38; G. Rougemont, *CID* i, no. 7) attests dealings between Delphi and Andros at roughly this period. See B. Smarczyk, *Untersuchungen zur Religions-politik und politischen Propaganda Athens im Delisch-attischen Seebund* (Munich, 1990), 513 n. 49: the historical significance of the text is hard to evaluate without a precise date. But it may have a bearing on the question of the relations between Delphi on the one hand and the Athenians and their allies on the other, i.e. there was evidently no actual exclusion of Athens' allies from Delphi in the war, as some have assumed. See *HSCP* 94 (1992), 192 and n. 83, and below 118. 1 n.

Νικίας ὁ Νικηράτου τρίτος αὐτός: 'Nikias son of Nikeratos, and two others'. See 27. 5 n. For expressions of the τρίτος αὐτός type see i. 61. 1 n. on *Καλλίαν* etc. and add Fornara, *Generals*, 29–37, agreeing with Dover that the person singled out has no more legal authority than his colleagues, but concluding (36) that 'the person named is in some sense more notable than his colleagues; that if one is to be named he is the logical one'.

2. μεταξὺ Χερσονήσου τε καὶ Ῥείτου: 'between the promontory Chersonesos and the stream Rheitos'. The words 'the promontory' and 'the stream' are not in the Greek, but 'stream' is what Ῥεῖτος ought to mean; the Ῥειτοί are sacred streams at Eleusis. The location of Chersonesos (again, the word just means a promontory, but is here a proper name) is agreed to be the baths of Helen (on the Saronic Gulf to the south of Kenchreai), now a much built-over seaside resort; the position of Rheitos is strictly uncertain but must be a few km. further south. See the maps at Stroud 1971, 231, or Salmon, 21. Stroud 1994, 286, notes, as part of an argument for special knowledge of Corinthian matters by Th., that these two place-names are of 'strictly local interest and are not found elsewhere in ancient literature. But there can be no doubt of their identity and location'. (This exaggerates a little in regard to Rheitos.)

ἐς τὸν αἰγιαλὸν τοῦ χωρίου ὑπὲρ οὗ ὁ Σολύγειος λόφος ἐστίν, ἐφ᾽ ὃν Δωριῆς τὸ πάλαι ἱδρυθέντες τοῖς ἐν τῇ πόλει Κορινθίοις ἐπολέμουν οὖσιν Αἰολεῦσιν· καὶ κώμη νῦν ἐπ᾽ αὐτοῦ Σολύγεια καλουμένη ἐστίν: 'to the part of the coast beneath the Solygeian ridge. In ancient times Dorian invaders had taken up position there and fought against their Aiolian enemies in Corinth, and today there is a village, called Solygeia, on the hill which they occupied'. For the site of Solygeia see Stroud 1971, 235 ff.: probably the hills west of Galataki, see his map at 231; also (for the shrine at Solygeia) C. Morgan, 'The Evolution of a Sacred Landscape: Isthmia, Perachora, and the Early Corinthian State', in S. E. Alcock and R. Osborne (eds.), *Placing the Gods: Sanctuaries and*

Sacred Space in Ancient Greece (Oxford, 1994), 104–42, at 135–8. Why the references to the battle and the Dorian invaders (for whom cp. i. 12. 3)? Morgan (137) may well be right that the battle was 'an episode of the greatest importance in the history of Dorian Corinth', and that the archaic poet Eumelus could have treated it also (was he Th.'s source?); nevertheless Th. surely included it for its incidental interest, cp. iii. 96 n. (Hesiod at Nemea). Sieveking (7 n. on Ἡιόνα etc.), for whom all geographical information in Th. serves a strict and immediate historical purpose, is one of those who see here a clue that the Athenians, like the Dorians of olden times, were planning a fort at Solygeia, see his 119 ff., and above, introductory n. Ridley, *Hermes* 1981, 37 (and cp. 45), comments that the Solygeian hill was 'admittedly not likely to be a well-known landmark' and that Th. gives 'historical background as usual'; the last two words are too strong. One might want to say that Th. sometimes likes to give historical background where (as here) Herodotus had, for whatever reason, been silent. Where by contrast some ancient topic had been treated by Herodotus, T.'s treatment can be very glancing and allusive, see e.g. v. 41. 2 and n. for the ancient Battle of the Champions between Argos and Sparta. For the noun αἰγιαλός, 'coast', 'beach', see Smith, *TAPA* 1900, 75.

Lewis, *Towards a Historian's Text*, 113, points out that the manuscripts have Σολύγιος, which is emended to Σολύγειος out of Stephanus of Byzantium. The OCT (contrast Hude) does not even register that the text has been emended.

δώδεκα σταδίους: 'nearly a mile and a half' [lit. 'twelve stades']. For stades see i. 63. 2 n. and iv. 3. 2 n. on ἀπέχει etc. Th.'s distances, here and elsewhere in the present section, are defended by Stroud 1971, 239 ff., cp. Stroud 1994, 286. Ridley, *Hermes* 1981, 37 rightly points out that the location details are very full. See previous n. for Th.'s treatment of Solygeia generally.

3. Κορίνθιοι δὲ προπυθόμενοι ἐξ Ἄργους ὅτι ἡ στρατιὰ ἥξει τῶν Ἀθηναίων: 'The Corinthians had had advance news from Argos of the intended Athenian invasion'. An interesting piece of lax security: how had the news reached Argos from Athens? Presumably there had been free talk by people who had attended the relevant Assembly meeting, and the news passed down to the Piraeus (cp. the story at Plut. *Nikias* 30: news of the Sicilian disaster reaches Athens when a man sits down for a haircut in the Piraeus; the barber runs to tell the authorities and the man is tortured before confirmation of his story arrives). Ordinarily, however, we must assume that the generals or the Council of 500 were able to make military plans with a reasonable expectation of confidentiality, see my *Greek World*, 121.

Stroud 1994, 287, seeing the episode from the Corinthian point of view, notes how much Th. seems to know about Corinthian plans and movements.

On military security generally see my n. on iii. 91. 4, citing Hermokrates at vi. 72. 5 for awareness of the problem, a passage which shows that J.-P. Vernant, *Myth and Society in Ancient Greece* (New York, 1990), 37, denied too absolutely the existence of a concept of military security in ancient Greek strategy.

πάντες πλὴν τῶν ἔξω Ἰσθμοῦ: 'except those who lived to the north of the Isthmus'. This seems to refer, not to the Perachora peninsula, but merely to the Saronic Gulf coastline immediately to the north of the Isthmus: see Stroud 1971, 239 ff.

4. ἦν ἄρα οἱ Ἀθηναῖοι ἐπὶ τὸν Κρομμυῶνα ἴωσιν: 'in case the Athenians attacked Krommyon'. The eastern outpost of Corinthian territory, once Megarian, see Strabo 380.

43. 1. Λυκόφρων: 'Lykophron'. For sling-bullets with this name on see introductory n.

2. καὶ πρῶτα μὲν τῷ δεξιῷ κέρᾳ τῶν Ἀθηναίων εὐθὺς ἀποβεβη-κότι πρὸ τῆς Χερσονήσου οἱ Κορίνθιοι ἐπέκειντο: 'The Corin-thians first attacked the Athenian right wing which had only just landed in front of the Chersonesos'. V. D. Hanson, 'Epameinondas, the Battle of Leuctra (371 BC) and the "Revolution" in Greek Battle Tactics', *CA* 7 (1988), 190–207, at 194, in the course of an argument designed to show that there was nothing new about Theban tactics at Leuctra, points out that the present passage is an example of the *left* wing taking the initiative, more than fifty years before Leuctra where Epaminondas con-centrated his best troops on the left.

3. πρὸς αἱμασιάν: 'behind a loose stone wall'. See Stroud, 242, for the location; as he says, the word, which is a homely one, occurs only here in Th.

καὶ ἐώσαντο μόλις: 'and shoved them back with some difficulty'. For the verb 'shove' here see J. F. Lazenby, 'The Killing Zone', in Hanson (ed.), *Hoplites*, 87–109, at 97; the noun for the act of shoving is ὠθισμός, which has been much discussed in arguments about what actually went on in a hoplite battle, see 96. 2 n. On the present passage see also Pritchett, *GSW* iv. 92.

ἦν γὰρ τὸ χωρίον πρόσαντες πᾶν: 'above a steep hill-side' [lit. 'for the whole place was steep']. Stroud 1971, 244, building on Sieveking (7 n. on Ἡιόνα etc.), 162 f., sees in the unusual imperfect here a sign that Th. interrogated a participant; otherwise Th. would have said 'the place *is* steep'. Cp. *Greek Historiography*, 165. For the possibility that what Th.

wrote was ἐπάναντες, see K. J. Dover, 'The Palatine Manuscript of Thucydides', *CQ* 4 (1954), 76–83, at 80 and 83. The meaning would be much the same.

παιανίσαντες: 'they raised the paean'. See 96. 1 n. on οἱ Βοιωτοί etc.

44. 1. ἦσαν γὰρ τοῖς Ἀθηναίοις οἱ ἱππῆς ὠφέλιμοι ξυμμαχό- μενοι, τῶν ἑτέρων οὐκ ἐχόντων ἵππους: 'the Athenians, who had the advantage of cavalry, whereas the Corinthians had none'. This parenthetical remark is a rare attestation by Th. of a cavalry achieve- ment in the Archidamian War (though see iii. 1. 2 n.); see Bugh (intro- ductory n. to 42–5), 90–3. It has been thought that the names of the hipparchs or cavalry commanders were Simon and Panaitios, who are mentioned in Aristophanes, *Knights* 242–3, and are said by the scholiast there to have been hipparchs. If so, Simon at least would be of great interest because under the name of Simon Hippikos ('Simon the horsey') he wrote a treatise on horsemanship and was the dedicatee of Xeno- phon's *On Horsemanship*. But Develin, *AO* 130, doubts whether the Aristophanic context allows us to say that they were real hipparchs.

4. τούτοις οὐ κατάδηλος ἡ μάχη ἦν ὑπὸ τοῦ ὄρους τοῦ Ὀνείου: 'could not see the battle because Mt. Oneion was in the way'. This, it is thought, shows that there was not yet a fort or observation post at Stanotopi, as there was later, in the fourth century: see R. S. Stroud, 'An Ancient Fort on Mt. Oneion', *Hesperia*, 40 (1971), 127–45, at 139.

κονιορτὸν δὲ ὡς εἶδον καὶ [ὡς] ἔγνωσαν: 'But when they saw the dust and realized what was going on'. See Hanson, *Western Way*, 147–8, for dust raised by armies, comparing e.g. Hdt. viii. 65; Plut. *Eum.* 16.

ἐβοήθησαν δὲ καὶ οἱ ἐκ τῆς πόλεως πρεσβύτεροι τῶν Κορινθίων αἰσθόμενοι τὸ γεγενημένον: 'The older men of Corinth also came out to help when they heard of the defeat'. Stroud 1994, 287, in course of an argument that Th. had special knowledge of Corinthian affairs, notes the specificity of this detail (with which cp. i. 105. 6).

6. τοὺς νεκροὺς οὓς ἐγκατέλιπον ... ἀνείλοντο: 'and recovered the two dead bodies which were missing' [Jowett has supplied the word 'two' from para. 5 above.]. For the importance of recovering the dead after a battle see generally chs. 97–8 below and nn. (the aftermath of Delion): incidents like these help to explain the Athenian feelings of outrage after the battle of Arginusai in 406, when the generals failed to pick up the dead: Xen. *Hell.* i. 6–7; Diod. xiii. 100 ff.

Plut. *Nikias* 6. 4–7 (perhaps merely an elaboration of Th., but possibly from the moralizing Ephorus) takes the present incident to show Nikias' piety because to ask for your dead was technically to admit defeat: Nikias was putting piety above success. But this cannot have comforted the

Corinthians much, so bad was their general situation. On this whole incident see P. Vaughn, 'Identification and Retrieval of Hoplite Battle Dead', in Hanson (ed.), *Hoplites*, 38–62, at 50, noting that 'the incident demonstrates the relative precision involved in the Athenians' reckoning of battle casualties'. But for the more usual chaotic position see Hanson, *Western Way*, 207.

ἀπέθανον δὲ Κορινθίων μὲν ἐν τῇ μάχῃ δώδεκα καὶ διακόσιοι, Ἀθηναίων δὲ ὀλίγῳ ἐλάσσους πεντήκοντα: 'The Corinthians lost two hundred and twelve men; the Athenians fewer than fifty'. See P. Krentz, 'Casualties in Hoplite Battles', *GRBS* 26 (1985), 13–20, at 16. The losses represent 2.5% of the winning Athenian side, and perhaps 12.1% of the losing Corinthian side (whose initial total has to be conjectured), compared to Krentz's averages of 5% for the winners and 14% for the losers.

As for the Athenian casualties, it used to be thought (see Gomme) that *IG* i³. 1184 (i². 949; *Syll.*³ 77) listed the casualties for 425, including Solygeia; but see the full arguments for 423 presented by D. Bradeen, 'The Athenian Casualty Lists', *CQ* 19 (1969), 145–59, at 151–4 (cp. below 103. 5 n. for Amphipolis and Argilos, and contrast 135. 1 n.); see also D. M. Lewis and D. Bradeen, 'Notes on Athenian Casualty Lists', *ZPE* 34 (1979), 240–6, at 242, and Pritchett, *GSW* iv. 194.

45. 2. ἐς Μέθανα τὴν μεταξὺ Ἐπιδαύρου καὶ Τροιζῆνος: 'to Methana, which is between Epidauros and Troizen'. For the volcanic Methana promontory see R. Baladié, *Le Péloponnèse de Strabon* (Paris, 1980; see i. 30. 2 n. on Κυλλήνην), 159 ff. Methana may have figured in an Athenian grand strategy which involved taking over the Megarid and using Epidauros (and Methana) as bridgeheads for offensives against the Peloponnese: see Lewis, *CAH* v². 388 and above, i. 67. 4 n.; also introductory n. to 66 ff. below.

Strabo 374 says that 'in some copies of Th., Μέθανα is spelt Μεθώνη'; he is presumably referring to the present ch. This is interesting evidence for the extent and closeness of Strabo's knowledge of Th., even though elsewhere he oddly prefers Ephorus for material available in Th.; see *Greek Historiography*, 56. On the text see Maurer *Interpolation*, 75 and n. 30: 'this is an abnormally convincing example of the kind of thing that caused Lewis, in his Princeton diss. [*Towards a Historian's Text*], to be suspicious of many place-names in Thuc. MSS; for they seem often 'corrected' (in the same way in which, today, a misspelling would be by an editor) to agree with Homeric scholarship.'

ἐλήστευον τὸν ἔπειτα χρόνον τήν τε Τροιζηνίαν γῆν: 'and continued for some time to devastate the territory of Troizen'. Troizen had been demanded back by the Athenians at Kleon's prompting earlier this summer, see 21. 3 n. on ἐλθόντων δέ etc. As a result, presumably, of the operations described in the present ch., Athens made definite territorial gains in Troizenian territory, see 118. 4 n. on καὶ τὰ ἐν Τροιζῆνι etc. And at some time between now and 423 (cp. next n. for Halieis) Athens made a separate agreement with Troizen, alluded to only at 118. 4, see n. there on καθ᾽ ἃ ξυνέθεντο etc. See M. H. Jameson, C. N. Runnels, and T. H. van Andel, *A Greek Countryside: the Southern Argolid from Prehistory to the Present Day* (Stanford, 1994), 78: 'Athens could force concessions for military use of Aktean territory [the area containing Troizen and Halieis, cp. next n.] because the local communities could not afford the constant damage to their crops and equipment.'

Ἁλιάδα: 'Halias' [the territory of Halieis]. Not long after this (424/3) the Athenians made an agreement with Halieis, *IG* i³. 88. See previous n.: as Jameson, Runnels, and van Andel say, 'Halieis, as much as Troizen, depended on its farmland for survival'.

From the absence in the present passage of Hermione from the list of places ravaged (contrast ii. 56. 5, describing events of 430), it has been ingeniously argued that Athens' treaty with Hermione, *SEG* x. 15, fell in 425 and explains the sparing of Hermione in 425. But this argument is not compelling, see B. D. Meritt and H. T. Wade-Gery, 'The Dating of Documents to the Mid-fifth Century, II', *JHS* 83 (1963), 100–17, at 103, replying to H. B. Mattingly, 'The Athenian Coinage Decree', *Historia*, 10 (1961), 148–88, at 173.

46–48. THE END OF THE CORCYRAEAN AFFAIR

This revolting piece of narrative immediately picks up the brief reference at 5. 2, but is really the first solid resumption of Corcyraean history since iii. 85. As in the book iii narrative (see iii. 81. 4 n.), Th. makes it clear that the Athenian commanders could have stopped the bloodshed if they had chosen to; and in the present section he adds that their attitude, which they did not conceal, made things worse, 47. 2. But the condemnation is not explicit.

46. 1. πολλὰ ἔβλαπτον: 'were doing a lot of damage'. See iii. 85. 3 for these oligarchs on Mt. Istone, who are there said to be inflicting 'death and destruction (ἔφθειρον) on the inhabitants of the city'.

4. οἱ δὲ τοῦ δήμου προστάται τῶν Κερκυραίων: 'the leaders of the Corcyrean democrats' [lit. the 'champions of the people']. For this expression see already iii. 75. 2, also about Corcyra (cp. ii. 65. 11 for 'championship of the people', ἡ τοῦ δήμου προστασία, in an Athenian context), and W. R. Connor, *The New Politicians of Fifth-Century Athens* (Princeton, 1971), 111–15 for discussion: the expression is commoner in Th. than δημαγωγός ('demagogue'), for which see 21. 3 n., and (Connor suggests) came in at Athens in the mid 420s.

47. 2. ὥστε ἀκριβῆ τὴν πρόφασιν γένεσθαι: 'This made the story convincing'. For πρόφασις see i. 23. 6 n.: here it must mean 'the excuse', the 'story' ('what was given out'); ἀκριβῆ means 'in conformity with reality', see i. 22. 1 n.

48. 1. ᾤοντο γὰρ αὐτοὺς μεταστήσοντάς ποι ἄλλοσε ἄγειν: they thought they were being taken somewhere else'. Multiple killing of prisoners, even when they are not armed, is difficult and may require deceit. For the same general idea on a more atrocious scale at Auschwitz see Primo Levi, *If This Is A Man* and *The Truce*, trans. S. Woolf (London, 1987), 'Afterword' at 388.

5. καὶ ἡ στάσις πολλὴ γενομένη ἐτελεύτησεν ἐς τοῦτο, ὅσα γε κατὰ τὸν πόλεμον τόνδε: 'the great revolution ended, at least for the duration of this war'. On the implications of this passage for the composition of Th.'s history see Dover, *HCT* v. 411. The problem is that Diod. xiii. 48. 1 mentions further *stasis* in 410/9. If Th. knew of this outbreak, the best explanation is that he wrote the present passage before and perhaps well before 410 and that he meant the Ten Years War by 'this war'. See, however, Introduction, 120, for other possibilities.

49. ATHENIAN CAPTURE OF ANAKTORION

Ἀνακτόριον Κορινθίων πόλιν ... ἔλαβον: 'made a successful expedition against Anaktorion, a Corinthian town'. See iii. 114. 3 n. As Salmon, *Wealthy Corinth*, 318, says, Corinth had now lost nearly everything on this coast-line.

50. THE ATHENIANS CAPTURE A PERSIAN EMISSARY

A rare glimpse of the Persian aspect to the Peloponnesian War, see Andrewes, 'Thucydides and the Persians', *Historia*, 10 (1961), 1–18, for Th.'s inadequate coverage of this topic; see further v. 1 n. on καὶ οἱ μὲν Δήλιοι etc.). For this disturbed phase of Persian history see Lewis, *Sparta and Persia*, 69 ff., calling it a 'Year of the Four Emperors' (see further below 3 n.), and above all M. Stolper, 'The Death of Artaxerxes I', *Arch. Mitt. aus Iran*, 16 (1983), 223–36, building and improving on Lewis, and more briefly in *CAH* vi². (1994), 237–8; also Pritchett, *TPOE* 174-7. On the Athenian aspect see A. E. Raubitschek, 'The Treaties Between Persia and Athens', *GRBS* 5 (1964), 151–9 (repr. in D. Obbink and P. A. Vander Waerdt, *The School of Hellas* (Oxford and New York, 1991), 3–10), at 156.

1. Ἀριστείδης ὁ Ἀρχίππου, εἷς τῶν ἀργυρολόγων νεῶν Ἀθηναίων στρατηγός: 'Aristides son of Archippos, one of the commanders of the money-collecting Athenian ships'. The other two were Demodokos and Lamachos, see 75. 1 and Fornara, *Generals*, 60, and Develin, *AO* 129.

For the money-collecting ships see ii. 69. 1 n. (the conclusion of which, however, I would now retract in light of a new treatment of the topic, see below). The rough coincidence in time between this mission and the reassessment of 425/4 (ML 69; see Introduction, above, p. 94) has always been one of the main arguments for the view that such 'money-collecting ships' (here, at ii. 69, and iii. 19) are to be associated with tribute reassessments. See, however, Kallet-Marx, 160–4, pointing out that this is the *only* one of the three Thucydidean occasions which can definitely be associated with a tribute reassessment; a candid reading of e.g. *ATL* iii.69–70 shows that the Thucydidean texts ii. 69 and iii. 19 have themselves exerted a powerful pull towards the dating (to, precisely, 430 and 428) of the two reassessments preceding that of 425. Those reassessments cannot therefore be used without circularity for the elucidation of Th. And although Th.'s word ἀργυρολόγος would, I continue to think, be *compatible* with the collection of tribute, Kallet-Marx is right to imply that it is tendentious actually to translate the prefix ἀργυρ- as 'tribute'—as do *ATL*, and as does Jowett, whom I have therefore changed. Warner fluctuates between 'money' (ii. 69, iv. 75) and 'tribute' (iii. 19, iv. 50). For the word ἀργυρολόγος as an adjective, in the same sense as Th., see Ar. *Knights* 1071. But the word was hardly technical, being a natural formation: it is found as a noun for an official at Samothrace: C. Habicht, *Chiron*, 24 (1994), 72 and n. 8.

Note also the compromise view of Lewis, *CAH* v². 5, apparently accepting that the expeditions here and at ii. 69 and iii. 19 had 'tribute-collecting' for their object, but wondering whether they were not 'regular annual events (cf. *Ath. Pol.* 24. 3), which Thucydides only reports when something of interest occurred'. (Cp. for a similar position Andrewes, *HCT* v. 362.) That is, Lewis suggests they were expeditions to extract tribute, but not specifically connected with reassessments.

See further iv. 75. 1 for the further adventures of these ships.

ἐν Ἠιόνι τῇ ἐπὶ Στρυμόνι: 'at Eion on the Strymon'. See 102. 3 n. on ὡρμῶντο etc.

2. οἱ Ἀθηναῖοι τὰς μὲν ἐπιστολὰς μεταγραψάμενοι ἐκ τῶν Ἀσσυρίων γραμμάτων ἀνέγνωσαν: 'the Athenians had his despatches translated and read. They were written in the Assyrian script'. In fact they were surely in Aramaic, see C. Nylander, 'ΑΣΣΥΡΙΑ ΓΡΑΜΜΑΤΑ: Remarks on the 21st "Letter of Themistocles"', *Opuscula Atheniensia*, 8 (1968), 119–36, at 122 n. 16, and J. A. O. Larsen, *CP* 53 (1958), 124 (review of Gomme), both correcting Gomme's view that they were in Old Persian cuneiform; see also Momigliano, *Alien Wisdom* (Cambridge, 1975), 9.

οὐ γιγνώσκειν ὅτι βούλονται: 'he could not understand what they wanted'. Perhaps this was indeed another manifestation of Spartan indecisiveness in foreign affairs, see Hodkinson (15. 2 n. on καὶ ὡς εἶδον etc.), 270. But it is also possible that Artaxerxes' protest was a diplomatic way of saying that if the Spartans wanted financial help (which was surely the object of the various embassies) they must make clear that they had no territorial claims in Asia Minor: see *Greek World*, 102.

3. τὸν δὲ Ἀρταφέρνην ὕστερον οἱ Ἀθηναῖοι ἀποστέλλουσι τριήρει ἐς Ἔφεσον: 'Later the Athenians sent Artaphernes in a trireme to Ephesos'. In translating ὕστερον, I have changed Jowett's tendentious and inaccurate 'shortly afterwards' to the vaguer 'later', in order to take account of Lewis, *Sparta and Persia*, 70 f., esp. 71 n. 140. See next n.

οἳ πυθόμενοι αὐτόθι βασιλέα Ἀρταξέρξην τὸν Ξέρξου νεωστὶ τεθνηκότα (κατὰ γὰρ τοῦτον τὸν χρόνον ἐτελεύτησεν): 'but they found that Artaxerxes the son of Xerxes had recently died; for he died about then'. About *when*? Lewis (introductory n.) discusses in detail the evidence of dated oriental documents, but his discussion has been superseded by that of Stolper 1983, who shows that Babylonian documents attest quite certainly that Artaxerxes I died in his forty-first regnal year, between December 424 and February 423. But Th. himself, by his mention of the eclipse of 52.1 (21 March 424) *after* his mention of Artaxerxes' death, has been thought to provide hard evidence for the king's death-date: the king must have died before 21 March 424. What then of the documents? Does Th. undermine them? The whole period was one of dynastic convulsion, and Lewis's preferred suggestion was that 'Artaxerxes' 41st year is in part or whole a chronological device protracted after his death to cover uncertainties about the succession'. That is, the oriental evidence could (Lewis thought) be forced into agreement with the assumed implications of Th., so as to produce a death-date earlier than 21 March 424. But from other Babylonian evidence Stolper 1983, 229–30, refutes this idea that year 41 of Artaxerxes was a fictional device; the better view (Stolper 1983, 230, taking his cue from the alternative offered at Lewis, 71 n. 140) is that Artaxerxes did indeed die in his 41st year and that the supposed argument from Th. is unsound: Th. is capable of giving material 'far beyond its chronological context'; cp. Andrewes, *HCT* v. 366, giving the present passage as an example of 'breaches of chronological order'. (Lewis, approved by Stolper 1983, 230 n. 38, compares iii. 68. 3 on Plataia; another example would be vii. 28. 2 on the results of the fortification of Decelea.) The king did indeed survive many months after 22 April 424 and thus into his 41st regnal year as conventionally computed. But there is no contradiction with Th. Stolper, 230–1, correctly puts it as follows:

> the most important issue is Thucydides. He is not in error, but he has been misunderstood. As Lewis suggests [this refers to *Sparta and Persia*, 71 n. 140], Thucydides has introduced a chronological parenthesis. The arrest of Artaphernes was duly entered in the sequential narrative as the first event of 425/4 BC. But the episode of Artaphernes and the Athenian mission to the Persian court proved to be without significant consequences or stages of development. Consequently, Thucydides narrates the whole episode at once, start to finish: Artaphernes was arrested in the winter before the eclipse; 'later' he was sent as far as Ephesus, where the story ended. The parenthesis beginning 'later' is actually fixed in time by reference to the king's death, which took place about a year later. Having completed the Artaphernes anecdote, Thucydides returns to his sequential narrative of the winter in which Artaphernes was arrested, then of the eclipse in March 424. The date of the king's death is not the aim of the narration. It is an assumed datum which closes the parenthesis beginning with the word 'later'.

Note finally that Stolper, 231–2, removes from the whole discussion the text discussed at Lewis, 72 n. 145, namely BM 33342, which appeared to show Darius II on the throne as early as August 424. The tablet has been misread: the true date is in March 423.

There are, it is true, historical difficulties about the new view. In particular, it is a consequence of Stolper's dating that the Athenians must be supposed to have waited nearly a year before sending their ambassadors to Ephesus with Artaphernes. Why should they have waited so long? We could follow up and adapt a suggestion of Lewis (*Sparta and Persia*, 77) and argue that the Athenians felt newly vulnerable after Delion (autumn 424), and so decided to approach Persia once again; see Introduction, p. 101 and n. 251.

The Athenian embassy has a bearing on the problem, when did Athens begin to support Amorges? (See i. 112. 2–4 n.) Surely not until after this embassy, which presupposes normal if not actually friendly relations between Athens and Persia, see Raubitschek (introductory n.), who thinks that the Athenians were 'shocked' (this is surely too strong, if it implies surprise) to hear that Sparta was trying to negotiate aid from Persia. There was in any case a rather less securely attested Athenian embassy sent, in 424/3, to renegotiate the Peace of Kallias, see ML 70 and comm., also Lewis in *Sparta and Persia*.

For Th.'s mention of Artaxerxes' death see 101. 5 n. on ἀπέθανε etc. giving other instances where he records deaths of non-Greeks.

51. THE CHIANS DISMANTLE THEIR NEW WALLS ON ATHENS' ORDERS

For this episode see J. Barron in J. Boardman and C. E. Vaphopoulou-Richardson, *Chios* (Oxford, 1986), 89–103 at 100 ff. Chios had been loyal in the war hitherto, see ii. 56. 2 and n. (military help). But after the suppression of the Mytilenean Revolt the Chians were, as Barron puts it, 'exposed as Athens' only remaining substantial naval ally'. What had aroused Athenian suspicions? Some Chians make payments to the Spartan war fund, on the evidence of ML 67 = Fornara 132, line 9, and if this inscription could be dated to 427 beyond any doubt, and the payments were made by 'a pro-Spartan party in Chios', that would, as ML say, help to explain Athenian suspicions in 425/4. But as we have seen (iii. 32. 2 n.), there are other possible dates for this inscription (B. Bleckmann, 'Sparta und seine Freunde im Dekeleischen Krieg: zur Datierung von IG v.i.i', *ZPE* 96 (1993), 297–308, argues for a date in the Ionian War; as does M. Piérart, 'Chios entre Athènes et Sparte', *BCH* 119 (1995), 253–82. It seems that the Chians of ML 67 were in exile, see ML (1989: paperback repr. of the 1988 edn.), addenda. Even exiled Chians could be relevant to Athens' alarm about the new Chian walls, if the exiles had allies in Chios itself: Loomis (8. 9 n.), 72 and 82. But perhaps no special explanation need be sought, beyond what Th. tells us (the new walls), for Athens' action; see n. below on τεῖχος etc. Piérart presses viii. 24 (Chios *stasis*-free before 411) very hard.

For further speculation see Barron, 101, suggesting that the writer Ion of Chios (for whom see K. J. Dover, in the same volume, 23–37) tipped Athens off. There is another possibly relevant inscription, *IG* i³. 70, Athenian honours to some Chian friends. Meritt, *Hesperia*, 14 (1945), 115–19, connected this with the present passage of Th., and Barron prefers this view to Lewis's scepticism in *IG*, partly because the word πίστεις, 'pledges', occurs both in Th. (see n. below) and in *IG* i³. 70.

H. Mattingly, 'Coins and Amphoras—Chios, Samos and Thasos in the Athenian Empire', *JHS* 101 (1981), 78–86 at 80 and n. 18, tries to relate the events of 425/4 and the changes in the sizes of Chian jars of the period; he sees one group of jars holding *either* 9 Chian *or* 8 Attic *choes* as evidence of Chian tact. (The Athenian decree ML 45 = Fornara 97, see 52. 3 n. on τάς τε, regulated allied use of weights and measures.)

For the possibility that the Athenian order of 425 was in Aristotle's mind when he spoke in the *Politics* of the 'humbling' of Chios, see i. 19 n.

τὸ τεῖχος . . . τὸ καινόν: 'their new walls'. As Barron says, the insurrectionist Mytilenean moves described at iii. 2 had included the building of walls; perhaps this action alone was considered tantamount to intended revolt. For the importance of walls in Th. see i. 2. 2 n.

τι νεωτεριεῖν: 'to rebel'. See below, n. on μηδέν etc.

ποιησάμενοι μέντοι πρὸς Ἀθηναίους πίστεις καὶ βεβαιότητα ἐκ τῶν δυνατῶν: 'But they first extracted from the Athenians the most reliable pledges and assurances they could get'. The word πίστεις, 'pledges', occurs at *IG* i³. 70 line 11, and since this is an Athenian decree honouring Chians, it is tempting to associate it with the present passage of Th., see introductory n. Piérart 262 f. prefers the very different tr. of Meiggs, AE 359: 'their leading men [δυνατοί] gave security that they would not change their policy towards Athens'. But see next n.

The Chians are docile when next heard of, providing ships for Athens against Mende and Skione at 129. 2. See n. there.

μηδὲν περὶ σφᾶς νεώτερον βουλεύσειν: 'to protect themselves against any sudden change in their position'. Here νεώτερον [lit. 'something new'] must refer to actions performed by the Athenians, whereas earlier in the sentence the related verb referred to hypothetical actions performed by the *Chians*, see n. on τι νεωτεριεῖν. But Gomme is surely right that this is how σφᾶς must be taken. *Contra*, Piérart (above).

On the reassessment of tribute in 425/4 BC, an item which Th. does not mention, see above, Introduction, pp. 94–8.

52. ANTI-ATHENIAN ACTIVITY BY REFUGEES FROM LESBOS

1. τοῦ τε ἡλίου ἐκλιπές τι ἐγένετο . . . καὶ . . . ἔσεισεν: 'there was a partial eclipse of the sun . . . there was an earthquake'. See i. 23. 3 n.:

Th. juxtaposes, but does not connect, the two phenomena, but the juxta-position tempts his readers to make a connection.

The eclipse is datable to 21 March 424.

2. καὶ οἱ Μυτιληναίων φυγάδες: 'the refugees who had escaped from Mytilene'. The narrative of iii. 50 is here resumed, but—despite '*the* refugees'—there was no specific mention of refugees in the Mytilene section of book iii. But no doubt they were people whose political sympathies (whether or not explicitly oligarchic as Classen/Steup suggest) meant that life in Mytilene was intolerable for them after the settlement imposed by Athens. The cleruchs of iii. 50 do not feature in the present ch., and this has (see n. there) been invoked as an argument that they were non-resident. But their absence from the military narrative in the present brief passage can be explained in various ways; perhaps any garrison was withdrawn, or perhaps they did act on the present occasion, but so ineffectively that Th. did not think it worth mentioning them. It is naïve to suppose that because Th. does not mention a particular group it does not exist, just as we should not assume that events Th. does not mention did not happen. The forthcoming publication by K. Hallof and C. Habicht in *Ath. Mitt.* of a Samian inscription dating from the mid fourth century, listing members of a 250-man *boule* or council of the Samian cleruchy, somewhat increases the probability that such cleruchs were basically resident.

αἱροῦσι Ῥοίτειον: 'took Rhoiteion'. For the site see J. M. Cook, *The Troad* (Oxford, 1973), 77 ff., 'The Rhoetean Coast', esp. 87 f.

δισχιλίους στατῆρας Φωκαΐτας: 'two thousand Phokaian staters'. Characteristically (see i. 63. 2 n.) Th. does not attempt to translate this sum into Attic or any other equivalent, although he purports to be writing for posterity, i. 22. 4.

The sum named seems to have amounted to 8 talents which (it has been suggested) was 'precisely the assessment' of Rhoiteion's tribute in 425 (*ATL* ii. 82, iii. 88), i.e. the Mytilenean exiles were helping themselves to Rhoiteion's tribute (as *ATL* put it, 'it looks very much as if the Mytilenaians timed their raids perfectly, and made off with Rhoiteion's tribute just when it had been gathered together for transportation to Athens'). But as Gomme already noted, the figure for Rhoiteion's tribute is no more than probable (all the stone has is ..TT, i.e. 2 talents, and this could be restored as 4 or 8), i.e. there is some circularity in the argument; for a much stronger attack see now Kallet-Marx, 155–9, suggesting other possible restorations of the assessment, and even doubting whether it relates to Rhoiteion at all (the name as well as the amount is restored). There seems no doubt that the authors of *ATL* were carried away by the neatness of their own argument. See above, Introduction, p. 7. In any case the figure of 2000 may be suspicious, see 80. 4 n.

Kallet-Marx (156) suggests that these exiles were trying to do what Alkidas had been urged to do at iii. 31, and that Th. relates the present incident in such detail as an 'intended and pointed' comparison; the money side, she suggests, is stressed because such naval plans were expensive. At the same time the present ch. prepares us for ch. 75, note esp. παρασκευάζεσθαι ἔμελλον at para. 3 below, and n. there.

3. καὶ μετὰ τοῦτο ἐπὶ Ἄντανδρον στρατεύσαντες: 'They then made an expedition against Antandros'. For Antandros, the hill-top site of which has long been fixed by epigraphic finds, see J. M. Cook (above, para. 2 n.), 267–71, calling it (269) a 'citadel of great strength and little amenity'; it commanded the important coastal road along the south coast of the Troad, from Adramyttion to Assos, cp. *ATL* i. 468. Antandros' tribute assessment is restored as 15 talents in 425 (ML 69), which if correct is evidence of wealth; the 421 assessment is said to be 8 talents, still a large sum. But it must be said that the assessment totals of these 'Aktaian cities' (see iii. 50. 3 n.) like Antandros and Rhoiteion are to an unusual degree based on conjecture (for Rhoiteion see para. 2 n. on δισχιλίους etc.). Neither place features on any tribute quota list as having actually paid; they are merely restored on two assessment lists, and the amounts are highly precarious, see Kallet-Marx, 157–8.

Antandros gave the Athenians trouble again in 411, see viii. 108. 4, with Andrewes's n. in *HCT*.

In *c.*410 the grateful Antandrians gave rights of potential citizenship to the Syracusans who had helped them with their fortifications, Xen. *Hell.* i. 1. 26, with W. Gawantka, '*Isopoliteia*', *Vestigia*, 22 (1975), 173–4. The Judgement of Paris happened on the mountain above Antandros (Cook, 270, for details).

For the Athenian recapture of Antandros see below, 75. 1.

τάς τε ἄλλας πόλεις τὰς Ἀκταίας καλουμένας: 'the so-called Aktaian cities' [lit. 'cities of the coast']. See iii. 50. 3 n., dealing with events of 427. To that note add now a ref. to the fragment of the coinage decree (ML 45) recently found at Hamaxitos, for which see H. B. Mattingly, 'New Light on the Athenian Standards Decree (*ATL* ii. D14)', *Klio*, 75 (1993), 99–102. Hamaxitos, for which see viii. 101. 3 and n., was one of the 'Aktaian cities'. Its appearance in a fragment of the decree makes more likely a date for the main decree in the 420s (because the place was not in the Athenian empire before then) rather than the ML date in the 440s. The alternative, recognized by Mattingly, is that as and when new places were added to the empire they were made to put up copies of the decree. See further 109. 3 n. on Olophyxos for the Aristophanic argument, which always indicated the 420s.

καὶ κρατυνάμενοι αὐτήν: 'which they wanted to strengthen'. This corresponds to κατασκευάζεσθαι at 75. 1, see n. there and below, n. on παρασκευάζεσθαι etc.

αὐτόθεν ξύλων ὑπαρχόντων καὶ τῆς Ἴδης ἐπικειμένης: 'Mount Ida was near and would provide timber for ship-building'. This region continued to be timber-rich, and so important, throughout Greco-Roman antiquity, cp. e.g. Xen. *Hell.* ii. 1. 10. See esp. M. Rostovtzeff, 'Notes on the Economic Policy of the Pergamene Kings', in W. H. Buckler and W. M. Calder (eds.), *Anatolian Studies Presented to W. M. Ramsay* (Manchester, 1923), 359–90, at 365: 'The possession of, or the command over, the region around Mount Ida was a question of life and death for the Pergamene kingdom, as Ida was the main, if not the only, source of timber and pitch for the shipbuilding activity of the Pergamene kings.' Hence (as Rostovtzeff says) the Attalid fortress of Philetairia on the slopes of Ida. (Strabo 606 mentions a timber-market there, and says (603) that King Attalos I of Pergamon wrote about a beautiful pine tree in the region.) For pitch see the Elder Pliny, *Natural History* xiv. 128. See generally D. Magie, *Roman Rule in Asia Minor* (Princeton, 1950), 1, 43 and n. 23; R. B. McShane, *The Foreign Policy of the Attalids of Pergamum* (Urbana, 1964), 56, 88, 167 n. 88, and R. Meiggs, *Trees and Timber in the Ancient Mediterranean World* (Oxford, 1982), 357, cp. 332. Meiggs (108) points out that Ida provided some of the wood for Patroklos' funeral pyre in Homer, see *Iliad* xxiii. 117 ff. See also R. Janko, commentary on *Iliad* xiv. 157–8.

τὰ ἐν τῇ ἠπείρῳ Αἰολικὰ πολίσματα: 'the Aiolian fortresses on the mainland'. In Th., a *polisma* (the termination -μα stresses the physical aspect, i.e. the buildings of the place, cp. LSJ) is said to be either (i) a city of non-Greeks or (ii) a fortified place. See Zahrnt, 60 n. 37, and Hansen, forthcoming. But we should not make Th. too precise: see 54. 1 n. for Skandeia, which is called by both names in very similar contexts; and see 78. 6 n. for Dion, which is called a *polisma* but is not obviously (i) or (ii). See also 103. 5 n. for Amphipolis at 103. 5. The whole topic is discussed, with reference to the *polismata* of the Bottiaians (Th. i. 65. 2), by Pernille Flensted-Jensen in a valuable appendix to an article on 'The Bottiaians and their *Poleis*', in M. H. Hansen and K. Raaflaub (eds.), *Studies in the Ancient Greek Polis* (*Historia Einzelschrift* 95, 1995), 103–32, at 129–32. She concludes, correctly, that the word does *not* (as is sometimes thought) mean 'small towns' but places which were either barbarian or located in border areas. The Aiolian fortresses in the present passage are, she thinks, an example of such Hellenic towns in border areas. Of

Skandeia in ch. 54 she suggests that it belongs to a small category of places which were admittedly 'Hellenic towns in the middle of Greece' but which were *dependent poleis*. She compares Prasiai in Lakonia (ii. 56. 6) and the towns in Doris, i. 107. 2. But even the barbarian/border areas/ dependent *poleis* taxonomy is too limited in view of the description of (part of?) Amphipolis as a *polisma* (iv. 103. 5 and see n. there): Amphipolis is certainly a *polis* at 102. 2 and the 103. 5 usage seems to be more geographically restricted, the 'citadel' as Pritchett says.

παρασκευάζεσθαι ἔμελλον: 'that was the plan'. Picked up by similar-*sounding* words at 75. 1 (see n. there), esp. μελλούσης κατασκευάζεσθαι, although the key *thought* there expressed, namely 'strengthen', corresponds to καὶ κρατυνάμενοι in the present ch., see above.

53–57. ATHENIAN EXPEDITION AGAINST KYTHERA

Kythera, the birth-place of Aphrodite, is the island off the southern tip of Lakonia, the nut almost caught between the crackers of Capes Malea (Matapan) and Tainaron. The Spartans colonized Kythera relatively late, see I. Malkin, 'Colonisation spartiate dans la mer égée: tradition et archéologie', *REA* 95 (1993), 365–81, at 379–80, and *Myth and Territory in the Spartan Mediterranean* (Cambridge, 1994), 82. For Kythera generally see J. N. Coldstream and G. L. Huxley (eds.), *Kythera: Excavations and Studies Conducted by the University of Pennsylvania Museum and the British School at Athens* (London, 1972). For Nikias' 424 campaign see Huxley's ch. 2, 'The History and Topography of Ancient Kythera', at 38. The present section of Th., esp. ch. 53, is a key text on Kythera's importance to Sparta, but see also Hdt. vii. 235 (which, though it purports to show the value already placed on Kythera by mid-sixth-century Sparta, may actually have been written under the influence of the events described in the present passage of Th., see C. W. Fornara, 'Evidence for the Date of Herodotus' Publication', *JHS* 91 (1971), 25–34, at 33–4, with *Hermes* 109 (1981), 151. Hostile occupation of Kythera in the late 390s (soon after the domestically alarming conspiracy of Kinadon, Xen. *Hell.* iii. 3), by a force under the Persian satrap Pharnabazos and the Athenian Konon, pressurized the Spartans into the dramatic change of foreign policy whereby they finally abandoned claims to Asia Minor, Lewis, *Sparta and Persia*, 144. See also below vii. 26. 2 (413): the risk, in the Peloponnesian War as in the 390s, was always that Kythera would become a sanctuary for disaffected helots. Th. brings out this aspect more clearly at vii. 26 than in the ostensibly more generalizing iv. 53.

53. 1. καὶ τῶν ξυμμάχων Μιλησίους καὶ ἄλλους τινάς: 'Milesian and other allied forces'. The only reason for singling out the Milesians seems to be that they constituted a large force and played a large part in the military operations, 54. 1.

ἐστρατήγει δὲ αὐτῶν Νικίας ὁ Νικηράτου καὶ Νικόστρατος ὁ Διιτρέφους καὶ Αὐτοκλῆς ὁ Τολμαίου: 'The commanders were Nikias son of Nikeratos, Nikostratos son of Diitrephes, and Autokles son of Tolmaios'. All three recur at 119. 2 as precisely the three *strategoi* who swore to the 423 truce on behalf of Athens. For Nikias (the famous Nikias) see iii. 51. 1 and iv. 27. 5 nn. For Nikostratos see iii. 75. 1 n., and for Autokles see ML 77 line 16 (he was *strategos* again in 418/17). On the order of names see 119. 2 n. on Ἀθηναίων δὲ οἱ στρατηγοί etc.: it happens to be the official tribal order, but I think that is chance.

On the correct form of the name Diitrephes see iii. 75. 1 n., but see also Dover, *CQ* 1954, 81: Dietrephes (Διετρεφοῦς) may be what Th. actually wrote, here and elsewhere. For Diitrephes see also N. Dunbar, *Aristophanes: Birds* (Oxford, 1995), on line 798.

2. Λακεδαιμόνιοι δ᾽ εἰσὶ τῶν περιοίκων: 'it is inhabited by Spartan perioikoi'. For perioikoi see i.101. 2 n. on καὶ τῶν περιοίκων etc., and iv. 8. 1 n.

κυθηροδίκης ἀρχή: 'an officer, the Kytherodikes' [lit. 'officer, the judge of Kythera']. I have deleted Jowett's insertion of the word 'called' ('an officer *called* the judge of Kythera') so as to bring out the bald way Th. introduces this technical term, which he does, however, go on to explain; see *Thucydides*, 97. See Ridley, *Hermes* 1981, 32. Contrast the treatment of Skandeia at 54. 2 below, 'one of the ... cities called Skandeia'.

For the Kytherodikes see D. M. MacDowell, *Spartan Law* (Edinburgh, 1986), 30, seeing it as essentially non-military. The office is not attested epigraphically before its revival in the 130's AD, for which see *SEG* xi. 492. 13 with K. Arafat, *Pausanias' Greece* (1996), 164; there is, however, a dedication at Kythera by 'Menander the harmost [military governor]' to the Tyndaridai (i.e. the Dioskouroi, Castor and Pollux), *IG* v. 937 = Michel, *Recueil d'inscriptions grecques* (Brussels, 1891-1927), no. 1078 (first half of the fourth century; this man is obviously a Spartan, but note Xen. *Hell.* iv. 8. 8: Pharnabazos and Konon instal an *Athenian* called Nikophemos as harmost on Kythera during their brief period of control in 393). See Ed. Meyer, *Theopomps Hellenika* (Halle, 1909), 269 f. n. 3. The relation of this Kytheran harmost to the Kytherodikes is unclear. By the fourth century, as Meyer says, Kythera had been in enemy hands for some years and Sparta perhaps treated it on its recovery 'like other conquered parts of the Athenian empire', giving it a harmost *instead* of the old Kytherodikes: it does not follow, from the inscription, that the old Kytherodikes was really a sub-species of harmost, a word known to Th., see viii. 5. 2. That is, the fourth-century occurrence of 'harmost' in a Kytheran context does not show Th. to have been *either* incorrect in talking about a Kytherodikes *or* misleading in not saying that the Kytherodikes was a kind of harmost. So much for the assumption that the fourth-century harmost replaced the fifth-century Kytherodikes. (MacDowell is right on this.) It may, however, be (Meyer again) that in Th.'s time, as in the fourth century, there was a harmost in charge of the garrison, working *alongside* the Kytherodikes. Again, Th. cannot reasonably be criticized for not saying so. His reason for mentioning the Kytherodikes is to bring out the peculiar relation of Kythera to Sparta; harmosts were not peculiar.

ἐκ τῆς Σπάρτης: 'from Sparta'. I have changed Jowett's 'a Spartan officer', the implication of which, made explicit by Gomme in his n., is that the officer was a Spartiate as opposed to a perioikos of the kind just mentioned. No doubt he was a Spartiate, but Gomme is surely wrong to say that this is the implication of the Greek phrase equivalent to 'from Sparta'. For ἡ Σπάρτη, 'Sparta', in a purely geographical sense see e.g. iv. 15. 1.

κατὰ ἔτος: 'every year'. See MacDowell, above n. on κυθηροδίκης etc.: this may mean either that the office was held by a different man each year, or that one assize was held each year, or probably both.

ὁπλιτῶν τε φρουρὰν διέπεμπον αἰεί: 'The Spartans kept there a garrison of hoplites. This was regularly replaced'. The garrison may have been commanded by a harmost, see n. above on κυθηροδίκης etc.

3. ἦν γὰρ αὐτοῖς τῶν τε ἀπ' Αἰγύπτου καὶ Λιβύης ὁλκάδων προσβολή: 'Kythera was important to them because merchant ships from Egypt and Libya used to put in there'. Huxley, *Kythera*, 33, produces evidence (including a vase bearing the name of a mid-third-millennium Pharaoh) to show that Kythera's importance as a port of call goes back to Minoan times and earlier.

For Th.'s occasional awareness of the importance, in the Archidamian war, of securing the sea lanes for merchant traffic see ii. 69. 1 and n.

For προσβολή as a place where ships put in see Andrewes, *HCT* on viii. 35. 1, discussing the verb προσβάλλω in naval contexts.

καὶ λῃσταὶ ἅμα τὴν Λακωνικὴν ἧσσον ἐλύπουν ἐκ θαλάσσης, ᾗπερ μόνον οἷόν τε ἦν κακουργεῖσθαι: 'and also as protection, because the only way in which Lakonia was physically vulnerable was from piratical attacks by sea'. Aigina, though distant to the north, may have been one base for such raiding, see ii. 27. 1 n., citing Figueira.

54. 1. καὶ δισχιλίοις Μιλησίων ὁπλίταις: 'and two thousand Milesian hoplites'. A large total, which may explain the separate mention

of the Milesians at 53. 1, see n. there. The Milesian allies are not, however, used for the main attack, only for the 'feint' (Huxley, 38) against Skandeia; were they not entirely to be trusted?

τὴν ἐπὶ θαλάσσῃ πόλιν Σκάνδειαν καλουμένην: 'one of the coastal cities called Skandeia'. Skandeia does, but the Kytherodikes (53. 2 n.) does not, qualify for an apologetic 'so-called'; para. 4 unnecessarily repeats, more or less, the location of Skandeia. On 'called' and 'so-called' in Th. see *Greek Historiography*, 162 and n. 81. Skandeia is here called a *polis*, but at para. 4 below, in a very similar context, it is a *polisma*; see 52. 3 n. on καὶ τὰ ἐν τῇ ἠπείρῳ Αἰολικὰ πολίσματα.

ἐχώρουν ἐπὶ τὴν [ἐπὶ θαλάσσῃ] πόλιν τῶν Κυθηρίων: 'marched against the city of the Kytherians'. The words in square brackets would mean that the city was 'on the sea-shore', and were rightly deleted by Krüger, with whom Huxley (38) agrees: they are repeated from the description of Skandeia four lines earlier. I have changed Jowett's translation accordingly, but it is possible that the corruption is more extensive and a place name has dropped out.

For the topography of this campaign see Huxley, 38, and the maps in *Kythera*. The Athenians perhaps landed at Diakophti, and then moved against Palaiokastro ('the city of the Kytherians') not from the steeper eastern side, but by going initially north of the city and then up the easier slopes to the west. For new excavations at Palaiokastro see I. Petrocheilos, *Ergon* 1993, 77–80.

2. καὶ ὕστερον ξυνέβησαν πρὸς Νικίαν: 'Later they surrendered to Nikias'. Huxley remarks of this that the eagerness of the Kytherians to capitulate suggests that the city may not have been strongly fortified; in which case (Huxley, 39) the surviving defensive system must be later, perhaps early fourth-century. Certainly it seems to be a 'Geländemauer' or contour-hugging circuit of a kind characteristic of that century, see S. Hornblower, *Mausolus* (Oxford, 1982), 298 with n. 31, and references.

4. τήν τε Σκάνδειαν τὸ ἐπὶ τῷ λιμένι πόλισμα: 'Skandeia, the fortified place near the harbour'. See 1 n. on τὴν ἐπὶ θαλάσσῃ etc.

ἔς τε Ἀσίνην καὶ Ἕλος: 'Asine, Helos'. This is more likely to be the Lakonian Asine (mentioned by Strabo 363 in the same breath as Gytheion) than to be that mentioned at 13. 1, see n. there. It is, as Gomme says, surprising that Th. does not distinguish the two places, but it does not follow that, as Gomme thinks, the text is corrupt.

Helos, somewhere east of the mouth of the river Eurotas (the site has not been exactly located), is already mentioned in the Homeric Catalogue of Ships, *Iliad* ii. 584, as an ἔφαλον πτολίεθρον, a 'city on the sea'. The ancient derivation of 'helot' from Helos, which was an early

Spartan conquest, is quite uncertain; a likelier root is the verb meaning 'to capture'.

C. Falkner, 'A Note on Sparta and Gytheum in the Fifth Century', *Historia*, 43 (1994), 495–501, comments that Gytheion was *not* attacked, and uses this to support her argument that Gytheion was not as navally important to Sparta in the fifth century as sometimes assumed.

55. *Low Spartan morale*

This is the second of the six excursuses on morale in iv–v. 24, see Introduction, p. 109 above. It most obviously resumes iv. 41, and anticipates 80 and v. 14. 3, but there is also a clear relation to the fourth excursus (iv. 108), see 55. 1 n. on Πύλου etc.; Classen/Steup, discussing ch. 108, note that it is a sort of [Athenian] counterpart, 'eine Art Gegenstück', to the account of low Spartan morale in ch. 55.

55. 1. φοβούμενοι μὴ σφίσι νεώτερόν τι γένηται τῶν περὶ τὴν κατάστασιν: 'because they were afraid of internal revolution'. See the more specific 41. 3, where the helots are mentioned. For 'fearing'-words in the excursuses see Introduction, above, p. 109.

γεγενημένου μὲν τοῦ ἐν τῇ νήσῳ πάθους ἀνελπίστου καὶ μεγάλου: 'They had suffered a severe and unexpected blow at Sphakteria'. Lit. 'on the island'.

Πύλου δὲ ἐχομένης καὶ Κυθήρων: 'Pylos and Kythera were in the hands of the Athenians'. Cp. (as well as 80. 2 for Πύλου ἐχομένης) 108. 1 ἐχομένης δὲ τῆς Ἀμφιπόλεως, 'now that Amphipolis was in enemy hands', and introductory n. above.

2. ὥστε παρὰ τὸ εἰωθὸς ἱππέας τετρακοσίους κατεστήσαντο καὶ τοξότας: 'unusually for them, they now raised a force of four hundred cavalry and archers'. For the normally low quality of Spartan cavalry see Xen. *Hell.* vi. 4. 19 (371, the Battle of Leuktra).

πρὸς Ἀθηναίους, οἷς τὸ μὴ ἐπιχειρούμενον αἰεὶ ἐλλιπὲς ἦν τῆς δοκήσεώς τι πράξειν: 'the Athenians, in whose eyes not to attempt a thing was to fall short of their expectations of achievement' (Gomme). This, as Jowett and Gomme note, is very close to the spirit of i. 70, esp. para. 7; but note that there as here the judgement is not Th.'s own. There he was putting thoughts into the mouths of the Corinthians, and here, into the minds of the Spartans. But the judgement at viii. 96. 5 *is* authorial and shows that Th.'s view was in fact close to that expressed in the present passage.

3. οἷα καὶ ἐν τῇ νήσῳ: 'like that on Sphakteria' [lit. 'on the island']. See 1 n. on γεγενημένου etc.

56. 1. περὶ Κοτύρταν καὶ Ἀφροδιτίαν: 'in the neighbourhood of Kotyrta and Aphrodisia'. Both these are perioikic places, whose location is not securely identified; but Gomme is wrong to say that only Aphrodisia (Th. uses the Doric form Aphroditia) is mentioned elsewhere (at Paus. iii. 22. 11): for Kotyrta, perhaps modern Daimonia, see the entry under that name in Stephanus of Byzantium (citing Th.); *SEG* ii. 173–5 and xi. 899 are from K. but do not name it.

2. ἐς Ἐπίδαυρον τὴν Λιμηράν: 'to Epidauros Limera'. Very close to modern Monemvasia; originally a colony of the better-known Epidauros, but by this time a perioikic dependency of Sparta.

Θυρέαν: 'Thyrea'. Much of what follows, about the Aiginetans settled in Thyreatis by Sparta, and the reasons for the settlement, is repeated closely from ii. 27; see nn. there, and note Andrewes, *HCT* v.364, for this repetition as a possible indication of incompleteness in the Ten Years War narrative; he thinks Th. might have eliminated it. See above, p. 119.

ἥ ἐστι μὲν τῆς Κυνουρίας γῆς καλουμένης: 'which is situated in the country called Kynouria'. For Kynouria, between Argos and Sparta, see Pieske, *RE* xii. 1, 42–3. Cartledge, *Sparta and Lakonia*, index, treats it as synonymous with Thyreatis.

57. 3. ὅσοι μὴ ἐν χερσὶ διεφθάρησαν: 'all the Aiginetans who had not been killed in the battle'. This episode appears unknown to Hdt., vi. 91. 1, and this led Jacoby, *RE* suppl. 2, 232, to conclude that Hdt.'s work was complete before 424; see also J. A. S. Evans, 'Herodotus' Publication Date', *Athenaeum*, 57 (1979), 145–9; above, Introduction, p. 145.

4. καὶ τοὺς ἄλλους Κυθηρίους οἰκοῦντας τὴν ἑαυτῶν φόρον τέσσαρα τάλαντα φέρειν: 'they allowed the other Kytherians to live in their own country, paying a tribute of four talents'. A large tribute, which may reflect the prosperity of Kythera through the trade in purple dye. Modern Kythera is very poor, and has lost much of its population through emigration to Australia. Kythera's four talents of tribute are restored at *IG* i³ 287. Kallet-Marx (159–60) notes that the levying of tribute on Kythera, 'a Lakedaimonian [better, perioikic] city, was an unprecedented act' and testimony to Athens' strength and Sparta's weakness at this time. Note that the singularity of Kythera's status helps to explain why Th., unusually, gives a hard detail about tribute.

Kallet-Marx (182) detects here a new sort of Athenian imperial pattern: tributary but non-allied status. See v. 18. 5 n. on τὰς δὲ πόλεις etc.

58-65. THE CONFERENCE AT GELA

A 'conference'—but we are given only one speech, see 58 n. on ἄλλαι τε πολλαί ... The Gela conference (which picks up the Sicilian narrative left at ch. 25) may have brought to a close the Sicilian history of Th.'s contemporary Antiochus of Syracuse, *FGrHist* 555; if so, Gela and Hermokrates' speech may already have featured in local tradition as epoch-making events even before Th. got hold of them. This would not guarantee the details of Th.'s version of the speech (which has often been thought to show knowledge of the Athenian invasion of 415, see esp. 60. 2 n.), but it *would* mean that the framework was authentic and that Th. was right to insist, by the length of his coverage, on the importance of the episode. These chapters are not, then, quite free invention. Note, however, that, if (as is often thought) Athenagoras has Hermokrates in mind when in 415 he denounces youthful politicians at vi. 38. 5, Th. has antedated the prominence of Hermokrates in 424, see *Thucydides*, 56 and n. 41. The fact that Timaeus (see below) also gave prominence to Hermokrates' speech does not prove that Th. was right to make Hermokrates prominent: Timaeus, who wrote much later than Th., may have taken from Th. the 'fact' that Hermokrates spoke at all.

Polybius xii. 25 (= *FGrHist* 566 F 22) says that Timaeus also handled the conference, but that he gave Hermokrates more of the kind of generalizing, about the preferability of peace to war, that Th. passes over rapidly at chs. 59 and 62. It is revealing, about ancient attitudes to speeches in historians, that Polybius does not criticize Timaeus on the simple grounds that his Hermokrates speech differs from that given by Th. This oddity has led some scholars to believe that Polybius did not know Th., but the issue is more complicated than that because Polybius is surely aware of e.g. Th. i. 23 on causation and his view on speeches; see *Greek Historiography*, 60 f. and *JHS* 115 (1995), 59, arguing that Polybius was more familiar with the methodological portions of Th. than with the routine narrative and the particular speeches it contained.

Gomme 516 (cf. *OCD*³ 1518 col. 1 and 1519 col. 2) heard echoes of Gorgias.

There is a break in Hermokrates' speech at 62. 1; the first part of the speech, from 59. 1 to the beginning of 62, deals with the immediate threat posed by the Athenians. From 62. 1 to the end of 64 the speaker moves to more general and distant considerations (though the Athenian menace is never lost sight of, 63. 1, 64. 5). The proem at 59. 1-4 gives the speaker's claim to be listened to and explains why now is a good moment for discussing peace. The nature of the Athenian threat is spelled out at 60; possible objections, on grounds of racial affinity, are dealt with at

61. 2–4. Instead of such delusive arguments, a better analysis (the speaker suggests) is in terms of straight power politics and the facts of human nature, 61. 5–6. After the break at 62. 1 (see above), the rest of ch. 62 is highly general, a disquisition on the nature of revenge and its unpredictability. The two main theses of the speech—the Athenian threat, and the more remote benefits of unity—are recapitulated at ch. 63 and again at 64. 5, with what for Th. is an unusual amount of 'signposting'. Ch. 64 is resumptive in other respects: the opening of 64. 1 has an explicit cross-reference to the beginning of the whole speech, 59. 1; and the racial theme recurs at 64. 3. But other parts of this ch. take us to the remoter and more general considerations of ch. 62: the impossibility of controlling fortune (64. 1, end of sentence) and the 'never again' language of 64. 4 (let us introduce no more allies or mediators from outside).

The speech is the subject of a dissertation to which the above brief analysis owes much, G. P. Landmann, *Eine Rede des Thukydides: Die Friedensmahnung des Hermokrates* (Kiel, 1932); see also the brief essay by Hammond, in P. Stadter (ed.), *The Speeches in Thucydides* (Chapel Hill, 1973), 49–59. On Hermokrates, and Th.'s attitude to him, see n. on him at 58.

58. Καμαριναίοις καὶ Γελῴοις ἐκεχειρία γίγνεται πρῶτον πρὸς ἀλλήλους: 'the people of Kamarina and Gela made a truce, in the first instance with each other only'. For Kamarina see 26. 7 n.; for nearby Gela see P. Orlandini, *Princeton Encyclopaedia*, 346–7, and Wilson, *Arch. Reps.* 1987–8, 129. In 422, Gela and Kamarina will respond in different ways to an approach by Phaiax of Athens, see v. 4. 6 and nn.

ἄλλαι τε πολλαὶ γνῶμαι ἐλέγοντο ἐπ᾿ ἀμφότερα: 'many opinions were expressed on both sides'. Compare i. 139. 4, where very similar language was used, and n. there for Th.'s clear statement of a selective method over the reporting of speeches: even the most literal believer in Th.'s claim at i. 22. 1, to have reported speeches authentically, must admit that by omitting entire speeches Th. has in a sense failed to report 'what was actually said'. There is another instance at 88. 1.

καὶ Ἑρμοκράτης ὁ Ἕρμωνος Συρακόσιος: 'Then Hermokrates son of Hermon, a Syracusan'. On Hermokrates and Th.'s admiration for him see Westlake, *Essays*, ch. 12; Bender, 85 ff.; F. T. Hinrichs, 'Hermokrates bei Thukydides', *Hermes*, 109 (1981), 46 ff.; *Thucydides*, 70 and n. 97 (discussing the role which Hermokrates might have played in a hypothetical book 9). Though he gives Hermokrates his patronymic, Th. doubly delays a full characterization of this man (see next n.): he gives it, not here, nor yet at his second major appearance at vi. 32. 3, but at his third, at vi. 72. 2, cp. G. T. Griffith, *PCPhS* 187 (1961), 30, and Dover's n.

on vi. 72. 2 in *HCT*; cp. above, iv. 21. 3 n. on Κλέων etc. The tribute to
Hermokrates, when it comes, is glowing: among other qualities,
Hermokrates is there said to have ξύνεσις, 'intelligence'; for this word in
Th. see i. 79. 2 n.

**ὅσπερ καὶ ἔπεισε μάλιστα αὐτοὺς ἐς τὸ κοινόν, τοιούτους δὴ
λόγους εἶπεν:** 'who had been chiefly responsible for bringing them
together, spoke as follows' [lit. 'who had persuaded them into a common
thing, i.e. meeting, spoke . . .']. I agree with Jowett (and Gomme, but not
Warner in the Penguin) that the words ἐς τὸ κοινόν, 'together', should be
taken closely with what precedes them. This requires moving the
comma from its OCT position before ἐς and putting it before τοιούτους.
The much weaker alternative (keeping the comma in its OCT position)
would be to take ἐς τὸ κοινόν with what follows: Hermokrates made his
speech 'to the assembled gathering' lit. 'to the common thing'. This
would change the meaning of what precedes, giving the word 'persuaded' an absolute sense: Hermokrates it was whose speech (as it
turned out) was to persuade them, i.e. he was the most persuasive
speaker. The point is not trivial: this second trans. would mean that Th.
was after all, see last n., characterizing Hermokrates (as 'persuasive', cp.
iii. 36. 6 on Kleon). But that second trans. is surely wrong, both because
of the way ἐς τὸ κοινόν is treated, and also because it would be unlike Th.
to say, of a speech yet to be reported, that it was effective; to say this
would remove any element of narrative surprise. The place to say that a
speech was successful is at its end, and this is exactly what Th. does, 65. 1
πειθόμενοι οἱ Σικελιῶται, 'the Sicilians took his advice', lit. 'were persuaded'. [Note: Jowett's trans. of 58, which I have changed, actually has it
both ways. He says Hermokrates was 'the chief agent in bringing them
together', ἐς τὸ κοινόν I suppose, but continues by saying that he 'stood
forward in the assembly', presumably ἐς τὸ κοινόν again. That is, ἐς τὸ
κοινόν is being made to perform an illicit double duty.]

59–64. *Hermokrates' speech*

59. 1. οὔτε πόλεως ὢν ἐλαχίστης: 'the city to which I belong is not
the least important in Sicily'. This opening is irresistibly reminiscent of St
Paul's way of saying he comes from Tarsus, 'I am a citizen of no mean
city', Acts 20: 15. The point will be repeated at 64. 1.

ἐς κοινόν: 'to the common good'. Yet another sense of this word, see
preceding n.; there was a similar cluster of meanings of κοινόν at i. 91. 4
and 7; 92. 1, see nn. there. Th. (like the rest of us) sometimes gets certain
phrases into his head and they whirl around for a while. Cf. p. 322.

2. τις . . . ἐν εἰδόσι μακρηγοροίη; 'You well know . . . and therefore

I shall not speak to you about it at length' [lit. 'why should anyone speak at length among those who know . . .?']. See i. 68. 3 n.: this is a very *Thucydidean* tag, and its occurrence here may be a sign of artificiality, evidence that the real Hermokrates did indeed (if Timaeus is right, see introductory n.) praise peace at greater length than Th. allows. The semi-proverbial Hdt. i. 87. 4 shows the kind of thing which might be said in this vein ('in peace sons bury their fathers, in war the other way round'; this itself calls to mind Nestor's famously pathetic lines at *Odyssey* iii. 108–12, listing the warriors lying dead at Troy, including his son Antilochos). And the scholiast, as Landmann (29) notes, cites the proverbial γλυκὺς ἀπείρῳ πόλεμος, 'war is sweet to those who have no experience of it', cp. Pindar fr. 110 Snell/Maehler γλυκὺ δὲ πόλεμος ἀπείροισιν.

ξυμβαίνει δὲ τοῖς μὲν τὰ κέρδη μείζω φαίνεσθαι τῶν δεινῶν: 'the aggressor thinks the advantage outweighs the risks'. With the thought in this section generally, H. D. F. Kitto, 'The *Rhesus* and Related Matters', *YCS* 25 (1977), 317–50, at 331, compares Eur. *Suppl.* 484–5.

60. 1. καίτοι . . . εἰ σωφρονοῦμεν: 'But . . . if we are sensible'. Repeated at 61. 1; the opening sentence of this ch. and that of ch. 61 (first three lines in OCT) are of approximately the same length, a deliberate balancing, see Landmann, 37.

ἐπιβουλευομένην τὴν πᾶσαν Σικελίαν, ὡς ἐγὼ κρίνω, ὑπ' Ἀθηναίων: 'all Sicily is at this moment threatened by the plots of the Athenians'. The key word here, 'plotted against', is a strong one which runs through the speech, see 61. 1, 64. 5; Landmann, 38 n. 1, 75.

ὀλίγαις ναυσὶ παρόντες: 'with a few ships' [Keeping ὀ.ν. A scholiast, acc. to OCT and Hude (but not Hude's ed. of the scholia!) says some copies of Th. omit the words; G. Alberti's ed. (1992) confirms this. See App. to my vol. iii.]. Dover, *HCT* v. 412, thinks sixty ships could be called 'few' only by comparison with 415. But see next n.

2. καὶ πλέονί ποτε στόλῳ ἐλθόντας αὐτούς: 'they are sure to come again with a larger force'. A reference to the even greater expedition of 415, and thus a sign that the speech is inauthentic? (The point is, see Dover as cited in preceding n., that sixty ships is a large total in absolute terms, but small relative to the 415 operation.) Perhaps, but the theme of the speech is the plotting of the Athenians, and it is not implausible that Hermokrates should conjure these plots into concrete and frightening form. Landmann (13) thought it 'beyond doubt', 'zweifellos', that the thought of a later expedition was a possibility to which the real-life Hermokrates would have been alive; G. De Sanctis, *Rivista di filologia*, 62 (1934), 108 f., reviewing Landmann, criticized him for not wrestling long enough with the questions whether, in the speech as a whole, Th. is talking, or Hermokrates; and whether Th. has antedated Hermokrates' importance. (For the second of these points see above, introductory n. Landmann (12) does actually say that the speech is generally 'too heavy for its context'.) It is easier to rebuke Landmann's brisk certainty than to replace it with anything subtler (though Gomme pointed out that the word τετρυχωμένους, 'exhausted', is not a particularly good description of Sicily in 415). The anachronism in the present passage, if anachronism it is, is the only thing quite of its kind in the speech, though the Thucydidean tag at 59. 2, see n. there, could also be used as an argument for inauthenticity, as could the antedating of Hermokrates' prominence. Against these points one must place the very different way in which Hermokrates handles the racial issue in 424 (ch. 61) and in 415, see the more urgent appeal to Dorianism at vi. 77 and n. This might be thought consistent with the passing of time (though Th. was enough of an artist to create a mood of gathering urgency, by deliberately having a speaker handle the same topic in different ways).

Whatever view we adopt, it is noticeable that Hermokrates' language is picked up by Euphemos at vi. 86. 2, where the speaker acknowledges that the Athenians arrived in 415 with a frighteningly large force, δυνάμει μείζονι πρὸς τὴν τῶνδε ἰσχύν. (Or we might want to turn that round and say that on the 'reader-response' view of Th. set out in Connor's *Thucydides*, the reader is being invited to detect in the present passage a 'pre-echo' of Euphemos.)

τετρυχωμένους: 'exhausted'. See preceding n.

61. 1. καίτοι ... εἰ σωφρονοῦμεν: 'And yet, if we are sensible'. See 60. 1, first n.

χρὴ τὰ μὴ προσήκοντα ἐπικτωμένους: 'we should increase our own possessions' [lit., 'what does not belong to us']. Alcibiades at vi. 18. 1 similarly envisages that Athenian expansion to the west may not be the only possibility: Sicilian (specifically, Syracusan) power might come east. There is not much about this in Th., but see Diod. xii. 30. 1 and above, iii. 86. 2 n., for Syracusan expansion and mobilization in the period before the Peloponnesian War. The thought is not an outrageous or anachronistic one for 424, so the present passage need not be seen as an anticipation of Alcibiades' speech, or as having any implications for the composition question (60. 2 n. on καὶ πλέονι etc.).

νομίσαι τε στάσιν μάλιστα φθείρειν τὰς πόλεις καὶ τὴν Σικελίαν: 'We should remember that internal quarrels more than anything else have ruined Sicily and her cities'. Cp. Athenagoras at vi. 38. 3 and n.

2. καὶ ἰδιώτην ἰδιώτῃ καταλλαγῆναι καὶ πόλιν πόλει: 'we should be reconciled man to man, city to city'. See i. 144. 3 n.

παρεστάναι δὲ μηδενὶ ὡς οἱ μὲν Δωριῆς ἡμῶν πολέμιοι τοῖς

Ἀθηναίοις: 'No one should say to himself, "The Dorians among us may be enemies of the Athenians"'. The line Hermokrates takes here ('never mind race! Sicily for the Sicilians!') is different from his more traditional disparagement of the Ionian invader at vi. 77. 1. This contradiction means that Hermokrates cannot straightforwardly be invoked either by those scholars who stress, or those who minimize, the continuing relevance of the Dorian/Ionian divide. For this argument see i. 95. 1 n. on κατὰ τὸ ξυγγενές. One can only conclude that, if Th. here gives a plausible speech for a fifth-century speaker, it was possible for rhetorical purposes either to assert or to deny the importance of the racial factor. This shows that deference to that factor was not mandatory, but equally it shows that a speaker would be expected to deal with the point.

4. κατὰ τὸ ξυμμαχικόν: 'by their alliance'. On the 'alliance' and 'treaty' (τῆς ξυνθήκης, below) here referred to see iii. 86. 3 n. There were certainly definite alliances and treaties, as inscriptions show; but there was a sense in which all Ionians were held to be 'allies' in virtue of their common Ionianism. Here both ideas are present: the Chalkidians—i.e., here, the Sicilian colonists of *Ionian* (Strabo 447) Chalkis on Euboia, cf. iii. 86. 2–3, iv. 25. 7, vi. 3–4, 44. 3, see also iv. 64. 3 below—had never taken their Ionian obligations ('their alliance') seriously enough to help the Athenians; but the latter eagerly exploited the foot in the Sicilian door which their 'treaty' gave them.

5. καὶ τοὺς μὲν Ἀθηναίους ταῦτα πλεονεκτεῖν τε καὶ προ-νοεῖσθαι πολλὴ ξυγγνώμη: 'The greed and ambition of the Athenians are pardonable enough'. See 21. 2 n. for these themes, which dominate the first half of book iv (πλεονεκτεῖν, 'to be greedy', lit. 'to have/claim more than one's due', recurs at 62. 3). Arguably Th. and his speakers put too much blame for this 'greed' on the Kleon generation and too little on Pericles and his generation, see *Thucydides*, 174. At least Hermokrates in the present passage does not seek to limit the indict-ment too narrowly to the immediate phase of Athenian policy.

For the general thought in these paras. ('it is human nature to rule where you can') see above all v. 105. 2; cp. Connor, 152.

62. 1. καὶ τὸ μὲν ... τοσοῦτον ἀγαθόν: 'That is the great advantage'. This point marks the transition from the first to the second half of the speech, see introductory n.

2. οὐχ ἡσυχίαν μᾶλλον ἢ πόλεμον: 'surely it is peace rather than war'. For this use of ἡσυχία, lit. 'quiet', to mean 'peace', see H. Lloyd-Jones, *The Justice of Zeus*² (Berkeley, 1983), 206 n. 68: it is often used by those who feared or hated Athenian imperialism; see e.g. Pindar, *Pyth.* viii. 1.

καὶ τὰς τιμὰς καὶ λαμπρότητας ἀκινδυνοτέρας ἔχειν τὴν

εἰρήνην: 'peace brings honours and glories of its own, free from the dangers of war'. For the thought compare Milton, Sonnet XVI 'To the Lord General Cromwell', lines 10 f.: '... peace hath her victories | No less renowned than war'. Gomme compares v. 16. 1 (Nikias).

3. πλεονεκτήσειν: 'to grab what does not belong to him'. See 61. 5 n. τοὺς δ' ἀντὶ τοῦ πλέον ἔχειν προσκαταλιπεῖν τὰ αὐτῶν ξυνέβη: 'have, instead of winning more, often ended up by losing what they had before'. For such 'instead' constructions in ἀντί, for which there are Homeric parallels, see *Greek Historiography*, 157–8 and n. 69, comparing vii. 75. 7, which concerns precisely the defeated Athenians in Sicily. This ('*x* instead of *y*') is, we may say, the rhetorically strongest form of 'presentation by negation' in that it conjures up the diametrical opposite of what is being said not to exist or happen; it is slightly stronger and more emphatic than 'not *x* but *y*' (where *y* may be a substitute for *x* but is of the same basic type as *x*, e.g. iii. 50. 2, the Athenians did not levy tribute on Lesbos but exploited it in a different way, or v. 70, on why the Spartans march to the sound of flutes). The weakest is the formulation 'not so much *x* as *y*', οὐ τοσοῦτον as at i. 9. 1 and ii. 65. 11, or '*y* rather than *x*' as at i. 22. 4 μᾶλλον ἢ ἀγώνισμα and n. there on κτῆμά τε etc.; the normal or neutral version is simply 'not *x*', e.g. iv. 38. 5, the battle was not of a regular sort. But this normal version may be strengthened by emphatic repetition, see e.g. iv. 94. 1 n. on ψιλοί etc.

4. τὸ δὲ ἀστάθμητον τοῦ μέλλοντος: 'the inscrutable future'. See iii. 59. 1. See Babut, 429: Th., in the mouth of Hermokrates, is reminding us of Athens' success so far in the book, and warning us that the pattern is about to change.

63. 1. διὰ τὸ ἤδη †φοβεροὺς παρόντας Ἀθηναίους: 'because the Athenians, who are extremely dangerous enemies, are already at our gates'. See Maurer, *Interpolation*, 129–35.

2. φίλοι μὲν ἂν τοῖς ἐχθίστοις, διάφοροι δὲ οἷς οὐ χρὴ κατ' ἀνάγκην γιγνοίμεθα: 'we may perhaps become the friends of our greatest enemies, but we will certainly become the enemies of our real friends'. On this passage in particular and on the friends/enemies theme in general see J. de Romilly, 'Amis et ennemis au v-ème siècle avant J.C.', in *ΦΙΛΙΑΣ ΧΑΡΙΝ: Miscellanea... Manni*, iii (Rome, 1979), 739–46.

64. 1. ἅπερ καὶ ἀρχόμενος εἶπον: 'As I said at the beginning'. At 59. 1. Internal cross-references in Thucydidean speeches are not usually as direct as this, though see i. 35. 5, with Landmann, 68. Much of this ch. is recapitulation, see introductory n. (For authorial or narrative cross-references see v. 1 n. on καὶ ἅμα ἐλλιπές etc.)

3. οὐδὲν γὰρ αἰσχρὸν οἰκείους οἰκείων ἡσσᾶσθαι, ἢ Δωριᾶ τινα Δωριῶς ἢ Χαλκιδέα τῶν ξυγγενῶν: 'There is no disgrace in people giving way to other people who are close to them, whether Dorians to Dorians, or Chalkidians to the others of their race'. That is, to other Ionians, cf. 61. 2 and 61. 4 n. On this passage see Curty 1994, 196–7. As part of his argument that οἰκειότης is always in Th. the weaker, ξυγγένεια the stronger term, and that ξυγγένεια is confined to Ionian links with Ionians and Dorian links with Dorians, Curty says that in the present passage Th. begins with a 'generalizing formula', a 'proverbial expression' ('constation proverbiale') including the οἰκ- concept; then he uses the more precise ξυγγενῶν at the end of the sentence when he really is talking about Dorians and Ionians in a precise way. This is ingenious; but see Introduction, p. 67.

4. τοὺς δὲ ἀλλοφύλους ἐπελθόντας: 'unite as one man against a foreign invader'. Despite 61. 2–3 and 64. 3 above, where Hermokrates minimizes Dorian/Ionian hostility, this choice of word hints at it, see i. 102. 3 and n., also iv. 86. 5 and 92. 3, and vi. 23. 2. (vi. 9. 1 is a reference to the Egestans, who are not Greeks but Elymiots.)

65. *The Sicilians follow Hermokrates' advice*

65. 1. τοῖς δὲ Καμαριναίοις Μοργαντίνην εἶναι: 'only Morgantina was to be handed over to the Kamarinaians'. On this passage see Andrewes, *HCT* v. 364, giving it as one of the 'indications of incompleteness' in Th.'s account of the Ten Years War. 'The special arrangement made for Morgantina presumably owes its place to the fact that it was the only, or the only substantial, exception to the rule that each side was to keep what it had; but Morgantina has not been mentioned earlier (and is not later), nor do the references to Kamarina show any reason why this exception should have been made in her favour.'

3. ὡς ἐξὸν αὐτοῖς τὰ ἐν Σικελίᾳ καταστρέψασθαι δώροις πεισθέντες ἀποχωρήσειαν: 'because they believed that they might have conquered Sicily but had been bribed to go away'. This statement of Athenian war aims in Sicily is very categorical; previously (iii. 86. 4; 115. 4) Th. had tended to give a more limited objective together with a more ambitious one; see iii. 86. 4 n. But Th. is anxious to make the point that Athenian ambitions had changed, under the influence of Pylos, even since the generals had set out. 'Bribed': see *OCD*³ under Bribery, Greek.

4. ἡ παρὰ λόγον τῶν πλεόνων εὐπραγία αὐτοῖς ὑπιτιθεῖσα ἰσχὺν τῆς ἐλπίδος: 'the unexpected success of most of their operations, which filled them with extravagant hopes'. A mood caught in Ar. *Knights*, esp. 1303 ff., with my *Greek World*, 136. I agree with Classen/Steup that the

text can stand; Babut, 429 n. 2, wishes to revive the old idea that εὐπραγία should change places with τῶν πλεόνων, producing the meaning
'hope for more'. See generally Babut, 430, for the links with Pylos, e.g. 17.
4. Cp. also H.-P. Stahl, *Thukydides*, 154–5.

For hope here see Macleod, 150, comparing the 'hope' motif in the
run-up to Sicily (e.g. at vi. 24. 3).

Athenian success, here commented on, is about to end, see Introduction, above p. 108, for Megara as the 'hinge' in Babut's conception.

66–135. BRASIDAS IN MEGARA AND THE NORTH

This long section (plus book v. 1–11) is, in Homeric terms, a kind of
ἀριστεία (feminine singular) of Brasidas, that is, it resembles one of
those books of the *Iliad* in which a single hero (see Fig. 1, above pp. 44 f.)
dominates the narrative for a period, like Diomedes, Agamemnon, and
Menelaos in books 5, 11, and 17 respectively. (There is the occasional
interlude such as ch. 75, Lamachos in the Black Sea, but even that has a
concealed Megarian aspect which links it with what precedes, see n.
there.) We can add that Brasidas has already briefly appeared in very
Homeric style (see 12. 1 n. on ἡ ἀσπίς ...) at iv. 11–12, so the *aristeia*
loosely extends from iv. 11–v. 11. See more fully Introduction, pp. 38–61.

For an interesting analysis of the construction of this second half of
the book see Gomme, *The Greek Attitude to Poetry and History* (Berkeley,
1954), 135–7 (less arrestingly at *HCT* iii. 540, 546), arguing that 'we hear
of Brasidas' doings in the same way as the Athenians themselves did' and
that the Athenians woke up culpably late to the importance of what
Brasidas was up to and did too little too late; see below, 82 n. It is
important to remember that the book culminates in the event (the loss
of Amphipolis) which led to Th.'s own exile; if the Athenian reaction to
the Brasidas phenomenon was inadequate, that would go some way to
exonerate Th. himself. But if this is apology it is very gently done.

Gomme's analysis is clever, and may well be right as a comment on
how Th. made his notes (writing up despatches and news items as they
arrived). Gomme's main point stands, despite Andrewes, *HCT* v. 366:
'the fact that the items come in the order of the impact they made at
Athens is surely a product of Th.'s method, not his reason for adopting
it.' I would make two additional comments or qualifications. First, if the
Athenians are the focalizers in this general, top-level, sense throughout
the long narrative, that does not prevent others being the focalizers in
the short term, see e.g. 72. 1 for Boiotian alarm for Megara, with n. there.
Second, on Gomme's view, Th.'s account of Megara is intended to

bring out the unwise way in which the affair was trivialized at Athens, see esp. *Greek Attitude*, 137, 'everything going not so well at Megara? a nuisance, ἐναντίωμά τι (69. 1), *un petit dérangement*'. This is witty, so it is almost tiresome to have to point out that the two Greek words quoted actually refer not to Athenian domestic reaction to the Megara affair as a whole but to the generals' assessment of the first episode in it, see 69. 1 n. Certainly, the narrative pace or rhythm hereabouts (see M. Bal, *Narratology: Introduction to the Theory of Narrative* (Toronto, Buffalo, London, 1985), 68–76) is artfully managed: Th. gives a great deal of fully-narrated detail by comparison with the short period of real time covered (see esp. chs. 67–8). This ample pacing is the more notable in view of Th.'s previous neglect of Megara, see below, introductory n. to 66–74: ch. 66 has to resume and expand several years of Megarian developments before Th. suddenly switches at 67. 1 to a very immediate, action-by-action, style of narration. The fullness of the 424 narrative has the effect of insisting on Th.'s own high view of the importance of Brasidas and (after much Thucydidean neglect) of Megara.

66–74. *Athenian attack on Megara*

See iii. 51 (427 BC) and nn. for the most recently reported Athenian operations against Megara. On Megara itself see R. Scheer, in Lauffer (ed.), *Griechenland*, 413–15.

The importance of Megara ('the key point', Lewis, *CAH* v². 387) in Athenian pre-war policy and war strategy has not until now come out clearly in Th.: see i. 67. 4 n. (end of n.), discussing the Megarian decrees, also ii. 31. 3 n. The problem is to know whether Th., as Lewis puts it, was not particularly interested in Megara (*CAH* v². 388), or whether he deliberately played down the extent of Athenian activity against Megara so as to make Periclean policy seem less aggressive. For this possibility see *Greek Historiography*, 146, and below, 66. 1 n. on αἰεί . . ., for the invasions of the Megarid. For a third possibility see the valuable article of T. J. Wick, 'Megara, Athens and the West in the Archidamian War: a Study in Thucydides', *Historia*, 28 (1979), 1–14, who notes Th.'s general 'de-emphasis' (see Wick, 2 and 6, for the word) on Megara, and suggests (see esp. 14) that Th.'s motive had to do with the *run-up* to the war: he did not want his readers to accept the common view that 'Athenian–Megarian relations [above all the Megarian decrees] . . . were the major factor responsible for the outbreak of the war'. A fourth possibility is suggested by Wick's own conjecture that the importance of Megara lay in its position on the Crisaean Gulf and with outlets on both sides of the Isthmus of Corinth: Wick thinks that the Athenian pressure on Megara

was in part motivated by the desire to stop western grain coming to the
Peloponnese, iii. 86. 4. Now, Th. is reticent on Athenian western expansion in the *pentekontaetia*, see i. 115. 1 n., at end. His reticence about
Megara could then be seen as part of a wider 'western' reticence. These
various motives do not exclude each other.

**66. 1. Μεγαρῆς οἱ ἐν τῇ πόλει πιεζόμενοι ὑπό τε Ἀθηναίων τῷ
πολέμῳ:** 'the Megarians in the city were hard pressed by the Athenians'
[lit. 'by the A. in/by the war']. For de Ste. Croix, *OPW* 243, this Athenian
pressure, maintained with the help of the blockade at Minoa (below, 67.
3, and iii. 51 with nn. there), was the chief reason for the Megarian slow
starvation referred to at Ar. *Ach.* 535. De Ste. Croix also cites Paus. i. 40.
4, which mentions Megarian tribulations as a result of the invasions, and
slightly amplifies Th. (The source is perhaps Ephorus, cp. Diod. xii. 66. 1,
which is, however, a contraction not an amplification of Th.) But in the
immediate Aristophanic context, the starvation is surely linked closely
and causally with the Megarian decrees, see i. 67. 4 n. See also Ar. *Peace*
483 (421 BC), with Sommerstein's n.

αἰεὶ κατὰ ἔτος ἕκαστον δὶς ἐσβαλλόντων: 'who invaded the
country twice a year'. This interestingly adds to what we were told at ii.
31. 3 ('they repeated the invasion of the Megarid, sometimes with
cavalry, sometimes with the whole Athenian army, every year during the
war until Nisaia was taken', i.e. until 424 and the events of the present
section). That passage was itself remarkable from the literary point of
view, as a piece of iterative presentation, i.e. the narrator, rather than
narrating every instance of an action, says that an action happened
repeatedly. See *Greek Historiography*, 145 and n. 40, for this device, which
can have the effect of masking the significance of a development. Admittedly, a historian like Th. with a great deal to pack in would naturally
find such a device convenient (see ii. 24. 1 n., ii. 34. 7 n., iii. 1. 2 n. on καὶ
προσβολαί etc. for other examples). But in that case why are the
Peloponnesian invasions of Attica up to 425 solemnly reported in full
every time? Perhaps because they were not quite repeated every year—
there was none in 429, presumably because of the plague—but Th. could
surely have found a way of making this qualification while still putting
things iteratively. But it may also be that, for whatever reason (see introductory n. above), Th. was reluctant to acknowledge the extent of
Athenian aggressiveness against Megara. See now Pritchett, *TPOE* 174.

The present passage takes that tendency further: now for the first
time we are told that the invasions happened *twice* a year. This can be
explained in literary terms as an example of what Homeric scholars call
the 'technique of increasing precision'; see O. Taplin, *Homeric Soundings*

(Oxford, 1993), 198, and B. Hainsworth, *The Iliad: A Commentary*, iii. *Books 9-12* (Cambridge, 1992), 144. The most famous Homeric example (Taplin) is the way information about Achilles' death is progressively revealed as the *Iliad* unfolds. But from the historical point of view the effect is to mask for as long as possible the full extent of what Athens was up to; for a good statement of this point see Wick (above, introductory n.), 3, Th. 'has easily and effectively ensured that the information as a whole has minimal impact on the reader'.

πανστρατίᾳ: 'with their whole army'. See 68. 5 n.

καὶ ὑπὸ τῶν σφετέρων φυγάδων τῶν ἐκ Πηγῶν, οἳ στασι-ασάντων ἐκπεσόντες ὑπο τοῦ πλήθους: 'as well as by their own exiles in Pegai, who had been driven out by the people in a revolution'. See the prolepsis or anticipation of this at iii. 68. 3 and n. (Megarian exiles settled at Plataia). At least, this is probably the same lot of exiles, see R. P. Legon, 'Megara and Mytilene', *Phoenix*, 22 (1968), 200-25, at 215, also Wick, 10 and n. 23; Legon says the alternative is to 'invent some prior, unrecorded bout of *stasis* . . . a far less sound procedure'. The conclusion may well be right, but when we know so little about the politics of classical Megara it can hardly be unsound to admit the possibility of ('invent' is too strong) an unrecorded phase of trouble. Th. does not, after all, flag his back-reference in any way. On this passage see Andrewes, *HCT* v. 364, giving the lack of proper background about the Megara situation as one of the 'indications of incompleteness' in Th.'s account of the Ten Years War; he adds that 'the brief reference to *stasis* and exiles at iii. 68. 3 does not help'.

Gomme took the reference to 'the people' here to imply that Megara was a democracy of some sort, but de Ste. Croix, *OPW* 243 n. 25, objected that the *probouloi* of Ar. *Ach.* 755 suggest a constitution more oligarchic than democratic (cp., for *probouloi* generally, Andrewes in *HCT* on viii. 1. 3, ἀρχήν τινα. De Ste. Croix and Andrewes cite Ar. *Pol.* 1298b29, 1299b31, 1323a7). De Ste. Croix then has to take the exiles of the present passage as 'extreme' oligarchs. But even if we accept that Aristophanes was an authority on the Megarian constitution, and that the generalizing Aristotelian passages require inflexibly that every Greek state with *probouloi* was more oligarchic than democratic (and neither proposition is sure), the final decision must be based on the detailed narrative, and it fits Gomme's view better. The situation was volatile but it looks as if the people (πλῆθος) had ousted some of its enemies (though the friends of the exiles still have a voice in public affairs, para. 2), and the democratic leaders still, in 424, have the support of the people (δῆμος this time), but that support is precarious (see below, 3 n. on οὐ δυνατόν etc.). Gomme noted that the narrative shows that the majority were not fanatical (cp. *Greek Attitude*, 135, 'the unfortunate Megarians would, all of them, have liked to be neutral, but their state lay right in the path between the combatants'); Gomme also remarked that the 'popular leaders' (οἱ τοῦ δήμου προστάται) did not 'carry the majority of the people with them' and concluded that the expression οἱ τ. δ. π. means they were leaders of a 'party', not leaders of the majority. (Legon, 220 n. 27, objects that leaders do not have to be followed and supported on every issue, but the narrative supports Gomme.) The significant thing about the present ch., for the study of Athens' popularity (not however in an imperial context, contrast Mytilene in book iii), is that the first thought of the Megarian regime was not to invite in the Athenians but to make conciliatory moves towards the exiles; cp. Lewis, *CAH* v². 423: 'the democrats in Megara ... had at first thought, not of returning to the democratic yoke of Athens which they had shaken off in 446, but of offering the exiles terms of return.' Cp. the situation at Mytilene, iii. 27. 3 n. See also Legon at 220 f., stressing that the secrecy with which the 'popular leaders' had to go about trying to switch to a pro-Athenian policy is evidence that they did not think the *demos* would approve an alliance with Athens under any circumstances.

Legon in his later book, *Megara: the Political History of a Greek City-State* (Ithaca, 1981), 236–47, takes it as uncontroversial that Megara was democratic in 424, but seems unaware that de Ste. Croix has put it in doubt. He mentions the *probouloi* at 237, without reference to de Ste. Croix on this point, and oddly takes them to be evidence that the Megarians may have had a democratic *boule* modelled on that of Athens, as if *probouloi* were a normal feature of the Athenian democracy rather than a product of the emergency of 413. As said above, I hesitate to follow de Ste. Croix in his inference from the *probouloi*, but they certainly cannot be used as evidence for the opposite conclusion. Legon also cites the scholiast on Ar. *Knights* 855 who refers to ostracism (a democratic feature) at Megara at some date, 'if we give credence to this source'. Better not.

2. τὸν θροῦν αἰσθόμενοι: 'became aware of the agitation'. For exactly this phrase see v. 7. 2 (Kleon) and n. there. For the (epic and poetic) noun see Smith, *TAPA* 1900, 73.

3. οἱ τοῦ δήμου προστάται: 'the popular leaders'. For this expression see generally 46. 4 n., and for its implications here see n. 1 on καὶ ὑπό . . .
οὐ δυνατὸν τὸν δῆμον ἐσόμενον ὑπὸ τῶν κακῶν μετὰ σφῶν καρτερεῖν: '[realized] that the people were in a bad way and could not be trusted to hold out in support of them much longer'. This passage, see above, 1 n. on καὶ ὑπό . . ., is most easily compatible with the assumption that Megara was still (precariously) democratic. Legon, *Megara*, 239 f.,

points out that the Athenian demands for Nisaia and Pegai in 425 (21. 3), and the Spartans' equivocal behaviour in response (22. 1), may have created fears at Megara that Sparta might at any moment make peace with Athens at Megara's expense. This is likely enough, and helps to explain why the dominant group at Megara were now, in 424, ready to reject Sparta.

τοὺς τῶν Ἀθηναίων στρατηγούς, Ἱπποκράτη τε τὸν Ἀρίφρονος καὶ Δημοσθένη τὸν Ἀλκισθένους: 'the Athenian generals, Hippokrates son of Ariphron, and Demosthenes son of Alkisthenes'. Hippokrates, the nephew of Pericles (*APF* 456), is here mentioned for the first time by Th., though he had been general in 426/5, see *IG* i³. 369 (= ML 72; Fornara 114) line 3, showing that Hippokrates and colleagues got 20 talents in late summer 426, 'possibly for an invasion of the Megaris': ML, p. 216, with a ref. to the present passage. See Develin, *AO* 127, 132, for the generalships of 426 and 424.

For Demosthenes see iii. 91. 1 n., and add Roisman (3. 1 n. on κατὰ τύχην etc.), esp. 42–6, on the present, Megarian, episode.

ξυνέβησάν τε πρῶτα μὲν τὰ μακρὰ τείχη ἑλεῖν Ἀθηναίους: 'So they agreed that the Athenians should first seize their Long Walls'. For Megara's Long Walls see i. 103. 4 n. and 107. 1 n. on καὶ τὰ μακρὰ τείχη etc. A section, including part of a tower, was uncovered in 1982–3, NW of Palaiokastro (?Minoa), about 316 metres from the sea: P. Zoridis, *A. Delt.* 38 Chron. 1983 (1989), 39–40 and plate 22B; cp. *Arch. Reps.* 1990–1, 12. See also 67. 1 n. below on ἐν ὀρύγματι etc.

ἦν δὲ σταδίων μάλιστα ὀκτώ: 'which were about eight stades in length'. Again (see 66. 1 n. on αἰεί etc.) Th. uses the technique of increasing precision: we were not told in book i (see previous n.) the length of the Megarian Long Walls, though we were told that they ran to Nisaia; admittedly, the book i mention was in the high-speed *Pentekontaetia* digression, which Th. elsewhere supplements in more leisurely style (see ii. 27. 2 n. on καὶ ὅτι ...) at the point in the later narrative where the information is most relevant. Th. is here operating with one of his longest stades, see i. 63. 2 n. and Bauslaugh there cited; Bauslaugh (6) reckons that in the present passage the Thucydidean stade is about 225 m. Cp. *Greek Historiography*, 27.

ἀπὸ τῆς πόλεως ἐπὶ τὴν Νίσαιαν τὸν λιμένα αὐτῶν: 'and ran from the city to their harbour Nisaia'. For Nisaia see i. 103. 4 n. on ἐς Νίσαιαν.

ἐν ᾗ αὐτοὶ μόνοι ἐφρούρουν βεβαιότητος ἕνεκα τῶν Μεγάρων: 'the garrison in Nisaia consisted of Peloponnesians only; their function was to protect Megara'. See H. W. Parke, 'The Second Spartan Empire', *JHS* 50 (1930), 37–79, at 39–40 (cited by Legon, *Phoenix* 1968, 215) for this, 'a different kind of Spartan force abroad', consisting of Peloponnesians only, i.e. not Megarians (so too Classen/Steup; I have changed Jowett's 'of which they formed the sole garrison'). Parke notes the ambiguity of βεβαιότητος ἕνεκα, 'for protection'—not only against Athens, but against the possibility of Megarian disloyalty to Sparta.

67. 1. ὑπὸ νύκτα πλεύσαντες: 'The Athenians sailed at nightfall'. Th. now switches to a dense and immediate narrative style after the resumé manner of the previous ch. See above, introductory n. to 66–135.

ἐς Μινῴαν τὴν Μεγαρέων νῆσον: 'the Megarian island of Minoa'. See iii. 51. 1 n. on ἐπὶ Μινῴαν τὴν νῆσον etc. for the topographical problem (no island fitting Th.'s description now exists).

ἐν ὀρύγματι … ὅθεν ἐπλίνθευον τὰ τείχη: 'a pit out of which the bricks for the walls had been dug'. The upper part of the tower discovered in the early 1980s (see 66. 3 n. on ξυνέβησαν etc.) was constructed of mud brick.

2. Πλαταιῆς τε ψιλοὶ καὶ ἕτεροι περίπολοι: 'Some light-armed Plataians and also some Athenian frontier guards'. The word ἕτεροι, 'others', here (see Classen/Steup) simply means 'in addition', 'und ausserdem'; the point is important, see third para. of this n., where I justify my addition of the word 'Athenian', which is not in the Greek. (At i. 2. 2 I would now translate the comparable expression τῇ ἄλλῃ παρασκευῇ as 'and no resources either' rather than 'and no other resources', as in the comm., vol. i).

The function of περίπολοι was to patrol the frontiers: L. Robert, *Hellenica*, 10 (Paris, 1955), 287 n. 2, and for a full discussion of the evidence, C. Pélékidis, *Histoire de l'éphébie attique* (Paris, 1962), 35–44. They probably anticipated the functions of the 18–20-year old males who would in the fourth century be called ephebes, and were normally stationed on the frontiers of Attica, see P. Vidal-Naquet, *The Black Hunter* (Baltimore, 1986, see iii. 22. 2 n.; French edn. *Le chasseur noir* (Paris, 1981)), at 107 of the English version; J. Ma, 'Black Hunter Variations. I: Damon le chasseur noir (Plutarque, Cimon 1–2)', *PCPhS* 40 (1994), 49–59, at 50; and P. J. Rhodes, *CAAP* on *Ath. Pol.* xlii. 4, a passage which uses the verb περιπολοῦσι, 'they patrol', about ephebes; cp., for the association, Aeschin. ii. 167. (Pélékidis is too reluctant to allow a connection between ephebes and *peripoloi*, though he is no doubt right to deny that they were formally identical.) For ephebes see i. 144. 4 n. on ἀμύνεσθαι etc. and ii. 39, introductory n.; the present passage, and the mentions in military contexts of 'the youngest' (νεώτατοι) at i. 105. 4 and ii. 13. 7, all support the notion that something like the system of ephebes went back to the fifth century, although the name does not antedate the fourth. See esp.

D. M. Lewis, *CR* 23 (1973), 254–6 (showing that there is no epigraphic attestation before 334/3; the first literary references, see Rhodes above, are Aeschin. i. 49 and ii. 167, mentioning Aeschines' συνέφηβοι, i.e. his fellow-ephebes; this looks back to perhaps the late 370s, depending when Aeschines was born, on which topic see R. Lane Fox, in *RFP*, 136–7). For περίπολοι see also viii. 92. 2 and 5 with Andrewes, *HCT* v. 310.

The *peripoloi* were Athenian citizens. Against the old view (see e.g. Westlake, *CR* 4 (1954), 93 n. 2) that they were foreigners see Gomme and (more firmly) Andrewes, above. (Westlake thought that *after a certain point* they started to be recruited from foreigners.) Pélékidis, 36 n. 4, seems to want to revive the old view on the basis of the present passage, arguing that 'the adjective ἕτεροι makes us think that the ψιλοί [the *Plataian* light-armed] were also περίπολοι', i.e. he takes the words to mean 'the Plataians and some other *peripoloi*'. But this is incorrect; for the trans. of the Greek words see first para. above (and note para. 5 below, where we have 'the Plataians and the *peripoloi*', more clearly distinguished). Nevertheless it is highly relevant to the status of *peripoloi* that they are found *in association* with foreigners, Plataians here and an Argive at viii. 92. 2. As Vidal-Naquet puts it, they resemble foreigners in being marginal, 'en marge de la cité' as the French edn. puts it, p. 154. These *peripoloi* were probably based at Eleusis (cp. 68. 5 below), though Phyle, on the Plataia road, or Panakton are other possibilities, cp. *Syll*³ 485, 957 and below, v. 3. 5 n.

ἐς τὸ Ἐνυάλιον: 'at the temple of Ares' [lit. 'at the Enyalion']. The building or sanctuary has not been archaeologically located, nor is it mentioned by Pausanias i. 39–44. For Enyalios as an epithet of or alternative name for Ares see R. M. Gais, *LIMC* iii. 1 (1986), 746–7, entry under ENYO I. Enyalios is sometimes a separate god, of similar character to Ares (see Ar. *Peace* 457; Tod 204, the ephebic oath, lines 17–18; M. Launey, *Recherches sur les armées hellénistiques* (Paris, 1949–50), 928–31), though W. Burkert, *Greek Religion* (Oxford, 1985), 171, says that it is only in a few late sources that there is any evidence of mythology attempting to differentiate. (Pollux viii. 21 identifies the two.) Since the present passage would be compatible with either view (same god as Ares, or different) I have kept Jowett's rendering.

3. ἀκάτιον ἀμφηρικόν: 'a sculling-boat'. See i. 29. 3 n. for the noun; LSJ⁹ fatuously says that the adjective means 'with oars on both sides', though a boat with oars on only one side would go round in circles. From the scholiasts' comments it evidently means that the rower or rowers each had a pair of oars, a δικωπία, by contrast with the arrangement in larger boats where the rowers had a single oar (that is the

implication of ii. 93. 2). J. S. Morrison and R. T. Williams, *Greek Oared Ships* (Cambridge, 1968), 245, say the epithet 'suggests it was rowed by pairs of sculls'. I am not sure why Pritchett, *GSW* v (1991), 324, has ἀφηρικόν.

ὡς λῃσταί: 'as if they were going out on privateering raids'. For Peloponnesian privateering (piratical) activity generally see ii. 69. 1 n. on καὶ τὸ λῃστικόν etc., and for the prevention of privateering as one reason for Nikias' original garrisoning of Minoa in 427 see iii. 51. 2.

This trick is reminiscent, in a general sort of way, of some of the stratagems in Aeneas Tacticus, e.g. xi. 3: by pretending to do repairs over a period of time, you ensure that there are ladders available. See also 68. 5 n. below on λίπα γὰρ ἀλείψεσθαι.

πείθοντες τὸν ἄρχοντα: 'by the permission of the commander'. A Spartan, as we learn from 69. 3. Parke (66. 3 n. on ἐν ᾗ αὐτοὶ μόνοι ἐφρούρουν etc.) stresses the closeness of Spartan control of an allied state, a departure as far as we know. (There were *archontes* at Herakleia in Trachis, iii. 93. 2, but as a new foundation that was different.) See Cartledge, *Agesilaos* (London, 1987), 91. See 132. 3 n. on καὶ τῶν etc.

ὅπως τοῖς ἐκ τῆς Μινῴας Ἀθηναίοις ἀφανὴς δὴ εἴη ἡ φυλακή: 'the intention behind this was to deceive the Athenian garrison at Minoa'. This must be the sense of the Greek, but in order to extract it some emendation is needed: the Greek as transmitted means 'so that the Athenian garrison would be invisible'. Ed. Schwartz, *Das Geschichtswerk des Thukydides²* (Bonn, 1929), 301–2, suggest ὅπως τῇ ἐκ τῆς Μινῴας ἀφανὴς δὴ εἴη φυλακῇ, 'so that it would be invisible *to* the garrison at Minoa'; Steup wanted to change the adjective to produce e.g. 'so that the Athenian garrison would be careless', ἀμελής; Gomme ingeniously suggested changing the noun from 'garrison' to 'excursion', φυλακή to ἐκδρομή.

5. Πλαταιῆς τε καὶ περίπολοι: 'the Plataians and the frontier guards'. See 2 n. above, at end.

οὗ νῦν τὸ τροπαῖόν ἐστι: 'where the trophy now stands'. See Pritchett, *GSW* ii (1974), 265: the trophy was 'presumably erected for the battle for the walls (4. 68. 1–3) in which the Peloponnesians fled'. Such an assumption of topographical familiarity as is here made by Th. would get *Xenophon* into trouble with his modern critics.

68. 4 ἄλλο μετ᾽ αὐτῶν πλῆθος, ὃ ξυνῄδει: 'a large number of others who were in the plot'. Something like this must be the meaning, despite Th.'s confusing use of πλῆθος (contrast 66. 1 where it means 'the people', 'the democracy').

5. λίπα γὰρ ἀλείψεσθαι: 'they themselves were to be smeared with

oil'. Again, I cannot find a precise parallel in Aeneas Tacticus to this unpromising ruse, but like the more successful ploy with the sculling-boat at 67. 3 above (see n. there) it is reminiscent of his collection of stratagems. (As editors point out, it is hard to see how it would work if the men smeared were wearing hoplite armour.) See J. Ma, 'Black Hunter Variations. II: Damon of Chaironeia: a Historical Commentary (Plut. *Kim.* 1–2)', *PCPhS* 40 (1994), 60–6, at 62, discussing Plut. *Kim.* 1. 4.

For Smith, *TAPA* 1900, 74, this is a reminiscence from Homer.

ἀπὸ τῆς Ἐλευσῖνος: 'from Eleusis'. On the military importance of Eleusis see ii. 19. 2 n. on καθεζόμενοι etc.

καὶ ἱππῆς ἑξακόσιοι: 'and six hundred cavalry'. Three fifths of the full 1000-strong Athenian complement, cp. Bugh (introductory n. to 42–45), 39, 76, and 86: 'with their whole army' at 66. 1 above cannot refer to the cavalry. Roisman (3. 1 n. on κατὰ τύχην etc.), 43–6, thinks that the meagre results achieved by this relatively large Athenian force are to be explained by Demosthenes' eagerness to get on with the Boiotian campaign, cf. 73. 4 n. on ἐπειδή etc., citing Gomme and Holladay.

69. 1. ὅτι ἐναντίωμά τι ἐγένετο: 'that there had been a hitch'. See introductory n. to 66–135 above: Gomme in *HCT* ('first obstacle met by the confident Athenians') is better than in *Greek Attitude*, where he transfers it to Athenian reactions at home.

παρεγένετο δὲ σίδηρός τε ἐκ τῶν Ἀθηνῶν ταχὺ καὶ λιθουργοὶ καὶ τἆλλα ἐπιτήδεια: 'They quickly fetched everything they needed from Athens, including iron and stonemasons'. For the use of Athenian stonemasons outside Attica cp. v. 82. 6 and Plut. *Alc.* 16 (help for Argos).

3. τοῖς δὲ Λακεδαιμονίοις, τῷ τε ἄρχοντι καὶ εἴ τις ἄλλος ἐνῆν: 'the Spartan commander and any other Spartan there'. For this commander see 67. 3 n. on πείθοντες etc. N. van der Ben, *Mnemosyne* 49 (1996), 57 urges retention of the mss. τοῖς τε. See my vol. 3, Appendix.

4. οἱ Ἀθηναῖοι τὰ μακρὰ τείχη ἀπορρήξαντες ἀπὸ τῆς τῶν Μεγαρέων πόλεως: 'the Athenians breached the section of the Long Walls running from the city of Megara'. Thus securing their own position from attack by still-hostile Megara. The Megarians later captured and destroyed the Long Walls completely, 109. 1.

καὶ τὴν Νίσαιαν παραλαβόντες: 'took possession of Nisaia'. In 421 the Athenians retained Nisaia because it was acquired by capitulation, not treachery or force; this specious point (the place was surrendered not by the Megarians but by the Peloponnesian garrison) enabled Athens to counter the Theban retention of Plataia: see v. 17. 2 n. on ἀνταπαιτούντων etc. See also 118. 4 n. on τοὺς δ' ἐν Νισαίᾳ etc. for the provisional arrangements in 423.

70. 1. Βρασίδας δὲ ὁ Τέλλιδος Λακεδαιμόνιος κατὰ τοῦτον τὸν χρόνον ἐτύγχανε περὶ Σικυῶνα καὶ Κόρινθον ὤν, ἐπὶ Θρᾴκης στρατείαν παρασκευαζόμενος: 'But it so happened that Brasidas, son of Tellis, the Spartan, who was equipping an expedition intended for the Thraceward region, was in the neighbourhood of Sikyon and Corinth at the time'. An interesting piece of narrative anachrony or deviation, in fact a delay: Brasidas' plans must have been formulated some time before but, as Lewis says (*CAH* v². 424), 'we have been given no warning', cp. Connor, *Thucydides*, 127. For such delays as an 'archaic narrative device' see E. Fraenkel, *Aeschylus: Agamemnon* (Oxford, 1950), 805, Appendix A, 'On the postponement of certain important details in archaic narrative' (discussing Hdt. i. 110–12): the significant item is held back until it will make most impact. But here the anachrony, though a strikingly casual way of introducing a Spartan plan, is innocuous in that it serves no very obvious purpose, either positive (nothing is gained by the delayed impact) or negative (Th. is not trying to 'bury' the significance of the item by misplacing it). Th. is, in fact, merely solving a problem of linearization (for this term cp. D. Fowler, 'Narrate and Describe, the Problem of Ekphrasis', *JRS* 81 (1991), 25–35, at 29). He has to decide how best to present a set of jumbled events as if they were a line. See *Greek Historiography*, 143. One way in which Th. signals that he is making an abrupt transition is by the full introduction of Brasidas as a Spartan, with patronymic; contrast the last mention of him at 11. 4 in the middle of an exciting piece of battle. There an elaborate introduction would have slowed the narrative down.

The *motives* for Brasidas' northern expedition are further delayed, until chs. 79–81, a reflective section written demonstrably late (it contains at 81. 2, see n. there, an explicit reference to the final, post-Sicily phase of the war). On the gradual way Th. unfolds Brasidas' plan see Connor, *Thucydides*, 128–9 and n. 48: despite ἐτύγχανε, 'it so happened', in the present passage, it would be wrong (cp. Pylos) to think that chance played much part. See also the good discussion by Andrewes, *HCT* v. 366, for the relation between 70 and 79–81 and Th.'s breach of strict narrative sequence in this episode.

καὶ ὡς ᾔσθετο τῶν τειχῶν τὴν ἅλωσιν, δείσας: 'When he heard that the Long Walls had been taken, he was anxious'. For the participially expressed motivation see 9. 1 n. on Δημοσθένης δὲ ὁρῶν. Brasidas gets more such expressions than any other individual in the History. Lang's study (*Mnemosyne* 1995) takes in only participles, like δείσας here ('he was anxious'), but the present passage is a reminder that motivation can be expressed in indicative constructions too ('when he heard', ὡς ᾔσθετο).

ἐπὶ Τριποδίσκον (ἔστι δὲ κώμη τῆς Μεγαρίδος ὄνομα τοῦτο ἔχουσα ὑπὸ τῷ ὄρει τῇ Γερανείᾳ): 'at Tripodiskos, a Megarian village below Mount Geraneia'. Tripodiskos was one of the five constituent villages from which the *polis* of Megara was synoikized or concentrated (for this notion see i. 10. 2 n. on οὔτε ξυνοικισθείσης πόλεως, and introductory n. on ii. 14. 2–16): see Plutarch, *Greek Questions* 17. For the site (said to be at Chani about 12 km. west of Megara) see Legon, *Megara*, 33 and his map 1, with Y. Nikopoulou, *A. Delt.* 25. Chr. 1, 1970 (1972), 99–120, and *AAA* 2 (1969), 339–43, with English summary at 342–3 (tomb finds).

τοὺς μεθ᾽ αὑτοῦ ὅσοι ἤδη ξυνειλεγμένοι ἦσαν: 'as well as the troops he had previously collected'. Gomme's n. here ('apparently not more than one hundred or two', etc.) is confusing because it contains a misprint, '5000' for '6000' (cp. already J. A. O. Larsen, *CP* 53 (1958), 124). Gomme says that Brasidas at 72. 2 had 5000 [read 'at least 6000'] hoplites in all, and adds the total in the present passage (3,700 Corinthians, Sikyonians and Phliasians) to the 2,200 Boiotians at 72. 2, making 5,900 in total, i.e. nearly 6000, which leaves not much over for the 'previously collected' troops. When he sets off through Thessaly at 78. 1 he has 1700 troops, see n. there on ἑπτακοσίοις: of the 1000 non-helots (see 80. 5 for the 700 helots and the statement that the rest were hired from the Peloponnese) some must have been drawn from the Corinthians etc. of the present ch.

71. 1. αἱ δὲ τῶν Μεγαρέων στάσεις: 'the two factions in Megara'. This is the only undisputed instance in Th. of στάσις in the sense of 'faction'; on ii. 22. 3 see G. Rechenauer, *Rh. Mus.* 136 (1993), 238–44, with my n. in the World's Classics trans.; on vii. 50. 1 see Dover's n.

οἱ δὲ μὴ αὐτὸ τοῦτο ὁ δῆμος δείσας ἐπίθηται σφίσι καὶ ἡ πόλις ἐν μάχῃ καθ᾽ αὑτὴν οὖσα ἐγγὺς ἐφεδρευόντων Ἀθηναίων ἀπόληται: 'the other group realized that the democrats were afraid of exactly that, and feared they would therefore attack them, and that the city would then be destroyed by internal fighting, with the Athenians lying in close wait'. Gomme remarked that the democrats are given a selfish motive only (fear that the exiles would be recalled and that they themselves would then be forced out), whereas the oligarchs are given both a selfish and a more disinterested one (wish to avoid the destruction of the city); but he rightly went on to signal the oligarchs' behaviour at 74. 3—the trick by which they ensured that their chief enemies were killed, thus incidentally removing one set of potential witnesses for inquirers like Th. See also de Romilly, 'Cities' (1. 1 n. on αὐτῶν ἐπαγαγομένων), 2 and 11 n. 4, generally impressed with the behaviour of both parties at Megara, 'particularly the oligarchs (at least those among them who were moderate, and therefore not in exile)'.

For the way Th. sets out the fears and calculations of the two sides in this ch., so typical of his method (people always act according to rationally-calculated self-interest), see Schneider, *Information und Absicht*, 135 f.

72. 1. ἅμα δὲ τῇ ἔῳ οἱ Βοιωτοὶ παρῆσαν, διανενοημένοι μὲν καὶ πρὶν Βρασίδαν πέμψαι βοηθεῖν ἐπὶ τὰ Μέγαρα, ὡς οὐκ ἀλλοτρίου ὄντος τοῦ κινδύνου: 'At dawn the Boiotians appeared. Even before they were summoned by Brasidas, they had intended to relieve Megara; for the danger was close to home [lit. 'not foreign to them']'. Gomme saw the present passage in purely military terms—the threat to Boiotia if Megara was in hostile hands, so that in the event of invasion help could not get through from the Peloponnese—and that primary meaning is undeniably present in the words οὐκ ἀλλοτρίου, 'close to home'. (Cp. also Lewis, *CAH* v². 387, citing the present passage in support of the proposition that Megara was 'essential for communications between the Peloponnese and Boeotia'.) With this aspect cp. 6. 1 n. on νομίζοντες etc. But there is, I suggest, another aspect to οὐκ ἀλλοτρίου as well. There was an old sentimental connection between Boiotia and Megara, based on the story that Megara was founded by Boiotia. See K. Hanell, *Megarische Studien* (Lund, 1934), 24–35, citing such evidence as *FGrHist* 4 F 78: Megareus the eponymous founder of Megara came from Boiotian Onchestos. So Th.'s expression here is comparable to οἰκήια κακά, 'troubles close to home', at Hdt. vi. 21. 2 (said of Athenian feelings about the fall of their daughter city Miletos). In other words, Th. is alluding to a relation of kinship, for which notion see i. 95. 1 n. on κατὰ τὸ ξυγγενές and above, Introduction, pp. 61–80. See also v. 31. 7, 38. 1.

Curty 1994 has nothing on the present passage in his study of relationships between cities in Th.; I think he confines himself to too restricted a set of Greek terms; see above, Introduction, pp. 68 f.

If the religious or sentimental aspect is relevant, cp. i. 107. 2 and iii. 92. 3: Sparta sends military help to Doris because Doris was Sparta's metropolis or mother-city.

Note the focalization here: Th. is saying that the Boiotians *felt* the danger was their own. He is not committing himself on the question whether Boiotians or Athenians (see Hanell, 35–48, and below, 118. 4 n. on τοὺς δ' ἐν Νισαίᾳ etc., for the *Athenian* claim) were really the founders of Megara. No doubt Athenian claims to be Megara's 'metropolis' were relevant, in some circles, to Athenian interest in Megara at all times.

It would be possible to see the present passage as a piece of 'presentation through negation': the Boiotians did *not* in the end take the view which some of them had advocated (or which you might have expected them to take given their insularity), namely that Megara was really no concern of theirs; for this sort of argument cp. 95. 2 n. on παραστη etc. and Luschnat there cited. But I prefer to see the present negative as a strengthened positive, 'Megara was very close to home'.

4. τὸν μὲν γὰρ ἵππαρχον τῶν Βοιωτῶν: 'the Boiotian cavalry-commander'. The word ἵππαρχος, though a simple and obvious linguistic formation (hipparchs are found in other contexts, see e.g. Tod 147, lines 15 and 24, for hipparchs at Athens and Thessaly; and cavalry units called hipparchies are familiar from the history of Alexander), occurs here only in Th. For this officer, the Boiotian federal cavalry commander, see P. Salmon, *Étude sur la confédération béotienne* (Brussels, 1978 = *Mém. de la classe des lettres, Acad. Royale de Belgique*, vol. 63 fasc. 3), 182–3. Boiotia was good cavalry country, and its cavalry had a high reputation, cp. Tod 197 for Alexander's Boiotian cavalry, and generally L. J. Worley, *Hippeis: the Cavalry of Classical Greece* (Boulder, Colo., 1994), 60–3. For Th. on federal Boiotia see below, 76. 2 n. on τὰ Βοιώτια etc.

οὐ μέντοι ἔν γε τῷ παντὶ ἔργῳ βεβαίως οὐδέτεροι τελευτήσαντες ἀπεκρίθησαν: 'But as far as the whole battle went, the two sides separated without a decisive result'. The Greek is difficult and it is possible that some word or words have dropped out which would give more clearly the required meaning that neither side was victorious. G. N. Bernardakis, 'Διορθωτικὰ καὶ Ἑρμηνευτικά', *Laografia* 7 (1923) (Memorial vol. for N. Politis), 1–18, at 2–3, suggested the original reading was τελευτήσαντες ἐπεκράτησαν, ἀλλ᾽ ἀπεκρίθησαν, οἱ μὲν Βοιωτοί, etc.

73. 2. ἐπειδή τε ἐν φανερῷ ἔδειξαν ἑτοῖμοι ὄντες ἀμύνεσθαι, αὐτοῖς ὥσπερ ἀκονιτὶ τὴν νίκην δικαίως ἂν τίθεσθαι: 'although they had clearly shown that they were ready to engage; and could, in view of this, reasonably claim to have won a victory without fighting'. Something like this must be the meaning; I follow Gomme in thinking the text needs emendation, and have changed the OCT ἐπειδή γε to ἐπειδή τε and deleted καί before αὐτοῖς.

4. ὅπερ καὶ ἐγένετο. οἱ γάρ Μεγαρῆς, ὡς οἱ Ἀθηναῖοι ...: 'And that is what happened. At first the Athenians ...'. The whole eleven-line Greek sentence from ὡς οἱ Ἀθηναῖοι down to ὡρμήθησαν is a parenthesis, and the main verb 'they opened the gates', ἀνοίγουσί τε τὰς πύλας, of which the Megarians (οἱ γὰρ Μεγαρῆς) are the subject, is delayed for a further three lines. ('And that is what happened' means that the Athenians did indeed refuse battle, and that the Megarians

behaved as Brasidas had foreseen. Jowett, to make the general meaning clearer, actually added some English words not in the Greek: 'for the Megarians did indeed receive Brasidas'.)

ἡσύχαζον δὲ καὶ αὐτοὶ μὴ ἐπιόντων: 'when they were not attacked they too did nothing'. See J. Wilkins, *Euripides, Heraclidae: A Commentary* (Oxford, 1992), on line 533. On such (unusual) refusals of battle see Hanson, *Western Way*, 137.

ἐπειδὴ καὶ τὰ πλείω αὐτοῖς προυκεχωρήκει: 'they had got most of what they wanted'. This is an important judgement or rather misjudgement: the Athenians' gains were surely *not* such as to justify this complacent verdict, because what they really wanted was (not Nisaia or the Long Walls but) Megara itself, the 'key point' to Athens' Archidamian War strategy as Lewis puts it, see introductory n. to 66–74, also 21. 3 n. on ἐλθόντων etc. Apart from the intrinsic desirability of making exertions for Megara, note Gomme's point (in his n. on 74. 2) that by holding on at Nisaia, the Athenians could have 'delayed decisively Brasidas' march into Thrace'. (Only T. Wick (introductory n. to 66–74), 12–13, attempts a partial justification of the generals' decision, on the grounds that after Sphakteria the importance of Megara was anyway less.)

It is therefore crucial to establish who is the focalizer here: Th. or the generals? The question does not seem to have been addressed in previous scholarship; historians and commentators assume one view or the other (and sometimes both). Those who think the focalizer is Th. include Wade Gery, *OCD*[3], entry under 'Thucydides', p. 1519 col. 1, who remarks (with a reference to the present passage) that when the Athenian effort against Megara 'nearly bore fruit at last, Thucydides suggests that the capture of Megara was of no great moment', and uses this as evidence of Th.'s poor strategic judgement. Similarly Lewis, *CAH* v[2]. 387: 'Th. suggests that this [the capture of Nisaia] was a sufficient gain and that the generals would not have been justified in taking risks to capture Megara.' Again, he draws damaging inferences about Th.'s strategic grasp.

The other view, that the judgement is that of the generals ('der Sinn der attischen Strategen'), is held by Steup and by Lewis on a later page (424) of *CAH* v[2]: '*the generals* [my italics] reckoned that they had got most of what they had come for.' Westlake, *Individuals in Thucydides* (Cambridge, 1968), 115, begins by saying that the claim attributed to the generals is surprising (because Nisaia and the Long Walls were valuable but their main objective was undoubtedly Megara itself) and continues 'Th. does not appear to imply any judgment, favourable or unfavourable, on the claim' by the generals to have been largely successful; in n. 1 he adds the speculation that the claim represents self-justification by the generals either to their disgruntled troops or in a report to their fellow-generals at home. (This picks up a hint in Gomme, *HCT* iii. 535, although I cannot make out from Gomme's otherwise good n. who he thought was making the claim or what Th. thought about it. Gomme, followed on this point by A. J. Holladay, *Historia*, 27 (1978), 418 n. 64, thinks the generals had their Boiotia plan of chs. 76-7 in mind, and were impatient to get on with it.) Oddly, in view of his caution about Th.'s attitude to the Athenian claim, Westlake (114-15) is convinced that Th. 'evidently believed that Brasidas was wise to remain on the defensive'. This conviction is possible but precarious; it is true that Th. says after the report of the calculations of Brasidas and co. that 'that is what happened', but that is a statement that Brasidas was right in the event, not a judgement that he was wise before it. In order to extract Westlake's conclusion we need the further assumption, which may indeed be correct, that for Th. wisdom was always and invariably proved by success—which brings us back to the Athenian generals and whether Th. thought *they* had been successful. T. Wick (introductory n. to 66-74), 12 n. 27, also thinks in terms of self-justification by the generals; pressing hard the word πλείω, 'most' of their objectives, he says that the generals could have claimed to have scored two out of three (seizure of Long Walls; Nisaia; Megara), but agrees that 'this is a very superficial criterion for success'.

Actually the crucial words seem to be Th.'s own focalization as well as that of the Athenian generals; i.e. Lewis was right. It is true that the choice of a construction in ἐπειδή committed Th. to an indicative verb, even in the course of a largely accusative-and-infinitive sentence i.e. one which reported the generals' thinking. (For this distinction see K. J. Dover, *The Greeks and their Legacy* (1988), 74-82, discussing vii. 42, which is not however on all fours with the present passage.) But if Th. had wanted to report it merely as the generals' thinking he could have found a way of putting it into the accusative and infinitive construction of the clauses which precede and follow, or else he could have expressed the thought with a participial expression in the dative (cp. ἄρξασι) meaning 'having gained what they wanted'. But instead he chooses a construction imposing an emphatic indicative verb, which leaves us—it certainly left Wade Gery and half of Lewis—with the impression that Th. accepted the generals' claim. (He does not explicitly rebuke the claim, but that is not always his way, so nothing can be built on that.)

The misjudgement is important because it reveals again (see above, introductory n.) that even after this lengthy narrative Th. could or would not bring out the strategic importance of Megara.

τοῖς δὲ ξυμπάσης τῆς δυνάμεως καὶ τῶν παρόντων μέρος

ἑκάστων κινδυνεύειν εἰκότως ἐθέλειν τολμᾶν: 'The Peloponnesians were more willing to risk only part of their whole army and of
each of the contingents supplied by the various states'. This sentence is
probably corrupt (the last four words include three infinitives, all of
similar meanings); of the various solutions (Classen; Steup; Gomme) I
have preferred Classen's, i.e. I have, without much confidence, changed
the OCT ἕκαστον to ἑκάστων. Maurer, *Interpolation*, 126–8, defends the
existing text; he is right that the focalization is complex (he compares iv.
117. 2): what we have here is the Athenian analysis of what the Spartans
were thinking.

74. 2. μηδὲν μνησικακήσειν: 'forget old quarrels'. This is the regular
expression for an amnesty; elsewhere it occurs in Th. only at viii. 73. 6,
but is often used for the famous Athenian amnesty of 403, see T. C.
Loening, *The Reconciliation Agreement of 403/402 in Athens* (*Hermes Einzelschrift* 53, 1987), 21 and n. 6. See also de Romilly, 'Cities' (1. 1 n. on
αὐτῶν ἐπαγαγομένων), 9, calling this 'a good example of the true reality
of the *polis* as a whole, even in a case of stasis'—a rather rosy view in the
light of what Th. goes on to describe.
3. ἐξέτασιν ὅπλων ἐποιήσαντο: 'they held a military review'. For a
similar trick, as a way of disarming your opponents, cp. Hippias at vi. 58
and the Thirty Tyrants at Xen. *Hell.* ii. 3. 20 and ii. 4. 8.
ἀναγκάσαντες τὸν δῆμον ψῆφον φανερὰν διενεγκεῖν: 'and
forced the people to sentence them by an open vote'. Cp. for such voting
N. Spivey, 'Psephological Heroes', in *RFP* 39–51, at 48.
**3–4. καὶ ἐς ὀλιγαρχίαν τὰ μάλιστα κατέστησαν τὴν πόλιν. καὶ
πλεῖστον δὴ χρόνον αὕτη ὑπ' ἐλαχίστων γενομένη ἐκ στάσεως
μετάστασις ξυνέμεινεν:** 'They then set up an extreme oligarchy in
Megara. No change of government carried out by so few people, and
based on a revolution, ever lasted such a long time.' For this oligarchy
see v. 31. 6 (421), but we have no other good evidence. The sentence is
contorted because there are two superlatives, the small number of
people involved and the length of time for which the regime lasted.
From the aorist ξυνέμεινεν, 'it lasted' (as opp. imperfect 'it has been lasting') it is usually inferred (Steup; Gomme; Legon, *Megara*, 247) that by
the time Th. wrote these words, the extreme oligarchy had fallen, and if
we knew (as we do not) when it fell or by what date it had fallen we
would know the date after which Th. wrote this. Th. seems, if we press
the passage, to be looking back from a considerably later date, so Dover,
HCT v. 411. But see above, p. 120. Cf. also Andrewes, *HCT* v. 300.

75. *The Athenians take Antandros in the Troad; Lamachos in the Black Sea area*

This ch. 'reminds us, in effect, of the variety of Athens' commitments': Lewis, *CAH* v². 425 n. 135. [Note: the Penguin translation wrongly makes the second half of this chapter part of ch. 76.]

1. ὥσπερ διενοοῦντο, μελλούσης κατασκευάζεσθαι: 'the Lesbian exiles were going to strengthen Antandros as they had planned'. This resumes 52. 3 with what is almost, but not quite, an explicit cross-reference (see v. 1 and vi. 94. 1 with nn. for the only explicit ones in Th.). See final n. on 52. 3; the wording is very similar, but there we had παρα- not κατασκευάζεσθαι; and there the word for 'strengthen' was κρατύνεσθαι.

For Antandros see 52. 3 n. on καὶ μετὰ τοῦτο etc. The Athenian cleruchs of iii. 50 do not feature here any more than at iv. 52, see nn. there.

οἱ τῶν ἀργυρολόγων νεῶν Ἀθηναίων στρατηγοὶ Δημόδοκος καὶ Ἀριστείδης: 'Demodokos and Aristides, two commanders of the Athenian money-collecting ships'. For these ships, and discussion of their function, see 50. 1 n.; again (see previous n.) we are given what is almost a cross-reference, '*the* money-collecting ships'. Fornara, *Generals*, 60, followed by Develin, *AO* 132, thinks that Demodokos and Aristides were *not* re-elected generals for 424/3 but merely allowed to complete their job, whereas Lamachos *was* elected for that year. Aristides was given his patronymic at 50.1; Demodokos never gets his; for Lamachos see next n.

On the text see Dover, *CQ* 1954, 81. The word for 'ships', νεῶν, is in only one manuscript but is right.

ὁ γὰρ τρίτος αὐτῶν Λάμαχος: 'a third, Lamachos'. Lamachos makes a memorably martial appearance in Ar. *Acharnians* 572 ff.; see Sommerstein's n. on 566. He had taken part in Pericles' Pontic (Black Sea) expedition of 436/5, for which see Plut. *Per.* 20 and Th. i. 115. 2–117, introductory n.; the crucial evidence for dating is *IG* i³. 1180, a casualty list now restored to yield a reference to ἐν [Σιν]όπει, 'in Sinope' (as opp. Alope, the previous reading, cp. ii. 26. 2 n.). See Stadter's n. on the Plutarch passage, and Lewis, *CAH* v². 146 n. 113. Was Lamachos an expert on the Black Sea region? For the way Lamachos is here described cp. 2. 2 n. on Εὐρυμέδοντα etc. He does not get his patronymic (Xenophanes) until vi. 8. 2, the formal vote to send sixty ships to Sicily in 415, a solemn moment. He probably swore to the Peace of Nikias, see v. 19. 2 and n. there on Λάμαχος, with Andrewes and Lewis, *JHS* 1957, 180.

δέκα ναυσὶν ἐς τὸν Πόντον ἐσεπεπλεύκει: 'had sailed with ten ships into the Pontus' [i.e. Black or Euxine Sea]. The authors of *ATL* (iii. 89) connect this visit with tribute collection in the region ('the Athenians also anticipated collection of tribute in the Euxine area'), as part of their view that the 'money-collecting ships' of 50. 1 were linked to the tribute re-assessment of 425; they note that Lamachos' base was Herakleia Pontike, which had been assessed in 425. But see 50. 1 n. on these ships: the whole squadron may have been raising funds other than tribute, and Lamachos may have chosen to take his detachment to the Black Sea region because of his special knowledge and contacts there, see previous n.

However, there is one further aspect to the Black Sea visit: both Kalchedon and Herakleia were Megarian colonies (Th. mentions that Kalchedon was, but so too was Herakleia, see below 2 n. on ἐν τῇ Ἡρακλεώτιδι, discussing Boiotia as well). It is striking that an Athenian commander should have been active in Megara's colonial region at just the time when Megara itself was under attack by Athens, as described in chs. 66–74, and it is tempting to connect the two episodes as part of a general pressure on Megara. See above, p. 75 n. 177.

καὶ ἐδόκει αὐτοῖς δεινὸν εἶναι μὴ ὥσπερ τὰ Ἄναια ἐπὶ τῇ Σάμῳ γένηται: 'they suspected that it would prove as much of a nuisance to Lesbos as Anaia had been to Samos'. The words 'to Lesbos' are not in the Greek but are inserted by Jowett to clarify the meaning. For the Samian refugees on Anaia see iii. 19. 2 and n. there on καὶ Ἀναιτῶν, also iii. 32. 2.

2. ἐν τῇ Ἡρακλεώτιδι: 'in the territory of Herakleia'. For Lamachos' visit as an episode in the history of Herakleia on the Black Sea (Herakleia Pontike), the flourishing and splendid port on the south coast of the Black Sea, cp. S. M. Burstein, *Outpost of Hellenism: The Emergence of Heraclea on the Black Sea* (Berkeley, 1976), 32–3, and *CAH* vi² (1994), 222 (S. Hornblower) and 492 (J. Hind). Diod. xii. 72. 4 adds nothing to Th., but from Justin (xvi. 3. 9–12), perhaps drawing on the Hellenistic writer Nymphis (see Jacoby, *FGrHist* iii.B. comm. on nos. 297–607 at p. 255), we are for once able to amplify Th. from a good independent literary source; Steup's dismissal of this as 'later elaboration' is not justified. Justin says that Lamachos, after losing his ships as in Th., *was escorted to Kalchedon by the people of Herakleia*. This was an unexpectedly friendly gesture, given that Herakleia had refused to join the Delian League (Justin xvi. 3. 9); it was, however, included in the Athenian tribute assessment of 425, ML 69, under the new 'Cities of the Euxine' rubric, for which see B. D. Meritt and A. B. West, *The Athenian Assessment of 425 BC* (Ann Arbor, 1934), 87–8. But there is no good evidence that it ever paid anything, certainly not the vague Eupolis 235 K/A, cited by Burstein.

Evidence for actual payment in 421 is 'extremely tenuous': *ATL* iii. 117, discussing *ATL* i. 152, list 34. The authors of *ATL* think that the renewal in 424 of the Peace of Kallias (see ML 70) must have put a stop to Athenian fund-raising in the southern Black Sea area; but though they are probably right that Athens got little financial benefit from places like Herakleia, the particular argument is weak because Persian control here was often desultory, as in the period of Herakleia's fourth-century tyranny, for which see *CAH* vi². 222. See also Badian, *From Plataea to Potidaea*, 195 n. 47, describing as 'fiction' *ATL*'s notion that Lamachos' adventure was contrary to the Peace of Kallias, and even doubting whether Lamachos' purpose was financial at all ('the purpose of the mission may be support for Heraclea and Amisus, not long after Pericles' intervention there').

Burstein explains Herakleia's helpfulness to Lamachos in his humiliation, by the hypothesis of a recent change of government there in a democratic direction. *IG* i³. 74 (M. Walbank, *Proxenies*, no. 46) confers proxeny on one Sotimos the Herakleiot in 424/3, and it is likely enough (Walbank, p. 257) that he is from Herakleia on the Black Sea and possible that he is being thanked for help to Lamachos (but his home place might be e.g. Herakleion in Pieria. Note, however, that W. Ameling includes Sotimos in his 'Prosopographia Heracleotica', in Lloyd Jonnes [*sic*], *The Inscriptions of Heraclea Pontica* (Bonn, 1994), 162, cp. n. 120).

Herakleia, like Kalchedon (below) was a Megarian colony, Xen. *Anab.* vi. 2. 1 (though there was a Boiotian element as well, Ps.-Skymn. 973, Paus. v. 26. 7, and cp. above 72. 1 n. for Boiotian–Megarian ties). For the possible significance of this see para. 1 n. on δέκα etc., and above, p. 75 n. 177.

Gomme's n. on Herakleia on the Black Sea is confined to a single reference to Xen. *Anab.* He was (cf. above, p. 5) much less interested in Greek sites in modern Turkey than in those of modern Greece, including the islands. Cp. iii. 19. 2 n. for the Σάνδιος λόφος, or iii. 33. 2 n. for Klaros, and iii. 31–3 generally for other western Asia Minor sites. On all these places Gomme's treatment is much sketchier than, say, his notes on the central and northern Greek place-names at iv. 78.

ἐς τὸν Κάλητα: 'at the mouth of the river Cales'. SW of the city of Herakleia, see Burstein, 32. The manuscripts' Κάληκα, 'Calex', was emended by Palmerius out of Arrian, *Bithynica* 20, cp. *Periplus of the Black Sea* 13. But Lewis, *Towards a Historian's Text*, 42, 151, thinks that the emendation is 'high-handed' and that 'there is no point in emending Th. in conformity with an extremely uncertain guess': the evidence of the geographers (Arrian is not the only one) is conflicting.

ἀφικνεῖται ἐς Καλχηδόνα τὴν ἐπὶ τῷ στόματι τοῦ Πόντου Μεγαρέων ἀποικίαν: 'and arrived at Kalchedon, the Megarian colony at the mouth of the Pontus'. But Herakleia was a Megarian colony too, though Th. did not bother to tell us so. For the possible significance of this Megarian aspect see 1 n. above on δέκα etc. The manuscripts have Χαλκήδονα, but this should probably be emended, see Lewis, *Towards a Historian's Text*, 149 and 197: 'there is no other evidence for the antiquity of this [the manuscript] form which seems influenced by Latin usage. Probably we ought to read Χαλχήδονα [*sic*] and blame the scribe...'

κατελθόντος αἰφνιδίου τοῦ ῥεύματος: 'a sudden flood'. For flash floods in the region see Burstein, 5.

διὰ Βιθυνῶν Θρᾳκῶν: 'through the country of the Bithynian Thracians'. See Burstein, 4-11.

76-77. *Athenian plans for an attack on Boiotia*

The Athenians had not forgotten their decade of control in Boiotia up to 446, see i. 108. 3 and n. (also iii. 91 and iii. 95. 1 and n., for attempts on Boiotia in 426). But as Holladay remarks of the present attempt, *Historia*, 27 (1978), 419, 'the lesson of 446 was ignored' in that the Athenians put too much faith in the strength and effectiveness of the pro-Athenian groups in Boiotia. In any case, this time the object was more limited, not to annex Boiotia but to 'take it out of the war and democratize it': R. J. Buck, 'Boiotians in the Peloponnesian War', in A. Schachter (ed.), *Essays in the Topography, History and Culture of Boiotia* (*Teiresias* suppl. 3, 1990), 4-55, at 55; see also R. J. Buck, *Boiotia and the Boiotian League 432-386 BC* (Alberta, 1994), 16. The hope seems to have been that revolutions in the individual cities of Boiotia would lead to a shake-up in federal Boiotia as a whole, see 2 n. below on τὰ Βοιώτια etc.

76. 1. Δημοσθένης Ἀθηναίων στρατηγὸς τεσσαράκοντα ναυσὶν ἀφικνεῖται ἐς Ναύπακτον, εὐθὺς μετὰ τὴν ἐκ τῆς Μεγαρίδος ἀναχώρησιν: 'immediately after the withdrawal of the Athenians from the Megarid, the Athenian general Demosthenes arrived at Naupaktos with forty ships'. For Naupaktos see i. 115. 1 n.: the Thirty Years Peace had ensured that Athens could use this crucial naval base from 446 and in the war, because Naupaktos was not strictly an Athenian possession.

Unusually, i.e. even more than at iii. 86 or iii. 92, Th. sets out in advance and in depth and detail the thinking behind a campaign, and this involves him in some (for him) experimental narrative technique: at 76. 1 he describes Demosthenes' arrival at Naupaktos, then in the rest of 76 he sets out the political and strategic planning which brought him there, then (77. 2) he resumes the narrative from 76. 1, so completing the ring (ἀφικόμενος resumes ἀφικνεῖται). The more obvious way of doing this (cp. ii. 80 and iii. 100) would have been to say 'In the same summer some Boeotians persuaded Demosthenes and Hippokrates to, etc.', and then unfold the story. One effect of the method Th. adopts here is to stress the active agency of the Athenian generals, rather than having them merely 'persuaded' by foreigners to do something, and that may be deliberate: the responsibility for Delion was no doubt controversial. But his willingness here to expand authoritatively on background planning may have something to do with his own inside knowledge acquired as a general or *strategos* this year, and the narrative method he adopts enables him to expand comfortably within the 'ring'. (By the time of the Delion campaign Th. may already have started for the north, though Pritchett, *SAGT* ii (1969), 24–36, at 34, argues that he took trouble to inform himself about the topography of Delion. Megara was earlier than Delion and Th. was in an even better position to keep himself informed, whether in the *strategeion* at Athens or via communiqués received in—I suggest—his privileged capacity as a general.) Finally, the method adopted grips the reader's attention better than a slow uncoiling from general considerations to particular actions.

The suggestion of Roisman (3. 1 n. on κατὰ τύχην etc.), 47, that Demosthenes was behind the whole plan is attractive, but we should be cautious about going beyond Th. here: see *CR* 44 (1994), 336.

2. τὰ Βοιώτια πράγματα ἀπό τινων ἀνδρῶν ἐν ταῖς πόλεσιν ἐπράσσετο, βουλομένων μεταστῆσαι τὸν κόσμον καὶ ἐς δημοκρατίαν ὥσπερ οἱ Ἀθηναῖοι τρέψαι: 'There were individuals in the cities of Boiotia who wanted to overthrow their constitution and set up a democracy like that of Athens'. The word 'cities' here is important for Hansen's argument about Siphai's *polis*-status, see 3 n. below on Σίφας μέν etc. Hansen thinks there were more *poleis* in Boiotia than those mentioned in *Hell. Oxy.* xix. Note the plural words for 'the cities' combined with the singular words for 'constitution', 'democracy'. This seems to be Th.'s non-technical way of referring to the federal arrangements in Boiotia: the conspirators surely wished to change these arrangements, as well as the internal political structure in their own cities. (At iv. 91 Th. refers to the boiotarchs, cp. also ii. 2. 1, v. 37 and 38, vii. 30. 3; see also iv. 72. 4 n. on τὸν μὲν ἵππαρχον etc. and v. 38. 2 n. for Th.'s knowledge of the federal set-up.)

καὶ Πτοιοδώρου μάλιστ' ἀνδρὸς φυγάδος ἐκ Θεσπιῶν ἐσηγουμένου: 'mainly at the instigation of Ptoiodoros, a Thespian exile'. I have changed the Oxford text ἐκ Θηβῶν ('a Theban exile'); the variant 'Thespian' is not recorded in the apparatus to the OCT, but in two manuscripts it is given as a variant, and Gomme was surely right to prefer it. For pro-Athenians at Thespiai cp. *IG* i³. 23 (Thespian proxenoi, one called Athenaios, line 7) with Lewis, *CAH* v². 116 n. 74; Th. iv.

133. 1, vi. 95. 2, and *IG* i³. 72 (about whose date, however, Lewis, the editor of *IG*, changed his mind: the positioning in *IG* implies 424, but he eventually preferred 414, the date of Th. vi. 95; see his commentary). For M. Walbank's unacceptable suggestion about the name Ptoiodoros see 3 n. below on καὶ οἱ Ὀρχομενίων etc. For Ptoiodoros as a good Boiotian name, derived from Apollo Ptoios, see *IG* vii. 2716. I. 9 (Akraiphnion); 2740 (ending lost, could be Ptoiodora); 2781. 28 (where it is a Boiotian patronymic in the form Πτωιοδώριος) and 4259. 2 (Oropos). *LGPN* will list nine from Boiotia (but no Thespian *or* Theban!). No need to emend Th. to the usual epigraphic Πτωιοδώρου.

3. Σίφας μὲν ἔμελλόν τινες προδώσειν (αἱ δὲ Σῖφαί εἰσι τῆς Θεσπικῆς γῆς ἐν τῷ Κρισαίῳ κόλπῳ ἐπιθαλασσίδιοι): 'Some of the democrats were to betray Siphai, which is a seaport on the Krisaian Gulf in Thespian territory'. For Siphai, modern Aliki, with fine post-fifth-century fortifications running down to the sea, see P. Roesch, *Thespies et la confédération béotienne* (Paris, 1965), 54–6, who says of the Thucydidean period that 'Siphai semble alors un point stratégique'; also J. M. Fossey, *Topography and Population of Ancient Boiotia* (Chicago, 1988), 167–75; H. Beister, in Lauffer (ed.), *Griechenland*, 682–3. Siphai does not feature by name in the description of the Boiotian confederacy in *Hell. Oxy.* xix, which gives the units which provided the boiotarchs (federal officials) and military contingents; but Siphai was presumably part of the unit which consisted of Thespiai, Eutresis, and Thisbai, and provided two boiotarchs. For this view see Grenfell and Hunt, *P.Oxy.* 5 (1908), 227, noting that Thespiai's two boiotarchs are not surprising in view of the city's extensive territory, which included Siphai on the evidence of the present passage of Th. (Actually Thisbai to the north-west is closer to Siphai than is Thespiai and one might be tempted to wonder whether Th.'s 'Thespiai' should not be corrected to some form of 'Thisbai', a name which does not otherwise occur in Th. and could have been ousted by what in Th. at least is the commoner name. But Stephanus of Byzantium says that Siphai was the harbour of Thespiai.) Siphai was later independent: *IG* vii. 207 (Michel 170: *c.*200 BC); Roesch thinks it got its autonomy in 338 or earlier. Pausanias (ix. 32. 4) calls Siphai Tipha and says the inhabitants claimed to be the best sailors in Boiotia and to have supplied a famous Argonaut, the actual steersman of the Argo, Tiphys.

For Thespiai see Fossey, 135–65, esp. 165 on its agricultural prosperity and 138 on its rich epigraphy (about 1400 inscriptions, which were to be published by the late P. Roesch); on Thespian territory see also P. Salmon, *Étude*, 92–4; P. W. Wallace, *Strabo's Description of Boiotia* (Heielberg, 1979), 98–9; J. Buckler and A. J. S. Spawforth in *OCD*³.

M. H. Hansen, 'Boiotian Cities—a Test Case', in M. H. Hansen (ed.),

Sources for the Ancient Greek Polis (Copenhagen, 1995), 12–63, at 19–21 and 32, argues that Siphai was a *polis* (strictly a 'dependent polis', in his terminology), notwithstanding its relationship of subordination to Thespiai (Thespiai represented federally, Siphai not, see Hansen, 34, except through Thespiai). He takes Th.'s reference to 'the cities of Boiotia' at para. 2 above to include Siphai and Chaironeia, for which see below. The conclusion may well be right, but since the plan was that Orchomenians were to betray Chaironeia, it is possible that Thespians were included among those who were to betray Siphai (i.e. the vague τινες, '*some* democrats', refers to or includes Thespians meddling in Siphan affairs, rather than or as well as Siphans proper, a possibility strengthened if Ptoiodoros came from Thespiai, see above). For Hansen's argument from 89. 2 see n. there. The reason for seizing Siphai and Chaironeia was their military and naval importance as key points, see next n.

Χαιρώνειαν δέ, ἣ ἐς Ὀρχομενὸν τὸν Μινύειον καλούμενον, νῦν δὲ Βοιώτιον, ξυντελεῖ, ἄλλοι ἐξ Ὀρχομενοῦ ἐνεδίδοσαν: 'and some people from Orchomenos were to hand Chaironeia over to the Athenians. Chaironeia is a dependency of Boiotian (what was once called 'Minyan') Orchomenos'. [Note: this lemma and the next overlap.] In *Hell. Oxy.* xix. 3, Orchomenos is linked to Hysiai, whereas Chaironeia is grouped with Akraiphnion and Kopai, having apparently achieved independence from Orchomenos since Th.'s time. Salmon, *Étude*, 91, speculates that Thebes helped Chaironeia to independence in an attempt to weaken the 'dangerous rival', Orchomenos.

Chaironeia, scene of Greek defeats at the hands of Philip II of Macedon in 338 BC and of Sulla in 86 BC, was a strategically crucial site controlling a main corridor (the Kephissos valley) into Boiotia and southern Greece for an invader from the north; Chaironeia, Siphai, and Delion were well chosen as the widely separated points of entry for a three-pronged penetration into Boiotia (so rightly Classen/Steup). For Chaironeia see Fossey (previous n.), 375–85; Wallace (previous n.), 146–9; Roesch (previous n.), 60–1; and J. M. Fossey and G. Gauvin, 'Les fortifications de l'acropole de Chéronée', in J. M. Fossey and H. Giroux (eds.), *Proceedings of the Third International Conference on Boiotian Antiquities* (Amsterdam, 1985), 41–75, esp. 41–2 on the city's position and 64 for some possibly fifth-century trapezoidal fortifications. Some interesting remarks in J. Ma, 'Black Hunter Variations. II: Damon of Chaironeia: a Historical Commentary (Plut. *Kim.* 1–2)', *PCPhS* 40 (1994), 60–9. For the status of Chaironeia (*polis* or not?) see previous n. Hansen believes it was a *polis*, but though this may be right, I am not sure that the conclusion can be extracted from Th. See further below.

'Minyan' is obscure. It is said to derive from the mythical individual 'Minyas' about whom E. Simon, *LIMC* vi. 1 (1992), 581–2, collects what can be said; but as she admits, Minyas is only known via his adjective!— which is sometimes used of the Argonauts as well as of Orchomenos. That is, the epithet is older even than the Trojan Wars, cp. G. S. Kirk, *The Iliad: A Comm.*, i. *Books 1–4* (Cambridge, 1985), 198, n. on *Iliad* ii. 511: Homer uses 'Minyan' to stress Orchomenos' legendary status. For Th.'s interest in a place name cf. iv. 3. 2 n. on καλοῦσι δέ etc.

For Orchomenos, in another strong position, on Lake Kopais, see Fossey, 351–65; also Wallace, 155–67, discussing Orchomenos' main tourist-attraction, the Mycenaean 'treasury of Minyas' (a well-preserved tholos tomb), for which see Paus. ix. 36. 5—indignant at Greek indifference to it in his own day, although possession of such a prize was surely relevant to classical Orchomenos' political pretensions.

The verb ξυντελεῖ with ἐς,'is a dependency of', is the correct expression in a Boiotian federal context, cp. *Hell. Oxy.* xix. 3, τότε δὲ συντελούντων εἰς τὰς Θήβας, of places dependent on Thebes. See C. J. Tuplin, 'The Fate of Thespiae during the Theban Hegemony', *Athenaeum*, 64 (1986), 321–41, at 322–4. The idea of financial contributions seems to be present, see LSJ[9] under συντελέω and Gomme, *HCT* iii. 667 on αὐτοτελεῖς at v. 18. 2 (although τέλος in a Boiotian context can simply mean a district, *SEG* iii. 354, about Koroneia).

Χαιρώνειαν δέ ... ἄλλοι ἐξ Ὀρχομενοῦ ἐνεδίδοσαν, καὶ οἱ Ὀρχομενίων φυγάδες ξυνέπρασσον τὰ μάλιστα: 'some people from Orchomenos were to hand Chaironeia over to the Athenians . . . Some Orchomenian exiles were the main people involved in this plot'. [Cf. previous lemma.] Are these two groups of people (the groups linked with Orchomenos) the same, or separate, or is one group a sub-class of the other? De Romilly in the Budé edn. identifies them, note the colon in her tr. I disagree; the first lot look like Orchomenian citizens, the second are exiles. It would be very cumbersome if by the second expression Th. was merely referring back to the immediately preceding expression. That is, Orchomenians (to use that word loosely) both inside, and exiled from, Orchomenos, were meddling in the affairs of Chaironeia.

As for the exiles, Th. keeps them anonymous, but from inscriptions we know two Orchomenian benefactors of Athens whom it is attractive to associate with the present episode, Potamodoros and his son Eurytion. After Delion they needed help from Athens and got it, including an immediate grant of 500 drachmae to Potamodoros. The main inscription is M. Walbank, *Proxenies*, no. 45 (*IG* i[3]. 73), part of which is dated securely to 424/3. But the family's proxeny goes back much earlier, perhaps as far as the early fifth century, the time of Potamodoros' grandfather (M. Walbank, no. 4). The evidence for this is a later inscription (412/11) honouring Eurytion and saying that he and his father are already proxenoi, and making it clear that Eurytion's ancestors were too: M. Walbank, *Proxenies*, no. 73 (*IG* i³. 97). Walbank (pp. 252–3) wonders if the text of Th. has suffered corruption because the name Potamodoros is 'remarkably like' Ptoiodoros at para. 1 above. This suggestion should be rejected: not only are both names perfectly good Boiotian names, and not particularly similar to each other, but we would need to suppose that Th. confused a man from Thespiai or Thebes with one from Orchomenos.

καὶ ἄνδρας ἐμισθοῦντο ἐκ Πελοποννήσου: 'and were trying to hire mercenaries from the Peloponnese'. From the fact that some of the exiles were wealthy enough to hire mercenaries, Buck 1990 (introductory n. to 76–7), 46, infers that 'there was support in the higher reaches of the hoplite census, presumably among some aristocrats'. These people may have been more concerned to bring about an alignment with Athens than to bring about democracy on an Athenian model (para. 2), whatever example that would mean in Boiotia. For individual wealthy Boiotians in the fourth century, see W. P. Wallace, 'Loans to Carystus about 370 BC', *Phoenix*, 16 (1962), 15–28.

(ἔστι δὲ ἡ Χαιρώνεια ἔσχατον τῆς Βοιωτίας πρὸς τῇ Φανοτίδι τῆς Φωκίδος, καὶ Φωκέων μετεῖχόν τινες): 'The town of Chaironeia is the last place in Boiotia near the territory of Panopeus in Phokis, and some Phokians also took part in the plot'. Like Gomme, I prefer Steup's punctuation to that of the OCT, which I have changed, i.e. the bracket should end after τινες, not after Φωκίδος, because the participation of the Phokians goes closely with the statement that Chaironeia is next to Phokis. The place-name I have translated as Panopeus is given as Phanotis by the manuscripts of Th., but Panopeus is the more familiar form, see *Iliad* ii. 520 and xvii. 307 (κλειτῷ Πανοπῆι, 'famous Panopeus') and Paus. x. 4. 1. It was a Phokian from Panopeus who later betrayed the plot, 89. 1.

Hecataeus of Miletos (*FGrHist* 1 F 116) had said that Chaironeia was the *first* city of Boiotia; so whereas Th.'s 'last place in Boiotia' implies an Attic perspective, Hecataeus' itinerary evidently brought him from Delphi and the other direction, see Jacoby's comm. This apart, the points are similarly put, and Hecataeus might be Th.'s 'source' here. But the fact is not out-of-the-way and Th. could have come up with it himself. Even if it is his own comment, note that it is phrased in ethnographic mode. Hellanicus (*FGrHist* 4 F 81) also mentioned the position of Chaironeia.

4. τοὺς δὲ Ἀθηναίους ἔδει Δήλιον καταλαβεῖν τὸ ἐν τῇ Ταναγραίᾳ πρὸς Εὔβοιαν τετραμμένον Ἀπόλλωνος ἱερόν: 'The

Athenians meanwhile were to seize Delion, a temple of Apollo which is in the district of Tanagra and looks towards Euboia'. The site of ancient Delion has been much disputed, but it is probably at modern Dilesi, see Pritchett, *SAGT* ii (1969), 24–36, and (with new evidence for the temple) *SAGT* iii (1980), 295–7; Fossey (3 n. on Σίφας μέν etc.), 62–6; P. Wallace (3 n. on Σίφας μέν etc.), 27–9. See also K. Braun, in Lauffer (ed.), *Griech-enland*, 181. Delion ought to be close to the sea because of 96. 7, 'towards Delion and the sea'; modern Dilesi is a sea-side resort for Athenians. The main difficulty with this identification is that Strabo says that Delion was 30 stades (perhaps 5 km.) from Aulis, but Dilesi is more like 12 km. Strabo's distance must be discarded; so apparently P. Wallace. See further below, 89 ff. for nn. on the battle itself, e.g. 96. 2 n. on καὶ ἑκατέρων etc. See also 95. 2 n. on ἐν γάρ etc.

For Tanagra see Fossey, 44–9, and Roesch (3 n. on Σίφας μέν etc.), 50–1. It was apart in eastern Boiotia and had one boiotarch to itself (*Hell. Oxy.* xix. 3).

5. εἰ καὶ μὴ παραυτίκα νεωτερίζοιτό τι τῶν κατὰ τὰς πολιτείας τοῖς Βοιωτοῖς: 'even if the constitutional units of Boiotia did not imme-diately break out in revolution'. The translation of τὰς πολιτείας is not easy. Jowett has 'the states of Boiotia', which is certainly more accurate than Warner's 'cities' as if the Greek were πόλεις. I have preferred the prosaic 'constitutional units' because the idea of 'constitution' is present; I believe that Th. is again thinking (cp. 2 n. above on τὰ Βοιώτια) of a conflagration of political change in all the federated cities of Boiotia, to be followed by federal change. For the significance of this point see 89. 1 n.

ἐχομένων τούτων τῶν χωρίων καὶ λῃστευομένης τῆς γῆς: 'they could hold the places which they had taken and plunder the country'. Hansen argues that Th. uses the word 'places' rather than 'cities' because Delion was not a *polis* though Siphai and Chaironeia were. I agree with Hansen's categorization but am not sure if Th. was as careful as that. For 'plundering the country' see further 92. 1 n. on μέλλουσι φθείρειν.

77. 1. ἡ μὲν οὖν ἐπιβουλὴ τοιαύτη παρασκευάζετο: 'That was the plot'. How realistic was it? Lewis remarks (*CAH* v². 425) that it 'depended on careful timing and secrecy, and secured neither'; this is of course based on Th., who however does not even offer that much by way of general comment. He tells us twice (76. 4, 77. 1) that Delion and Siphai had to happen on the same day and then at 89. 1 that there was a mix-up about the day; this repetition is emphatic and may imply censure of such elementary incompetence. (It is true that there was a three-month gap in time between Demosthenes' original departure from

Athens and the arrival of Hippokrates at Delion, see 89. 1 n.; but Greek calendars were sophisticated enough to make such precise co-ordination possible and easy in principle, see J. D. Mikalson, *OCD*³, entry under 'calendars, Greek'.) Note, however, that Demosthenes' too-early arrival at ch. 89 was in a sense irrelevant because the plot had already been betrayed. As for secrecy, that was bound to be more of a problem, see 42. 3 n. for security in Greek warfare generally; and Boiotian politics in particular were so messy and divided that the plan was probably over-optimistic (although it was actually a Phokian who betrayed it).

τὸν δὲ Δημοσθένη προαπέστειλε: 'He had sent Demosthenes ahead'. By itself this would suggest that Hippokrates was Demosthenes' superior officer, but they were both generals on a board of ten, and any-way one would have expected Demosthenes, with his greater military experience, to have the greater prestige. The reality behind the Greek may be that it was part of the arrangement for Demosthenes to go ahead. But a doubt remains. As Lewis says of this passage (*CAH* v². 425 n. 136), its 'clear implication . . . is that Thucydides thought of Hippo-crates as the senior partner, surprisingly to us'.

2. Οἰνιάδας τε ὑπὸ Ἀκαρνάνων πάντων κατηναγκασμένους καταλαβὼν ἐς τὴν Ἀθηναίων ξυμμαχίαν: 'he found that the com-bined Akarnanian groups had already forced Oiniadai to enter the Athenian alliance'. I have followed Poppo and Stahl, basically approved by Gomme, and changed the Οἰνιάδας δὲ ὑπό τε Ἀκαρνάνων of the OCT. For Oiniadai see i. 111. 3 n., and for the present incident see E. Oberhummer, *Akarnanien, Ambrakia, Amphilochia, Leukas im Altertum* (Munich, 1887), 114. The Athenians now at last take Oiniadai, which had eluded them in 429: ii. 102. The fragmentary inscription *IG* i³. 180 (previously *IG* i². 67) was for long supplemented to give a reference to Oiniadai, and brought into connection with the present episode; but Lewis in *IG* i³ preferred a rather later date, perhaps 415-410.

ἐπὶ Σαλύνθιον καὶ Ἀγραίους στρατεύσας πρῶτον: 'and first marched against Salynthios and the Agraians'. For Salynthios see iii. 111. 4 and 114. 2. For the Agraians and their territory on the right bank of the River Acheloos see W. J. Woodhouse, *Aetolia* (Oxford, 1897), 81-4: they are not proper Aitolians because they have a king, whereas the Aitolians were already federally organized, see ML 67 bis (*SEG* xxvi. 461).

78–88. *Brasidas' expedition to Thrace*

This, in Th.'s conception, was already envisaged at iii. 92. 4 (the motive for the founding of Herakleia in Trachis, cp. 78. 1 n. on ἐπειδὴ ἐγένετο etc. below), unless that passage was written with knowledge of Brasidas' operations i.e. with hindsight. Connor, *Thucydides*, 127 n. 44, cites with approval D. W. Knight, 'Thucydides and the War Strategy of Pericles', *Mnemosyne*, 23 (1970), 150–61, at 154, 157, for the view that Brasidas' ultimate motive was to interrupt the Athenian grain supply. Even P. D. Garnsey, *Famine and Food-supply in the Graeco-Roman World* (Cambridge, 1988), though generally reluctant to put concern for foreign grain at the centre of Athenian foreign policy, accepts at 132–3 that after the beginning of the Peloponnesian War Athens tightened its hold on the Hellespont. Brasidas' campaign would then be a response to a newly heightened Athenian dependence on Black Sea grain.

78. 1. Βρασίδας δὲ κατὰ τὸν αὐτὸν χρόνον τοῦ θέρους: 'During this summer, and about the same time, Brasidas'. After two chapters on the Athenians in Boiotia, Th. gives eleven on Thrace before reverting to Boiotia, then (ch. 102) back to Thrace. The main precedents for switching between theatres like this were Homer and Herodotus. Homer in the *Iliad* alternates between Troy and the Greek camp (and Olympus); the *Odyssey* is more complicated because much of it is action reported by Odysseus. Herodotus moves the narrative towards the Persian Wars by alternating action in Greece and Persia. Various techniques were available; one rather crude Homeric device is to pick up a narrative exactly where it had been abandoned, as if no time had passed in between; this principle of narration is called Zielinski's law, see T. Zielinski, *Philologus* suppl. 8 (1901), 419 ff., with the good discussion of R. Janko, *The Iliad: A Commentary*, iv. *Books 13–16* (Cambridge, 1992), 150: 'a scene which the poet sets aside is frozen into immobility.' (The most famous example, see Janko, is Nestor's drinking-bout which begins at *Iliad* xi. 624 ff. and is still going on at xiv. 1.) Th. by contrast and by an improvement makes it clear (as here) when one set of actions is simultaneous with another set, already described; for another example see 129. 2 n. on ὑπὸ γὰρ τὸν αὐτὸν χρόνον etc. (The present passage is vague in its indication of simultaneity, by comparison with 129. 2, where we have a definite jump back or analepsis.) Herodotus in book vii (where he is most clearly interweaving Greek and Persian affairs) is somewhere in between. He is perfectly capable of saying categorically 'while this was happening', e.g. vii. 26. 1 and 178. 1, cp. 174. But some of the main transitions from Persia (or rather, from the Persian army on the move) to Greece are more artfully, if more vaguely, done. Thus 133, Xerxes didn't send to Athens or Sparta for earth and water, enables a smooth transition to Sparta, then Athens and the oracles given to the Athenians, then the decisions to send envoys to Argos, Gelon, Crete. And so on.

See the interesting remarks of Babut, 434–6, for the interlacing of the

Boiotian and Thracian/Chalkidic narratives. The whole Delion plan was a blunder with the Brasidas menace looming in the north, and interlacing helps Th. to bring this out.

ἑπτακοσίοις καὶ χιλίοις ὁπλίταις: 'with one thousand seven hundred hoplites'. At 80. 5 we shall be told, by the technique of increasing precision, that this force included 700 helots and that the rest were hired troops from the Peloponnese; see Connor, *Thucydides*, 128 n. 46, and above, 70. 1 n. on τοὺς μεθ᾽ αὑτοῦ etc. (the 1000 will have included some of the Corinthians etc. there mentioned).

ἐπειδὴ ἐγένετο ἐν Ἡρακλείᾳ τῇ ἐν Τραχῖνι: 'When he arrived at Herakleia in Trachis'. See iii. 92. 4 for access to Thrace as one of the Spartan motives for founding Herakleia in 426; but see introductory n. above (there may be hindsight at iii. 92). See Malkin, *Myth and Territory*, 219–35 on the founding of Herakleia: Herakles, he suggests, was presented to the Trachinians not as an arbitrary 'Spartan' imposition from above, but as the Trachinians' own local hero *par excellence* (234). Noting the present passage of Th., Malkin (224) suggests that Brasidas may have been one of the promoters of the colony, precisely with a view to this northward march on Thrace. See 81. 1 n. on αὐτόν τε Βρασίδαν etc.

ἐς Φάρσαλον παρὰ τοὺς ἐπιτηδείους: 'to Pharsalos, where he had friends'. Cp. Xen. *Hell.* vi. 1 for another Pharsalian with Spartan connections, Polydamas. For the word ἐπιτήδειος see below 2 n. on ἐκ Λαρίσης Νικονίδας etc. G. Herman, *Ritualized Friendship and the Greek City* (Cambridge, 1987), 119, uses the present passage to illustrate the duties of guest-friends: they are expected to escort Brasidas in an awkward situation. Herman (119 n. 7) notes that Brasidas' friends are called his ξένοι at para. 4 below; this is another word for the relationship.

Πάναιρος: 'Panairos'. Cf. *IG* ix. 2. 247. The fullness of detail about these good Thessalian names is remarkable; it could reflect either Th.'s conversations with people on Brasidas' staff, or high-grade local Thessalian information: Nikonidas (below) is an obvious candidate. Cf. above, p. 103.

Ἱππολοχίδας: 'Hippolochidas'. A nice, aristocratic, 'horsey' Thessalian name for this Pharsalian. The name 'Hippolochos' was common in Thessaly, esp. in Larisa.

Τορύμβας: 'Torymbas'. Emended by Masson 1486–8 [328–30] from OCT Τορύλαος, 'Torylaos'; cf. Dion. Hal. x. 1. 1, *IG* ix. 2. 6a. 6. Probably scribal corruption.

Στρόφακος πρόξενος ὢν Χαλκιδέων: 'Strophakos who was the proxenos of the Chalkidians'. On this and other proxenies see ii. 29 introductory n., and 29. 1 n. on καὶ ἐν τῷ αὐτῷ θέρει etc. The importance of the Chalkidian connection becomes properly clear only at 79. 2 where we learn that the Chalkidians (and Perdikkas) had already summoned Brasidas, cp. next n. for Nikonidas. See Connor, *Thucydides*, 128, for Th.'s delaying of this 'essential information'. 'Strophakos', though also found at Miletos, is a good Thessalian name. One might be tempted to change the OCT Στρόφακος to Στρώφακος in the light of *IG* ii². 2406 line 7, Μένων Στρωφάκο[υ, 'Menon son of Strophakos'. Christian Habicht has (see *ZPE* 101 (1994), 221 n. 4) recognized this Attic inscription as a list of Thessalians (note Menon, cp. ii. 22. 3 and n.); see S. V. Tracy, *Athenian Democracy in Transition: Attic Letter-cutters of 340–290 BC* (Berkeley, 1995), 88. See also *SEG* xv, no.370c line 46, for a Στρωφακίδης from Thessalian Skotoussa, and *SEG* xxxv, no. 798, for a Στρώφακος Στρωφακίδ[ο]υ on a gravestone from Vergina in Macedonia. On the other hand, there is an epigraphically attested Στρόφακος at, precisely, Pharsalos (*IG* ix. 2. 234 line 89), so after all it may be safer to leave Th.'s Pharsalian Strophakos spelt with an omicron. As Professor Tracy kindly observes to me in a letter dated 30 November 1994, 'concerning the spelling of Strophakos with omikron/omega, I supposed they were dialectual variants and did not give the matter much thought. I do not think I would regularise the spelling'. I am grateful to Christian Habicht for help with this n.

2. ἐκ Λαρίσης Νικονίδας Περδίκκᾳ ἐπιτήδειος: 'Nikonidas a friend of Perdikkas from Larisa'. See above, n. on Πάναιρος ... Again (see previous n., on Στρόφακος etc.) the Perdikkas connection becomes clear only at 79. 2. The word ἐπιτήδειος, something of a favourite with Th., seems to have been particularly appropriate for these political friendships, cp. para. 1 above and e.g. ii. 18. 3; Herman (1 n. on ἐς Φάρσαλον etc.), 119 n. 7; Eernstman (above, Introduction, p. 66 n. 152) 66, 133–4. With the present passage cp. 132. 2 n. on παρασκευάσας etc.: Th. generalizes about Perdikkas' friendships with leading Thessalians.

Krüger changed the spelling Νικονίδας to Νικωνίδας because Plut. *Luc.* 10 has the form Νικωνίδης (a Thessalian siege-engineer). But see *IG* ix. 2. 211 for the form Νικονίδου (patronymic of a Thessalian called Stratippos; from Melitea in Phthiotic Achaia). Outside Thessaly, the name is very rare (*LGPN* files). But see, from *Larisa*, n.b.: *SEG* xiii. 391; xxix. 534, 540, cf. *IG* ix. 2. 519. 80 (Gyrton). Sometimes the spelling is -ουνίδας.

τὴν γὰρ Θεσσαλίαν ἄλλως τε οὐκ εὔπορον ἦν διιέναι ἄνευ ἀγωγοῦ καὶ μετὰ ὅπλων γε δή, καὶ τοῖς πᾶσί γε ὁμοίως Ἕλλησιν ὕποπτον καθειστήκει τὴν τῶν πέλας μὴ πείσαντας διιέναι: 'It was always difficult to cross Thessaly without an escort, and particularly difficult with an army. In general, crossing a neighbouring country without permission was something which aroused suspicion anywhere in Greece'. For the generalization about Greece see D. J. Mosley, 'Crossing Greek Frontiers Under Arms', *Rev. Int. des Droits de l'Antiquité*, 20 (1973), 161–9, a valuable collection of the evidence. He shows that it was legitimate and normal to cross someone else's country under arms unless you were at war with that country, and gives instances ('Greece was so fragmented that it was difficult to move far in any direction without encountering the frontier of a state . . . free rights of access could be assumed': p. 164, cp. 167 for the difficulty of sending an army any distance if you really had to 'make all the official requests for passage' in advance); this does not of course invalidate Th., who is merely talking about the suspicions which would be aroused. See also R. Bauslaugh, *The Concept of Neutrality in Classical Greece* (Princeton, 1992), 46 n. 47. Ridley, *Hermes* 1981, 39, echoing Gomme perhaps, calls this sentence of Th. a 'strange explanation', something 'it is hard to imagine any able-bodied Greek who had served in his army not being aware of'. But Mosley's material proves that the position was complex, so that Th.'s remark was not stupid or unnecessary; see also J. A. O. Larsen, *CP* 53 (1958), 124–5 (review of Gomme), who suggested against Gomme that καθειστήκει means that it *had* (i.e. recently) become less usual to grant free passage, and cited Th. v. 47. 5, clause in a treaty of 420 which restricted the passage of forces under arms. (Gomme thought the verb meant it was once *mal vu* to cross frontiers under arms but war had now made it commonplace.) See also 4 n. below.

τοῖς τε Ἀθηναίοις αἰεί ποτε τὸ πλῆθος τῶν Θεσσαλῶν εὔνουν ὑπῆρχεν: 'Besides, the ordinary people of Thessaly were always well disposed to the Athenians'. See ii. 29, introductory n.: despite the implications of the present passage, Athens had friends among the Thessalian upper classes. With the sentiment that the ordinary people of Thessaly were well disposed to Athens, compare Diodotos at iii. 47. 2 (the *demos* everywhere said to be well disposed to Athens) with my n. there. The echo makes me reluctant to follow Gomme in taking πλῆθος to mean 'the majority of full Thessalian citizens' rather than what Gomme calls 'the common people in the ordinary sense'. I agree with Gomme that *isonomia* in the next sentence does not imply democracy, but nor on the other hand does it imply the non-existence of something which could be called the common or ordinary people. The point of mentioning the ordinary people here is military: they were the people whom Brasidas would come across as he passed through Thessaly. I suspect that Th. was so accustomed (see next n.) to operating with the opposition between δυναστεία and ἰσονομία that he inserted the latter without giving it much thought, i.e. we should not worry about it to the extent of forcing an unnatural sense on πλῆθος.

3. ὥστε εἰ μὴ δυναστείᾳ μᾶλλον ἢ ἰσονομίᾳ ἐχρῶντο τὸ ἐγχώριον οἱ Θεσσαλοί, οὐκ ἄν ποτε προῆλθεν: 'And if Thessaly had not been traditionally run by a narrow oligarchy rather than a more

equal form of government, Brasidas could never have gone on'. See previous n. For ἰσονομία, 'a [more] equal form of government' see iii. 62. 3 n. on ἡμῖν μὲν γάρ etc. and for δυναστεία, 'narrow oligarchy' or 'small family clique' ibid. on δυναστεία etc. There (where the context is Theban), as here, the two concepts are opposed to each other, in a way that suggests that Th. was well versed in oligarchic theory, cp. iii. 65. 3 n. on καὶ πλείω etc.

The expression τὸ ἐγχώριον is adverbial, 'according to the traditions of the country'; the scholiast explains it thus (ἐγχωρίως). But he may have read τῷ ἐπιχωρίῳ with Dionysius of Halicarnassus, p. 799.

For the political situation in Thessaly in the fifth century see Rechenauer (71. 1 n. on αἱ δέ etc.), 240–1.

ἀδικεῖν ἔφασαν ἄνευ τοῦ πάντων κοινοῦ πορευόμενον: 'saying that he had no right to go further without the consent of the whole Thessalian people'. For the translation of κοινόν adopted here (basically, 'community'), see J. Tréheux, '*KOINON*', *REA* 89 (1987), 39–46, at 39–41, discussing and rejecting earlier interpretations, e.g. those which, like Gomme's, presuppose a meeting of the federal Thessalian assembly (there was surely no time for that) or which see here a reference to a federal executive.

4. αἰφνίδιόν τε παραγενόμενον ξένοι ὄντες κομίζειν: 'he had suddenly appeared and they were doing their duty as guest-friends in accompanying him'. See 1 n. above on ἐς Φάρσαλον etc. for guest-friendship, its obligation and its vocabulary, citing Herman.

Θεσσαλοῖς τε οὐκ εἰδέναι καὶ Λακεδαιμονίοις ἔχθραν οὖσαν ὥστε τῇ ἀλλήλων γῇ μὴ χρῆσθαι: 'He had never heard that there was any enmity between the Thessalians and Spartans which prevented either of them from passing through the territory of the other'. This is noticeably muted; the day was long past (so rightly U. v. Wilamowitz-Moellendorff, *Pindaros* (Berlin, 1922), 124) when one could have made positive appeal to the mythical links between Sparta and Thessaly, as alluded to by Pindar in the pairing at the beginning of *Pythian* 10 (*c*498 BC): ὀλβία Λακεδαίμων, μάκαιρα Θεσσαλία, 'happy Sparta, blessed Thessaly', both possessing royal lines descended from Herakles. For persistent Spartan interest in Thessaly and the north see A. Andrewes, 'Two Notes on Lysander', *Phoenix*, 25 (1971), 206–26, at 217–26, esp. 219 and 225.

Bauslaugh (2 n. above on τὴν γὰρ Θεσσαλίαν etc.), 47 n. 20, argues, against Gomme and on the basis of the present passage, that the Thessalians at this time were (not allied to Athens but) neutral.

Brasidas' remark is used by Larsen, 124–5, cp. Mosley, 161–2 (see 2 n. above on τὴν γὰρ Θεσσαλίαν etc.) as part of an argument that to refuse passage would normally be an act of hostility; the conclusion may well be right, but the particular argument from Th. perhaps makes insufficient allowance for Brasidas' very tricky situation, which called for some blustering rhetoric amounting to bluff (either Brasidas' own rhetoric or some put into his mouth by Th.).

5. δρόμῳ: 'at full speed' [lit. 'at a run']. Connor, *Thucydides*, 128 n. 45, notes that Th. often (e.g. ii. 25. 2, Brasidas' first mention) uses the vocabulary of 'running' about Brasidas, a characterization 'all the more striking when the reader remembers the repeated criticism of the Spartans for their slowness', e.g. i. 71. 4.

Brasidas' long and rapid journey has been thought to have a bearing on the date of the *Old Oligarch*, see 85. 4 n.

ἐκεῖθεν δὲ ἐς Φάκιον: 'From there he went on to Phakion'. Phakion was the last site in Thessaly proper, 'in the north-east corner of the western plain of Thessaly' (Gomme). The site is strictly unknown, but there is a possible ancient site, suggested by Stählin (n. on 6 below), 133–5, a little to the south of the line of the road between Trikka and Larisa, see his end-map. More recent commentators, such as Gomme, and Briscoe on Livy xxxii. 13. 9, go along with this.

6. οἱ δὲ Περραιβοὶ αὐτόν, ὑπήκοοι ὄντες Θεσσαλῶν: 'the Perrhaibians, who are subjects of the Thessalians'. Perrhaibia and the Perrhaibians are mentioned here only in Th. Perrhaibia was a border area between Thessaly and Macedonia, usually (as in the present passage) controlled by Thessaly, and geographically part of it, see H. D. Westlake, *Thessaly in the Fourth Century BC* (London, 1935), 15 and 85 n. 2; F. Stählin, *Das hellenische Thessalien* (Stuttgart, 1924), 5–39; G. Kip, *Thessalische Studien* (Neuenhaus, 1910), 111–28; Walbank, *HCP* ii. 613 (on Pol. xviii. 46. 5); B. Helly, *L'état Thessalien* (1995). A Latin inscription (*BSA* 17 (1910–11), 193–204), may imply that it formed part of Macedonia in the time of Amyntas III (early fourth cent.) and this might lie behind Diod. xv. 57. 2, which says that Jason of (Thessalian) Pherai conquered it (i.e. recovered it for Thessaly?). But the inscription is hard to interpret, see M. Crawford and D. Whitehead, *Archaic and Classical Greece* (Cambridge, 1983), no. 321B, comm. Gomme notes that Brasidas' route by the Petra pass avoided Larisa, 'doubtless for political reasons', by crossing the river Peneios higher up than Larisa, the usual crossing-point (but there was one friendly Larisan, Nikonidas, see 2 above).

κατέστησαν ἐς Δῖον τῆς Περδίκκου ἀρχῆς, ὃ ὑπὸ τῷ Ὀλύμπῳ Μακεδονίας πρὸς Θεσσαλοὺς πόλισμα κεῖται: 'brought him to Dion in the territory of Perdikkas. Dion is a town of Macedonia lying under Mount Olympus on the Thessalian side'. For Macedonian Dion, mentioned here only in Th., see Strabo vii, frag. 17; Walbank, *HCP* i. 516

(on Pol. iv. 62. 1–2, Skopas of Aitolia's raid on Dion in 219 BC); Hammond, *HM* i.125; P. A. Mackay, *Princeton Encyclopaedia*, 276. It was the scene of a festival to Zeus (the name Dion indicates the Zeus connection). The festival was possibly moved there from Aigai by King Archelaos (i.e. not many years after Brasidas' time), cf. Bosworth on Arr. *Anab.* i. 11. 1 (Arrian wrongly puts the festival at Aigai, but see Diod. xvii. 16. 3–4). Excavations by D. Pantermalis in the 1980s, reported in *Arch. Reps.*, seem to have turned up nothing earlier than the fourth cent.

The word πόλισμα here is puzzling on the view (which I doubt) that Th. always distinguishes it carefully from *polis*, see 52. 3 n. on καὶ τὰ ἐν τῇ ἠπείρῳ Αἰολικὰ πολίσματα. Dion was not obviously a strong place/fortress; nor, one would have thought, did its population (in Th.'s view) contain so large a non-Greek element as the small πολίσματα at 109. 3–4 (which include another place called Dion). But I suppose—without going into the large question whether Th. thought the Macedonians were Greeks, for which see 124. 1 nn. on καὶ ἦγον etc., and ἱππῆς etc.—that we must accept, on the evidence of the present passage, that he did not think Dion was a Greek-style *polis*.

79. 1. Βρασίδας Θεσσαλίαν φθάσας διέδραμε πρίν τινα κωλύειν παρασκευάσασθαι: 'Brasidas succeeded in getting through Thessaly fast before anybody could do anything to stop him'. This is very emphatic; φθάσας (lit. 'he anticipated') is not easy to translate elegantly, but means much the same as πρίν τινα κωλύειν παρασκευάσασθαι, 'before anybody could do anything to stop him'. For διέδραμε, another 'running' word, see 78. 5 n. on δρόμῳ.

2. ὡς τὰ τῶν Ἀθηναίων ηὐτύχει, δείσαντες: 'alarmed at Athens' recent successes'. That is, Pylos and Sphakteria. This generalizing reference to Athenian success is balanced by the generalization, at the end of the chapter, about the way things were going badly for Sparta (κακοπραγία); the two generalizations enclose the particular material about Perdikkas and the Chalkidians.

οἵ τε ἐπὶ Θράκης ἀφεστῶτες Ἀθηναίων καὶ Περδίκκας ἐξήγαγον τὸν στρατόν: 'Perdikkas and the Athenian allies in revolt in the Thraceward region had . . . summoned the army from the Peloponnese'. At last we are given, by an analepsis or flashback, the background and motive for an expedition which was first sprung on us at 70. 1, see n. there. The invitation must have preceded 70. 1 because Brasidas' operations are under way, but even then the explanation is a long time coming, so the whole section is an example both of narrative delay and of increasing precision. The effect (and presumably the aim) is to render Brasidas' arrival in Thrace highly dramatic. The Thessalians in the exciting ch. 78 do not know exactly what he is up to, and nor (unless we are reading Th. 'backwards') do we.

The tribute record of Thrace in the 420s is studied by M. Piérart, '*IG* i³. 281–282 et le *phoros* de Thrace', in D. Knoepfler (ed.), *Comptes et inventaires dans la cité grecque* (Neufchâtel, 1988), 309–31, esp. 310 and n. 5.

It may be helpful at this point to review and recapitulate the position in the north. Olynthos, the centre of a new Chalkidic league ('the Chalkidians'), the Bottiaians, and Potidaia had revolted in 432 (i. 58). Potidaia had been recovered with difficulty in winter 430/29 (ii. 70), but the Olynthians and Bottiaians remained in revolt despite all Athens' efforts. However, the revolt never included the whole of the Chalkidike in the geographical sense: see Zahrnt's map 2, between pp. 56 and 57, showing that the revolt did not include by any means all of the three Chalkidic prongs. Much of Pallene, the western prong, remained in Athenian control, including Mende and Skione. And the southern part of Sithonia, the central prong, was held by Athens, above all the important city of Torone. Most of Akte, the eastern prong, was still pro-Athenian, including Akanthos near the narrowest point. So Brasidas' efforts (abetted by 'the Chalkidians' i.e. above all the citizens of synoikized Olynthos) will be directed at Akanthos, Torone, Skione, and Mende.

Περδίκκας δὲ πολέμιος μὲν οὐκ ὢν ἐκ τοῦ φανεροῦ, φοβού-μενος δὲ καὶ αὐτὸς τὰ παλαιὰ διάφορα τῶν Ἀθηναίων: 'Perdik-kas was not an open enemy of Athens, but was afraid because of the old differences between himself and the Athenians'. One of the Methone decrees, ML 65 = *IG* i³. 61 lines 46–51, shows that Perdikkas was right to feel worried: the Athenians say that Methone's complaints against Perdikkas for his alleged unjust treatment will be considered when the two embassies sent to Macedon report to the people; for the significance of this see Lewis, *CAH* v². 426 n. 139. The relevant decree is securely dated to 426/5, cp. ML 72 line 5 (Megakleides is secretary both in the relevant Methone decree and in ML 72, but ML 72 has the archon name Euthynos).

On Perdikkas' behaviour at this time see J. T. Chambers, 'Perdiccas, Thucydides and the Greek City-States', *ΑΡΧΑΙΑ ΜΑΚΕΔΟΝΙΑ* (*Ancient Macedonia*), 4 (1986), 139–45, at 143–5, stressing that Perdikkas' motives seem to have had little to do with Athens or the war, but a lot to do with Lynkos. Certainly modern criticisms of Perdikkas for his switches of side are inappropriate because unconsciously made from the standpoint of Athens (or Sparta). Cp. Badian, *From Plataea to Potidaea*, 176, rightly chiding the usual presentation of Perdikkas as an 'unreliable liar' (though Badian's main concern is the narrative of books i and ii).

For the participially expressed motivation (φοβούμενος, 'was afraid'), see 9. 1 n. on Δημοσθένης δὲ ὁρῶν. Perdikkas is perhaps the only surprise among the six highest-scoring Thucydidean agents in Mabel Lang's list.

Ἀρραβαῖον τὸν Λυγκηστῶν βασιλέα: 'Arrhabaios, king of the Lynkestians'. He is more fully introduced at 83. 1, see n. there. The name Arrhabaios (for which see Masson 1480 f. [322 f.]) recurs in the fourth-century inscription Tod 148 as the patronymic of a Menelaos who is probably identical with the 'Menelaos the Pelagonian' of Tod 143. Tod accepted the view that this Menelaos was the grandson of the Lynkestian king mentioned in the present passage by Th. But Pelagonia and Lynkos are not the same, though close, and the suggestion of direct ancestry should probably be rejected, see Hammond, *HM* ii. 20, and M. Osborne, *Naturalization in Athens*, iii and iv (Brussels, 1983), 61 n. 174 on T56, also F. Papazoglou, *Les villes de Macédoine à l'époque romaine* (*BCH* suppl. 16, 1988), 278-9 (cp. *SEG* xxxviii. 58).

For Lynkos and Arrhabaios' territory see 83. 2 n.

3. ἡ τῶν Λακεδαιμονίων ἐν τῷ παρόντι κακοπραγία: 'The Spartans . . . because they themselves were doing so badly at the time'. See 2 n. above on ὡς τὰ τῶν Ἀθηναίων ηὐτύχει etc.

80. 1. τῶν γὰρ Ἀθηναίων ἐγκειμένων τῇ Πελοποννήσῳ καὶ οὐχ ἥκιστα τῇ ἐκείνων γῇ: 'now that the Athenians were applying pressure to the Peloponnese, and especially Lakonia'. The reference is to Pylos, Methana, and Kythera, see 41. 2, 45. 2 and 55. 1.

Chs. 80-1 form the third of the six digressions on morale in iv–v. 24, see Introduction, above, p. 109.

2-3. καὶ ἅμα τῶν Εἱλώτων βουλομένοις ἦν ἐπὶ προφάσει ἐκπέμψαι, μή τι πρὸς τὰ παρόντα τῆς Πύλου ἐχομένης νεωτερίσωσιν· ἐπεὶ καὶ τόδε ἔπραξαν φοβούμενοι αὐτῶν τὴν νεότητα καὶ τὸ πλῆθος (αἰεὶ γὰρ τὰ πολλὰ Λακεδαιμονίοις πρὸς τοὺς Εἵλωτας τῆς φυλακῆς πέρι μάλιστα καθειστήκει): 'They were also glad of a pretext for getting temporarily rid of some of the helots: they were afraid of a helot rising now that Pylos was occupied. (Spartan policy towards the helots was largely determined by considerations of security.) They were so afraid of the number and youthful vigour of the helots that . . .'. There is a textual crux here, νεότητα or σκαιότητα? Both have some manuscript authority. The first (which I agree with Gomme is preferable) would mean 'youthfulness'; the obvious objection to this is that not all helots were young. (But the formidable ones presumably were.) The OCT has σκαιότητα, 'awkward-ness', 'stupidity'(cf. Hdt. ix. 80), which is defended by W. E. Thompson,

'The Corruption at Thucydides 4.80.3', *Anc. Hist. Bulletin*, 1 (1987), 61–4, who suggests that the Spartans refused to acknowledge that others cherished their autonomy, and so put down the persistence of the helots to stupidity. On this view 'stupidity' is embedded focalization: the judgement is not Th.'s but that of the Spartans. This is ingenious, but I suspect the Spartans regarded helot aspirations as all too rational; in any case it seems odd to fear rather than despise helot stupidity.

There is also a problem of translation a little further on. With Gomme, but against Jowett, I take the generalization in the bracketed Greek words to mean that most Spartan relations with the helots were precautionary in character (rather than 'most of the Lacedaemonian institutions were specially intended to guard them against this source of danger': Jowett). So K. Welwei, *Unfreie im antiken Kriegsdienst* (*Forschungen zur antiken Sklaverei* 1: Wiesbaden, 1974), 109 n. 7.

For helots see i. 101. 2 n. Th.'s generalization here, about Spartan policy towards them, has been much discussed in connection with the Spartan social system, and is equally important for the historian however the Greek be translated. R. J. A. Talbert, 'The Role of the Helots in the Class Struggle at Sparta', *Historia*, 38 (1989), 22–40, argued that tension between Spartiates and helots was limited, but P. Cartledge, in his reply, insisted (rightly in my view) that the present passage of Th. points firmly the other way: *Historia*, 40 (1991), 379–81. As Cartledge notes against Talbert, Spartan willingness (para. 5 below) to use helots as hoplites does not indicate indifference to the helot threat: Spartan policy to the helots was always a cunning mixture of repression (as in the Kinadon affair, Xen. *Hell.* iii. 3) and inducements. (The sociologist H. Marcuse, in *One-Dimensional Man*, described this sort of thing as 'repressive tolerance'.) The effectiveness of Spartan methods is seen most clearly after Leuktra (371 BC) when large numbers of helots astonishingly enlisted in aid of Sparta when it was militarily on its knees: Xen. *Hell.* vi. 5. 29. On the inconsistency between fearing helots and using them note the acute comment of Y. Garlan, 'War and Peace', in J.-P. Vernant (ed.), *The Greeks*, trans. C. Lambert and T. L. Fagan (Chicago and London, 1995), 53–85, at 74: 'it is significant that the helots, who were considered particularly treacherous, were clearly more in demand than Athenian slaves: this is because their residual vocation as a formerly free people explained both their defiant spirit and their relative military aptitude.' See also v. 23. 3 n.

3–4. προεῖπον αὐτῶν ὅσοι ἀξιοῦσιν ἐν τοῖς πολέμοις γεγενῆσθαι σφίσιν ἄριστοι, κρίνεσθαι, ὡς ἐλευθερώσοντες, πεῖραν ποιούμενοι καὶ ἡγούμενοι τούτους σφίσιν ὑπὸ φρονήματος, οἵπερ καὶ ἠξίωσαν πρῶτος ἕκαστος ἐλευθεροῦσθαι, μάλιστα ἂν

καὶ ἐπιθέσθαι. καὶ προκρίναντες ἐς δισχιλίους, οἱ μὲν ἐστε-
φανώσαντό τε καὶ τὰ ἱερὰ περιῆλθον ὡς ἠλευθερωμένοι, οἱ δὲ
οὐ πολλῷ ὕστερον ἠφάνισάν τε αὐτοὺς καὶ οὐδεὶς ᾔσθετο ὅτῳ
τρόπῳ ἕκαστος διεφθάρη: 'they proclaimed that a choice would be
made of those helots who claimed to have done the best service to
Sparta in war, and promised them freedom. The announcement was
meant to test them; they thought that those among them who were
most keen to win their freedom would also be the most high-spirited,
and most likely to rise against their masters. So they chose about two
thousand, who crowned themselves with garlands and went in procession round the temples: they were supposed to have been freed, but
not long afterwards the Spartans did away with them and nobody knew
how any of them was killed'. Th. leaves the date of this incident timeless,
floating in the air; it is, in fact, an 'achrony': for this term see M. Bal, *Narratology* (introductory n. to 66–135), 66, and G. Genette, *Figures* III (Paris,
1972), 119, trans. *Narrative Discourse* (Oxford, 1980), 84. (Another
example is the Athenian alliance with Akarnania at ii. 68. 8.) B. Jordan,
'The Ceremony of the Helots in Thucydides IV. 80', *L'Ant. Class.* 59
(1990), 37–69, at 55, in the course of an exhaustive discussion of the
whole section, suggests that the liquidation of the helots happened
before, but not long before, Brasidas' expedition, 'perhaps during the
year following the Sphacteria surrender'. But much earlier dates are
possible (C. D. Hamilton, 'Social Tensions in Classical Sparta', *Ktema*, 12
(1987), 34 ff., thinks the warfare referred to by ἐν τοῖς πολέμοις could be
that of the 470s and 460s). Hence Jowett's trans. introduced the story
with the word 'Once', i.e. 'Once upon a time'. But this is not in the Greek,
so I have removed it. In any case, we must agree with Andrewes, *HCT* v.
366, that the present passage breaches Th.'s normal habit of indicating
events within a 'firm chronological framework' (365): 'no indication is
given of the date of this earlier murder of helots (contrast iii. 34. 1).' That
is a good contrast: iii. 34 gives a precise retrospective dating of Itamenes'
capture of Kolophon.

There is nothing implausible about the promise of freedom, see i. 132.
4, iv. 26. 5, and Xen. *Hell.* vi. 5. 28. For the significance of helot 'high-
spiritedness' see Garlan, cited in previous n.

For the crowning or garlanding see M. Blech, *Studien zum Kranz bei
den Griechen* (Berlin, 1982), 364, showing that garlanding was particularly appropriate to free men, and citing Artemidorus i. 77 ἴδιον γὰρ
ἐλευθέρων οἱ στέφανοι, 'garlands are characteristic of free men'. On the
processing and garlanding see also Jordan, who concludes that the helots
were presumptuously imitating the ceremony of election to the *gerousia*
or council of Spartan elders, see Plut. *Lyc.* 26 and Ar. *Pol.* 1271a9–18;
hence their punishment. (Cp. J. Bremmer, *Greek Religion* (*Greece and Rome*

New Survey 24: Oxford, 1994), 40, 'processions were particularly suited to make symbolic statements about power relations, since they often drew large audiences'.) The circumambulation of the temples, Jordan thinks, fits Nilsson's type of procession in which a circle is created which protects everything inside it, see M. Nilsson, 'Das Prozessionstypen im griechischen Kult', *Opuscula Selecta*, i (Lund, 1951), at 179–88, for such magical processions. If Jordan is right, what we have here is a change of mind or failure of nerve, perhaps evidence of divided opinion among the Spartiates; the less plausible alternative is to see the entire incident as coldly planned from the start.

The above is written on the assumption that the whole extraordinary story is true. But there are grounds for unease, most obviously the sheer difficulty of doing away with so many able-bodied men, without modern methods. But what of the details? One might be troubled by the figure 2000, of which Th. was fond, see ii. 70. 2 (cost in talents of the siege of Potidaia); vii. 48. 5 (the Syracusans had spent more than 2000 talents); iv. 52. 2 (2000 Phokaian staters). See D. Fehling, trans. J. G. Howie, *Herodotus and his 'Sources'* (Liverpool, 1989), 229–30, for (?suspicious) frequency of 2000 in Hdt. But the figure 2000 is common in Th., and no doubt also in real life, for a large hoplite force, see e.g. i. 29. 1, 61. 1; iii. 91. 1; iv. 42.1, 53. 1, 100. 1; v. 6. 5, 57. 2; so 2000 helots was a militarily plausible total. We are left with the more basic implausibility of killing so many people in such a way as to leave no trace. But note that Th. uses no distancing formula such as 'it is said', λέγεται, that would strictly justify Lewis, *CAH* v². 426 n. 141, 'it was said that the first two thousand to volunteer mysteriously disappeared . . .'

5. καὶ τότε προθύμως τῷ Βρασίδᾳ αὐτῶν ξυνέπεμψαν ἑπτα-κοσίους ὁπλίτας, τοὺς δ᾽ ἄλλους ἐκ τῆς Πελοποννήσου μισθῷ πείσας ἐξήγαγεν: 'So they were only too eager to send seven hundred helots with Brasidas as hoplites. He hired the rest of his army from the Peloponnese'. See 70. 1 n. on τοὺς μεθ᾽ αὑτοῦ etc. Only now are we given the means to calculate how Brasidas' forces were made up in detail. The word for 'eager', here used in its adverbial form (προθύμως) to describe Spartan feelings about helots, is repeated (as a verb) in the next sentence (81. 1) to describe Chalkidian feelings about Brasidas; the repetition prepares us for the presentation of Brasidas as someone expected to be dynamic and positive. (In the language of C. Gill, see Introduction, p. 42, he is defined in terms of character rather than personality, i.e. actively not passively.) At 81. 2 we have the related word ἐπιθυμία, used of the attraction Brasidas exerted on Athens' allies.

On the hiring of troops here see Parke (66. 3 n. on ἐν ᾗ αὐτοί etc.), 40: it anticipates fourth-century methods.

Andrewes, in Garnsey and Whittaker (eds.), *Imperialism* (87. 5 n. on
οὐδ᾽ αὖ etc.), 99 with 305 and n. 20, notes that the *neodamodeis*, helots
liberated in advance of military service, were presumably not yet available in 424, at least not for use by Brasidas. They first appear at v. 34. 1.

**81. 1. αὐτόν τε Βρασίδαν βουλόμενον μάλιστα Λακεδαιμόνιοι
ἀπέστειλαν (προυθυμήθησαν δὲ καὶ οἱ Χαλκιδῆς):** 'He himself
was very keen to go, and the Chalkidians were eager to have him. So the
Spartans sent him.' See previous n. for the tense and insistent words for
desire and eagerness; they lead naturally into the character-sketch that
follows, which is expressed largely, though not wholly, in terms of anti-
cipations of or reactions to him (so that the reiterated words for desire
are appropriate). For such 'indirect narration' in Th. see J. Lothian (ed.),
Adam Smith, *Lectures on Rhetoric and Belles Lettres* (London, 1963), 88–90.
The device is Homeric, cp. the *teichoskopia* in *Iliad* iii, which enables the
poet to present the Greek heroes through Helen's eyes, as she points
them out to Priam from the walls of Troy; we are after all in the *aristeia*
of Brasidas, see Introduction, pp. 38–61. The indirectness about Brasidas
is more than a literary device: it (*almost*) buries Th.'s own view of him,
see Connor, *Thucydides*, 131 (against earlier views which see ch. 81 as
giving Th.'s own assessment): 'there is relatively little [but see above
pp. 55 f., and 2 n. below on ἑαυτόν etc.] in the passage that indicates the
author's own view and a great deal concerning contemporary reaction to
him.' The reason for this is not, presumably, that Th. disapproved of
Brasidas or thought him a fraud (though see 108. 5 and n.), but that the
real 'long-run importance' (Connor) of his qualities lay in the expectations and the pro-Spartan feelings he excited.

This para. raises the question of Brasidas' relationship to the home
government and of his attitude to the sending of the expedition. See
generally Kallet-Marx, 171, who argues trenchantly that Brasidas does
not represent official policy, and that the Spartan leadership as a whole
may still not have grasped the necessity of striking at Athens' financial
power (see 87. 3 and n.). First Brasidas. It is surely reasonable to suppose
that Brasidas favoured the sending of the expedition, but (i) strictly the
Greek just means that he personally was keen to go and (ii) the initiative
was in any case not merely Spartan because Perdikkas and the
Chalkidians 'summoned', ἐξήγαγον, the Spartan army (79. 2), and
indeed the present passage reminds us of the Chalkidians' eagerness.

As for the home government or Spartan leadership, (i) we have just
been told that because of the helot problem they were only too glad to
see the back of the 700 helots, and (ii) they seem to have wanted at the
outset what they eventually got, namely conquests to bargain with, see

81. 2 with Raaflaub, *Freiheit*, 252 n. 172; cp. also 108. 7. (iii) Brasidas himself will say at 86. 1 that he has extorted sworn guarantees from the authorities at Sparta that they will respect the autonomy of places he wins over. This claim, which is corroborated by the narrative at 88. 1, see n., implies not just that the authorities had reservations, but that these reservations had been discussed and overcome; that is, *he was carrying out agreed policy*. If it were not for the narrative corroboration we would probably conclude that in view of Sparta's actual treatment of e.g. Amphipolis and Torone the oaths look like merely seductive rhetoric. The Thucydidean Brasidas is an unusual type of Spartan, and Kallet-Marx may well be right that other Spartans did not see the importance of removing revenue-producing cities; note esp. the jealousy of Brasidas felt by 'the first men' at Sparta, 108. 7: as Lewis says (*CAH* v². 426): 'his ambitious plans found no welcome at Sparta.' Can we then conclude that his successes do not reflect 'official Spartan policy'? The evidence is ambiguous. In the fourth century the Spartans sometimes found it convenient to disapprove of or distance themselves from policies or actions of their nationals while profiting from those actions or policies; one thinks of Phoibidas' seizure of Thebes in the 380s, when the Spartans 'punished the offender but condoned the offence' (Plut. *Pel.* 6). The same may have been true in the fifth century. Thus (to return to Brasidas), there is on the one hand the *phthonos* or jealousy of him mentioned at 108. 7, and 132. 3 may imply a Spartan wish to curb Brasidas. On the other hand there is full co-operation between him and the Spartan commissioners at 122. 4 over Skione, cp. 117, where we are told that the Spartans were happy to go on benefiting from Brasidas' achievements, cp. above on 81. 2. Had Brasidas been less successful it would no doubt have been different. Literary considerations are also relevant: part of Th.'s object is to present him as a romantic 'loner', but he was not as cut off from home as, say, Hannibal in Italy. Note esp. v. 12–13, Rhamphias' reinforcements, and esp. 13. 1 n. on νομίσαντες etc. See Introduction, p. 50–61.

     Note that if Malkin is right (*Myth and Territory*, 224) that Brasidas was one of those behind the sending of the colony to Herakleia in Trachis, and that he already had his northern mission in mind at that time, this would be evidence that Brasidas was on the same wavelength as the Spartan authorities as early as 426. But Malkin's idea is conjectural.

ἄνδρα ἔν τε τῇ Σπάρτῃ δοκοῦντα δραστήριον εἶναι ἐς τὰ πάντα: 'at Sparta he was thought an energetic man in every way'. For this device ('a man who . . .') as a way of emphasizing an individual's importance see Connor, 130 n. 52; the last occurrence was 21. 3, Kleon. The word δραστήριος, lit. a [successful] 'doer', is rare in Th., being used elsewhere only at ii. 63. 3. Diodorus' word for 'energetic' is δραστικός on which see

J. Hornblower, *Hieronymus of Cardia* (Oxford, 1981), 279 and n. 21: he uses it three times in fourteen chapters, all about Agesilaos (xv. 19. 4; 31. 4; 33. 1).

This sentence about Brasidas the *doer* is complemented at 84. 2 below by the favourable assessment of Brasidas the *speaker*, see n. there.

πλείστου ἄξιον ... γενόμενον: 'he proved invaluable'. For the expression cp. ii. 65. 4 (said about Pericles); see Connor, 130 n. 52. The past participle γενόμενον may indicate that the end of the sentence was inserted later than the rest, see Griffith, *PCPhS* 187 (1961), 29–30 and n. 1.

2. ἑαυτὸν παρασχὼν δίκαιον καὶ μέτριον ἐς τὰς πόλεις: 'he showed himself just and moderate to the cities'. For the 'moderation of Brasidas' theme (Babut, 431–3) see 105. 2 n. on καὶ τὴν ξύμβασιν etc., and 108. 2 n. on ὁ γὰρ Βρασίδας, etc. where we have ἑαυτὸν παρεῖχε, cp. ἑαυτὸν παρασχών here, the same expression for 'showing oneself' to be something. Jowett translates the present passage 'he gave an impression of justice and moderation', but 108. 2 'he showed himself moderate'. Where the two passages are so nearly identical, one ought to translate the same way both times. But which? Bétant renders the expression 'se gerere'; LSJ⁹ under παρέχω A.II.3 has 'show, exhibit oneself so-and-so'. I therefore prefer 'showed himself' to the more obviously cynical 'gave an impression': Th. thought Brasidas *really had these qualities*. This is not to deny that Th., esp. at 108. 5, expresses cynicism about Brasidas and his image. See Introduction, pp. 55 f., discussing Connor's view.

With Th.'s formulation here Connor, 130 n. 52, compares and contrasts both i. 130. 2, Pausanias the Regent δυσπρόσοδόν τε αὐτὸν παρεῖχε, 'he made himself [lit. 'showed himself'] difficult to approach', and i. 77. 6, the Athenians' generalizing comment on the unacceptable behaviour of Spartans abroad: see S. Hornblower, 'The Fourth-Century and Hellenistic Reception of Thucydides', *JHS* 115 (1995), 47–68, at 66–7, for the series of Spartans from Alkidas on (iii. 32. 2) who behave badly, οὐ καλῶς, before and after Brasidas. Th. is insisting on the singularity of Brasidas' methods, compared to other (not just earlier) Spartans; see also para. 3 n. below and 84. 2.

τὰ δὲ προδοσίᾳ εἷλε τῶν χωρίων: 'while others were betrayed to him'. Jowett's trans., which I have not changed, smooths over the difficulty that the verb here is active, '*he took* places by treachery', and this does not look much like justice or moderation. But the point is, I suppose, that his perceived justice and moderation were what gave rise to pro-Spartan factions.

ἀνταπόδοσιν καὶ ἀποδοχὴν χωρίων: 'they had places to give in return for what they hoped to recover'. For Raaflaub's plausible suggestion that this was the Spartan thinking behind the sending of Brasidas see 81. 1 n. above on αὐτόν τε etc. This is a nice example of a modern historian reasoning like Th., i.e. inferring motivation from results! Lewis, *Sparta and Persia*, 69 n. 121 (with refs. to Brunt and de Ste Croix), sees the difference between intending a result and capitalizing on it: 'bargaining counters' may merely be what Brasidas' gains turned out to be.

τοῦ πολέμου ἀπὸ τῆς Πελοποννήσου λώφησιν: 'to lighten the pressure of war on the Peloponnese'. The abstract noun λώφησις is used here only in Th.; as in the character-sketch of Themistokles, i. 138, Th.'s style becomes more abstract hereabouts, cp. ἀνταπόδοσιν above for the return of territory.

ἔς τε τὸν χρόνῳ ὕστερον μετὰ τὰ ἐκ Σικελίας πόλεμον ἡ τότε Βρασίδου ἀρετὴ καὶ ξύνεσις: 'And at a later period of the war, after the Sicilian expedition, the honourable conduct and ability of Brasidas'. This passage was evidently written late (cp. Dover, *HCT* v. 411–12), and like para. 3 below it implies a long and (from the point of view of disillusioned enthusiasts for Sparta) not very pleasant perspective. (Gomme thought the whole chapter was written in a manner foreign to the context of the narrative, and so written late like ii. 65. This may be right, but Th. was capable of varying his register to suit the subject matter, cp. above on τοῦ πολέμου etc.)

Note the interesting reference to the Ionian or Decelean War as merely the war which followed the Sicilian Expedition: Th. had no special expression for it, cp. v. 26. 3 n., with De Ste. Croix, *OPW* 295, and my article in *JHS* 115 (1995), at 60 n. 65.

The combination of ἀρετή and ξύνεσις, albeit only in the perception of others, puts Brasidas in a select category: for ξύνεσις, 'intelligence', see i. 79. 2 n. with references, to which add A. Cook, 'Particular and General in Thucydides', in *History/Writing* (Cambridge, 1988), 43; and for the combination with ἀρετή cp. vi. 54. 5 (the Pisistratids; see further below). The Greek quality *arete* is impossible to translate satisfactorily. Much has been written about it since the time of Gomme, who did not think it worth stopping for. LSJ[9] lists 'goodness', 'excellence', 'valour', but also registers the sense 'moral virtue', and it is debatable how far and how often the latter sense is present, cp. A. W. H. Adkins, *Merit and Responsibility* (Chicago, 1960), but for a better view, stressing that *arete* had an ethical flavour early and often, see H. Lloyd-Jones, *The Justice of Zeus* (Berkeley, 1971), 2, 136–7, 158, and generally. Good discussions by Andrewes in *HCT* on v. 105. 4 (with reservations about Adkins' views) and by Dover in *HCT* on vi. 54. 5 and vii. 86. 5 (on which cp. also Adkins, 'The *Arete* of Nikias: Thucydides 7.86', *GRBS* 16 (1975), 379–92). It is a word of high praise, but sometimes denotes excellence in an almost functional way. Thus at the highly problematic (and too often neglected) Th. viii. 68. 1 it is used of Antiphon, a discreditable figure in some ways and by Greek standards; and there, see Andrewes's n., it hardly refers to more than Antiphon's excellence as a forensic speaker (though Andrewes concedes a possible moral sense: Antiphon was loyal to his friends). Returning to Brasidas, the judgement is complicated by the fact, already noted, that we are here dealing with Brasidas as he appeared, not as Th. necessarily judged him to be. As always with an abstract noun which Th. pairs with another or to which he attaches an adjective, it is important to look at what company the noun is keeping (cp., for *philotimia*, ii. 65. 7 n. on κατὰ τὰς ἰδίας etc. and iii. 82. 8 n. on πάντων etc.). Here the association with ξύνεσις suggests (in the light of Th.'s own application of ξύνεσις elsewhere) that the word *arete* is commendatory at a higher level than viii. 68 (Antiphon); but (it may be said) ξύνεσις is an intellectual rather than a moral term, and we must still enquire how far there is an ethical flavour at iv. 81. The context (Brasidas' dealings with those with whom he came into contact) is crucial, and shows that we are concerned with perceived standards of interpersonal behaviour (so J. L. Creed, 'Moral Values in the Age of Thucydides', *CQ* 23 (1973), 213-31, at 220, firmly putting the present passage among 'quiet' i.e. non-competitive uses of ἀρετή, to use Adkins' terminology). The Penguin 'gallantry' is therefore not quite right for Brasidas, because to the modern reader it suggests behaviour on the battlefield or towards women. Bétant lists the present passage as an instance of *arete* in the sense of 'probitas', 'innocentia', and this resembles Jowett's 'honesty'. These renderings perhaps emphasize the ethical content too exclusively, so I have (with some indebtedness to Andrewes in his n. on v. 105) offered 'honourable conduct' as (i) indicating that Brasidas' behaviour was thought to conform to the highest Greek values to be looked for in a male military leader, while (ii) allowing that those values allotted esteem to an amalgam of soldierly, ethical, and functional qualities.

Finally, we may glance forward to vi. 54 and the Pisistratids, who are also said to combine ξύνεσις and ἀρετή. 'Honourable conduct' suits the sense of *arete* there reasonably enough (Dover remarks that the unobtrusive and lenient exercise of power was 'good' in as far as refraining from forcing the will of others is good); but the contexts are different and we need not feel obliged to adopt precisely the same tr. for vi. 54 as for iv. 81. The combination of ἀρετή and ξύνεσις is also attributed by implication to Antiphon (viii. 68. 1 and 4) but at different points in the ch.; at viii. 68. 4 the active oligarchs collectively (and including Antiphon) are said to be ξυνετοί.

The present passage begins as if categorically and authorially attributing *arete* and *xynesis* to Brasidas, and this attribution is not cancelled; but (see next n.) Th. immediately slides to an emphasis on what people heard about it and their experience of it. See Introduction, pp. 56–60.

τῶν μὲν πείρᾳ αἰσθομένων, τῶν δὲ ἀκοῇ νομισάντων: 'which some had experienced, and which others knew about by reputation'. The word for 'knew about' (*νομίζω*) here really means 'believed in', as one could be said to *νομίζειν* the gods, cp. Steup citing Krüger. The opposition experience/hearsay looks Herodotean, cp. autopsy vs. hearsay at Hdt. ii. 99. 1. But I would not claim this as a Herodotean allusion.

μάλιστα ἐπιθυμίαν ἐνεποίει τοῖς Ἀθηναίων ξυμμάχοις: 'mainly attracted the Athenian allies'. Gomme thought that this remark about enthusiasm for Sparta, and for Brasidas, was not written at the same time as ii. 8. 4–5: enthusiasm at the beginning of the Ten Years War. But as Dr. Rood points out to me, enthusiasm is not the same as *eunoia* (good will).

3. πρῶτος γὰρ ἐξελθὼν καὶ δόξας εἶναι κατὰ πάντα ἀγαθὸς ἐλπίδα ἐγκατέλιπε βέβαιον ὡς καὶ οἱ ἄλλοι τοιοῦτοί εἰσιν: 'For he was the first Spartan who had been sent to them, and he won himself a good reputation in every way. This left in their minds a firm conviction that the others would be like him'. As Lewis drily remarks of the second part of this (*Sparta and Persia*, 29) 'we are surely meant to understand that they were not'; so too de Ste. Croix, *OPW* 158. Some have seen here a specific contrast with Lysander, see de Romilly, *Thucydides and Athenian Imperialism* (introductory n. to 1–16), 46; Raaflaub, *Freiheit*, 257 n. 198.

On 'conviction' here [lit. 'hope', *ἐλπίς*] see Connor, 131 n. 57, who argues that because, for Th., hope is never secure (*βέβαιος*), we must take the adjective here to mean 'persistent', 'long-lasting'. But there is irony here: it seemed secure, but they were fooled. So I have kept Jowett's 'firm'. For *ἐλπίς* here see also A. Cook (2 n. above on *ἔς τε τὸν χρόνῳ* etc.), 42.

82. καὶ τῶν ταύτῃ ξυμμάχων φυλακὴν πλέονα κατεστήσαντο: '[the Athenians] kept a closer watch over their allies in that region'. Whether this refers to attitude or to actual military steps or (most likely) both, it sounds a little 'perfunctory' (Gomme, *HCT* iii. 540); but we need not see it as a gentle hint by Th. that more could have been done in advance to protect Amphipolis, the cause of his own banishment.

83. 1. στρατεύει ἐπὶ Ἀρραβαῖον τὸν Βρομεροῦ Λυγκηστῶν Μακεδόνων βασιλέα ὅμορον ὄντα: 'marched against Arrhabaios son of Bromeros, king of the Lynkestian Macedonians, a neighbouring people' [lit. 'king']. A fuller introduction, with patronymic, of a man already mentioned at 79. 2: cp. the handling of Pericles and Archidamos in book i, see i. 127. 3 n. on ὧν γάρ etc. and ii. 19. 1 n. on ἡγεῖτο δέ etc. For the name Bromeros ('noisy') see Masson 1481 [323].

2. ἐπὶ τῇ ἐσβολῇ τῆς Λύγκου: 'at the pass leading into Lynkos'. For the identification of this pass from Eordaia to Lynkos see Hammond, in *HM* i. 104 and ii. 129, arguing (against Gomme, for whose view see his n. on 127. 2) for the Kirli Dirven pass.

For Lynkos (the area west of Lake Prespa) and Arrhabaios' territory see Hammond, *HM* i. 103, suggesting, in view of Arrhabaios' military strength—he could contemplate facing Brasidas' and Perdikkas' combined forces—that he possessed more than just Lynkos proper: maybe the area of Resen or Ochrid (for these places see his map 6 on p. 40) in addition. See ii. 99. 2 n.

3. καὶ γὰρ τι καὶ Ἀρραβαῖος ἐπεκηρυκεύετο, ἑτοῖμος ὢν Βρασίδᾳ μέσῳ δικαστῇ ἐπιτρέπειν: 'He was partly influenced by messages which came from Arrhabaios, saying he was willing to submit to Brasidas as intermediary and arbitrator'. The last three words of English represent Greek which means literally 'a judge', δικαστῇ, 'in the middle', μέσῳ. By para. 5, the softening effect of μέσῳ has disappeared, so that Perdikkas can say angrily that he had not brought Brasidas to Macedon as a *judge*. But I have kept the trans. 'arbitrate': δικαστής can mean 'arbitrator' as well as 'judge'; on the word see also next n.

5. Περδίκκας δὲ οὔτε δικαστὴν ἔφη Βρασίδαν τῶν σφετέρων διαφορῶν ἀγαγεῖν: 'But Perdikkas answered that he had not brought Brasidas there to arbitrate in the quarrels of Macedonia' [lit. 'as an arbitrator', δικαστής, see 3 n.]. See 3 n. above. This lively exchange is surely not Th.'s invention: some speeches in Th. are more authentic than others. Classen/Steup detected some characterization ('the half-barbarian vanity of the Macedonian') in the language here, esp. Perdikkas' arrogant claim to have 'brought' Brasidas north (which ignores the role of the Chalkidian cities, 79. 2). For the almost metaphorical use of δικαστής here cp. vi. 87. 3 (the Athenian Euphemos at Kamarina).

6. τρίτον μέρος ἀνθ' ἡμίσεος τῆς τροφῆς ἐδίδου: 'and paid only a third instead of half the expenses of the army'. Gomme asks, why did Perdikkas pay anything? His own answer was that Perdikkas must have got something worth having out of the deal and he went on to speculate exactly what. But even when angry, Perdikkas was surely too shrewd to deny himself further bargaining chips, i.e. the possibility of cutting his contribution still further (or cancelling it), like Tissaphernes in 411 (book viii). Parke (66. 3 n. on ἐν ᾗ αὐτοί etc.), 40 n. 10, suggests that up till now the other half had been paid by the Chalkidic League.

84. 1. ἐπὶ Ἄκανθον τὴν Ἀνδρίων ἀποικίαν: 'Akanthos, a colony of Andros'. Gomme has no note on the colonial aspect of this at all, any more than on 88. 2 (similar information about Stagiros); he waits for no obvious reason until ch. 109. 3, where he gives a list of the places in book iv where Th. records the colonizing state, cp. Ridley, *Hermes* 1991, 39. These colonial relationships, and Th.'s punctilious flagging of them, should, however, be given their proper importance, see Introduction, pp. 74–80. For the Akanthos–Andros connection in particular sée Plutarch, *Greek Questions* 30, describing the curious tale of the race between the Andrians and the Chalkidians for Akanthos at the time of its foundation.

Meiggs, *AE* 335, notes acutely that Akanthos, Stagiros (88. 2), and Argilos (103. 3) were all colonies of Andros, and all came over to Brasidas (and cp. 103. 2 for the pro-Spartan Argilians in Amphipolis). Meiggs concedes that this might be coincidence, since all three were on Brasidas' route, but conjectures attractively that 'Andrian ill-feeling against Athens', as a result of the cleruchy imposed *c*450, could have influenced these Andrian colonies. Note, however, that Sane, yet another Andrian colony, *resisted* Brasidas, 109. 3 and 5. See Introduction, pp. 76–8. And 42. 1 (see n. there on καὶ Ἄνδριοι) shows that the Andrians were loyal at the time of the Solygeia campaign.

For Akanthos at the top of the Akte (Athos) peninsula, north-east of the isthmus linking the peninsula to the mainland, see M. Zahrnt, *Olynth*, 146–50, and in Lauffer (ed.), *Griechenland*, 89, my entry 'Acanthus' in *OCD*[3], and S. N. Miller, *Princeton Encyclopaedia*, 23. For excavations in the 1980s at the city site, 600 m. SE of Ierissos, see E. Trakasopoulou, *ADelt* 39 Chron. 222–3, summarized at *Arch. Reps.* 1991–2, 43: an imposing building has conjecturally been identified as the prytaneion, and there are fortifications. (There were excavations at a separate cemetery site through the 1970s and 1980s, but I forbear to give all references; for the most impressive finds see E. Yiouri, *ADelt* 26 Chron. 2, 393–5, cp. *Arch. Reps.* 1975–6, 21: Attic black—and red-figure pottery, including an Attic black-figure column crater depicting the death of Aigisthos.) Akanthos usually paid 3 talents tribute to Athens after 446/5, but perhaps 5 talents in 450. From 124. 1, where the Chalkidian troops of Brasidas are mentioned separately from the Akanthian, Zahrnt and others infer that Akanthos was not a member of the Chalkidic league, as it was at the time of Amyntas III (early fourth century): Tod 111 line 19. 'No other state of the Chalkidic peninsula is so rich in coin hoards' (Zahrnt); for the coinage see Kraay, *ACGC* 135–6 (the change to the Phoenician standard probably not connected with the revolt from Athens but with the need to conform to the dominant coinage of the region). The statement in modern books that Akanthos depended primarily on agriculture is based on the present passage of Th. with its stress on the grape harvest, see next n. But it is nearby Mende, not Akanthos, whose coins draw attention to the city's wine-production, by depicting bunches of grapes, see Kraay, 136.

ὀλίγον πρὸ τρυγήτου: 'a little before the grape harvest'. Not so much a chronological indicator as a statement about the Akanthians' state of mind (para. 2 below and 88.1); as Lewis puts it (*CAH* v². 427), 'they were very worried about their grapes'.

2. καταστὰς ἐπὶ τὸ πλῆθος: 'So he went before the people'. That Akanthos was some sort of democracy is argued (partly on the basis of the present passage) by C. H. Grayson, 'Two Passages in Thucydides', *CQ* 22 (1972), 63–73, at 64.

ἦν δὲ οὐδὲ ἀδύνατος, ὡς Λακεδαιμόνιος, εἰπεῖν: 'he was not a bad speaker for a Spartan'. This is almost that rare thing, a Thucydidean joke. The perspective is emphatically Athenian; in fact the Spartans placed a high value on succinct but good conversation, see P. Cartledge, 'Literacy in the Spartan Oligarchy', *JHS* 98 (1978), 25–37, at 33. As for public oratory, see 17. 2 and n. The characterization of Brasidas here as a good or not-un-good speaker balances 81. 1, where he was a 'doer', δραστήριος, see n. there. Brasidas thus combines the two halves of the Homeric ideal as set out by Phoinix at *Iliad* ix. 443, quoted at i. 139. 4 n. on λέγειν καὶ πράσσειν δυνατώτατος, 'a very able man in speech and action' (Th.'s characterization of Pericles, less guarded than that of Brasidas). *Iliad* ix displays Achilles, Brasidas' prototype (see Introduction, pp. 38–61), at his most rhetorically forceful. See 85. 1 n. below.

85–87. *Brasidas' speech to the Akanthians*

This speech has not been much studied, but on its 'specious oratory' see A. B. Bosworth, *JHS* 113 (1993), 36–7, and see E. D. Francis (introductory n. to 17–20), 210–11; there are also good remarks scattered in Raaflaub, *Freiheit*, and I cite these as appropriate. The ostensible theme is liberation (see Babut, 433–4), and the word ἐλευθερία and cognates occur no less than 8 times in the speech (85. 1, 5, 6; 86. 1, 4; 87. 2, 4, 6; see Kallet-Marx, 171 and n. 49; add that the end of 87. 3 is a reference to liberation without using the word). But there is clear menace too, and Raaflaub, *Freiheit*, 252, aptly speaks of 'Zwangsbefreiung', 'freeing by force'. The style is forceful and lucid (except for the complicated thought at 86. 6) though there is a noticeable fondness for abstract nouns, see 85. 1 n. on ἡ μὲν ἔκπεμψις etc. and nn. on 85. 3 and 87. 1 (the very unusual and quasi-Homeric word περιωπή); see Francis, 211, for Brasidas' use of -σις abstracts, for which see also 17–20 introductory n.: the Spartans at

Athens). There is also, in Brasidas' speech, a noticeable amount of repetition of key words and expressions; such repetition is characteristic of propaganda in all periods (if we can speak of 'propaganda' in the strict sense in the ancient world, see my entry on the word in *OCD*[3]. J. Ellul, *Propaganda* (London, 1973), distinguishes between 'agitation' propaganda and 'integration' propaganda. The second kind is perhaps exemplified by the Spartan *agoge* which encouraged conformism. Sparta's liberation propaganda is an example of the first type, i.e. propaganda designed to change a given state of affairs). For the repetitions of ἐλευθερία see above; and see also 85. 6 n. for ἐπιφέρειν and 86. 2 n. on οὐδὲ τιμωρὸς ἀδύνατος.

But these repetitions are of literary interest too. Is it Th.'s aim to give the 'Spartan Achilles' an individual oratorical manner? For the linguistic individuality of Brasidas' epic prototype see Parry, Reeve, Griffin and Martin, cited above p. 43 n. 110, esp. Martin 220–2 for Achilles' special use of repetition. Francis (212) cites Plato's comparison of Brasidas to Achilles, cp. 205, but stops short of drawing an actual parallel.

Brasidas' speech is important for its bearing on the question of authenticity, of the sort claimed at i. 22. At the most important but least surprising level, iv. 108. 2 confirms (as Dr. Rood reminds me) that Brasidas did indeed speak about liberation. Then there are details. On the one hand there is a statement (85. 7, about Nisaia) which, very unusually, can be shown to have been uttered by a Thucydidean speaker in real life; and 86. 1 (the oaths) gets confirmation from the narrative at 88. 1. On the other hand, 85. 1 (ἔκπεμψις) recalls a speech in book i, and it has been claimed that 86. 4 and 5 should be regarded as Thucydidean generalizations. See my nn. on all these passages. The conclusion has to be, that the speech is a mixture of genuine Brasidas and Thucydides. Note that at 120. 3 we are told that at Skione Brasidas repeated what he had said at Akanthos and Torone, and at 114. 3 that at Torone he more or less repeated what he said at Akanthos, i.e. the Akanthos speech is specially important for Th.'s purposes (which does not quite prove authenticity, but it suggests that Brasidas really made the Akanthos pledges). See Introduction, above, p. 87.

The speech's first main theme is liberation, the second main theme is force. The first is stated and developed immediately, the second (violence) is introduced obliquely at first and then explicitly; at the end the two themes are recapitulated on a footing of equality.

Brasidas begins with an emphatic assertion of the liberation theme— necessary because it is some time since we heard anything about it (nothing so far in book iv), and the Spartan attitude reported at 20. 4 was tantamount to a sell-out, see n. there. He then (85. 2) apologizes for

Spartan slowness to act, and follows this by a pained expression of surprise (85. 3) at being shut out of Akanthos. He complains (85. 6) that people will think either that there is something wrong with the freedom he is bringing, or else that he lacks the capacity to 'protect' them against Athens. This allows him (85. 7) to expand on his military strength—and thus indirectly to warn the Akanthians what they are up against if they do not co-operate. As if recoiling from this menacing posture he begins the next section (86. 1) with a protestation that he comes not to harm the Greeks but to free them, and claims, remarkably, to have made 'the authorities' at Sparta swear solemn oaths to respect the autonomy of any places he should win over. He insists (86. 2) on the strength of his own pledges, and on his capacity for protection (the Greek echoes 85. 6, see above, and similarly draws subtly menacing attention to his strength). He now turns aside to answer a possible worry, that he will favour one faction over another (86. 3–4), but says he will leave that sort of thing to the Athenians. The ch. ends (86. 6) with a complicated (and hardly Spartan) statement of the preferability of violent over hypocritical methods—a sinister adumbration of the direct, though elaborately introduced, threat of violence in the next ch. (87. 2). Brasidas claims by way of justification that he owes it to the Spartans not to let them be damaged financially by continued Akanthian payments to Athens, and to the Greeks at large not to let their chance of freedom be frustrated (87. 3). The speech ends (87. 6) with a neat summary of the speech's two messages ('Zwangsbefreiung', see above, introductory n.): by submitting, the Akanthians will avoid unpleasant consequences, and they will get credit for helping the great task of liberation.

Luschnat, *Feldherrnreden*, 65–6, notes similarities between this speech and Brasidas' speech before Amphipolis, from the beginning and end of his Thracian expedition: specifically, several phrases in v. 9. 9 pick up phrases in iv. 86. 1 and 87. 3; see nn. on v. 9 .9.

85. 1. ἡ μὲν ἔκπεμψίς μου καὶ τῆς στρατιᾶς ὑπὸ Λακεδαιμονίων: 'The Spartans have sent me out at the head of this army' [lit. 'the sending-out of me and the army']. The abstract noun, found here only in Th. (though we do have πέμψις at vii. 17. 3), makes for a striking and digni-fied opening; cp. the beginning of the Athenian speech at i. 73, ἡ μὲν πρέσβευσις ἡμῶν οὐκ . . . ἐγένετο, 'we were not sent here . . .' [lit. 'this embassy of ours did not happen . . .'], where again the noun is unique in Th. If the echo is deliberate, the aim may (cp. 17. 2 n.)be to show that Brasidas could match the best orators in Greece. But this is not the only place in the speech where an abstract expression is used where a simpler locution would have done the job, see introductory n. (For a similar opening—abstract noun + verb—see also iii. 53. 1, τὴν μὲν παρά-δοσιν τῆς πόλεως . . . ἐποιησάμεθα, 'we surrendered our city . . .'.)

τὴν αἰτίαν ἐπαληθεύουσα ἣν ἀρχόμενοι τοῦ πολέμου προείπο-μεν, Ἀθηναίοις ἐλευθεροῦντες τὴν Ἑλλάδα πολεμήσειν: 'to make good the declaration which we made at the beginning of the war: we said that we were going to fight the Athenians in order to free Greece'. Not just the thought but the language closely echoes ii. 8. 4, προειπόντων ὅτι τὴν Ἑλλάδα ἐλευθεροῦσιν, 'they professed to be the liberators of Greece'; but this slogan was no doubt widely broadcast and tells us little about Th.'s compositional methods. For the liberation theme see introductory n. Note 'Greece', not 'the Greeks'. When writing a Greek prose one is told to avoid putting things as Th. does here. But see 88. 2 n. (Whitehead).

2. διὰ τάχους ... ἠλπίσαμεν Ἀθηναίους καθαιρήσειν: 'we thought we could crush the Athenians quickly'. For the thought and language cp. v. 14. 3 and n. there on ἐν ᾧ etc.

3. θαυμάζω δὲ τῇ τε ἀποκλῄσει μου τῶν πυλῶν: 'So I am surprised that you close your gates against me' [lit. 'I am surprised at your gate-shutting-out of me']. Again an abstract noun where the job could have been done with an active verb.

4. διὰ τῆς ἀλλοτρίας πολλῶν ἡμερῶν ὁδὸν ἰόντες: 'marching for many days through a foreign country'. *Old Oligarch* ii. 5 talks of the impossibility of long land journeys if you are a land power, and this has been thought to prove that the treatise must have been written before 424 and Brasidas' expedition: see G. W. Bowersock, 'Pseudo-Xenophon', *HSCP* 71 (1966), 33–55, at 36 f. (but J. de Romilly, 'Le Pseudo-Xénophon et Thucydide, étude sur quelques divergences de vues', *Revue de Philologie*, 36 (1962), 225–41, at 234, notes that Pericles at Th. i. 141. 4 had already made a point similar to the *Old Oligarch*'s). I agree with Gomme, *More Essays*, 50, that the argument is weak; as Gomme says 'the difficulties of Brasidas illustrate and do not contradict' the statement in *Old Oligarch*. See generally my entry 'Old Oligarch' in *OCD*3.

5. τῇ τε ὑμετέρᾳ αὐτῶν ἐλευθερίᾳ καὶ τῶν ἄλλων Ἑλλήνων, δεινὸν ἂν εἴη: 'It would be monstrous . . . the freedom of your own city and that of the rest of Greece'. The words underlined are a hexameter, though not a very obtrusive one. On this sort of metricality see *Greek Historiography*, 65–9. Th. normally avoids it, but it is evoked at solemn moments of narrative or would-be solemn moments in speeches.

6. ἢ ἄδικον τὴν ἐλευθερίαν ἐπιφέρειν: 'that there is something wrong with the freedom I am offering'. The alternative trans., preferred by Gomme without giving reasons, is 'that it is wrong to bring freedom'. But I follow Classen/Steup in taking ἄδικον [lit. 'unjust'] adjectivally with 'freedom', balancing the two adjectives in the second half of the sentence (ἀσθενής, ἀδύνατος). Also, the bracketing of 'unjust' and 'freedom' is a harsh oxymoron anyway, but harsher when the suspicion imputed to the Akanthians is that bringing freedom of *any* kind might be wrong; it makes good sense to have them suspect that Brasidas' freedom might be of a suspect variety (the Penguin has 'unreal').

As we have seen (introductory n.), the word 'freedom' is often repeated in this speech; but so is the verb ἐπιφέρειν, 'bringing', cp. (with Gomme) 86. 4, 87. 2 and 5. This is a nice instance of 'clustering': Gomme, pp. 555 f. suggests that there is a deliberate ambiguity, because the verb can often mean 'inflict', 'impose' something unpleasant.

ἀσθενὴς καὶ ἀδύνατος τιμωρῆσαι: 'too weak to be able to protect you'. See introductory n.: rebuttal of the idea that he is too weak to be effective against the Athenians allows Brasidas to expand, intimidatingly, on his own strength. See also 86. 2 n. (the present passage repeated).

7. καίτοι στρατιᾷ γε τῇδ᾽ ἦν νῦν ἔχω ἐπὶ Νίσαιαν ἐμοῦ βοηθήσαντος οὐκ ἠθέλησαν Ἀθηναῖοι πλέονες ὄντες προσμεῖξαι: [I follow Gomme and others who omit ἐγώ after νῦν or after ἔχω]: 'But in fact when I helped Nisaia with the army which I have brought with me now, the Athenians refused to fight me despite their superior numbers'. There are several inaccuracies here, as Gomme notes: Brasidas' army now was not the same as at Megara, and it outnumbered the Athenians (Gomme cites 67. 1–2, 68. 5, 72. 2, 74. 1, 84.1, to which add πρὸς πλέονας at 73. 4). It is a less serious distortion that, as Gomme notes, Brasidas had also refused to fight on that occasion.

Gomme rightly cross-refers to 108. 5, where Th. explicitly says that this statement about Nisaia was false; 108. 5 is (see Gomme on that passage) hard evidence that the present passage gives what Brasidas really did say, ἀληθῶς λεχθέντα. For this point see Lewis, *CAH* v². 426 n. 142, 'this is the only Thucydidean speech which is demonstrably not free composition'. (It would be slightly better to say 'not entirely free composition', in view of the reminiscence at 85. 1 of i. 73, ἔκπεμψις/ πρεσβευσις.) For another sentence which was actually spoken by Brasidas see 86. 1 and n.

ὥστε οὐκ εἰκὸς νηίτῃ γε αὐτοὺς τῷ ἐν Νισαίᾳ στρατῷ ἴσον πλῆθος ἐφ᾽ ὑμᾶς ἀποστεῖλαι: 'they are not likely now, given that their troops must be brought by sea, to send an army against you of the size which they had at Nisaia'. The Greek would be easier if we emended to νηίτην, but I am not sure the emendation is unavoidable.

86. 1. ὅρκοις τε Λακεδαιμονίων καταλαβὼν τὰ τέλη τοῖς μεγίστοις ἦ μὴν οὓς ἂν ἔγωγε προσαγάγωμαι ξυμμάχους ἔσεσθαι

αὐτονόμους: 'I have made the authorities at Sparta swear the most solemn oaths to respect the autonomy of any allies I bring over to their side'. Without corroboration from the narrative, this would be hard to believe, coming as it does straight on top of an identifiable lie (see above on Nisaia), quite apart from the extraordinary prestige it implies Brasidas enjoyed at Sparta. But if it is true, and 88. 1 (see n. there) does imply that the oath-taking at Sparta was a historical fact, it is very relevant to the problem of Brasidas' relations with the home government at Sparta. On that topic see 81. 1 n. on αὐτόν τε etc. and Introduction pp. 50 f.: he was carrying out agreed policy (and this is true even if we think oaths *were* sworn, but not through, or solely through, Brasidas' agency). The narrative corroboration also proves that, like 85. 7 (above), this part of the speech was actually delivered; see introductory n.

Neither here nor at the corresponding passage 88. 1 does Gomme comment on the oaths; this is consistent with his general tendency to neglect religion in Th. Cf. above, p. 10.

Whether or not these oaths were sworn at Sparta (and the evidence indicates that they were), the autonomy of the places in question was soon violated; see Raaflaub, *Freiheit*, 252, citing e.g. 132. 3, Spartan commanders installed at Amphipolis and Torone.

With 'autonomy of any allies ...', ξυμμάχους ἔσεσθαι αὐτονόμους, Luschnat, *Feldherrnreden*, 65, compares v. 9. 9, Λακεδαιμονίων ξυμμάχους κεκλῆσθαι, 'the name of Spartan allies, which you will deserve ...', etc. But see next n.: there is contrast as well as similarity.

οὐχ ἵνα ξυμμάχους ὑμᾶς ἔχωμεν ἢ βίᾳ ἢ ἀπάτῃ προσλαβόντες: 'I do not want to win your alliance by force or fraud'. Gomme notes that the meaning of ξυμμάχους seems literally to be 'to have you fighting in our ranks' and notes that Brasidas adopts a rather different tone (i.e. one of exhortation) at Skione, 120. 3, and before the second battle of Amphipolis, v. 9. 9 (not very surprising before a battle). See previous n.

ἀλλὰ τοὐναντίον ὑμῖν δεδουλωμένοις ὑπὸ Ἀθηναίων ξυμμαχήσοντες: 'but to fight alongside you and free you from your Athenian slavery' [lit. 'to fight alongside you who have been enslaved by the Athenians']. Cp. v. 9. 9, ἢ Ἀθηναίων τε δούλοις, with n. there; see introductory n. above.

2. οὐδὲ τιμωρὸς ἀδύνατος νομισθῆναι: 'nor should you think I am an inadequate protector'. The language corresponds to that at the end of 85. 6; for the significance of such repetitions see introductory n.

4. οὐ γὰρ ξυστασιάσων ἥκω, οὐδὲ ἂν σαφῆ τὴν ἐλευθερίαν νομίζω ἐπιφέρειν, εἰ τὸ πάτριον παρεὶς τὸ πλέον τοῖς ὀλίγοις ἢ τὸ ἔλασσον τοῖς πᾶσι δουλώσαιμι: 'I have not come here to take part in factional politics. It would be a dubious sort of liberation if I were

to go against Spartan tradition and either enslave the many to the few or the minority to the whole people'. The Greek has just 'go against tradition', and this could mean 'against Akanthian tradition', i.e. Brasidas would on that trans. be promising not to disturb existing constitutional arrangements at Akanthos; so (apparently) Steup; A. Fuks, *The Ancestral Constitution* (London, 1953), 60; and K. R. Walters, 'The "Ancestral Constitution" and Fourth-Century Historiography', *AJAH* 1 (1976), 129–44, at 133–4. But I have (in effect) preferred Jowett's trans., which is also reported by Grayson (84. 2n. on κατασάς etc.), 64 n. 5, to be the trans. preferred by Andrewes. The Greek means 'putting aside' the tradition; if forcible change of government were meant, we would expect a stronger verb. It is no objection, in this rhetorical context, that Brasidas' claim is untrue as a description of Spartan practice. Grayson (65) notes that Brasidas' promise was too broadly framed, in that 'there was no possibility (or likelihood in view of the Spartan record) of any *oligarchy* being ousted in favour of a puppet democracy', and concludes that the remark is in effect a comment by Th. himself, of an entirely general kind, on the priorities of Greek politics. See introductory n., at end.

On the two kinds of 'enslavement' see K. Raaflaub, 'Contemporary Perceptions of Democracy in Fifth-century Athens', in W. R. Connor and others, *Aspects of Athenian Democracy* (*Cl. et Med.* Dissertations 11, 1990), 33–70, at 38, and above all in *Freiheit*, 283, noting that the enslavement of the majority by the few is opposed to that of the few by the *whole* (not just the majority), and explaining this by the ambiguity of *demos* as 'populus' and as 'plebs'. (But *demos* is not actually used here.) At *Freiheit*, 304, he notes that Brasidas' formulation is most unusual, implying as it does an *oligarchical* conception of internal political freedom. On 'the whole' here, and on the ambiguities of *demos*, see also de Romilly, 'Cities' (1. 1 n. on αὐτῶν ἐπαγαγομένων), 7–8; of the present passage she remarks 'in everybody's eyes at that time, there was not a great difference between majority and total amount'. Cp. also de Romilly, 9, for freedom as the 'bait' offered by Brasidas.

5. χαλεπωτέρα γὰρ ἂν τῆς ἀλλοφύλου ἀρχῆς εἴη: 'That would be worse than foreign rule'. I. Plant, 'Thuc. viii. 48. 5: Phrynichus on the Wishes of Athens' Allies', *Historia*, 41 (1992), 249–50, sees a contradiction between this and viii. 48. 5, where domestic politics takes second place to foreign policy; he suggests that both passages represent Th.'s own thinking (see introductory n. for the significance of this) and that Th.'s priorities had developed by the time he wrote book viii, when he had started to think inter-state relations more important than domestic politics. This is a surprising conclusion, given the amount of domestic politics in book viii. I doubt if the supposed contradiction needs any explanation other than the rhetorical need of the speaker.

On the word for 'foreign', ἀλλοφύλου, see 64. 4 n. (Brasidas is probably hinting at the Ionian/Dorian divide.)

6. ἀπάτῃ γὰρ εὐπρεπεῖ: '... by hypocrisy and deceit'. This difficult sentence is out of line with the rest of the speech; see introductory n.

87. 1. οὕτω πολλὴν περιωπὴν ... ποιούμεθα: 'We are careful ...' [lit. 'so much carefulness do we show']. The word for 'carefulness' is another abstract noun found only here in Th., see introductory n., indeed it is unique in this sense in all Greek literature. For the word itself cp. *Iliad* xiv. 8 and xxiii. 451; *Odyssey* x. 146; but in Homer it is not abstract, it means 'vantage-point'.

2. μάρτυρας μὲν θεοὺς καὶ ἥρως τοὺς ἐγχωρίους ποιήσομαι: 'I shall first call the gods and heroes of your country to witness'. See ii. 74. 2 and n. for such an ἐπιθειασμός or invocation of protective gods and heroes.

ἐπ' ἀγαθῷ ἥκων: 'I have come here for your good'. Classen/Steup rightly refer back to 86. 1, where Brasidas says he has not come to harm but to free; that is, 'for good' here means liberation. See Y. Nakategawa, 'Forms of Interstate Justice in the Late Fifth Century', *Klio*, 76 (1994), 135–54, at 149 and 153. The Penguin trans. of the present passage has 'to help you' which does not quite capture the flavour.

γῆν δὲ τὴν ὑμετέραν δῃῶν πειράσομαι βιάζεσθαι: 'I shall then use force and ravage your land'. At last the mailed fist; see introductory n.

3. τῶν μὲν Λακεδαιμονίων, ὅπως μὴ τῷ ὑμετέρῳ εὔνῳ, εἰ μὴ προσαχθήσεσθε, τοῖς ἀπὸ ὑμῶν χρήμασι φερομένοις παρ' Ἀθηναίους βλάπτωνται: 'I must not allow the Spartans to be damaged by letting you be merely sympathetic to me without actually joining me, and they *will* be damaged by the revenues which the Athenians will continue to get from you'. References in speeches to the tribute paid to the Athenians by their allies are always of interest: this is one of the most explicit. See, for a good discussion, Kallet-Marx, 172. But note that even here, tribute is not said to be an allied grievance against Athens, but a source of Athenian strength. On the trans. of τῷ ὑμετέρῳ εὔνῳ I follow J. de Romilly, 'Eunoia in Isocrates or the Political Importance of Creating Good Will', *JHS* 78 (1958), 92–101, at 92, against what she takes to be Gomme's view that the Greek means 'lest Sparta, through her good will towards you, be injured', etc. Actually Gomme equivocates. He starts by saying (without explaining his reasons) that 'editors' are 'probably right' to take it to refer to good will felt by Athens' allies towards Sparta, i.e. he and de Romilly are in agreement; but then he goes on to give reasons for the other trans. (Sparta would not actually be injured by good will felt for Sparta by Athenian allies; this difficulty can be got rid of by translating as in the trans. adopted above, i.e. 'to be merely sympathetic', etc.). And he says this trans. would 'ordinarily' be easier. So one is left wondering why he did not adopt it (and de Romilly evidently thought he *did* adopt it). I think de Romilly is right to adduce, as a parallel, 114. 4 (Torone), where the good will is definitely felt towards, not by Sparta, see n. there. Brasidas in Chalkidike seeks to capitalize on the general good will or *eunoia* towards Sparta so strongly emphasized by Th. at ii. 8. 4. (I do not mean that *eunoia* was some sort of Spartan monopoly. The name *Eunoia* was used for Athenian triremes in the fourth cent. and no doubt the fifth as well, though navy-lists do not survive from before the last years of that century: see K. Schmidt, *Die Namen der attischen Kriegschiffe* (Engelsdorf-Leipzig, 1931), 12, no. 41. Such ship-names, for which see also Casson, *Ships and Seamanship* (25. 4 n.), 350 ff., are an under-exploited source of evidence for Athenian values.)

οἱ δὲ Ἕλληνες ἵνα μὴ κωλύωνται ὑφ᾽ ὑμῶν δουλείας ἀπαλλαγῆναι: 'Second, the Greeks must not lose their hope of liberation just because of you'. Cp. v. 9. 9 τοῖς δὲ λοιποῖς Ἕλησι etc. with n. there, and see introductory n. above.

5. οὐδ᾽ αὖ ἀρχῆς ἐφιέμεθα: 'we do not want an empire'. Did they or didn't they? A. Andrewes, 'Spartan imperialism?', in P. Garnsey and C. Whittaker (eds.), *Imperialism in the Ancient World* (Cambridge, 1978), 91–100, examines two of the best claimants to be Spartan imperialists (Pausanias the Regent; Lysander), but the question-mark in his title makes the point that there was always something reluctant about Spartan imperialism.

ξύμπασιν αὐτονομίαν ἐπιφέροντες: 'bring autonomy to all'. See A. B. Bosworth, 'Autonomia: The Use and Abuse of Political Terminology', *Studi ital. fil. class.* 10 (1992), 122–52, at 129: 'autonomy was too important to be left wholly to the people made autonomous.'

88. 1. πολλῶν λεχθέντων πρότερον ἐπ᾽ ἀμφότερα: 'after much had been said on both sides'. Cp. i. 139. 4 and iv. 58 with nn.

διά τε τὸ ἐπαγωγὰ εἰπεῖν τὸν Βρασίδαν καὶ περὶ τοῦ καρποῦ φόβῳ: 'partly because what he said was attractive, partly because they were afraid of losing their grape vintage'. At 108. 5 Th. repeats that what Brasidas said was seductive (this time ἐφολκά), but adds that it was untrue. The word used here for 'attractive', ἐπαγωγός, is found elsewhere in Th. in powerful contexts, always with the additional idea that the attraction is treacherous: v. 111. 3 (the Melian Dialogue) and vi. 8. 2 (the 'attractive but false' promises of the Egestans).

Cp. Aeneas Tacticus vii. 1 with Whitehead's n. for exploitation of defenders' fear for their crops (γλιχομένους τοῦ καρποῦ) at harvesttime; Aeneas says this fear will make people tend to stay out in the fields, but Th. does not suggest the Akanthians did so.

Note the impartial way Th. gives the two motives; he does *not* say 'but they were really afraid for their vintage'. It is important that Brasidas' propaganda worked.

ἔγνωσαν οἱ πλείους ἀφίστασθαι Ἀθηναίων: 'They decided, by a majority, to revolt from Athens'. Plutarch (*Lys.* 1) saw a treasury at Delphi dedicated by 'Brasidas and the Akanthians from the Athenians', *Syll.*³ 79, not mentioned by Gomme (see above, p. 11); for the probable position see J. Bommelaer, *Guide de Delphes: le site* (Paris, 1991), 160–2. It is not possible to say precisely where it fits into the sequence of events in Th., but it must refer to some joint success soon after the revolt here described. On this dedication and its implications see further 134. 1 n. on τροπαῖά τε etc., discussing A. H. Jackson's study of Greek dedications of spoils taken from Greeks.

καὶ πιστώσαντες αὐτὸν τοῖς ὅρκοις οὓς τὰ τέλη τῶν Λακεδαιμονίων ὀμόσαντα αὐτὸν ἐξέπεμψαν, ἦ μὴν ἔσεσθαι ξυμμάχους αὐτονόμους οὓς ἂν προσαγάγηται: 'They made Brasidas give pledges to stand by the oaths which the authorities at Sparta had sworn before they sent him out, to respect the autonomy of new allies' [as Classen/Steup say, ὀμόσαντα goes with 'the authorities', not with Brasidas, i.e. it is neuter plural not masculine singular]. This sentence has not detained commentators (though see de Ste. Croix, *OPW* 18), but it is very remarkable, for two main reasons. First, for the absence of any distancing verb like 'which *he had said* [at 86. 1] the authorities', etc. That is, Th. seems (see above, p. 50) to accept as a minimum that the oaths were a fact, and probably also that Brasidas' prestige was indeed great enough to enable him to force the Spartan authorities to swear them (see also 81. 1 n.). This, if Th. was correctly informed, has the further consequence that the later Spartan breaches of autonomy (see 86. 1 n.) were instances not merely of aggression but of actual impiety. (For occasional Spartan cynicism about oaths see Parker, *Miasma* 187.) If these oaths were historical, they help to explain the clause in the Peace of Nikias which guaranteed 'autonomy' for Akanthos etc., see v. 18. 5 n. on τὰς δὲ πόλεις etc., and Introduction, pp. 50 f.

Second, the present piece of narrative implies that Brasidas did indeed report, as Th. makes him do at 86. 1, that oaths were taken at Sparta. 86. 1 was therefore 'really said', ἀληθῶς λεχθέν, cp. i. 22. 1; cp. 85. 7 n. for another para. which can be shown to have been 'really said'.

For the Homeric verb πιστόω see Introduction, p. 48.

2. Στάγιρος Ἀνδρίων ἀποικία ξυναπέστη: 'Stagiros, a colony of Andros, revolted as well'. Again (see 84. 1 n.) Gomme has no note on this (though he does, in his n. on v. 6. 1, notice the strange repetition of the same colonial fact there, see my n., and cp. 107. 3 n. on καὶ Γαληψός etc.). For the possible significance of the Andrian connection see 84. 1 n. on ἐπὶ Ἄκανθον etc. For Stagiros or Stagira, the birth-place of Aristotle, probably situated on the coast SE of Lake Bolbe between Akanthos and Bormiskos, see Zahrnt, 238–43 and my entry 'Stagira' in *OCD*3. (The site is the modern Olympiada. The modern inland town of Stagira, which has a statue of Aristotle, is not the ancient Stagira.) There are fine walls to be seen round the acropolis and a public building, perhaps a temple, further down. For press reports of excavations there see *Arch. Reps.* 1991–2, 45. For 'Stagiros' (not 'the Stagirans') see D. Whitehead, *Mus. Helv.* 53 (1996), 7 f.

89–101. *The Delion campaign*

The narrative is resumed from chs. 76–7 where the strategic plan was given. For the battle and its site see Pritchett, *SAGT* ii. 24–36 and iii. 295–7. I retain the usual name 'battle of Delion', which has the authority of Th. himself at v. 14. 1 and 15. 2 (cp. iv. 108. 5 and n. on ἐν τοῖς Βοιωτοῖς etc.); although it is not mere pedantry to insist that, though the sanctuary of Delion was in Boiotia, the main battle was fought (as Th. himself appears to accept at 91) in the Oropia, on Attic soil. For the significance of this see 95. 2 n. on ἐν γὰρ τῇ τούτων etc. and 99 n. on νομίζοντες etc.

89. 1. γενομένης διαμαρτίας τῶν ἡμερῶν: 'But there was a mistake about the day' [lit. 'days']. See 77. 1 n. G. Wylie, 'Demosthenes the General—Protagonist in a Greek Tragedy?', *G & R* 40 (1993), 20–30, at 25, points out that the 'suggested mistake in dates . . . is almost a red herring. If the plot was betrayed [see below], the dates agreed on were irrelevant.' Even Gomme equivocates, though he sees the point: 'the principal cause of the failure . . . was the leakage of information *as much as* the mistiming' (my italics); better to say '*rather than* the mistiming'.

μηνυθέντος τοῦ ἐπιβουλεύματος ὑπὸ Νικομάχου ἀνδρὸς Φωκέως ἐκ Φανοτέως: 'the plot was betrayed by a Phokian called Nikomachos from the town of Panopeus'. See 76. 3 and n. on ἔστι δέ . . .

2. προκαταλαμβάνονται αἵ τε Σῖφαι καὶ ἡ Χαιρώνεια. ὡς δὲ ᾔσθοντο οἱ πράσσοντες τὸ ἁμάρτημα, οὐδὲν ἐκίνησαν τῶν ἐν ταῖς πόλεσιν: 'they were able to forestall the Athenians by seizing Siphai and Chaironeia. When the conspirators saw that there had been a mistake, they made no revolutionary move in the Boiotian cities'. I interpret this to mean that the failure of the *military* attempt on Siphai and Chaironeia (places chosen for their military strength) led to the abandonment of the *political* attempt at revolution there and elsewhere. That is, 'the cities' in the present passage is more than just a way of referring back to Siphai and Chaironeia: it means 'the cities of Boiotia' generally, and is more or less (see below) a way of describing the constituent members of the Boiotian confederacy. But Hansen (76. 3 n. on Σίφας μέν etc.), 20–1, may well be right to claim that Siphai and Chaironeia are *included* in 'the cities', i.e. they may have had *polis* status although they were dependent on Thespiai and Orchomenos respectively, and although Siphai was not listed in *Hell. Oxy.* as one of the federal cities. On the issue of Boiotian *polis* status see 76. 3 n. on Σίφας μέν etc.

If ἁμάρτημα picks up διαμαρτίας, Th. continues to insist that it was the mistake in the days, rather than the betrayal of the plot, which was fatal; see para. 1 nn. Gomme criticizes Th. for not making it clear there were two causes of the failure, but one might want to say that there was only one real cause and Th. chose the wrong one. (But Dr. Rood suggests to me that ἁμάρτημα just means general failure.)

90. 1. ὁ δὲ Ἱπποκράτης ἀναστήσας Ἀθηναίους πανδημεί: 'Hippokrates had called out the Athenians in full force'. Th. makes no mention of any involvement by the Assembly (or *boule*, the Council of Five Hundred) and this probably reflects the reality when a levy had to be ordered out at short notice: see A. Andrewes, in E. Badian (ed.), *Ancient Society and Institutions* (Oxford, 1966), 11 and n. 19, who notes that 'the lack of notice will account for the fact that a levy πανδημεί produced only some 7000 men (iv. 94. 1; 93. 3)'.

αὐτοὺς καὶ τοὺς μετοίκους καὶ ξένων ὅσοι παρῆσαν: 'metics as well as citizens, and all the foreigners who were then in the city' [lit. 'of the foreigners, those who were present in the city'; 'in the city' is not in the Greek]. That some metics were hoplites is stated at ii. 13. 7, cp. iii. 16. 1 for metics used on sea-borne raids. But they were used primarily for defence. The present use of them for fighting outside Attica was unusual, see D. Whitehead, *The Ideology of the Athenian Metic* (*PCPhS* suppl. 4, 1977), 82–3 and 96. (But Delion was only just outside Attica.) Cp. also Bradeen, *CQ* 1969 (see 44. 6 n. on ἀπέθανον δέ etc.), 153.

Who are the 'foreigners then in the city'? Probably allies, rather than 'non-resident foreigners' as Gomme thought. See Whitehead, 42 f., and P. Gauthier, 'Les ΞΕΝΟΙ dans les textes Athéniens de la seconde moitié du vᵉ siècle av. J.-C.', *REG* 84 (1971), 44–79, at 51–2, pointing out that the partitive genitive ('*of* the foreigners . . .') requires that some of these foreigners should *not* be present in Athens; therefore, only allies can be

meant. Gomme conjectured, and Gauthier agreed, that the foreigners
were used only for the wall-building. At 94. 1 the three categories here
mentioned have collapsed into two, foreigners and citizens. To which of
the two, then, should the metics be assimilated? Probably the foreigners
(rather than, as Wilamowitz thought, the citizens), so Whitehead, 61.

2. **τάφρον μὲν κύκλῳ περὶ τὸ ἱερὸν καὶ τὸν νεὼν ἔσκαπτον:** 'His
army dug a trench round the temple and the sacred precinct'. With this
rapid wall-building Hainsworth, *The Iliad: A Commentary*, iii. *Books 9-12*,
p. 345, compares the logs and stones used at *Iliad*, xii. 258-60.

καὶ λίθους ἅμα καὶ πλίνθον ἐκ τῶν οἰκοπέδων τῶν ἐγγύς: 'stones
and bricks from the houses nearby'. οἰκόπεδον here means 'house' or
'building' (not 'building site'); see M. I. Finley, *Studies in Land and Credit in
Ancient Athens* (New Brunswick, 1951), 253 n. 50.

4. **τὸ μὲν στρατόπεδον προαπεχώρησεν ἀπὸ τοῦ Δηλίου οἷον
δέκα σταδίους ὡς ἐπ' οἴκου πορευόμενον:** 'the army withdrew
about ten stades distance from Delion, intending to go home'. This withdrawal took them inside Attica, to the borders of the territory of Oropos
(91. 1); Pritchett (*SAGT* ii. 34) suggests that their position would have
been on the upper plateau of Paliokhani, for which see his plate 17.

91. **οἱ δὲ Βοιωτοὶ ἐν ταῖς ἡμέραις ταύταις ξυνελέγοντο ἐς τὴν
Τάναγραν:** 'Meanwhile the Boiotians were gathering at Tanagra'. For
Tanagra see i. 108. 1 n. and iv. 76. 4 n.; also iii. 91. 3-5 for an Athenian
attack on Tanagra earlier in the war (426).

τῶν ἄλλων βοιωταρχῶν, οἵ εἰσιν ἕνδεκα: 'most of the boiotarchs, of
whom there are eleven' [lit. 'the other b.']. Here Th. reveals his knowledge of Boiotian federal institutions, see my paper in *Proc. 2nd Int.
Congress of Boiotian Studies 1992* (forthcoming); also 72. 4 n. on τὸν μὲν
γὰρ ἵππαρχον etc. and 76. 2 n. on τὰ Βοιώτια etc. Jowett's tr. (contrast
Penguin, 'ten out of the eleven') allows the possibility that Arianthidas
backed Pagondas.

ἐπειδὴ οὐκ ἐν τῇ Βοιωτίᾳ ἔτι εἰσί: 'because the Athenians had left
Boiotian territory' [lit. 'are no longer in Boiotia']. I have changed Jowett's
'the enemy' to 'the Athenians', although he is quite right that the main
focalizers are the boiotarchs; note that Th.'s own focalization is introduced by 'for', γάρ, immediately following; see next n. But the 'for'
sentence expands and explains the boiotarchs' reasoning, i.e. Th. seems
to accept the factual point that the Athenians were now out of Boiotia.
This is important, not least for the understanding of the rhetoric of the
speeches, see next n., and 95. 2 n. on ἐν γὰρ τῇ τούτων etc.

μάλιστα γὰρ ἐν μεθορίοις τῆς Ὠρωπίας ... ἦσαν: 'For ... they
were just on the borders of the territory of Oropos'. At this time Oropos

was in Athenian hands (see ii. 23. 3 n. on ἦν νέμονται etc.), so the Athenians were now on the borders of Attica. The word here rendered 'borders', μεθορίοις, really means 'lying between as a boundary' (LSJ), but there was no policed line of frontier. The Athenians could thus be out of Boiotia but not quite in Attica, so that Hippokrates can assert and Pagondas deny that the Athenians are in Boiotia, see 95. 2 and 92. 1, with nn. In normal circumstances the two generals might each be expected to say they were defending home territory, i.e. we would expect Hippokrates to assert and Pagondas to deny that the Athenians were in *Attica*.

Παγώνδας ὁ Αἰολάδου βοιωταρχῶν ἐκ Θηβῶν: 'Pagondas son of Aioladas . . . He was one of the two boiotarchs from Thebes'. Thebes had four boiotarchs at the time described by the Oxyrhynchus Historian xix, two for Thebes and two for Plataia and some smaller places nearby. But Th. should not be read as implying that in 424, the date of the present passage, Thebes had control of *only* two boiotarchs. On the contrary the arrangement described in *Hell. Oxy.* was probably already in force i.e. Thebes had the two boiotarchs mentioned by Th. (these were 'from Thebes' in a strong sense) and also the two from Plataia etc. On this view the 'Thebans and the Boiotians grouped with them' (Θηβαῖοι καὶ οἱ ξύμμοροι αὐτοῖς) at 93. 4 came from the four boiotarch-supplying districts controlled by Thebes. See P. Salmon, *Étude*, 82–3.

For the name Pagondas (for the ending cp. the even more famous Theban Epaminondas) see Pindar fr. 94b Snell/Maehler, a *partheneion* or maidens' song; the poem (written for Pindar's own kinsman) mentions an Agasikles son of Pagondas who may be Th.'s Pagondas; see Wilamowitz, *Pindaros* (Berlin, 1922), 436, and C. M. Bowra, *Pindar* (Oxford, 1964), 99 f.: Pindar's father's name is supposed to have been Pagondas, in which case he and the victor of Delion may have been related. There is a Theban called Pagondas at *SEG* xxxii. 436; see also Moretti, *Olympionikai* no. 33; there is a Pagon at *IG* vii no. 2466 line 4, and note that the Παγω- at no. 3656 could be supplemented to yield Pagondas rather than Pagon. For the name Pagondas see also E. Rawson, *Roman Culture and Society: Collected Papers* (Oxford, 1991), 136 n. 32.

μετ' Ἀριανθίδου τοῦ Λυσιμαχίδου: 'the other being Arianthidas son of Lysimachidas'. See ML 95d with commentary at p. 288: the name [....]θιος [Λυσι]μαχίδαο [Βοιω]τῶν ν[αύαρχος] ('...thios son of Lysimachidas, Boiotian admiral') appears on one of the statue-bases which formed part of the monument at Delphi celebrating Lysander's victory at Aegospotami (405). Whatever the exact form of the name (Paus. x. 9. 9 has Erianthes, Plut. *Lys.* 15 Erianthos, the scholiast on Dem. xix. 65 Euanthos), 'the identification with the Theban Boiotarch of 424 . . . seems highly probable' (ML). See n. above on τῶν ἄλλων.

καὶ ἡγεμονίας οὔσης αὐτοῦ: 'and he was in command at the time'. Th. does not tell us what rules governed the command; it is possible that the commander was always a Theban (in which case Pagondas and Arianthidas may have alternated); see Roesch (76. 3 n. on Σίφας μέν etc.), 98, who also asks whether the commander was chosen for a whole year or just for one campaign; also P. Salmon, 139–40 (who thinks it 'very probable' that a Theban was always commander). Bruce (105) cites Paus. ix. 13. 6 (Leuktra, 371) to show that decisions were normally taken by a majority vote of the boiotarchs, so that Pagondas' action was 'highly irregular'. But even if Paus. is decisive, Th. does go on to say (93. 1) that Pagondas' speech *persuaded* the Boiotians (including his reluctant colleagues? see next n. and 92. 1 n.) to fight. See also 93. 1 n. on τοιαῦτα etc.

προσκαλῶν ἑκάστους κατὰ λόχους: 'He therefore called up one brigade at a time'. Hansen, *Historia* 1993, 168, calls this 'an interesting piece of information'; it seems to be one of the supports for his view (169) that ancient generals 'exhorted the units successively' (but in Hansen's view the exhortation merely consisted of a few encouraging apophthegms; see below). Hansen is no doubt right that surviving accounts give too smooth and stylized an impression of speeches before battles, but may Th. not have mentioned Pagondas' procedure precisely because it was unusual? The other boiotarchs may by now have been included in the groups so addressed, see previous n.

92. *Speech of Pagondas*

Little has been written on this speech (no entry in W. West's bibliography at P. Stadter (ed.), *The Speeches in Thucydides* (Chapel Hill, 1973), 158); the fullest treatments are by Luschnat, *Feldherrnreden*, 44–53, and Leimbach, 64–71.

Pagondas' speech and the incomplete one of Hippokrates at ch. 95 go together; in fact, despite Leimbach, 76 n. 20, the second roughly 'answers' the first, so that Rutherford, *RFP* 60, is right to call them an antilogy and a matching pair. But Hippokrates' speech does not answer Pagondas' in ways that tell seriously against the authenticity of either, because the content of the two speeches is hardly contrived or recherché—Hippokrates, in particular, does not have time for that—nor are the correspondences between them very detailed, see further introductory n. to 95. (In both respects, contrast ii. 87–9, the rather closer and subtler correspondences between Phormio's speech and that of the Peloponnesian commanders.) A more fundamental attack on the authenticity of Pagondas' speech is implied by M. H. Hansen's thesis (*Historia* 1993) that battle exhortations in ancient historiography were always fictional. For general discussion of this see Introduction, above pp. 82 ff. As for Pagondas' speech, Pritchett, *EGH* 58, points out that it was delivered *at Tanagra*, not to 'an army drawn up in battle order' as Hansen (168) says.

Pagondas' speech is not merely a speech of encouragement, but one in criticism of (or argument against, see 92. 1 n.) his ten (or nine?) fellow-boiotarchs (see ch. 91 and n. on τῶν ἄλλων); so Luschnat, 45, and Leimbach, 65. A scholiast says the speech is divided into arguments from expediency and justice, τὸ δίκαιον and τὸ σύμφερον, cp. Pritchett, 57 (but of how many Thucydidean speeches is this *not* true?). Pagondas begins by challenging the view (which had presumably been urged by his colleagues) that the Boiotians should not fight unless they caught the Athenians on Boiotian soil: after all, they have built a fort on our territory (para. 1). Then follows (paras. 2–6) what the scholiast calls the 'abuse of the Athenians', διαβολὴ Ἀθηναίων, cp. Luschnat, 44). Greedy invaders should be resisted unhesitatingly (para. 2). Boiotian tradition requires it of you (para. 3). Look at their treatment of Euboia: you risk being absorbed into one vast Attica (para. 4). Against arrogant aggressors, attack is the best security (para. 5). Our victory at Koroneia proves as much (para. 6); show yourselves worthy sons of your fathers who fought there. God will be on our side against these impious temple-desecrators (para. 7). Pagondas ends by appealing to his men's 'noble nature', which now replaces the 'tradition' of para. 3; or as Leimbach (71) puts it, Pagondas now adds 'can' to 'ought' ('damit ergänzt er das Sollen durch das Können').

Apart from the polemical beginning, the speech is a fine example of what Th. vii. 69. 2 calls 'old-fashioned speaking', ἀρχαιολογεῖν. There are some characteristically Thucydidean twists (paras. 2 and 5), but otherwise the appeals to history and to piety, and the exhortation to the Boiotians to be worthy of their fathers, are straightforward. One might be tempted to think that Th. was attempting to represent Pagondas as an old-fashioned Boiotian, or rather as old-fashioned because Boiotian, if it were not that the Athenian Hippokrates in ch. 95 is made to speak in the same way. Nor should the more subtle paras. 2 and 5 be forgotten: perhaps Pagondas, or the Thucydidean version of Pagondas, was not so different from his (?) kinsman Pindar; against the usual view that Pindar was a 'backward Boiotian' see L. Kurke, *The Traffic in Praise* (Ithaca, 1991), 255. Pagondas may himself have been a survivor of Koroneia.

Note that although the battle is now fairly close this is still not Pagondas' last word, see 96. 1 for his second short speech, and see 92. 7 n. on πιστεύσαντας etc., end of n.

1. χρῆν ... μηδ᾿ ἐς ἐπίνοιάν τινα ἡμῶν ἐλθεῖν τῶν ἀρχόντων ὡς οὐκ εἰκὸς Ἀθηναίοις, ἢν ἄρα μὴ ἐν τῇ Βοιωτίᾳ ἔτι καταλάβωμεν

αὐτούς, διὰ μάχης ἐλθεῖν: 'no one among us commanders should ever have allowed the thought to enter his head that we ought not to fight the Athenians unless we catch them on Boiotian soil'. A curious way to open a speech supposedly delivered (mainly) to the rank and file, because it is criticism of, and so risks undermining confidence in, the officers who are about to lead them. Perhaps a sign of inauthenticity? Note '*us* commanders', ἡμῶν, implying perhaps that Pagondas is still represented as engaged in an argument with his colleagues; for the significance of this see 91 n. on καὶ ἡγεμονίας etc.

The clear implication is that the Athenians are no longer in Boiotia, indeed μὴ ἐν τῇ Βοιωτίᾳ picks up οὐκ ἐν τῇ Βοιωτίᾳ at 91 line 24, see n. there. Contrast 95. 2 n. on ἐν γάρ etc.: Hippokrates.

μέλλουσι φθείρειν: 'with the intention of devastating Boiotia'. Luschnat (45) compares 76. 5, see n. there on ἐχομένων etc. Pagondas could have heard about Athenian plans from Nikomachos of Panopeus, see 89. 1.

2. οὐ γὰρ τὸ προμηθές, οἷς ἂν ἄλλος ἐπίῃ, περὶ τῆς σφετέρας ὁμοίως ἐνδέχεται λογισμὸν καὶ ὅστις τὰ μὲν ἑαυτοῦ ἔχει, τοῦ πλέονος δὲ ὀρεγόμενος ἑκών τινι ἐπέρχεται: 'When a man's own possessions are secure but he nevertheless goes out of his way to attack others out of greed for more, he should weigh the consequences very carefully; but it is quite different when he is the victim of an attack and is fighting for what is rightfully his' i.e. that is no time for prudent reflection. For the thought cp. i. 86. 4. τοῦ πλέονος δὲ ὀρεγόμενος, 'out of greed for more', is the language of Th. himself about Athens, see 21. 2. As for *Theban* aspirations, G. L. Cawkwell, 'Agesilaus and Sparta', *CQ* 26 (1976), 62–84, at 81, notes that in the whole speech Pagondas manifests 'no concern with anything more than the integrity of Boiotia'; that is, there is no trace of the larger Theban ambitions of the 360s and Epaminondas, for which see J. Roy, *CAH* vi² (1994), ch. 7. On Thebes' fifth-cent. (as opp. Thebes' more aggressive fourth-cent.) policies see also Connor, 'Polarization in Thucydides' (below 5 n. on εἰώθασι etc.), 55.

3. πάτριόν τε ὑμῖν στρατὸν ἀλλόφυλον ἐπελθόντα καὶ ἐν τῇ οἰκείᾳ καὶ ἐν τῇ τῶν πέλας ὁμοίως ἀμύνεσθαι: 'It is a Boiotian tradition to resist foreign invaders, inside and outside Boiotia'. Luschnat, 46, (followed by Leimbach, 67 n. 11) cautiously identifies here a somewhat overblown allusion to 72. 1, Boiotian help to Megara (outside Boiotia but close in more than one sense, see my n. there). But there is a lot we do not know about earlier Boiotian history, and the allusion is no doubt multiple.

Leimbach (67) and Luschnat (47) also see in the word for 'foreign', ἀλλόφυλον, an allusion to the Dorian/Ionian distinction, cp. 64. 4 n.

Speech of Pagondas

(Hermokrates) and 86. 5 n. (Brasidas); for other parallels between
Brasidas at Akanthos and Pagondas see Luschnat, 49, detecting a shared
preoccupation with the theme slavery/freedom.

4. παράδειγμα δὲ ἔχομεν τούς τε ἀντιπέρας Εὐβοέας καὶ τῆς
ἄλλης Ἑλλάδος τὸ πολὺ ὡς αὐτοῖς διάκειται: 'Look at the way
they treated the Euboians over the water, and look at the way they have
treated most of Greece' [lit. 'we have as an example the way ...']. On
Euboian resentment against Athens in the last quarter of the fifth cent.
see G. L. Cawkwell, 'Euboea in the 340s', *Phoenix*, 32 (1978), 42–67, at
43. Note, with Lewis *CAH* v². 427 n. 144, the two Eretrians (i.e.
Euboians) who may have fought at Delion on the Boiotian side: *IG* vii.
585 with 96. 3 n. below; as Lewis says, 'the defeat at Delion will certainly
have had some effect on opinion there', i.e. on Euboia. Lewis adds 'somewhere we have to fit in the mysterious expedition to Euboea ... of Philochorus 328 F130'. On this kind of παράδειγμα, 'example', see R. B.
Rutherford, 'Learning from History: Categories and Case-histories', in
RFP, 53–68, at 60, and see 6 n. below on Koroneia.

εἰς ὅρος ... παγήσεται: 'there will be one fixed frontier'. What does
horos mean here? Wade-Gery, *Mélanges Glotz* (Paris, 1932), 881, wanted
it to mean a stone recording a mortgage rather than a boundary stone.
This would be a bold metaphor, 'a single stone recording our absorption
in Athenian territory'. Gomme registered this interpretation without
comment, merely giving it as a (less desirable?) alternative to the more
obvious trans. 'frontier', which he gave first; T. C. W. Stinton, 'Solon,
Fragment 25', *JHS* 96 (1976), 159–62, at 161 and n. 20, positively
accepted Wade-Gery's view, translated Pagondas 'if we are beaten we
will have one *horos*-pillar stuck up affecting our land', and said the word
here 'cannot mean boundary-stone'. This view is extraordinary, and
J. V. A. Fine, *Horoi* (*Hesperia* Suppl. ix, 1951), 50 n. 40, was right to reject
it. Fine observed that our evidence for *horoi* of the Wade-Gery type is
fourth-century; the present tricky and flowery passage of Th. would be
the only fifth-century evidence, and it is hardly compelling. With the
present passage Fine compares instead the inscriptions bearing e.g. ὅρος
μνήματος, 'the boundary of the tomb'. Add the obvious point that Th.
has just used *horoi* in the sense of 'boundaries' a few words earlier, περὶ
γῆς ὅρων τὰς μάχας, 'fights about frontiers', cp. para. 5 ἔξω ὅρων
προαπαντῶντα, 'crosses the boundary of his own country to meet them'.
On the Wade-Gery view, two normal senses of the word sandwich one
use of it in a different, metaphorical and specialized sense. This is
improbable. I suggest that there is a kind of concealed negative here,
'there will not be a boundary *between* Attica and Boiotia but one single

boundary delimiting a big territorial unit Attica + Boiotia as that unit existed in 457–446'.

For the idea that the boundaries or *horoi* of Attica might be extendable in the way Pagondas implies cp. Tod 204 line 19, ephebic oath sworn by the 'boundaries of the fatherland', ὅροι τῆς πατρίδος, a phrase followed by the list 'wheat, barley, vines, olives, figs'. (Cf. now Parker, *ARH* 253.) On the elucidation of this see J. Ober, 'Greek Horoi: Artifactual Texts and the Contingency of Meaning', in D. Small (ed.), *Methods in the Mediterranean: Historical and Archaeological View on Texts and Archaeology* (*Mnemosyne* Suppl. 135: Leiden, 1995), 91–123, at 107, comparing Plut. *Alc.* 15. 4, Alcibiades argues that the Athenians had sworn to treat as their own fatherland anywhere in which wheat, barley, vines, olives, and figs were grown (cp. Th. vi. 13. 1, the sea the *horos* between Athens and Sicily). Ober therefore suggests that in the oath as interpreted (or distorted) by Alcibiades, the agricultural products are themselves in a sense '*horoi*' of the fatherland', rather than being listed alongside those *horoi* (a 'metonymic' rather than a 'paratactic' interpretation). Pagondas is of course a Boiotian not an Athenian, but it would not be surprising if Th. allowed him to betray awareness of Athenian ideology.

As for παγήσεται, it is odd to find a verbal form in *pag-* in the mouth of *Pag*ondas. Not likely to be deliberate, in this least ludic of writers, but at some level there may have been a mental association. Note the iambic jingle. There may be Solonian influence at some level, cp. the verbally similar Solon F 36 W line 6, ὅρους ἀνεῖλον πολλαχῆ πεπηγότας, 'I uprooted the *horoi* which were fixed in many places'.

5. τοσούτῳ ἐπικινδυνοτέραν ἑτέρων τὴν παροίκησιν τῶνδε ἔχομεν: 'They are far more dangerous than ordinary neighbours' [lit. 'we have a more dangerous propinquity of these people than of others']. Leimbach (68) detects an illogicality in this section of the argument: Pagondas does not need to show that the Athenians are unusually dangerous, but that they will become less dangerous by reason of an immediate Boiotian attack. (But the aim of a speech like this is to raise the level of aggression among one's hearers, perhaps at the price of some illogicality.)

The word παροίκησιν, 'propinquity', is unusual, but cp. iii. 113. 6 for a similar thought about the Athenians, expressed by the simple form πάροικοι. The proverbial expression Ἀττικὸς πάροικος, 'Attic neighbour' (aptly cited by Classen/Steup), meant 'cuckoo in the nest', see G. T. Griffith, in *Imperialism* (87. 5 n. on οὐδ' αὖ etc.), 140, 303 n. 40: it was used about the Athenian cleruchy (settlement) on Samos.

εἰώθασί τε οἱ ἰσχύος που θράσει τοῖς πέλας, ὥσπερ Ἀθηναῖοι

νῦν, ἐπιόντες τὸν μὲν ἡσυχάζοντα καὶ ἐν τῇ ἑαυτοῦ μόνον ἀμυνόμενον ἀδεέστερον ἐπιστρατεύειν: 'Men like the Athenians, who wantonly attack others, will not hesitate to invade the territory of people who remain quietly at home and make no move except to defend themselves'. On the quietist position here criticized by Pagondas see the good remarks of W. R. Connor, 'Polarization in Thucydides', in R. Lebow and B. S. Strauss (eds.), *Hegemonic Rivalry from Thucydides to the Nuclear Age* (Boulder and San Francisco, 1991), 53–69, at 55 (but his ref. to 4. 95 is to be corrected to 4. 92. 5): 'if the policy Pagondas criticized was in fact traditional in Thebes, its rationale is easy to conjecture: given the constant difficulties Thebes faced in maintaining control over Boeotia and the recurrent problems with Phocis, Thessaly, and other neighbouring states, it would be wise to avoid excessive entanglement in the Peloponnesians' war with the Athenians.' See also above 2 n. on οὐ γάρ etc.

6. νικήσαντες γὰρ ἐν Κορωνείᾳ αὐτούς, ὅτε τὴν γῆν ἡμῶν στασιαζόντων κατέσχον: 'Once, they were able to occupy Boiotia, because of our internal dissensions, but we defeated them at Koroneia'. The 'occupation' referred to is the decade of Athenian control of Boiotia, for which see i. 108. 3 and n.; for the battle of Koroneia see i. 113. 2. The main piece of information here conforms to the rule for which I argue in Annex A above, pp. 132–4, namely that references in Thucydidean speeches to past events tend to be drawn *either* from Herodotus *or* from Th.'s own narrative, like the present reference, and like the similar references to Koroneia at iii. 62. 5 and 67. 3 (the Theban and Plataian speeches at Plataia). But for one detail *not* in Th.'s narrative elsewhere see on *stasis* below.

Rutherford (4 n. on παράδειγμα etc.) points out that the weakness of such appeals to history is that they are 'available on both sides of an argument', cp. 95. 2 for Hippokrates on Oinophyta. For appeals to past successes in a specifically *military* context see next n.

The 'internal dissensions' are interesting. Dissensions between Boiotian cities, or inside Boiotian cities? Lewis, *CAH* v². 116, citing Ar. *Rhet.* 1407a2, which quotes Pericles on conflict *between* Boiotian cities, takes the reference here and at iii. 62. 5 (where the Greek is κατὰ στάσιν) to be to inter-city *stasis*. H.-J. Gehrke, *Stasis* (Munich, 1985), 166 n. 16, by contrast, appears to take it to refer to struggles inside the cities (though he cites Ar. *Rhet.*). See above, p. 85, for Lewis's sense of στασιάζειν or στάσις (the closest parallel is Hermokrates at iv. 61. 1). Alternatively one would have to say that Pagondas was for rhetorical purposes treating federal Boiotia as a unit so that struggles between its members were a kind of *stasis*. This is just possible, though I incline to

Gehrke's view. On either interpretation, the passage is remarkable as a
reference, in a speech, to a factual detail *not* given in the relevant piece of
narrative, and it and iii. 62. 5 should be added to my list of exceptions in
Annex A above (see p. 133, cf. 132). But Pagondas is perhaps inventing
the fact for a rhetorical purpose, namely to extenuate the military implications of the Athenian takeover ('a convenient fiction for any
defeated state', Gomme); in which case the present passage would be
like the Theban claim about 'isonomous oligarchy' at iii. 62. 3, which is
not from Hdt., but is suspect because it suits the Thebans' case so neatly,
cp. my n. on that passage and Annex A above, p. 131.

7. ὧν χρὴ μνησθέντας ἡμᾶς τούς τε πρεσβυτέρους ὁμοιωθῆναι
τοῖς πρὶν ἔργοις: 'the older men among us should try to match their
own earlier achievements'. See Hanson, *Western Way*, 93: it is perfectly
possible that there were veterans of Koroneia present (including perhaps Pagondas himself), and their presence would be an enormous
psychological boost to their juniors.

πιστεύσαντας δὲ τῷ θεῷ πρὸς ἡμῶν ἔσεσθαι, οὗ τὸ ἱερὸν
ἀνόμως τειχίσαντες νέμονται, καὶ τοῖς ἱεροῖς ἃ ἡμῖν θυσαμένοις
καλὰ φαίνεται, ὁμόσε χωρῆσαι τοῖσδε: 'The god whose temple
they have sacrilegiously fortified and occupied will be on our side, and
the sacrifices are favourable to us; so let us advance to meet them in the
confidence of divine favour'. R. Syme, 'Thucydides', *PBA* 48 (1962), 39–
56 (above, p. 111 n. 284), at 52, exclaimed 'look what happens to those
characters in his History who make appeal to the gods—the unfortunate
Plataians, the people of Melos, Nicias in the retreat from Syracuse'. But
Pagondas in the present passage is a counter-instance: the Boiotians go
on to win at Delion. (Syme's remark works better for the Athenians'
sadly optimistic claim at 98. 6, to the effect that the god will pardon
wrongs done under duress.)

Gomme rightly remarked that it is unusual for Th., as opp. Xenophon,
to mention battle sacrifices, on which see M. H. Jameson, 'Sacrifice
Before Battle', in Hanson (ed.), *Hoplites*, 197–227. (But note Th. vi. 69. 2,
with Jameson, 204, the description of the Athenian sacrifices before the
first battle at Syracuse, with the only occurrence of σφάγια in Th.) The
word *hiera*, used by Th. in the present passage, covers both (i) *hiera* in
the narrow sense, the leisurely sacrificing and burning of the victim and
then examination of the innards, perhaps in camp or on the march, and
also (ii) *sphagia*, the 'rites focussed on bloodletting' (Jameson, 201) i.e. on
the slaughter by throat-cutting of the animal shortly before engaging the
enemy, with attention on the part of the *mantis* or seer to signs like how
the blood spurted or how the animal fell. The *sphagia* (ii) happened very
shortly before the battle and in view of the time-lapse implied at 93. 1 is

less likely than (i) to be what Pagondas is here referring to. (See also introductory n., citing Pritchett for the location of the speech, and noting 96. 1 for Pagondas' absolutely final speech.) That is, Th. here refers to *hiera* in the narrower sense. (It is tempting to press his language in the present passage, so as to reach the same conclusion. He does after all call the sacrifices *hiera*, and as we saw he uses the distinct word *sphagia* in book vi. But this argument is not quite decisive because of the confusing double meaning of *hiera*—general and particular.) Gomme's comment, that Pagondas 'must have managed the sacrifice rapidly and cleverly', will not do. See Introduction, p. 10.

93. 1. τοιαῦτα ὁ Παγώνδας τοῖς Βοιωτοῖς παραινέσας ἔπεισεν ἰέναι ἐπὶ τοὺς Ἀθηναίους: 'That was Pagondas' speech of encouragement, and it persuaded the Boiotians to attack the Athenians'. Th. does not quite say that this was a successful appeal to the generality of Boiotians over the heads of his colleagues, who themselves may have been among those 'persuaded', see 92. 1 n. That is, Pagondas was not necessarily acting irregularly, see 91 n. on καὶ ἡγεμονίας etc.

ἤδη γὰρ καὶ τῆς ἡμέρας ὀψὲ ἦν: 'because it was late in the day'. Gomme (in his n. on ch. 91) considered, but rightly rejected, the possibility that this was evidence that supreme command changed daily, i.e. Pagondas had to act (for the command problem see 91 n. on καὶ ἡγεμονίας etc.). He just wanted to 'catch the Athenians' (Gomme).

ἐς χωρίον καθίσας ὅθεν λόφου ὄντος μεταξὺ οὐκ ἐθεώρουν ἀλλήλους: 'he took up a position where a hill interrupted the view'. Not certainly identifiable.

3. ὁπλῖται ἑπτακισχίλιοι μάλιστα καὶ ψιλοὶ ὑπὲρ μυρίους, ἱππῆς δὲ χίλιοι καὶ πελτασταὶ πεντακόσιοι: 'they had about seven thousand hoplites, more than ten thousand light-armed troops, a thousand cavalry, and five hundred peltasts'. Diodorus (xii. 70. 1) adds that there were ἡνίοχοι, which should mean 'charioteers', and L. H. Jeffery, *CAH* iv². (1988), 360, apparently accepts this; but see G. L. Huxley, 'Boiotian Charioteers in Diodoros', *Philologus*, 135 (1991), 320–1: chariots in Greek warfare of 424 BC are incredible; the title 'chariot-driver' may however (Huxley suggests) have survived as a title in classical Boiotia; for a similar suggestion see already P. Salmon, *Étude*, 97. Diodorus' cavalry battle before the main battle of Delion (xii. 70. 2) is generally disbelieved.

As for the approximately 7000 hoplites, Salmon (96) thinks this merely shows that the 11000 of *Hell. Oxy.* xix (i.e. 1000 from all the eleven districts, cp. Th.'s 'eleven boiotarchs' at 91) was an exaggerated paper total. Alternatively it has ingeniously been supposed that the *c.*7000 represents roughly a 2/3 turnout from the ten districts other than Tanagra, which as the area invaded had to provide a full levy (10 × 666 = 6660, + 1000 = 7660; see Gomme citing (but rejecting) P. Seymour, 'Note on . . .' and 'Further Note on the Boeotian League', *CR* 36 (1922), 70, and 37 (1923), 63, and Bruce, 109; 162. The 1000 cavalry are roughly in line with what we would expect from *Hell. Oxy.*, i.e. 1100 (100 from each of the 11 areas of Boiotia). Gomme thought some garrison troops might have been left behind in Boiotia, which could explain the discrepancy 7000/11000. Pritchett, *EGH* 58–9 n. 20, thinks it possible that although all eleven boiotarchs had come to Tanagra, not all were persuaded i.e. some went home with their men. But Th. 93. 1 says 'the Boiotians' *were* persuaded.

On the 10000 light-armed see Bruce, 162, suggesting they lacked political franchise as being of less than hoplite status. For peltasts see 28. 4 n. on καὶ πελταστάς.

4. εἶχον δὲ δεξιὸν μὲν κέρας Θηβαῖοι καὶ οἱ ξύμμοροι αὐτοῖς· μέσοι δὲ Ἁλιάρτιοι καὶ Κορωναῖοι καὶ Κωπαιῆς καὶ οἱ ἄλλοι οἱ περὶ τὴν λίμνην· τὸ δὲ εὐώνυμον εἶχον Θεσπιῆς καὶ Ταναγραῖοι καὶ Ὀρχομένιοι: 'The Thebans and the Boiotians who were grouped with them held the right wing. In the centre were the troops from Haliartos, Koroneia, and Kopai, and the other people who live round Lake Kopais [lit. 'round the lake']. On the left wing were the Thespians, Tanagraians, and Orchomenians'. This ch., together with ch. 76, is priceless evidence for the fifth-century organization of the Boiotian league and for Th.'s knowledge of that organization. Th.'s picture generally bears out that given by *Hell. Oxy.* xix, but there are differences.

Over Thebes and its dependencies, Th. is merely vague where *Hell. Oxy.* is precise (cp. Hansen, 'Boiotian Cities' (76. 3 n. on Σίφας μέν etc.), 16, for Th. as 'characteristically vague' in this ch., both about the Theban dependencies and about the 'people round the lake'). The places which Th. says were 'grouped with' Thebes surely included Plataia, see 91 n. on Παγώνδας etc.; the others given by *Hell. Oxy.* are Skolos, Erythrai, and Skaphai. Th.'s exact word ξύμμοροι is not used by *Hell. Oxy.* in ch. xix, and indeed is found nowhere else at all. It is said to be derived from the military word μόρα, used in the Spartan army. *Hell. Oxy.* does, however, use μέρη for the 'divisions' of Boiotia, and it is surely possible that Th.'s word is related to μέρος. Some mss. of Th. have the easier (but not necessarily correct) ξύμμαχοι, 'allies', lit. 'fighters with'. The literal sense would suit the context well.

Th.'s second group is 'Haliartos, Koroneia, and Kopai, and the other people round Lake Kopais'. The first two are grouped together by *Hell. Oxy.*, but with Lebadeia (a place nowhere mentioned by Th.) as the third instead of Th.'s Kopai. Lebadeia, as Bruce (107) says, would be among those said by Th. to have been 'around the lake'. Kopai in *Hell. Oxy.* is grouped with Akraiphnion and Chaironeia. At first these look like significant differences, but actually, as Salmon (*Étude*, 97) says, Th. has simply enumerated the chief cities bordering Lake Kopais, *without distinguishing the two districts* (i.e. the two districts separately given by *Hell. Oxy.*).

For Haliartos, mentioned here only by Th., see M. Holleaux, 'Pausanias et la destruction d'Haliarte par les Perses', *Études d'épigraphie et d'histoire grecques*, 1 (Paris, 1938), 187–93, at 188: Pausanias (ix. 32. 5 and x. 35. 2) claimed that Haliartos was destroyed by the Persians, and that he himself saw its ruins, but the present passage of Th. proves its existence in the Peloponnesian War. Pausanias may have mistaken the ruins left by C. Lucretius in 171 BC for Persian War devastation; the mistake, Holleaux cleverly suggested, may have arisen because Pausanias misunderstood a reference somewhere to ἐν τῷ Περσικῷ πολέμῳ as 'in the Persian War' rather than 'in the war against Perseus'. Even a scholar as generally sympathetic to Pausanias as C. Habicht accepts that Pausanias made a 'major error' here, see *Pausanias' Guide to Ancient Greece* (Berkeley, 1985), 99 and n. 14. For Haliartos see also Roesch (76. 3 n. on Σίφας μέν etc.), 63–4; Salmon, *Étude*, 95–6; Fossey (76. 3 n. on Σίφας μέν etc.), 301–8; S. Lauffer, in Lauffer (ed.), *Griechenland*, 254–5; Snodgrass, 'Survey Archaeology and the Rural Landscape of the Greek City', in O. Murray and S. Price (eds.), *The Greek City* (Oxford, 1990), 113–36, at 129–30. For Koroneia, which otherwise features in Th. only as the site of the battle of 446, see Roesch, 63, and Salmon, 96; and for Kopai Roesch, 64, and Salmon, 98.

Th.'s third and final group (the left wing) consists of Thespiai, Tanagra, and Orchomenos, for which places see the refs. at 76. 3 and 4 nn. Unlike Th.'s other two main divisions, these three places do not go together geographically. In *Hell. Oxy.* Tanagra is on its own, Thespiai is grouped with Eutresis and Thisbai, and Orchomenos is grouped with Hysiai. As we saw on 76. 3, Th. says that Chaironeia was subordinate to Orchomenos, whereas in the time described by *Hell. Oxy.* it was apparently independent and grouped with Kopai (see above) and Akraiphnion.

To conclude, Th.'s account (taking chs. 76 and 93 together) differs from that of *Hell. Oxy.* in significant details, e.g. over the status of Chaironeia; otherwise it is a looser version of the same basic arrangements. Here as elsewhere Th. avoids unnecessary political and institutional technicality, see my paper in *Proc. 2nd Int. Conference of Boiotian*

Studies, forthcoming. But he is essentially faithful to the facts, if we assume (as is usually done) that *Hell. Oxy.* gives high-grade material.

ἐπ' ἀσπίδας δὲ πέντε μὲν καὶ εἴκοσι Θηβαῖοι ἐτάξαντο, οἱ δὲ ἄλλοι ὡς ἕκαστοι ἔτυχον: 'The Thebans were drawn up twenty-five deep; elsewhere the depth varied'. Th. comments on the depth of the Theban line, because it was unusual; the normal or original depth (the 'Urtiefe') seems to have been eight, see Pritchett, 'Depth of Phalanx', *GSW* i. 134-43, with chart at 135; Pritchett suggests that the 25 of the present passage represent three files of eight plus one ἐνωμόταρχος. The twenty-five at Delion anticipated the deepened Theban *left* at Leuktra, see V. D. Hanson, *CA* 1988 (see 43. 2 n.), 194 (who sees nothing remarkable about Leuktra in this respect, given the number of other pre-Leuktra deepenings collected by Pritchett). But in the Peloponnesian War it was still normal for the best troops to be posted on the right for the reason implied by Th. at v. 71. 1, see n. there.

The motives behind the deepening of the file were, it has been suggested, to increase confidence, to give greater momentum and (sometimes) to cope with the exigencies of rough terrain: Pritchett, *GSW* i. 141; Hanson, *CA* 1988, 194; P. Krentz, 'The Nature of Hoplite Battle', *CA* 4 (1985), 50-61, at 59-60; D. M. Lewis, *CAH* v². 425 ('it [the Theban right] had a depth of twenty-five men to the normal Athenian eight and pushed correspondingly harder'). G. L. Cawkwell, 'Epaminondas and Thebes', *CQ* 22 (1972), 261, and *Philip of Macedon* (London, 1978), 154-5, suggested that the aim of very deep files was to provide a strategic reserve, because the 'tail' could fan out to attack the enemy in flank. This is attractive, but critics have objected that there is no specific evidence for such use of the tail, see Lazenby, in V. D. Hanson (ed.), *Hoplites*, 98-9.

94. 1. Ἀθηναῖοι δὲ οἱ μὲν ὁπλῖται … ὄντες πλήθει ἰσοπαλεῖς τοῖς ἐναντίοις: 'The Athenians had the same number of hoplites as the Boiotians'. That is, 7000; not a high total for what was supposed to be a full levy. For the reason, see 90. 1 n. on ὁ δὲ Ἱπποκράτης etc.

ψιλοὶ δὲ ἐκ παρασκευῆς μὲν ὡπλισμένοι οὔτε τότε παρῆσαν οὔτε ἐγένοντο τῇ πόλει: 'They had no regular light-armed troops with them on this occasion, nor did Athens ever have an organized force of this kind'. A nice example of 'presentation through negation', for which technique see *Greek Historiography*, 152-6: why does Th. bother to tell us something the Athenians did *not* have? The fact that Boiotians *did* have ψιλοί, 'light-armed' (93. 4), helps to explain, though it does not completely explain, why he tells us the Athenians did not have them on this occasion; but he goes further and adds in effect a second negative, saying emphatically that Athens *never* had such a force. Gomme remarked that Th. 'writes as though he were contradicting a popular misconception', to which Ridley, *Hermes* 1981, 30, replied 'obviously one which could hardly have been held by Athenians'. Possibly Th. is contradicting a statement in some other (non-Athenian) *writer*. But other explanations are available. Perhaps the second negative here means 'they did not, as you might expect, have such a force'. If so, it might be thought an implied rebuke by an Athenian of his own city's arrangements (but ch. 96 does not suggest that a proper force of light-armed would have made much difference to the outcome of the battle). Or perhaps Th. is simply taking the opportunity to be didactic (with a non-Athenian readership in view), at the military level discussed by Rutherford, *RFP* 55.

πανστρατιᾶς ξένων τῶν παρόντων καὶ ἀστῶν: 'a complete call-out of foreigners and citizens'. See 90. 1 n. on αὐτούς etc.

2. Ἱπποκράτης ὁ στρατηγὸς ἐπιπαριὼν τὸ στρατόπεδον τῶν Ἀθηναίων παρεκελεύετό τε καὶ ἔλεγε τοιάδε: 'Hippokrates the general went along the lines and encouraged them like this'. Again (cp. introductory n. on 92, Pagondas' speech), the detail that Hippokrates walked along the front of the line can be taken to support the view of Hansen, *Historia* 1993, 168–9, that generals did not deliver one set speech to the entire army. But again one might wish to ask, why did Th. mention the fact unless it was unusual? Hippokrates got only half way along the line, see 96. 1. See also Pritchett, *EGH* 57, arguing that the way Hippokrates is described as addressing his troops is plausible.

95. *Speech of Hippokrates*

For this speech see Luschnat, 53–7, and Leimbach, 72–6. For its relation to Pagondas' speech see introductory n. to 92. Both speeches deal with the point that the Athenians are outside Attica (92. 1; 95. 2), and Hippokrates counters Koroneia (92. 6) with Oinophyta (95. 3). But these are not troubling correspondences. Rutherford, *RFP* 60, suggests that Th. deliberately makes Hippokrates break off his speech as a way of indicating that the Athenians are about to lose the battle (but note the possibility that the speech was originally written for delivery at *Delion*, see below 2 n. on ἐν γάρ etc.). Luschnat (54) had suggested that Th. did not want to make Hippokrates' speech too long, so that it would not detract from the effect of Pagondas'.

1. ὑπόμνησιν μᾶλλον ἔχει ἢ ἐπικέλευσιν: 'I don't want to hector you, just to remind you of things you already know'. With this thought, Jowett compares the description of the Spartans' behaviour before the battle of Mantinea at v. 69. 2, see n. there.

2. παραστῇ δὲ μηδενὶ ὑμῶν ὡς ἐν τῇ ἀλλοτρίᾳ οὐ προσῆκον τοσόνδε κίνδυνον ἀναρριπτοῦμεν: 'You should not think that because we are on foreign soil we are facing dangers we ought never to have incurred'. On the wider implications of 'we ought never' here (οὐ προσῆκον) see Leimbach, 73, who suggests that Hippokrates here replies to 'Periclean' objections to a forward, extra-Attic strategy. See next n. for the question, were they on foreign or home soil? With the imagined objection ('we should not get involved') Luschnat (55) compares 72. 1 (Megara, see n. there) and vi. 84. 1 (Euphemos at Kamarina).

ἐν γὰρ τῇ τούτων ὑπὲρ τῆς ἡμετέρας ὁ ἀγὼν ἔσται: 'It is true that we are in Boiotian [lit 'their'] territory, but we shall be fighting for our own'. Lazenby, in Hanson (ed.), *Hoplites*, 105, citing the present passage, discusses the motives which impelled hoplites to fight, and stresses the need to feel that you were in effect about to 'defend your home and loved ones' even if you were actually in somebody else's territory as an aggressor. This is generally true and important (we may compare the double motive attributed to the Athenians in Sicily at vi. 69. 3). But in the present instance, there was an easier rhetorical move open to Hippokrates, which oddly he does not choose to avail himself of, namely to assert that the Athenians *were* inside, and thus defending, Athenian territory. At 91, line 24 of the OCT we were, in contradiction of the present passage, told that the Athenians were no longer in Boiotia (οὐκ ἐν τῇ Βοιωτίᾳ ἔτι εἰσί), and this is accepted by Pagondas in his argument at 92. 1. The battle was in fact 'on the borders', ἐν μεθορίοις, 91 line 25, with n. there, and 99 line 10, but all parties except Hippokrates (that is, the boiotarchs, Pagondas, and Th. himself in ch. 91, though see below) seem to accept that the fighting was in Athenian rather than Boiotian territory, see 99 lines 9–11, and n. on νομίζοντες etc. I suppose that Hippokrates and his troops are uneasily aware that Delion, which they had fortified, *was* in Boiotian territory (76. 4), hence the rhetorical need to face that issue boldly. But Hippokrates has certainly left Delion and joined the main part of his army by now, see 93. 2. The point has not had the attention it deserves, though Gomme's n. on 95. 2 briefly and correctly says 'contrast 91, οὐκ ἐν τῇ Βοιωτίᾳ ἔτι εἰσί'. At ch. 91 Th. seems, as we have seen, to accept that the battle was not in Boiotia, but in the retrospective reference at 108. 5 he refers to the defeat 'in Boiotia' (actually 'among the Boiotians'). This is compatible with his other retrospective references (v. 14. 1 and 15. 2) where the battle is 'at Delion', but it is loose. See also Introduction, p. 92: was Hippokrates' speech originally written for delivery at Delion?

καὶ ἢν νικήσωμεν, οὐ μή ποτε ὑμῖν Πελοποννήσιοι ἐς τὴν χώραν ἄνευ τῆς τῶνδε ἵππου ἐσβάλωσιν: 'If we win, the Peloponnesians will be deprived of the Boiotian cavalry and will never invade Attica again'. The Peloponnesian invasions of Attica did indeed stop after 425 (see iv. 2. 1), although Athens *lost* the battle of Delion (in 424); but the reason why Sparta stopped invading was fear for the prisoners taken at Sphakteria (iv. 41. 1), see Leimbach, 74. See Connor, 'Polarization in Thucydides' (92. 5 n. on εἰώθασι etc.), 55.

3. οἳ τούσδε μάχῃ κρατοῦντες μετὰ Μυρωνίδου ἐν Οἰνοφύτοις τὴν Βοιωτίαν ποτὲ ἔσχον: 'who in times gone by were led by Myronides to victory over these Boiotians at Oinophyta, and then occupied Boiotia'. See i. 108. 3 for the battle of Oinophyta in 457; the *Pentekontaetia* narrative is here echoed with verbal closeness (ἐστράτευσαν ἐς Βοιωτοὺς *Μυρωνίδου* στρατηγοῦντος, καὶ *μάχῃ ἐν Οἰνοφύτοις* τοὺς Βοιωτοὺς νικήσαντες τῆς τε χώρας ἐκράτησαν τῆς Βοιωτίας). Such echoes by Thucydidean speakers of Th.'s own narrative may weaken belief in the authenticity of the relevant section of a speech, see Annex A above, p. 134.

See 92. 6 and n. for Pagondas' matching appeal to the battle of Koroneia, esp. Rutherford, there cited. Unlike Pagondas in his reference to Koroneia (see 92. 7 n. on ὧν χρή etc.), Hippokrates does not say that there were veterans of Oinophyta actually present in the Athenian army: this is careful of Th., because Oinophyta was over a decade earlier than Koroneia. See Introduction, p. 86. Leimbach (76) notes that Hippokrates ignores the Athenian defeat at the battle of Tanagra, which immediately preceded Oinophyta.

96–97. 1. *The battle of Delion*

Delion (with Mantinea at v. 70 ff.) is one of 'the only two encounters of infantry of any magnitude' in the Peloponnesian War: Hanson, *Western Way*, 219. It is one of the more fully and reliably described hoplite battles of classical Greek history, and features correspondingly often in the extensive modern literature on hoplite warfare; see esp. 2 n. on τὸ δὲ ἄλλο etc. for *othismos* or 'shoving'.

On the name 'battle of Delion' see introductory n. to 89–101.

96. 1. μέχρι μὲν μέσου τοῦ στρατοπέδου ἐπελθόντος, τὸ δὲ πλέον οὐκέτι φθάσαντος: 'he was able to work along half the army, but had no time for the rest'. See 94. 2 n. and introductory n. to 95.

οἱ Βοιωτοί, παρακελευσαμένου καὶ σφίσιν ὡς διὰ ταχέων καὶ ἐνταῦθα Παγώνδου, παιανίσαντες ἐπῆσαν ἀπὸ τοῦ λόφου. ἀντεπῆσαν δὲ καὶ οἱ Ἀθηναῖοι καὶ προσέμειξαν δρόμῳ: 'the Boiotians, to whom Pagondas had been making a second short speech, raised the paian, and came down on them from the hill. The Athenians moved forward in their turn and met them at a run'. I have changed Jowett's 'the two armies met at a run'; the subject of the verb is the Athenians. This is significant: see Pritchett, *GSW* iv. 73, 'it was disadvantageous to remain stationary and receive the onset of the enemy. When the Boiotian hoplites were seen advancing down the hill at Delion, the Athenian phalanx, although in a downhill position, charged on the double to engage them', etc. (See also Pritchett, 78, though I do not see why he says 'we can deduce' that the Boiotians occupied an uphill position. Th. says they did, there is no need for deduction.) Contrast Hanson, *Western Way*, 138, who calls this Athenian charge at Delion a 'misguided attack', and speaks in this connection of generals 'exhausting their troops in an *uphill* run'. But in fact the Athenian wing was victorious (though the Athenians lost the whole battle), so Pritchett's view seems preferable: if charged from above it was better to get up some momentum oneself.

For the paian (in naval contexts) see i. 50. 5 n. on ἐπεπαιάνιστο, and for land warfare add Dover, *HCT* on vii. 44. 6, distinguishing the paian as war-cry (never Athenian or Ionian, but rather e.g. Boiotian as here) from the paian as prayer or hymn (universal among Greeks); Pritchett, *GSW* i. 107; Lazenby, in Hanson (ed.), *Hoplites*, 90; Hanson, *Western Way*, 100 (who suggests that the paian dispelled the 'hypnotic trancelike state' experienced by soldiers before a battle); and Burkert, *Greek Religion*, 44. In the situation here described, an additional idea or at any rate effect must have been to increase the terror caused by surprise as the Boiotians came over the hill.

With Pagondas' additional encouragement compare Nikias at vii. 69. 2.

2. καὶ ἑκατέρων τῶν στρατοπέδων τὰ ἔσχατα οὐκ ἦλθεν ἐς χεῖρας, ἀλλὰ τὸ αὐτὸ ἔπαθεν· ῥύακες γὰρ ἐκώλυσαν: 'The extreme right and left of the two armies never engaged, for the same reason: they were both prevented by water-courses'. On these water-courses or ravines see Pritchett, *SAGT* ii. 32 and iii. 297.

τὸ δὲ ἄλλο καρτερᾷ μάχῃ καὶ ὠθισμῷ ἀσπίδων ξυνειστήκει: 'But the rest clashed, and there was a fierce struggle and shoving of shields'. The concept of *othismos*, 'shoving', has been much debated in recent years. The orthodox view is that 'hoplites in the rear ranks literally put their shields against the backs of those in front and pushed'; so Lazenby, in Hanson (ed.), *Hoplites*, 97, citing V. D. Hanson, *Western Way*, 174–5, who says 'each hoplite pressed with the centre of his shield against the back of the man in front'. It has been objected that this would throw the front ranks off balance; R. D. Luginbill, '*Othismos*: the Importance of the Mass-Shove in Hoplite Warfare', *Phoenix*, 48 (1994), 51–61, at 53, therefore suggests that the pressure was on the shoulder and side of the man in front, who would be better able to brace himself.

For the orthodox view, see also A. J. Holladay, 'Hoplites and Heresies', *JHS* 102 (1982), 94-103; Pritchett, 'The Pitched Battle', in *GSW* iv (1985), 1-93.

Two 'heretical' views have been proposed. The more extreme, and in my view not persuasive, is that *othismos* should generally be understood metaphorically, meaning something like 'compelling the other side to retreat': P. Krentz, 'The Nature of Hoplite Battle', *CA* 16 (1985), 50-61 (who however admits at p. 52 that in the present passage of Th., *othismos* must mean a literal shoving), and 'Continuing the *Othismos* on *Othismos*', *Anc. Hist. Bulletin*, 8.2 (1994), 45-9, where Krentz still concedes that the present passage has the literal sense, but says it does not require a mass shove: 'as they dueled, individual hoplites might have shoved other individuals in an attempt to knock them off balance.' Against Krentz, see Luginbill (above).

The other heretical view is that the *othismos* was indeed literal, but it was a feature only of the final phase of hoplite battles, after there had been prolonged individual fighting. The phrase 'until it came to shoving', ἐς ὃ ἀπίκοντο ἐς ὠθισμόν, at Hdt. ix. 62 (battle of Plataia) is undoubtedly support for this view. See G. L. Cawkwell, *Philip of Macedon* (London, 1978), 150-7, and 'Orthodoxy and Hoplites', *CQ* 39 (1989), 375-89. Cawkwell discusses the present passage of Th. at *CQ* 1989, 376-8; he thinks the Theban 'shoving' came at a point well on in the battle and suggests that in the present para. Th. 'is making a general summation of the action, which he proceeds to describe in detail'. This is strained; the word καί, which opens para. 3, looks as if it describes the next event in a sequence. For Cawkwell's view γάρ would be preferable. So the shoving at Plataia was late in the proceedings, that at Delion was early, and one cannot feel confident that Cawkwell is right to see Plataia as normal. Generally, it has been objected against Cawkwell that the evidence for individual duels is slight, see esp. Pritchett, *GSW* iv. 85-9 and n. 255, against Cawkwell's use of *promachoi* as evidence for individual prowess in front of the phalanx or personal combat before shock action: the word is found in poetic rather than historical contexts. (Though see Th. vi. 69. 2 for the verb προυμάχοντο.)

Not all the arguments on each side can be gone into here. I mention one argument because Delion has been invoked. It has been urged against the traditional view that prolonged shoving would call for impossible stamina, on the assumption that battles went on for a long time. Luginbill, 55-6 (who does, however, believe in the compatibility of literal shoving and long battles) cites Delion as an example of a long battle, because it went on till nightfall, see para. 8 below. But at 93. 1 Th. says the battle began 'late in the day'. Hanson's view, argued for throughout *Western Way*, is that hoplite battles were generally short, and I believe this should be accepted.

Only an unusually arrogant scholar could claim to know exactly what kind of thing went on in a hoplite battle, but as things stand at present I do not think the orthodox view has been overthrown.

3. καὶ ἐπίεσαν τούς τε ἄλλους ταύτῃ καὶ οὐχ ἥκιστα τοὺς Θεσπιᾶς ... οἵπερ διεφθάρησαν Θεσπιῶν, ἐν χερσὶν ἀμυνόμενοι κατεκόπησαν: '[the Athenians] pressed hard on this part of the army, and on the Thespians in particular ... the Thespians who died were cut down fighting hand to hand'. For the likely mass grave of these Thespians, see *IG* vii. 1888, with C. Clairmont, *Patrios Nomos* (Oxford, 1983), 232–4, and Pritchett, *GSW* iv. 132–3. (Lewis, *CAH* v². 425 n. 137, says this inscription was 'unknown to Gomme'. It was certainly perverse of Gomme not to cite it when commenting on 96. 3, but in fact he merely delays mention of it until the bare and misprinted reference in his first n. on 101. 2, the general statement of Boiotian casualties.) There were perhaps 300 Thespians buried in all, although there are only 101 names on the stelai, including a Pythian and an Olympic victor labelled as such, Tisimeneis and Polynikos respectively. The case for associating the grave with Delion is circumstantial, and rests largely on the present passage of Th. But there are many grave gifts and there were funerary lions, indicating a very special occasion. On the Thespian losses see further 133. 1. That para. also says that Thebes demolished Thespiai's walls because of its alleged Athenian sympathies. On this see Buck, 'Boiotians in the Peloponnesian War' (introductory n. to 76–7), 47, who suggests that Delion had wiped out the Thespian hoplite class with its pro-federal, pro-oligarchic sympathies; cp. also Hanson, *Western Way*, 201.

Cp. also *IG* vii. 585 from Tanagra, which 'may also refer to this battle' (Lewis); it lists sixty-one citizens and two Euboians from Eretria, for the relevance of whom cp. 92. 4 n. The alternative but less attractive context is the fighting at Th. iii. 91, as my comm. there ought to have mentioned. In favour of Delion see also Clairmont, 230–1, and Pritchett, *GSW* iv. 190–2 (= *SEG* xxxv. 411): we should recall that the Tanagraians were on the left wing along with the badly-mauled Thespians (93. 4). It makes sense to suppose that they too suffered heavy losses.

The Thespians and Tanagraian losses are compatible with Th.'s figure of 'fewer than 500' at ch. 101.

ἠγνόησάν τε καὶ ἀπέκτειναν ἀλλήλους: 'killed each other by mistake'. A reminder that Greeks did not wear uniforms; though blazons on shields (like the famously frightening letter 'lambda' for 'Lakedai-monioi', i.e. Spartans) would sometimes enable you to tell friends from enemies. See Hanson, *Western Way*, 185–8, cp. 65 and 99.

4. τὸ δὲ δεξιόν, ᾗ οἱ Θηβαῖοι ἦσαν, ἐκράτει τῶν Ἀθηναίων, καὶ ὠσάμενοι κατὰ βραχὺ τὸ πρῶτον ἐπηκολούθουν: 'But the right wing, where the Thebans were stationed, was mastering the Athenians; they shoved them back gradually at first, and followed them closely' [in the Greek, as in my trans., there is a change of subject from singular, 'the right wing', to plural, i.e. 'the Thebans']. For 'shoving' here, see 2 n.; Cawkwell thinks *othismos* at para. 2 looks forward to the shoving here, as part of his view that 'shoving' happened in the late stages of a battle.

5. καὶ ξυνέβη, Παγώνδου περιπέμψαντος δύο τέλη τῶν ἱππέων ἐκ τοῦ ἀφανοῦς περὶ τὸν λόφον, ὡς ἐπόνει τὸ εὐώνυμον αὐτῶν, καὶ ὑπερφανέντων αἰφνιδίως, τὸ νικῶν τῶν Ἀθηναίων κέρας, νομίσαν ἄλλο στράτευμα ἐπιέναι, ἐς φόβον καταστῆναι: 'But Pagondas now sent two squadrons of cavalry round the hill because his left wing was in trouble. They started from a point out of sight and sud-denly appeared over the ridge; the victorious wing of the Athenians thought that another army was attacking them, and panicked'. Note that Th. does not say 'Pagondas *saw* what was happening and therefore sent . . .', he says 'because the left wing *was* in trouble, Pagondas sent', etc. Generally the Athenians are the focalizers in this para., cp. the ref. to what the temporarily victorious Athenians *thought*. But Th. surely inter-rogated both sides; so why the different handling? The effect of describ-ing Pagondas' reasoning so impersonally is to enhance our sense that he is completely in control of events (as indeed he was, cp. Cawkwell, 382, also Pritchett, *EGH* 117, for Pagondas' 'deliberate pre-battle planning'), rather than merely acting on a hunch. The Athenians by contrast appear as more human and fallible, appropriately for the defeated side.

6. φυγὴ καθειστήκει παντὸς τοῦ στρατοῦ τῶν Ἀθηναίων: 'the Athenian army was completely routed'. Socrates fought bravely at Delion, Plat. *Symp.* 221a, see also *Apol.* 28e, and led a small group of escapers to safety, thanks to the ferocity of his manner towards Theban pursuers. (Cf. Introduction, above p. 59 n. 139.) See Hanson, *Western Way*, 180–1, on this incident, which rubs in the point that you stood a much better chance of survival in a group than alone.

7. καὶ οἱ μὲν πρὸς τὸ Δήλιόν τε καὶ τὴν θάλασσαν ὥρμησαν: 'Some fled to the sea at Delion'. This is an important indicator for the position of Delion, cp. Pritchett, *SAGT* iii (1980), 295.

οἱ δὲ ἐπὶ τοῦ Ὠρωποῦ: 'others towards Oropos'. Like Socrates (above 6 n.): Plut. *Mor.* 581d–e.

8. Βοιωτοὶ δὲ ἐφεπόμενοι ἔκτεινον, καὶ μάλιστα οἱ ἱππῆς οἵ τε

αὐτῶν καὶ οἱ Λοκροί: 'The Boiotians pursued and slaughtered them. This was done mainly by their cavalry and that of the Lokrians'. For this function of cavalry (harassing escaping hoplites) see L. Worley, *Hippeis* (72. 4 n. on τὸν μὲν γάρ etc.), 96, and Hanson, *Western Way*, 183.

97. 1. σκυλεύσαντες: 'stripped'. For the word (appropriate to removal of arms from *dead* troops) see Pritchett, *GSW* i. 55 and v. 132–47.

Diodorus (xii. 70. 5) is more informative than Th. on what was done with the booty which the Thebans acquired at Delion: they built the great stoa in the agora of Thebes, put up bronze statues there, and used the captured armour to decorate the statues in the other stoas in the agora. See Pritchett, *GSW* i. 62 n. 61. But Gomme (567), discussing the Diodorus passage, is incautious in his acceptance of Diod.'s furher statement that the Boiotians 'also instituted a Delian πανήγυρις'. This looks suspiciously like some sort of confusion by Diod. with his own xii. 58. 7, discussing the *Athenian* re-establishment of the festival on *Delos* (cp. Th. iii. 104); note the verbal similarity between ἐποίησαν δὲ καὶ πανήγυριν τὴν τῶν Δηλίων (xii. 58) and τήν τε τῶν Δηλίων πανήγυριν . . . ἐνεστήσαντο ποιεῖν (xii. 70).

97. 2–99. *Exchange between Boiotians and Athenians*

The manner of this section represents a departure for Th.: as Andrewes, *HCT* v. 365, remarks, 'it is a far longer piece of *oratio obliqua* [indirect speech] than is to be found elsewhere, even in viii'. Andrewes's remark is found in a section on 'indications of incompleteness' in Th.'s account of the Ten Years War; he believes that the narrative quality drops in the latter part of the Ten Years War (but see below, introductory n. to 102–8 and above, pp. 110–13), and connects this with Th.'s exile. Andrewes apparently regards an innovation like the present piece of indirect speech as part, or an anticipation, of the post-Delion deterioration in quality. And yet he himself notes that Brasidas has two speeches of normal type (i.e. in direct speech) to deliver, at iv. 126 and v. 9. Following this hint, we should consider whether the present section is (not a clumsy aberration to be rectified later, but) a deliberate experiment, just as the Melian Dialogue at the end of book v is an experiment. Orwin (98. 1 n.) has compared the content of 97–9 to that of the Melian Dialogue; perhaps there is a parallel to be made at the level of presentation also. Th., that is, was feeling towards an impersonal and dialectical mode of argument, more suitable than formal speeches to his immediate purpose. See Introduction, p. 89–93; 116. (But see 97. 4 for a peculiarly Boiotian word.)

2. ἐκ δὲ τῶν Ἀθηναίων κῆρυξ πορευόμενος ἐπὶ τοὺς νεκροὺς ἀπαντᾷ κήρυκι Βοιωτῷ, ὃς αὐτὸν ἀποστρέψας καὶ εἰπὼν ὅτι

οὐδὲν πράξει πρὶν ἂν αὐτὸς ἀναχωρήσῃ πάλιν: 'The Athenian herald, as he was on his way to ask for their dead, met a Boiotian herald, who turned him back, saying that he would get no answer until he himself had returned'. Many think that Euripides' *Suppliants*, which deals with the Theban refusal to let the Argive women recover their male relatives, was inspired by this episode. See C. Collard (ed.), *Euripides: Supplices* (Groningen, 1975), introduction, 10–11, esp. 10 and n. 32. Collard regards 424 and Delion as the upper limit chronologically for the play; cp. Collard, 10: 'it would be very remarkable indeed if a play which other indications place in the middle or late 420s, and which dramatises refusal of burial to slain warriors as a moral issue between Thebes and Athens, should not have been prompted by, and therefore be later in date than, the Theban refusal to relinquish the Athenian dead for burial after the campaign at Delium in November of 424.' See also Boegehold (v. 16. 1 n. on πόνων etc.), 152, and the very full treatment by A. Bowie, 'Tragic Filters for History: Euripides' *Supplices* and Sophocles' *Philoctetes*', in C. Pelling (ed.), *Greek Tragedy and the Ancient Historian* (Oxford, 1996), for whom the similarities between the events at Delion and the plot of the play are 'striking' and whose discussion is predicated on the assumption of a close connection, but who concludes that the dramatic 'replay' of Delion represents 'as it were a mythical/theatrical "rectification" of recent events'; that is (to borrow Pelling's summary of Bowie in the same volume), 'the parallel with Delium is close but not exact'. In any case, the similarity of theme between Euripides' play and the Delion episode in Th. has undoubtedly exerted a strong pull on those who date the play close to 424 (perhaps 423); note the sarcasm of G. Zuntz, *The Political Plays of Euripides* (Manchester, 1955), 4: 'if the battle of Delion is taken to be re-enacted on the stage, Aeschylus, in the *Eleusinians*, had managed to visualise the same situation nearly fifty years before it became reality'. It is true that there are other kinds of argument, e.g. the prevalence of metrically resolved syllables, and on these criteria a date in the late 420s would be roughly right, but this sort of indicator can only be approximate.

2–3. καταστὰς ἐπὶ τοὺς Ἀθηναίους ἔλεγε τὰ παρὰ τῶν Βοιωτῶν, ὅτι οὐ δικαίως δράσειαν παραβαίνοντες τὰ νόμιμα τῶν Ἑλλήνων· πᾶσι γὰρ εἶναι καθεστηκὸς ἰόντας ἐπὶ τὴν ἀλλήλων ἱερῶν τῶν ἐνόντων ἀπέχεσθαι: 'He then went before the Athenians, and on behalf of the Boiotians accused them of violating Greek norms by their outrageous behaviour. Invaders, he said, always refrained from violating the temples'. Note *Greek* as opposed to barbarian norms; if there is a particular implied contrast, it is with the Persian sack of the Athenian acropolis in 480 (but note Hdt. vi. 118 and Paus. x. 28. 6, aptly cited by Mikalson, *GRBS* suppl. 10 (1984), 224 n. 28: the Persian Datis behaved scrupulously towards the sanctuary of, precisely, Delion). For the idea here expressed by the Boiotian herald see Walbank's nn. on Pol. iv. 62 (the Aitolian raid on Dion) and v. 11 (Philip V's retaliatory raid on Thermon, with Polybius' censorious remarks); cp. also (on the present passage) Pritchett, *GSW* v. 162. P. Ducrey, *Le traitement des prisonniers de guerre dans la Grèce antique* (Paris, 1968), 294 n. 1, collects the evidence for such 'general laws of the Greeks'; cp. also J. Wilkins (ed.), *Euripides: Heraclidae* (Oxford, 1991), on lines 963 ff. and 1010 ff. However, some distinctions should perhaps be made: M. Ostwald, *From Popular Sovereignty to the Sovereignty of Law* (Berkeley, 1986), 101, sees a difference between the νόμιμα here, which he renders 'the norms of the Greeks', and the νόμος appealed to by the Athenians at 98. 2 below. This, says Ostwald, is a 'general principle', whereas 'the *nomima* of the Boeotian herald consist in specific acts that in this case have not been observed'. For these acts see 3 below and n. See *OCD*[3] under 'law, international'.

3. Ἀθηναίους δὲ Δήλιον τειχίσαντας ἐνοικεῖν, καὶ ὅσα ἄνθρωποι ἐν βεβήλῳ δρῶσι πάντα γίγνεσθαι αὐτόθι: 'whereas the Athenians had fortified Delion and were now occupying it, and generally doing the things that people do in unconsecrated places'. The expression 'the things that people do in unconsecrated places' is, I suppose, reticent rather than merely vague; normally Th. does not talk explicitly about the bodily functions (ii. 49. 6 is in a medical context), but he presumably means that the Athenians had been using the sacred space as among other things a latrine. (Cf. vii. 87. 2, OCT lines 3–4). See B. Jordan, 'Religion in Thucydides', *TAPA* 116 (1986), 119–47, at 129 n. 18, citing Parker, *Miasma*, 162. Compare *IG* i[3]. 4, early fifth-cent. regulations about behaviour on the Athenian acropolis, including a prohibition at line 11 μεδ' ὄνθο[ν] ἐγβ[αλέν . . .], no throwing out of excrement and waste from the processing of sacrificial animals (I follow the interpretation of G. Németh, 'Μεδ' ὄνθον ἐγβαλεῖν: Regulations Concerning Everyday Life in a Greek Temenos', in R. Hägg (ed.), *Ancient Greek Cult Practice from the Epigraphical Evidence* (Stockholm, 1994), 59–64); see also *IG* xii Suppl. 353 (Thasos) lines 6, 9.

ὕδωρ τε ὃ ἦν ἄψαυστον σφίσι πλὴν πρὸς τὰ ἱερὰ χέρνιβι χρῆσθαι, ἀνασπάσαντας ὑδρεύεσθαι: 'They were even drawing and using the water which the Boiotians themselves were forbidden to use except as holy water for the sacrifices'. For the use of the sacred water see above all S. Guettel Cole, 'The Use of Water in Greek Sanctuaries', in R. Hägg, N. Marinatos, and G. C. Nordquist (eds.), *Early Greek Cult Practice* (Stockholm, 1988), 161–5: water used in sanctuaries had to be pure because it was used for sacred rituals, though not all water from sanctuaries was restricted to ritual use: sometimes sanctuaries sold water for domestic use (Cole, 162 n. 14, citing *BCH* 91 (1967), 92–5 (Delphi); *IG* ii². 1361 (Attic orgeones of Bendis); *IG* xii supp. 353 (Thasos)). See also U. Sinn, in N. Marinatos and R. Hägg, *Greek Sanctuaries* (London, 1993), 106 and n. 48; Parker, *Miasma*, 226 f. For the noun χέρνιψ 'holy water', 'water of purification', see Smith, *TAPA* 1900, 75.

4. ἐπικαλουμένους τοὺς ὁμωχέτας δαίμονας καὶ τὸν Ἀπόλλω: 'they called on the Athenians in the name of Apollo and all the other deities worshipped in the temple'. The word ὁμωχέτας is found here only, and in glosses on Th. (TLG): the scholiast, Hesychius, Photius' *Lexicon*, and the Suda (ὁμαιχ-). The last two, drawing on a common source, say it is Boiotian (cf. LSJ⁹, 'prob. Boeot.'). It apparently means that the other deities 'share in' the cult offered in the temple.

98. 1. τοσαῦτα τοῦ κήρυκος εἰπόντος οἱ Ἀθηναῖοι πέμψαντες παρὰ τοὺς Βοιωτοὺς ἑαυτῶν κήρυκα τοῦ μὲν ἱεροῦ οὔτε ἀδικῆσαι ἔφασαν οὐδέν: 'That is what the Boiotian herald said. The Athenians sent a herald of their own to the Boiotians. He said that the Athenians had done no wilful damage to the temple'. What follows is in effect a speech, though reported indirectly. It is usefully discussed by C. Orwin, *The Humanity of Thucydides* (Princeton, 1994), 91–6, who calls it a 'neglected passage' (96) and sees in it a foreshadowing of the Athenian attitudes expressed in the Melian Dialogue. (Orwin's 'Piety, Justice and the Necessities of War: Thucydides 4. 97–101', *American Political Science Review*, 83 (1989), 233–9, differs hardly at all from his 1994 treatment, by whose page nos. I cite). Most recent critics have protested against the special pleading involved in Gomme's view (p. 571) that Th. spread himself over the aftermath of Delion because he deplored the Boiotian refusal to allow the Athenians to collect their dead and regarded this refusal as 'another evil resulting from war' (as if the Athenians were blameless): apart from Orwin, see G. Eatough, 'The Use of *Hosios* and Kindred Words in Thucydides', *AJP* 92 (1971), 238–51, at 245, the Athenians are 'derisively exposed' by the underlying facts of the situation; B. Jordan (97. 3 n.), 130 (whose talk of blatant Athenian sophistry 'goes too far', according to A. Bowie, above 97. 2 n.); J. D. Mikalson, 'Religion and the Plague in Athens, 431–423', *GRBS* Monograph 10 (1984), 217–45, at 224, quotes Gomme's strictures on the Boiotians and comments 'much the same could be said of the Athenian desecration of the sanctuary and of the specious, sophistical arguments by which they defended their action'. (By contrast, in *Honour Thy Gods: Popular Religion in Greek Tragedy* (Chapel Hill, 1991), 125 and 275 n. 300, Mikalson is concerned only with the behaviour of the Thebans.) Pritchett comes

closest to Gomme: he first cites Gomme without comment, then notes
that the Boiotians do eventually give up the dead unconditionally, and
ends by citing Jowett's remark that the Theban surrender of the bodies,
without insisting on the Athenians quitting Oropia, proves that 'the
Thebans were wrong, according to Hellenic international law' (*GSW* iv.
191-2). Parker, *Miasma*, 44, notes that 'in declaring themselves only con-
ditionally willing to return these corpses the Thebans were obviously
defying pollution'; see also his valuable n. 46 for other ancient texts. (But
Parker's main point is that both in Th.'s account of the post-Delion argument and in Euripides' *Supplices*, see above 97. 2 n., pollution is not mentioned although we would expect it to be.)

The Athenians begin by denying that they have caused or intend to
cause intentional damage to the sanctuary; they take their stand on their
right of possession, asserting what for the classical period (see 8 n.) is an
unusually brash claim, that of 'spear-won territory'. Any offences they
have committed have been done under necessity and will therefore be
pardoned by the gods (para. 6).

2. τὸν δὲ νόμον τοῖς ῞Ελλησιν εἶναι, ὧν ἂν ᾖ τὸ κράτος τῆς γῆς
ἑκάστης ἤν τε πλέονος ἤν τε βραχυτέρας, τούτων καὶ τὰ ἱερὰ
αἰεὶ γίγνεσθαι, τρόποις θεραπευόμενα οἷς ἂν πρὸς τοῖς
εἰωθόσι καὶ δύνωνται: 'Greek custom dictated that the temples on a
given piece of land, large or small, belonged to the people in possession
of that land, who were expected to carry out the usual religious observ-
ances as far as possible'. For νόμος here see above, 97. 2-3 n. For the
principle enunciated see R. Parker, 'Athenian Religion Abroad', in *RFP*
339-46, at 342, comparing (with acknowledgement to B. Smarczyk) Th.
iii. 68. 3 (the Spartans take over Plataia in its cultic aspect). So also
W. Burkert, 'Greek *poleis* and Civic Cults', in Hansen and Raaflaub (eds.),
Studies in the Ancient Greek Polis (52. 3 n. on τὰ ἐν τῇ ἠπείρῳ etc.), 201-10,
at 202-6. So far so good, but lurking here, and explicit at para. 8 below
(see n. there), is the anachronistically broad notion of 'spear-won
territory'.

3. καὶ γὰρ Βοιωτοὺς καὶ τοὺς πολλοὺς τῶν ἄλλων, ὅσοι ἐξανα-
στήσαντές τινα βίᾳ νέμονται γῆν: 'There was a time when the
Boiotians themselves and most other people who had driven out the
earlier inhabitants of the land which they now occupied ...'. 'Other
people' is vague, but the speaker presumably means 'other Greeks'. As
for the historical allusion (Boiotians expelling previous inhabitants), this,
like the comparable statement at iii. 61. 2 (see n. there on ξυμμείκτους
etc.) is taken over from Th.'s own narrative (or rather from the *Archaeology*), see i. 12. 3. Since the present ch. is in effect a speech, this
conforms to the principle argued for in Annex A above, pp. 132-4, that

speeches rarely introduce factual material, about past events, not already known from Hdt. or from Th.'s own narrative.

5. ὕδωρ τε ἐν τῇ ἀνάγκῃ κινῆσαι: 'as for interfering with the water'. See 97. 3 n. on ὕδωρ τε etc.

6. πᾶν δ' εἰκὸς εἶναι τὸ πολέμῳ καὶ δεινῷ τινὶ κατειργόμενον ξύγγνωμόν τι γίγνεσθαι καὶ πρὸς τοῦ θεοῦ: 'The god would surely forgive offences committed under the constraint of war or some other extremity'. Critics have pounced on the speciousness of the argument: the Athenians are not in Boiotia (see 76. 4: Delion in Tanagraian territory) as a result of some involuntary lapse: they are invaders, see Orwin, 94. The Athenian appeal to what the god would 'surely', or 'very probably' (πᾶν εἰκός) do resembles the pathetic language of Nikias at vii. 77. 4; cp. Orwin, 93 and n. 93. But Orwin sees mainly an anticipation of the Athenian position at v. 105 (Melian Dialogue): the gods are subject to laws of behaviour which amount to a kind of necessity. See also 92. 7 n. on πιστεύσαντες etc. (Syme).

καὶ γὰρ τῶν ἀκουσίων ἁμαρτημάτων καταφυγὴν εἶναι τοὺς βωμούς: 'If you do wrong involuntarily, you are allowed to take refuge at an altar'. Altars were places of refuge for more than involuntary offences, but there is no need to emend to ἑκουσίων, which would produce the meaning 'if you do wrong voluntarily': the sentence is a rhetorical amplification of the notion just expressed, about doing wrong under pressure of emergencies. For sanctuaries, in general, as places of asylum for suppliants see U. Sinn, 'Das Heraion von Perachora: eine sakrale Schutzzone in der korinthischen Peraia', *AM* 105 (1990), 53–116, at 108, citing Eur. *Ion* 1312 f.; Pol. iv. 35. 3, and other refs. (See also U. Sinn, 'Greek Sanctuaries as Places of Refuge', in N. Marinatos and R. Hägg (eds.), *Greek Sanctuaries: New Approaches* (London, 1993), 88–109, esp. 106 for the present episode.) For altars in particular see W. Burkert, trans. J. Raffan, *Greek Religion* (Oxford, 1985), 59 and n. 33, explaining the peculiar sanctity of altars in terms of blood ritual: 'the asylum of the altar stands in polar relation to the shedding of blood', because the altar is the sacred spot where blood is shed by a sacrificer enjoying exceptional status in accordance with the divine ordinances. Thus 'a man who sits on or next to an altar cannot be harmed or killed: this would be a perversion of the sacred and would inevitably plunge the whole city into ruin'. (Burkert cites the killing of Kylon, who took refuge at an altar; see i. 126. 10 ff.).

7. ἢ τοὺς μὴ ἐθέλοντας ἱεροῖς τὰ πρέποντα κομίζεσθαι: 'than the Athenians who refused to give up the sanctuary in order to get what was rightfully theirs' [lit. 'than those who were not willing to take what was fitting (i.e. what was owed to them) in exchange for temples']. The Greek is not easy but does not need to be emended, as the scholiast

wanted, by inserting μή before πρέποντα, which would mean 'to get back, at the price of a sanctuary, what it is not proper so to get back' (Gomme's trans. of the reading he rightly rejects). I have changed Jowett, who seems to be following the scholiast (his trans. is 'who refused to make such an unseemly exchange').

8. οὐ γὰρ ἐν τῇ ἐκείνων ἔτι εἶναι, ἐν ᾗ δὲ δορὶ ἐκτήσαντο: 'for in fact they [the Athenians] were not in Boiotia at all, but on land which they had fairly won by the spear'. (Delion *was* in Boiotia, see 6 n. on πᾶν . . .) This is a reference to the Homeric concept of 'spear-won territory', δορίκτητος χώρα. We hear a lot about this in the Hellenistic period, but much less in the classical; see W. Schmitthenner, 'Über eine Form-veränderung der Monarchie seit Alexander d. gr.', *Saeculum*, 19 (1968), 31–46, with the qualifications of A. Mehl, '*Δορίκτητος χώρα*. Kritische Bemerkungen zum Speererwerb im Politik und Völkerrecht der hellenistische Epoche', *Anc. Soc.*, 11/12 (1980/1981), 173–212, and J. K. Davies, *CAH* vii². 1 (1984), 296 and n. 238, cp. 66 (F. W. Walbank). See also J. Hornblower, *Hieronymus of Cardia* (Oxford, 1981), 53; R. R. R. Smith, 'Spear-won Land at Boscoreale: on the Royal Paintings', *JRA* 7 (1994), 100–27. In the classical period we find occasional mentions of it, e.g. Diod. xii. 83. 6 (Nikias), but that passage may be contaminated in advance by the vocabulary of Hieronymus of Cardia, whom Diod. was to use for the period of Alexander's Successors and had already digested. That is, the Athenians in the present passage of Th. are making a claim which is out of line with contemporary fifth-cent. notions but which looks simultaneously back to Homer and forward to the exorbitant and 'Homeric' pretensions of the Hellenistic rulers. On the poetic word δορί here see i. 128. 7 n. and Smith, *TAPA* 1900, 77.

99. νομίζοντες, τὴν μὲν Ὠρωπίαν, ἐν ᾗ τοὺς νεκροὺς ἐν μεθο-ρίοις τῆς μάχης γενομένης κεῖσθαι ξυνέβη, Ἀθηναίων κατὰ τὸ ὑπήκοον εἶναι: 'The battle had taken place on the borders, and the Boiotians knew [lit. 'thought'] that the territory of Oropos, in which the dead lay, was actually subject to Athens'. There is some unclarity here, but it reflects the lack of clarity about border areas in general (see 91 n. on μάλιστα γὰρ ἐν μεθορίοις etc.) and also the marginality of Oropos (ii. 23. 3 n.), currently subject to Athens (see now Parker, *ARH* 146–9) but not an integral part of Attica with deme status etc. If the battle was on the borders, the dead should be on the borders too, rather than on territory definitely subject to Athens. But in fact all parties except Hippokrates (see 95. 2 n. on ἐν γὰρ τῇ τούτων etc.) do take the view that the battle was in Attica, or at any rate not in Boiotia. The present passage is the most explicit indication that the battle site was positively in Attica; the negative view that as a border area it was 'not in Boiotia' (91; 92. 1) is easier to understand than the positive. (All this concerns the legal position; there is, as Classen/Steup say, no doubt that for the moment the Boiotians are in actual control of the battle-field, see 97. 1, where they leave a contingent to guard it.) Gomme comments on the present passage that the dishonesty of the Boiotian reply, namely that if the disputed territory was spear-won by Athens there was nothing to stop them coming to get their dead back, 'lay simply in the fact that the field of battle was not Delion. They admit in fact that the field of battle is Athenian territory, κατὰ τὸ ὑπήκοον.' This is good, but it simplifies a little, in that it takes the location of the battle-field (in Boiotia? in Attica?) to be uncontroversial. And it is not actually clear how much the Boiotians 'admit' out loud, beyond the simple reply that the Athenians can have the bodies if they quit Boiotia; that is, the whole section about what the Boiotians 'knew' or 'thought' may include a good deal of inter-pretation by Th. rather than being his account of what they said. (οὐδ᾽ αὖ ... ἐκείνων, 'and they pretended ... belong to them', see next n., is probably Th.'s comment, as Classen/Steup and Gomme say.)

καὶ οὐκ ἂν αὐτοὺς βίᾳ σφῶν κρατῆσαι αὐτῶν· οὐδ᾽ αὖ ἐσπένδοντο δῆθεν ὑπὲρ τῆς ἐκείνων: 'But [lit. 'and'] they reckoned that the Athenians could not take the dead away without their permission [lit. 'by force']. And they pretended to be unwilling to make a truce about territory which did not belong to them'. This (with small changes) is Jowett's rendering of these difficult sentences, that is, I accept that 'but' is needed, producing the sense 'although they accepted that Oropos was in Attica, nevertheless they thought the Athenians could not take their dead away from Oropos by force; they themselves could therefore get away with making the reply that the Athenians could have their dead back if they left Boiotia' i.e. if they abandoned Delion. For the unclear focalization see p. 91, and previous n.

ὁ δὲ κῆρυξ τῶν Ἀθηναίων ἀκούσας ἀπῆλθεν ἄπρακτος: 'The Athenian herald left without getting what he had come for'. Cp. the similar language at iii. 113. 5: the Ambrakiot herald who (for different reasons) went away without getting permission to remove the bodies of the dead, ὁ δὲ κῆρυξ ὡς ἤκουσε ... ἀπῆλθεν εὐθὺς ἄπρακτος. If this reminiscence is intentional (and the two passages are separated by over a hundred chapters, which reduces the likelihood that this is accidental recall of a recently-used phrase), Th. is reminding us of that Ambrakiot disaster, whose scale he commented on forcefully. This is a Homeric way of making a comparison. For another ignorant herald, reminiscent of the Ambrakiot one, see iv. 101. 1 n. See p. 16 n. 50: nothing in *HCT*.

100–101. 2. *The Delion campaign concluded*

100. 1. καὶ τῶν ἐκ Νισαίας ἐξεληλυθότων Πελοποννησίων φρουρῶν: 'and by the Peloponnesian garrison which had evacuated Nisaia'. See iv. 69. 3.

καὶ μηχανὴν προσήγαγον, ἥπερ εἷλεν αὐτό, τοιάνδε: 'and finally took it with a machine constructed like this'. For Th.'s reasons for including the description which follows, see Rutherford, *RFP* 55 f.: this sort of detail belongs in Rutherford's most basic category of Thucydidean instruction, namely the giving of practical aid via descriptions of tactics, ruses, and military innovations. But as Rutherford says, Th. is throughout concerned not only with the practical details but with the pressures which bring these changes about.

4. φλόγα ἐποίει μεγάλην καὶ ἧψε τοῦ τείχους: 'these made a huge flame, and set fire to the rampart'. The machine was 'really a gigantic bellows': E. W. Marsden, *Greek and Roman Artillery*, i (Oxford, 1969), 51, making the point that Th.'s interest in this sort of machine shows that artillery did not yet exist or he would have mentioned it (cp. introductory n. to ii. 71–8); see also Y. Garlan, 'Les machines incendiaires', *Recherches de poliorcétique grecque* (Paris, 1974), 140–1. Marsden and Garlan both compare the machine Brasidas uses at Lekythos (Torone), below, iv. 115. Lewis, *CAH* v². 425, calls the Delion machine a 'primitive, but terrifying, flame-thrower'.

101. 1. τοῦ δὲ Δηλίου ἑπτακαιδεκάτῃ ἡμέρᾳ ληφθέντος μετὰ τὴν μάχην: 'Delion fell seventeen days after the battle'. So the bodies were not returned until at least this period had elapsed. See P. Vaughn (44. 6 n.), in Hanson (ed.), *Hoplites*, 52, for the 'amazing' implications of this: decomposition and corruption of the bodies would have set in well before this, and she suggests that the Boiotian guards must have provided some rudimentary care and protection from the animals and the elements. (But the time of year is relevant: it was the beginning of winter, 89. 1, so that decomposition was surely much slower than in one of the hot Greek summers in which battles usually took place.) See also Hanson, *Western Way*, 205, though he is not quite right to say that Th. 'presents a picture of the rotting corpses of Athenians killed at Delion'. To the attentive reader, Th. *suggests* such a picture by his 'seventeen days', but he characteristically declines to present it directly.

καὶ τοῦ ἀπὸ τῶν Ἀθηναίων κήρυκος οὐδὲν ἐπισταμένου τῶν γεγενημένων ἐλθόντος οὐ πολὺ ὕστερον αὖθις περὶ τῶν νεκρῶν: 'Not knowing this, the Athenian herald came shortly afterwards to ask again for the dead'. Another ignorant herald, cp. iii. 113, and for another reminiscence of the Ambrakiot herald see above, 99 n. on ὁ δὲ κῆρυξ etc.

2. ἀπέθανον δὲ Βοιωτῶν μὲν ἐν τῇ μάχῃ ὀλίγῳ ἐλάσσους πεντακοσίων, Ἀθηναίων δὲ ὀλίγῳ ἐλάσσους χιλίων καὶ Ἱππο-κράτης ὁ στρατηγός, ψιλῶν δὲ καὶ σκευοφόρων πολὺς ἀριθ-μός: 'In the battle the Boiotian losses came to rather less than five hundred; the Athenian losses were rather less than a thousand, including Hippokrates their general. They also lost a great number of light-armed troops and baggage-bearers'. These casualties amount to 7.1% for the Boiotians and 14.3% for the Athenians. This is more or less in line with the averages established by P. Krentz (44. 6 n. on ἀπέθανον etc.), who reckons 5% for the winners and 14% for the losers; see Krentz, 16, for Delion in particular. The Boiotian casualties here given are compatible with the 300-odd Thespian dead (see 96. 3 n.); Lewis, *CAH* v². 425-6, shrewdly comments that very few of the dead can have been Thebans, and that the Delion victory 'did wonders for Theban self-esteem, so badly dented in the Persian Wars'.

On the loss of the Athenian general Hippokrates see Hanson, *Western Way*, 113, 'the battlefield commander of any defeated army inevitably perished along with most of those stationed in the front rank that met the charge of the enemy'; he goes on to give a long list. Cp. also Lazenby, in Hanson (ed.), *Hoplites*, 98. Finally, the unnumbered light-armed etc. (What follows assumes that the text is sound. But Classen/Steup, followed by Bradeen, *CQ* 1969 (44. 6 n. on ἀπέθανον δέ etc.), 153, preferred to emend to οὐ πολύς, '*not* many', rather than 'a great number'.) For the vagueness about these cp. iii. 87. 3 n. on τοῦ δὲ ἄλλου etc. also *Greek Historiography*, 150 f.; note also iii. 113. 6 (Ambrakia again, see above 99 n. on ὁ δὲ κῆρυξ etc.), 'I have not written down the number of those who died because it would seem incredible'. For the baggage-bear-ers see Pritchett, *GSW* i (1971), 42. I follow the view that the Athenian casualty list *IG* i³. 1163 does not give the Delion dead but the dead from Koroneia in the 440s; see Bradeen, *CQ* 1969, 151-4, against H. Mat-tingly, 'The Growth of Athenian Imperialism', *Historia*, 12 (1963), 257-73, at 261-3, cp. D. W. Bradeen and D. M. Lewis, 'Notes on Athenian Casualty Lists', *ZPE* 34 (1979), 240-6, at 242; Pritchett, *GSW* iv. 184, and Lewis, *CAH* v². 133 n. 60.

So ended the campaign of Delion, which Beloch called 'the most frightful defeat that Athens had so far suffered in this war': *Gr. Gesch.* ii². 1. 335.

101. 3–4. *Demosthenes' failure in Sikyonian territory*

3. ὁ Δημοσθένης ... ἀπόβασιν ἐποιήσατο ἐς τὴν Σικυωνίαν:
'Demosthenes ... made an attack on the Sikyonian coast'. See Lewis,
CAH v². 426 n. 138: the effect of this incident was 'to round the troubles
of the [Delion] campaign'; we are being prepared for 108 with its
account of Athenian setbacks and associated anti-Athenian feeling in
Greece. Roisman (3. 1 n. on κατὰ τύχην etc.), 50, suggests Demosthenes
was pushed back because he landed in stages rather than with his full
force.

Demosthenes now disappears from the military scene until his
Epidaurian command at v. 80. 3; but he swears the Peace of Nikias, see v.
19. 2; cp. Andrewes and Lewis, *JHS* 1957, 180.

101. 5. *Death of Sitalkes*

**5. Ἀπέθανε δὲ καὶ Σιτάλκης Ὀδρυσῶν βασιλεὺς ὑπὸ τὰς αὐτὰς
ἡμέρας τοῖς ἐπὶ Δηλίῳ, στρατεύσας ἐπὶ Τριβαλλοὺς καὶ νικη-
θεὶς μάχῃ:** 'During the days of the Delion affair, Sitalkes the Odrysian
king died; he had been taking part in an expedition against the Triballi
but was defeated in battle'. See Z. Archibald, *CAH* vi². 454 with n. 23,
and her forthcoming book on Thrace, *Orpheus Unmasked* (Oxford): the
story of the assassination of a Sitalkes in Ps.-Dem. xii. 9 should probably
not be connected with the death of this, the best-known Sitalkes. Kallet-
Marx (171) asks why Th. here 'judges it important to inform us of his
death', and suggests an answer: 'most likely, his intention is to under-
score implicitly, as he had done earlier, Athens' loss of a powerful friend
with enormous resources in the very region now threatened by Brasidas'.
With this, cp. previous n. for the general darkening, in ch. 101, of the
Athenian picture. His successor Seuthes' exact policies are unclear, but
Gomme was probably right that the change of Thracian ruler was of
indirect help to Brasidas (and 'might increase the difficulties of Thucydides in securing the aid of his Thracian friends'). For Seuthes' coinage,
with the legends ΣΕΥΘΑ ΚΟΜΜΑ and ΣΕΥΘΑ ΑΡΓΥΡΙΟΝ, see
Archibald, *CAH* vi² (1994), 454.

A death notice like the present item is oddly Tacitean, although it
does not come at the end of a year; it also looks forward to the way the
chronographic source of Diodorus records the deaths of rulers. What is
unusual about the present item is that the notice of Sitalkes' death is not
immediately occasioned by the narrative, though it is certainly relevant
to it, see above. Th. records deaths, especially of non-Greek rulers, elsewhere, but they are tied in to the narrative rather than introduced with

an 'about this time' formula. See for instance iv. 50. 3 (Artaxerxes); 107. 3 (Pittakos); vii. 1. 4 (Archonides the Sikel king). The deaths of prominent Greeks tend to go unrecorded, causing difficulties; even Pericles' death is not recorded in its place (ii. 65. 6), and Archidamos' not at all; for the problem about Phormio see iii. 7. 1 n.; for Hyperbolos at viii. 73 see n. there. We are told about Kimon's death at i. 112 because it is directly relevant to the end of the Cyprus campaign. Naturally Th. covers the deaths of military leaders killed in battle or on campaign, such as Brasidas, Kleon, Nikias, though Nikias is exceptional in getting an obituarial statement about the kind of life he led, vii. 86. 5. Perhaps Sitalkes falls into this category: he does after all die while on campaign (though Th. stops short of saying he was killed in battle). But even so, the present para. is strictly disconnected from the surrounding narrative. We should not rule out desire on Th.'s part to vary the menu a little, cp. introductory n. to 133–4. As Tacitus says (*Ann.* iv. 33), the deaths of famous men refresh the mind. Cf. A. Pomeroy, *The Appropriate Comment* (Frankfurt, 1991), 23–31. For the Triballi or Triballians see ii. 96. 4 n.

102–108. *Brasidas captures Amphipolis*

Andrewes, *HCT* v. 364, comments that the narrative after Delion is 'markedly selective'; thereafter 'it is only the northern narrative of iv. 102–v. 13 that exhibits the real finish'. For instance Andrewes included the items at 133–4 in his list of 'sporadic and mostly scrappy' references, but see nn. below on those chs., which have some structural point.

102. 1. Βρασίδας ἔχων τοὺς ἐπὶ Θρᾴκης ξυμμάχους ἐστρά-τευσεν ἐς Ἀμφίπολιν τὴν ἐπὶ Στρυμόνι ποταμῷ Ἀθηναίων ἀποικίαν: 'Brasidas and his allies from the Thraceward region made an expedition against Amphipolis on the river Strymon, the Athenian colony'. The historical sketch of Amphipolis which follows is unusual; Gomme (584) justly remarks that in this whole section Th. does not exaggerate either his own role or the importance of the campaign; nevertheless, a whole 18-line chapter to 'introduce' a single city (there was a brief mention at i. 100. 3) is unparalleled in Th.'s whole work. Kallet-Marx (173) is right to say that Th. 'underscores the importance of the region by noting all the attempts to found the colony'. (But all this still, we may want to say, does not constitute an exaggeration: Amphipolis *was* important, 108. 1.) For the colonial 'flagging' see p. 76.

L. Pearson, *Local Historians of Attica* (Philadelphia, 1942), 40, thought that the dates in the present ch., for the various attempts to colonize Amphipolis, 'are likely to come from an Amphipolitan source'. But why should Th. not have done the arithmetic himself? (I shall argue that there is some indebtedness to Hdt. for the *facts*.)

Important excavations were conducted at Amphipolis by the late D. Lazaridis (died 1985) from 1956, and especially in the 1970s and early 1980s. The results of these can now best be found in D. Lazaridis (ed. K. and T. Lazaridis), *Amphipolis* (Athens, 1994), an excellent and well-illustrated 154-page account of the site and its history, with special reference to recent finds and helpful maps. See Fig. 2 of the present work, based (with permission; see Preface) on Lazaridis' two maps at 22 f. (fig. 5) and 70 f. (fig. 39). See also Z. Archibald, *CAH* vi². 453 and nn. 17 and 18, giving full refs.; also Lazaridis' own entry on Amphipolis in *Princeton Encyclopaedia*, 51-2, and his 'La cité grecque d'Amphipolis et sa système de défense', *CRAI* 1977, 194-214, and 'Les fortifications d'Amphipolis', in P. Leriche and H. Tréziny (eds.), *La fortification dans l'histoire du monde grec* (*CNRS Colloque International 614, December 1982*: Paris, 1986), 31-8 and figs. 140-52. On Lazaridis' findings and views about the fortifications see below, 3 n. on ἦν Ἀμφίπολιν etc. (In some editions of Th. this is part of a para. 4 which the OCT does not recognize, see 3 n. on ὡρμῶντο etc.) See also N. Jones, 'The Topography and Strategy of the Battle of Amphipolis in 422 BC', *CA* 10 (1977), 71-104; Pritchett, 'Amphipolis Restudied', *SAGT* iii (1980), 298-346; B. M. Mitchell, 'Kleon's Amphipolitan Campaign: Aims and Results', *Historia*, 40 (1991), 170-92.

Th. goes on in the rest of the ch. to amplify his statement that Amphipolis was an Athenian colony. It was a valuable source of revenue but was not tributary in the normal sense, see 108. 1 n.

2. τὸ δὲ χωρίον τοῦτο ἐφ᾽ οὗ νῦν ἡ πόλις ἐστὶν ἐπείρασε μὲν πρότερον καὶ Ἀρισταγόρας ὁ Μιλήσιος φεύγων βασιλέα Δαρεῖον κατοικίσαι, ἀλλὰ ὑπὸ Ἡδώνων ἐξεκρούσθη: 'The city stands on the site which Aristagoras of Miletos once attempted to colonize, when he was fleeing from King Darius; he was driven out by the Hedonians'. Aristagoras was one of the instigators of the unsuccessful revolt of Ionia from King Darius I of Persia in 500-499 BC. He and his fellow-instigator Histiaios tried to establish themselves in Thrace (for Histiaios see Hdt. v. 23-4 and 124. 2). The present passage is one of only two (indirect) allusions in Th. to the Ionian Revolt, the other being vi. 4. 5 (Samian occupation of Zankle). Commentators (Classen/Steup, Gomme) note correctly that the story of Aristagoras' Thracian failure is also told by Hdt., v. 126, cp. 11. But that raises the question, was Hdt. the source for Th. here? See above, Annex A at p. 124: the cautious and sceptical view is that the verbal similarity is not striking—as I said in 1992 and as Kennelly (Introduction, p. 25 n. 73), 100, now repeats—and that the fact given by both authors could (especially in view of Th.'s

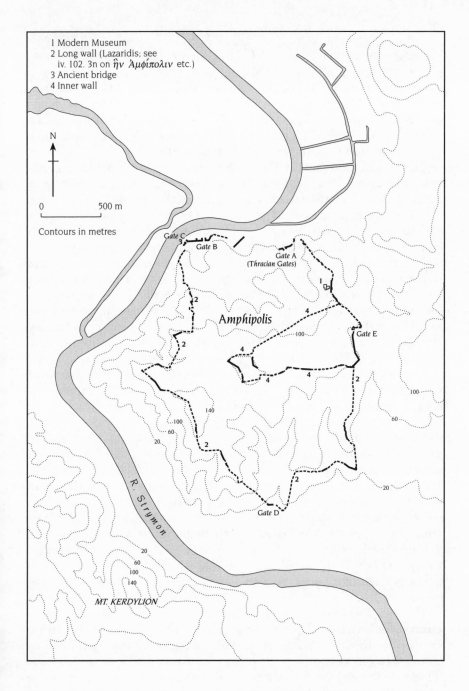

Within the figure:

1 Modern Museum
2 Long wall (Lazaridis; see
   iv. 102. 3n on ἦν Ἀμφίπολιν etc.)
3 Ancient bridge
4 Inner wall

N

0   500 m

Contours in metres

Gate C
3
Gate B

Gate A
(Thracian Gates)

1

2

Amphipolis

4

2

Gate E

4

4

100

2

4

4

100

60

140

100

60

20

2

20

2

2

Gate D

20

60
100
140

R. Strumon

MT. KERDYLION

FIG. 2 Plan of Amphipolis (based on D. Lazaridis, *Amphipolis* (1994), figs. 5 and 39)

321

Thracian connections) be put down to common knowledge or to awareness of authors other than Hdt. (The revolt featured in the works of
authors other than Hdt., such as Lysanias of Mallos, *FGrHist* 426, on
whom see O. Murray, *CAH* iv². 468; not to mention the Athenian tragic
poet Phrynichus, for whom see Hdt. vi. 21. 2, though Phrynichus' theme
seems to have been the end of the revolt and he may not have mentioned or featured Aristagoras who helped start it.) Macan in his comm.
on Hdt. v. 126 thought that Th. was here correcting or amplifying Hdt.'s
version, which is less full; for a similar view see Schneege, 52–53, who
thought that the reference to 'fleeing from Darius', φεύγων βασιλέα
Δαρεῖον, presupposed Hdt. (See Hdt. v. 124. 1: Th.'s word φεύγων is
perhaps pejorative and a sign that Th. followed or at least agreed with
Hdt.'s view, v. 124. 1, that Aristagoras was a poor-spirited creature who
fled for that reason, ψυχὴν οὐκ ἄκρος . . . δρησμὸν ἐβούλευε.) And Lisa
Kallet-Marx has pointed out to me a point I missed in 1992, namely that
for Th.'s purposes in this ch., which is about *Athenian* attempts to colonize the site, the actions of the *Milesian* Aristagoras were strictly irrelevant. This makes it likelier that Th. was going out of his way to amplify
Hdt. Note that the Drabeskos disaster, which Th. goes on to mention,
also featured in Hdt., see next n. For Hedonians see i. 100. 3 n.

The verb for 'was driven out' is ἐκκρούειν; this is not a common word
in Th. (the literal meaning is 'knock out'), but of its five occurrences in
his History, four are in book iv and three of those are in the last forty
chapters of the book (the present passage; 128. 1; and, very shortly afterwards, 131. 2; note also ἀπεκρούσθη at 107. 2, cp. 115. 2). This looks like
what Homeric scholars call 'clustering', i.e. repetition of a word or
formula several times within a brief space but hardly at all outside it.
This presumably happens because the author has the word on the mind.
In order to be significant I suppose it is necessary that the word should
not be excessively technical (which might explain limited local occurrence) nor specially rhetorical (which might explain repetition). See
B. Hainsworth, *The Iliad: A Commentary*, iii. *Books 9–12* (Cambridge,
1993), 27 f., 98, and N. J. Richardson, *The Iliad: A Commentary, vi. Books
21–24* (Cambridge, 1993), 89, 198. It is interesting to find such an 'oral'
feature in Th. For Th. as the product of a partly oral culture see
R. Thomas, *Literacy and Orality in Ancient Greece* (Cambridge, 1992), 102.

ἔπειτα δὲ καὶ οἱ Ἀθηναῖοι ἔτεσι δύο καὶ τριάκοντα ὕστερον,
ἐποίκους μυρίους σφῶν τε αὐτῶν καὶ τῶν ἄλλων τὸν βουλόμενον πέμψαντες, οἳ διεφθάρησαν ἐν Δραβήσκῳ ὑπὸ Θρᾳκῶν:
'Thirty-two years later the Athenians also made an attempt; they sent a
colony of ten thousand, made up partly of their own citizens, partly of
any others who wanted to join; but these also were attacked by the

Thracians at Drabeskos, and wiped out'. For this disaster see i. 100. 2–3, and nn. It is also probably mentioned at Hdt. ix. 75, cp. previous n.; though Schneege, 53, thought that there might be two disasters (Th. has Drabeskos as the location, Hdt. has Daton. Or is Th. correcting Hdt. on the name?—the usual methodological problem). For the chronology see further vol. iii of this commentary, Appendix I; see also next n. for Th.'s 'thirty-two'.

On the whole the present ch. is a kind of postponed introduction of Amphipolis, and gives material not given at i. 100. 3 where the place was first mentioned. But the Drabeskos disaster is an exception to this: it has already been described at i. 100. 3 in roughly the same degree of detail as here (but this time Th. waits until para. 3 and Hagnon's colonization before telling us that the place was previously called 'Nine Ways').

The expression 'any others who wanted ...' is reminiscent of the language of Athenian official decrees.

3. καὶ αὖθις ἑνὸς δέοντι τριακοστῷ ἔτει ἐλθόντες οἱ Ἀθηναῖοι, Ἅγνωνος τοῦ Νικίου οἰκιστοῦ ἐκπεμφθέντος, Ἠδῶνας ἐξελάσαντες ἔκτισαν τὸ χωρίον τοῦτο, ὅπερ πρότερον Ἐννέα ὁδοὶ ἐκαλοῦντο: 'Twenty-nine years later the Athenians came again, under the leadership of Hagnon the son of Nikias, drove out the Hedonians, and colonized the same spot, which was previously called "The Nine Ways"'. See i. 100. 2–3 n. The date (437) of Hagnon's foundation is certain, from the evidence of a good source, the scholiast to Aeschines ii. 31 = Fornara 62, cp. Diod. xii. 32. 3, archonship of Euthymenes. The Diodorus item is from the chronographic source, see Ed. Schwartz, *Griechische Geschichtschreiber* (Leipzig, 1959), 42. For this source see *CAH* vi². 8 (it is perhaps not as reliable as Schwartz believed, but is good enough to act as useful confirmation of the Aeschines scholiast). Th. gives no 'absolute' dates (how could he? The system of dating by Olympiads did not become general until Timaeus in *c*.300 BC). He could, however, have dated Amphipolis by reference to the beginning of the Peloponnesian War, cp. ii. 21. 1. He presumably here forgot posterity and assumed, as Gomme supposes, that the foundation of Amphipolis was a well-known event (it occurred in the lifetime of his readers), and gave his other dates (twenty-nine, thirty-two) by reference to that event.

The successful foundation of Amphipolis was a triumph, given the series of earlier disasters and Hedonian resistance. In addition to the purely military story there were religious and symbolic aspects which Th. naturally does not tell us about, but which may have helped Athens to prevail in the end. The Athenian Hagnon returned the bones of the local Thracian hero Rhesus from Troy to Amphipolis (Polyain. vi. 53). But the Polyainus story, for what it is worth, is clear that the bones were brought back in the teeth of opposition from the local 'barbarians' (did they have any idea what was going on?). For Rhesus' bones and their connection with the founding of Amphipolis, see also Parker, in *RFP* 340 with n. 4, and P. Bourgeaud, 'Rhésos et Arganthoné', in Borgeaud (ed.), *Orphisme et Orphée, Mél. Rudhardt* (Geneva, 1991), 51–9. Superficially, the 'bones of Kimon' look similar (for this episode see i. 98. 2 n.), but as Parker says, that was different because there 'the island [Skyros] did not gain but lost a precious relic'. Cp. I. Malkin, *Religion and Colonization in Ancient Greece* (Leiden, 1987), 81–4, and *Myth and Territory*, 28 and 137.

For archaeological traces of the Hedonians at 'Nine Ways' or Ennea Hodoi (esp. at Hill 133) see Lazaridis, *Amphipolis*, 72–3, also 31 and 36 for pre-437 evidence of occupation at Amphipolis itself.

For Hagnon as a 'northern expert' see ii. 58. 1 n., and for him as oikist of Amphipolis and recipient of oikist cult there see v. 11. 1 n. on καταβαλόντες etc. On Th.'s language in the present passage see J. de Wever and R. van Compernolle, 'La valeur des termes de "colonisation" chez Thucydide', *L'Ant. Class.* 36 (1937), 461–523, at 468.

The foundation of Amphipolis in 437 falls at the end of the *pentekontaetia*. It was not, however, mentioned in book i, although it was highly relevant to Th.'s theme in the *pentekontaetia* excursus, namely the growth of Athenian power and the fear it inspired in Sparta. Amphipolis was, we may conjecture, alarming to Sparta's ally Corinth (and thus indirectly to Sparta), because Corinth had colonial connections not far away, especially at Potidaia. See introductory n. to i. 56–66 for the omission of the founding of Amphipolis in book i, and the bearing of that event on the *Potidaiatika*. The external analepsis or 'flashback', which the present passage represents, has the effect of masking Athenian aggression in the run-up to the war, in a way I discuss in *Greek Historiography*, 143–4: by postponing this item and others like it to books later than book i, Th. keeps some material episodes out of sight. The only controversial question, surely, is whether this is evidence of deliberate and sinister pro-Athenian bias, or whether Th. merely holds back information until it is most relevant (not everything could go into the already distended i. 89–117). On any view, it is remarkable that Th.'s narrative of the *pentekontaetia* ends without covering the years 439–434, precisely the period when tension between Athens and (especially) Corinth was increasing dangerously. For the omissions in this, what we may call the 'great gap', see introductory n. to i. 115–17 at p. 188: Amphipolis is only one of these omitted events, and they all, if they had been included, would have tended to inculpate Athens and exculpate Sparta.

[The OCT marks no para. 4, but in Classen/Steup's and other edns. it begins here.]

ὡρμῶντο δὲ ἐκ τῆς Ἠιόνος, ἣν αὐτοὶ εἶχον ἐμπόριον ἐπὶ τῷ στόματι τοῦ ποταμοῦ ἐπιθαλάσσιον, πέντε καὶ εἴκοσι στα-δίους ἀπέχον ἀπὸ τῆς νῦν πόλεως: 'Their base of operations was Eion, a market and seaport which they already possessed. It was at the mouth of the river, twenty-five stades from the site of the present town of Amphipolis'. Like Amphipolis, Eion has featured before (i. 98; iv. 50. 2), but like Amphipolis it gets the 'full treatment' only here.

As i. 98. 1 reports, Eion was taken from the Persians by Kimon in the 470s, see n. there, and add *LSAG*² 479–80 no. C, funerary epigram for one Tokes, killed at Eion, perhaps in this fighting (illustration at Lazaridis, *Amphipolis*, 16–17, plate 3). For the location of Eion see Ch. Koukouli-Chrysanthaki, *ADelt.* 35 (1981, but published 1988), Chron. 423–4, summarized at *Arch. Reps.* 1988–1989, 83: the acropolis of Eion is said to be on Profitis Elias hill 6 km. east of the Strymon bridge at Amphipolis; cp. also *Arch. Reps.* 1991–2, 51. If this is right, it would mean Th. was using a stade of 240 m. (Bauslaugh, *JHS* 1979 (8. 6 n. on ἡ γὰρ νῆσος etc.), 6, has 160 m., but that is because he assumed Eion was 4 km. from Amphipolis.) As Thucydidean stades go, 240 m. is on the long side (see Bauslaugh's list), but not impossible.

Eion did not, on the evidence of the extant tribute lists, pay tribute to Athens (though the example of Amphipolis, 108. 1, shows that that evidence is not decisive against payment of some sort); payments 'to Eion' are thought to be payments by other places to generals stationed at Eion, Meiggs, *AE* 158.

ἦν Ἀμφίπολιν Ἅγνων ὠνόμασεν, ὅτι ἐπ' ἀμφότερα περιρ-ρέοντος τοῦ Στρυμόνος [διὰ τὸ περιέχειν αὐτὴν] τείχει μακρῷ ἀπολαβὼν ἐκ ποταμοῦ ἐς ποταμὸν περιφανῆ ἐς θάλασσάν τε καὶ τὴν ἤπειρον ᾤκισεν: 'Hagnon called the new foundation "Amphi-polis" ("City on Both Sides") because the Strymon flowed round it on both sides: [because he planned to enclose it,] he cut it off by a long wall from river to river, and made it a conspicuous landmark by sea and land'. [The words in square brackets, deleted by Dobree, are defended and explained by Pritchett, *SAGT* iii. 308–9, whom I follow. The text is also defended by Maurer, *Interpolation*, 53–4, who does not, however, cite Pritchett. I do not think it necessary to follow de Romilly in the Budé and emend περιφανῆ 'conspicuous from' to περιφερῆ, 'surrounded by'.] The last part of the sentence is a flowery way of saying it was on a hill. As Gomme says, the Strymon in fact flows on three (not two) sides, north, west, and south or south-west of the hill; but Th.'s expression makes sense as a way of saying that the hill was enclosed by two lines forming an angle of the river. Th. here shows an interest in a place-name (cf. iv. 3. 2 n. on καλοῦσι δέ etc.). For the interesting formation 'Amphipolis' see M. Casevitz, '*Astu* et *polis*: les composés: Quelques composés en -*polis* et leurs dérivés', *Ktema*, 10 (1985), 91–103, at 100: at Aesch. *Cho.* 75, ἀμφίπ(τ)ολις means 'which embraces the city', but in the present passage of Th. it means 'a city on both sides' (of the Strymon river), 'ville de part et d'autre, de tous côtés (du Strymon)'. That is, in technical philological language, the word is formed not by hypostasis (as in the Aeschylus example) but by 'determination', i.e. *polis* keeps its grammatical status as a substantive. Gomme seemed to think that the opposition sea/ mainland also helped to explain the 'both' contained in ἀμφ- (the first component of the city's name); but this is over-ingenious: Th.'s ἀμφότερα ('both sides') is surely intended, by itself, to explain the name.

Pritchett, *SAGT* iii. 302, fig. 30, and 308–16, suggested that the Long Wall ran (or was planned to run) in a rough semi-circle from a point on the northern bend of the Strymon near the bridge, to the top of the Amphipolis ridge, then down to another point on the Strymon near the Thracian gates. For the bridge (Fig. 2, feature no. 3) see 103. 4 n. and for the Thracian gates (Fig. 2, Gate A) see v. 10. 1 n. I follow the view which puts both (bridge and gates) in the northern sector. See, however, below, for Lazaridis' suggestion that the outer circuit (as opposed to the walls round the citadel) was considerably more ambitious than this.

The classical fortifications have recently been elucidated by archaeology: see Lazaridis 1986 and 1994 (see 1 n. above), esp. the maps at 1994, plates 5 and 39 (see Fig. 2 at p. 321 above). In particular the excavation of the two gates discussed below (v. 10. 1 and 6 nn.) and of the splendid bridge (for which see iv. 103. 4 n. on ἐπὶ τὴν γέφυραν etc.) has clarified the look of the fortifications in the northern area, where it is now clear that much of the action described at v. 6 ff. took place. As for the circuit as a whole, this is perhaps less secure. Lazaridis believed that the line of fortifications was much larger than had previously been assumed, by Gomme (649), Pritchett (*SAGT* i. 33; iii. 298–346) and others (though Gomme in the note to his map opp. 654 says the line of the city walls which he marks is 'formal only', so it is a little unfair of Lazaridis to cite that page as if it gave his definite view). In particular, Lazaridis claims that the 'Long Wall' of the present passage (see Fig. 2 above, where the Long Walls are marked as no. 2) was not a simple arc, but a contour-hugging, 'Geländemauer' type of enceinte. See esp. Lazaridis 1986, 33, 'une enceinte qui entourait une très grande partie du complexe formé par les collines'. This is a fourth-century type of wall (54. 2 n.), and for that reason and the well-known difficulty of assigning dates to fortifications, one might be tempted to question Lazaridis' implied fifth-century date for the line of the original circuit (he himself says it recalls, 'rappelle', Messene and Megalopolis, but it can be said to recall them only in the sense that they might come to the mind of a modern student familiar with those later foundations. Note that Lazaridis (1986, 32) suggests that the 'Long Walls' were repaired in Hellenistic times). A date in the fourth century for the fortifications would make perfectly good military and political sense, given that Amphipolis was as important in that century as in the previous one; thus it was under powerful pressure from Athens in the 360s, see J. Roy, *CAH* vi² (1994), 195. In support of his view about the extent of the fifth-century wall, Lazaridis (1986, 33) points to 103. 5, 104. 1, and 106, large numbers of Amphipolitans flee inside the wall; that is, the circuit needed to be large. This is hardly decisive because as Pritchett says (*SAGT* iii. 313), the Amphipolitans fled to the enclosed *citadel* area. For scepticism about Lazaridis' 1986 claims, whose truth is assumed in the posthumous 1994 book as well, see B. Mitchell, *Historia* 1991, 190. But Lazaridis was the excavator, and a very distinguished archaeologist, so I defer to his view.

The statement that Hagnon (not 'the Athenians') gave the colony its name has not attracted much comment, but it is striking in this period of Periclean democracy, although it is true that in the archaic period 'the names of colonies were usually given to them by their founders': Malkin, *Myth and Territory*, 134. See also Malkin, 'What's in a Name? The Eponymous Founders of Greek Colonies', *Athenaeum* 63 (1985), 114–30, at 126 (disagreeing with the tentative suggestion of D. Asheri, 'Studio sulla storia della colonizzazione di Anfipoli sino alla conquista Macedone', *Riv. Fil* 95 (1967), 5–30, at 19 n. 4, that Amphipolis might once have been called Hagnoneia, a suggestion based on an entry in Steph. Byz., which seems to be referring to a place *near* Amphipolis, and looks terribly like a misunderstanding of Th. v. 11. 1).

103. 1. ἄρας ἐξ Ἀρνῶν τῆς Χαλκιδικῆς: 'Starting from Arnai in Chalkidike'. Arnai is not precisely identified, but is probably in the hinterland of Sithonia (the central prong of the three Chalkidian promontories). See Zahrnt, 161–2, against earlier speculations (including the unpublished suggestion of T. J. Cadoux mentioned by Gomme).
καὶ ἀφικόμενος περὶ δείλην ἐπὶ τὸν Αὐλῶνα καὶ Βορμίσκον, ᾗ ἡ Βόλβη λίμνη ἐξίησιν ἐς θάλασσαν: 'towards evening he reached the Aulon and Bormiskos, at the point where Lake Bolbe flows into the sea'. The narrative pace (what narratologists call the 'rhythm') changes suddenly: after reviewing 75 years in one ch., Th. now tells us the time of day and the weather (snowing slightly, para. 2). Aulon (the Greek word

means a 'kind of trough, with a level bottom and steep sides': R. Syme, *Anatolica: Studies in Strabo*, ed. A. R. Birley (Oxford, 1995), 197, 340-3) was not a city but a geographical feature of the kind defined by Syme, without however discussing the present passage; for this Aulon or aulon see Zahrnt, 167, and Hammond, *HM* i. 186. It was the pass of Rendina, through which Lake Bolbe emptied into the Gulf of Strymon. For Bormiskos, on the coast to the east of Lake Bolbe, near the village of Stavros, and to the north of the Aulon, see Zahrnt, 170-1, and Hammond, *HM* i. 196. Euripides was supposed to have died there, see Steph. Byz., entry under the name. It paid 1000 drachmas to Athens in 421 and *may* (but see Hammond, *HM* ii. 132-3 and n. 3) have been assessed for the same amount in the reassessment of 425; but it did not, as far as we can see, pay anything before that. Even if it was included in the very optimistic 425 reassessment, that would not be evidence that it was securely Athenian, rather than Macedonian, at the time of Brasidas' journey past it. Zahrnt is agnostic.

2. χειμὼν δὲ ἦν καὶ ὑπένειφεν· ᾗ καὶ μᾶλλον ὥρμησε: 'The weather was wintry and it was snowing slightly, so he pushed on all the quicker'. Again (see previous n.) note the detail. Babut (423) compares 3. 1 (Pylos), see n. there on κατὰ τύχην χειμών etc.

3. ἦσαν γὰρ Ἀργιλίων τε ἐν αὐτῇ οἰκήτορες (εἰσὶ δὲ οἱ Ἀργί-λιοι Ἀνδρίων ἄποικοι): 'There were settlers at Amphipolis from Argilos, a place originally colonized from Andros'. The Andrian connection may be significant for the anti-Athenian attitudes of these Argilians: see 84. 1 n. on ἐπὶ Ἄκανθον etc.; but it is claimed that there were other factors, see next n.

4. μάλιστα δὲ οἱ Ἀργίλιοι, ἐγγύς τε προσοικοῦντες καὶ αἰεί ποτε τοῖς Ἀθηναίοις ὄντες ὕποπτοι καὶ ἐπιβουλεύοντες τῷ χωρίῳ: 'The town of Argilos is very near Amphipolis; the Athenians had for a long time regarded the Argilians as suspect, and indeed the Argilians were always plotting against Amphipolis'. For Argilos, *c*3 km. west of the mouth of the Strymon, see Zahrnt, 158-60, citing earlier work. The tribute record of Argilos (see below) has often been invoked to help explain its attitude towards Athens, but even if this is right, Th. typically does not say anything about this aspect: only at 87. 3 (Brasidas' speech at Akanthos, see n. there) does tribute feature in the story of Brasidas' successes in the north. The tribute record of Argilos is in any case problematic: it paid $10\frac{1}{2}$ talents in 454/3, one talent in 446/5 to 438/7, and 1000 drachmas in 433/2. *ATL* iii. 5-6 and 62, following a suggestion of Perdrizet, thought that the 454/3 total of $10\frac{1}{2}$ was impossible (absolutely too large, and also out of line with the rest of Argilos' record) and emended it to $1\frac{1}{2}$; Zahrnt (159) approves the change. Against the emendation see Gomme, iii. 576 n. 1, and Meiggs, *AE* 159 n. 3, with whom I agree. Meiggs pointed out that the mistake is not a natural one for the cutter to make, and conjectured that 'if Brea [for this topographically mysterious Thracian colony see ML 49] was carved out of the territory of Argilos', the 'sharp reduction' between 454/3 and 446/5 is intelligible. This argument is also used by the emenders to explain the hypothetical drop from 1½ to one. All parties agree that the final drop to 1000 drachmas was compensation for the founding of Amphipolis. It will be seen that the tribute record of Argilos can hardly be used, without circularity, for the elucidation of Th. Gomme for instance writes that 'successive reductions of the tribute payable by Argilos did not appease her jealousy of Amphipolis', but without knowing the scale of the reductions we cannot say whether they were relevant at all. See Introduction, p. 98 f. Note that other considerations than tribute, or resentment about Amphipolis, may have operated: 84. 1 n. on ἐπὶ Ἄκανθον etc.

πρὸς τοὺς ἐμπολιτεύοντας σφῶν ἐκεῖ: 'with the other Argilians inside Amphipolis'. The meaning of the verb ἐμπολιτεύω, used also of the Athenians at 106. 1, is controversial; M. Casevitz (102. 3 n. on ἦν Ἀμφίπολιν etc.) 99 and n. 51 rightly complained that it did not interest Gomme. But Casevitz's own idea, that it denotes living in a city without losing one's status in one's home city, is less likely than the alternative, viz. that these Argilians (and Athenians) had forfeited their original citizenship when they joined the colony. See A. J. Graham, *Colony and Mother City in Ancient Greece*[2] (Chicago, 1983), 245–8; D. Asheri (102. 3 n. on ἦν Ἀμφίπολιν etc.), 20–1. Casevitz cites neither Graham nor Asheri.

καὶ ἀποστάντες τῶν Ἀθηναίων ἐκείνῃ τῇ νυκτί: 'Argilos now revolted from Athens that very night'. D. M. Lewis, in D. W. Bradeen and D. M. Lewis, 'Notes on Athenian Casualty Lists', *ZPE* 34 (1979), 240–6, at 244 (cp. Pritchett, *GSW* iv. 194 and *SEG* xxix. 60) suggested reading the name Argilos in the casualty list *IG* i[3]. 1184 line 76. That would imply Athenian losses at Argilos around this time, but we cannot pin them to a definite episode in Th. For the list see further below, 5 n. on ἦν βιασάμενος etc.

πρὸ ἕω: 'before dawn'. Most manuscripts have πρόσω, but see Dover, *CQ* 1954, 81, discussing the Palatine manuscript's reading, adopted in OCT.

ἐπὶ τὴν γέφυραν τοῦ ποταμοῦ: 'the bridge over the river'. The discovery by Lazaridis of the remains of a considerable bridge, with fossilized stakes, now makes it very likely (Pritchett, *SAGT* iii. 307, 312–19, 342, with maps at 302, 306, and at B. Mitchell, *Historia* 1991, 190) that the bridge was to the north of the town, rather than in the south (Pritchett, *SAGT* i (1965), 37f.) or west (Gomme). For the location of the bridge see above, Fig. 2, feature no. 3. For the remains of the bridge see Lazaridis 1986, 36 and fig. 148, and 1994, 40–1 and plates 19 and 20; see 5 n. below on καὶ οὐ etc.

5. ἀπέχει δὲ τὸ πόλισμα πλέον τῆς διαβάσεως: 'the place where it crosses is at some distance from the town'. Here Amphipolis is a *polisma*, but elsewhere in the present narrative it is a *polis*, see e.g. 102. 2. For the problem of these two words see 52. 3 n. on τὰ ἐν τῇ ἠπείρῳ Αἰολικὰ πολίσματα. One solution is to conclude that the present passage resembles Skandeia at 54. 1 and 4 in showing that Th.'s language in this department was not always as precise as modern scholars would like. But the better solution is to follow Classen/Steup and Pritchett, *SAGT* iii. 313, and assume that Th. here seeks to distinguish the city of Amphipolis inside the wall from the area outside, τὰ ἔξω as he calls it later in the present para., cp. below, n. on καὶ τὰ ἔξω etc. The distance between the excavated bridge and the citadel area is large enough for Th.'s statement to be valid. Flensted-Jensen (52. 3 n. on τὰ ἐν τῇ ἠπείρῳ etc.), 131, wrongly takes the present mention of πόλισμα to refer to Argilos. On the contrary, Classen/Steup and Pritchett are right to take it to refer to (part of) Amphipolis.

καὶ οὐ καθεῖτο τείχη ὥσπερ νῦν: 'At that time there were no walls down to the river, as there are now'. That is, the bridge 'had not been brought within the fortification system of the town' (Gomme). Th. forgets posterity here: the reader is assumed to be a rough contemporary—perhaps an Athenian one: the present passage resembles v. 10. 6 and 11. 1 in indicating changes to Amphipolis since the days of Athenian control. That is, Th. (for whose visits see above, p. 23) is giving an update to Athenian readers who might have visited the place before 424. Lazaridis 1986, 36, and 1994, 38, says that in 422 the bridge was within the fortification system, so the fortifications must have been extended between 424 and 422; see v. 10. 6 n.

Westlake (*Essays*, 130) remarks that it was not the fault of Th.'s colleague Eukles, for whom see 104. 4 and n., that the bridge was not yet included in the fortification system. (This is part of Westlake's speculative case that Th.'s narrative was subtly slanted against Eukles.) Whoever was at fault, Brasidas uses surprise and profits by negligence, cp. Babut, 422, comparing 32. 1 (Sphakteria), half-asleep garrison.

ἦν βιασάμενος ῥᾳδίως ὁ Βρασίδας: 'Brasidas easily overwhelmed the guard'. The Athenian (called Philophron) who was killed at Amphipolis according to the casualty list *IG* i³. 1184 line 45 may have died in this fighting; see Bradeen, *CQ* 1969, 156, regarding this as strong evidence that the list relates to 423.

καὶ τὰ ἔξω τῶν Ἀμφιπολιτῶν οἰκούντων κατὰ πᾶν τὸ χωρίον:

'the possessions of all the Amphipolitans living over the whole area outside the walls'. See Snodgrass, in Murray and Price (eds.), *The Greek City*
(93. 4 n. on εἶχον δὲ δεξιόν etc.), 113–36, at 127, for the living habits here
implied: ancient Greeks, he concludes, 'actually did prefer to reside
permanently on farmsteads built on their lands, even when these lay
quite close to their city'. Gomme's objection, that for Th. to imply that
the citizens lived outside the walls would be to state the obvious, is
unwarranted (and his alternative view requires emendation). Th. does
sometimes tell us 'obvious' things: see Larsen's review of *HCT* ii–iii (78.
2 n. on τὴν γὰρ Θεσσαλίαν etc.). And Snodgrass's discussion makes it
clear that the general point about settlement habits is not obvious but
highly controversial. As for Amphipolis in particular, Snodgrass takes
Th. to be referring to the area between the bridge over the Strymon and
the city. Given this proximity, it is surely possible that these Amphipolitan possessions were examples of rural buildings used as 'secondary
or temporary residences of a stable population in a nearby town'; see
M. H. Jameson, 'Class in the Ancient Greek Countryside', in P. N.
Doukellis and L. G. Mendoni (eds.), *Structures rurales et sociétés antiques*
(Paris, 1994), 55–62, at 57.

**104. 2. καὶ λέγεται Βρασίδαν, εἰ ἠθέλησε μὴ ἐφ᾽ ἁρπαγὴν τῷ
στρατῷ τράπεσθαι, ἀλλ᾽ εὐθὺς χωρῆσαι πρὸς τὴν πόλιν, δοκεῖν
ἂν ἑλεῖν:** 'It is said that opinion at the time was that Brasidas would
have taken Amphipolis if he had attacked it immediately, instead of
allowing his army to plunder'. On this view (Classen/Steup, and Jowett
in a footnote), the elaborate way in which the thought is introduced ('it is
said that . . .') is supposed to be Th.'s way of distancing himself from the
judgement. (Gomme, though apparently approving the above trans.,
suggested that δοκεῖν might just mean 'it is said that Brasidas thought
he could have taken Amphipolis'.) The main difficulty editors feel with
the Greek is that the expression is tautological if λέγεται and δοκεῖν are
taken to be a double distancing device ('it is said'; 'it was thought'). See,
however, H. D. Westlake, '*ΛΕΓΕΤΑΙ* in Thucydides', *Mnemosyne*, 30
(1977), 345–62, at 355–6: λέγεται is best taken as meaning 'there is
information that' i.e. it does not here indicate uncertainty. He thinks that
Th. on his arrival at Eion may have interrogated some of the Athenian
refugees of 106. 1, who perhaps sought to justify their speedy acceptance
of Brasidas' terms (see n. there).

The language of v. 7. 5 is curiously similar, see n. there on ἑλεῖν γὰρ
ἂν etc.

**4. πέμπουσι μετὰ Εὐκλέους τοῦ στρατηγοῦ, ὃς ἐκ τῶν Ἀθηνῶν
παρῆν αὐτοῖς φύλαξ τοῦ χωρίου:** 'Then they and Eukles, the

general who had come from Athens to protect Amphipolis, sent jointly
. . .'. Nothing is known of Eukles beyond the command here mentioned
by Th. We do not know if he was punished like Th.: as Kallet-Marx (173
n. 56) says, it is interesting that Th. does not (explicitly) blame Eukles,
the man on the spot and therefore a more legitimate target for Athenian
anger. Westlake (*Essays*, 127-9) thought that Th.'s narrative *was*
intended to be condemnatory of Eukles, in particular by not making it
clear that his forces were too small to be of much use. But we do not
know that they were small. Or large. Or anything else about them.

ἐπὶ τὸν ἕτερον στρατηγὸν τῶν ἐπὶ Θράκης, Θουκυδίδην τὸν
Ὀλόρου, ὃς τάδε ξυνέγραψεν, ὄντα περὶ Θάσον (ἔστι δὲ ἡ
νῆσος Παρίων ἀποικία, ἀπέχουσα τῆς Ἀμφιπόλεως ἡμίσεος
ἡμέρας μάλιστα πλοῦν), κελεύοντες σφίσι βοηθεῖν: '. . . for help
to the other general of the Thraceward region, Thucydides son of
Oloros, who wrote this history. He was then at Thasos, an island colonized from Paros, and about half a day's sail from Amphipolis'. Th.'s command, and activity against Brasidas, are familiar facts to us, but the
introduction of his own name must have been a shock to readers or
listeners (not however on Connor's 'reader-response' view, cf. 60. 2 n. on
καὶ πλέονι . . .)

The expression 'the other general of the Thraceward region' [lit. 'the
other general of the ones of the Thraceward region'] is curiously not
cited by Fornara, *Generals*, 79, in support of his thesis that already in the
fifth century, Athens developed a system of 'special competencies', in
particular a Thraceward command. Fornara believes this system came in
only after the Sicilian disaster and offers the Thracian command of
Diitrephes at viii. 64. 2 as an example. But why are Th. and Eukles not
relevant? Surely the present passage proves that, even in the Archidamian War, generals were thought of as having particular provinces or
theatres, if only in informal discourse. Th.'s command surely shows, at
the least, that the Athenians operated a system of regional experts, cp.
Greek Historiography, 148 and n. 45; Badian, *From Plataea to Potidaea*, 242
n. 18 (Hagnon is, as we have seen at 102. 3 n., another northern expert).
See also v. 26. 5 n. on μετὰ τὴν ἐς Ἀμφίπολιν στρατηγίαν.

Here only does Th. give his father's name, Oloros. It is an unusual and
interesting one which strongly suggests that he was descended from the
Thracian king Oloros, mentioned at Hdt. vi. 39 and 41 as the father of
Hegesipyle who married the younger Miltiades. Thus, as Hobbes
famously remarked, Th. had in his veins the blood of kings. As always
when Hdt. and Th. interconnect on a point of fact, it is worth asking
whether one of Hdt.'s motives for including it was awareness of its
topical, Thucydidean, interest, i.e. did Hdt. go out of his way to mention
the earlier Oloros because of his knowledge of his own contemporary

Th.'s military and literary activities? Note Hdt. vi. 41, where another wife of Miltiades is mentioned, 'not the daughter of Oloros the Thracian but somebody else'—who is unnamed, i.e. Oloros was worth mentioning but the other woman's father was not. Perhaps Miltiades' Thracian marriage was remarkable enough by itself to account for the different treatment, but I think that Hdt.'s Athenian listeners would have picked up the significance of the name Oloros. I have not however listed it in my Annex B.

The exact affinity has been much discussed. Davies (*APF* 234-5) thinks that Oloros of Halimous, father of Th., was a son of a daughter of Miltiades (IV, i.e. Miltiades the younger) and of Hegesipyle, 'born to her in the 480s and given his maternal great-grandfather's name'. He conjectures that Oloros' father may have been closely connected with the cult of Demeter Thesmophoros.

Th. can surely have had few or no precedents for mentioning himself as an agent in a narrative work, thus eliding the difference between author or narrator on the one hand and character or *personnage* on the other; see G. Genette, *Fiction et diction* (Paris, 1991), ch. 3, and my *Greek Historiography*, 31 and 132. Was he to use the first person or the third? When speaking of himself as an agent in the present section he invariably uses the third person, thus conferring detachment on the narrative. (True, at v. 26. 5 he refers to his Amphipolitan command again, using the *first* person; but this is a historiographic context, where he is giving his credentials as a recorder of the war). When speaking of himself as an author he fluctuates, thus (to take two passages close to each other) contrast iii. 113. 6 ἀριθμὸν οὐκ ἔγραψα, 'I have not written down the number', with iii. 116. 3, ὃν Θουκυδίδης ξυνέγραψεν, 'which Thucydides recorded', a habitual phrase echoed in the present passage. See generally, for Th.'s techniques of self-reference, i. 1. 1, first n.

For Thasos generally see i. 100. 2 n. on διενεχθέντας, and for its colonization by Paros in *c*650 BC see Strabo x. 478. The best modern discussion is by A. J. Graham, 'The Foundation of Thasos', *BSA* 73 (1978), 61-98 (esp. 97 for the concluding suggestion that before the Greek colonization, Thracians occupied Thasos and the coast opposite, and lived in a 'mutually beneficial relationship with Phoenicians').

For the distance between Amphipolis and Thasos see Gomme's addendum on p. 734 as well as his main n. The distance was *c*.50 miles or 80 km., and could have been done in perhaps 5½ hours (taking 50 miles to be 43½ nautical miles, at 6080 feet per nautical mile, see *OED* under 'mile'). According to J. Morrison and J. Coates, *The Athenian Trireme* (Cambridge, 1986), 103-6, at 106, 8 knots [i.e. nautical miles per hour] is a 'possible average speed for an oared warship in a hurry'. See further 106. 3. Morrison and Coates do not consider Th.'s voyage specifically.

Th. has been much criticized in modern times for being at relatively far-off Thasos, not Eion, see e.g. Westlake, *Essays*, 133 ff. Speculation is futile: our only evidence is what Th. himself tells us, which on this point is nothing at all.

5. καὶ ὁ μὲν ἀκούσας κατὰ τάχος ἑπτὰ ναυσὶν αἳ ἔτυχον παροῦσαι ἔπλει: 'As soon as he heard the message he sailed to Amphipolis at full speed with the seven ships which were on the spot'. If Th. the historian were not here talking about Th. the general, nobody would pounce on 'at full speed' as a piece of self-justification. But the fact is that on the evidence of his own—admittedly partisan—narrative, Th. did move at top speed, as is clear from 106. 4 (he saved Eion, see n. there). As for the seven ships, I have changed Jowett's 'which happened to be on the spot', because it exaggerates the degree of chance implied by the verb τυγχάνω. But Gomme's suggested trans., 'seven ships, all that were at the moment under his command', seems to go beyond the Greek in a different way. Gomme is right that seven is surprisingly few, but Th. does not labour this, nor can we be sure whose fault it was that there were not more, or whether a larger number would have made any difference.

καὶ ἐβούλετο φθάσαι μάλιστα μὲν οὖν τὴν Ἀμφίπολιν, πρίν τι ἐνδοῦναι, εἰ δὲ μή, τὴν Ἠιόνα προκαταλαβών: 'he wanted to get to Amphipolis before it surrendered, or failing that, to occupy Eion'. Kallet-Marx (175 n. 60) acutely detects 'an element of apologia' here: Th. is quietly making the point that Eion was 'part of the original plan'.

In the next ch. Th. switches from his own, Th.'s, calculations and plans, to those of Brasidas; see Schneider, *Information und Absicht*, 20, for the artful 'dialectical opposition/antithesis' ('dialektische Gegenüberstellung') between Th.'s plans on the one hand and Brasidas' on the other.

105. 1. καὶ πυνθανόμενος τὸν Θουκυδίδην κτῆσίν τε ἔχειν τῶν χρυσείων μετάλλων ἐργασίας ἐν τῇ περὶ ταῦτα Θρᾴκῃ καὶ ἀπ' αὐτοῦ δύνασθαι ἐν τοῖς πρώτοις τῶν ἠπειρωτῶν, ἠπείγετο προκατασχεῖν, εἰ δύναιτο, τὴν πόλιν: 'He had learned that Thucydides had the right of working gold mines in the neighbouring district of Thrace and consequently had great influence with the leading men on the mainland. So he did his utmost to get possession of Amphipolis before Thucydides appeared'. I have changed Jowett's incorrect 'Th . . . was consequently one of the leading men of the country', not least because it would, improbably, make the Athenian Th. describe himself as an ἠπειρώτης or mainlander; see Classen/Steup.

The autobiographical information is precious—for instance it tells us that Th. was a very rich man—but not gratuitous, and it is important to realize precisely why it is included. See Kallet-Marx, 174–5: Th. generally believed that wealth was a source of power, and is here insisting that Brasidas 'reasoned that Thucydides would be better able to levy troops, and to do so more quickly, than any other general because of his influence'. See also Lewis, *CAH* v². 427: 'Brasidas was told that he owned gold mines there and had great influence in Thrace ... and was convinced by this that speed was essential'.

In fact, despite Lewis's formulation about *ownership* of the mines, it is more likely that he merely had the right to work them; see Luschnat, 'Thukydides', *RE* Suppl. 12 (1970), 1095–7, and Graham *BSA* 1978 (104. 4 n. on ἐπὶ τὸν ἕτερον etc.), 93 n. 106. It is usually and surely rightly assumed that Th. acquired these rights by inheritance, see 104. 4 n. on ἐπὶ τὸν ἕτερον etc. for the Oloros connection. In particular, Graham argues against Davies, *APF* 236–7, who (while not excluding the family connection) thought that the family could not have acquired its property in the mines before 463 when the Thasians lost possession of its mainland holdings to Athens, see i. 101. 3. But Thasos' mainland possessions are not likely to have extended as far as the Eion/Amphipolis region where Th.'s property surely was (see below); and in any case, as Graham says, concessions like that of Th. may have been the result of private arrangements with Thracian owners (i.e. unaffected by the Athenian takeover of the 460s). Presumably Th.'s property was unaffected by his exile i.e. he continued to be rich, cf. above, p. 22 and n. 66.

For Thucydides' Thracian 'mineral rights' as an example of Athenian property-holding abroad in the time of the empire (an important aspect of Athenian imperialism) see J. K. Davies, *Wealth and the Power of Wealth in Classical Athens* (New York, 1981), 58.

Marcellinus 47 locates Th.'s property at Skapte Hyle, but this is generally discounted as a guess based on Hdt. vi. 46. We simply do not know more than Th. chooses to tell us here, namely that the mines were in the 'neighbouring district' of Thrace (ἐν τῇ περὶ ταῦτα Θρᾴκῃ) i.e. near Amphipolis/Eion.

Th. here tells us a lot about what Brasidas feared and reckoned; see the good analysis of Schneider, *Information und Absicht*, 14–20. But despite Schneider's emphasis (20) on Th.'s 'compositional' or literary motives as against 'authenticity', it is not all likely to be merely inferred motivation: surely the two men talked between 424 and 422. Did that artful speaker Brasidas flatter Th. a little by telling him (no doubt truthfully) that Th.'s influence and wealth was in part relevant to the speed with which he himself had moved in 424? But only in part: see Westlake, *Essays*, 133.

τὸ πλῆθος τῶν Ἀμφιπολιτῶν: 'the people of Amphipolis'. Amphipolis was evidently a democracy of some sort, as one would expect given that it was an Athenian foundation, cp. J. Papastavru, *Amphipolis: Klio Beiheft* 37 (1936), 47. For De Ste. Croix, *OPW* 37, Amphipolis was an example of a democracy which was strong enough to maintain itself without needing to stay inside the Athenian empire. Certainly the Amphipolitans after the Peace of Nikias showed the opposite of enthusiasm for a return to Athenian control, see v. 21. 1 f. and 35. 5.

2. καὶ τὴν ξύμβασιν μετρίαν ἐποιεῖτο: 'So he offered moderate terms'. The 'moderation' of Brasidas is stressed again, cp. 81. 2 n. on ἑαυτὸν παρασχών etc. (also 108. 2 n. on ὁ γὰρ Βρασίδας etc.). See p. 56.

κήρυγμα ... ἀνειπών: 'He made a proclamation'. For the word see B. Knox, *The Heroic Temper* (Berkeley, 1964), 95, taking it to be appropriate for an emergency decree, and comparing ii. 2. 4 (and add iv. 37. 1); but the closest parallel to the present passage is i. 27. 1 where the noun is not used at all, see next n. (That is, there is nothing magic about the *noun*.) On *kerugma* see also C. Sourvinou-Inwood, 'Assumptions and the Creation of Meaning: Reading Sophocles' *Antigone*', *JHS* 109 (1989), 134–48, at 138, though she slightly overdoes its democratic connotations; the present passage, which she cites, is after all a proclamation by the Spartan Brasidas (as is 114. 1 and 4, where *kerugma* is used of Brasidas at Torone; cp. also 116. 2 n. on καὶ ἔτυχε κηρύξας etc.).

Ἀμφιπολιτῶν καὶ Ἀθηναίων τῶν ἐνόντων τὸν μὲν βουλόμενον ἐπὶ τοῖς ἑαυτοῦ τῆς ἴσης καὶ ὁμοίας μετέχοντα μένειν: 'that any Amphipolitan or Athenian in the city could either remain in Amphipolis and keep his property and political rights on an equal footing'. Cp. i. 27. 1, ἐκήρυσσον ἐπὶ τῇ ἴσῃ καὶ ὁμοίᾳ τὸν βουλόμενον ἰέναι, the terms of the Corinthian proclamation of a colony to Epidamnos, with a very similarly worded guarantee of equal political rights. See my n. on that passage for epigraphic parallels.

Most translations simply ignore τῶν ἐνόντων, 'in the city', but the words are important. If they refer to the Athenians only, we need to ask: are these the same as the group mentioned at 106. 1 below, who are said to ἐμπολιτεύειν? See n. there, and, for the verb, see 103. 4 n. on πρὸς τοὺς ἐμπολιτεύοντας etc. Asheri (102. 3 n. on ἦν Ἀμφίπολιν etc.), 22, suggests that the reference in the present passage is to the members of an Athenian garrison ('epoikia-presidio'), and that these are distinct from the people in 106. 1. His interpretation assumes that τῶν ἐνόντων refers to the 'Athenians' only, not the 'Amphipolitans and Athenians'. It is true that we need an explanation of 'in the city'—redundant words on the face of it if applied to both Amphipolitans and Athenians, but meaningful if they refer to a special group of Athenians only. However

Graham (244) supplies a different explanation: 'those in the city' are opposed to those outside, who are already in Brasidas' control. If this is right, and I think it is, we must make the further assumption that Brasidas' edict (unnecessarily but understandably) distinguished between Amphipolitans of Athenian origins, and other Amphipolitans. τὸν δὲ μὴ ἐθέλοντα ἀπιέναι τὰ ἑαυτοῦ ἐκφερόμενον πέντε ἡμερῶν: 'or if he preferred not to stay, he could have five days to leave, taking his property with him'. For the five-day provision cp. vii. 3. 1. The Athenian Pisistratids were given five days to leave Attica, Hdt. v. 65. 2; and compare the ten days allowed to people ostracized from Athens.

106. 1. ἄλλως τε καὶ βραχὺ μὲν Ἀθηναίων ἐμπολιτεῦον, τὸ δὲ πλέον ξύμμεικτον: 'very few of the citizens were Athenians, the majority being of mixed origin'. For the meaning of the verb ἐμπολιτεῦον see 103. 4 n. on πρὸς τοὺς ἐμπολιτεύοντας etc., and for the status of these people, see 105. 2 n. on Ἀμφιπολιτῶν etc., esp. Graham there cited. These people are Amphipolitans of Athenian origin, who lost their Athenian citizenship when they joined the colony, but are singled out by Th. as (in a sense) Athenians because of their obvious sympathies. For the mixed character of Amphipolis see Tod, p. 150, on his no. 150. Some of the mix, as we know from 103. 4, were Argilians.

καὶ τὸ κήρυγμα: 'the proclamation'. See 105. 2 n. on κήρυγμα . . .

2. τοῦ παρόντος Ἀθηναίων στρατηγοῦ: 'the Athenian general in the city'. That is, of course, Eukles. But why is he not named? This (cf. above p. 18) is an example of what narratologists call attributive discourse or denomination, see *Greek Historiography*, 160, citing I. de Jong, *Narrative in Drama: The Art of the Euripidean Messenger Speech* (Leiden, 1991), 94 ff., and 'Studies in Homeric Denomination', *Mnemosyne*, 46 (1993), 289–306. Westlake (*Essays*, 132) suggests that the roundabout expression in the present passage is chosen, in preference to the name, so as to underline Eukles' responsibility for safeguarding Athenian interests at Amphipolis.

3. ὁ δὲ Θουκυδίδης καὶ αἱ νῆες ταύτῃ τῇ ἡμέρᾳ ὀψὲ κατέπλεον ἐς τὴν Ἠιόνα: 'The same evening Thucydides and his ships sailed into Eion'. In his main n. (p. 579) Gomme thought that Eukles must have sent a message by signal, because he could not have sent his message off much before dawn (103. 4, 104. 4), and the journey from Amphipolis to Thasos at speed 'could hardly have taken less than seven or eight hours' of a short winter's day. But Gomme changed his mind at p. 734, convinced by T. J. Cadoux that a boat could have done the journey Amphipolis–Thasos in about five hours; nevertheless he was dubious: 'if so we must adjust our notions' about the speed of ancient ships and boats. It is now clear that a signal is improbable (cf. Pritchett *SAGT* iii (1980) 314

n. 25) and that Gomme's second thoughts about the timetable were right and that, for a trireme at least, older notions must indeed be adjusted. At a fast average speed for a trireme, the journey could have been done in 5½ hours, see 104. 4 n. on ἐπὶ τὸν ἕτερον etc. Th., who sailed from Thasos to Eion rather than the more distant Amphipolis, could have taken rather less than this. We do not, however, know how the message of 104. 4 was brought (if it *was* brought, rather than transmitted by signalling). But if we allow time for Th. to make hasty preparations for putting to sea, the two journeys could have been made in, say, 12 hours. On the evidence he provides, Th. moved fast.

4. καὶ τὴν μὲν Ἀμφίπολιν Βρασίδας ἄρτι εἶχε, τὴν δὲ Ἠιόνα παρὰ νύκτα ἐγένετο λαβεῖν· εἰ γὰρ μὴ ἐβοήθησαν αἱ νῆες διὰ τάχους, ἅμα ἕῳ ἂν εἴχετο: 'but not before Brasidas had taken possession of Amphipolis. Brasidas missed taking Eion by just one night: if the ships had not come to the rescue at top speed, Eion would have fallen to Brasidas at daybreak'. We can call this self-justification if we like, but the facts (see previous n.) support Th.'s claim. A more cynical way of putting that would be to say that Th.'s narrative is compatible with his judgement here. See also 104. 5 n. on καὶ ἐβούλετο etc. for Eion as part of Th.'s original agenda. On Th.'s conduct and its relation to his own narrative much has been written; apart from Gomme, 584-8, see H. D. Westlake, *Essays*, 123-37 (= H. Herter (ed.), *Thukydides* 620-38), who is severe on Th., and Schneider, *Information und Absicht*, 11-28.

The final sentence is a classic 'if . . .not' type of formulation, as de Jong calls this suspenseful way of telling a story; see *Narrators and Focalizers* (Amsterdam, 1987), 68-81. (H.-G. Nesselrath calls these 'Beinahe-Episoden', see his *Ungeschehene Geschehen* (Stuttgart, 1992).) For the whole topic, and for other Thucydidean and Homeric examples, see *Greek Historiography*, 158: cp. esp. Th. iii. 49 and vii. 2, Mytilene and Syracuse both saved by a whisker, i.e. the implied thought is 'if the second Athenian trireme/Gylippos had not arrived, it would have been disastrous for Mytilene/Syracuse'. But in those two places the actual words 'if . . . not' are not used, as they are in the present passage, which is thus (see p. 18) a very good example.

107. 1. δεξάμενος τοὺς ἐθελήσαντας ἐπιχωρῆσαι ἄνωθεν κατὰ τὰς σπονδάς: 'He received those who had left Amphipolis according to the agreement and wished to come into Eion'. These people are obvious possible sources of information for Th. the historian, though not necessarily unbiased ones: cp. 104. 2 n. on καὶ λέγεται etc. for the possibility that when interrogated by Th. they felt the need to exculpate themselves for taking Brasidas up on his offer so quickly and so making him a present of Amphipolis.

2. ἀμφοτέρωθεν ἀπεκρούσθη: 'in both attempts he was foiled'. For the verb here see 102. 2 n. on τὸ δὲ χωρίον etc., discussing ἐξεκρούσθη and Th.'s fondness hereabouts for κρου- verbs.

3. καὶ Μύρκινος: 'Myrkinos'. Myrkinos, north of Amphipolis and about half-way between Amphipolis and Drabeskos, was where Histiaios of Miletos tried to found a colony (cp. 102. 1 n.): see Hdt. v. 11. 2; 23. 1; 124. 2; 126. 1. See further below, v. 6. 4 and v. 10. 9 n.: Myrkinian peltasts.

Πιττακοῦ τοῦ Ἠδώνων βασιλέως ἀποθανόντος ὑπὸ τῶν Γοάξιος παίδων καὶ Βραυροῦς τῆς γυναικὸς αὐτοῦ: 'Pittakos the king of the Hedonians had been assassinated by the children of Goaxis and by his own wife Brauro'. Th., the Thracian and northern expert (105. 1, cf. 104. 4 n. on ἐπὶ τὸν ἕτερον etc.), suddenly throws some unexplained Thracian detail at us, including a most uncharacteristic mention by name of a female agent in his history. On Brauro see the good study by T. E. J. Wiedemann, 'ἐλάχιστον . . . ἐν τοῖς ἄρσεσι κλέος': Thucydides, Women, and the Limits of Rational Analysis', *G & R* 30 (1983), 163–70, at 166: she belongs (like Stratonike at ii. 101. 5) to a group of Thucydidean women 'whose marriages result in political links between rulers on the fringes of the Greek world', cp. 167 for Brauro as 'marginal' and 168 for her alleged irrationality. The weather, says Wiedemann with appropriate references to Pylos, is one irrational factor in Th.'s narrative, and women, like the murderous Brauro, are another. But without knowing what Brauro had to put up with from Pittakos, or what she thought of his presumably pro-Athenian policies, I do not see how we can be sure that what she did was actually irrational. What remains true is that Th. was more prepared to treat women as agents in non-Greek areas. Note that the order children–women conforms to Th.'s usual practice as noted by Wiedemann, see 123. 4 n. on ὑπεκκομίζει etc.

For Pittakos see Hammond, *HM* 130, suggesting that he had succeeded to a numismatically attested king Demetrios, for whom see Hammond, 112.

Cp. K.-L. Elvers, 'Der "Eid der Berenike und ihrer Söhne": eine Edition von IGBulg. III 2, 1731', *Chiron*, 24 (1994), 241–66, for joint activity by the wife of a Thracian king and her *own* 'children' (who could of course have been mature adults, both in Th. and in the inscription).

For Th.'s mention of Pittakos' death see 101. 5 n. on ἀπέθανε etc. giving other instances where he records deaths of non-Greeks.

καὶ Γαληψὸς οὐ πολλῷ ὕστερον καὶ Οἰσύμη· εἰσὶ δὲ αὗται Θασίων ἀποικίαι: 'Soon afterwards Galepsos and Oisyme (both colonies of Thasos) came over to him' [but the name may be Syme, see below]. Galepsos (not to be confused with the Sithonian Galepsos of Hdt. vii. 122, more usually called Gale, see Zahrnt, 178–9) was on the

coast south-east of Eion. Homer, *Iliad* viii. 304, mentions a place called
Aisyme, which Steph. Byz. identifies with Oisyme; 'speculative', according to G. S. Kirk in his *Iliad* commentary. But there is a problem of considerable complexity and importance lurking here. Lewis, *Towards a
Historian's Text*, 44–6, 164, 166–7, 197, noting that the manuscripts of
Diod. xii. 68. 4, from Ephorus, have Σύμη, suggested that what Th.
wrote was Σύμη, 'Syme', and that this was 'emended' in antiquity to
something like the Homeric form of the name. 'The vast body of theorising on the Homeric corpus touched the name. I suggest that at some
time this theorising affected an ancient editor's view on the text of Thucydides.' Lewis also speculated ingeniously that the Syme attested in the
Tribute List for 434/3 as one of the places whose names were added by
private individuals to the list of tributary places (*IG* i³. 278 = list 21, col.
VI line 28) was not, as usually thought, the island off Caria—it would be
in strange company if it were—but Th.'s Thracian [Oi]syme. If so,
Gomme's n. ('not mentioned in the tribute-lists') is wrong. (Lewis
discusses more ancient testimony than I have given in the above
summary.)

Galepsos certainly paid tribute to Athens, varying between 3 talents in
442 and 1000 drachmas in 428. Note, with Meiggs, *AE* 537, that
although these minor places went over to Brasidas, the more important
Neapolis (modern Kavalla) stayed loyal. The manuscripts have Γαψη-
λός, 'Gapselos', which is to be emended not just because of the evidence
of Stephanus of Byzantium (see OCT apparatus) but because of
Diodorus (as above), who has Γαληψός.

The colonial relationship is specified as often (Introduction, p. 74) but
here it indicated, at least until the 460s, a closer relationship than might
be guessed from Th.: Hdt. (vii. 109. 2) speaks of 'the mainland cities of
Thasos' as if they were actual dependencies in the Persian War period. At
v. 6. 1, on which see my n., Th. will oddly repeat the information (more
relevant here) that Galepsos was a Thasian colony (and that Stagiros was
an Andrian one, something we have already been told at 88. 2).

παρὼν δὲ καὶ Περδίκκας εὐθὺς μετὰ τὴν ἅλωσιν ξυγκαθίστη
ταῦτα: 'Perdikkas arrived soon after the capture of Amphipolis and
helped him to settle the newly-acquired places'. See Hammond, *HM* ii.
130, though it is a slight misrepresentation to say that Perdikkas 'helped
Brasidas to win over' Myrkinos, Galepsos, and Oisyme. Hammond himself notes that Perdikkas does not seem to have gained from Brasidas'
successes in the Strymon basin.

108. 1. ἐχομένης δὲ τῆς Ἀμφιπόλεως οἱ Ἀθηναῖοι ἐς μέγα δέος
κατέστησαν, ἄλλως τε καὶ ὅτι ἡ πόλις αὐτοῖς ἦν ὠφέλιμος
ξύλων τε ναυπηγησίμων πομπῇ καὶ χρημάτων προσόδῳ: 'The

Athenians were seriously alarmed now that Amphipolis was in enemy hands: it was very useful to them because it provided timber which they imported for ship-building, and also financial revenue'. This ch. is the fourth of the six excursuses on morale, see Introduction, p. 109. In particular, as Classen/Steup say (cp. also Babut, 420 and n. 1, with refs. to ch. 41 as well), this important ch. parallels digression no. 2 at ch. 55, on Spartan morale, in general and in detail (with the opening words cp. 55. 1 Πύλου δὲ ἐχομένης καὶ Κυθήρων, 'Pylos and Kythera were in the hands of the Athenians'). And see below 2 n. on ὁ γὰρ Βρασίδας etc. for the relation to 81. 2 and the 'moderation of Brasidas' theme. The focalization in the chapter is complex: we begin with the Athenians, then there is a natural transition to the allied view at para. 2, because one of Athens' fears is of allied revolt. Towards the end of para. 6 (ὧν αἰσθανόμενοι) we return to Athenian awareness of allied opinion, and the ch. ends with Spartan feelings about Brasidas. Cp. Connor, 133 and n. 65 (but we must add 'allied attitude' to Connor's 'Athenian attitude' and 'Spartan attitude'). Westlake (*Essays*, 123–4) remarks that such sketches of opinion 'have a function similar to that of the speeches'.

Th. presents this material about the usefulness of Amphipolis to Athens here, rather than in ch. 102 where, as Gomme complained, it 'might well have been inserted'. He does so not just because, as Gomme eventually noted, it is only now that the Athenians realize what they have lost, although that is no doubt true. (Cp. also Ridley, *Hermes* 1981, 37, Th.'s 'extensive notes on Amphipolis': the economic and strategic notes on the place are 'kept back some chapters, to serve, more dramatically, as an indicator of Athenian alarm on its fall'.) Th. also needs the 108. 1 material where it is because it rubs in the effect of the capture of Amphipolis on allied opinion. Note para. 2, where they are said to have heard about the taking of Amphipolis and about Brasidas' promises and his mildness, in that order. And finally there is the effect back home at Sparta: the taking of Amphipolis is surely a large part of the reason for the *phthonos* or jealousy of Brasidas felt by the leading men at Sparta, para. 7.

On Amphipolis as a source of ship-building timber, see R. Meiggs, *Trees and Timber in the Ancient Mediterranean World* (Oxford, 1982), 357–8: the timber was probably from Mount Pangaion, now very bare; it is also possible that logs were brought down the Strymon from the interior.

Amphipolis does not appear on the Athenian tribute lists, but the present passage is important evidence that there were rich revenue-providing places which do not feature in the epigraphic record at all; we should therefore be careful not to assume that a complete account of

Athenian resources can be obtained from inscriptions alone. See Kallet-Marx, 175–6: the implication of πρόσοδος, 'income' or 'revenue', is that 'wealth from Amphipolis flowed into Athens regularly'. She suggests that the bulk of this derived from the gold and silver mines of Pangaion; though she accepts that there could have been subsidiary wealth accruing from sacred precincts in what was after all a colony, where such precincts were normal (see above, p. 97).

On δέος as the word for fear see Introduction, p. 109.

2. ὁ γὰρ Βρασίδας ἔν τε τοῖς ἄλλοις μέτριον ἑαυτὸν παρεῖχε: 'This was because Brasidas showed himself so generally moderate'. The key word here, 'moderate', μέτριον, was used of Brasidas at 81. 2, see n. there on ἑαυτὸν παρασχών etc., discussing the right trans. of the Greek: Th. thought Brasidas *really was moderate* (cf. p. 56); cp. also 105. 2 n. on καὶ τὴν ξύμβασιν etc., and Babut, 431, for the 'moderation-of-Brasidas' theme; cf. above, pp. 55 f. For the thematic resumption of ch. 81 see Connor, 133–5, suggesting (134) that 'the similarities are designed to return us to the ideas and themes of [ch. 81]'. Like that ch. (on which see 81. 1 n. on αὐτόν τε Βρασίδαν etc.), the present assessment is not all Th.'s own: both chapters are more concerned (apart from the vital παρέχω clauses) with the effect produced on people by Brasidas, than with his real character or intentions. However ch. 108 is more obviously loaded against Brasidas; this raises the question of 'date of composition', see 4 n.

ὡς ἐλευθερώσων τὴν Ἑλλάδα ἐκπεμφθείη: 'that he had been sent to free Greece'. See the Akanthos speech (whose general authenticity the present passage confirms), esp. 85. 1, where all the components of the present expression are present in some form.

3. καὶ αἱ πόλεις πυνθανόμεναι αἱ τῶν Ἀθηναίων ὑπήκοοι τῆς τε Ἀμφιπόλεως τὴν ἅλωσιν καὶ ἃ παρέχεται, τήν τε ἐκείνου πραότητα: 'When the cities subject to Athens heard of the capture of Amphipolis, and of Brasidas' promises and of his mildness'. Westlake, *Essays*, 140, observes that 'the cities' appears at first to refer to the whole Athenian empire but must in fact refer only to the Chalkidike.

The word for mildness, πραότητα, occurs here only in Th., and the simple adjective πρᾶος never. The vocabulary Th. uses about, or puts into the mouth of, Brasidas, seems to be distinctive, see pp. 42–9 and introductory n. to 85–7 and (for πραότης) de Romilly, *Phoenix* 28 (1974), 99 f.

The motives attributed to the northern allies in their secession from Athens are as notable for what they do not include as for what they do. Nothing, for instance, about the recent increase in the tribute. As we have seen (see Introduction above, p. 96), Lewis, *CAH* v². 420, found it 'more than surprising' that the reassessment does not feature in the discussion of allied attitudes in the present ch. Given that Th. had not mentioned the reassessment itself in its place, it is (one might wish to say) merely consistent of him not to mention it here. But the 'failure' to include it among allied grievances supports the view of Kallet-Marx (see above pp. 94–8) that the reassessment was after all not that important.

See Babut, 420, for the parallel with the results of Pylos, e.g. 41. 3.

μάλιστα δὴ ἐπήρθησαν ἐς τὸ νεωτερίζειν: 'they were more impatient to revolt than ever'. On the verb ἐπήρθησαν see Connor, 135 (with n. 68), glossing it as 'mightily lifted up' to revolt, and commenting that 'it regularly conveys not mere excitement but the exaltation that precedes a disaster'; he compares iii. 45. 1, iv. 121. 1 (Skione), and v. 14. 2.

4. καὶ γὰρ καὶ ἄδεια ἐφαίνετο αὐτοῖς, ἐψευσμένοι μὲν τῆς Ἀθηναίων δυνάμεως ἐπὶ τοσοῦτον ὅση ὕστερον διεφάνη: 'They thought that there was no danger; but in fact Athenian power was afterwards proved to be as great as their own mistake in underestimating it'. A much-discussed sentence. The first words mean literally 'it seemed to them that there was a state of not-fear', i.e. no occasion for fear; but Connor (135) thinks (if I interpret him correctly) that the noun 'not-fear', ἄδεια, had by this time come to mean 'immunity' e.g. from prosecution, so that Th. is putting his point very strongly by a kind of legal metaphor: the allies thought they had a kind of 'grant of immunity of prosecution'. This is ingenious, but vii. 29. 3 shows that the literal sense was still felt to be present; so I have not tried to reflect Connor's point by changing Jowett's trans.

Translation is not easy; as Westlake (*Essays*, 140) says, Th. here runs together two ideas, the allied miscalculation which made them think they could revolt with impunity, and their failure to realize that Athenian power was as great as it was; as Westlake rather testily says, it is daring of Th. to compare the size of Athens' power with the size of an allied mistake. Jowett's 'Athenian power, which afterwards proved its greatness and the magnitude of their mistake' gets the point but is not idiomatic today and in revising it I have shamelessly borrowed from Warner.

To what period does 'afterwards' (ὕστερον) refer? The question has a bearing on the difference in flavour between the present ch. and 81, which contains a definite allusion (at para. 2) to the period after the Sicilian disaster. Westlake (*Essays*, 138–44) argues (against Gomme, cp. also Dover, *HCT* v. 412) that the subject of the sentence is the Chalkidic cities, not the whole empire (see above, 3 n. on καὶ αἱ πόλεις etc.), and that 'afterwards' refers to the period 423–421 (as being the only period for which the remark is true of those cities), not to the Ionian War, i.e. the period after the Sicilian Disaster of 413. If that is right, the present passage was written before ch. 81; and Th. changed his mind, in a favourable direction, about Brasidas (who at para. 5 below is more explicitly and authorially said to be insincere than anywhere in ch. 81, which is mostly focalized through others). This is all too strict. Even if Gomme is wrong about the meaning of 'afterwards', he could still be right that the sentence is an insertion. In any case there is a fallacy in Westlake's reasoning: even if the passage *refers* to 423-421, it could nevertheless have been written, or thought, at a much later date (including the composition date of 81. 2, whenever exactly after 413 that was). So nothing follows about the relation to ch. 81, and we can follow Connor, 134, who sees the resumption of themes as deliberate: 'the reader is now [after hearing Brasidas and seeing him in action] prepared for a more explicit and more critical analysis of Brasidas' claims.' This is an attractive approach, but it remains uncomfortably true that 81 is 'not fully co-ordinated' with 108. 2-6: so Andrewes, *HCT* v. 364, for whom the lack of co-ordination is one of the 'indications of incompleteness' in Th.'s account of the Ten Years War. See above, Introduction, pp. 121 f.

I have changed the OCT ἐψευσμένοις to ἐψευσμένοι, the reading of the Palatine manuscript, in view of Dover, *CQ* 1954, 81 and 83. The sense is the same.

εἰωθότες οἱ ἄνθρωποι οὗ μὲν ἐπιθυμοῦσιν ἐλπίδι ἀπερισκέπτῳ διδόναι, ὃ δὲ μὴ προσίενται λογισμῷ αὐτοκράτορι διωθεῖσθαι: 'Men are always incautiously optimistic about getting what they want, but if they dislike a possible outcome, they discount it by arbitrary reasoning'. We are suddenly catapulted into a style of discourse much more characteristic of the speeches or the Corcyraean *stasis* than of the routine narrative even at its most reflective; cp. Diodotos on hope at iii. 45, or the Athenians at Melos, v. 103. There is a bold metaphor in 'arbitrary reasoning'; the word is αὐτοκράτωρ, a word from the military/political vocabulary meaning 'possessed of full or absolute powers'; cp. 126. 5 n. on αὐτοκράτωρ δὲ μάχη etc.

5. ἐν τοῖς Βοιωτοῖς νεωστὶ πεπληγμένων: 'had recently been defeated in Boiotia'. A loose reference to what we call the Delion campaign—and what Th. in two other retrospective passages (v. 14. 1 and 15. 2) also calls 'Delion'. Delion itself was in Boiotia (76. 4 n.), whereas the battle was on the borders of Attica and Boiotia. For the abiding unclarity on this point see 95. 2 n. on ἐν γὰρ τῇ τούτων etc. and Introduction, pp. 91-3.

καὶ τοῦ Βρασίδου ἐφολκὰ καὶ οὐ τὰ ὄντα λέγοντος, ὡς αὐτῷ ἐπὶ Νίσαιαν τῇ ἑαυτοῦ μόνῃ στρατιᾷ οὐκ ἠθέλησαν οἱ Ἀθηναῖοι ξυμβαλεῖν: 'and Brasidas told the allies what was attractive but untrue, namely that at Nisaia the Athenians had refused to fight against unaided Spartan troops'. See 85. 7 for the corresponding part of Brasidas'

Akanthos speech, and n. there for the important implications of the two passages combined: this is one speech, or part of a speech, which we can be confident really was delivered. See Introduction, p. 86.

The word ἐφολκά is found here only in Th., and is more evidence that Brasidas is described in very singular language; cp. 3 n. on καὶ αἱ πόλεις etc. for πραότητα.

καὶ ἐπίστευον μηδένα ἂν ἐπὶ σφᾶς βοηθῆσαι: 'and were confident that no army would ever reach them'. Irony: Kleon did reach them. See Connor, 135.

6. καὶ αὐτὸς ἐν τῷ Στρυμόνι ναυπηγίαν τριήρων παρεσκευ- άζετο: 'and he himself began to build triremes on the Strymon'. For the timber see 1 above and n.

7. φθόνῳ ἀπὸ τῶν πρώτων ἀνδρῶν: 'because their leading men were jealous of him'. For Brasidas' relations with the home authorities see 81. 1 n. on αὐτόν τε etc. and Introduction, pp. 50–61, esp. 52.

109. 1 (first part). *The Megarians recapture and destroy their Long Walls*

For the Long Walls (now archaeologically attested) of Megara see iv. 66. 3 n. on ξυνέβησαν etc.; also i. 103. 4 n.

109. 1 (second part)–116. *Brasidas in Chalkidike*

In the Greek, the resumption of the Brasidas narrative is as closely tied as it could possibly be ('in the same winter the Megarians recaptured . . . and Brasidas', using a 'both . . . and' construction, τε . . . καί) to the preceding half-sentence about Megara. It is as if Th. does not wish to lose momentum.

109. 1. ἐπὶ τὴν Ἀκτὴν καλουμένην: 'the so-called Akte'. The Chalkidic peninsula furthest to the north-east. It is not obvious why Akte should get a 'so-called' whereas Pallene, the most south-western of the three promontories, did not get one at its first mention (i. 56. 2, contrast Hdt. vii. 123. 1, giving old name as well), unless it is because Th. feels in didactic vein: he is about tell us some Persian-War background. Macan in his n. on the comparable passage of Hdt. (vii. 22, see next n.) gives Th. a good mark for giving the name of the Akte peninsula as Hdt. had not.

2. ἔστι δὲ ἀπὸ τοῦ βασιλέως διορύγματος ἔσω προύχουσα, καὶ ὁ Ἄθως αὐτῆς ὄρος ὑψηλὸν τελευτᾷ ἐς τὸ Αἰγαῖον πέλαγος: 'a peninsula which runs out from the canal made by the Persian King, and culminates in Athos, a high mountain which projects into the Aegean Sea'. Note '*the* canal'; perhaps just because it was a familiar fifth-century landmark. But perhaps we are expected to know our Herodotus (vii. 22; with Th.'s ἔσω προύχουσα Gomme rightly compares Hdt. vii. 22. 3 αἱ δὲ ἐκτὸς Σάνης, ἔσω δὲ τοῦ Ἄθω οἰκημέναι). On the other hand, 'so-called' (1 n. above) treats the readers as if they are fresh to the subject; and some of the factual material (Athos a big mountain which runs into the sea) is close to Hdt. vii. 22. 2, as if after all we needed reminding of what Hdt. says. Whatever the reason for this uncertainty of manner, Th.'s indebtedness to Hdt. in the present ch. as a whole seems clear, see the following notes, and above, Introduction, pp. 34 f. For the remains of the canal see now B. S. J. Isserlin, R. E. Jones, S. Papamarinopoulos, and J. Ure, 'The Canal of Xerxes on the Mount Athos Peninsula: Preliminary Investigations in 1991–2', *BSA* 89 (1994), 277–84, with refs. to earlier work. It is still uncertain whether the canal went all the way through the peninsula as Hdt. implies, or only part of the way as Demetrius of Skepsis says, Strabo vii fr. 35. Where the canal crossed the higher ground, it was located in a deep man-made trench. This would surely have still been visible in Th.'s time.

3. **πόλεις δὲ ἔχει Σάνην μὲν Ἀνδρίων ἀποικίαν:** 'The cities on Akte include Sane, an Andrian colony'. Sane features in Hdt. (vii. 23. 1), but Th. has added the colonial point. See 84. 1 n. citing Meiggs for the anti-Athenianism of most of the Andrian colonies in this region; but Sane is an exception (para. 5 below) and so tells against Meiggs's suggestion. See Introduction, p. 78. For Sane, on the narrow point of the Akte pensinula, see Zahrnt, 219–21. Zahrnt follows the emendation of Sane to Gale at v. 18. 6, but see n. there.

τὰς δὲ ἄλλας Θυσσὸν καὶ Κλεωνὰς καὶ Ἀκροθῴους καὶ Ὀλόφυ-ξον καὶ Δῖον: 'the others are Thyssos, Kleonai, Akrothooi, Olophyxos, and Dion'. Hdt.'s order of these places (vii. 22. 3) is almost the reverse: Dion, Olophyxos, Akrothoon, Thyssos, Kleonai. This looks like silent correction by Th. of Hdt. on the detail of Thyssos-then-Kleonai, whether or not Th. was right. But was he? Care is needed here because Th.'s order has itself evidently been influential on the speculative identifications preferred by e.g. Zahrnt, 184, cp. 182, 191, 194 (Thyssos at Zographu, Kleonai at Xiropotamu). But the argument is not circular because Ps.-Skylax 66 has Th.'s order, except for putting Dion at the other end of the list, and as the authors of *ATL* remark (i. 464), he was writing a *periplous* or account of a coasting voyage, and must have known what he was talking about i.e. he did not just transcribe Th. I conclude (see p. 35 above) that Th. was correcting Hdt. (Lest it be thought an eccentricity of my own to see a Herodotean aspect here, I note that Gomme says that Hdt.'s description 'looks like Thucydides' authority', while adding 'though he repeats the information doubtless because he knew the country himself'. Gomme does not, however, discuss the small discrepancy which is my reason for arguing not merely dependence on but correction of Hdt.) A final point: I noted above that Thucydides more or less reverses Hdt.'s order, i.e. he works round the peninsula in the opposite direction. This fits the brilliant observation of Maurer, *Interpolation*, 74 n. 28, that Th. prefers to enumerate places *counter*-clockwise.

The only reasonably secure identification is Akrothooi on the site of the monastery of Agia Lavra.

All these places paid small amounts of tribute to Athens; Olophyxos, Sane, and Dion paid together, Kleonai at first paid together with the larger Thyssos and was then separated.

Olophyxos, 'a small place of little economic or political importance' (Meiggs, *AE* 587), features in Ar. *Birds* of 415 (line 1041, requirement to 'use the same weights and measures as the Olophyxians') as part of a parody of the Athenian coinage decree, ML 45. It is obviously chosen (apart from for its ridiculous smallness) to set up the 'Ototyxioi' joke in the next line, cp. Meiggs's rendering 'return to the goad standard', and N. Dunbar, *Aristophanes: Birds*, n. on the passage (who adds that Ar. may also have had in mind the epic ὀλοφυδνός, 'lamenting', see e.g. *Iliad* v. 683). The reasonable assumption that this was a more or less topical joke (i.e. prompted by the military activity in the N. Aegean described in Th. iv and v) always made attractive a date in the 420s or 410s (rather than the 440s) for the main coinage decree, and this has now been rendered likely on entirely different grounds, see (for the new Hamaxitos fragment) 52. 3 n. on τάς τε ἄλλας πόλεις τὰς Ἀκταίας etc. It was unlike Gomme to miss commenting on an Aristophanic point, but he has nothing to say on this aspect of Olophyxos, a place mentioned here only in Th. Cf. Introduction, above, p. 13.

4. αἳ οἰκοῦνται ξυμμείκτοις ἔθνεσι βαρβάρων διγλώσσων: 'They are inhabited by a mixed population of barbarians, speaking Greek as well as their own language' [lit. 'bilingual barbarians']. Cp. Hdt. vii. 22. 2 on Mount Athos, οἰκημένον ὑπὸ ἀνθρώπων, 'inhabited by men', where Macan attractively suggested adding ⟨βαρβάρων⟩ or ⟨διγλώσσων⟩ ('barbarian' or 'bilingual') precisely on the basis of the present passage of Th. This suggestion appears in the apparatus to the 1926 reissue of Hude's OCT of Hdt., having appeared too late for the original printing. Either of these emendations, but especially the more striking διγλώσσων, would increase the similarities between Hdt. and Th., though obviously it would be circular to invoke the emended text as further 'proof' of Th.'s dependence on Hdt., see preceding nn. Macan's n. is amusing: the transmitted text, he says, is 'almost impossible ("not by wild beasts, as you might expect from my description") ...'. However,

Powell's lexicon to Hdt. finds no difficulty in taking ἄνθρωποι here in the sense 'inhabitants', i.e. 'human beings'. See above, pp. 35 f.

καί τι καὶ Χαλκιδικὸν ἔνι βραχύ, τὸ δὲ πλεῖστον Πελασγικόν, τῶν καὶ Λῆμνόν ποτε καὶ Ἀθήνας Τυρσηνῶν οἰκησάντων, καὶ Βισαλτικὸν καὶ Κρηστωνικὸν καὶ Ἠδῶνες: 'A few of them are from Euboian Chalkis, but most are either Pelasgians (descended from the Tyrrhenians who once inhabited Lemnos and Athens) or else Bisaltians, Krestonians, or Hedonians'. For the 'elusive Pelasgians' (J. Boardman, *CAH* iii². 1 (1982), 773) see W. Albright, *CAH* ii² (1975), 512–13, tentatively accepting an identification with the Philistines [?].

Pelasgians are said to occupy Lemnos at Hdt. v. 26, but the Tyrrhenian, i.e. Etruscan, presence on Lemnos is (see above, p. 36) Th.'s own contribution (though Hdt. i. 57. 1 connects Pelasgians and Tyrrhenians and Krestonians). Modern philology supports Th. over the Etruscan–Lemnian connection, by detecting Etruscan features in a fifth-cent. stele from Lemnos. See H. Rix, 'Eine morphosyntaktische Übereinstimmung zwischen Etruskisch und Lemnisch: die Datierungsformel', in *Studien zur Sprachwissenschaft und Kulturkunde: Gedenkschrift für W. Brandenstein* (Innsbruck, 1968), 213–22; J. Heurgon, 'À propos de l'inscription "tyrrhénienne" de Lemnos', *CRAI* 1980, 578–600; J. Penney, *CAH* iv². 725. See also P. Stadter (ed.), *Plutarch On the Virtue of Women* (1966), 66, and on Th.'s spelling Τυρσ- see D. Briquel, *Les Tyrrhènes: peuple des tours: Denys d'Halicarnasse et l'autochthonie des Étrusques* (Rome, 1993), 198.

For the Bisaltians see Hammond, *HM* i. 192–3; for Krestonia 179–82; for the Hedonians 427–8 and above, 323 f.

κατὰ δὲ μικρὰ πολίσματα οἰκοῦσιν: 'They all live in small citadels'. For *polismata*, see 52. 3 n. The present passage would also suit the other meaning (other than 'fortified place') which *polisma* is said to bear in Th., namely a non-Greek town. But Th. here seems to have his eye on the physical aspect.

5. Σάνη δὲ καὶ Δῖον ἀντέστη: 'but Sane and Dion held out'. See 3 n. above for the significance of Sane's resistance. We are not told *why* they held out; contrast the detail with which Akanthos' submission is described. For Th., Brasidas' story is a success story.

110. 1. εὐθὺς στρατεύει ἐπὶ Τορώνην τὴν Χαλκιδικήν: 'so he promptly made an expedition against Torone in Chalkidike'. For Torone near the tip of the middle Chalkidic prong (i.e. Sithonia, never named by Th., contrast Hdt. vii. 122) see Zahrnt, 247–51, and in Lauffer (ed.), *Griechenland*, 689, and my entry in *OCD*³ (there is no entry in the *Princeton Encyclopaedia*); B. D. Meritt, 'Scione, Mende and Torone', *AJA*

27 (1923), 447–60, is still also worth consulting. (Gomme for some reason does not mention Meritt's article here, referring only to Leake for Torone; but oddly enough, he does mention it when he comes to Mende, in his n. on 121. 2). The site of Torone (esp. the fort and promontory which Th. calls the Lekythos or 'oil-bottle', see 113. 2) has been excavated since 1975 by a Greek and Australian team led by A. Cambitoglou. At the time of writing, publication of A. Cambitoglou and J. K. Papadopoulos, *Torone* i (the first volume of the final publication) is awaited. Meanwhile, the fullest reports (also by Cambitoglou and Papadopoulos) are to be found in the Australian journal *Mediterranean Archaeology*, as follow: 1 (1988), 180–217 (though called 'Excavations at Torone, 1986: a Preliminary Report', this covers earlier years as well, and is thus specially important. Note esp. 214, architectural fragments which may derive from the temple of Athena on the Lekythos promontory, including a potsherd inscribed with the first three letters of the name Athena, see below 116. 2 n. on ἔστι γάρ etc.); 3 (1990), 93–142 (covers 1988; note esp. 139: buildings found under a late- or post-Byzantine tower are 'probably' those referred to in Th.'s account of the battle between the Athenians and Spartans in 424 BC, see below, chs. 115–16 and nn. See also 138: a digamma carved on a rock has a non-Euboian letter-form, which may suggest the early settlers were not Euboians after all); 4 (1991), 147–71 (covers 1989); 7 (1994), 141–63 (covers 1990). It may also be helpful to give references here to the briefer summaries which have appeared over the past twenty years in *Arch. Reps.*: 1975–6, 21; 1976–7, 43–4; 1979–80, 43; 1982–3, 42–4; 1985–6, 58–60; 1986–7, 37–8 (with a good photograph of the promontory at 38, fig. 59); 1988–9, 74; 1989–90, 52; 1990–1, 50–1; 1992–3, 55 (very brief); 1993–4, 52, underwater ashlar blocks 'may mean that Th.'s description of the site needs reassessment'. See also *Ergon* 1993, 61–5.

ἄνδρες ὀλίγοι: 'a few of the inhabitants'. *Only* a few? That is, were the rest basically pro-Athenian? We can hardly say. Gomme speculates on the attitudes of the Toronaians, and notes that the city's tribute had risen from 6 to 12 to 15 talents in the period up to 425 (see also Zahrnt, 249, who thinks this tribute increase was displeasing to the propertied classes at Torone and inclined them to Brasidas); but Th. refuses to adduce this kind of consideration (cp. 108. 3 n.), and we should not assume we know better, i.e. insist that tribute levels were relevant.

καὶ ἀφικόμενος νυκτὸς ἔτι καὶ περὶ ὄρθρον: 'He arrived when it was still night, in fact just about daybreak'. Connor (127 and n. 43) sees hereabouts a general parallelism with Pylos, which was also a dawn operation (31. 1). Cp. generally Babut.

πρὸς τὸ Διοσκόρειον: 'the temple of the Dioskouroi'. The second of the two such temples in Th., see iii. 75. 3 for Corcyra. For the Dioskouroi or Dioscuri, Castor and Polydeukes (Pollux), see above all the multi-author article at *LIMC* iii. 1 (1986), 567–635 (with plates in iii. 2). In established Greek mythology they were sons of Leda, and so brothers of Clytemnestra and Helen, and are also called the 'Tyndaridai'; but it is thought that they go back very far indeed, to the original Indo-European family (five gods and goddesses) which arrived in Greece at the begin-ning of the second millennium BC: J. Bremmer, *Greek Religion* (Oxford, 1994), 98. The cult of the Dioskouroi is widespread through the Greek world (cp. Macaulay in *The Battle of Lake Regillus*: 'By many names men call us, In many lands we dwell: | Well Samothracia knows us; Cyrene knows us well. | Our house in gay Tarentum is hung each morn with flowers: | High o'er the masts of Syracuse Our marble portal towers . . .'). But though Macaulay was right about the importance of their cult at Tarentum (R. Parker, *CAH Plates to vols. v and vi* (1994), no. 157), their mythological home was Sparta ('. . . But by the proud Eurotas is our dear native home; | And for the right we come to fight Before the ranks of Rome'): see Malkin, *Myth and Territory*, 62–4. It would therefore be strange if the Spartan Brasidas did not now sacrifice, however briefly, to the Dioskouroi (cp. his sacrifice at v. 10. 2), but typically Th. does not say so (any more than he mentions that Brasidas sacrificed *after* success at Lekythos, 116. 2 n. on καὶ ἔτυχε etc., though considering what else Brasidas did there to honour the epiphany by Athena, it would be aston-ishing if he did not).

For the possible site of the Dioskoureion see Meritt, *AJA* 1923, 457–8, blocks at 500 m. distance from Torone. This would mean that Th.'s stade here is about 167 metres, because he gives the distance as 3 stades. This is a reasonable figure for a Thucydidean stade. (Bauslaugh, *JHS* 1979 (8. 6 n. on ἡ γὰρ νῆσος etc.), 6, in his good study of Th.'s stades, gives the true distance from Torone to the temple as 'unknown', but this is because he does not take account of Meritt's suggestion. Nor, as we have seen, did Gomme, who was not interested in the temple of the Dioskouroi anyway.)

2. ἦρχε δὲ αὐτῶν Λυσίστρατος Ὀλύνθιος: 'commanded by Lysi-stratos of Olynthos'. An informant of Th.? We cannot here applaud Th. for accuracy or verisimilitude (contrast the Chalkidian proxenos Strophakos of Thessaly, 78. 1) because no other Lysistratos appears in the prosopo-graphy in M. Gude, *A History of Olynthus* (Baltimore, 1933), at 47. The name is not unusual. (For a Macedonian, see *SEG* i. 268, cf. xxvii. 247: Amphipolis.) The Olynthian origin of Lysistratos is significant evidence for tension between Olynthos and Torone: Zahrnt, 59, 249. In the fifth cen-tury, at least, wealthy and important Torone stayed aloof from the

Chalkidic League, centred on Olynthos. See v. 3. 4 n. on καὶ τῶν Τορωναίων etc. and my article on Torone in *OCD*³. How this factor affected internal politics at Torone is anybody's guess.

καὶ τὴν κατὰ Καναστραῖον πυλίδα διῄρουν: 'they then began to break down the postern-gate towards the promontory of Kanastraion'. Kanastraion was the tip of Pallene, the Chalkidic promontory to the west of Sithonia (Torone was situated on Sithonia): Hdt. vii. 123. 1; Ps.-Skylax 66; Strabo vii frgs. 25 and 32. A πυλίς (diminutive of πύλη, 'gate') is a postern, and a postern or postern-gate is defined by *OED* as 'a back door, a private door, any door or gate distinct from the main entrance'. (A wicket-gate, i.e. a small gate cut out of a larger one, such as can still be found in the medieval cathedrals and universities of Europe, is an ἐκτομάς, cp. Aen. Tact. xxiv. 5.) The Spartans were not expected from the seaward side, so Brasidas gained surprise. As Gomme remarks, it is surprising ('inexcusable' is his word) that with Brasidas in Chalkidike there were gaps in the walls, as there must have been for Lysistratos and his group to enter. See also 112. 2 n.

111. 1. ἑκατὸν δὲ πελταστὰς προπέμπει: 'sent forward a hundred peltasts'. For peltasts see 28. 4 n. on καὶ πελταστάς. With the use of the light-armed here, Connor, 127 and n. 43, compares 32. 4 (Pylos).
2. καὶ αἱ κατὰ τὴν ἀγορὰν πύλαι τοῦ μοχλοῦ διακοπέντος ἀνεῴγοντο: 'and cut down the bar of the gates near the agora [marketplace] and opened them'. That is, the main city gates, on the side of the town away from the sea. With the action here described Classen/Steup and Gomme compare ii. 4. 4 (Plataia). Such bars were important enough to have a section to themselves in Aen. Tact., see xix and xx, including (unusually for him) advice for attackers, not defenders: pour oil on the cross-bar as you are sawing through it, so as to save time and prevent noise (xix. 1).

ὅπως κατὰ νώτου καὶ ἀμφοτέρωθεν: 'in their rear and thus on both sides at once'. Babut (422) compares 32. 3 (Sphakteria), πανταχόθεν κυκλωμένοις, 'completely surrounded'.

τὸ σημεῖόν τε τοῦ πυρός: 'the fire-signal'. For such signals generally see D. Whitehead, *Aineias Tacticus: How to Survive under Siege* (Oxford, 1990), 113.

τοὺς λοιποὺς ἤδη τῶν πελταστῶν ἐσεδέχοντο: 'and brought in the rest of the peltasts'. The addition of the prefix ἐς-, 'in', is not redundant from the point of view of sense, but it also breaks up what would otherwise have been a hexameter, at the end of a vigorous narrative para. which gallops along in lively dactyls (ἐγγιγνομένου . . . θαυμάζοντες κατὰ μικρόν . . . τῆς πόλεως . . . τῶν ἐσεληλυθότων . . . ἥ τε πυλίς . . . αἱ

κατὰ τὴν ἀγορὰν ... μὲν κατὰ τὴν πυλίδα ... ὅπως κατὰ νώτου καὶ
ἀμφοτέρωθεν ... εἰδότας ἐξαπίνης ... τοῦ πυρός ... καὶ διὰ τῶν κατὰ
τὴν ἀγοράν ...).

112. 1. καὶ ἔκπληξιν πολλὴν τοῖς ἐν τῇ πόλει παρασχόντας: 'and
striking terror into the inhabitants'. Again, Connor, 127 and n. 43, and
Babut, 422, compare 34. 2 (Pylos), but the word ἔκπληξις is something
of a favourite with Th.

**2. οἱ δὲ κατὰ δοκοὺς τετραγώνους, αἳ ἔτυχον τῷ τείχει πεπτω-
κότι καὶ οἰκοδομουμένῳ πρὸς λίθων ἀνολκὴν προσκείμεναι:**
'others went in at a place where the wall had fallen down and was being
repaired: they climbed up [these words are inserted to make the
presumed meaning clear] by some planks which had been placed against
it for pulling up stones'. Again (cp. 110. 2 n. on καὶ τήν etc.) the
Toronaians had been careless, in a way which would later be warned
against by Aen. Tact. viii. 3, cp. xxi (referring to another work of his, on
military preparations): city-defenders should render useless anything
lying around in the countryside.

3. ὁ δὲ ἄλλος ὅμιλος κατὰ πάντα ὁμοίως ἐσκεδάννυντο: 'the rest
of his soldiers overran the town'. The subject [lit. 'the rest of the crowd']
is surely Brasidas' troops, though LSJ⁹ under σκεδάννυμι ('scatter, dis-
perse ...; of a routed army') seem to take it to refer to the defeated
Toronaians.

**113. 2. οἱ δὲ Ἀθηναῖοι (ἔτυχον γὰρ ἐν τῇ ἀγορᾷ ὁπλῖται καθεύ-
δοντες ὡς πεντήκοντα):** 'The Athenians had a force of hoplites, of
whom about fifty were sleeping in the agora'. I have adopted Gomme's
rendering of this (it does not mean 'there happened to be fifty hoplites
sleeping', etc.).

ἐς τὴν Λήκυθον τὸ φρούριον: 'a fort called Lekythos'. For this place,
evidently both a fort and the promontory on which it was situated, see
110. 1 n. on εὐθύς etc., with *Med. Arch.* 1988, 180. Gomme rightly notes
that here, as elsewhere in the Torone narrative, the detail is introduced
as it is relevant or as the actors became aware of it; but the present
passage is not quite like, say, 104 (Thasos) or 108 (Amphipolis), postponed detail about a place already mentioned.

114. 1. κήρυγμα ἐποιήσατο: 'made a proclamation'. For the noun
κήρυγμα see 105. 2 n. on κήρυγμα ...

τὸν βουλόμενον ἐπὶ τὰ ἑαυτοῦ ἐξελθόντα ἀδεῶς πολιτεύειν:
'anyone who wanted could come out and go home; they could exercise
their citizen rights without fear'. Another moderate proclamation by
Brasidas, cp. 105. 2 with nn. See pp. 56 f.

For the terms cp. Diod. xviii. 56. 4.

2. ὁ δὲ ἐσπείσατο δύο: 'he granted them two days'. More moderation, cp. Babut, 432: the Athenians had asked for a truce of only one day.

**3. καὶ ξύλλογον τῶν Τορωναίων ποιήσας ἔλεξε τοῖς ἐν τῇ
Ἀκάνθῳ παραπλήσια:** 'He then called a meeting of the Toronaians
and addressed them in much the same terms which he had used at
Akanthos'. The word ξύλλογος here means an ordinary gathering, not a
military meeting, i.e. it has the sense it has at ii. 59. 3, not that argued for
by Christensen and Hansen for ii. 22. 1, see n. there, and add a ref. to
R. M. Errington, 'ἐκκλησία κυρία at Athens', *Chiron*, 24 (1994), 135-60,
at 138 n. 7, rejecting the Christensen–Hansen view.

On the present passage see Introduction, pp. 86-9 and introductory n.
to 85-7: Akanthos is the basic blueprint (cp. 120. 3 for Skione), and this
does suggest, as does 108. 5, that Brasidas did indeed make the pledges
he is represented as making to the Akanthians. What follows in 114. 3-5
is not a précis of 85-7, but adds the arguments particularly appropriate
to the new situation, cp. the new material at 120. 3. At Torone, where
the citizens were split, he needs to include a section (114.3) urging no
reprisals. And the proclamation of 114. 1 calls for a special section (para.
4). But there are parallels to Akanthos even in what Th. does report: the
claim to have come to Akanthos in a spirit of impartiality (86. 4) has
some resemblance to 114. 3, see n. there; *eunoia*, good will towards
Sparta, features at both 87. 3 (see n. there for the trans.) and para. 4
below; most important, Akanthos-style 'Zwangsbefreiung', 'freeing by
force' (cp. introductory n. to 85-7) recurs at Torone: para. 5 below, the
Toronaians must expect to be punished for acts of disloyalty.

This is a new Thucydidean technique for handling speeches: he gives
in full the basic Brasidan patter (Akanthos) and thereafter adds the
variants. (It is true that at ii. 13. 9, after the detailed financial exposé
which fills much of the ch., we were told that Pericles added his more
usual optimistic arguments designed to show that the Athenians would
win through; this is not, however, an explicit reference to i. 140-4,
optimistic though some of that speech was. Contrast the explicit refs. to
Akanthos here and in iv. 120.) With this new technique one might compare modern campaign speeches, see e.g. T. H. White, *The Making of the
President 1960* (New York, 1961), 291, 367: the candidate has a basic
speech which he or she adapts to the particular place of delivery.
Brasidas, unlike other Thucydidean speakers but like a modern political
candidate with a programme, travels around a good deal within a short
space of narrative. Hence the new technique for reporting him. In the
language of iii. 82. 2, the essential phenomenon varies in form, τοῖς
εἴδεσι διηλλαγμένα, according to circumstances.

ἀφῖχθαι γὰρ οὐ διαφθερῶν οὔτε πόλιν οὔτε ἰδιώτην οὐδένα: 'because he had not come to destroy either the city or any individuals'. Implicit here is a claim to impartiality, cp. 86. 4 at Akanthos, with preceding n. above.

4. τὸ δὲ κήρυγμα ποιήσασθαι: 'he had made the proclamation'. See 1 n. on κήρυγμα.

τούτου ἕνεκα: 'he had made it because'. That is, Steup and Gomme are right (against Warner and Jowett, whose trans., 'in this spirit', I have changed) to take this to refer forwards, rather than backwards to para. 3 with its claim about not destroying city or individuals.

πολλῷ μᾶλλον . . . εὔνους ἂν σφίσι γενέσθαι: 'feel even more good will towards them'. See 87. 4 and n.; also 3 n. above on καὶ ξύλλογον etc. for the motif of *eunoia* towards Sparta.

5. ὅτι ἂν ἁμαρτάνωσιν αἰτίαν ἕξοντας: 'and expect henceforward to be punished for acts of disloyalty'. As at Akanthos, the mailed fist, see 87. 2 and n. on γῆν δέ etc., and introductory n. to 85–7; also 3 n. above on καὶ ξύλλογον etc. (There is a slight difference in that here at Torone the threat relates to hypothetical future acts of disloyalty by citizens of a place already in his power; at Akanthos the threat was designed to bring the place into his power.)

115. 2. μηχανῆς μελλούσης προσάξεσθαι αὐτοῖς ἀπὸ τῶν ἐναντίων, ἀφ' ἧς πῦρ ἐνήσειν διενοοῦντο ἐς τὰ ξύλινα παραφράγματα: 'the Spartans were bringing up a siege engine, from which they planned to throw fire on the wooden breastwork'. For such engines see 100. 4 n.

3. τὸ δὲ οἴκημα λαβὸν μεῖζον ἄχθος ἐξαπίνης κατερράγη καὶ ψόφου πολλοῦ γενομένου: 'The weight was too heavy for the building and it suddenly collapsed with a loud crash'. Babut (423), always alert to parallels between the Pylos/Sphakteria and Chalkidike narratives, compares the accidental fire at Sphakteria, see 34. 2 n. on καὶ ὁ κονιορτός etc. The parallel is not specially striking, but Babut is no doubt right to remind us that Th. is fully aware, throughout his narrative, of the workings of the unexpected. For archaeological evidence bearing on this episode see above 110. 1 n. on εὐθύς etc., citing *Med. Arch.* 1990, 139.

116. 2. (ἔστι γὰρ ἐν τῇ Ληκύθῳ Ἀθηνᾶς ἱερόν . . .: 'There was [lit. 'is'] a temple of Athena in Lekythos'. For the discovery on Lekythos of a potsherd (amphora fragment), inscribed with the first three letters of the name 'Athena', see *Med. Arch.* 1988, 214; *Arch. Reps.* 1990–1, 50–1; for a photograph of the potsherd see the *Med. Arch.* publication or *Ergon* 1986, plate 30, or *BCH* 111 (1987), 548 plate 52. The inscription is *SEG*

xxxvii no. 589: Ἀθη[νᾶ or -νᾶς. (Or, I suppose, Ἀθη[νᾶι.) For architectural fragments of what in view of the sherd seems overwhelmingly
likely to be the temple see *Arch. Reps.* 1988–9, 74, cp., for other archaeological refs., 110. 1 n. on εὐθὺς etc.

... καὶ ἔτυχε κηρύξας, ὅτε ἔμελλε προσβαλεῖν, τῷ ἐπιβάντι
πρώτῳ τοῦ τείχους τριάκοντα μνᾶς ἀργυρίου δώσειν): 'and
when Brasidas was about to storm the place he had made a proclamation that the first man to scale the wall should receive thirty minae'.
Note the small narrative dislocation: Brasidas' promise must in fact
antedate the collapse of the tower recorded in ch. 115.

For the reward see Pritchett, *GSW* ii (1974), 277 n. 6, in the course of
a discussion of ἀριστεῖα (rewards for bravery, neuter plural) in Greek
warfare. Pritchett adduces the present passage in refutation of Adcock's
view (*Greek and Macedonian Art of War*, 4–5) that *aristeia* were foreign to
phalanx warfare. See also Pritchett 289 n. 55, conceding that the amount
of the proposed reward (3000 drachmae or half a talent) was 'remarkably
large' (Gomme), but resisting attempts, with which Gomme appears to
sympathize, to emend it. (Lewis, *Towards a Historian's Text*, 130, thought
'thirty' should perhaps be emended to 'three', τριάκοντα to τρεῖς, by
analogy with viii. 29. 2, see my n. there.) As Pritchett says, 'the fact that
this is the only case where Th. refers to an award bespeaks an exceptional prize. The assignment involved unusual peril and merited unusual
recompense.' Pritchett gives examples from other sources, e.g. Diod. xi.
76. 2, where 600 men are each given a mina after a battle, and xiv. 53. 4,
where the first man up a wall is given 100 minae. (Both these are from
Sicilian warfare. We are not told that any promise was made in advance,
and that does seem to distinguish the present passage of Th. from the
others cited in this n.) The more usual reward for valour was a panoply
or suit of armour and weapons (Isoc. xvi. 29), though Timoleon got a
house (Plut. *Tim.* 36. 4). Hdt. ix. 80–1 does not specify the nature of the
awards after Plataia, other than those to Pausanias the commander, but
is sure they were given. To Pritchett's examples add Arr. *Anab.* ii. 18. 4,
financial rewards given by Alexander for work of outstanding merit,
ἀρετή, on the mole built by the Macedonians in connection with the
siege of Tyre.

νομίσας ἄλλῳ τινὶ τρόπῳ ἢ ἀνθρωπείῳ τὴν ἅλωσιν γενέσθαι,
τάς τε τριάκοντα μνᾶς τῇ θεῷ ἀπέδωκεν ἐς τὸ ἱερὸν καὶ τὴν
Λήκυθον καθελὼν καὶ ἀνασκευάσας τέμενος ἀνῆκεν ἅπαν: 'But
now he decided that the capture had been brought about by some more
than human power, so he gave the thirty minae to the goddess for the
temple. He then pulled down Lekythos, cleared the ground, and turned
the whole place into a sacred precinct'. A very interesting passage; here

as elsewhere (see iv. 121. 1 n. on καὶ τὸν Βρασίδαν etc. discussing προσήρχοντο, and v. 11. 1 nn.) Brasidas prompts Th. to make some (for him) uncharacteristically full remarks of a religious sort. See above, Introduction, p. 49. This incident is, in fact, a sort of epiphany, or divine manifestation: see Pritchett, *GSW* iii (1979), 26, in the course of a section on military epiphanies. As Pritchett says, Brasidas believed Athena had intervened in the siege (the beliefs of Th. himself remain inscrutable). This does not necessarily mean some actual vision of the goddess. See also Pritchett, 330–1 (adducing the present passage to show that many strategoi were genuinely pious men) and 187, discussing sacrifices after battles: Th. does not specifically mention one here, but says that Brasidas consecrated the whole cape to Athena. If Pritchett means that Brasidas probably sacrificed to Athena as well as everything else he did, I agree (cp. above 110. 1 n. on πρὸς τὸ Διοσκόρειον).

For such epiphanies see also W. Speyer, 'Die Hilfe und Epiphanie einer Gottheit, eines Heros, eines Heiligen in der Schlacht', in E. Dassmann and K. Suso Frank (eds.), *Pietas: Festschrift für B. Kotting* = *Jhrb. f. Ant. u. Christ. Ergänzbd.* 8 (1980) (Münster, Westfalen, 1980), 55–77; for epiphanies generally see R. Lane Fox, *Pagans and Christians* (London, 1986), 102–23, and A. Henrichs, *OCD*[3], entry under 'epiphany'.

For such precincts, τεμένη, as Th. mentions here, see I. Malkin, *OCD*[3] entry under 'temenos'. Cambitoglou and Papadopoulos, *Med. Arch.* 1988, 214, note that (despite the welcome confirmation of the temple's existence provided by the Ath- potsherd, for which see above, n. on ἔστι γάρ etc.) nevertheless 'the lack of better preserved Classical architectural remains' of the temple may be the result of Brasidas' action in dedicating the ground after dismantling the fortifications.

Note that Th. might perfectly well have used the noun κήρυγμα here (cp. 105. 2 n.), in which case the present passage would no doubt feature in modern discussions of that word, in which there is no particular magic.

117–119. *One-Year truce between Athens and Sparta*

For this truce, whose main object was to enable more lasting terms to be settled (117. 1, 118. 13, v. 15. 2), see J. Steup, *Thukydideische Studien* (Freiburg i. B. and Tübingen, 1881), 1, 1–28, and above all A. Kirchhoff, *Thukydides und sein Urkundenmaterial* (Berlin, 1895), 3–27, hereafter Kirchhoff; Gomme's general discussion at 606–7; and C. Meyer, *Die Urkunden im Geschichtswerk des Thukydides*[2] (Munich, 1970), hereafter C. Meyer, *Urkunden*; but on the first (1955) and not very different edn. of this book, barely signalled by Gomme in an addendum (734) where he called it a 'good general discussion', see A. Andrewes's severely critical review, *JHS* 77 (1957), 328. See also a discussion not for some reason mentioned by Gomme, namely U. v. Wilamowitz-Moellendorff, 'Der Waffenstillstand von 423 v. Chr.', *Kl. Schr.* iii (Berlin, 1969), 362–79, originally in *S.B. Berlin* 1915, 607–22; I cite as 'Wilamowitz', and by the pages of the reprint.

Kirchhoff's discussion is as admirable now as when Gomme (596) praised it forty years ago, and I have followed a number of Kirchhoff's suggestions without always discussing them, e.g. where they have already been adopted in the OCT. But on one main point raised by Kirchhoff, Gomme was surely right. Kirchhoff believed, on the grounds that the narrative seems ignorant of the detailed stipulations and clauses of the truce, that Th. visited the Metroon and saw the archival text of the truce (and of the Peace of Nikias, v. 18) only after 404. (See Kirchhoff, 22, on the need for access to the Athenian state archives in the Metroon, 'Zugang zum Attischen Staatsarchive im Metroon'.) But Th. died, Kirchhoff thinks, before he had time to adjust his narrative to the newly incorporated material. Gomme retorted by appealing to the 'apparent capriciousness' in Th.'s choice of events worth narrating. Gomme went on to stress 'apparent', and books like Connor's *Thucydides* have taught us to be wary of regarding anything in Th. as 'capricious', but it is right that Kirchhoff's position demands too high a level of consistency and uniformity of texture from Th. We can add one or two particular arguments against Kirchhoff; see detailed nn. on 118 below, e.g. 4 n. on τοὺς μὲν ἐν τῷ Κορυφασίῳ, 5 n., and 119. 3 n. Wilamowitz also thought the whole truce text an insertion. But his detailed discussion is valuable.

Something should be said about the 'archives' mentioned above, on the assumption (but see below) that Th. had access to the Athenian copy only. Gomme's addendum at 734 referred to A. R. W. Harrison in *JHS* 75 (1955), 26–35. But much work has been done on this topic in recent years, and the result has been to make still less probable Kirchhoff's implied assumption that the truce document (a very temporary and provisional affair) was sitting in an orderly archive in the Metroon for twenty years waiting for Th. to come along and transcribe it. See above all R. Thomas, *Oral Tradition and Written Record in Classical Athens* (Cambridge, 1989), 34–94, e.g. 47: 'document-mindedness' a feature of the fourth century more than of the fifth. She holds (90) that historians used documents infrequently if at all: 'Thucydides cited contemporary documents only in book v [this is an obvious slip for 'books iv and v', not to mention book viii], probably realizing that the exact texts were necessary.' This is a very different picture from Kirchhoff, who thought that Th. managed to write his entire iv. 1–v. 24 narrative *without* the exact texts.

Finally, a word should be said about the exact location of the notional 'archive text' of the truce. Kirchhoff's talk of 'access' to the state archive has a whiff of the modern public records office or national archive, to which access may be granted—or (in the case of sensitive material) refused. But decrees concerning Athens' relations with other states were more usually put up 'on the Acropolis' i.e. for all to see: Thomas, 76. However, the truce text as transmitted by Th. contains nothing about publication at Athens, and so temporary a document would not, it may be thought, have been carved in stone and erected on the Acropolis. This is, however, not absolutely certain. Athenian motives for carving and erecting inscriptions were various and inscrutable, see R. Thomas, in A. K. Bowman and G. D. Woolf (eds.), *Literacy and Power in the Ancient World* (Cambridge, 1994), 33–50. The provisions about Delphi, 118. 1–2, were obviously a topic on which Athens felt strongly, perhaps strongly enough to give them maximum publicity; and they could have wanted their allies to know the provisions in para. 4 about Kythera, etc. If so, then it is just conceivable that whoever looked at the copy on Th.'s behalf, some time after 423 but not necessarily after any great interval, need only have walked up the Acropolis rather than gaining 'access' to an 'archive'. But I emphasize that I think it unlikely that the truce was carved in stone and displayed on the Acropolis.

But all this discussion of the Athenian copy may be beside the point: as Gomme (606) said, following Steup, the Athenian copy was not the only one; note 122. 1 for the copy taken to Chalkidike. Cp. Tod, i. 177 on no. 72, the alliance between Athens and Argos, etc.

For Babut, 424, this truce near the end of the book corresponds to that at ch. 16, near the beginning of the book: both register the marked superiority of one side (Athens at 16, Sparta now), while saving the face of the other [in ch. 16 the face-saving is not very prominent to my eye, though 118. 4 did leave Athens in possession of Pylos, Kythera, and Minoa]; after both treaties expire, a more decisive victory follows: Sphakteria; the defeat of the Athenians before Amphipolis.

As we saw at 15. 2 n. on σπονδάς etc. the truce at ch. 16 anticipates in a small but interesting and portentous way the most striking innovation of 118–19 (and, we must add, v. 18–19 and 23, the Peace of Nikias and the consequent alliance), namely the inclusion of documentary material in the narrative. But as we saw at 15. 2 n., the difference is (to quote Andrewes, *HCT* v. 365, there cited) the combination of (*a*) absolutely 'verbatim transcription' and (*b*) the fact that (unlike iv. 16) these verbatim documents contain material dealing with issues not alluded to in the narrative. (Andrewes instances 118. 2, the reference to 'those present', implying absentees; 118. 3, the issue of Delphic funds;

and 118. 4, Troizen. See nn. on those passages.) Once we have rejected, as we must, the Kirchhoff theory of wholesale interpolation, and the associated dogma that there was a stylistic law prohibiting ancient historians from including such documents (see for good remarks, Andrewes, *HCT* v. 374 f., with modern refs.), we are left with the problem, *why* did Th. include these documents? Andrewes's general view (see introductory n. to 102–8) was that the quality of the narrative had begun to deteriorate towards the end of the Ten Years War, partly because Th. was now in exile. Andrewes's discussion of the truce treaty in the context of incompleteness leads one to suppose that he thought the documents (and under this head we must include v. 18–19 and 23) would eventually have disappeared when Th. gave the narrative the final polish; and at *HCT* v. 383 Andrewes makes this belief explicit. There he says the choice is between belief that Th. was deliberately adopting a new method, and belief that 'the full verbatim documents might in the final version have been replaced by shorter summaries'. He adds that 'the latter appears to me very much more likely'. (On this view the documents were left where they are *either* by Th. himself *or* by an editor who found two versions, the full text and a brief summary, and opted for the text.) Perhaps the 'incompleteness' theory is right. But despite the occasional difficulties of reconciling treaty texts and narrative, the 'innovation' view seems to me preferable to the 'incompleteness' view. (i) Not only is the Melian Dialogue at the end of v an innovation; there is also the long exchange in indirect speech as early as iv. 97. 2–99, see introductory n. there. And iv. 16 with the 425 truce terms is innovative, as we have seen, though we may readily concede that its inclusion is explicable in a way that 118 is not. It may have attracted Th. that there was an almost literal concreteness about a truce, treaty, or alliance text about to be recorded on stone. By the late 420s both sides were reaching near-exhaustion; but what stood in the way was a reluctance to be cheated territorially or in other ways. The discussions must have been extremely concrete. (In the run-up to the Peace of Nikias, v. 17. 2, see n. there, may mask the preliminary work of two ten-man commissions whose existence is almost totally concealed by Th.) Both in 423 and 421, the treaties give the hard nuggets of diplomacy in a form which could certainly have been more elegantly and more briefly paraphrased. But some concreteness and immediacy would have been forfeited—and some clarity too. By clarity I do not mean that the texts make everything instantly clear; on the contrary they raise (as we shall see) abundant problems of their own. But Th. may have decided that, for instance, by not giving the terms of the Thirty Years Peace in book i, some big issues were left obscure (as they certainly were). (ii) Another reason for including the 421 treaty and alliance (but not the 423 truce) is their emphasis on oaths, cp. D. T. Steiner, *The Tyrant's Writ: Myths and Images of Writing in Ancient Greece* (Princeton, 1994), 66–7, for a good discussion of the importance, from the ritual aspect, of the oaths in Thucydidean and other treaties, and of the connection between oath-taking and the act of inscription. At v. 56. 3 we are told that Alcibiades persuaded the Athenians to write under their inscribed copy that 'the Spartans have not kept their oaths'. Th. wishes to rub in the inefficacy of these oaths. (iii) Structurally, too, the inclusion of documents can be justified: see Connor, *Thucydides*, 146, 'they help mark out the stages in an otherwise complex and amorphous diplomatic narrative. Their placement emphasizes the major stages in the rapidly changing patterns of Greek diplomacy ... The armistice in 4. 118–19 follows swiftly after the setbacks at Delium and Amphipolis. As a sequel to the battle of Amphipolis two documents, the treaty and the alliance between Athens and Sparta, proclaim co-operation between the two rivals.' Connor rightly stresses (145) that Th.'s narrative is not homogeneous: it allows him for instance to include the Homeric Hymn at iii. 104 and the language of the oracle at v. 16. (iv) Finally there is the possibility, as Philip Stadter suggests to me in a letter (8 March 1995), that Th. 'feels that [treaty texts] tell us as much as any speech about the thinking of the two parties'. See above, Introduction, pp. 113–19.

The personal names attached to the truce of 423, and to the treaty and the alliance of 421, have been felt peculiarly problematic (for a strong statement that Th.'s hypothetical final version would not have repeated them, see Andrewes, *HCT* v. 374). On this see Introduction, pp. 107, 118 f.

Ch. 117, which introduces the truce, is the fifth and penultimate of the six excursuses on morale which punctuate iv–v. 24, see Introduction, above, p. 109. Like the sixth and last (v. 14 ff.) which prepares us for the Peace of Nikias, it pays attention to both sides. See 117. 2 n. at end for a specific verbal parallel, and note that both passages have ἐδέδισαν ('they were afraid'), iv. 117. 1 and v. 14. 2.

117. 1. νομίσαντες Ἀθηναῖοι μὲν οὐκ ἂν ἔτι τὸν Βρασίδαν σφῶν προσαποστῆσαι οὐδὲν πρὶν παρασκευάσαιντο καθ᾽ ἡσυχίαν, καὶ ἅμα, εἰ καλῶς σφίσιν ἔχοι, καὶ ξυμβῆναι τὰ πλείω: 'The Athenians hoped to prevent Brasidas from winning over any more of their allies for the moment; the interval would give them time to make preparations at leisure. If things went well they could make a proper peace later'. The Athenian hope was not fulfilled, see chs. 120 ff. for Brasidas' successes at Skione and Mende. Gomme, following de Romilly, *Thucydides and Athenian Imperialism* (Oxford, 1963), 58 ff. (57–62 of the original French edn.), has a good n. on the monolithic way Th. here speaks of 'the Athenians' as if there were no differences of opinion between them. One way of looking at this sort of phenomenon is to call it deliberate simplification (Gomme, 593, 614; cp. also de Romilly, 'Cities' (1. 1 n. on αὐτῶν ἐπαγαγομένων), 10, who says, discussing the related attitude to Athens of the subject cities, that Th. simplifies on this topic 'even more than elsewhere'). Another related way is to see it with Lewis as selectivity, see 27. 5 n. on ἐχθρὸς ὢν etc. In any case, the largeness of the generalization means it is a spectacular piece of inferred motivation, cp., for an even more spectacular one, ii. 8. 4 n. on ἡ δὲ εὔνοια etc. Th. doubtless had his Athenian informants, about whose motives he could speak confidently; but how many of them were there? **καὶ τοὺς ἄνδρας σφίσιν ἀποδόντας:** 'return the Sphakteria prisoners'. The Greek just has 'return the men'.

2. τοὺς γὰρ δὴ ἄνδρας περὶ πλέονος ἐποιοῦντο κομίσασθαι, ὡς ἔτι Βρασίδας ηὐτύχει· καὶ ἔμελλον ἐπὶ μεῖζον χωρήσαντος αὐτοῦ καὶ ἀντίπαλα καταστήσαντος τῶν μὲν στέρεσθαι, τοῖς δ' ἐκ τοῦ ἴσου ἀμυνόμενοι κινδυνεύσειν καὶ κρατήσειν: 'Their main object was to recover their prisoners while the good fortune of Brasidas lasted; if he made still more spectacular gains or brought about something like parity, the Spartans would have to acquiesce in the loss of their prisoners, and fight an equal struggle with their remaining forces, with all the risks of such a struggle as well as its possibilities of success'. This is the best trans. I can manage of the transmitted text of an extremely difficult, almost certainly corrupt and certainly much disputed sentence. (For instance, Steup in the latest edn. of Classen/Steup disagrees with Classen's views as expounded in his second edn., where Classen followed Herbst; see further below. Gomme has a long n. in which he considers and seems to approve a number of emendations.) The best attempt to make sense of the text as transmitted is in the Budé edn., which I have followed for its rendering of the last few words ('pour mener, avec les autres, une lutte à égalité, avec ses risques et ses succès').

But there are serious problems. As the Budé edn. says (*note complémentaire*, p. 184), 'the chief difficulty remains ... in the fact that the principal idea is contained in the element introduced by μέν ...' [that is, in the words 'the Spartans would have to acquiesce in the loss of their prisoners'].

The Budé bravely deals with what some editors (Steup; Gomme) have felt to be the worst difficulty, which lies in the first sentence. (The Budé translates τοὺς γὰρ ... ὡς ἔτι Βρασίδας ηὐτύχει as 'leur plus grand souci était ces hommes, qu'ils voulaient recouvrer tant que la fortune souriait à Brasidas'; for this the old emendation ἕως, i.e. '*while* Brasidas' success lasted', might help; this goes back to the scholiast on Ar. *Peace* 479, though Lewis, *Towards a Historian's Text*, 88, noted that the Ravenna ms. of the scholiast actually has ἕως ὅτε not ἕως ὅτ' ὁ as the OCT apparatus says. Lewis anyway preferred ὡς to ἕως as the more difficult reading.) But the literal meaning of the Greek is 'they attached more importance to getting their men back, because of the continuing success of Brasidas', and this is an odd thing to say. Probably (Steup; Gomme) half a dozen or so words have dropped out, and the original sense was 'they attached more importance to getting their men back [than to entertaining extravagant hopes] because of the continuing success of Brasidas'.

The final words of the whole lemma (κινδυνεύσειν καὶ κρατήσειν) are also very hard, and have attracted many emendations, e.g. Wilamowitz (375) was one of those who wanted to delete καὶ κρατήσειν. Though I have followed the Budé trans., it is worth re-stating the view of Classen (ultimately Herbst) according to which the 'reflections about motivation are given from the *Athenian* [not the Spartan] standpoint, but with the words of the author [Th.] himself'. Here is what I take to be Classen's trans., with the added thought in square brackets: 'Their main object was to recover their prisoners while Brasidas' good luck lasted at its present level; [the Athenians were worried that] if he made still more gains and restored something like parity, the Spartans would be tempted to acquiesce in the loss of the prisoners taken on Sphakteria, fight an equal struggle with their remaining forces and win'. On any view the focalization of the ch. is complex. Much of it is concerned with what Th. thought not only about what A thought but about what A thought B thought, and so on: the Spartans in para. 1 realized what the Athenians were afraid of, and now, on Classen's view, we are told what the Athenians thought the Spartans were thinking. The Spartans are presumably the subjects of para. 3, so if the Athenians are tacitly understood to be the focalizers of the present sentence, they disappear again very soon.

The word ηὐτύχει looks forward to the final excursus on morale, v. 16. 1, also about Brasidas.

Maurer, *Interpolation*, 125–6, defends the existing text.

3. γίγνεται οὖν ἐκεχειρία αὐτοῖς τε καὶ τοῖς ξυμμάχοις ἥδε: 'So they made a truce for themselves and their allies on the following terms'. What follows, to the end of 118. 10, is a document drawn up as if by Spartan representatives at Athens (Kirchhoff, 5), hence the 'you and we' (ὑμεῖς καὶ ἡμεῖς) of 118. 3. It begins very abruptly, and Gomme (p. 598) thought that some introductory formula has dropped out at the beginning of 118. 1, perhaps 'This is what the Spartans and their allies have decided'.

118. 1. περὶ μὲν τοῦ ἱεροῦ καὶ τοῦ μαντείου τοῦ Ἀπόλλωνος τοῦ Πυθίου δοκεῖ ἡμῖν χρῆσθαι τὸν βουλόμενον ἀδόλως καὶ ἀδεῶς κατὰ τοὺς πατρίους νόμους: 'We have agreed that anyone who wishes may use the temple and oracle of Pythian Apollo, without fraud or fear, according to ancestral custom'. The reference is to Delphi. Religion comes first, as in the Peace of Nikias, v. 18. 2 (though see n. there on περὶ μὲν τῶν ἱερῶν τῶν κοινῶν etc. for the different and wider scope of the religious provisions of 421). This order of topics may do more than simply reflect normal Greek priorities: the 423 stipulation perhaps indicates particular Athenian vexation on the subject of Delphi (and as we shall see at v. 18. 2 n., the stipulations there are also likely to have been the result of Athenian pressure). The present passage should not be taken as evidence that there had been any formal restriction on access to or attendance at the Panhellenic sanctuaries and festivals. I have discussed this point in vol. i of this commentary (see pp. 390 and 521-2) and at *HSCP* 94 (1992), 191-3, where I conclude that, despite the absence of evidence for any formal or actual ban, it may have been hazardous for Athenians to visit Delphi during the Ten Years War. Gomme speaks of 'exclusion, in practice if not in theory, of Athenians and their allies from the shrine owing to Peloponnesian domination'. This is much better than those like Grote who assumed outright exclusion, but I think that, though the nuance is hard to get right, both 'exclusion in practice' and 'domination' are too strong here (see for instance 42. 1 n. on καὶ Ἄνδριοι for epigraphic evidence about Athens' allies the Andrians at Delphi at about this period; ML 74, the Delphi and Olympia dedication of the Messenians from Naupaktos, Athenian allies, may also be relevant, see *HSCP* 1992, 193; and note, with Parker *CRUX*, 325 n. 98, Paus. x. 11. 6, Athenian dedication at Delphi, apparently in 429). The Spartans never dominated Delphi as the Aitolians were to do in the third century. The Spartans' efforts to increase their amphictionic representation by the foundation in 426 of Herakleia in Trachis show that their influence at Delphi was not as great as they would have liked. For these efforts see my n. on iii. 92, also *HSCP* 1992, 189-90; the idea argued for in those places is now judged convincing by Malkin, *Myth and Territory*, 233 n. 65.

Parker, 'Greek States and Greek Oracles', *CRUX*, 298-326, at 325-6, notes that here and in the Peace of Nikias (v. 18. 2), the guarantee of free access illustrates general belief in (though not the fact of) Apollo's basic fairness.

Ar. *Birds* 188-9, rightly cited by Gomme, shows that it was from the Boiotians that trouble for Delphi-bound pilgrims could be expected; see

Sommerstein's good n. and G. Zeilhofer, *Sparta, Delphoi und die Amphiktyonen im 5. Jahrhundert vor Christus* (Diss. Erlangen, 1959), 67 f. Hence the Boiotian aspect to the specific statement in para. 2 below.

For 'ancestral custom' in this sort of context cp. ML 73 (inscription about the bringing of first-fruits to Eleusis), where offerings are to be brought 'in accordance with ancestral tradition' (κατὰ τὰ πάτρια) and in accordance with a Delphic oracle, lines 4–5. 'Ancestral custom' features twice in para. 3, which is also about Delphi.

2. καὶ τοῖς ξυμμάχοις τοῖς παροῦσιν: 'and their allies here present'. We do not know who all the absentees were (they presumably rejected the truce). It is only from the need for special attention to Delphi, see next n., that we know that the Boiotians and Phokians were not included. For those Spartan allies present see 119. 2: Corinth, Sikyon, Megara, Epidauros. As Gomme saw, these places controlled the Isthmus of Corinth, i.e. they could make possible or impossible an invasion of Attica; and they had fleets. The absentees were less important.

See introductory n. to 117–19: the preceding narrative has not prepared us for the mention of 'those present' with its implication of absentees; nor does the subsequent narrative settle the question.

Βοιωτοὺς δὲ καὶ Φωκέας πείσειν φασὶν ἐς δύναμιν προσκηρυκευόμενοι: 'and we will send heralds to the Boiotians and Phokians, and do our best to persuade them to agree also'. That is, the Boiotians and Phokians had not agreed to the truce; between them they controlled the whole territory between Athens and Delphi, hence this stipulation. The present passage is not evidence that the Boiotians and Phokians were not members of the Peloponnesian League: so rightly de Ste. Croix, *OPW* 337, against Larsen, *GFS* 133 and n. 4.

Kirchhoff (25) makes the general point that Th.'s narrative does not betray knowledge of the detailed clauses of the truce; for instance (cp. Gomme, 606, summarizing Kirchhoff) 'it is only from the document that we learn that the Boeotians, Lokrians and Phokians take no part in the negotiations at all'. But I agree with Gomme that Kirchhoff's argument is not generally compelling, for instance (Gomme, 607), 'most of his surprising omissions about its [the truce's] details, for example, the absence of so many enemy states from the final confirmation are just those which he should have had no difficulty in learning, from his usual sources of information'. See also, for a particular argument against Kirchhoff, below 4 n. on τοὺς μὲν ἐν τῷ Κορυφασίῳ.

3. περὶ δὲ τῶν χρημάτων τῶν τοῦ θεοῦ ἐπιμέλεσθαι ὅπως τοὺς ἀδικοῦντας ἐξευρήσομεν, ὀρθῶς καὶ δικαίως τοῖς πατρίοις νόμοις χρώμενοι καὶ ὑμεῖς καὶ ἡμεῖς καὶ τῶν ἄλλων οἱ βουλόμενοι: 'As for the treasures of the god, both you and we and any others who wish, according to our and their ancestral customs, will see to it that the culprits are detected, using all fair and just means'. This surely refers to some particular incident, so by implication Wilamowitz (363) and others. At i. 121. 3 the Corinthians had suggested using the treasures of Delphi and Olympia, and it is not impossible that some were indeed used (see my n. on that passage). Privateering like that mentioned at ii. 69. 1 (see n. there on καὶ τὸ ληστικόν) cost money, some of which could have come from the 'fixed sums of money' at ii. 7. 2, see n. there on καὶ ἀργύριον ῥητόν. But some Delphic money may have been diverted. See also Kallet-Marx, 177–8, citing Parke–Wormell's suggestion that Delphic money might have been used to hire Arkadian mercenaries in 426, cp. iii. 101. 1 and 109. 2. If any of this had happened, it would, as Gomme says, be diplomatic for all parties to speak merely of criminals who must be caught.

Again (cp. 2 n.) see introductory n. to 117–19.

4. Λακεδαιμονίοις καὶ τοῖς ἄλλοις ξυμμάχοις: 'The Spartans and their allies'. Strictly, 'the Spartans and their *other* allies', but the reference can hardly be to a group distinct from 'the allies here present', though the reference here may be larger, i.e. it notionally includes absent allies as well.

τοὺς μὲν ἐν τῷ Κορυφασίῳ: 'the Athenians at Koryphasion' [lit. 'those at K.']. That is, at Pylos, for which 'Koryphasion' was the Spartan name. See 3. 2 and n. on καλοῦσι δέ etc.: Th.'s explanatory words there presuppose the mentions, here and at the equally documentary v. 18. 7, of Koryphasion. This is a small piece of evidence tending against Kirchhoff's view that the documents were later insertions.

ἐντὸς τῆς Βουφράδος καὶ τοῦ Τομέως μένοντας: 'shall stay between Bouphras and Tomeus'. Not certainly identified. Pritchett (*EGH* 157–8) now rejects the old identification (Gomme, 599) of Bouphras with Voidokoilia, the small bay north of Pylos; the identification was partly based on the similarity of name (Bouphras = 'Ox-ford', and Voidokoilia has a similar meaning). He now suggests that Tomeus or Mt. Tomaios was a rock on the Profitis Elias hill to the north of Voidokoilia, while Bouphras was a real ford across a river (the river Karia?) which flowed through the area now occupied by the lagoon called Divari. Thus by the 423 truce the Athenians 'were restricted to Mount Tomeus in the north and the region of the Karia River in the east. They retained their fortifications and a long stretch of the sandbar for their ships, i.e. what they had seized at the outset. With the sandbar as an anchorage, their ships controlled Sphakteria, which in any case was uninhabited' (Pritchett, 158).

τοὺς δὲ ἐν Κυθήροις μὴ ἐπιμισγομένους ἐς τὴν ξυμμαχίαν, μήτε

ἡμᾶς πρὸς αὐτοὺς μήτε αὐτοὺς πρὸς ἡμᾶς: 'They shall remain at Kythera, but shall not communicate with the Peloponnesian League, neither we with them nor they with us'. See chs. 53–4; as Gomme remarks, Athens could presumably go on collecting the 4-talent tribute mentioned at 57. 4.

τοὺς δ' ἐν Νισαίᾳ καὶ Μινῴᾳ μὴ ὑπερβαίνοντας τὴν ὁδὸν τὴν ἀπὸ τῶν πυλῶν τῶν παρὰ τοῦ Νίσου ἐπὶ τὸ Ποσειδώνιον, ἀπὸ δὲ τοῦ Ποσειδωνίου εὐθὺς ἐπὶ τὴν γέφυραν τὴν ἐς Μινῴαν (μηδὲ Μεγαρέας καὶ τοὺς ξυμμάχους ὑπερβαίνειν τὴν ὁδὸν ταύτην): 'The Athenians who are in Nisaia and Minoa shall not cross the road which leads from the gates of the shrine of Nisus to the temple of Poseidon, and goes straight from the temple of Poseidon to the bridge leading to Minoa; nor shall the Megarians and their allies cross this road'. See 69. 4 n. on καὶ τὴν Νίσαιαν etc. for the Athenian acquisition of Nisaia; the present arrangement is provisional but the Peace of Nikias confirmed Athenian possession of it, see v. 17. 2 n. on ἀνταπαιτούντων etc. See iii. 51 for Minoa, with n. there; for the bridge in particular see iii. 51. 3.

Nisus, one of the four sons of Pandion, was given the Megarid at the time of the mythical division of Attica, when Lykos got NE Attica, Pallas the Paralia (ii. 55. 1 n.), and Aigeus the Pedias or plain-region and the city of Athens: Soph. *TrGF* 24; *FGrHist* 329 F 2. See E. Kearns, *The Heroes of Attica* (*BICS* supp. 57, 1989), 115–17 and 188; G. Berger-Doer, *LIMC* vi. 1 (1992), 304–5, entry under 'Lykos II'. Nisus was probably a Megarian hero originally, but was later grafted onto the family of Pandion so as to support Athenian claims to the Megarid. This is clearly provocative, as Kearns says; the alternative version made Megara a Boiotian foundation, see 72. 1 n.

καὶ τὴν νῆσον, ἥνπερ ἔλαβον οἱ Ἀθηναῖοι, ἔχοντας: 'the Athenians shall keep the island which they have taken'. Steup and Gomme find it hard to believe that this is Minoa, the island most recently mentioned. Steup therefore emended so as to produce a reference to Atalante, cp. ii. 32 for its fortification by Athens. For this we need to emend to τὴν νῆσον, ἥνπερ ἔλαβον οἱ Ἀθηναῖοι ⟨ἐπὶ Λόκροις, τοὺς Ἀθηναίους⟩ ἔχοντας, because Atalante off Lokris is described as being ἐπὶ Λόκροις at ii. 32 and iii. 89. 3. This is daring, especially since Atalante is plainly referred to by its name at v. 18. 7; and equally daring is Gomme's attempt to produce a reference to Methana (cp. again v. 18. 7); this too involves emendation, mainly, but not only, the insertion of the word 'Methana'. Neither of these suggestions is compelling (for one thing, Methana is not strictly an island but a peninsula) and we should revert to

Minoa. At the end of his n., Gomme relented and said that if the island *is* Minoa we should delete καί before τὴν νῆσον.

καὶ τὰ ἐν Τροιζῆνι, ὅσαπερ νῦν ἔχουσι: 'what they now hold near Troizen'. Troizen had been an Athenian ally before 446, but was one of the territorial concessions made in the Thirty Years Peace, see 115. 1 n. Kleon then persuaded the Athenians to demand it back in 425, see 21. 3 n. on ἐλθόντων etc. This demand came to nothing and we next find Athens raiding Troizenian territory later in the summer of 425, see 45. 2 n. on ἐλῄστευον etc. Noting that Troizen was not represented in the truce negotiations of the present ch. (see 119. 2), Gomme suggested that Troizen may have objected to the present clause as giving Athens too much.

καθ' ἃ ξυνέθεντο πρὸς Ἀθηναίους: 'according to the agreement concluded between the Athenians and Troizenians'. No such agreement is mentioned by Th. (see introductory n. to 117–19, citing Andrewes); an obvious context would be 45. 2, see nn. there on ἐλῄστευον etc. and Ἁλιάδα. This is one of the omissions in Th.'s narrative which led Kirchhoff (26) to argue that Th. cannot have known of the separate Troizen treaty when he wrote the main narrative of 46–116. But the omission is not all that large or serious.

5. καὶ τῇ θαλάσσῃ χρωμένους, ὅσα ἂν κατὰ τὴν ἑαυτῶν καὶ κατὰ τὴν ξυμμαχίαν, Λακεδαιμονίους καὶ τοὺς ξυμμάχους πλεῖν μὴ μακρᾷ νηί, ἄλλῳ δὲ κωπήρει πλοίῳ, ἐς πεντακόσια [τάλαντα] ἄγοντι μέτρα: 'As for the use of the sea, the Spartans and their allies may sail along their own coasts and the coasts of the Peloponnesian League, not in warships, but in any other rowing boat whose tonnage does not exceed five hundred measures' [lit. 'not in a long boat, but . . .']. Nothing is said about ordinary sailing boats and ships, which could probably be used, see Gomme (also Wallinga, see below), who must also be right that the restriction can hardly have affected allies like Syracuse; it must affect only the Peloponnesian League proper. On the present passage see above all H. T. Wallinga, 'The Unit of Capacity for Ancient Ships', *Mnemosyne*, 17 (1964), 1–40, esp. 12–13, 22–3, and esp. Appendix II at 37–40 on 'The talents in Thukydides IV 118'; see also his *Ships and Sea-Power Before the Great Persian War* (Leiden, 1993), 25 n. 33. I follow Wallinga in deleting τάλαντα, 'talents'. Certainly we do not need μέτρα, 'measures', as well as 'talents'. Some earlier scholars (e.g. Wilamowitz, 366 n. 1) have argued for the deletion of 'measures'. But Wallinga argues that it is τάλαντα which should be deleted, so that the Greek merely contains a reference to measures, which (Wallinga argues) here simply means *amphorae*. Wallinga generally challenges the idea that the talent was the unit of capacity for ancient ships. (At 37 n. 1 Wallinga calls Gomme's n. on the present passage 'strangely muddled'. I think that Wallinga, if I have followed him correctly, has misunderstood Gomme's English at the relevant point. When Gomme says 'the ordinary merchant vessel could not be used, even as an auxiliary, in a battle unless supplied with oars', his word 'could' does not—as Wallinga wrongly assumes—refer to the restrictions in the present treaty, but to the ordinary conditions of naval warfare, i.e. Gomme is in effect saying 'was not as a matter of fact ordinarily used', etc. Wallinga agrees with Gomme that there was no ban on ordinary 'sailing vessels'.) Cp. also Dover's n. in *HCT* on the 'ten-thousand carriers' of vii. 25. 6.

'Long boats' or 'warships' are triremes, cp. Eupolis cited at 129. 2 n. on ὧν ἦσαν δέκα Χῖαι.

On the relevance of the present passage to viii. 56. 4 and the question of the restriction of a state's right to use its own coasts see Lewis, *Sparta and Persia*, 102 n. 74; cp. my n. on the book viii passage.

8. κατὰ τὰ πάτρια: 'according to ancestral custom'. See Ostwald, *Autonomia*, 4: in the roughly corresponding arbitration clause in the Peace of Nikias, this clause was replaced by something more realistic, see v. 18. 4 n. on δικαίῳ χρήσθων etc.

10. ἧπερ καὶ ὑμεῖς ἡμᾶς ἐκελεύετε: 'as you asked us'. I have adopted the suggestion of Kirchhoff (13), approved by Steup and Gomme, to read ἐκελεύετε (imperfect) for κελεύετε (present), although the emendation does not feature even in the apparatus criticus in the OCT. The Spartan delegates must have come with powers to treat; the Athenians cannot now be asking for those delegates to be given those powers at some future date.

αἱ δὲ σπονδαὶ ἐνιαυτὸν ἔσονται: 'This truce shall be for a year'. Cp. 117. 1; this is one of the few details contained in the truce which is also featured in the narrative, though the fact was so basic that it must have been generally known.

11. ἔδοξεν τῷ δήμῳ: 'The Athenian people passed the following decree'. What follows in paras. 11-14 is, with one main exception about to be discussed, in the regular form of an Athenian decree, with the name of the 'tribe or *phyle* in prytany' (i.e. that sub-division of the citizen body, in this case the tribe Akamantis, which in the persons of fifty of its members presided, for one tenth of the administrative year, over the Council of 500 or *boule* and over the Assembly); the name of the secretary; the name of the *epistates* or temporary president; the name of the proposer (Laches); the introductory formula invoking good luck.; and the contents of the decision.

The exception mentioned above concerns the Council of 500 or *boule*. The normal formula (though see Tod 114 line 2) is ἔδοξεν τῇ βουλῇ καὶ τῷ δήμῳ, 'it seemed good to the Council and the People' i.e. the *ekklesia* or Assembly. What has happened to the Council? Kirchhoff and Steup believe that Th. has correctly represented the position: the motion (it is said) had been duly considered by the Council some days earlier, i.e. it was not ἀπροβούλευτον and thus it was not unconstitutional (see *Ath. Pol.* 45. 4). On the Kirchhoff view, the formula transmitted by Th. ignores this stage because it was purely formal (Kirchhoff, 16, 'seine Bedeutung lediglich formale war'). Gomme was surely right to protest against this: 'the essence of a formula is that it makes clear that a resolution has been formally, that is constitutionally, passed'. Gomme also rejected the idea that Laches' motion was an amendment (for something like this idea see Wilamowitz, 367–8, arguing that the assembly rejected the proposal of the *boule*). Laches' was the 'principal motion'. Gomme therefore believed that we should read ἔδοξεν ⟨τῇ βουλῇ καὶ⟩ τῷ δήμῳ, that is, he believed the omission to be a purely scribal error. Perhaps. But the manuscript tradition is unanimous, and we should consider seriously whether the omission goes back to Th. himself. As we have seen (i. 139. 3 n. on ἅπαξ etc. and iii. 36. 5 n.) Th. is very coy about mentioning the *boule* at all. This is part of his general impatience with constitutional procedures and details. Did he, perhaps unconsciously, omit mention of the *boule* in the present decree?

(There is actually a second exception, which commentators have not stopped to notice, the omission of the annual eponymous archon or magistrate. The archon-date is more common in Athenian decrees after 421 (see E. S. Roberts and E. A. Gardner, *Introduction to Greek Epigraphy*, ii (Cambridge, 1903), 3, and Pritchett, *Mnemosyne*, 26 (1973), 384) though it does occasionally appear before then, see ML 63 and 64 of the 440s and 430s = Fornara 124 and 125, the alliances with Rhegion and Leontini; also ML 37 = Fornara 81, though the date of this is disputed, see *SEG* xxxix no. 1. But plenty of decrees earlier than 423, the date of the present passage, do not have the archon-date, see e.g. ML 31, 65, 68, 71 = Fornara 68, 128, 133, 139. The omission of this feature is therefore not abnormal. On Th.'s omission here see above, p. 118.)

Λάχης εἶπε: 'Laches moved that . . .'. For Laches see iii. 86. 1 n. At v. 43. 2 he is bracketed with Nikias as one of the authors of the Peace of Nikias, through whom the Spartans had negotiated. On the other hand he had been one of the commanders in Sicily from 427, and would be one of those at Mantinea, v. 61. 1—two aggressive campaigns. So Gomme was right that nothing can be inferred from the present passage about his general attitude to peace.

12. ἄρχειν δὲ τήνδε τὴν ἡμέραν, τετράδα ἐπὶ δέκα τοῦ Ἐλαφη-βολιῶνος μηνός: 'beginning from today, the fourteenth day of the month Elaphebolion'. At the end of March, on what Gomme confidently stated to be the day after the City Dionysia. But the timetable of the festival is not known for sure, and the present passage of Th. is one of the key pieces of evidence. It is not quite certain that the assembly could not have met to ratify the truce *during* the festival. See *DFA*³ 59 and n. 71, 64 (allowing the possibility that the ratification happened *during* the festival, since only legal and some other business was prohibited by the law of Euegoros), and 66 (concluding, after all, that the Dionysia of 423 was probably over by the 14th, which was chosen for the Assembly meeting precisely because the Dionysia was over and the Pandia, another festival, had not yet begun). Taking all the evidence, including Th., into account, the revisers of *DFA* believe that in the Peloponnesian War period the main part of the festival lasted from 10–13 Elaphebolion. The festival was shorter during the war; at other times it lasted up to and including the 14th.

But whether or not the Dionysia was actually over, we must surely, as Gomme said, allow a couple of days for the Peloponnesian delegates to confer with the *boule* before the festival began. If so, the delegates very likely attended the festival, and this would also be likely even if the ratification happened during the festival. Gomme noted that the plays they would have seen (Cratinus' *Pytine*, Aristophanes' *Clouds*, and Ameipsias' *Konnos*) 'had, for the time, less of politics in them than might have been expected'. This may be true, but the festival itself, especially the pre-play ceremonial, was a very assertive occasion at which the *polis* in its imperial and military aspects was on show in the most literal sense. Thus there was a display of the tribute, and those orphans of the war-dead who had recently come of age paraded in full armour (Isoc. viii. 82; Aischin. iii. 154, and other evidence cited at *DFA*³ 59). See S. Goldhill, 'The Great Dionysia and Civic Ideology', in J. Winkler and F. Zeitlin (eds.), *Nothing To Do With Dionysos?* (Princeton, 1990), 97–129; C. Sourvinou-Inwood, 'Something To Do With Athens', *RFP* 269–90, at 271–2. Gomme is right that the delegates' reactions to a Dionysia would have been interesting, but we should remember that they would be getting the full City Dionysia experience—food for thought, surely—not just the plays. (I do not mean to suggest that Gomme was ignorant of the features which more recent scholars have stressed, but he either did not think them worth mentioning specifically, or took it for granted that his readers knew what they were.)

Th. in his narrative or authorial person (122. 6) evidently knew the exact day on which the truce began. This does not quite prove that the relevant details of the truce treaty, i.e. the present passage and 119. 1, were available to him when he wrote the narrative, but it makes it likelier. (Gomme (607) seemed to regard this, I would say rightly, as an argument against Kirchhoff's general position, but was less sure at 612 when discussing 122. 6, see my n. there.)

14. ἐκκλησίαν δὲ ποιήσαντας τοὺς στρατηγοὺς καὶ τοὺς πρυ-τάνεις πρῶτον περὶ τῆς εἰρήνης ... βουλεύσασθαι Ἀθηναίους καθ' ὅτι ἂν ἐσίῃ ἡ πρεσβεία περὶ τῆς καταλύσεως τοῦ πολέμου: 'The generals and the prytaneis shall proceed to hold another assembly, first of all about the question of peace ... the people shall discuss any proposal the embassy may make about the ending of the war'. Kirchhoff established that there is a gap in the text, and he was followed by OCT and later editors: the *generals* cannot have been told to do the discussing. The words καθ' ὅτι ἂν ἐσίῃ are also very likely corrupt. Gomme's καθ' ὅτι ἂν εἴπῃ, 'whatever proposals the embassy may make' produces an attractive sense, but I am not sure how something so straightforward could have been corrupted into what we have. Whether the embassy envisaged is Spartan or Athenian is uncertain; Kirchhoff's conjecture εἶσιν (3rd person singular of εἶμι *ibo*, 'I shall go'), would mean 'shall decide how the embassy *shall go* ...'; this presupposes an Athenian embassy to Sparta. On the constitutional role of the *prytaneis* and generals see M. H. Hansen, *The Athenian Assembly* (Oxford, 1987), 24f.

119. 1. ταῦτα ξυνέθεντο Λακεδαιμόνιοι [καὶ ὤμοσαν] καὶ οἱ ξύμμαχοι: 'These were the terms agreed on by the Spartans and their allies'. The square-bracketed words ('and they swore an oath') were deleted by Kirchhoff, and the OCT follows. A manuscript variant ὡμολόγησαν (*sic*) gives a clue to how they came to be inserted; this means 'they agreed' and was (Kirchhoff (21) suggested) the explanatory marginal addition of an officious hand ('ich glaube die Worte καὶ ὡμολόγησαν für den erklärenden Zusatz eines Unberufenes').

Kirchhoff (18–19) was right to insist that both chs. 118 and 119 (not 118 only) be enclosed in inverted commas; ch. 119 is not yet Th.'s own words, which resume at 119. 3.

Kirchhoff (19) notes that the formula, recording that something has been carried out in the terms of the original motion, resembles e.g. ML 65 (Methone), lines 29–32, cp. 5–9. Gomme adds ML 69 (tribute re-assessment), line 58, and ML 87 (Selymbria), lines 28–31 (refs. up-dated).

μηνὸς ἐν Λακεδαίμονι Γεραστίου δωδεκάτῃ: 'on the twelfth day of the Spartan month Gerastios'. That is, the same day as the fourteenth of the Athenian month Elaphebolion. For the precise detail and its bearing on the question of Th.'s knowledge of the truce see 118. 12 n. on ἄρχειν δέ etc.

The Spartan month-name Gerastios is of interest. It must be related to

Geraistios, one of the cult titles for Poseidon (on whom see generally M. Jameson, *OCD*[3] entry under Poseidon). See Ziehen, 'Sparta: Kulte' *RE* iiiA (1928), 1502, and S. Wide, *Lakonische Kulte* (Leipzig, 1893), 32 and 43 n. 5. The title is derived from Geraistos on the southern tip of Euboia, where there was a temple of Poseidon Geraistios, see *Odyssey* iii. 178 (no note in S. West's comm.), and *IG* xii. 9. 44 line 14 + T. W. Jacobsen and P. M. Smith, 'Two Kimolian Dikast Decrees from Geraistos in Euboia', *Hesperia*, 37 (1968), 184–99, with J. and L. Robert, *RÉG* 1969, *Bull. Épig.* no. 447. According to Steph. Byz., entry under Tainaros, Geraistos was a brother of Tainaros and Kalauros; for Tainaron in southern Lakonia and the Poseidon temple there, see i. 128. 1 nn. This Lakonian connection via Tainaron means that the month-name, which we owe to Th.'s reporting of the truce, is an authentic detail.

The month-name Gerastios also occurs at Dorian Cos, *Syll.*[3] 1012 line 15 and *LSCG* 161 (*Syll.*[2] 940) line 4; also at Kalymnos, M. Segre, *Tituli Calymnii* (Bergamo, 1952) = *ASAA* 22–3 [NS 6–7] (1944–5), nos. 88 line 86; 89A lines 17 and 25; 89B lines 11–12; 93B line 5; for cult of Poseidon Gerastios at Cos see S. M. Sherwin-White, *Ancient Cos* (Göttingen, 1978), 167 n. 81 and 98. Geraistios (with an extra *iota*) was a month-name both at Troizen (Karystios, *FHG* iv. 359 = Ath. 639 B–C) and nearby Kalaureia, *Syll.*[3] 993, with n. 1 for a possible connection between these two places and Euboia.

2. Λακεδαιμονίων μὲν οἵδε· Ταῦρος Ἐχετιμίδα, Ἀθήναιος Περικλείδα, Φιλοχαρίδας Ἐρυξιλαΐδα: 'for Sparta, Tauros son of Echetimidas, Athenaios son of Perikleidas, Philocharidas son of Eryxilaidas'. The patronymics here and throughout the list of names, are remarkable; Gomme was surely right to think that they featured in the original list, i.e. are not Th.'s own carefully researched insertion. But in any case they conform to one of Th.'s categories for inclusion of patronymics, namely that they all (one assumes) held important offices of state: G. T. Griffith, *PCPhS* 187 (1961), 21–33, at 21.

The name Echetima (feminine name) occurs at Sparta's colonies Melos (*IG* xii. 3. 1133) and Thera (*IG* xii. 3. 888, cp. also 785: Ἐχετιμ-).

For the pro-Athenian family of Athenaios son of Perikleidas, see Ar. *Lys.* 1137 ff., with the commentaries of J. Henderson (1987) and Sommerstein: Perikleidas asked Athens for help against the helots in the 460s. (Cp. i. 45. 2 n. discussing Lakedaimonios son of Kimon, the Athenian mirror-image of Athenaios.) For Athenaios see further 122. 1, where he is sent with Aristonymos of Athens to announce the truce. For the name Athenaios in a pro-Athenian family outside Athens cp. the Thespian in *IG* i[3]. 23, with Lewis, *CAH* v[2]. 116 n. 74; cp. above, 76. 2 n.

Philocharidas recurs in the same capacity at the end of the Peace of

Nikias, v. 19. 2, and is sent with Leon and Endios on an embassy to Athens at v. 44. 3 because he and they were thought at Sparta to be likely to be acceptable to Athens. See n. there.

Κορινθίων δὲ Αἰνέας Ὠκύτου, Εὐφαμίδας Ἀριστωνύμου: 'for Corinth, Aineas son of Okytos, Euphamidas son of Aristonymos'. For the 'influential and anti-Athenian' Corinthian family of Aineas see Wilamowitz, *Kl. Schr.* iii. 371: he may be a grandson of Adeimantos son of Okytos, the Corinthian leader mentioned by Hdt. viii. 5, 59 etc.; this Adeimantos was father of the well-known Aristeus of Hdt. vii. 137 and Th. i. 60. 2, see my n. there. I suppose Wilamowitz assumes an Okytos II, son of Adeimantos, brother of Aristeus and father of Aineas. Apart from Hdt. and Th., the name Okytos is not attested in the Peloponnese.

'Aineas', Αἰνέας, is not a rare name. In Homer, the name Aeneias is normally Αἰνείας, i.e. with an extra *iota*, but is spelt in Th.'s way—Αἰνέας, two syllables—at *Iliad* 13. 541; the Corinthian delegate is in any case spelt Ἐνέας, Ἐννέας, 'Eneas', 'Enneas', in some of the manuscripts of Th., so we cannot be sure that we have exactly what Th. wrote or the correct form of the man's name. Some form of the Homeric Aineias surely lies behind it. Lewis, *Towards a Historian's Text*, 90, pointed out that the scholiast on Ar. *Knights* 794 has Αἰνείας. The question, whether to emend Th.'s names to more 'correct' forms, is tricky. He keeps Doric forms like Lich*as*, Epitad*as*, contrast Leonid*es* in Hdt. But this does not (cf. p. 105) mean we should regularize Boiotian and Thessalian names like those at iv. 76 and 78. See v. 18. 6 n.

For Euphamidas see ii. 33. 1, where he and other Corinthians restore the tyrant Euarchos to Astakos; he also attends and makes an intervention at a conference held at Mantinea, v. 55. 1 (probably the same person, though he is not there given his patronymic). See R. Stroud, 'Thucydides and Corinth', *Chiron*, 24 (1994), 267–304, at 267 (and 289, describing the Mantinea intervention as an 'inconsequential detail'; this is a slight exaggeration given the detailed diplomatic character of book v generally. Euphamidas' suggestion is after all taken up and might well have been remembered by those present). Stroud argues that such 'apparently trivial' (268) information needs a special explanation, in fact an explanation in terms of Th.'s close knowledge of and perhaps residence at Corinth during his exile. See above, pp. 21 f.

For the name Euphamidas at Corinth cp. J. H. Kent, *Corinth VIII.III: The Inscriptions 1926–1950* (Princeton, 1966), no. 366, a Latin inscription, after 44 BC: line 3 has EUPHAMI [dots under the E, the M, and the I], which 'seems to contain part of a proper name, possibly Euphami[das]'. If so, this would increase the probability that Th. got the name right, if that were considered doubtful. It is not however an uncommon name if we include variants; thus there are two Euboians and four Athenians called Euphemides, see Fraser and Matthews, *LGPN* i, and M. Osborne and S. Byrne, *LGPN* ii; and see *IG* iv. 1. 184 (Aigina): Euphamides.

Σικυωνίων δὲ Δαμότιμος Ναυκράτους, Ὀνάσιμος Μεγακλέους: 'for Sikyon, Damotimos son of Naukrates, Onasimos son of Megakles'. For the name Damotimos in the Peloponnese see *IG* iv. 801 (Troizen) line 1; v. 1. 1385 (Messenia) line 36; v. 2. 35 (Tegea in Arcadia) line 24. There is a Naukrates at *IG* iv. 734 (Hermione) line 6. Onesimos is a reasonably common name in the Peloponnese.

Μεγαρέων δὲ Νίκασος Κεκάλου: 'for Megara, Nikasos son of Kekalos'. Nikas- names are common, but the precise form Nikasos is very unusual (*LGPN*). Wilamowitz (371 and n. 2) thinks Kekalos corrupt (no Peloponnesian matches in *LGPN*); he notes an Argive Kaiklos (Καίκλος) at Ath. 13b.

Ἐπιδαυρίων δὲ Ἀμφίας Εὐπαΐδα: 'for Epidauros, Amphias son of Eupaiidas'. Again Wilamowitz thinks Eupaiidas' name is corrupt; he comments, 'Hude's suggestion Εὐπαλίδας [Eupalidas] is only one possibility among many'. The *LGPN* files for the Peloponnese suggest no obvious solution to the corruption, if it is one.

Ἀθηναίων δὲ οἱ στρατηγοὶ Νικόστρατος Διιτρέφους, Νικίας Νικηράτου, Αὐτοκλῆς Τολμαίου: 'and for Athens, the generals Nikostratos son of Diitrephes, Nikias son of Nikeratos, Autokles son of Tolmaios'. For all three men see 53. 1 n. on ἐστρατήγει etc. (they served together against Kythera). None of them (contrast Athenaios, 2 n. above) is sent round to announce the truce at 122. 1: Aristonymos is sent instead. Wilamowitz (370-1) said that the names were in the official Athenian tribal order, Nikostratos probably from I (Erechtheis, 'Nikostratos wird aus der Erechtheis gewesen sein'), Nikias from II (Aigeis), Autokles from X (Antiochis). But this is not right, because Nikostratos is now believed to be from the deme Skambonidai which is in Leontis (tribe IV). (See iii. 75. 1 n. and M. Osborne and S. Byrne, *LGPN* ii entry under Νικόστρατος no. 146, to which add Fornara, *CQ* 1970, 40). For Wilamowitz's point about tribal order to be right we would have to suppose that the order of the first two names has been transposed. In favour of this (it might be said), is the order at 53. 1: Nikias, Nikostratos, Autokles. That is, as things stand, Th.'s narrative preserves the correct tribal order, the truce text not! But the order at 53. 1 is more likely to be the result of putting the famous man (Nikias) first; I cannot believe Th. in his narrative bothered about the tribal order, which he disregards at e.g. ii. 23. 2 (V, VII, II). The official list of names of swearers to the Peace of Nikias is a different matter; Andrewes and Lewis, *JHS* 1957, showed that the sixth to fifteenth Athenian names at v. 19. 2 are in tribal order, see n. there.

3. περὶ τῶν μειζόνων σπονδῶν: 'about a more lasting peace'. See

118. 6 and 13–14, also v. 15. 2. The present passage is one of those in Th.'s own narrative which are consistent with the detail of the truce treaty; but it does not quite require knowledge of the treaty, because the negotiations about a more lasting peace were an independently ascertainable fact. See introductory n. to 117–19.

120–123. *Skione and Mende go over to Brasidas*

120. 1. περὶ δὲ τὰς ἡμέρας ταύτας αἷς ἐπήρχοντο: 'About the time when the delegates were going to and fro'. The meaning of the verb is disputed; it depends whether it derives from ἀρχ- ('begin'), or from ἐρχ- ('come'). If the first is right, the meaning is said (see e.g. C. Meyer, *Urkunden*, 15–17, following Steup) to be 'about the time of the [ritual beginning of the] pouring of libations'; editors compare e.g. *Odyssey* xviii. 418 f., οἰνοχόος μὲν ἐπαρξάσθω δεπάεσσιν, ὄφρα σπείσαντες κατακείομεν, 'let him begin by pouring wine into the cups, that we may pour a libation and recline'. But note that in Homer the 'libation' idea is made explicit by σπείσαντες. I think Gomme and Wilamowitz (*Kl. Schr.* iii. 374 n. 1) were right to reject Steup here. A search in TLG provides no support for the supposed sense of ἐπάρχεσθαι. (The word is certainly found epigraphically in ritual contexts, as a synonym for ἀπάρχεσθαι, 'offer first-fruits to'; see *LSCG Suppl.* no. 46 line 10, and the texts about Theogenes/Theagenes, no. 72 B lines 4–5, cp. A line 2 for ἀπάρχεσθαι; see R. Martin, *BCH* 64–5 (1940–1), 176, and J. Pouilloux, *BCH* 118 (1994), 199–206, at 202, also on Theagenes, on whom see further 121. 1 n. on καὶ τὸν Βρασίδαν etc., at end. On ἐπάρχεσθαι see also L. Robert, *Études épig.* 38–75. But none of this material supports the sense wanted by Steup and Meyer.) In any case, as Robert Parker points out to me, the supposed derivation from ἐπάρχομαι produces bad sense: 'pouring libations to ratify a treaty doesn't take *days*.'

If the second derivation is right, we have an unusual imperfect of ἐπέρχομαι, 'I come to, approach'. That is how the scholiast took it, by saying in explanation 'each side to one another', εἰς ἀλλήλους ἑκάτεροι. Hence Jowett's 'to and fro'. This is also not very good sense if we press it in detail, but the scholiast (in my view) shows roughly what sense we want.

But Gomme offered a third possibility. He thought that the word transmitted in our manuscripts is merely an explanatory gloss which has displaced a lost word for what the delegates were doing i.e. leaving Athens or Sparta to announce the truce. (I am not forgetting that Gomme (610), discussing 121. 1, referred to his Addendum, i.e. p. 734.

But here the only relevant thing is a citation of C. Meyer's then new book.)

The question whether the word derives from ἐπαρχ- or ἐπερχ- matters not just for itself but for a more interesting and important question: the meaning of the related word προσήρχοντο at 121. 1, where the two different possibilities (προσαρχ-, προσερχ-) produce startlingly different meanings. If the original word at 120. 1 (the present passage) has been lost, 120. 1 cannot help with 121. 1; see n. there. As I have said, I do not, in connection with 120. 1, accept the ἐπαρχ- theory: *either* we have an unusual imperfect *or* (the solution I slightly prefer) Gomme is right and the original word is irrecoverable. It therefore follows (and this will be crucial, hence the length of this n.) that the present passage does not support the theory that προσήρχοντο at 121. 1 derives from προσαρχ-. Note that if we accept the unusual imperfect at both 120 and 121 the unusualness of both would be reduced, but I cannot make use of this given that I follow Gomme as above.

Σκιώνη ἐν τῇ Παλλήνῃ πόλις ἀπέστη ἀπ' Ἀθηναίων πρὸς Βρασίδαν: 'Skione, a town of Pallene, revolted from the Athenians and joined Brasidas'. For Skione, on the south-west of Pallene, see Hdt. vii. 123 and viii. 128; Oberhummer, *RE* iiiA 529–30; Zahrnt, 234–6, referring to Meritt (110. 1 n.), who found traces of ancient settlement between Nea Skioni (which is north-east of the ancient Skione) and Hagios Niko- laos. (Gomme does not cite this suggestion, any more than he did Meritt's work at Torone, though he did cite him for Mende at 122. 2.) M. H. McAllister, *Princeton Encyclopaedia*, 845, has eight lines on Skioni (contrast Torone on the one hand (no entry at all) and Mende on the other (nearly a column, see below 123. 1 n.)). On Skione see also Zahrnt, in Lauffer (ed.), *Griechenland*, 623–4, and my entry in *OCD*[3], under 'Scione'.

From 450/49 to 447/6 Skione's tribute was amalgamated with that of Mende, cp. 123. 1 n. on Μένδη etc. On Skione's tribute thereafter, *ATL* iii. 64–5 (followed by Gomme, 608, Meiggs, *AE* 528–9, Zahrnt, 235 n. 355), made a suggestion which I have already discussed at i. 56–67, introductory n., giving other modern refs: *ATL* believe that the tributes of Skione and Potidaia in 434 were mixed up by the stonecutter, and that Skione paid its usual 6 talents in that year (not 15 talents as the entry appears to say; this is said to be Potidaia's tribute, increased from 6 talents, and a possible cause of its revolt). I was doubtful about this when I wrote the first vol. of this commentary but in the end accepted the *ATL* view. However I would now (cf. p. 6 above) reject it, even though it involves an inexplicably fluctuating record for Skione. As I said then, '... "inexplicable", in a patchily-documented period like the 430s, does not mean "impossible"', and I should have followed the implications of this.

After this, Skione paid 4 talents in 432–431, then 9 talents in 430–429–428. Gomme and others explain these changes in terms of Skione's loyalty at the time of the siege of Potidaia (the drop to 4 talents) and then the expenses of the siege of Potidaia (the increase to 9). This postulated treatment of Skione seems a little unfair and illogical (the same basic event is being used to explain both a fall and a rise). We should do better to admit ignorance. We do not know how much Skione was assessed for in 425. But (see 108. 3 n.) Th. does not encourage us to assume that the tribute increases of that year were relevant to Brasidas' successes.

φασὶ δὲ οἱ Σκιωναῖοι Πελληνῆς μὲν εἶναι ἐκ Πελοποννήσου, πλέοντας δ' ἀπὸ Τροίας σφῶν τοὺς πρώτους κατενεχθῆναι ἐς τὸ χωρίον τοῦτο τῷ χειμῶνι ᾧ ἐχρήσαντο Ἀχαιοί, καὶ αὐτοῦ οἰκῆσαι: 'The Skionaians, according to their own account, came originally from Pellene in the Peloponnese, but on their return from Troy their ancestors were blown off course to Skione by the storm which hit the Achaian fleet; and they settled there'. An uncharacteristic mention by Th. of one of the *nostoi* (returns from Troy) of which Odysseus' was the most famous. For the traditions about the Italian foundations of Diomedes (hero of *Iliad* v) see P. M. Fraser, at *Greek Historiography*, 183. In Th. the only other mention of foundations by people wandering after the fall of Troy is at vi. 2. 3, though the founders there are not returning Achaians, i.e. Greeks like Odysseus or Diomedes, but displaced Trojans like Aeneas.

The particular oikist or founder (see i. 4 n. on οἰκιστής) of Skione is known from an unexpected source, a *coin* of c.480 depicting the 'Achaian', i.e. Greek, hero Protesila(o)s: see Kraay, *ACGC* 134; G. F. Hill, *NC* 1926, 120; J. Babelon, 'Protésilas à Sioné', *RN* 13 (1951), 3; Zahrnt, 234; F. Cancioni, *LIMC* vii. 1 (1994), 554–5. This is confirmed, more or less, by *FGrHist* 26 Konon F 1 (xiii), who says that Protesilaos returned from the Trojan War with Priam's sister Aithilla as his prisoner, and landed between Skione and Mende. But there is a difficulty: Protesilaos, famously, was the first Greek to be killed in the Trojan War, and therefore did not return home, let alone found Skione *en route*. To the Konon problem at least, the solution (for which Hill cites a work I have not seen, U. Hoeffer, *Konon* (Greifswald, 1890), 62 f.) is that Protesilaos founded Skione after the *first* expedition against Troy, under Herakles and Telamon. (For a different approach see D. Boedeker, 'Protesilaus and the End of Herodotus' *Histories*', *CA* 7 (1988), 30–48, at 36 n. 22.) Cancioni in *LIMC* does not discuss this possibility, or the relation of Konon and the coins to the present passage of Th. In any case, Protesilaos the

'Achaian' (in the broad Homeric sense) is easily reconcilable with the story of a foundation from Achaia (in the narrow geographical sense of Achaia, i.e. the northern Peloponnese).

On Skione's link with Pellene in Achaia (in the narrow sense of Achaia) see Oberhummer, 529: the story may be based merely on the similarity of name Pallene/Pellene; but he cited C. Robert, 'Alkyoneus', *Hermes*, 19 (1884), 479, on the transfer of the Alkyoneus legend from the Isthmus to Pallene, as showing that the Achaia/Skione connection might have some basis. See also H. Lloyd-Jones, *Academic Papers* 2 (1990), 146.

Gomme (whose only comment on any of the above was to tell the reader to 'note the usual interest taken' in the colonial aspect) was troubled by φασὶ δέ, 'the Skionaians say', which Jowett renders 'according to their own account'. After all (Gomme points out), the male Skionaians were put to death in 421: v. 32. 1. I cannot feel that the difficulty is enormous (Gomme worried about whether Th. wrote the words in question before 421, and if after, whether he simply did not bother to change them; or whether Steup was right that Th. meant that he interrogated the surviving but enslaved Skionaian women and children). Surely the present tense is timeless; Th., who describes Skione's enthusiasm in these chapters so well, never touching on the menace round the corner from Kleon, could hardly write: 'the Skionaians say (or they used to before they were wiped out by Athens) ...'. See above, Introduction, p. 77.

2. ἐν κελητίῳ ... κέλητος: 'A small boat ... a boat'. For these terms see 9. 1 n. on ἐκ λῃστρικῆς etc.

3. περαιωθεὶς δὲ καὶ ξύλλογον ποιήσας τῶν Σκιωναίων ἔλεγεν ἅ τε ἐν τῇ Ἀκάνθῳ καὶ Τορώνῃ: 'He succeeded in crossing, and summoned a meeting of the Skionaians. He repeated what he had said at Akanthos and Torone'. For 'meeting', ξύλλογος, see 114. 3 n., and see the same n. for the way Th. refers us to the Akanthos speech when covering Brasidas at Torone, and to the Akanthos and Torone speeches when covering Brasidas at Skione; and the reasons for Th.'s handling. In the present passage the cross-reference does not mean 'what Brasidas said at Skione was the basic Akanthos speech plus the extra Torone material at 114' (which was appropriate to Torone only); it surely means that the basic Akanthos message was repeated *both* at Torone *and* again at Skione, with appropriately different new material each time. See above, Introduction, p. 88. Skione differs from both Akanthos (where he needed to win over the populace as a whole) and from Torone (where the place was already his when he made his speech, but where there had been a sharp political division); Skione by contrast had already come over of its own accord. The Skionaians therefore get congratulated.

There is strong irony in what follows, given the casual way Skione was abandoned by Sparta after the Peace of Nikias; see A. B. Bosworth, *JHS* 113 (1993), 37: the 'fine words' at Skione 'meant little'.

καὶ προσέτι φάσκων ἀξιωτάτους αὐτοὺς εἶναι ἐπαίνου: 'adding that they deserved the highest praise'. Are we meant to recall the (possibly formal) praise, ἔπαινος, awarded to Brasidas on his first appearance? See ii. 25. 2 n. on καὶ ἀπὸ τούτου etc.

ὑπὸ Ἀθηναίων Ποτείδαιαν ἐχόντων: 'for although the Athenians were holding Potidaia'. Potidaia has not featured since ii. 79, if we leave the problematic iii. 17 out of account.

καὶ ὄντες οὐδὲν ἄλλο ἢ νησιῶται αὐτεπάγγελτοι ἐχώρησαν πρὸς τὴν ἐλευθερίαν: 'so that ... Skione was ... as exposed as if it were an island, it had nevertheless chosen freedom without prompting' [lit. 'being nothing other than islanders']. Bosworth, *JHS* 113 (1993), 37 n. 37, notes that this 'fatally echoes and inverts the Athenian declaration at Melos (v. 97) and recalls Cleon's indictment of Mytilene' (iii. 39. 2).

For the connotations of 'islands'/'islanders' see my *OCD*3 entry under 'islands'; and J. Wilkins on *Eur. Heraclidae* 84 (islands contemptible—because vulnerable?). See further 121. 2 n. on ἡγούμενος etc. and 122. 5 n. on ὀργήν etc.

Brasidas' comparison of Skione to an island may, as Bosworth suggests in his Arrian commentary (Oxford, 1980), explain why Arrian, in his catalogue of Athenian frightfulness at *Anab.* i. 9. 5, inaccurately describes Skione as an island. This would suggest that on this point Arrian used Th. directly rather than going to Isoc. iv. 100. Cp. my paper on Th.'s reception, *JHS* 115 (1995), at 54 n. 29.

καὶ οὐκ ἀνέμειναν ἀτολμίᾳ ἀνάγκην σφίσι προσγενέσθαι περὶ τοῦ φανερῶς οἰκείου ἀγαθοῦ: 'They were not such cowards as to wait until they were forced to do what was obviously in their own interests'. As Gomme says, this is not very polite about Akanthos, Torone, etc. The idea 'forced' is expressed by the noun ἀνάγκη, on which see generally M. Ostwald's useful study, *ANAΓKH in Thucydides* (Atlanta, 1987), though he does not discuss the present passage specifically.

καὶ τἄλλα τιμήσειν: 'and pay them the highest honour'. The irony is intense. The strong final word τιμήσειν also closed (in the form τιμήσει) the Spartan speech exactly 100 chapters earlier, at 20. 4, see n. there. (More fuel for the Babut theory summarized above, Introduction pp. 108 f.?) At 20. 4 the word was used for a proposed deal by which Sparta would betray its allies ('the rest of Greece will pay both of us the greatest honour'). We are perhaps meant to reflect that neither of these Spartan rhetorical invocations of 'honour' is, in the end, honourable.

121. 1. καὶ οἱ μὲν Σκιωναῖοι ἐπήρθησάν τε τοῖς λόγοις: 'This speech raised the spirits of the Skionaians'. For the verb see 108. 3 n. on μάλιστα δὴ ἐπήρθησαν etc.

καὶ τὸν Βρασίδαν τά τ᾽ ἄλλα καλῶς ἐδέξαντο καὶ δημοσίᾳ μὲν χρυσῷ στεφάνῳ ἀνέδησαν ὡς ἐλευθεροῦντα τὴν Ἑλλάδα, ἰδίᾳ δὲ ἐταινίουν τε καὶ προσήρχοντο ὥσπερ ἀθλητῇ: 'They received Brasidas warmly, and in the name of the city they crowned him with a golden crown as the liberator of Greece; in addition, many people showed their personal admiration by putting ribbons round his head, and going up to greet him as if he were an athlete'. [The alternative translation, representing the orthodoxy among commentators, is 'they offered him first-fruits, as if he were an athlete'; see below. To sum up a long discussion, I reject this view because it requires us to postulate a verb προσάρχομαι for which there is no other evidence. It is better to suppose either that προσήρχοντο is an unusual imperfect of the common verb προσέρχομαι, 'I approach' or that the quotation—which is what it is—of Th. by Pollux (below) preserves the correct form of what Th. wrote, namely προσῆσαν, the usual imperfect of προσέρχομαι. The unexpected form of the imperfect has a close parallel at 120. 1, as transmitted, but that is itself problematic.]

There is a distinction here between public and private. The public honour, a golden crown, is attested at Athens in 410, ML 85 (honours to the assassins of Phrynichos) line 10, and frequently in the fourth century, see e.g. Tod 133 (sons of Dionysius of Syracuse), 152 (Androtion), etc. Remarkably, whole peoples could be so crowned, see *IG* ii². 456, the people of Kolophon. At Soph. *Antigone* 699 we find οὐχ ἥδε χρυσῆς ἀξία τιμῆς λαχεῖν; 'does she not deserve to receive an honour of gold?', but Jebb denies that this conceals a reference to golden crowns. There was plenty of gold in Thrace, see ii. 97. 3 n. on καὶ δῶρα etc. For crowns see M. Blech (80. 3–4 n.), and N. Dunbar, *Aristophanes: Birds* (Oxford, 1995), comm. on line 1274, and for the liberation motif see ii. 8. 4 n. and introductory n. to iv. 85–7.

Then there are the honours by private persons, which look like semicultic attention, see end of this n. ταινίαι are headbands or ribbons of a type found in exactly such contexts as the present, namely honours paid by individuals, see L. Robert, *OMS* vii (1990), 728–9 with n. 5, discussing the epigraphic and literary evidence both for the noun and for the verb ταινιόω, which is used here by Th. (add a ref. to Dover on Ar. *Frogs* 393, rendering the word 'ribbons'; see also Arr. *Anab.* vi. 13. 3, where, however, Brunt's 'wreaths' is slightly misleading, cp. below where I reject 'garlands' for the present passage). The ταινία is inferior to a crown and 'trop banal'; Robert notes that the ταινία tends to be, as here, a 'manifestation émanant des particuliers' i.e. conferred by private individuals. That suits Th.'s distinction exactly, cp. Blech (80. 3–4 n.), 113–14, on the present passage. The word does not quite mean 'garland' (as the Penguin and Jowett render it) any more than does στέμματα, see 133. 2 and n.

Brasidas (see above, p. 49) prompts Th. to unusual richness of religious description elsewhere (iv. 116, the Torone 'epiphany'; v. 11. 1, the cult honours Brasidas had enjoyed at Amphipolis, an item absolutely unique in Th., though what we learn about Hagnon there is more startling still). These crowns and ribbons are semi-religious, and very much *not* in Th.'s usual style; contrast Xen. *Hell.* v. 1. 3, the reception of Teleutias. It is therefore peculiarly frustrating that there should be a serious problem about the translation of one crucial word, προσήρχοντο. (The problem has to be taken in conjunction with ἐπήρχοντο at 120. 1, see n. there.) *What* did the Skionaians do to Brasidas 'like an athlete'? The issue is interesting partly because Th. is not often as informative on religious issues in general as he is here, partly because his handling of athletics in particular is so generally sparing, see iii. 8. 1 n. on ἦν δὲ Ὀλυμπιάς etc.; also v. 49–50 nn. And yet, although the present passage, despite its difficulties, is an early prose attestation of Greek attitudes to athletes and athletics, it does not feature in sourcebooks on Greek athletics, such as W. Sweet, *Sport and Recreation in Ancient Greece: A Sourcebook with Translations* (Oxford and New York, 1987), or S. Miller, *Arete: Greek Sports from Ancient Sources* (Oxford, 1991). But athletics were a pervasive feature of Greek *polis* life; cp. the casual simile used of Agesipolis at Xen. *Hell.* iv. 7. 5, 'like a pentathlete', for which word see *OCD*[3] entry under 'pentathlos'. (I assume in the above and in what follows that the words 'like an athlete', ὥσπερ ἀθλητῇ, were written by Th. himself. It is, however, conceivable that an ancient commentator or reader added 'like an athlete' as a marginal gloss on the verb, and this gloss was then incorporated into the text. This must however have happened—if it did happen, which I do not believe—before the time of Pollux, see below.)

The problem is to know whether the imperfect verb προσήρχοντο derives from προσέρχομαι, a common verb meaning to 'go to', 'approach', 'go up to', in which case we have an unusual imperfect (προσῆσαν is the expected form); or whether it derives from the extremely rare (I shall argue non-existent) verb προσάρχομαι, which is said to mean something like 'offer first-fruits to', a word which would be related to e.g. ἀπαρχή, for which see i. 96. 2 n. on ταμιεῖον etc., and to προκαταρχόμενοι at i. 25. 4, for which see n. there on οὔτε Κορινθίῳ etc. This is an exciting possibility and I would like to be able to accept it. But I shall conclude that the probabilities are against it, and that Herbst,

Bétant, Steup, Gomme, and C. Meyer (*Urkunden*, 15 f.) are all wrong to think of 'first-fruits'; and that the Penguin trans. of Warner is right to translate the word 'used to come up to him'. Jowett's 'congratulated him' is a fudge which leaves me unclear which verb he thought he was translating. Connor (136) adopts 'set out ritual offerings' in his text, though conceding at n. 72 that 'the verb is ambiguous and might be translated "crowded around"'; but he goes on 'but see C. Meyer', etc., that is, he does in the end believe in the derivation from προσάρχομαι. Robert Parker points out to me that προσάρχομαι might (on the assumption that the verb exists, and he thinks my arguments against it existing are very strong) mean something less specific than 'first-fruits': it could have 'one of a wide range of ritual "beginnings", not all of which would necessarily entail treating the recipient as semi-divine.'

The first piece of evidence is Pollux, iii. 152, entry under πένταθλος: Ξενοφῶν γὰρ εἴρηκεν ἐταινίουν τε καὶ προσήεσαν ὥσπερ ἀθλητῇ, 'Xenophon says they put ribbons round his head and went up to him like an athlete'. This is certainly a reference to the present passage of Th. i.e. the attribution to Xenophon is simply a mistake, a slip of memory—and/ or perhaps a confusion with Teleutias, see above? (Xen.'s *phrasing* (v. 1. 3) is quite different.) But the slightly different form of the verb, with the more normal imperfect προσήεσαν (this ought to be προσῆσαν), enables us to see that Pollux remembered Th. as having used the imperfect of the verb προσέρχομαι, 'they went up to him'. See Wilamowitz, *Kl. Schr.* iii. 374 n. 1. It is very tempting to suppose that Pollux's version of the verb counts as a textual variant; if Pollux had said 'Thucydides' not 'Xenophon' his προσῆσαν would certainly appear in modern critical apparatuses of Th. Robert Parker notes of ερχ- verbs that 'the ηρχ- forms certainly become commoner with time (W. Veitch, *Greek Verbs Irregular and Defective* (Oxford, 1886), 276–7), and biblical reminiscence [see below for Acts] could perhaps have encouraged substitution'.

So far the derivation from προσέρχομαι is ahead, and that would be especially true if we were to accept (as I fear I do not) that ἐπήρχοντο at 120. 1 (see n. there) is the correct reading and that it too derives from a verb in -ερχομαι. This might be held to support προσήρχοντο because it would reduce the force of the argument that the imperfect is unusual. (Two 'strange' imperfects in rapid succession are less strange than one. Note that Bétant, in his entry under ἐπάρχεσθαι, was prepared, in a bracket, to accept the alternative possibility that 120. 1 was from ἐπέρχομαι, i.e. he thought it might mean 'went to'. But for some reason his entry προσάρχεσθαι, '*auspicari*', allowed no alternative derivation from προσιέναι ('approach', the infinitive of προσέρχομαι) for 121. 1. This was inconsistent.)

But by now it should be clear where my argument is tending. I believe that at both 120 and 121 Th. wrote a word meaning 'they came'; at 120 I think the scholiast entitles us to say that the original word was an irrecoverable word meaning 'they went', i.e. they went to announce the truce; at 121. 1 Pollux entitles us to say that the original word was προσῇσαν, 'they went up to', which has been corrupted to προσήρχοντο.

But what of the alleged verb προσάρχομαι, and does προσήρχοντο derive from it? LSJ⁹ allow both possibilities. In the course of the long entry under προσέρχομαι ('come or go to', infinitive προσιέναι) they give the present passage of Th., but add an instruction to see the entry under προσάρχομαι. Under προσάρχομαι they give the meaning 'offer, present' and cite just two passages, Plato, *Theaetetus* 168c (to which we shall have to return in a moment) and the present passage of Th., on which they say 'so perh. τὸν Βρασίδαν . . . ἐπαινίουν τε καὶ προσήρχοντο ὥσπερ ἀθλητῇ *paid* him the *tributes* due to an athlete (for which see Plut. *Caes.* 30), Th. 4. 121'. (On this Plutarch passage see further below; it is not decisive.)

The Plato passage is clearly important; Steup appeals to it, as does C. Meyer. Unfortunately (as Steup shows awareness, though Meyer does not) it has itself been the subject of violent emendation by baffled editors, commentators and translators. It runs τῷ ἑταίρῳ σου εἰς βοήθειαν προσηρξάμην κατ᾽ ἐμὴν δύναμιν, σμικρὰ ἀπὸ σμικρῶν. The usual emendation is προσήρκεσα μὲν κατ᾽ ἐμὴν δύναμιν, 'I helped you as far as was in my power . . .' This is accepted by Lewis Campbell and by Jowett in his Plato trans.; J. McDowell in his Oxford edn. (1973) does not discuss the point and I am not clear from his trans. what reading he prefers.

At this point the search must be widened. Is the verb προσάρχομαι attested anywhere in Greek literature, apart from the disputed Plato and Th. passages? Searches in TLG, the computerized thesaurus, result in the answer 'No'. A search under προσαρχ- threw up no instances whatever. A search under προσήρξ- produced just one attestation: precisely the doubtful passage of Plato, *Theaetetus*, already discussed. A search under προσηρχ- produced fifteen attestations of either προσήρχετο or προσήρχοντο, including the present passage of Th. All of them simply and obviously mean 'he/they approached', i.e. they are from προσέρχομαι. Most of them are from very late Christian writers, some of them commenting on Acts of the Apostles 28: 9, προσήρχοντο καὶ ἐθεραπεύοντο, 'others came also and were cured'—which is itself, of course, one of the fifteen. The only classical attestation is Aesop, ed. Hausrath, Teubner edn. i. 2, p. 117, (*fabulae tabulis ceratis Assendelftianis servatae* i. 8) where the word is restored: π)ροσήρ(χετο. The lateness of most of the writers does confirm that the imperfect in προσήρχετο or προσήρχοντο is unusual in Attic Greek like that of Th. But as we have seen 120. 1 (ἐπήρχοντο) reduces the difficulty of προσήρχοντο, and vice versa.

It must be concluded that there is no certain instance of προσάρχομαι in all Greek (and I may add that I have been unable to find a single epigraphic instance, e.g. in the indexes to the various vols. of Sokolowski, *Lois Sacrées* and Robert, *Bullétin Épigraphique*. I have also consulted the P. H. I. Pandora epigraphic database. There is a ghost instance of the active form προσάρχοντα at *IG* vii. 4143 line 4. But this is a mere stone-cutter's slip for προάρχοντα, i.e. a reference to the previous ταμίας or official, cp. *IG* vii. 303 line 38). If Th. was using it in the sense 'bring first-fruits to' he was using an extremely rare word, if not coining it. It is true that where the religious context requires it Th. is capable of using a word once and never again, thus σφάγια at vi. 69. 2 (cp. iv. 92. 7 n. citing Jameson). But σφάγια is a common Greek word, although found only at vi. 69 in Th., while the alleged word meaning 'bring first-fruits to' is found nowhere else for certain in all Greek literature. I conclude that in the present passage the disputed verb derives from προσερχ- and means 'they came up to Brasidas'. That is, we should read προσῇσαν or (less satisfactory) retain προσήρχοντο and the unusual imperfect. It will be seen that both at 120. 1 and 121. 1 we have rejected a rather arcane religious sense of a word in favour of a more everyday sense. This seems a reasonable outcome: there is evidence for Greek religion in Th. but it is not as pervasive as in, say, Xenophon. It would not be like Th. to throw highly unusual technical religious terms at us. The closest parallels would perhaps be ἐντέμνουσι at v. 11. 1 (used of the sacrifices to, precisely, Brasidas, see n. there), or βοταμίων at v. 53, see n. there, if that word has been correctly transmitted.

So far the discussion has been purely linguistic. But we must ask whether 'bringing first-fruits' is intrinsically plausible as a way of treating athletes, because this might settle the issue after all in favour of 'first-fruits'. The closest parallel seems to be Paus. iv. 16. 6: Aristomenes when he returned to Andania after his victory over the Spartans was pelted by women with ribbons *and seasonal flowers*, ταινίας αἱ γυναῖκες καὶ τὰ ὡραῖα ἐπιβάλλουσαι τῶν ἀνθῶν. This might be thought close to 'first-fruits'. (For the words ὡραῖα, 'seasonal produce', and ἀπαρχαί, 'first-fruits', in combination, see Th. iii. 58. 4.) Aristomenes is not an athlete; he is more like Brasidas, a liberator (which strengthens the parallel in one way but weakens it in another); and there are serious problems about the usability of Pausanias' Messenian material. On φυλλοβολία or flower-throwing at athletes see Callim. *Hecale* fr. 69. 11 Hollis, and E. N. Gardiner, 'The Alleged Kingship of the Olympic Victor', *BSA* 22 (1916–

17/1917–18), 85–106, at 92. Neither there nor in his books *Greek Athletic Sports and Festivals* (London, 1910) or *Athletics of the Ancient World* (Oxford, 1930) does Gardiner discuss the present passage of Th. The evidence for bringing fruit, flowers, etc. to athletes, or adorning them with such agricultural produce, is plentiful (some think that the custom betrays the agricultural origin of the festivals); but the Th. passage, if it did mention first-fruits, would be the most specific. Plut. *Caes.* 30, the passage adduced by LSJ[9] under the phantom verb προσάρχεσθαι, merely turns out to be evidence for garlanding athletes, for which see also Plut. *Per.* 28, cp. *Timol.* 8 (not actually an athlete but an instance of garlanding of a prominent person); D. Sansone, *Greek Athletics and the Origins of Sport* (Berkeley, 1988), 80. I conclude that though the 'first-fruits' interpretation of Th. iv. 121 is compatible with the rest of the evidence, it goes slightly if excitingly beyond it, and that normal Greek practice towards athletes cannot actually be adduced in favour of a linguistically doubtful interpretation.

We are left with the idea of going up to or approaching an athlete. Contained here is, I suggest, the idea of *adventus* i.e. of going *out* to greet a *homecoming* athlete, cp. e.g. Pindar, *Nemean* ii. 24–5, σὺν εὐκλέϊ νόστῳ, 'with glorious return', cp. L. Kurke, *The Traffic in Praise: Pindar and the Poetics of Social Economy* (Ithaca, 1991), 40. According to Diod. xiii. 82, Exainetos of Akragas in the late fifth century was drawn into the city in a four-horsed chariot, attended by 300 citizens. See Gardiner, *Athletics*, 99, and perhaps cp. such New Testament passages as Mark 11: 8–10 and John 12: 12–13, parallels I owe to Dr J. F. Coakley.

For the semi-religious aura of athletes, attested by such 'star treatment' as garlanding them, if not actually giving them first-fruits, see above all the evidence about Theagenes (Theogenes) of Thasos: J. Pouilloux, *Recherches sur l'histoire et les cultes de Thasos*, i (Paris, 1954), 62–106, with Pouilloux, 'Théogénès de Thasos ... quarante ans après', *BCH* 118 (1994), 199–206; J. Fontenrose, 'The Hero as Athlete', *CSCA* 1 (1968), 73–104; R. Seaford, *Reciprocity and Ritual: Homer and Tragedy in the Developing City-State* (Oxford, 1994), 184 and n. 152. (Gardiner, *Greek Athletic Sports and Festivals*, 77, was too ready to dismiss such 'extravagances' as belonging to 'a later period'.) It is remarkable that Brasidas, for whose posthumous cult at Amphipolis see v. 11. 1 n., should also get rapturous and semi-religious treatment at Skione during his lifetime. For a firm statement of the connection between iv. 121. 1 (Skione) and v. 11. 1 see Habicht, *Gottmenschentum*[2], 206 n. 51.

2. διέβη πάλιν καὶ ὕστερον οὐ πολλῷ στρατιὰν πλείω ἐπεραίωσε: 'he returned, but soon afterwards again crossed the sea with a larger army'. That is, Brasidas went back from Skione to Torone, and then back again to the Pallene promontory on which Skione was situated. Gomme noted that this suggests some Athenian negligence. In whose hands was the northern command now that Th. and Eukles were (presumably) back home standing trial?

βουλόμενος: 'he wanted'. Not necessarily inferred motivation; Th. could have spoken to Brasidas not long after.

τῆς τε Μένδης καὶ τῆς Ποτειδαίας ἀποπειρᾶσαι: 'to try to take Mende and Potidaia'. A proper introduction of Mende is delayed until 123. 1, at the beginning of the main Mende narrative. For Potidaia see 120. 3 n. on ὑπὸ Ἀθηναίων etc.

ἡγούμενος καὶ τοὺς Ἀθηναίους βοηθῆσαι ἂν ὡς ἐς νῆσον καὶ βουλόμενος φθάσαι: 'He was sure that the Athenians would send a force to Skione, which he reckoned they would think of as an island; and he wanted to forestall them'. [The words 'he reckoned' are not in the Greek, which means literally 'would send force as if to an island'. But the Athenian thought about the island is framed inside Brasidas' reasoning, hence my expansion. Jowett has 'he made sure', which is just a slip, unless it is a Victorian idiom I am unfamiliar with.] This sentence recalls 120. 3 above and prepares us (to some extent) for the startling 122. 5 below where the Athenians are angry that even the islanders are now in revolt. See n. there.

122. 1. Ἀθηναίων μὲν Ἀριστώνυμος, Λακεδαιμονίων δὲ Ἀθήναιος: 'Aristonymos from Athens, and Athenaios from Sparta'. For Athenaios see on 119. 2. Aristonymos (a common name) is otherwise unknown, and Th.'s omission of his patronymic (perhaps only to balance Athenaios, whose patronymic had already been given) has ensured that he remains so. Not an important officer of state (Develin, *AO* 134, calls him an 'envoy'), Aristonymos did not qualify for a patronymic on Griffith's most obviously relevant criterion (119. 2 n.).

3. Ἀριστώνυμος δὲ τοῖς μὲν ἄλλοις κατήνει, Σκιωναίους δὲ αἰσθόμενος ἐκ λογισμοῦ τῶν ἡμερῶν ὅτι ὕστερον ἀφεστή-κοιεν, οὐκ ἔφη ἐνσπόνδους ἔσεσθαι: 'Aristonymos agreed to everything with one exception: he made a calculation of the days and worked out that Skione had revolted after the conclusion of the truce. So he refused to include them'. Th. shared the view of Aristonymos the Athenian: see 6 n. below.

4. οἱ Ἀθηναῖοι εὐθὺς ἕτοιμοι ἦσαν στρατεύειν ἐπὶ τὴν Σκιώνην: 'The Athenians were immediately ready to send an expedition against Skione'. For 'immediately', εὐθύς, see 123. 3 n.

καὶ τῆς πόλεως ἀντεποιοῦντο Βρασίδα πιστεύοντες: 'They laid claim to Skione, relying on the evidence of Brasidas'. This passage is relevant to Brasidas' relations with Sparta, see 81. 1 n. on αὐτόν τε Βρασίδαν etc. and Introduction, p. 52. Despite the jealousies mentioned at 108. 7, the Spartans were happy to take their cue from Brasidas when territorial gains were in question.

5. οἱ δὲ δίκῃ μὲν οὐκ ἤθελον κινδυνεύειν: 'But the Athenians did not want to risk arbitration'. Contrast 118. 8: the Athenians had just agreed to exactly that. See next n.

ὀργὴν ποιούμενοι εἰ καὶ οἱ ἐν ταῖς νήσοις ἤδη ὄντες ἀξιοῦσι σφῶν ἀφίστασθαι, τῇ κατὰ γῆν Λακεδαιμονίων ἰσχύι ἀνωφελεῖ πιστεύοντες: 'they were furious at discovering that even the islanders were now daring to revolt from them, in futile reliance on Spartan land power'. At 120. 3, see n. there on καὶ ὄντες etc. Brasidas had *compared* Skione (on the Pallene promontory) to an island, and at 121. 3 we were told that Brasidas thought that the Athenians themselves would actually regard Pallene as an island. Steup says that in the eyes of the Athenians the thought at 120. 3 has become fully real, but 121. 3 is more relevant.

The word 'futile' here, ἀνωφελεῖ, is Athenian focalization (Classen/Steup: the adjective is in predicative position, and is therefore offered as an Athenian judgment). The emphasis, as Gomme says, is on *land* power, which could not force its way past Athenian-held Potidaia; Brasidas himself had come by sea. Gomme compares the Melian Dialogue, v. 104–10.

Dr Rood comments: 'By the way, 122. 4–5 looks like another passage where knowledge of the truce text is presupposed: we could see in the negative of para. 5 [they did '*not* want to risk arbitration'] a 'not (as they should have done by the terms of the treaty)' as well as a 'not (as they discussed doing in an assembly debate)' of the sort you discuss in your *Greek Historiography* article [153]. You remark (*inter alia*) on the absence of that debate (below, 388): 'there would (contrast Mytilene) be not much of a debate if feeling was unanimous'; is this the sort of thing Th.'s selectivity and talk of 'the Athenians', allows us to speculate about?' Rood's first point may be right, though the existence of an arbitration clause could have been common knowledge.

6. εἶχε δὲ καὶ ἡ ἀλήθεια περὶ τῆς ἀποστάσεως μᾶλλον ἢ οἱ Ἀθηναῖοι ἐδικαίουν· ... δύο γὰρ ἡμέραις ὕστερον ἀπέστησαν οἱ Σκιωναῖοι: 'The facts were on their side; for the truth was that the Skionaians had revolted two days after the truce was made'. It is most unusual for Th. to adjudicate emphatically in this way between competing claims; see *Greek Historiography*, 152 n. 57.

The present passage is most easily taken to mean that Th. had done his own calculations and endorsed those of Aristonymos, see para. 3

above. It would be just possible to say (a possibility which Gomme considered) that it only means that Th. was absolutely convinced by his Spartan and other informants, but this is surely less likely. This has a bearing on the relation of ch. 118 to its narrative context, see introductory n. to 117-19, i.e. the narrative presupposes knowledge of the truce text; but the dates were surely widely discussed.

Note that even if the Athenians were in the right on the dates, they were not right (in another sense of 'right') to refuse arbitration, see para. 5 above and 123. 1 n. on ἔστι γάρ etc.

ψήφισμά τ' εὐθὺς ἐποιήσαντο, Κλέωνος γνώμῃ πεισθέντες, Σκιωναίους ἐξελεῖν τε καὶ ἀποκτεῖναι: 'On Kleon's proposal they immediately passed a decree to destroy Skione and put the citizens to death'. And were as good as their word, v. 32. 1, thus ensuring that the name of Skione (like Torone: v. 3. 4 n. on καὶ τῶν Τορωναίων etc.) sat on Athenian consciences and blackened Athens' reputation in time to come, see Xen. *Hell.* ii. 2. 3, Isoc. iv. 100. Skione was often bracketed with Melos; the obvious difference is that there was no Skionaian Dialogue; and no Skionaian Debate (as at Mytilene). The Athenian decision here and its execution in book v are alike recorded as briefly as possible. Thucydidean selectivity is part of the explanation, but there are others. With Delion out of the way (a campaign which called for some complicated splicing of narration), Th. keeps Brasidas in centre stage till his death. A narrative switch to Athens now would reduce the momentum of Brasidas in the north, cp. 109. 1 n. for the rapidity with which Megara is disposed of. Moreover there would (contrast Mytilene) be not much of a debate if feeling was unanimous; nor were the Skionaians (unlike the Melians) being offered a way out. Nevertheless Bosworth is right (*JHS* 113 (1993), 37 n. 37) to say 'it is no surprise that Cleon proposed slaughter and enslavement for Scione', cp. 120. 3 n. on καὶ ὄντες etc.

For 'immediately', εὐθύς, see 123. 3 n.

123. 1. Μένδη ἀφίσταται αὐτῶν, πόλις ἐν τῇ Παλλήνῃ, Ἐρετριῶν ἀποικία: 'Mende, a city of Pallene and an Eretrian colony, revolted from Athens'. For Mende, west of Skione and south of Potidaia and Sane, see Zahrnt 200-3, and in Lauffer (ed.), *Griechenland*, 421; S. G. Miller, *Princeton Encyclopaedia*, 572, and my entry in *OCD³*; and Meritt (109. 1 n. on εὐθὺς στρατεύει etc.). The ancient site was probably located south of the modern village Kalandra. In addition there are extensive remains of a temple to Poseidon close to the beach at the promontory of modern Possidi, see 129. 3 n. on ἄραντες etc. Mende was (at least until the early Hellenistic foundation of Kassandreia nearby) a prosperous place, paying 8 talents tribute to Athens in 451/0 and 438/7, and varying amounts between 5 and 9 talents subsequently. (From 450/49 to 447/6 its tribute was amalgamated with that of Skione.) Mende's wine exports are indicated by its coinage, see Kraay, *ACGC* 136 (also 137 for inconclusive discussion of Mende's coinage in relation to the coinage decree, ML 45, premissed on a date for that decree in the 440s; but for a date in the 420s see above 52. 3 n. on τάς τε ἄλλας πόλεις τὰς Ἀκταίας etc.). Mende founded the Chalkidic Eion mentioned at ch. 7. It is famous as the place of origin of the sculptor Paionios, for whose sculpture of Nike at Olympia, paid for out of spoils won by Messenians and Naupaktians in alliance with Athens, see iii. 114. 1 n. on τὰ μὲν τῶν Ἀθηναίων etc. B. A. Sparkes in J. Boardman (ed.), *Plates to CAH v and vi* (1994), 30 (discussing the Nike, which is pl. 31) notes that Mende was also an Athenian ally. (Apart, that is, from the present brief flirtation with Brasidas.)

ἔστι γὰρ ἃ καὶ αὐτὸς ἐνεκάλει τοῖς Ἀθηναίοις παραβαίνειν τὰς σπονδάς: 'he, for his part, claimed that the Athenians had broken the treaty in a number of respects'. [I have substituted the clumsy 'for his part' for the 'too' in Jowett's 'he too charged the Athenians with violating', so as to make the meaning clearer: the Greek does not imply that anybody else had been charging the Athenians with violations, but that Brasidas' claims answered those of the Athenians.] See C. Meyer, *Urkunden*, 20: the only thing in Th.'s narrative that this can refer to is 122. 5, the refusal of arbitration. As Connor (137) notes, 'legally, there is little justification for Brasidas' action' at Mende.

2. τεκμαιρόμενοι καὶ ἀπὸ τῆς Σκιώνης ὅτι οὐ προυδίδου: 'and they drew inferences from his refusal to hand over Skione to the Athenians'. More irony, considering how Brasidas abandoned Pallene, see Bosworth, *JHS* 1993, 37 and n. 39.

καὶ ἅμα τῶν πρασσόντων σφίσιν ὀλίγων τε ὄντων: 'the people who negotiated with him were a small minority'. Connor (137 n. 76) has a good n., prompted by Mende, on attitudes to Brasidas, which were perhaps less enthusiastic than Th. suggests. As Connor says, Th.'s narrative may have been partly shaped by desire to emphasize how mistaken was the enthusiasm for Brasidas, and this 'may have led him into deemphasizing those groups that had early reservations about his promises'. See further 130. 1 and 7 and nn.

3. οἱ δὲ Ἀθηναῖοι εὐθὺς πυθόμενοι: 'Immediately the Athenians heard'. The word 'immediately', εὐθύς, occurs for the third time in two chapters to describe and stress Athens' instant reactions to events at Skione and Mende, see 122. 4 and 6.

4. ὑπεκκομίζει ἐς Ὄλυνθον τὴν Χαλκιδικὴν παῖδας καὶ γυναῖκας τῶν Σκιωναίων καὶ Μενδαίων: 'by taking away the Skionaian and Mendaian children and women to Olynthos in Chalkidike'. I have changed Jowett's 'wives and children' because Th.'s order of words is of interest and worth preserving, see Wiedemann (107. 3 n. on Πιττακοῦ etc.), at 163-4: Th. mentions 'women and children', thus bracketed together, on twenty occasions in all. On fourteen of those occasions he puts children first; Wiedemann thinks they are given priority over women because it was the fact that they could provide citizens with legitimate children that gave 'wives' a special status above that of other women. C. Rehdantz in his edn. of Xenophon's *Anabasis* (edn. 5, Berlin, 1882), commenting on vii. 8. 9, interestingly notes that Xenophon in the *Anabasis* has the order women–children when talking about barbarians, cp. iv. 1. 8 and vii. 8. 9, but children–women when talking about Greeks, e.g. i. 4. 8, iii. 4. 46, v. 3. 1. Th. does not conform to this, cp. e.g. v. 3. 4 (Torone: order is women–children). But Xenophon's order when speaking of Greeks would fit Wiedemann's hypothesis about Greek priorities as reflected by Th.'s usual order.

Gomme, and Bosworth, *JHS* 1993, 37 n. 38, note that this (humanitarian) evacuation seems to have been far from complete, see v. 32. 1.

For Olynthos see i. 58. 2 n. on καὶ Περδίκκας etc.

τῶν Πελοποννησίων αὐτοῖς πεντακοσίους ὁπλίτας διέπεμψε: 'sent across five hundred Peloponnesian hoplites . . . to help Skione and Mende'. A paltry force; Bosworth, *JHS* 1993, 37 n. 39, thinks Brasidas 'irreparably weakened the resistance to Athens of Pallene' by taking so many troops away at 124. 1. See also 129. 2 for the Athenian expeditionary force, which at perhaps 3000 was far larger than what Brasidas left behind on Pallene, but not much, if at all, larger than Brasidas' *whole* force including those taken to Macedon. As Gomme (on 124. 1) and Bosworth say, this was reckless division of forces on Brasidas' part.

ἄρχοντά τε τῶν ἀπάντων Πολυδαμίδαν: 'all under the command of Polydamidas'. Not a very good choice as it turned out, see 131. 4. For Polydamidas' appointment see 132. 3 n. on καὶ τῶν ἡβώντων etc., citing Parke.

124-128. *Brasidas and Perdikkas campaign in Lynkestis*

124. 1. καὶ ἦγον ὁ μὲν ὧν ἐκράτει Μακεδόνων τὴν δύναμιν καὶ τῶν ἐνοικούντων Ἑλλήνων ὁπλίτας: 'Perdikkas led his own Macedonian army and a force of hoplites supplied by the Greek inhabitants of the country'. On the face of it a simple opposition between Macedonians and Greeks, with the implication that Th. thought the Macedonians were not Greeks. See further below, n. on ἱππῆς etc.

Χαλκιδέας καὶ Ἀκανθίους: 'Chalkidians, Akanthians' [i.e. Chalkidians *and* Akanthians]. I have changed Jowett who seems to have taken it as a hendiadys, 'Chalcidians from Acanthus'. The point is material; as Zahrnt (148) notes, the separate mention of Chalkidians and Akanthians indicates that Akanthos, like Torone, was not a member of the Chalkidic League.

ξύμπαν δὲ τὸ ὁπλιτικὸν τῶν Ἑλλήνων τρισχίλιοι μάλιστα: 'The entire Greek hoplite force came to about three thousand'. On the serious implications, for the defence of Pallene, of this removal of Greek troops, see 123. 4 n. on τῶν Πελοποννησίων etc.

ἱππῆς δ' οἱ πάντες ἠκολούθουν Μακεδόνων ξὺν Χαλκιδεῦσιν ὀλίγου ἐς χιλίους, καὶ ἄλλος ὅμιλος τῶν βαρβάρων πολύς: 'the Chalkidian and Macedonian cavalry [came to] nearly a thousand, and there was also a large mass of barbarians'. καὶ ἄλλος ὅμιλος means 'and there was besides a great multitude of barbarians' (Smith: Loeb) or 'and there was also a great crowd of native troops' (Warner: Penguin). The interest of Th.'s formulation here is that it has a bearing on what in the late twentieth century is a much-discussed question of ethnicity: were the Macedonians Greeks? (On which see now O. Masson, *OCD*[3] entry under 'Macedonian Language', which Masson concludes was a form of North-West Greek.) Or rather, it has a bearing on the narrower question, did Th. think of the Macedonians as Greeks or as barbarians? The nub is καὶ ἄλλος ὅμιλος. A few lines earlier (see above, n. on καὶ ἦγον etc.) Th. made a straightforward binary distinction between Macedonians and Greeks. But now it looks as if he is sorting into three (not two) categories: Greeks (see above, n. on ξύμπαν etc.), Macedonians, and barbarians. This seems to make Macedonians intermediate between Greeks and barbarians, always with the proviso that we are dealing merely with Th.'s own view. Or did Th. think the Macedonians were barbarians too? Steup thought so, and he believed that the reference in the final part of the sentence was to the Macedonian *infantry*, i.e. we have Greek hoplites, Macedonian and Chalkidian cavalry, and in addition a great mass of barbarians (i.e. Macedonian infantry). Steup's reasoning was as follows: the fact that the Macedonians are here straightforwardly called barbarians is completely consistent both with the opposition Greeks/barbarians earlier in 124. 1 [see above, n. on καὶ ἦγον etc.] and with 126. 3 [that is, in 126. 3 the word 'them' in the expression 'the Macedonians among them', τοῖς Μακεδόσιν αὐτῶν, refers to 'the barbarians', βαρβάρους, just mentioned]. So far Steup (though see below for 126. 3, which is from a speech). Gomme (whose summary of Steup is not at all clear, partly because he fails to bring out that Steup wanted to read the Macedonian-cavalry/Macedonian-infantry distinction into 124. 1 as well as into 125. 1) said 'Steup may be right'. But Gomme noted that others took the barbarians in the present passage to be 'allies of the barbarians', i.e. to be people other than the Macedonians. It is a weakness of Steup's general position that he had to emend yet another passage, namely 125. 1 (see n. there), by inserting ἱππῆς, 'cavalry', after Μακεδόνες. He had to do this so as to make sense (on his own premiss that Macedonians were themselves barbarians) of the apparent opposition at 125. 1 between 'the Macedonians' and the 'mass of the barbarians' (τὸ πλῆθος τῶν βαρβάρων), i.e. Steup wanted to introduce an opposition at 125. 1 between 'Macedonian cavalry' and 'Macedonian infantry' i.e. the mass of foot-soldiers. See my n. on οἱ μέν etc. at 125. 1.

I suggest that Th.'s view was not absolutely rigid or consistent. If he had to choose between saying whether Macedonians were Greeks or barbarians, he would say they were barbarians, hence the binary opposition in the sentence beginning καὶ ἦγον near the beginning of 124. 1; hence too the use at 126. 3 (though we must be careful about that because it is a speech of Brasidas, where a slighting reference to a recently defeated sub-group of Macedonians, namely the Lynkestians, as 'barbarians' is rhetorically appropriate and says nothing about Th.'s own categorization). But at the same time he thought there were degrees of barbarian-ness, so that it was possible for him to distinguish between Macedonians and e.g. Illyrians by saying 'the Macedonians' and 'the barbarians'. So in the present passage, I do think that Th. meant to suggest that the Macedonians were intermediate between Greeks and (utter) barbarians, and that Th. did not operate with an undifferentiated concept 'barbarian'. This avoids the need to emend 125. 1.

I suggest that ii. 100. 5, with its distinction between Thracians on the one hand and 'excellent Macedonian cavalry, well protected with breast-plates', ἄνδρας ἱππέας τε ἀγαθοὺς καὶ τεθωρακισμένους, supports the idea of a military distinction between Macedonians and outright barbarians, at the cavalry level; this distinction is additional to the distinction between Macedonians and Greeks, for which see above. According to this second distinction the Macedonians were themselves barbarians.

On the view I take of 124. 1, there were Macedonian cavalry but not Macedonian infantry, or at least Th. thought there were not or has not specifically mentioned any. I believe we should accept this consequence. The army of Brasidas and Perdikkas was strong in cavalry (the Macedonians and Chalkidians) and also in infantry (the Greek hoplites). In addition there were motley barbarians to inspire terror.

P. A. Brunt, 'Anaximenes and King Alexander I of Macedon', *JHS* 96 (1976), 151–3 at 151, discussing the present passage, says 'Th. speaks with contempt of Perdiccas' foot as "a numerous barbarian rabble"'. It follows from the above that I think this is a misinterpretation, if Brunt is talking about Macedonian infantry proper at this point, and he surely is.

See generally the excellent study by E. Badian, 'Greeks and Macedonians', in *Studies in the History of Art*, 10 (Washington, DC, 1982), 33–51.

2. **ἐσβαλόντες δὲ ἐς τὴν Ἀρραβαίου καὶ εὑρόντες ἀντεστρατο-πεδευμένους αὐτοῖς τοὺς Λυγκηστάς:** 'They entered the territory of Arrhabaios, where they found the Lynkestians ready for battle'. For Arrhabaios and Lynkos see 79. 2 n. on Ἀρραβαῖον etc. and nn. on 83. 1 and 2.

3. **καὶ ἐχόντων τῶν μὲν πεζῶν λόφον ἑκατέρωθεν, πεδίου δὲ τοῦ μέσου ὄντος, οἱ ἱππῆς ἐς αὐτὸ καταδραμόντες ἱππομάχησαν πρῶτα ἀμφοτέρων:** 'The infantry of the two armies was drawn up on two opposite hills, and between them was a plain. First, the cavalry forces of each side rode down into the plain and fought'. For this kind of preliminary cavalry engagement see C. J. Tuplin, *The Failings of Empire: A Reading of Xenophon's Hellenica 2.3.11–7.5.27* (*Historia Einzelschrift 76*: Stuttgart, 1993), 187, comparing the battle of Leuktra in 371, and citing (186) passages from Xenophon's cavalry writings, namely *On Horsemanship* viii. 12 and *Cavalry Commander* viii. 23.

τῶν Λυγκηστῶν ὁπλιτῶν: 'the Lynkestian hoplites'. Brunt (1 n. above on ἱππῆς etc.) notes that the mention of Lynkestian hoplites is unexpected (in view, I suppose, of the fact that we are nowhere told that Macedon proper had any. And in view of Lynkestian settlement patterns, see next n.).

4. **ἐπὶ τὰς τοῦ Ἀρραβαίου κώμας:** 'against the villages of Arrhabaios'. Hammond, *HM* i. 103, citing the inscription at *BCH* 21 (1897), 161 f., notes that the Lynkestians were still a 'tribal state' (ἔθνος) in the second century AD, and adds 'we can imagine that they still lived in the *komai* or villages [he then quotes the present passage] which were the only objectives left to Perdiccas to destroy, when the defeated Lyncestae took to the heights'. Archaeological investigation, cited by Hammond, tends to confirm this (unwalled village near Florina). The Lynkestian hoplites (see preceding n.) are thus a little surprising, since hoplites tend to be associated with the *polis*.

125. 1. **οἱ Ἰλλυριοὶ μετ' Ἀρραβαίου προδόντες Περδίκκαν γεγένηνται:** 'the Illyrians had just betrayed Perdikkas and joined Arrhabaios'. An Athenian inscription, *IG* i³. 162, honours Grabos the Illyrian (perhaps the grandfather of the man of the same name at Tod 153 line 13). These honours may have something to do with the present passage of Th., unless Grabos did his service to Athens at the time of the Epidamnos affair, i. 24 ff.

οἱ μὲν Μακεδόνες καὶ τὸ πλῆθος τῶν βαρβάρων: 'The Macedonians and the mass of the barbarians'. On the face of it a clear opposition between Macedonians on the one hand and the barbarians on the other, to set against 124. 1 (see n. there on καὶ ἦγον etc.) with its distinction between Macedonians and Greeks. Steup, as we have seen (124. 1 n. on ἱππῆς etc.) wished to emend the present passage by the insertion of the word ἱππῆς, 'cavalry', after Μακεδόνες. This (he hoped) would produce the sense 'the Macedonian cavalry and the Macedonian infantry'. But the text of the present passage is not in any way disturbed, and the emendation is only called for by Steup's idea that Th. unequivocally categorized the Macedonians as barbarians. But I have argued (124. 1 n. on ἱππῆς etc.) that this view is incorrect and I therefore believe that the emendation of the present passage is undesirable. I note that the OCT does not register the emendation at all, not even in the apparatus criticus. (I am not clear what Gomme thinks; at 125. 1 he merely registers Steup's idea neutrally, whereas at 124. 1 he says Steup may be right. But Steup's two interpretations really go together, so I suppose Gomme thinks the emendation may be right.)

εὐθὺς φοβηθέντες, ὅπερ φιλεῖ μεγάλα στρατόπεδα ἀσαφῶς ἐκπλήγνυσθαι: 'were instantly seized with one of those unaccountable panics to which large armies are liable'. Cp. vii. 80. 3. The word ἀσαφῶς, 'unaccountable', is perhaps a piece of presentation by negation, for which see 94. 1 n. on ψιλοὶ δέ etc. The implied thought is 'not, as you might superstitiously think, due to the intervention of Pan'. I agree with Steup and against Gomme that W. Schmid ('Das Alter der Vorstellung vom panischen Schrecken', *Rh. Mus.* 50 (1895), 310–11) may well be right to see here concealed Thucydidean polemic against popular superstition; see also Pritchett, *GSW* iii (1979), 45, 148, 163. For 'panic' see P. Borgeaud, *The Cult of Pan in Ancient Greece* (Chicago, 1988), ch. 5. Compare the more obviously polemical v. 70, the Spartans march to the sound of flutes, *not* for religious reasons but to keep in step.

ἠνάγκασαν πρὶν τὸν Βρασίδαν ἰδεῖν ... προαπελθεῖν: 'he was forced to go away without seeing Brasidas'. See Ostwald, *ANAΓKH*, 47, calling this a contrapuntal use of the 'necessity' concept, because of the proximity to 128. 5, see n. there.

2. Βρασίδας δὲ ἅμα τῇ ἔῳ: 'At dawn Brasidas'. See 128. 3 n.

ξυναγαγὼν καὶ αὐτὸς ἐς τετράγωνον τάξιν τοὺς ὁπλίτας καὶ τὸν ψιλὸν ὅμιλον ἐς μέσον λαβὼν διενοεῖτο ἀναχωρεῖν: 'So he decided to retreat. He formed his hoplites into a square, and placed his light-armed troops in the centre'. A kind of 'hollow' square formation; inverted commas because the centre was not literally hollow but contained light-armed. The technical word for a hollow square or rectangle is πλαίσιον, cp. vi. 67. 1, though note that even there the centre is occupied, by baggage-bearers. See too vii. 78. 2, the retreating Athenians adopt it. For the hollow square formation see the good discussion by J. K. Anderson, *Xenophon* (London, 1974), 129, citing Xen. *Anab.* iii. 2. 36 where Xenophon advocates it in a speech, iii. 3. 6 where it is adopted, and iii. 4. 19 ff. where its deficiencies are remedied. (Anderson is concerned to make the point that the formation is not Xenophon's idea but is found in the Peloponnesian War, used by both Spartans and Athenians.)

3. ἐκδρόμους δέ, εἴ πῃ προσβάλλοιεν αὐτοῖς, ἔταξε τοὺς νεωτάτους: 'he ordered his youngest troops to charge the enemy wherever they attacked'. By running out between narrow gaps in the formation, as Gomme says following Stahl. Stahl compares ii. 83. 5: the fast Peloponnesian ships were supposed to do this in the sea-battle against Phormio, cp. the similar language εἴ πῃ προσπίπτοιεν. See also 127. 2 for the way Brasidas' provisions and prevision correspond to what actually happens, with Hunter, 25: '*logoi* and *erga* [words and deeds] form a closely-knit unity and, forewarned by the former, the reader is well aware how events will happen and why.'

καὶ αὐτὸς λογάδας ἔχων τριακοσίους τελευταῖος γνώμην εἶχεν ὑποχωρῶν: 'he himself intended to bring up the rear with three hundred picked men'. See 126. 1 n. on ἄνδρες Πελοποννήσιοι for the view that these picked men, and these only, are the intended audience of the speech which follows.

4. καὶ πρὶν τοὺς πολεμίους ἐγγὺς εἶναι, ὡς διὰ ταχέων παρεκελεύσατο τοῖς στρατιώταις τοιάδε: 'Time was short, but before the Illyrians came up he exhorted his soldiers as follows'. *All* the soldiers, as the Greek implies (it simply means 'the soldiers')? Or only the 300 élite Peloponnesians just mentioned? See 126. 1 n. on ἄνδρες Πελοποννήσιοι. For the context of the speech which follows see Pritchett, *EGH* 59, and Hansen, *Historia* 1993, 168.

126. *Speech of Brasidas*

For this speech see Luschnat, 57–63; Leimbach, 77–83; Hunter, 23–30, who is concerned to show how the 'predictions' in the speech (and at 125. 3, see n. there on ἐκδρόμους etc.) are borne out by the subsequent narrative in ch. 127; note, however (cf. above, p. 15), that Luschnat, 59–60, not cited by Hunter, already makes exactly the same point, with similar parallel layout of passages (predictions in speech/fulfilment in narrative; Luschnat's scheme goes: (i) first defence, 126. 5–6 προσμεῖξαι ... and τὴν πρώτην ... corresponding to 127. 2 ὅπῃ ... ἀντέστησαν; (ii) retreat, 126. 6 ὅταν καιρός ... corresponding to 127. 2 ἡσυχαζόντων ...;

(iii) energetic counterattack, 126. 5 (οὐκ) αἰσχυνθεῖεν ... corresponding to 128. 2 προσπεσόντες ... Hunter (29) believes that 'Brasidas' arguments are only those with which the historian has supplied him in order to make his success purposeful'. Sure, the correspondences between speech and narrative are over-neat. But non-Greek fighting techniques were no secret, cp. ii. 81 (did Knemos talk to Brasidas? see 3 n. below); and Brasidas' general line of encouragement ('this frightening rabble, however numerous, will be no match for you men') is plausible generalship in a tight spot.

Hansen, *Historia* 1993, thinks the speech made up, while Pritchett, *EGH*, ch. 2, thinks it authentic, each in keeping with his general position (see Introduction, pp. 82 f.). I agree with Pritchett that Brasidas spoke.

Steup, followed by Luschnat, thinks that there are three basic points arising from the army's situation, all of which Brasidas has to deal with or answer: (i) your allies have fled, (ii) the enemy are barbarians, (iii) there are a lot of them; but Brasidas takes these in the order (i) and (iii) together (paras. 1–2), then (ii) at length (paras. 3–6). In more detail, Brasidas starts by saying that he must instruct as well as encourage because his troops have been abandoned and are probably fearful (para. 1). The enemy numbers are not so formidable, rightly judged (para. 2). He knows something of these barbarians, if only by hearsay, which he can add to his own shrewd appraisal (para. 3). Appearances are not everything (para. 4); the Illyrians look threatening enough but will not stand their ground (para. 5); but you must stand yours when attacked or they will soon be at your heels (para. 6).

The speech in general opposes appearance to reality, note esp. para. 6 where reality (ἔργῳ) is opposed to sight and hearing, ὄψει δὲ καὶ ἀκοῇ. With this compare perhaps vi. 31. 4 on the Athenian naval preparations for the Sicilian expedition where, remarkably, it is all said to look like a display of power and resources *rather than* a preparation for war, ἐπίδειξιν μᾶλλον εἰκασθῆναι τῆς δυνάμεως καὶ ἐξουσίας ἢ ἐπὶ πολεμίους παρασκευήν. There is some illogicality in all this; display is not by itself incompatible with, but can be a manifestation of, real power; cp. v. 60. 3: the fine-looking army assembled at Nemea really was fine. As Leimbach (82) says with reference to the present speech, the threatening appearance of the barbarians does not actually exclude their fighting bravely; and Brasidas' implied opposition is thus not entirely logical, however rhetorically appropriate and encouraging. The implied premiss of the whole second half of the speech is that only orderly Greek hoplite armies both *look* fine and threatening and actually *are* so. Cp. 5 n. on καὶ γὰρ πλήθει etc.

1. ἄνδρες Πελοποννήσιοι: 'Peloponnesians!' A problem arises imme-diately because the army was not just Peloponnesian. (For its composi-tion see Luschnat, 61 n. 2: of the 3000 Greek hoplites, the Peloponnesians amounted to at most 1200, because 500 of the original 1700 at 78. 1 (including 700 helots, 80. 5) had stayed behind at Mende, 123. 4. That means there were about 1800 Chalkidian hoplites.) There are three possible solutions. (i) Some have supposed that Brasidas is using 'Peloponnesians' in a purely conventional and extended sense. So apparently Pritchett, following Gomme, though Gomme offered the additional suggestion that the simplification was deliberate and compar-able to the way Th. speaks of 'the Athenians' as if there were no differ-ences of opinion, see 117. 1 n. on νομίσαντες etc. This parallel is not particularly close. For Th. himself to generalize about 'Athenians' is very different from making a speaker address an audience as 'Pelopon-nesians', especially when, as Luschnat (61) points out, there is a perfectly good precedent at ii. 11. 1 for starting a speech 'Peloponnesians and allies!', ἄνδρες Πελοποννήσιοι καὶ ξύμμαχοι. Leimbach (77 n. 8) also compares, for a fuller form of address, vii. 61. 1, 66. 1, and 77. 1. And Brasidas himself differentiates at v. 9. 1 and 9 between Peloponnesians and allies (Leimbach, 78). (ii) The second possibility (Luschnat, 61; Leimbach, 78) is that in the present passage *only* the Peloponnesians are being addressed, i.e. the 300 élite troops at the rear, see 125. 3. Against this is the completely general expression τοῖς στρατιώταις, 'the soldiers', for the audience Brasidas is said, in 125. 4, to address. (iii) A third possib-ility might be to insert ⟨καὶ ξύμμαχοι⟩ on the analogy of ii. 11. 1, see above, i.e. to suppose that a reference to allies had dropped out of the text. But there is no manuscript justification for this, and it would be awkward—given that Brasidas goes on at para. 2 to minimize the need for the presence of allies, ξυμμάχων παρουσία (referring to the Mace-donians)—for him to begin the speech by acknowledging that other allies (the Chalkidians) *were* present. And this brings us back to the choice between (i) the view of Gomme and Pritchett that 'Peloponnesians' is purely conventional and (ii) the view of Luschnat and Leimbach that only the 300 picked troops of 125. 3 are being addressed. I incline more to view (i), without being happy about the word 'conventional'. (The convention is hardly a well-established one, given all the instances, already cited above, where words 'and allies' are added as part of the address.) It might be better to say the usage was honorific, that for rhetorical purposes Brasidas is treating the army as a cohesive unit (as opposed to the rabble they are faced with), in fact as a wholly Peloponnesian army. Contrast the situation reached by 421, see v. 18. 7 n. on καὶ τοὺς ἄλλους etc.

See also n. on the difficult sentence at para. 2 below, καὶ μηδὲν πλῆθος πεφοβῆσθαι ἐτέρων, οἵ γε μηδὲ ἀπὸ πολιτειῶν etc.

διδαχήν: 'instruction'. See 4 n. below.

νῦν δὲ πρὸς μὲν τὴν ἀπόλειψιν τῶν ἡμετέρων: 'but now that we are left alone by our allies' [lit. 'in view of the desertion by our people'; not easy Greek, and Classen/Steup wonder if a word for allies e.g. ξυμμάχων, has dropped out]. The force of νῦν here is almost 'but as it is'. The abstract noun ἀπόλειψις, 'desertion', is elsewhere found only at vii. 75. 2 in all Th. For another unusual abstract noun in the mouth of Brasidas see 85. 1 n. on ἡ μὲν ἔκπεμψίς μου etc. and for other examples of unusual vocabulary ('language of Brasidas') in the present speech see below 5 n. καὶ γὰρ πλήθει etc.

2. ἀγαθοῖς γὰρ εἶναι ὑμῖν προσήκει τὰ πολέμια οὐ διὰ ξυμμάχων παρουσίαν ἑκάστοτε, ἀλλὰ δι᾽ οἰκείαν ἀρετήν: 'you ought to fight bravely not just when you have allies with you, but because of your own native courage'. Cp. ii. 89. 2 n. for the idea that Peloponnesian courage is somehow innate. Brasidas is on rhetorically thin ice on the present occasion: he is addressing part or all (I would say all, see preceding n.) of an army which included some allies, namely Chalkidians; but he is now saying 'you can do without allies' (Macedonians). I believe this difficulty helps to explain why in para. 1, see n. on ἄνδρες Πελοποννήσιοι, he chooses to address the troops *as if they were all Peloponnesians.*

καὶ μηδὲν πλῆθος πεφοβῆσθαι ἐτέρων, οἵ γε μηδὲ ἀπὸ πολιτειῶν τοιούτων ἥκετε, ἐν αἷς οὐ πολλοὶ ὀλίγων ἄρχουσιν, ἀλλὰ πλεόνων μᾶλλον ἐλάσσους, οὐκ ἄλλῳ τινὶ κτησάμενοι τὴν δυναστείαν ἢ τῷ μαχόμενοι κρατεῖν: 'In particular, do not be scared of the enemy's numbers. Remember that in the cities from which you come, the many govern the few, but where these people come from, the few govern the many, and have acquired a cliquish predominance simply by success in war'. A difficult sentence. I follow Gomme in his commentary and at *CR* 1 (1951), 135-6, who makes sense of the passage without recourse *either* to emendation e.g. of οὐ πολλοί to οἱ πολλοί *or* to strained interpretations of the unemended Greek. Gomme rightly sees a contrast between the Peloponnesians on the one hand (among whom the many rule over the few, i.e. this is a kind of claim to democratic government), and on the other hand their enemies—and I would add, their unreliable and now departed Macedonian allies—among all of whom the few tyrannize over the many. (Gomme is followed by Hammond, *HM* i. 103 n. 5, who goes further and suggests that Th. may well have in mind the specific circumstances by which

Arrhabaios came to power, i.e. by 'force of arms'. This would be to read too much into a rather vague rhetorical contrast.)

Others (e.g. Steup; Luschnat, 61; and now apparently Hunter, 24 and n. 2) think that the states in which 'the many do not rule the few' (but the few the many) are the Peloponnesian ones, i.e. Brasidas is saying that his addressees are a brave few Peloponnesian oligarchs who hold down a majority by force, in contrast with the enemy among whom the many rule over the few. This is an improbable way of addressing Peloponnesians and can be extracted only by emendation or what Gomme rightly calls a 'strained construction'. The unemended Greek literally and clumsily means 'you do not come from states/constitutions in which the following is true: they [the states you do not come from, i.e. the Illyrian, Macedonian states] are not states in which the many rule the few [a respect in which they are unlike the good democratic Peloponnese], on the contrary they are states in which people have acquired cliquish predominance through nothing other than fighting'. For δυναστεία see iii. 62. 5 n. on δυναστεία ὀλίγων ἀνδρῶν. It means a family clique.

The presence of the helots (see above) makes the claim to democracy rather hollow, but that problem is not entirely solved by adopting the Luschnat/Leimbach view according to which only the picked 300 men are being addressed (see 1 n. on ἄνδρες Πελοποννήσιοι). As Gomme says, these picked men may themselves have included some helots.

For Sparta as a democracy of sorts, see (as well as Gomme) Andrewes, in *Ehrenberg Studies*, 16.

3. τοῖς Μακεδόσιν αὐτῶν: 'the Macedonians among them'. Cf. 124. 1 n. on ἱππῆς etc.

ἀφ᾿ ὧν ἐγὼ εἰκάζω τε καὶ ἄλλων ἀκοῇ ἐπίσταμαι: 'from my own estimate of them, and what I have heard from others'. For εἰκάζειν here ('guessing', 'conjecturing', on which notion see i. 138. 3 n. on ἄριστος εἰκαστής) see Hunter, 27–30. As for what Brasidas has 'heard from others', I suggest that the experiences of Knemos the Spartan nauarch at ii. 80–2 would have been most relevant. But not everything that happened in the fifth century BC was recorded by Th., and there were no doubt other sources of information.

4. διδαχὴ ἀληθὴς προσγενομένη: 'when they are properly understood' [lit. 'a truthful teaching being applied']. The word διδαχή is found twice in the present speech (see para. 1 above) and elsewhere only in the Corinthians' speech at i. 120–4, where again it occurs twice, 120. 2 and 121. 4. Two curious and widely separated examples of clustering. For the orator as instructor see L. Kallet-Marx, *RFP* 233–5, though she is not there concerned with military matters.

5. καὶ γὰρ πλήθει ὄψεως δεινοὶ καὶ βοῆς μεγέθει ἀφόρητοι, ἥ τε διὰ κενῆς ἐπανάσεισις τῶν ὅπλων ἔχει τινὰ δήλωσιν ἀπειλῆς:

'Their numbers are a terrifying spectacle, the noise of their shouting is hard to bear, and they brandish their weapons in the air in a threatening way' [lit. 'the brandishing of arms has a show of threat']. S. Mitchell, *Anatolia: Land Men and Gods in Asia Minor*, i (Oxford, 1993), 44 n. 29, calls this a rhetorical *topos* or commonplace.

The word ἐπανάσεισις, 'brandishing', is unique in Th. Similarly, the word for 'threat', ἀπειλή, is uncommon in Th., though it occurs again in the present speech at para. 6. (After that only at viii. 40. 3; the verb ἀπειλεῖν is found in book viii only: 33. 1; 84. 2; 92. 6.) For the idiosyncratic 'language of Brasidas' see pp. 43-8 and introductory n. to 85-7.

οὔτε γὰρ τάξιν ἔχοντες αἰσχυνθεῖεν ἂν λιπεῖν τινὰ χώραν βιαζόμενοι: 'they are drawn up in no regular order, and so are not ashamed to desert any position under pressure'. As borne out by 128. 2, where they are dislodged from the summit of the hill, see n. there citing Luschnat.

αὐτοκράτωρ δὲ μάχη: 'The style of fighting in which every man is his own commanding officer' [lit. 'battle in command of itself']. Another bold metaphorical use of the adjective αὐτοκράτωρ, cp. the authorial 108. 4 with n. there on εἰωθότες etc. See above, Introduction, p. 48.

μάλιστ' ἂν καὶ πρόφασιν τοῦ σῴζεσθαί τινι πρεπόντως πορίσειε: 'gives each man the opportunity to protect himself without disgrace'. There is an obvious contrast with hoplite methods, see Pritchett *GSW* ii (1974), 211; and esp. L. Pearson, 'The *Prophasis* of Desertion', *CQ* 36 (1986), 262-3, to whom I am indebted both generally for the interpretation of the passage and for the translation of πρόφασις here as 'opportunity'. (Pearson is chiefly concerned with vii. 13. 2.)

6. ἔργῳ ... ὄψει δὲ καὶ ἀκοῇ: 'really ... eyes and ears only'. The combination ὄψις and ἀκοή is unlike Hdt., who opposed them with each other (81. 2 n. on τῶν μὲν πείρᾳ etc.). For the opposition of these two senses with reality see introductory n.

ἄπωθεν ἀπειλαῖς: 'threaten from a distance' [lit. 'through threats from afar', so correctly Classen/Steup]. For ἀπειλαῖς, 'threats', see 5 n. on καὶ γὰρ πλήθει etc. Maurer, *Interpolation*, 112, defends the existing text by citing Cassius Dio's imitation at xxxix. 45. 2.

127-128. *Brasidas extricates his army*

A first-class piece of professional soldiering under pressure; everything said by Hammond, *HM* i. 108 and n. 1, is right. Connor may be right to warn us generally against seeing Th. as Brasidas' encomiast, but Th. the *strategos* surely wants us to admire this achievement at the purely military level.

**127. 1. οἱ δὲ βάρβαροι ἰδόντες πολλῇ βοῇ καὶ θορύβῳ προσ-
έκειντο:** 'When the barbarians saw this they attacked with a lot of
noise'. As predicted or 'predicted' by Brasidas, see Hunter, 25.

**2. καὶ ὡς αὐτοῖς αἵ τε ἐκδρομαὶ ὅπη προσπίπτοιεν ἀπήντων καὶ
αὐτὸς ἔχων τοὺς λογάδας ἐπικειμένους ὑφίστατο, τῇ τε πρώτῃ
ὁρμῇ παρὰ γνώμην ἀντέστησαν καὶ τὸ λοιπὸν ἐπιφερομένους
μὲν δεχόμενοι ἠμύνοντο, ἡσυχαζόντων δὲ αὐτοὶ ὑπεχώρουν:**
'But, wherever they attacked, the soldiers whose function it was ran out
and met them, and Brasidas himself with his picked men received their
charge. So the first onslaught of the barbarians met with a resistance
which surprised them, and whenever they renewed the attack the
Spartans withstood them and drove them back, and when the attacks
ceased, they proceeded with their march'. Again (see n. 1) much as
Brasidas had anticipated and arranged, see 125. 3 and 126. 6, with Luschnat, 59, and Hunter, 25, claiming Th. has 'converted results into purposes'. The scholiast, Steup, and LSJ[9] think ἐκδρομαί, 'runnings out', is
abstract for concrete, 'parties of skirmishers' (LSJ).

**καὶ τὴν ἐσβολήν, ἥ ἐστι μεταξὺ δυοῖν λόφοιν στενὴ ἐς τὴν
Ἀρραβαίου:** 'a narrow pass between two hills, which led into the
country of Arrhabaios'. The Kirli Dirven pass; see 83. 2 n.

128. 1. ὁ δὲ γνούς: 'Brasidas realized what was going on'. For the confident participially expressed statement of perception and motive, see 9.
1 n. on *Δημοσθένης δὲ ὁρῶν*, citing Mabel Lang (Brasidas the highest-
scoring agent about whom such expressions are used by Th.).

ἐκκροῦσαι: 'to dislodge'. For the 'clustering' of the verb *ἐκκρούω* in
the latter part of book iv see 108. 2 n. on *τὸ δὲ χωρίον* etc.

**2. καὶ οἱ μὲν προσπεσόντες ἐκράτησάν τε τῶν ἐπὶ τοῦ λόφου,
καὶ ἡ πλείων ἤδη στρατιὰ τῶν Ἑλλήνων ῥᾶον πρὸς αὐτὸν
ἐπορεύοντο:** 'They attacked and defeated them; and the main body of
the Greek army reached the summit without trouble'. This is Luschnat's
'energetic counterattack' (see introductory n.), corresponding to 126. 5,
barbarians are 'not ashamed to desert any position under pressure'.

**οἱ γὰρ βάρβαροι καὶ ἐφοβήθησαν ... νομίζοντες καὶ ἐν με-
θορίοις εἶναι αὐτοὺς ἤδη:** 'the barbarians ... took fright ... they
realized that the enemy were already on the borders of the country' [lit.
'they realized that 'they were already', etc.]. I have followed Jowett in
changing the second 'they' to 'the enemy' for clarity's sake. But this
conceals the shift in focalization at the beginning of this sentence; the
Illyrians are the focalizers throughout it, down to and including the
statement that the barbarians stopped pursuing when they realized the
Greeks had got away.

3. αὐθημερὸν ἀφικνεῖται ἐς Ἄρνισαν: 'on the same day he arrived at Arnisa'. For which see Hammond, *HM* i. 108: 'close to the Eordaean frontier at the Kirli Dirven pass, not on the road but either at Sotir or at Petres'. Hammond (108 n. 1) notes that 'on the same day' picks up 'at dawn', ἅμα τῇ ἕῳ at 125. 2: a remarkable journey of about 27 miles.

4. ὅσοις ἐνέτυχον κατὰ τὴν ὁδὸν ζεύγεσιν αὐτῶν βοεικοῖς: 'when they came upon ox-carts'. For such supply trains see Pritchett, *GSW* i (1971), 42.

5. ἀπὸ τούτου τε πρῶτον: 'From that time on' [lit. 'from that time first']. Para. 5 is a mild prolepsis or anticipation of future developments. **καὶ ἐς τὸ λοιπὸν Πελοποννησίων τῇ μὲν γνώμῃ δι' Ἀθηναίους οὐ ξύνηθες μῖσος εἶχε, τῶν δὲ ἀναγκαίων ξυμφόρων διαναστὰς ἔπρασσεν ὅτῳ τρόπῳ τάχιστα τοῖς μὲν ξυμβήσεται, τῶν δὲ ἀπαλλάξεται:** 'and developed a hatred of the Peloponnesians, which was not habitual because of his dislike of the Athenians. Nevertheless he took steps to come to terms with the Athenians and get rid of the Peloponnesians, so disregarding his own best interests'.

Gomme thinks the sentence corrupt; it is certainly very difficult; see his note in *CR* 1 (1951), 136–7, as well as his comm. The approximate sense is not, however, in doubt. Gomme's suggested emendation is attractive: τῇ δὲ ἀναγκαίῳ ξυμφορᾷ, 'owing to the unavoidable clash of events'.

On the words τῶν δὲ ἀναγκαίων ξυμφόρων διαναστάς, lit. 'distancing himself from what was necessary to his self-interest', see Ostwald, *ΑΝΑΓΚΗ*, 47, calling this a 'contrapuntal' use of an ἀνάγκη ('necessity')-word, because it picks up 125. 1: Th. is using the two related words to show 'how circumstances made Perdiccas give up his alliance with Brasidas and turn instead to the Athenians'. But as Ostwald says, Th. curiously 'does not attribute Perdiccas' breach with Brasidas to necessity; necessity involves the Macedonians alone, first in motivating the flight of their troops and then in explaining the policy that necessity should have dictated for Perdiccas'.

129–132. *The Athenians take Mende and blockade Skione; Perdikkas changes sides and joins Athens*

129. 1. καταλαμβάνει Ἀθηναίους Μένδην ἤδη ἔχοντας: 'he found the Athenians already in possession of Mende'. See next n. for the way Th. presents the sequence of events. Th. must now backtrack to tell us *how* the Athenians came to be in possession of Mende; the last we heard, they were merely angry and making preparations (123. 3).

2. ὑπὸ γὰρ τὸν αὐτὸν χρόνον τοῖς ἐν τῇ Λύγκῳ ἐξέπλευσαν ἐπί τε τὴν Μένδην καὶ τὴν Σκιώνην οἱ Ἀθηναῖοι, ὥσπερ παρεσκευά-

ἵοντο: 'During his Lynkestian campaign, the Athenians had carried out their plan to sail against Mende and Skione' [lit. 'they sailed, as they had prepared/were preparing to do'; Jowett has 'having completed their preparations']. The reference to the plan or preparations is a back-reference to the angry decisions recorded at 122. 4-6 and 123. 3. Note the 'meanwhile' arrangement of the narrative, comparable to but much more abruptly dislocating than 78. 1, see n. there on Βρασίδας δέ etc. discussing how Th. (and sometimes Hdt.) move beyond Zielinski's law by which poets like Homer 'freeze scenes into immobility'. The present passage (unlike 78. 1, where the temporal connection was left vague) involves a sharp and definite analepsis or jump backwards in time, rather in the manner of book viii (e.g. viii. 63. 3): Brasidas arrives at Torone and finds Mende occupied by Athens; we then get a full account of how the Athenians recovered it. I think that it is only at the beginning of 132 that Th. picks up again from the point reached at the end of 128: both places deal with Perdikkas' change of side. Then later in 132 (para. 3) Brasidas starts to act again, appointing governors in Amphipolis and Torone, and (135) attacking Potidaia. Th.'s attention to the sequence of events in the final part of book iv is noticeably close, perhaps because chronology mattered to an exceptional degree and for non-academic reasons in this period, see 122. 3-4 for the political fuss about the relation of the truce to the Spartan takeover of Skione.

Note that the expedition is against Mende and Skione only. The Athenians can do nothing about Torone, because Brasidas took it before the truce of 118.

ὧν ἦσαν δέκα Χῖαι: 'of which ten were Chian'. Gomme notes Chians are obedient, and adds 'especially just now', citing a fragment of Eupolis' contemporary comedy, *The Cities* (K/A, *PCG* v (Berlin and New York, 1986), 437 F 246, with a ref. to the present passage of Th. at their n. 2), where Chios is said to be a fine city which provides Athens with long ships and men when needed, and is generally obedient like a horse that does not need the whip. (αὕτη Χίος, καλὴ πόλις ⟨   ⟩ πέμπει γὰρ ὑμῖν ναῦς μακρὰς ἄνδρας θ᾽ ὅταν δεήσῃ, καὶ τἆλλα πειθαρχεῖ καλῶς, ἄπληκτος ὥσπερ ἵππος). We should certainly recall the disciplinary measures at 51; perhaps that is part of what Gomme meant by 'especially just now'. See also T. J. Quinn, *Athens and Samos, Lesbos and Chios 478-404 BC* (Manchester, 1981), 42.

καὶ Θρᾳξὶ μισθωτοῖς χιλίοις: 'a thousand Thracian mercenaries'. B. M. Lavelle, 'Herodotus on Argive *misthotoi*', *LCM* 11 (1986), 150, notes that the noun μισθωτοί is found only here and at v. 6. 4 in Th., both times about Thracian fighters 'whose martial character [Th.] did not admire'. Lavelle suggests that it is a pejorative word ('hireling'), by contrast with ἐπίκουροι and μισθοφόροι. But the present context looks neutral enough.

καὶ ... πελτασταῖς: 'and peltasts'. V. D. Hanson, in *Hoplites*, 81, says the present ch. demonstrates the 'unsuitability of hoplites outside the phalanx'. I take this to mean that he is noting the use of peltasts and other light-armed.

ἐστρατήγει δὲ Νικίας ὁ Νικηράτου καὶ Νικόστρατος ὁ Διιτρέφους: 'Nikias son of Nikeratos and Nikostratos son of Diitrephes were the commanders'. See 53. 1 and 119. 2 and nn. Although these men have already been given their patronymics twice in the present book alone, they get them again as important officers of state, by 'Griffith's law', see 119. 2 n. on Λακεδαιμονίων etc.

One possible restoration of ML no. 72 lines 55–6 is a payment to these commanders.

3. ἄραντες δὲ ἐκ Ποτειδαίας ταῖς ναυσὶ καὶ σχόντες κατὰ τὸ Ποσειδώνιον: 'They sailed from Potidaia and disembarked at the Poseidonion'. For this use of ἔχω ('put in, land') see LSJ⁹, under ἔχω, A.II.8, citing the present passage. The Poseidonion was surely the promontory (modern Possidi) near Mende, with a temple of Poseidon on it, the excavated remains of which can be seen at the northern end of Possidi beach. See 123. 1 n. on Μένδη etc. and J. A. Alexander, *Potidaea, its History and Remains* (Athens, 1963), 80 and n. 114.

ξύμπαντες [δὲ] ἐπτακόσιοι ὁπλῖται: 'seven hundred hoplites in all'. I have printed Jowett's trans. unchanged, but the passage is probably corrupt. The word δέ was deleted by Krüger. But it seems likely (Steup, Gomme) that the problem is more serious and a reference to peltasts has dropped out. (Polydamidas had 300 peltasts at 124. 3, and Mende probably provided some too.) The original sense may have been that there were seven hundred hoplites *and six, seven or eight hundred peltasts*. The hoplite total is itself suspect (too small), given that Polydamidas had 500 Peloponnesians at 123. 4 and 300 Skionaians, not to mention people from Mende. It is tempting to go further and suggest that the number 700 relates to the *peltasts* and that it is the hoplite total which has been lost.

καὶ Πολυδαμίδας ὁ ἄρχων αὐτῶν: 'under the command of Polydamidas'. See 123. 4.

4. Νικίας μὲν Μεθωναίους τε ἔχων εἴκοσι καὶ ἑκατὸν ψιλούς: 'Nikias took with him a hundred and twenty Methonaian light-armed troops'. For Athens' good relations with (geographically) Macedonian Methone see ML 65; for the place see my entry 'Methone (1)' in *OCD*³. It was a Greek city on the Thermaic Gulf, north of Pydna. Th. alludes to it (glancingly) only here and at vi. 7. 3 (where he calls it a neighbour of Macedonia): see Dover's n.

κατὰ ἀτραπόν τινα του λοφου: 'by a path running up the hill'. For ἀτραπός see 36. 3, the only other occurrence in Th.; I suggested in my n. there (cf. p. 32 f.) that the use of the word in the context of a comparison with Thermopylai indicates contamination from Hdt. vii. 175, the famous path, τήν δὲ ἀτραπόν. But the present passage shows that ἀτραπός was not alien to Th.'s normal vocabulary.

καὶ τραυματιζόμενος: 'but he suffered casualties'. I have changed Jowett's 'he was wounded', for which the Greek, as editors and commentators have accepted since Graves, would be τραυματισθείς.

ἄλλη ἐφόδῳ ἐκ πλέονος: 'by another and more circuitous route'. Gomme remarks that Nikostratos had further to go, and asks if Th. means to imply that the two attacks failed to synchronize as they should have done. Note also Pritchett *GSW* iv (1985), 79, instancing the present passage as showing the advantages of terrain, i.e. of possession of the higher ground.

καὶ ἐς ὀλίγον ἀφίκετο πᾶν τὸ στράτευμα τῶν Ἀθηναίων νικηθῆναι: 'and the whole Athenian army was nearly defeated'. This sort of favourite Thucydidean saved-by-a-whisker locution resembles such 'if . . . not' constructions as I discussed at 106. 4 n., except that we are not told *what* saved the Athenians. That is, Th. does not say 'the Athenians would have been defeated if such-and-such had not happened'. He leaves it unexplained why they were *not* defeated, though here Gomme's and Pritchett's points (4 n. above on ἄλλη etc.) are relevant to the question why they *were* so nearly defeated.

5. οἱ Ἀθηναῖοι ἀναχωρήσαντες: 'the Athenians retired'. Gomme has a good n. on the implications of this passage for Greek siege-warfare: with the Peloponnesians outside the city undefeated, the Athenians could not simply begin the siege.

νυκτὸς ἐπελθούσης: 'when night came on'. See Pritchett, *GSW* ii. 163 for such battles broken off at nightfall.

130. 1. ἦν γάρ τι καὶ στασιασμοῦ ἐν τῇ πόλει: 'because of political divisions in the city'. See 123. 2 n. on καὶ ἅμα etc.

2. κατὰ τὰς ἄνω πύλας, ᾗ ἐπὶ Ποτειδαίας ἔρχονται: 'the upper gates of Mende, where the road to Potidaia begins'. That is, on the north side of the city.

3. τοῖς Μενδαίοις καὶ ἐπικούροις: 'the Mendaians and their allies'. For this sense of *epikouroi* see B. M. Lavelle, '*Epikouroi* in Thucydides', *AJP* 110 (1989), 36–9.

4. καὶ ὡς ἀντεῖπεν ἐπισπασθέντος τε τῇ χειρὶ ὑπ' αὐτοῦ καὶ θορυβηθέντος: 'as soon as he had spoken he was seized by Polydamidas and roughly handled'. Harsh Spartan liberation in action; this

incident recalls the reasons given at iii. 93.2 for the failure of Herakleia in Trachis: the 'severe and often unjust' (χαλεπῶς τε καὶ ἔστιν ἃ οὐ καλῶς) behaviour of the governors sent out by Sparta. Brasidas, we are perhaps meant to reflect, would not have lost his temper in this (for Sparta) disastrous way. For the physical violence, very much a feature of Spartan upbringing (cp. e.g. Xen. *Lak. Pol.* ii. 3), compare viii. 84. 2 (Astyochos) or Hdt. vi. 75: Kleomenes I goes round hitting in the face with his staff any Spartiate he meets; on this see Forrest, *History of Sparta*[2] (London, 1981), 91 ('even the Spartans found this extension of their youthful habits irksome'). See the excellent remarks by J. Redfield, 'Homo Domesticus', in J.-P. Vernant (ed.), *The Greeks* (80. 2–3 n.), 153–83, at 173: Spartiates were 'raised predominantly by women, then evicted into the male world of asceticism and competition, and we may attribute to the abruptness of this change the rigid and yet uncertain self-control of the Spartans; for all their discipline, they were certainly (as we meet them in the histories) more than other Greeks subject to fits of rage and violence.' Cf. i. 95. 1.
ὁ δῆμος εὐθὺς ἀναλαβὼν τὰ ὅπλα περιοργής: 'This angered the democrats, who grabbed their arms'. Jowett and Warner in the Penguin have 'the people', which is not wrong, because δῆμος as often is ambiguous between 'the people' and 'the democrats'; but the sentence goes on to talk of their opponents who were collaborating with the Peloponnesians, τοὺς τὰ ἐναντία σφίσι μετ' αὐτῶν πράξαντας.

Note 'angered': when we seek to elucidate the sympathies of 'Mende', 'the Mendaians', or even of particular factions among the Mendaians, cp. 123. 2 n. on καὶ ἅμα etc. we should bear in mind that in a few moments the sympathies of individuals and groups can be changed, or their determination hardened, by small incidents like Polydamidas' behaviour as described here (behaviour which, despite Th.'s formulation, could have angered others besides committed pro-Athenians and democrats).

5. τοῖς Ἀθηναίοις τῶν πυλῶν ἀνοιγομένων: 'the gates were thrown open to the Athenians'. Diodorus' brief summing up of the Athenian retaking of Mende merely says they took the place by treachery, προδόντων τινῶν αὐτήν, xii. 72. 9.

6. καὶ μόλις οἱ στρατηγοὶ κατέσχον ὥστε μὴ καὶ τοὺς ἀνθρώπους διαφθείρεσθαι: 'the generals had difficulty restraining their men from slaughtering the population'. Lewis, *CAH* v[2]. 429 n. 147, observes of this sentence: 'it is not often that we get an insight into the ordinary Athenian's attitude to revolting allies.'

7. πολιτεύειν ἐκέλευον ὥσπερ εἰώθεσαν: 'were then told that they were to keep their constitution unchanged'. Some sort of democracy, judging from the statement at 123. 2 that the pro-Brasidas faction was small and from its need for outside help: Classen/Steup; Zahrnt, 201;

Larsen, *GFS* 68. Gomme's 'restoring to Mende full autonomy' is not an accurate paraphrase of the present passage.

ἐπειδὴ δὲ τὰ περὶ τὴν Μένδην κατέσχον: 'After securing Mende in this way'. See Kraay, *ACGC* 137, for an attempt to link the discontinuation of Mende's coinage with the Athenian recapture, though I do not see how one can tell when the discontinuation of a coinage was 'forcible'.

131. 2. ἐκκρούσαντες: 'dislodged'. For the word see 102. 2 n. on τὸ δὲ χωρίον etc.

3. οἱ . . . πολιορκούμενοι ἐπίκουροι: 'the Peloponnesian auxiliaries who were besieged'. The word 'Peloponnesian' is inserted by Jowett to make it clear that the reference is to 130. 6. For the word *epikouroi* see 130. 3 n.

132. 1. Περδίκκας τοῖς τῶν Ἀθηναίων στρατηγοῖς ἐπικηρυκευσάμενος ὁμολογίαν ποιεῖται πρὸς τοὺς Ἀθηναίους διὰ τὴν τοῦ Βρασίδου ἔχθραν περὶ τῆς ἐκ τῆς Λύγκου ἀναχωρήσεως, εὐθὺς τότε ἀρξάμενος πράσσειν: 'Perdikkas, who now hated Brasidas, because of what had happened in the retreat from Lynkos, sent heralds to the Athenian generals and came to an understanding with them (he had begun negotiations immediately after the retreat)'. See 128. 4–5. For the interpretation of the last four words of Greek [lit. 'beginning immediately then'] I have followed the version which Jowett relegates to a footnote; in the text he has 'came to an understanding with them, which without loss of time he took measures to carry out'. Of the relegated version Jowett says that if we adopt it, 'εὐθὺς τότε ἀρξάμενος and ἐτύγχανε τότε [see next n.] must refer to different times', that is, 'then', τότε, refers in the present passage back to the retreat from Lynkos (ch. 128) and in the next sentence to the point reached in ch. 132. This is slightly awkward but not impossible; whereas the alternative version contributes virtually nothing worth having: Jowett's 'took measures to carry out' sounds plausible but extracts a good deal from πράσσειν. The version I have adopted is that preferred by Classen/Steup and Warner; Gomme does not discuss the problem.

Note that we are now back where we were at the end of 128, see nn. on 129. 1–2. On the resumptive interpretation of εὐθὺς τότε ἀρξάμενος which I have adopted (see above), the present passage is a further narrative signpost. The unified narrative (Brasidas and Perdikkas; the Athenians) can now proceed.

The statement about Perdikkas' feelings is not here participially expressed (διὰ τὴν τοῦ Βρασίδου ἔχθραν, lit. 'through hatred of

Brasidas'), but it is worth recalling Mabel Lang's finding (*Mnemosyne* 1995) that Perdikkas is one of the six Thucydidean agents to whom Th. most often ascribes participially expressed motives.

For an Athenian alliance with (some of) the Bottiaians, usually dated about now, see Tod 68 (not in ML), *IG* i³. 76, with Lewis, *CAH* v². 429 n. 148. (Spartolos remained at war with Athens, see v. 18. 5.) But Lewis there dissociates *IG* i³. 89, Athens' treaty with Perdikkas and Arrhabaios, from the present context. 'It seems best to put it towards the end of Perdikkas' reign' (died 413).

On Perdikkas' behaviour see J. Chambers, 'Perdikkas, Thucydides and the Greek City-States', *Ancient Macedonia*, 4 (Thessalonike, 1986), 139–45: Perdikkas' decision to abandon Brasidas helped prevent a Spartan victory in the north and contributed to the stalemate which produced the Peace of Nikias; cp. the same author's 'Macedonia and the Peace of Nikias', *Ancient Macedonia*, 5 (1993), 323–35.

2. (ἐτύγχανε γὰρ τότε Ἰσχαγόρας ὁ Λακεδαιμόνιος ... μέλλων): 'Ischagoras the Spartan was then just about to'. See previous n. This description ('Lakedaimonian' rather than 'Spartiate') does not fit Andrewes's comment (*HCT* v. 70 f.) that Th. slightly (but note 'slightly') prefers 'Spartiate' to 'Lakedaimonian' on first introductions. For Ischagoras see further v. 19. 2 and 24. 1 (the peace and alliance of 421). **παρασκευάσας τοὺς ἐν Θεσσαλίᾳ ξένους, χρώμενος αἰεὶ τοῖς πρώτοις:** 'So by his influence over the leading Thessalians, with whom he was always on terms of friendship'. [P. 'now worked upon his friends in Thessaly, with the foremost of whom he was always on good terms'— Forster Smith in the Loeb trans. But the real meaning of the last four words of Greek must be that he was always on good terms with the leading men in Thessaly, not that he was always on good terms with a subdivision of his friends there. For χράομαι with the dative in the sense of 'treat as a friend', i.e. 'be intimate with' see LSJ⁹ under χράω C(IV).]

There is selectivity here, see 27. 5 n. on ἐχθρὸς ὤν. For a particular Thessalian friend of Perdikkas, Nikonidas, see 78. 2. For such (guest-)friendships and the duties they implied see Herman, *Ritualized Friendship* (78. 1 n. on ἐς Φάρσαλον etc.), 119, citing the present passage at n. 7.

ὥστε μηδὲ πειρᾶσθαι Θεσσαλῶν: 'indeed, the Spartans did not even try to get permission from the Thessalians'. For such permissions see 78. 2 n. on τὴν γὰρ Θεσσαλίαν etc., and 78. 4 n.; also v. 13. 1.

3. καὶ τῶν ἡβώντων αὐτῶν παρανόμως ἄνδρας ἐξῆγον ἐκ Σπάρτης, ὥστε τῶν πόλεων ἄρχοντας καθίστανται καὶ μὴ τοῖς ἐντυχοῦσιν ἐπιτρέπειν: 'They brought with them, quite illegally, some young Spartans, intending to make them governors of the cities, instead of leaving them to be run by chance appointments'. For this new and sinister development, see Connor, 138 and n. 77: 'the first sign of the Spartan harmost system' (though Th. does not use the word harmost until viii. 5. 2). Parke (66. 3 n. on ἐν ᾗ αὐτοί etc.), 42, observes that these governors resemble the *archon* in Megara (67. 3 n. on πείθοντες etc.) rather than Polydamidas in Mende, who is left behind only temporarily so that Brasidas can go off to join Perdikkas, 123. 4. See also Andrewes, in Garnsey and Whittaker, *Imperialism*, 99 and 305 n. 19, noting the way such appointments enabled Sparta to deal with distant commitments without resort to the full military levy.

The expression παρανόμως implies the existence of a law. A. D. Knox, 'A Strange Law at Sparta', *CR* 43 (1929), 52–3, suggested that the law was directed against favouritism of one's own kin (he supposed that the offensive feature was that the commissioners appointed younger relatives). See, however, the reply by J. A. Nairn, 'A Law at Sparta', *CR* 43 (1929), 114, more plausibly adducing Isoc. xi. 18, a Spartan law making it illegal for men of military age to leave Sparta without permission. Mac-Dowell, *Spartan Law* (Edinburgh, 1986), is no help on the problem.

This resembles presentation by negation (for which technique see 94. 1 n. on ψιλοί etc.), lit. 'and not to hand them over to just anybody'. Here 'not' perhaps means 'not, as you might have expected from Sparta'; but the focalization is interesting: presumably (as Gomme says) somebody said 'we can't have the cities run by just anyone'. But it is not clear if it was Brasidas who said this, or if it was rather Brasidas' enemies at home (108. 7) who said 'we can't leave it to Brasidas to make the appointments'. I do not (though see next n.) see how we can go further than what Th. tells us, frustrating though that is. A full account of what lies behind the present passage would help with the problem of Brasidas' relations with the Spartans at home, see above, Introduction, p. 52. On the obscurity of the thought here see Andrewes, *HCT* v. 364, for whom it is one of the 'indications of incompleteness' in Th.'s narrative of the Ten Years War.

καὶ Κλεαρίδαν μὲν τὸν Κλεωνύμου καθίστησιν ἐν Ἀμφιπόλει, Πασιτελίδαν δὲ τὸν Ἡγησάνδρου ἐν Τορώνῃ: 'So Brasidas appointed Klearidas son of Kleonymos governor of Amphipolis, and Pasitelidas [but perhaps this should be Epitelidas, see below] son of Hegesander governor of Torone'. That Brasidas makes the appointments perhaps suggests (see previous n.) that they were his idea in principle; so much for his pledges at 87. 5 about not being interested in imperialism. Cartledge, *Agesilaos* (London, 1987), 92, thinks they were probably Brasidas' protégés.

Pasitelidas is usually emended from the manuscripts' Epitelidas,

'Ἐπιτελίδαν, see v. 3. 1 and 2; but Lewis, *Towards a Historian's Text*, 142, protested that 'this is just the sort of conjecture that ought not to be made. We know from iv. 132. 3 that Brasidas had several Spartiates available. Are we really entitled to say (1) that Brasidas could not have changed the governor of Torone during the winter, and (2) even if he did not, it is Epitelidas that is wrong and not Pasitelidas?' For Klearidas see H. D. Westlake, 'Thucydides, Brasidas and Clearidas', *GRBS* 21 (1980), 333–9 = *Studies*, 78–83, suggesting that he was a source for Th. for events after Brasidas' death and even before; Th. (Westlake thinks) treats Klearidas much as he treats Brasidas himself (he acts like Brasidas, pursues policy divergent from the Spartan government, uses deceit, is contrasted with conventional Spartans). See further v. 21. 1 n. and Introduction, p. 58 f.

Unlike the commissioners Ischagoras, Ameinias, and Aristeus, the two governors get patronymics. If we want an explanation, we can say that the permanent officials will recur in the narrative and are more important; but (though patronymics were hardly a valuable state secret) we should recall that it was not easy for Th. to find out about Sparta, v. 68. 2.

133–4. *Events at Thespiai, Argos, Skione; Battle between Mantinea and Tegea*

Wilamowitz, *Kl. Schr.* iii. 376 and n. 1, thought that the bittiness of chs. 133 and 134, and Th.'s failure to make clear the significance of the Thespiai and Tegea/Mantinea incidents in particular, was evidence that Th.'s information about Greek affairs was beginning (now that he 'had retreated to the fastness of his Thracian possessions', see Introduction, p. 110) to be patchy; he thought the section lacked the final authorial elaboration. (This was all part of Wilamowitz's argument that the truce at 118 was an insertion.) See, in similar vein, Andrewes, *HCT* v. 364, on these chs. as illustrating the 'sporadic and mostly scrappy' quality of the references to non-northern events in the post-Delion narrative (Andrewes is discussing 'indications of incompleteness' in Th.'s narrative of the Ten Years War). But this is not the only place where Th., in a manner foreshadowing Tacitus in the *Annals*, lumps together a number of disparate items at the end of a year, or becomes more expansive; the motive may partly be to vary the handling after a long narrative of uniform texture; Th. is 'mixing up his shots' as they say of tennis-players. See ii. 102–3; iii. 114–16; vi. 7; vii. 18. In such sections (this is conspicuously true of ii. 102 with its mythical content, and iii. 116 on the eruption of Etna), he allows himself to relax his customary austerity. This may be relevant to the Chrysis story below. Finally, we should not forget that after the truce military activity was meagre, so that he allows in material which might not normally qualify for inclusion. (But 'padding' is not habitual with Th.: v. 82–3, a whole year covered in two chapters, shows that if he had litle to say he was happy to be suitably brief.) See Introduction, pp. 110–13.

As for the function of 134, see n. there.

133. 1. ἐν δὲ τῷ αὐτῷ θέρει Θηβαῖοι Θεσπιῶν τεῖχος περιεῖλον ἐπικαλέσαντες ἀττικισμόν, βουλόμενοι μὲν καὶ αἰεί, παρεσχη-κὸς δὲ ῥᾷον ἐπειδὴ καὶ ἐν τῇ πρὸς Ἀθηναίους μάχῃ ὅτι ἦν αὐτῶν ἄνθος ἀπωλώλει: 'During the same summer the Thebans dismantled the walls of Thespiai, because of the alleged pro-Athenian tendencies of the Thespians. They had wanted to do this for some time, and now they had their opportunity, because the flower of the Thespian army had fallen in the battle against the Athenians'. That is, at Delion, though we should not, with Jowett, actually translate 'in the battle of Delion', because the focalization makes a difference: although the Thespians had actually fallen alongside the Thebans, and fighting against the Athenians, they were all now to be punished for the pro-Athenian politics of some of their citizens. There is perhaps some criticism of the Thebans contained in Th.'s emphasis here and in his avoidance of 'at Delion' (which he uses at v. 14. 1); just as there certainly is criticism contained in 'now they had their opportunity', παρεσχηκὸς δὲ ῥᾷον [lit. 'and it was now more easily in their power to do this'], of which Gomme laconically remarked 'Th. does not spare the Thebans'.

For the crushing Thespian casualties at Delion see 96. 3 n. on καὶ ἐπίεσαν etc. and Buck there cited, for the likelihood that the pro-federal hoplite class at Thespiai was particularly badly hit. (Note, however, that although Buck says 'the Thebans, and the rest of the Boiotian federation', now acted against Thespiai, Th. mentions only the Thebans.) For pro-Athenian sentiments at Thespiai see 76. 2 n. On the present passage see also Hanson, *Western Way*, 101.

For the formation *attikismos* for pro-Athenian sympathies see iii. 62. 2 n. on ἀττικίσαι. I there discuss, and express reservations about, Colin Macleod's idea that the word was a neologism. Note also *FGrHist* 4 Hellanicus F 81 for the word ὀρχομενίζω meaning 'I have sympathies with [Boiotian] Orchomenos'. This further strengthens the idea that such coinages were common, and a verb to express sympathies with Athens in particular would surely have many uses in fifth-century Greece.

2. καὶ ὁ νεὼς τῆς Ἥρας τοῦ αὐτοῦ θέρους ἐν Ἄργει κατε-καύθη, Χρυσίδος τῆς ἱερείας λύχνον τινὰ θείσης ἡμμένον πρὸς τὰ στέμματα καὶ ἐπικαταδαρθούσης, ὥστε ἔλαθεν ἀφθέντα πάντα καὶ καταφλεχθέντα: 'During the same summer the temple of

Hera near Argos was burnt down; Chrysis the priestess had put a light too near the woollen fillets, and had then gone to sleep, so that they all caught fire and were burnt before she noticed'. For the Argive Heraion, an important sanctuary 10 km. from Argos and 5 from Mycenae, see R. S. Mason's entry 'Argive Heraion' in *Princeton Encyclopaedia*, 90. It was once thought that it was after this conflagration in 423 that the temple was rebuilt. (So Classen/Steup and more recent scholars, e.g. S. G. Miller, 'The Date of the West Building at the Argive Heraion', *AJA* 77 (1973), 9–18 at 11, but see his n. 16. Gomme has nothing to say about the temple at all.) See, however, P. Amandry, 'Observations sur les monuments de l'Héraion d'Argos', *Hesperia*, 21 (1952), 222–74, at 272, denying that the fire of 423 marked an epoch in the history of the shrine: 'l'incendie du Vieux Temple en 423 n'a pas eu l'influence déterminante qu'on lui prête'; see also Amandry, 'Sur les concours Argiens', in *Études Argiennes* (*BCH* Suppl. 6, 1980), 211–53, at 236, in much the same vein, followed by J. des Courtils, 'L'Architecture et l'histoire d'Argos dans la première moitié du Vᵉ siècle', in M. Piérart (ed.), *Polydipsion Argos* (*BCH* Suppl. 22, 1992), 241–51, at 245. Th., says Amandry, restricts himself to mentioning the fact of the fire without stating a connection between the burning of the temple and the rebuilding of the sanctuary; it has been left to modern scholars to do that (this is sarcastically meant, the point being that the modern scholars are wrong). Amandry 1952, 272, suggests that the Argives exploited the period of peace and prosperity between 450 and 420, the Thirty Years Peace with Sparta (see i. 115. 1 n. and v. 14. 4 n.), to rebuild the temple lavishly—and slowly: he thinks the work went on into the fourth century. Naturally, after reading all this, one turns back to see what Th. actually says. Even if the last words [lit. 'all/everything caught fire and was consumed'] refer only to the burning of the fillets, as Warner takes it (Jowett had 'the whole place took fire and was consumed'), we are left with κατεκαύθη, 'burned down', earlier in the sentence. LSJ⁹ gives the meaning of κατακαίω as 'burn completely'. The other uses in Th. listed by Bétant do not solve the question how total a fire is meant in the present passage. At Hdt. i. 50. 3 the temple at Delphi burns down (κατεκαίετο), but a gold lion is evidently saved. When the fourth-century temple at Delphi was destroyed by fire, it was rebuilt completely, see Tod 205, the Parian Marble, line 83, κατεκάη 'it was burnt down' (though another tradition spoke of an earthquake); 133 (honours to Dionysius) lines 9–10; and 140. We must conclude either (i) that Th. has exaggerated the extent of the fire, or else (ii) that the archaeologists are wrong and the fire of 423 was after all a bigger event in the history of the sanctuary than they are prepared to acknowledge. (I am not competent to assess the specialist archaeological arguments, but it is hard to believe that a fire which was serious enough to make Chrysis make such a spectacular departure should not also have been serious enough to make a considerable difference to the building history of the temple. I suppose there could have been a visually impressive blaze which nevertheless left the stone walls more or less intact.) The final and preferable possibility (iii) is that perhaps the old temple went on being used while a new one slowly arose nearby. This would not be possible at a place like Delphi where there was one and one only site for the main temple of Apollo; but elsewhere it is feasible, cp. *Syll*³ 756 (Asklepieion at Athens).

It has been claimed that unpublished epigraphic evidence has a bearing on the present passage, and I therefore quote Lewis, *CAH* v² (1992), 109 n. 46 in full: citing P. Amandry 1980 (as above), he notes that 'strong arguments have been produced ... for supposing that the Argive decision to reshape the Heraeum site had already been taken around 460 in the euphoria at regaining control of the Argolid. The archaeological evidence shows that work there long antedated the burning of the temple in 423 (Thuc. iv. 133. 2) and there is unpublished epigraphic evidence pointing to the same conclusion.' I gather from Marcel Piérart (to whom I am grateful for discussion of various points dealt with in the present n.), that this must be a reference to the subject-matter of C. Kritzas, 'Aspects de la vie politique et économique d'Argos au Vᵉ siècle avant J.-C.' in Piérart (ed.), *Polydipsion Argos* (1992; see above), 231–40. This article discusses (see 236) new epigraphic evidence for enormous revenues distributed by the 'twelve', οἱ Δυώδεκα, to phratries. It thus confirms the picture of mid-century Argive prosperity. But it does not bear specifically on the Heraion.

For Chrysis see ii. 2. 1 n. on ἐπὶ Χρυσίδος etc., quoting Syme and also (for long-serving priestesses) ML p. 109. Syme's statement that she is the only female agent in Th. is a slight exaggeration. Wiedemann (107. 3 n. on Πιττακοῦ etc.), 168, says that it is tempting to see the explanation for her disappearance as 'due to a subconscious feeling on the historian's part that this is the kind of chance calamity for which women are to blame'. Perhaps, but to make this point he did not need to give us, in addition, the name of her successor Phaeinis (3 n. on οἱ δὲ ἄλλην etc.). For another suggested motive for allowing the admittedly untypical Chrysis incident into the history see below 3 n. on ἔτη δέ etc. See also introductory n. to 133–4.

The word στέμματα deserves comment. I have changed Jowett's 'garlands' to 'woollen fillets', that is, bands or strips worn by priests (Hdt. vii. 197 and see below), or used to decorate statues or put round the heads of sacrificial animals (cp. Hdt. i. 132. 1). Warner also has the translation 'garlands', which suggest wreaths made of flowers, leaves (olive; laurel etc.); but such things are not easy to set on fire, unless we suppose (but why should we?) that they were in dried form. By far the best discussion of the present passage is J. Servais, *'ΣΤΕΜΜΑΤ' ΕΧΩΝ ΕΝ ΧΕΡΣΙΝ* (*Iliade* A 14)', *L.'Ant. Class.* 36 (1967), 415–53, at 449 n. 106, in the course of an argument that στέμματα are usually woollen fillets ('bandelettes de laine') rather than objects made of vegetable matter; the Budé trans. of the present passage of Th. rightly has 'bande-lettes'. (LSJ⁹ briefly acknowledges the existence of this meaning, giving it as sense (2); but the same entry firmly gives Th. iv. 133 as an example of sense (1), 'wreath, garland, chaplet'.) As Servais says of the present passage, if στέμματα, made of wool and full of fat and probably also sacred oil, were hung with their ends close to a flame, it would be hard to imagine a better torch. He cites *Batrachomyomachia* 179–80, where lamps and στέμματα are again juxtaposed (ἐπεὶ κακὰ πολλὰ μ᾽ ἔοργον | στέμματα βλάπτοντες καὶ λύχνους εἵνεκ᾽ ἐλαίου) and Ar. *Wealth* 685–6. For στέμματα in religious contexts see also *LSCG* 17B line 22 (Athens), with comm. on p. 36; 151A (Cos) lines 30, 37–8; *LSCG Suppl.* 22 (Epidauros) line 6; 109 (Rhodes), line 3 (heavily restored). For an interesting use of the title στεμματη[φόρος ('fillet-wearer') as an equivalent for the more normal *stephanephoros*, 'wreath-wearer', see J. and L. Robert, *Bull. Ép.* 1976, no. 721 (Syrian Apameia). For priestly fillets see also *IDidyma* 282 with Robert, *Hellenica*, 11–12 (1950), 450–1 and the illustration at pl. XXVIII. Cf. also Pol. xvi. 33. 4 and Plut. *Pel.* 12. See Introduction, pp. 8 f.

3. καὶ ἡ Χρυσὶς μὲν εὐθὺς τῆς νυκτὸς δείσασα τοὺς Ἀργείους ἐς Φλειοῦντα φεύγει: 'Fearing the reaction of the Argives, she fled that very night to Phleious'. Pausanias (ii. 17. 7; iii. 5. 6) adds some details about Chrysis' flight (as well as telling us that the Argives did not destroy her statue—for fear of supernatural reprisals?). She ended up at Tegea, taking sanctuary at the temple of Athena Alea. (For such 'sanctuary' in the modern sense see 98. 6 n. on καὶ γὰρ τῶν ἀκουσίων etc.) Gomme notes that the detour via Phleious was a long one; the direct way from the Heraion to Tegea would be via Argos, which she avoids for obvious reasons. Pausanias seems to have got hold of some information not in Th. Perhaps he was told a story about the statue, which no doubt had an inscription.

οἱ δὲ ἄλλην ἱέρειαν ἐκ τοῦ νόμου τοῦ προκειμένου κατεστήσαντο Φαεινίδα ὄνομα: 'and the Argives appointed another priestess named Phaeinis, selecting her in the way provided by law'. Steup is surely right that the reference to legality in the expression ἐκ τοῦ νόμου τοῦ προκειμένου refers to the manner, not the fact of appointment. I have therefore changed Jowett's 'the Argives, as the law provided, appointed'. Th. does not bother to tell us what exactly was the 'way provided by law'. J. D. Smart, 'Thucydides and Hellanicus', in I. S. Moxon, J. D. Smart, and A. J. Woodman (eds.), *Past Perspectives* (Cambridge, 1986), 19–35, at 32 f. suggests, over-ingeniously, that Th. is here anxious to stress the 'inefficacy of *nomos*', i.e. law or convention, as against the reality of *physis* or nature. The words 'in the way provided by law' are, Smart says, 'contextually redundant and seem intended simply to show the basis of eponymic schemes [i.e. chronological schemes based on the office-holding periods of magistrates, see next n.] in *nomos*.'

ἔτη δὲ ἡ Χρυσὶς τοῦ πολέμου τοῦδε ἐπέλαβεν ὀκτὼ καὶ ἔνατον ἐκ μέσου, ὅτε ἐπεφεύγει: 'Chrysis had been priestess for eight and a half years of the war when she went into exile'. Since Hellanicus wrote a 'Priestesses of Argos', and since Th. criticizes Hellanicus at i. 97, scholars have reasonably felt that Hellanicus is somehow the key to the inclusion of the whole of the present uncharacteristic passage. J. D. Smart, 'Thucydides and Hellanicus' (see previous n.), 23–4, as part of his argument that Th. had a strong desire to improve on Hellanican chronology, thinks that part of Th.'s motive in this para. is 'to indicate that the relationship between such eponymous schemes [as Th. rejects at v. 20. 2–3] and the events they encompassed was contingent not natural'. Smart suggests that the present passage about Chrysis makes this 'beautifully clear': the 'chance event of her leaving a burning lamp occurred in the middle of a natural seasonal unit [here he quotes the present passage] and resulted in a ludicrous division of a naturally connected series of events, i.e. the ten-year war, between two priestesses and so between two chronological eras.' The clumsiness of the formula here used about Chrysis is certainly effective preparation for the methodological polemic at v. 20, though 'ludicrous' is perhaps too strong. K. J. Dover, 'La colonizzazione della Sicilia in Tucidide', *Maia*, 6 (1953), 39–56, at 41, German trans. in Herter (ed.), *Thukydides* (Darmstadt, 1968), 344–68, wondered if Th. was prompted to include the Chrysis story because Hellanicus' account of the priestesses of Argos had only recently been published and it stopped before 423, i.e. Th. was continuing Hellanicus' work rather than criticizing his methodology. To which Gomme replied that Th. may have inserted the present passage later. This bears on 'recently published', but it might still be true that Th. was giving an item not covered by Hellanicus.

Another motive for including the present passage may be to prepare us for the importance of Argos in book v, starting with v. 14. 4; cp. below 134. 1 n. on Μαντινῆς etc.

134. 1. ἐν δὲ τῷ ἐπιόντι χειμῶνι: 'In the following winter'. That is, the Mantinea–Tegea engagement was fought out of campaigning season.

See Lazenby, in Hanson (ed.), *Hoplites*, 88, for the rarity of such winter battles.

Μαντινῆς δὲ καὶ Τεγεᾶται καὶ οἱ ξύμμαχοι ἑκατέρων ξυνέβαλον ἐν Λαοδοκείῳ τῆς Ὀρεσθίδος: 'But the Mantineans and Tegeans and their respective allies fought a battle at Laodikeion in the territory of Oresthis'. For Th.'s presentation of this episode, so disconnected from its surroundings, see introductory n. to 133–4. But though it is isolated from its immediate context, it prepares us for the Peloponnesian events which take up so much of book v; cp. Wilamowitz, *Kl. Schr.* iii. 376–7 n. 1: the Mantinea–Tegea battle 'is connected with the break-up of the Peloponnesian League, about which book v has much to say'. So too H. R. Immerwahr, in P. Easterling and B. Knox (eds.), *Cambridge History of Classical Literature* (paperback edn.), 1.3 (1989), 41, for whom this short account has a 'paradigmatic significance'; it 'illustrates the confusion reigning in the Peloponnese'.

Laodokeion is in south-western Arkadia, south of the later Megalopolis; see Andrewes, *HCT* iv. 92, discussing v. 64. 3 and map opp. p. 34; but note that Andrewes's conclusions, esp. his acceptance of E. Meyer's idea that the place called Oresthasion/Orestheion/Oresteion is the centre of the district Oresthis mentioned in the present passage, are criticized by Pritchett. At *SAGT* iv (1982), 42, Pritchett observes that Th.'s use of Ὀρέσθειον τῆς Μαιναλίας at v. 64. 3 ('Orestheion in Mainalia') and of Λαοδοκείῳ τῆς Ὀρεσθίδος ('Laodokeion in Oresthis') imply that Mainalia and Oresthis were two different districts. At *SAGT* v (1985), 74, Pritchett suggests that Mainalia is east of Mt. Tsemberou, whereas the plain west of Tsemberou was perhaps called Oresthis. For the Mt. Tsemberou region see also E. Drakopoulos, 'Orestheum or Oresthasion in Arcadia', *L'Ant. Class.* 60 (1991), 29–41, though this is mainly concerned with Oresthasion; I defer further discussion until my n. on v. 64. 3.

In view of the above, I have changed Jowett's 'Orestheum' to 'Oresthis'.

Lewis, *CAH* v². 429, calls this battle 'an extreme case of return to local priorities' after the truce; he notes that it is evidence of the common tendency of Tegea and Mantinea to expand into western Arkadia; see also his remarks earlier in the volume (104), where he conjectures that the battle recounted in the present passage was not the first attempt either city had made to extend its influence in that direction, and notes other such evidence for Peloponnesian mini-imperialisms. Gomme suggested that the Mantineans' allies were the Parrhasioi (he adduced v. 33. 1; see also Andrewes in *HCT* on v. 29. 1), and the Tegeans' allies were the Heraians and Mainalioi. (It would be better to say, 'and most of the

Mainalioi', because the northern Mainalioi were perhaps allies of Mantinea: Gomme adduced v. 67. 1, but see Andrewes's n. on Μαινάλιοι at v. 67. 1.)

καὶ νίκη ἀμφιδήριτος ἐγένετο: 'the victory was disputed'. A TLG search confirms Gomme's view that the adjective is not specially poetical, the opposite if anything; in addition to Pol. iv. 33. 8 and xxxv. 2. 14, it is used by Cornutus *de nat. deorum* lvi. 15. It is striking that although ἀμφιδήριτος μάχη would be the second half of an iambic line, the word is *not* found in the tragedians.

κέρας γὰρ ἑκάτεροι τρέψαντες τὸ καθ᾽ αὑτούς: 'For the troops of both sides defeated those on the wing opposite them'. Jowett has 'the allies on the wing opposed', but though this is a likely enough formation, it goes beyond the Greek. See further 2 n. on καὶ ἀγχωμάλου etc.

τροπαῖά τε ἀμφότεροι ἔστησαν καὶ σκῦλα ἐς Δελφοὺς ἀπέπεμψαν: 'both sides erected trophies, and sent spoils to Delphi'. See *Syll.*³ 78, not mentioned by Gomme (cf. pp. 11 f.): Mantinean victory dedications, very probably from this battle, at (*a*) Mantinea and (*b*) Delphi (does not survive; restored from Paus. x. 13. 6). For (*a*) [ἀπὸ Τεγεατᾶν] Ἀπόλλονι καὶ συνμάχον δεκόταν [*sic*], 'tithe to Apollo [from the Tegeans] and their allies', see also *LSAG*² 213 and 216 no. 32 with plate 41, accepting the association with the present passage of Th. (There is some risk of circularity, because 'Tegeans' has been restored, and Th. iv. 134 has clearly influenced the restoration. But if we ask, 'would the Tegeans have been restored, as an obvious Mantinean enemy, even *without* this passage of Th.?' the answer is probably Yes; and note the allies who feature in both Th. and the inscription. The less attractive alternative, see Hiller's n. on *IG* v. 2. 282, is to relate the inscription to Th. v. 29. 1, Mantinean reduction of an unspecified 'part' of Arkadia.) As Th. describes things (para. 2), the Tegeans had slightly the better of it, but the present passage is explicit that the Mantineans also dedicated victory spoils. For σκῦλα here see Pritchett, *GSW* i (1971), 155. A. H. Jackson, in Hanson (ed.), *Hoplites*, 246, says it is 'not surprising' that both sides choose to send their spoils to Delphi, rather than to Olympia which was closer; he thinks this may have something to do with feelings of unease at dedicating spoils taken from Greeks. But at 244, where he likewise says it was 'no wonder' that on the present occasion both sides sent spoils 'all the way to Delphi', his rather different point is that both Olympia and Delphi were simply 'famous and much-frequented panhellenic shrines'. Jackson (246) may be right that after 423 very few offerings of spoils taken from Greeks are reliably reported from Delphi, but there does not seem to be much sign of unease in the Ten Years War itself, cp. *Syll.*³ 79 with 88. 1 n. on ἔγνωσαν etc., spoils taken by Brasidas and the Akanthians from the Athenians; and (from Olympia) ML 74, Messenians at Naupaktos from the enemy, i.e. presumably the Peloponnesians. So Jackson's emphasis at 244 seems preferable to that at 246. See also Parker, *CRUX*, 325 n. 98, cp. above 118. 1 n.

2. διαφθαρέντων μέντοι πολλῶν ἑκατέροις: 'There were certainly heavy casualties on both sides'. P. Krentz, *GRBS* 1985 (44. 6 n. on ἀπέθανον etc.), 20, notes that 'heavy' was a matter of perception; he suggests that even 5% losses could be felt as heavy.

καὶ ἀγχωμάλου τῆς μάχης γενομένης: 'the outcome was still undecided'. See Lazenby, in Hanson (ed.), *Hoplites*, 91, for such stalemates, perhaps the result of the drift-to-the-right phenomenon which Th. notes at v. 71. 1, which could produce 'a tendency for each side to create an overlap on the right', cp. above, 1 n. on κέρας γάρ etc.

ἀφελομένης νυκτὸς τὸ ἔργον: 'night put an end to the conflict'. Cp. Aesch. *Persians* 428, ἕως κελαινῆς νυκτὸς ὄμμ' ἀφείλετο, 'until the eye of black night removed [the battle] from view', with Broadhead's comm.

135. *Brasidas foiled at Potidaia*

1. προσελθὼν γὰρ νυκτὸς καὶ κλίμακα προσθείς: 'He approached it by night and planted a ladder against the walls'. For such scaling-ladders see Aen. Tact. xxxvi. 1, with Whitehead's n. As Gomme says 'this rare attempt at surprise attack by night on a fortified town' is easily foiled; cp. Pritchett, *GSW* ii (1974), 163.

The three Athenians killed at Potidaia according to the casualty list *IG* i³. 1184 cannot have been killed in this episode of 422, if that list is rightly dated to 423; see Lewis, in D. W. Bradeen and D. M. Lewis, *ZPE* 34 (1979), 242, against an earlier idea of Bradeen. Cf. 44. 6 n. on ἀπέθανον . . .

τοῦ γὰρ κώδωνος παρενεχθέντος οὕτως ἐς τὸ διάκενον, πρὶν ἐπανελθεῖν τὸν παραδιδόντα αὐτόν, ἡ πρόσθεσις ἐγένετο: 'because the ladder was placed at a point which the guard who was passing on the bell had just left, and before he had returned to his post'. Sommerstein on Ar. *Birds* 842 suggests that some time before 414 (the date of the play) the usual system was changed, as a result of the sort of incident Th. here describes. After the change, the duty of sentry and bell-man were separated. N. Dunbar in her *Birds* commentary (Oxford, 1995) merely notes that Th. iv. 135 'seems to reflect a different system' from that in *Birds*.

ἀπήγαγε πάλιν κατὰ τάχος τὴν στρατιάν: 'he withdrew his army in haste'. Presumably to Torone, see v. 2. 3 n. on οὔτε Βρασίδας etc.

BOOK V. 1–24

1. THE TRUCE (?) EXTENDED; ATHENS EXPELS THE DELIANS FROM DELOS

1. τοῦ δ' ἐπιγιγνομένου θέρους αἱ μὲν ἐνιαύσιοι σπονδαὶ διελέλυντο† μέχρι Πυθίων: 'At the beginning of summer the year's truce expired [but another was made, lasting] up to the Pythian games'. The Greek as it stands is extremely difficult, and it seems almost inescapable that something has dropped out at the point I have marked with a dagger. I follow Steup and Gomme who conjecture that some words like ἄλλαι δὲ ἐπεγεγένηντο (Steup, pluperfect, 'another had been made'), or ἐπεγένοντο (Gomme, aorist, 'was made') have dropped out, corresponding to my square-bracketed addition in the trans. The point of conjecturing the disappearance, during the process of textual transmission, of another verb (ἐπεγεγένηντο, ἐπεγένοντο) ending (like διελέλυντο) in -ντο is to explain why the eye of the copyist jumped straight to μέχρι.

The Pythian games were held at Delphi every four years, in the third year of each Olympiad, i.e. half way between Olympic festivals, and take their name from Apollo Pythios. They were one of the four Panhellenic festivals, the others being the Olympic games, the Nemean, and the Isthmian. The Pythian games ranked second in prestige to the Olympic games. See N. J. Richardson, *CAH* v². 224, 231, and in *OCD*³. The local Delphic month Boukatios, in which the games were held, corresponded to the Athenian month Metageitnion, and this year Metageitnion ran from 25 July to 23 August, see the tables at Meritt, *AFD* 178. There was therefore a gap between spring 422 when the truce expired (iv. 117. 1 shows that it was made at the beginning of 'spring of the following summer', i.e. in spring 423, and 118. 12 shows that it came into immediate effect) and the games at the end of summer 422. Hence the need for an extension of the truce, see above.

The alternative sense, compatible with Th.'s narrative and presumed intention, would be 'there were no actual hostilities until after the Pythia, but no formal extension of the truce either', but that can hardly be extracted from the Greek as it stands, and it would require some very radical supplementation to produce it.

Even if we assume, as we surely must, that Th. is here merely echoing the terms of the truce, it is unusual for him to mention any of the four Panhellenic festivals. The Olympic festival of 428 was the location of the meeting at which the Mytileneans spoke, iii. 8 ff., but Th.'s silence about the 432 Olympic festival is striking, see *HSCP* 94 (1992), 170–1; the only Olympic games he reports at all fully are those of 420, see v. 49–50. In addition he tells us that Kylon and Alcibiades were Olympic competitors or victors, see iii. 8. 1 n. on ἦν δὲ Ὀλυμπιάς etc. (Dorieus). For the Isthmian games see *HSCP* 1992, 193. The Nemean games are nowhere mentioned.

As Gomme says, there was no automatic general truce during the games, though competitors and others attending were considered privileged persons, see *HSCP* 1992, 191–2, and iv. 118. 1 n. and v. 18. 2 n. **καὶ ἐν τῇ ἐκεχειρίᾳ Ἀθηναῖοι Δηλίους ἀνέστησαν ἐκ Δήλου, ἡγησάμενοι κατὰ παλαιάν τινα αἰτίαν οὐ καθαροὺς ὄντας ἱερῶσθαι:** 'During the armistice the Athenians removed the Delians from Delos; they had now decided that at the time when they had been consecrated they were impure because of some ancient offence'. Maybe the massacre of Aiolian pilgrims: Hyperides fr. 70 with Parker, *ARH* 225.

What prompted the Athenians to take this step? Surely not an oracle from Pythian Apollo, because at 32. 1 we learn that the Athenians had to reinstate the Delians partly because Pythian Apollo told them to. B. Jordan (iv. 97. 3 n.), 137–9, suggests, following Nilsson, that there were military purposes to the whole purification process, including esp. that described at iii. 104 (on which see my long n. there); on this view, which can at most be part of the truth, the present decision might reflect a moment at which more secular, 'hard-headed' thinking was uppermost, whereas the reversal at 32. 1 would indicate religious qualms. But such sharp secular/religious distinctions are always treacherous, and this would probably be too cynical a view of the present passage. On Diod. xii. 73. 1 (Delians in secret negotiations with Sparta) see Parker, *ARH* 151: either rationalizing invention, or Th. 'has been culpably economical with the truth'. See also Parker, *Miasma*, 203.

καὶ ἅμα ἐλλιπὲς σφίσιν εἶναι τοῦτο τῆς καθάρσεως, ᾗ πρότερόν μοι δεδήλωται ὡς ἀνελόντες τὰς θήκας τῶν τεθνεώτων ὀρθῶς ἐνόμισαν ποιῆσαι: 'The island had been purified before, when they removed the tombs of the dead, as I have already narrated; but this purification, which seemed adequate at the time, was now thought unsatisfactory because the inhabitants had been allowed to remain' ['because ... remain' amplifies the Greek a little]. The words 'as I have already narrated' (which are a back-reference mainly to iii. 104, but cf. also i. 8. 1) are a most unusual explicit, self-referential, internal cross-reference in Th.'s narrative (for *speeches* see iv. 64. 1 n.; and note that 114. 3 and 120. 3 are not self-referential); the only other is vi. 94. 1, ὥσπερ καὶ πρότερόν μοι εἴρηται, which refers to vi. 4. 2. The form of words here adopted is Herodotean, see Hdt. vii. 108. 1, ὡς καὶ πρότερόν μοι δεδήλωται. For ancient cross-refs. see R. J. Starr, 'Cross-references in Roman Prose', *AJP* 102 (1981), 431–7 (an item I owe to A. J. Wood-man), noting that (*a*) cross-refs. in Latin writers tend to use a limited vocabulary e.g. 'ut supra diximus'; this is relevant to Th.'s echoing of Hdt., see above. (*b*) The author often, as here and at vi. 94, gives the basic fact, despite the cross-ref., so that 'even if [the reader's] memory fails, he need not consult the other passage'. (*c*) Cross-referencing can allow the author to assert his presence and control over his material (Starr, 437). Add that Th. was particularly interested in and anxious to emphasize this purification, and this provides yet another motive for the cross-ref., namely desire for emphasis; this is, however, not true of vi. 94. 1. Note that there is yet another reference to the Delos purification, at viii. 108. 4 (see next n.), though there Th. uses no cross-referencing device. This means that, by a 'ring', the purification of Delos comes near the beginning (i. 8), and near the end, of the work as we have it; the emphasis is pronounced.

καὶ οἱ μὲν Δήλιοι Ἀτραμύττιον Φαρνάκου δόντος αὐτοῖς ἐν τῇ Ἀσίᾳ ᾤκησαν, οὕτως ὡς ἕκαστος ὥρμητο: 'Pharnakes gave the Delians refuge at Adramyttion in Asia, and whoever wanted to went and settled there' [or, 'as each set out, he settled . . .']. A. Andrewes, 'Thucyd-ides and the Persians', *Historia*, 10 (1961), 1–18, at 1, notes that this is the only mention of the Persians in Th. between iv. 50 and viii. 5. 4 (Tissa-phernes' mission), a remarkable gap which he thinks Th. would have put right by subsequent revision. I postpone discussion of the distribution of attention in v. 25–116 until vol. iii of this commentary, but the focus (Peloponnese; Melos) is certainly narrow, and something in that section about Pissouthnes and/or Amorges (see below) would have prepared us for viii. 5. 5 where we are told that Tissaphernes has orders to bring Amorges in dead or alive.

For the Persian satrap Pharnakes, satrap of Hellespontine Phrygia, and his family see i. 129. 1 nn. and ii. 67. 1 and n.; Lewis, *Sparta and Persia*, 59. For Adramyttion see Andrewes, *HCT* on viii. 108. 4: Adramyttion (modern Edremit, a reasonably important town) on the gulf of the same name, is on the evidence of the present passage clearly inside the Persian sphere of control, i.e. not in the Athenian empire, although Strabo xiii. 606 calls it a 'colonial city of the Athenians', Ἀθηναίων ἄποικος πόλις, and although the nearby 'Astyrene Mysians' (Ἀστυρηνοὶ Μυσοί) did pay tribute to Athens, *ATL* i. 473. (And, we can add, although the Athenians took pains to keep Antandros in their hands, see iv. 52 and 75 for this place, which controlled the Assos–Adramyttion road.)

This action of Pharnakes has a bearing on the question, when did the Persian satrap Pissouthnes (for whom see i. 115. 4 nn.; he was satrap of the more southerly satrapy of Sardis) begin his revolt? (For which see Andrewes above.) It is usually thought (though see Westlake, *Studies*, 105) that this revolt was connected with the subsequent revolt of Pissouthnes' natural son Amorges, an important development because it ultimately led Persia to help Sparta to victory in the Peloponnesian War; see i. 112. 2–4 n. At viii. 108. 4, under 411, there is a long (ten-year) back-reference to the present short Delian presence at Adramyttion (which ended in 421 when the Athenians reinstated the Delians on Delos, thus reversing the present action: v. 32. 1). At viii. 108. 4 we shall be told retrospectively that Arsakes, at that time described as hyparch (some kind of satrapal subordinate) of Tissaphernes, had committed an atrocity against these Delians (or some of them; others survived to be reinstated in 421, as we have seen). But Adramyttion on the evidence of the present passage was in Pharnakes' satrapy (which by 411 had passed to his son Pharnabazos). One way out of this difficulty is to assume that in the late 420s Arsakes was an agent of Pharnakes, and only subsequently entered the employment of Tissaphernes. On this view Pharnakes' treatment of the unfortunate Delians, assuming that he authorized Arsakes' action, was treacherous in the extreme. A more attractive and interesting possibility, aired by Andrewes, *HCT* on viii. 108. 4, n. on Ἀρσάκου etc., is that Pissouthnes' revolt fell precisely in 422–421, and that Tissaphernes, 'sent down as the king's general to deal with the revolt, had then authority extending outside Pissouthnes' own satrapy; and that, if the speculation could be confirmed, would give us the date for the revolt which at present we lack. The service for which the Delians were to be conscripted [this is a ref. to the episode described at viii. 108] might indeed be service against Pissouthnes.' See also Lewis, *Sparta and Persia*, 80 n. 198.

2–3. KLEON IN CHALKIDIKE

A. G. Woodhead, 'Thucydides' Portrait of Kleon', *Mnemosyne*, 13 (1960), 289–317, at 304–6, argued that Th., misled by disgruntled informants (see esp. 7. 2) and activated by personal malice, seriously underrated Kleon's achievement on this campaign, in particular by failing to mention that he reconquered a number of Thracian places listed in *IG* i³. 77, the assessment of 421 (or 422? see below). See, however, the rebuttal by

W. K. Pritchett, 'The Woodheadean Interpretation of Kleon's Amphipolitan Campaign', *Mnemosyne*, 26 (1973), 373–86: the places in question are trivial (though see 18. 6 n.), with the exception of Trailos whose location Pritchett shows Woodhead to have mistaken; and the assessment list in question (*IG* i³. 77) may (*a*) belong to 422, not 421, and thus be too early to be relevant to Kleon's activities and (*b*) be unrealistically optimistic. See further 6. 1 n.

I. G. Spence, 'Thucydides, Woodhead and Kleon', *Mnemosyne*, 48 (1995), 411–37, curiously covers much of the same ground as, but in apparent ignorance of, Pritchett's 1973 article in the same journal!

2. 1. Κλέων δὲ Ἀθηναίους πείσας ἐς τὰ ἐπὶ Θρᾴκης χωρία ἐξέπλευσε: 'Kleon got the permission of the Athenians to lead a naval expedition to the Thraceward regions' [lit. 'Kleon, after persuading the Athenians, sailed out ...']. Kleon was last heard of at 122. 6 as the proposer of the decree against Skione. Note the (?tendentious) way Th. represents the present expedition as Kleon's initiative, merely endorsed by the Assembly. Cp. next n.

Ἀθηναίων μὲν ὁπλίτας ἔχων διακοσίους καὶ χιλίους καὶ ἱππέας τριακοσίους: 'with twelve hundred Athenian hoplites, three hundred Athenian horsemen'. At 7. 2, a retrospective passage, we learn that the troops were unwilling to serve on this expedition; Pritchett, *Mnemosyne* 1973, 385, puts this down to a combination of political dislike and a feeling that the force was too small: if Nikias or some other general (he suggests) set out with the entire hoplite force, feeling might have been different.

2. σχὼν δὲ ἐς Σκιώνην πρῶτον ἔτι πολιορκουμένην: 'He put in first at Skione, which was still being besieged'. The contemporary Ar. *Wasps* 209–10 mentions the siege; see nn. on 210 by Sommerstein and D. M. MacDowell in their edns.

κατέπλευσεν ἐς τὸν Κωφὸν λιμένα τῶν Τορωναίων: 'he sailed into the Still Harbour in the territory of Torone'. I have changed Jowett's 'so-called Colophonian port'. The manuscripts do indeed have 'of the Kolophonians', Κολοφωνίων. But Κωφόν (which is simply a common adjective meaning 'dumb', 'dull', 'muffled', 'quiet', i.e. 'sheltered') is the ingenious and surely correct emendation of Pluygers, *Mnemosyne*, 6 (1857), 287; but see already W. M. Leake, *Travels in Northern Greece*, iii (London, 1835), 119 and n. 2: Leake's name deserves to be in the apparatus to the *OCT* instead of or in addition to that of Pluygers (cp. Pritchett, *EGH* 1). The emendation can be defended by appeal to four items of evidence. (i) Strabo vii fr. 32 mentions a Κωφὸς λιμήν in the right area. (ii) The harbour of Torone was proverbially noted for its tranquillity, and the word used for 'tranquil' in the proverbs is, precisely, κωφός. See Suid. κ 2310 Adler, κωφότερος τοῦ Τορωναίου λιμένος, 'quieter than the harbour of Torone', cp. Zenobius iv. 68 in Leutsch and Schneidewin, *Corp. Paroem. Graec.* i, p. 103, explaining the proverb by reference to the sheltered nature of the harbour, from which you could not hear the roar of the sea. There was an analogous but more famous 'Still Harbour', κωφὸς λιμήν, at the Piraeus near Athens: Xen. *Hell.* ii. 4. 31. This was probably the 'bight attaching to the northern side of the Grand Harbour': R. Garland, *The Piraeus from the Fifth to the First Century* BC (London and Ithaca, NY, 1987), 151, 153, 217 (whose trans. 'Still Harbour' I have borrowed), drawing on J. Day, 'The *Kophos Limen* of the Piraeus', *AJA* 31 (1927), 441-9 (who discusses Torone at 443). LSJ⁹, entry under κωφός, less plausibly suggests that Munychia is meant, 'as opposed to the noisy Piraeus'. (iii) There is a superb natural harbour near Torone to the south, for which see Meritt, *AJA* 1923 (iv. 110. 1 n. on εὐθὺς στρατεύει etc.; as we saw there, Gomme ignores this article in its Torone aspect), 453, with photograph, also 455. (iv) The harbour area is now called Koupho, a modern version of the ancient name (Meritt).

3. αἰσθόμενος ὑπ' αὐτομόλων: 'where he learnt from deserters'. Lang (*Mnemosyne* 1995), 52, includes this among participial expressions of motivation relating to Kleon; but it is not quite on all fours with absolute uses of the participle αἰσθόμενος, 'realizing', 'perceiving' that *x*; here it is offered as a factual statement that Kleon interrogated deserters and learnt the correct fact that Brasidas was not at Torone. Note the military intelligence-gathering.

ὅτι οὔτε Βρασίδας ἐν τῇ Τορώνῃ οὔτε οἱ ἐνόντες ἀξιόμαχοι εἶεν: 'that Brasidas was not at Torone, and that the garrison was too weak to resist'. On 'not at Torone' Gomme remarks 'though it was apparently his headquarters (iv. 122. 2, 129. 1)'. So this is a significant piece of presentation by negation (iv. 94. 1 n. on ψιλοὶ δέ etc.): the point is 'finding that Brasidas was not at Torone, as might have been expected given that it was his headquarters'. The passages adduced by Gomme antedate the appointment of Pasitelidas (or Epitelidas? see n. there) at iv. 132. 3, but even with a lieutenant in usual control of Torone, Brasidas' absence (presumably denuding the town's defences of good troops) was surely rash. We do not know how far away he was, see 3. 3 n.

⟨ἐς⟩ τὸν λιμένα: 'into the harbour'. This must be the harbour of Torone itself (near the Lekythos promontory and to the north of the hill on which Torone proper stood) as distinct from the Still Harbour to the south, which is 'in Toronaian territory' (above, para. 2). See Meritt's plan at 453; for Torone generally see iv. 110. 1 n. on εὐθὺς στρατεύει etc.

4. καὶ πρὸς τὸ περιτείχισμα πρῶτον ἀφικνεῖται, ὃ προσπερι-

ἔβαλε τῇ πόλει ὁ Βρασίδας: 'He first came to the new line of wall
which Brasidas had built round the city . . .'. This analepsis or flashback
is not a precise back-reference to anything we have been told in the
Torone narrative in book iv (110–16). Th. delays telling us about it until
now when he needs it for the resumed narrative.

3. 1. Πασιτελίδας τε ὁ Λακεδαιμόνιος ἄρχων: 'Pasitelidas the
Spartan governor'. See iv. 132. 3 and n. on καὶ Κλεαρίδαν etc.

καὶ αἱ νῆες ἅμα περιέπλεον ⟨αἱ⟩ ἐς τὸν λιμένα περιπεμφθεῖσαι:
'the Athenian ships that had been sent round were sailing into the
harbour'. For these ships, and for the harbour (not the Still Harbour), see
2. 3 and n. on ⟨ἐς⟩ τὸν λιμένα.

**3. ἀποσχὼν τεσσαράκοντα μάλιστα σταδίους μὴ φθάσαι
ἐλθών:** 'He was within about forty stades of arriving in time to prevent
it'. Perhaps 8 km., though we do not know what stade Th. was operating
with here, cp. Bauslaugh, *JHS* 1979 (iv. 8. 6 n. on ἡ γὰρ νῆσος etc.), 6.
With this item cp. iv. 106. 4 where Brasidas just beats Th. to Amphipolis
but misses taking Eion by a night. This is a counterfactual (not quite an
'if . . . not' because the protasis is not negative, contrast iv. 106. 4 n.): 'if
Brasidas had managed to cover these forty stades in less time / . . . he
had been slightly closer when he set out, the city would not have fallen'.
Where *did* he set out from? Th. does not say. We last saw Brasidas in
action at Potidaia, iv. 135, but after that he 'withdrew his army', presumably
to Torone, see n. there and 2. 3 n. on οὔτε Βρασίδας etc. That is, he
was now only temporarily absent from Torone.

    Gomme, *More Essays*, 114, remarks that Kleon's celerity at Torone
recalls, precisely, Brasidas himself at Amphipolis in book iv.

4. τροπαῖά τε ἔστησαν δύο: 'erected two trophies'. See Pritchett,
GSW ii (1974), 265 f.: more than one trophy was sometimes erected, as
here, cp. vii. 24. 1 (three).

καὶ τῶν Τορωναίων γυναῖκας μὲν καὶ παῖδας ἠνδραπόδισαν,
αὐτοὺς δὲ καὶ Πελοποννησίους καὶ εἴ τις ἄλλος Χαλκιδέων ἦν,
ξύμπαντας ἐς ἑπτακοσίους, ἀπέπεμψαν ἐς τὰς Ἀθήνας· καὶ
αὐτοῖς τὸ μὲν Πελοποννήσιον ὕστερον ἐν ταῖς γενομέναις
σπονδαῖς ἀπῆλθε, τὸ δὲ ἄλλο ἐκομίσθη ὑπ' Ὀλυνθίων, ἀνὴρ
ἀντ' ἀνδρὸς λυθείς: 'They enslaved the women and children of
Torone, and sent a total of seven hundred male prisoners to Athens,
made up of Toronaians, any other Chalkidians taken in Torone and
Peloponnesians. The Peloponnesian prisoners were released at the
peace which was concluded shortly afterwards; the rest were recovered
by the Olynthians in exchange for a corresponding number of prisoners
held by them'. This passage provides full and valuable information about

the treatment of a captured town: Pritchett, *GSW* iv (1990), 156, and elsewhere: see below. With the formula ἀνὴρ ἀντ' ἀνδρός ('in exchange for a corresponding number of prisoners held by them', lit. 'man for man') cp. ii. 103: Pritchett, 253. Against Gomme's view that the woman and children would have been ransomed automatically by private individuals see Pritchett, 284 n. 106 (also *GSW* i (1971), 91 n. 35); Pritchett notes that ransom, λύτρωσις, is 'relatively infrequent in many hundreds of proxeny and honorary decrees'. The mention of the Olynthians is a puzzle: we are not told how they came to have so many Athenian prisoners. Gomme suggested Spartolos (ii. 79) or Eion (iv. 7); Pritchett (256 and n. 370, cp. 298), noting that Potidaia was an Athenian base, suggested that some Athenians had been captured in an unrecorded engagement. For sale on the spot see Pritchett, 433, comparing e.g. Diod. xiii. 104. 7 (Lysander and Iasos in Caria). (At 256 and n. 370 Pritchett cites Oberhummer *RE*, entry under 'Torone', for the population of Torone, an estimated 3000, but adds that the assessment of 15 talents in 425 might suggest a higher figure. That hopeful assessment is however a precarious basis for such reasoning.)

Note the proleptic reference to the Peace of Nikias: Th. is not particularly concerned to maintain suspense, cp. the forward refs. to the plague at i. 23 and ii. 31. 2, see n. there on οὔπω νενοσηκυίας. The clause about the Peloponnesian garrison at Torone seems to be v. 18. 7, see n. there on εἴ τις τῶν ξυμμάχων etc. C. Meyer, *Urkunden*, 27, notes that the present passage is one of those which indicate knowledge by Th. of a particular paragraph of the peace treaty, and thus tells against the 'Kirchhoff thesis' according to which chs. 18–19 are a late insertion.

Here the women are mentioned before the children, contrary to the more normal Thucydidean pattern observed by T. Wiedemann, see iv. 123. 4 n. on ὑπεκκομίζει etc. Diodorus (xii. 73. 3) reverses Th.'s order.

From the separate mention of Toronaians and Chalkidians, Zahrnt (248) plausibly infers that Brasidas had not incorporated Torone into the Chalkidian League (*contra*, Gomme, *HCT* iii. 591). For Olynthian/Toronaian tension in this period see iv. 110. 2 n. on ἦρχε etc.

Torone was remembered like Skione (iv. 122. 6 n. on ψήφισμα etc.): Xen. *Hell.* ii. 2. 3.

5. εἷλον δὲ καὶ Πάνακτον Ἀθηναίων ἐν μεθορίοις τεῖχος Βοιωτοὶ ὑπὸ τὸν αὐτὸν χρόνον προδοσίᾳ: 'About the same time Panakton, a fortress on the Athenian frontier, was betrayed to the Boiotians'. For the important fort of Panakton, overlooking the Skourta plain, see M. H. Munn, *The Defense of Attica: The Dema Wall and the Boiotian War of 378–375 BC* (Berkeley, 1993), 7, with map at 6 and fig. 2 at end of book. (A list of ephebes has now been discovered there, which as Munn says clinches the identification; see Munn forthcoming in J. Fossey (ed.), *Boeotia Antiqua* (6). I am grateful to Prof. Munn for an advance sight of this paper.) Panakton is mentioned alongside Eleusis and Phyle in *Syll*.³ 485; see also Dem. lii. 3.

The mention of Panakton here is not only abrupt but interrupts a narrative which otherwise deals with Chalkidike (para. 6 follows on naturally from para. 4). But we do not need to suppose, with Gomme that this is due to imperfect revision.

6. [On *IG* i³. 76, Athenian alliance with some Bottiaians, which Gomme discussed at this point, see iv. 132. 1 n.]

4-5. PHAIAX IN SICILY AND ITALY

Th. resumes the Sicilian narrative from iv. 65. The present short section prepares us (see pp. 108 and 120 n. 304) for the main Sicilian expedition of books vi–vii, most obviously at v. 4. 5 (Syracusans said to be aiming at supremacy; see n. there for the way events at Leontini strengthened Syracuse still further). Note also that v. 4. 3 (the depopulation of Leontini by Syracuse) anticipates vi. 6. 2; 8. 2; 33. 2; 44. 3, etc.; and there may be a reference to v. 4. 6 (Phaiax wins over Kamarina and Akragas) at vi. 6. 1, καὶ τοῖς προσγεγενημένοις ξυμμάχοις, see Jowett's footnote (but text and meaning are uncertain, see Dover in *HCT*). The mention of Kamarina looks forward to the great Kamarina debate at vi. 75 ff. (cf. iv. 60. 2 n. on καὶ πλέονι, end of n.). And finally, v. 5. 1, cp. 4. 1, stresses the Italian aspect to Athens' interest in the west; for this important dimension to the great Sicilian expedition see vi. 34. 1; 44. 2–3; 88. 6–7; vii. 33. 4–5; 57. 11.

Phaiax has limited success in Sicily and gives up (4. 6 nn.), but he deserves more credit than he usually gets for his diplomatic success, however short-lived, at Italian Lokri (usually hostile to Athens), where he was able to take advantage of the Lokrians' local difficulties with their Tyrrhenian colonists, see 5. 3 n.

On the peculiar arrangement of Phaiax's mission in Th.'s narrative (esp. the postponement of the Lokrian agreement) see 5. 2 n.

4. 1. Φαίαξ δὲ ὁ Ἐρασιστράτου: 'Phaiax son of Erasistratos'. Phaiax, of good birth (Plut. *Alc.* 13) and son of a strategos (Diog. Laert. ii. 63) features in Aristophanes, see *Knights* 1377 with Sommerstein's n. (Phaiax admired by the young for his clever oratory; contrast Eupolis F116 Kassel/Austin, where he is said to be good at chatting, but no good at speaking, λαλεῖν ἄριστος, ἀδυνατώτατος λέγειν). Phaiax is also known from Plutarch for his collusive role in the ostracism of Hyperbolus, see viii. 73. 3 n. and Rhodes, *RFP* 85-6; for ostraka cast against Phaiax see M. Lang, *Agora*, xxv (1990), 98-9, and F. Willemsen and S. Brenne, 'Verzeichnis der Kerameikos-Ostraka', *AM* 106 (1991), 147-56, at 155; *LGPN* ii, 'Phaiax' no. 1.

ἐς Ἰταλίαν καὶ Σικελίαν: 'to Italy and Sicily'. The Italian dimension to Athens' interest in the west should never be forgotten; see below ch. 5 and above, Introductory n. to 4-5.

2. Λεοντῖνοι: 'the Leontines'. For Athens' ally Leontini see iii. 86. 2 n. on οἱ γὰρ Συρακόσιοι etc. and iii. 86. 3 n.; iv. 25. 9 n.

ἀπελθόντων Ἀθηναίων ἐκ Σικελίας μετὰ τὴν ξύμβασιν: 'After the general peace and the withdrawal of the Athenians from Sicily'. See iv. 65. 1-2 (425). Th. might have inserted this piece of information somewhere in the second half of book iv. See further 5. 2 n.

πολίτας τε ἐπεγράψαντο πολλοὺς καὶ ὁ δῆμος τὴν γῆν ἐπενόει ἀναδάσασθαι: 'the Leontines had enrolled many new citizens, and the democratic party were planning a redistribution of land'. This is the only mention in Th. of the important notion of γῆς ἀναδασμός, 'redistribution of land', the desire or demand for which (often coupled with cancellation of debts, χρεῶν ἀποκοπή) was a feature of the fourth century and Hellenistic periods: D. Asheri, *Distribuzioni di terre nell' antica Grecia* (*Memorie dell'accad. delle scienze di Torino, Classe di scienza morali, storiche e filologiche*, 4 no. 10: Turin, 1966), see further below; J. K. Davies, *CAH* vii² (1984), 294; A. Fuks, 'Social Revolution in Greece in the Hellenistic Age', in *Social Conflict in Ancient Greece* (Leiden and Jerusalem, 1984), 40-51, noting that in the fifth century, by contrast with the following centuries, there was little striving for change of the kind expressed by demands for redistribution of land. Actual redistributions were rare at all periods, see, for one example, Fuks, 'Redistribution of Land and Houses in Syracuse in 356 BC', *CQ* 18 (1968), 207-23, repr. in *Social Conflicts* (above), 213-24. For such evidence (not entirely negligible) as there is for social and economic tensions in the classical period see M. M. Austin, *CAH* vi² (1994), 528-9 and 533 (adducing evidence from the fifth century as well as the fourth); D. Asheri, *CAH* iv² (1988), 754, notes that, as a colonial region, Sicily was always specially prone to social upheaval.

With the redistribution of land Gomme, following Arnold, compares Hdt. iv. 159 (Cyrene, another colonial context), where we hear that settlers were invited by Delphi to go to Cyrene for a redistribution of land, ἐπὶ γῆς ἀναδασμῷ. This certainly causes resentment and leads to outside intervention, but some other features look very different from the present passage, e.g. the involvement of Delphi, and above all the difference in the kind of land to be redistributed. At Leontini it was privately owned land, at Cyrene it was hitherto unallocated land. Asheri, *Distribuzioni* (above), 41, discussing the present passage of Th., rejects Gomme's comparison outright.

The enrolment of new citizens is not always or necessarily a sign of social unrest, cp. Hdt. viii. 75. 1 (Thespiai), but it was surely liable to exacerbate tension in a context of deportations, mass evictions, etc., such as characterize Sicilian history (cp. e.g. Th. v. 5. 1; vi. 4. 2; 5. 3). Asheri, *CAH* v². 158, notes that the resettlement (by the middle of the fifth cent.) of Naxos and Katana, whose populations had been decanted to Leontini (iv. 25. 7 n. on ἐστρατευσαν etc.), must have been a relief to Leontini, which thus saw the departure of large numbers of deportees and could look forward to a period of prosperity. He is speaking of the mid cent., but Leontini's history became troubled again with the war against Syracuse (iii. 86: 427), and the present passage shows that the citizenship and land issues became problematic again after the Gela congress of 424.

3. οἱ δὲ δυνατοὶ αἰσθόμενοι Συρακοσίους τε ἐπάγονται καὶ ἐκβάλλουσι τὸν δῆμον. καὶ οἱ μὲν ἐπλανήθησαν ὡς ἕκαστοι, οἱ δὲ δυνατοὶ ὁμολογήσαντες Συρακοσίοις καὶ τὴν πόλιν ἐκλιπόντες καὶ ἐρημώσαντες Συρακούσας ἐπὶ πολιτείᾳ ᾤκησαν: 'The oligarchs realized this, called in the Syracusans, and drove out the democrats, who dispersed over Sicily. The oligarchs then made an agreement with the Syracusans whereby they abandoned and dismantled Leontini, and settled in Syracuse as citizens'. For the destruction of Leontini see M. Dreher, 'La dissoluzione della *polis* di Leontinoi dopo la pace di Gela (424 a.C.)', *ASNP* 16 (1986), 637–60, suggesting (654) that the depopulation of Leontini fell in winter 424/3; S. Berger, 'Great and Small Poleis: Syracuse and Leontinoi', *Historia*, 40 (1991), 129–42, at 137.

Numismatic evidence may suggest that some of the refugees may have gone to mainland Greece (Euboia): P. R. Franke, 'Leontinische *ΦΥΓΑΔΕΣ* in Chalkis? Ein Hortfund sizilischer Bronzemünzen des 5 Jhrdt. v. Chr. aus Euboia', *Arch. Anz. (Beiblatt zum JDAI)*, 81 (1966), 395–407, esp. 404–5.

4. Φωκαίας τε τῆς πόλεώς τι τῆς Λεοντίνων χωρίον καλούμενον καταλαμβάνουσι καὶ Βρικκινίας ὃν ἔρυμα ἐν τῇ Λεοντίνῃ: 'seized a place called Phokaiai, which was part of the town of Leontini, and Brikinniai, a fortress in the territory of Leontini'. Not securely located. Steph. Byz. mentions Brikinniai.

5. ὡς Συρακοσίων δύναμιν περιποιουμένων ἐπιστρατεῦσαι: 'that the Syracusans were aiming at hegemony'. See iii. 86. 2 n. on οἱ γὰρ Συρακόσιοι etc., citing J. K. Davies, and for the growth of Syracuse see now Asheri, *CAH* v². 166–8. See above, introductory n. to 4–5. Beloch *Gr. Gesch.* ii² 1. 354 concludes his discussion of the present episode by

saying 'the territory of Leontini was incorporated in the Syracusan state', and cites only Th. This goes slightly beyond what Th. tells us, but is no doubt right. Syracuse was, then, stronger and more powerful still as a result of the events between 424 and 422, and part of the point of these two chapters is to rub that in.

6. **τοὺς μὲν Καμαριναίους πείθει καὶ Ἀκραγαντίνους:** 'Phaiax won over the Kamarinaians and Akragantines'. Andrewes, *CAH* v². 447-8, notes that these two cities which received Phaiax well were both *Dorian*: 'hostility to Syracuse was not simply based on that [the Ionian/Dorian] antithesis'. (Andrewes omits to mention Phaiax's success at Italian Lokri, see 5. 2 n. on ἐγεγένητο etc.)

For Kamarina, a small place, but one which had prospered in recent decades, see iv. 25. 7 n. on Καμαρίνης etc.

Akragas, mentioned here for the first time by Th., was a much bigger catch; for its prosperity and size see esp. Diod. xiii. 81-4 and for its superb natural site see Pol. ix. 27. 1-10, with Walbank's nn. See generally P. Orlandini, *Princeton Encyclopaedia*, 23-6; R. Wilson, *Arch. Reps.* 1987-8, 126-8, and *OCD*³, entry under 'Acragas', and in *CAH* plates vol. to iv² (1988), no. 266 (the enormous temple to Olympian Zeus); Kraay, *ACGC* 226 (Akragantine silver perhaps derived from Spain via Carthage, with which Akragas certainly traded extensively, Diod. xiii. 81. 4); D. Asheri, *CAH* v². 168-70, calling Akragas an 'affluent plutocratic republic'; and Lewis, *CAH* vi². 124, Akragas 'evidently the second city of Sicily' after Syracuse. For Akragas' population see Diod. xiii. 84. 3, with J. de Waele, 'La popolazione di Acragas antica', in *ΦΙΛΙΑΣ ΧΑΡΙΝ: Miscellanea in honore di E. Manni*, iii (Rome, 1979), 744-60: Diodorus' figures of up to 20,000 citizens and a total population of 200,000 may not be far wrong, though the second figure cannot be controlled.

ἐν δὲ Γέλᾳ ἀντιστάντος: 'he failed at Gela'. For Gela see iv. 58 n. on Καμαριναίοις καὶ Γελῴοις etc. At iv. 58 we were told that Kamarina and Gela made a truce with each other; note that they respond in different ways to Phaiax's overtures.

οὐκέτι ἐπὶ τοὺς ἄλλους ἔρχεται: 'so did not approach them' [the other states]. I have changed Jowett's 'went no further' because it is misleading to make Th. say Phaiax succeeded at Kamarina and Akragas but failed at Gela so went no further: Gela is between Kamarina and Akragas, so Phaiax's order of visits was presumably Kamarina, Gela, Akragas. Andrewes, *CAH* v². 447, describes Phaiax's mission thus: he 'encouraged the Leontine remnant on the spot and hoped to help them further by building a coalition against Syracuse. This got nowhere ...'

ἐς Κατάνην: 'at Katana'. The Katanans have already been mentioned at iii. 116. 1, though not in a military or political context, but because the eruption of Mt. Etna damaged their territory. On the site, which briefly became a new and renamed city Aitna earlier in the century, see G. Rizza, *Princeton Encyclopaedia*, 442–3, and R. Wilson, *Arch. Reps.* 1987–8, 117, and in *OCD*³, entry under 'Catana'; D. Asheri, *CAH* v². 157.

5. 1. καὶ ἐν τῇ Ἰταλίᾳ τισὶ πόλεσιν: 'several Italian cities'. See, for the Italian factor, introductory n. to 4–5.

καὶ Λοκρῶν ἐντυγχάνει τοῖς ἐκ Μεσσήνης ἐποίκοις ἐκπεπτω- κόσιν: 'some Lokrian settlers who had been driven out of Messina'. Again (see 4. 2 n.) this is material which might have been recounted in its right chronological place somewhere in book iv. For Lokri see iii. 86 and iv. 1. 1 n. on Συρακοσίων etc.

καὶ ἐγένετο Μεσσήνη Λοκρῶν τινὰ χρόνον: 'so for a while Messina was held by the Lokrians'. On this episode see Musti, in *Locri Epizefirii* (iv. 1. 1 n. on Συρακοσίων etc.), 89–90, calling it 'qualitatively different' from the brief takeover at iv. 1.

2. ἐγεγένητο γὰρ τοῖς Λοκροῖς πρὸς αὐτὸν ὁμολογία ξυμβά- σεως πέρι πρὸς τοὺς Ἀθηναίους: 'for the Lokrians had already agreed with him to enter into a treaty with the Athenians'. This was quite a coup for Phaiax, given Lokri's hostility to Athens and Athens' allies, and its political closeness to Syracuse, both before and after 422 (iii. 86, 103; iv. 1, 24. 2; vi. 44. 2, see below). Andrewes in *CAH* (cp. above 4. 6 n. on τοὺς μὲν Καμαριναίους etc.) passes over the Lokri success, and the Italian dimension to Phaiax's visit generally, when he merely writes of Phaiax being well received at Kamarina and Akragas (he does, however, discuss Rhegion's attitude in 415). See Frederiksen, in *Locri Epize- firii*, 205–6 (cp. above, iii. 86. 2 n. on Λοκροί etc.) for the suggestion that the brief reconciliation achieved by Phaiax may have increased Athens' desire for S. Italian timber. Frederiksen further cites the mention, in the Hellenistic 'Lokri tables', of pitch, another desirable commodity for a naval power: see A. de Franciscis, *Stato e società in Locri Epizefiri (L'Archivio dell' Olympieion Locrese)* (Naples, 1972), no. 15 line 14, τᾶς [*sic*; genitive] πίσσας. The Lokri tables are inscriptions recording money raised by the sanctuary of Olympian Zeus at Lokri for King Pyrrhus in his war against Rome, see P. Franke, *CAH* vii². 2 (1989), 471–2; D. Musti (ed.), *Le tavole di Locri: Atti del colloquio sugli aspetti politici, economici, cultuali e linguistici dei testi dell'archivio locrese 1977* (Naples, 1979).

Th.'s formulation is cautious: in effect the Lokrians agreed to make an agreement. Evidently they were hostile again by 415, see vi. 44. 2. See also next n.

It is striking that Th. records this Lokrian agreement with Phaiax in this retrospective, anachronic (chronologically deviant), way; see

Andrewes's good discussion at *HCT* v. 366–7, in a section on breaches of chronological sequence as one possible category of 'indications of incompleteness' in Th.'s account of the Ten Years War. Andrewes accepts that some such breaches are due to Th.'s preference for giving material where it becomes most helpful or relevant; but he regards the present passage (together with iv. 70 and 79–81, Brasidas' expedition to Thrace; and iv. 80. 3–4, the liquidation of the helots) as one of the more serious 'breaches of chronological order'. As for Phaiax's agreement with Lokri, it must, as Andrewes says, precede his negotiations in Sicily, 'and it might have been expected that Th. would have put this in its chronological place'; Th. might even have split Phaiax's mission 'into two or more parts'.

3. οὐδ᾽ ἂν τότε, εἰ μὴ αὐτοὺς κατεῖχεν ὁ πρὸς Ἱππωνιᾶς καὶ Μεδμαίους πόλεμος: 'And they would have continued to hold out if they had not been constrained by a war against the Hipponians and Medmaians'. [The manuscripts have Ἰτωνέας and Μελαίους, hence Jowett's 'Itoneans and Melaeans' which I have, without much confidence, changed in accordance with A. Weidner, 'Zu Thucydides', *Rh. Mus.* 19 (1864), 140–1, who emended on the basis of Strabo vi. 256. Weidner must have been basically right; Beloch, *Neue Jahrb. f. Philol.* 123 (1881), 392, preferred Ἱππωνιέας on the evidence of the coins, cp. *HN*² 100, but it is unsafe to assume Th. had precisely that form; cp. Lewis, *Towards a Historian's Text*, 151, discussing Μελαίους: 'I do not see that there is any great profit in making the alteration. Thucydides was just wrong'.] Both places were colonies of Lokri (Strabo, as above), on the other side of the Bruttium peninsula, i.e. the toe of Italy. For Hipponion (later Vibo Valentia), whose naval installations were developed by Agathokles (Strabo), see L. Richardson, Jr., *Princeton Encyclopaedia*, 394; N. Purcell, *CAH* vi². 396 n. 55 and 399 n. 69; K. Lomas, *Rome and the Western Greeks 350 BC–AD 200: Conquest and Acculturation in Southern Italy* (London, 1993), 21 (it had more cultivable land than its neighbour Rhegion). The most exciting recent find from Hipponion is the 'Orphic' text, *SEG* xxvi (1976), 1139 (*c*.400 BC), on which see H. Lloyd-Jones, *Academic Papers* i (Oxford, 1990), 82, and M. Gigante, in *Locri Epizefirii*, 646–51. The old Greek name Hipponion was used by Appian, *BC* v. 91; for this piece of apparent cultural archaism Lomas (183) cites E. L. Bowie, in M. I. Finley (ed.), *Studies in Ancient Society* (London, 1974), 201 n. 95.

For Medma see Philipp, *RE* xv. 107–8; M. Paoletti and S. Settis, *Medma e il suo territorio* (Bari, 1981); K. Rutter, *HN*³ (forthcoming).

This was a colonial war, in that respect like that between Corinth and its daughter-city Corcyra at i. 25 ff. Its nature has been much discussed, though there is perilously little evidence for Lokri's relations with its daughter-cities. For those relations see Graham, *Colony and Mother-City* (iv. 103. 4 n. on πρὸς τοὺς ἐμπολιτεύοντας etc.), 86 and 94–5; J. Seibert, *Metropolis und Apoikie* (diss. Warburg, 1963), 81–7; D. Musti, 'Sui rapporti tra Locri e le colonie Locresi sul Tirreno', in *Locri Epizefirii*, 108–20. The main items of ancient evidence are: (i) *SEG* xi. 1121, which Jeffery and Johnston, *LSAG*² 285–6, no. 2, put *c.*525–500 BC: a dedication at Olympia by the Hipponies [*sic*], together with the Medmaians and Lokrians, of spoils taken from the people of Kroton; (ii) The present passage of Th.; (iii) *SGDI* 2840 or *FD* iii. 1. 176, an inscription mentioning a 'Lokrian Hipponian' in (?) the third cent. BC. Of these, (i) is an alliance (which might however have been temporary), (ii) is a war, and (iii) implies very close relations indeed between Lokri and Hipponion, almost identity. But as Seibert, 85 n. 1, points out, Hipponion's fourth-century history had been stormy and (iii) is thus not evidence for the fifth-century position. Colony/mother-city relations are very diverse, and we cannot mechanically take a model of such relations and impose it on the Lokrian case. Seibert, 83 and n. 4, sees the war of *c.*422 as an attempt by Lokri to *get* control of its colonies. W. Oldfather, *RE* xiii. 6332, thinks the war was undertaken by the Lokrians, to win back their revolted colonists which had long been free (he thinks it improbable that they chose precisely this time to rebel, when Lokri looked strong after the annexation of Messina. This goes beyond what we can possibly know). Musti (113) thinks the colonies were trying to *escape* from a relationship unfavourable to themselves, and that the initiative for the war came from the colonies. I do not see how we can decide. If we have to do so, then in view of the physical propinquity, Musti's view seems likelier. Cp. Graham, 84, discussing this war: colonies which were neighbours of the metropolis had more opportunity for wars, but such wars were still shameful.

The seriousness of the war can be measured by the (temporary) effect it had on Lokrian foreign policy, causing them to reverse a consistent anti-Athenianism, see previous n. Th.'s 'if . . . not' presentation makes this emphatically, 'they would not have done it now if they had not been constrained'.

6-13. KLEON'S AMPHIPOLITAN CAMPAIGN; DEATHS OF KLEON AND BRASIDAS

For this campaign see Gomme, 'Thucydides and Kleon: the Second Battle of Amphipolis', *More Essays*, 112–21 (Th.'s account factually reliable but slanted in its judgement against Kleon, who cannot be convicted of cowardice); Pritchett, *SAGT* i (1965), 30–45; J. K. Anderson, 'Cleon's Orders at Amphipolis', *JHS* 85 (1965), 1–4 (mainly on 10. 3–4, see n. there); N. Jones, *CA* 1977 (iv. 102. 1 n.), 71–104; Pritchett, *SAGT* iii (1980), 298–346, and briefly *EGH* (1994), 61. (Pritchett's lengthy 1980 study seems to be in part a reply to Jones, who is, however, explicitly cited only once and briefly, at 327 n. 63, but who is presumably the author of the 'recent reconstruction of the battle' mentioned by Pritchett without citation at 337, see below, 10. 6 n. on ἔθει etc.; Jones is also, I think, one of those in Pritchett's mind at 332, where he rejects Kromayer's Hill of the Macedonians—calling it 'the other candidate in the literature'—as the site of Kleon's *lophos* at 7. 4, see n. there. There is also an apparent reference to Jones, 93–4, at Pritchett, 301, where he says that a site on the eastern wall 'has been favoured by some' as a candidate for the Thracian Gates; cp. also Pritchett, 340. See 10. 1 n.) Pritchett also reconsiders and alters his 1965 views on the topography and strategy, in the light of Lazaridis' findings; see below. But note that Lazaridis 1986 rejects Pritchett's 1980 views, though Lazaridis' own idea that *fifth*-century Amphipolis was surrounded by a Geländemauer circuit should be accepted with caution, see iv. 102. 3 n. on ἦν Ἀμφίπολιν etc., where however I defer to Lazaridis' authority. See also B. Mitchell, *Historia* 1991, 170–92 (Kleon's career an unsuccessful attempt to combine the roles of politician and military leader; his behaviour at Amphipolis in particular demonstrates his lack of experience). Full refs. to all these studies are given at iv. 102. 1 n., as also to the various publications of D. Lazaridis. Lazaridis' excavations have converted most investigators to the view that the bridge over the Strymon (see iv. 103. 4 and final n.) was on the northern, not the southern or western side of the city, and that the Thracian Gates of v. 10. 1 were on the northern part of the wall. The 'first gate' of 10. 6 (see n. there on καὶ ὁ μέν etc.) should also be located in the north (not, as Gomme thought, the south-east), near the bridge but to the west of the Thracian Gates.

For the battle of Amphipolis as part of the *aristeia* of Brasidas see Howie (Introduction, p. 39 n. 99), 441–4 and 448.

6. 1. Σταγίρῳ μὲν προσβάλλει Ἀνδρίων ἀποικίᾳ καὶ οὐχ εἷλε, Γαληψὸν δὲ τὴν Θασίων ἀποικίαν λαμβάνει κατὰ κράτος: 'attacked Stagiros, a colony of the Andrians, but failed to take it. He succeeded, however, in storming Galepsos, a Thasian colony'. But we have already been told that Stagiros was an Andrian, and Galepsos a Thasian, colony, see iv. 88. 2 and 107. 3 and nn.; see Introduction, pp. 74 ff., 80, 119. For Andrewes, *HCT* v. 364, this repetition is an 'indication of incompleteness' in Th.'s Ten Years War narrative.

Against Woodhead's idea that Th. has here concealed significant territorial gains made by Kleon, and attested by inscriptions, see Pritchett, *Mnemosyne* 1973, 373–86 (above, introductory n. to 2–3), and

Mitchell, *Historia* 1991, 170–82; cp. already Gomme, *More Essays*, 115 and n. 2. Mitchell (192) suggests that Th. specifies the Thasian origins of Galepsos because he was aware of a confusion with Gale/Galepsos (see iv. 107. 3 n. on καὶ Γαληψός etc.); I doubt this, partly because it does not account for Stagiros, nor does it allow for Th.'s habitual inclusion of such colonial descriptions (above, p. 74), even to the extent of repeating himself on the subject of Galepsos, see above for iv. 107. 3.

2. κατὰ τὸ ξυμμαχικόν: 'according to the terms of the alliance'. See iv. 132. 1.

καὶ ἐς τὴν Θρᾴκην ἄλλους παρὰ Πολλῆν τὸν Ὀδομάντων βασιλέα: 'and another to Polles the king of the Odomantian Thracians'. For the Odomantians, east of the Strymon, see N. Jones, *CA* 1977, 83 and 101 n. 59; Pritchett, *SAGT* iii. 329 and n. 66; cp. Hammond, *HM* 193.

αὐτὸς ἡσύχαζε: 'he made no further move' [lit. 'he remained quiet']. See Schneider, *Information und Absicht*, 21 f.: by declining, here and at 7. 1, to tell us (as he so often does tell us about his agents) what Kleon's plan was, Th. gives the impression that Kleon was drifting aimlessly.

3. Βρασίδας δὲ πυνθανόμενος ταῦτα ἀντεκάθητο καὶ αὐτὸς ἐπὶ τῷ Κερδυλίῳ· ἔστι δὲ τὸ χωρίον τοῦτο Ἀργιλίων ἐπὶ μετεώρου πέραν τοῦ ποταμοῦ, οὐ πολὺ ἀπέχον τῆς Ἀμφιπόλεως: 'When Brasidas heard all this, he took up a counter-position on Kerdylion. This is high ground on the right bank of the river, not far from Amphipolis, in Argilian territory'. For the most probable identification of Kerdylion as Hill 339 see Pritchett, *SAGT* i. 39 and iii. 323–8 with plate 41b. It is marked on N. Jones's map at 78 or Mitchell, 190. Jones himself prefers St Catherine's Hill (Hill 152), but see Pritchett, *SAGT* iii. 327–8. Pritchett (323) notes that Kerdylion was a hill, not a town as some interpreters have taken it. For Argilos see iv. 103. 4 n. on μάλιστα δὲ οἱ Ἀργίλιοι etc.

καὶ κατεφαίνετο πάντα αὐτόθεν, ὥστε οὐκ ἂν ἔλαθεν αὐτὸν ὁρμώμενος ὁ Κλέων τῷ στρατῷ: 'From here he had an excellent view of the country all round, so that he would be sure to see Kleon if he made a move with his army'. N. Jones (83), as part of his argument for the low-lying St Catherine's Hill, takes πάντα ('the country all round; lit. 'everything') restrictively, 'the entire extent of the approach to Amphipolis from Eion'. But this seems strained. Jones may be right that ὥστε, 'so that', is a clause of result not purpose.

ὑπεριδόντα σφῶν τὸ πλῆθος: 'he reckoned that Kleon would despise the numbers opposed to him'. Contrast 8. 2, where we are told that numbers were equal, but Brasidas is the focalizer of the present passage, which merely purports to tell us what, at this early point in the episode, Brasidas thought Kleon would be thinking. The present passage is alluded to by Brasidas at 9. 3.

4. Θρᾷκας τε μισθωτούς: 'Thracian mercenaries'. For the noun see Lavelle, cited at iv. 129. 2 n. on καὶ Θρᾳξί etc.

Μυρκινίων ... πελταστάς: 'Myrkinian ... peltasts'. Cf. iv. 107. 3, first n., v. 10. 9 n.

5. μετὰ Κλεαρίδου: 'under Klearidas'. For whom see iv. 132. 3 n. on καὶ Κλεαρίδαν etc.

7. 1. ὁ δὲ Κλέων τέως μὲν ἡσύχαζεν: 'Kleon made no move for a time'. We shall shortly be told that this inaction (on Th.'s presentation of which see 6. 2 n. on αὐτὸς ἡσύχαζε) caused restlessness; however, Kleon's behaviour was not cowardly but prudent: he was waiting for the reinforcements mentioned at 6. 2. See Gomme, *More Essays*, 114.

ἔπειτα ἠναγκάσθη ποιῆσαι ὅπερ ὁ Βρασίδας προσεδέχετο: 'but he was soon compelled to make the movement which Brasidas expected'. That is, to go up against Amphipolis. Gomme says in *HCT* that what Kleon now does (carry out a reconnaissance forced on him by his men) is not quite what Brasidas is said at 6. 3 to expect (namely that Kleon would despise his, Brasidas', numbers and go up against Amphipolis). But Th. is speaking in general terms.

2. τῶν γὰρ στρατιωτῶν ἀχθομένων μὲν τῇ ἕδρᾳ, ἀναλογιζομένων δὲ τὴν ἐκείνου ἡγεμονίαν πρὸς οἵαν ἐμπειρίαν καὶ τόλμαν μετὰ οἵας ἀνεπιστημοσύνης καὶ μαλακίας γενήσοιτο καὶ οἴκοθεν ὡς ἄκοντες αὐτῷ ξυνῆλθον: 'For the soldiers were disgusted at their inaction, and drew comparisons between the generals, and between the skill and daring to be expected from Brasidas, and the ignorance and cowardice to be expected from Kleon. And they remembered how unwilling they had been to follow Kleon when they left Athens'. For the attitude of the troops on setting out see 2. 1 n. on Ἀθηναίων μέν etc., citing Pritchett, *Mnemosyne* 1973. As for their present mood, the focalization in the present passage is artful: the opinions and comparisons are offered as the soldiers' but the reader is left feeling that Th. endorses the unfavourable comparison.

αἰσθόμενος τὸν θροῦν καὶ οὐ βουλόμενος ...: 'He was aware of their grumbles and did not want ...'. See Lang, *Mnemosyne* 1995, for this participially expressed motivation; to her point at 50 (Th. openly hostile to Kleon, who is unlikely to have confided in him) we can now add that Kleon, like Brasidas, would very soon not be in a position to confide in anyone, see ch. 10. Cp. also Hunter (33) on the concentration, in the present ch., of statements—not always plausible—about what Kleon wanted or thought. For αἰσθόμενος τὸν θροῦν, 'aware of their grumbles', cp. iv. 66. 2 and n., citing C. F. Smith for the noun.

3. καὶ ἐχρήσατο τῷ τρόπῳ ᾧπερ καὶ ἐς τὴν Πύλον εὐτυχήσας ἐπίστευσέ τι φρονεῖν: 'He acted in the same confident spirit which had already been successful at Pylos, and had given him a high opinion of his own shrewdness'. I follow Jowett, Gomme, and Arnold in taking τρόπῳ to mean 'spirit', 'mood', rather than technique. See Hunter (33) for the confident statements about Kleon's state of mind.

κατὰ θέαν δὲ μᾶλλον ἔφη ἀναβαίνειν τοῦ χωρίου: 'He said that he was only going to reconnoitre the place'. See Pritchett, *SAGT* iii (1980), 328–31, arguing that this was reconnaissance in force, and comparing Xen. *Hell.* vi. 5. 52. The phrase κατὰ θέαν, 'to reconnoitre', lit. 'for a view', recurs in Brasidas' speech (9. 3), exactly as if Brasidas had heard Kleon.

ὡς κύκλῳ περιστὰς βίᾳ αἱρήσων τὴν πόλιν: 'because he hoped to surround the city completely and take it by storm'. See N. Jones, 84–5, suggesting that Kleon's insistence on waiting for his allies (1 n. on ὁ δὲ Κλέων etc.) is partly to be explained by his intention to carry out 'multiple simultaneous assaults' along the course of the Long Walls.

4. ἐπὶ λόφου καρτεροῦ πρὸ τῆς Ἀμφιπόλεως: 'on a steep hill in front of Amphipolis'. Probably Hill 133, at about 1 o'clock from Amphipolis on a map orientated north–south, see Pritchett, *SAGT* i (1965), 41–2 and iii (1980), 331–3; N. Jones (86–90) concludes (90) in favour of Kromayer's Hill of the Macedonians, but see Pritchett, iii. 332. See further 10. 2 n.

5. ὥστε καὶ μηχανὰς ὅτι οὐκ ἀνῆλθεν ἔχων, ἁμαρτεῖν ἐδόκει: 'He even thought he had made a mistake in coming up against the city without siege-engines'. N. Jones (85 n. 67) says that a fortification begun as early as 437/6 is 'unlikely to have been constructed in such a way that it could withstand the newly evolving techniques of Greek siegecraft', and cites (n. 67) Pericles' siege of Samos in 440/39 and his use there of siege-machines. But the technology of fortification did not develop really fast until artillery began to be used by besiegers, and this did not happen until after about 400 or even the mid fourth century when torsion artillery came in, see Y. Garlan, *CAH* vi² (1994), 682–6, 689–90. Kleon's machines will have been simple rams or scaling-ladders, cp. iii. 51. 3 n. on μηχαναῖς, also ii. 71–8, introductory n.

ἑλεῖν γὰρ ἂν τὴν πόλιν διὰ τὸ ἐρῆμον: 'Amphipolis was, he thought, deserted, and he could have captured it there and then'. The words 'he thought' are my addition to make clear that the focalization is purely Kleon's; the irony is pronounced (Th. knows, and we know, that no place with Brasidas nearby could be called militarily deserted). Gomme in *HCT* is right that despite the ostensible similarity to iv. 104. 2 (see n. there on καὶ λέγεται Βρασίδαν etc.), the only criticism here is Kleon's (misguided) criticism of himself.

8. 2. καὶ νομίζων ὑποδεεστέρους εἶναι, οὐ τῷ πλήθει (ἀντίπαλα γάρ πως ἦν), ἀλλὰ τῷ ἀξιώματι: 'because he thought his own troops were inferior, not in their numbers, which were about the same as the enemy, but in their quality'. Contrast both 6. 3, see n. there on ὑπεριδόντα etc., and para. 3 below, see n. there on εἰ γάρ etc. Brasidas had 2000 hoplites and 300 Greek cavalry (6. 5) whereas Kleon had 1200 Athenian hoplites, 300 Athenian cavalry, and an unspecified number of allies (2. 1). The reference to Peloponnesian inferiority in quality is remarkable ('a notable tribute to the Athenian hoplite': Gomme, *More Essays*, 116), especially given that Brasidas' force included men seasoned in northern fighting.

τῶν γὰρ Ἀθηναίων ὅπερ ἐστράτευε καθαρὸν ἐξῆλθε: 'for the Athenian forces were undiluted citizen troops'. Gomme in *HCT* and *More Essays*, 116 n. 4, is probably right that καθαρόν means 'pure' in the sense of Athenians only, rather than 'picked troops' (Steup). Nevertheless the word has strongly favourable connotations and we should not regard it as too neutrally descriptive.

καὶ Λημνίων καὶ Ἰμβρίων τὸ κράτιστον: 'and they were supported by the best of the Lemnians and Imbrians'. See iv. 28. 4 n. on Λημνίους etc.

3. εἰ γὰρ δείξειε τοῖς ἐναντίοις τό τε πλῆθος καὶ τὴν ὅπλισιν ἀναγκαίαν οὖσαν τῶν μεθ᾽ ἑαυτοῦ: 'he thought that if he let them see how few and badly armed his soldiers were . . .'. But we were told at para. 2 above that the two armies were equal in numbers, see n. there. For ὅπλισιν ἀναγκαίαν, 'badly armed', see Ostwald, *ΑΝΑΓΚΗ*, 10; the relevant sense of ἀνάγκη, 'necessity', is 'minimum requirement'.

οὐκ ἂν ἡγεῖτο μᾶλλον περιγενέσθαι ἢ ἄνευ προόψεώς τε αὐτῶν καὶ μὴ ἀπὸ τοῦ ὄντος καταφρονήσεως: 'he would be less likely to succeed than if he attacked before they had had time to see him coming, and before they had any real grounds for their contempt of him'. The negative μή here has been thought redundant (ἄνευ, lit. '*without* them seeing him coming', already contains a negative idea). See, however, A. Boegehold, 'Thucydides' Representation of Brasidas Before Amphipolis', *CP* 74 (1979), 148–52, at 150: the elliptical thought can be expressed thus: 'Brasidas thought he would not more likely prevail than he would without their seeing his troops beforehand and not with ⟨their having seen his troops beforehand, which would result in⟩ their becoming contemptuous as a result of their awareness of his true position.' Boegehold is suggesting that Brasidas is 'relinquishing one possible advantage, a feeling of contempt on the enemy's part, in favour of another, the element of surprise'.

4. μεμονωμένους: 'on their own' [lit. 'abandoned', 'isolated']. A rather odd way of describing the absence, on the Athenian side, of Thracian and Macedonian allies who are merely expected or hoped for; Gomme, *More Essays*, 116, and in *HCT* thinks it inconsistent that Brasidas is here implied to have the advantage, whereas at para. 3 he is implied to be in a tight spot through lack of numbers.

ξυγκαλέσας δὲ τοὺς πάντας στρατιώτας καὶ βουλόμενος παρα-θαρσῦναί τε καὶ τὴν ἐπίνοιαν φράσαι, ἔλεγε τοιάδε: 'So he called together all his troops, and wishing to encourage them and to explain his plan, he spoke as follows'. Note *all* his troops; see 9. 1 n. on Ἄνδρες Πελοποννήσιοι.

9. *Brasidas' speech to his troops and to Klearidas*

See Luschnat, *Feldherrnreden*, 64–72; Leimbach, 84–91; Hunter, 30–41. This lively speech derives some of its effect from our knowledge (was Th. banking on this?) that Brasidas is about to disappear from the scene for ever: it is a specially effective touch, given that he will go down fighting (10. 8 and 11), to end the speech (9. 10) with a promise that he will carry out his own advice, i.e. fight bravely. This is not the only respect in which the battle narrative of ch. 10 fulfils the expectations created by the speech in ch. 9; for this 'technique of preparation' see Luschnat, 68 (9. 6 is fulfilled by 10. 6, Brasidas' rush at the Athenian centre; and 9. 7 by 10. 7, Klearidas' attack). See also Hunter's chart at 37 for very similar points about *logoi/erga* correspondences (she makes the additional points that 9. 7 is fulfilled by 10. 6, the Athenians panic; and less strikingly 9. 8, 'this is the way to terrify them' is made good in an approximate way by 10. 7). Luschnat rightly says that we have met this technique before, see introductory n. to iv. 126. As with iv. 126, Luschnat in 1942 anticipated Hunter in 1973, but she does not cite him either in her text or in her bibliography. Gomme on 9. 3 (cp. Hunter, 37) adds that the speech also conforms to the *earlier* narrative, see n. there.

On the structure of the speech (general remarks at paras. 1 and 9–10 enclose the battle plan at paras. 2–8) Luschnat ingeniously appeals to iv. 81. 2, the ἀρετὴ καὶ ξύνεσις, 'honorable standards and intelligence' of Brasidas: the intelligence, Luschnat suggests, is illustrated by his battle plan, the *arete* (for this untranslatable word of commendation see iv. 81. 2 n. on ἔς τε τὸν χρόνῳ etc.) by the rest, especially, I suppose, by the talk of Dorian fighting qualities at the opening, and of liberation at the close, of the speech. In this connection (liberation) note Luschnat's good point, already mentioned above at introductory n. to iv. 85–7, that there are thematic responsions between Brasidas' Akanthos speech at the beginning, and the present speech at the end, of his Thracian expedition. These will be noted as they arise.

441

In detail, Luschnat (64) distinguishes between three main sections: (1) opening address to Peloponnesians (para. 1), stressing the strengths of Dorianism; (2) battle plan (2–8), subdivided into (*a*) reasons for dividing forces (2–5), (*b*) what Brasidas himself proposes to do (6), (*c*) what Klearidas is to do (7–8); finally (3) exhortation to Klearidas and the allies.

The present speech, the eighth in the whole long section iv–v. 24, is not quite the last speech of all; see 10. 5 for Brasidas' final brief speech, after which there is no direct discourse until the Melian Dialogue and the trio of speeches before the Sicilian Expedition (v. 85–113; vi. 9–23).

There is no reason to doubt that Brasidas made a speech on the present occasion, see Introduction, above pp. 82 f. for the argument between Hansen and Pritchett, and for the present speech specifically see Pritchett, *EGH* 61. It is a separate question whether Brasidas said just what Th. makes him say. The element of justified prediction (see above on Luschnat and Hunter) is hardly an argument for inauthenticity. Brasidas had a plan. He then implemented that plan.

A notable feature of the speech is that para. 8 is virtually quoted by Aeneas Tacticus (xxxviii. 2) in the mid fourth century; see n. there for the implications of this for Th.'s reception after his own time.

9. 1. Ἄνδρες Πελοποννήσιοι: 'Peloponnesians!' Cp. iv. 126. 1 and n.: again, Brasidas opens his address, to an army which is partly Peloponnesian partly not, as if the men were all Peloponnesians. But at para. 9 he will address the allies separately (contrast iv. 126, which is thus more problematic). Gomme seems to have thought that there was 'conventional simplification' here; Steup and Leimbach (85 n. 8), more troubled than was Gomme by the impoliteness of addressing the initial remarks about Dorians to an audience which included many Ionians, think that Brasidas' remarks were addressed to different sections of his audience. Gomme represents Steup as saying that Brasidas 'turns from one part of his forces to another' at para. 9, but any 'turning' envisaged by Steup— who does not use the word, but speaks of 'addressing', 'Anrede'—is purely metaphorical; or rather, it is compatible with 'turning' on the spot, in the sense that a conductor on a podium 'turns' towards different sections of the orchestra. Leimbach goes further: he says that the assumption that Brasidas *changed his position* ('die Annahme, Brasidas wechsle während seiner Rede seinen Platz') is easier than supposing he allowed Ionians to hear the anti-Ionian boost he was giving the Dorians, and Leimbach cites Steup with approval, i.e. he seems more categorically to attribute to Steup the view that Brasidas actually changed position. But Steup does not quite go this far, nor is Leimbach's further assumption necessary. Gomme adds, rather feebly, that 'it is better not to visualize these addresses too clearly'. On the contrary, this and other speeches in Th. gain from being visualized, see Dover, *HCT*, introduction to vi. 8. 3–26 and his particular nn. on vi. 9. 2 and 23. 1 (p. 260, foot). Why should we not imagine Brasidas putting his hand on Klearidas' shoulder at para. 7? Steup's view that he addressed the opening and closing remarks primarily to different sections of the audience, but that everybody was meant to hear the plan (2–8) revealed in the central section, is simplest and best (cp. also Pritchett, *EGH* 61–2: 'as to passages relating to any one part of the army, this is a matter of gesture and direction of voice'). After all, 8. 4 is explicit that Brasidas summoned *all* his troops and addressed them, see n. there on ξυγκαλέσας etc.

καὶ ὅτι Δωριῆς μέλλετε Ἴωσι μάχεσθαι, ὧν εἰώθατε κρείσσους εἶναι: 'you are Dorians, and are about to fight with Ionians, whom you have beaten again and again'. Cp. viii. 25. 3 and J. Alty, 'Dorians and Ionians', *JHS* 102 (1982), 1–14, at 3 and 5 with n. 26.

2. ἵνα μή τῳ τὸ κατ' ὀλίγον καὶ μὴ ἅπαντας κινδυνεύειν ἐνδεὲς φαινόμενον ἀτολμίαν παράσχῃ: 'so that you will not be discouraged at the apparent disproportion of numbers, because we are going into battle not with our whole force but with a handful of men'. As Luschnat says, the reference is not to the overall inferiority implied at 8. 3 (but denied at 8. 2). The 'handful' is the force of 150 (8. 4) which Brasidas will command personally, see 9. 6. Hude wanted to read κατ' ὀλίγους, accepting that the sense is 'not with our whole force', but this is not necessary, cp. (with Luschnat, 69 n. 1) iv. 10. 4. Luschnat missed some Greek equivalent of 'initially', to make it clear that the handful would soon be joined by others.

3. τοὺς γὰρ ἐναντίους εἰκάζω καταφρονήσει τε ἡμῶν καὶ οὐκ ἂν ἐλπίσαντας ὡς ἂν ἐπεξέλθοι τις αὐτοῖς ἐς μάχην ἀναβῆναί τε πρὸς τὸ χωρίον καὶ νῦν ἀτάκτως κατὰ θέαν τετραμμένους ὀλιγωρεῖν: 'Our enemies, I think, despise us; they believe that no one will come out to attack them, and so they have climbed the hill, where they are busy looking at the view in complete disorder, and disregarding us'. This, as Gomme notes (see introductory n.), picks up 6. 3, 7. 3 (note esp. κατὰ θέαν), also 8. 3, esp. καταφρονήσεως, which is echoed by καταφρονήσει here, 'despise us'.

Leimbach (87) remarks that there is disparagement ('Herabsetzung') in the plural κατὰ θέαν τετραμμένους, '*they* are busy looking at the view'. The narrative of 7. 4 spoke of Kleon alone inspecting the terrain, but Brasidas makes out that the Athenians are collectively behaving like a group of tourists, 'als eine Art Touristengruppe'.

On εἰκάζω, 'I think', 'I conjecture', see i. 138. 3 n. on ἄριστος εἰκαστής, and J. Gommel, *Rhetorisches Argumentieren bei Thukydides* (*Spudasmata* 10, 1966), 18–20 and 28; V. Hunter, 28–30 and 35.

4. πλεῖστ᾽ ἂν ὀρθοῖτο: 'The successful general . . .' [lit. 'he is most likely to succeed who . . .']. As Steup, Gomme, and Luschnat (70) note, the language is exactly that of Teutiaplos trying to galvanize Alkidas at iii. 30. 4 (Jowett's footnote ref. to iii. 29 is a slip), and the thought is also comparable: exploit the moment when the enemy is off his guard. Luschnat is right that the similarity has a point: Alkidas would not be persuaded; a new sort of Spartan was needed.

5. τὰ κλέμματα: 'those stratagems'. Steup compares the use of κλέπτειν, lit. 'to steal', at Xen. *Anab.* iv. 6. 11 ff., a *Spartan* context; see Leimbach, 88 n. 16. See also Dem. xviii. 31 (where the word means 'fraud', 'deception'), with H. Wankel, *Demosthenes Rede für Ktesiphon über den Kranz* (Heidelberg, 1976), 266.

6. προσπεσοῦμαι δρόμῳ κατὰ μέσον τὸ στράτευμα: 'charging straight at the centre of the army'. See 10. 6, which corresponds in content and language (κατὰ μέσον τὸ στράτευμα): see introductory n.

7. σὺ δέ, Κλεαρίδα: 'Then, Klearidas'. An unusual and lively exhortation to an individual; see introductory n. Luschnat (67), followed by Leimbach (89 n. 21), notes that at vii. 69. 2, Nikias exhorts the trierarchs *by name*.

8. τὸ γὰρ ἐπιὸν ὕστερον δεινότερον τοῖς πολεμίοις τοῦ παρόντος καὶ μαχομένου: 'reinforcements are always more formidable to an enemy than the troops with which he is already engaged'. Gomme compares Demosthenes' success at Olpai, iii. 108. 1, and this is certainly apt; but the sentence is of great interest for a completely different reason. The present passage is reproduced very closely by Aeneas Tacticus xxxviii. 2 in the mid fourth century: τὸ γὰρ ἐπιὸν μᾶλλον οἱ πολέμιοι φοβοῦνται τοῦ ὑπάρχοντος καὶ πάροντος ἤδη, 'an enemy is more fearful of reserves than of the forces already there'; see Whitehead's n. and Hunter and Handford's edn., p. lxxxi. This shows that one not very famous or obvious bit of Th. was known to one not specially intellectual reader, and this has implications for our view of the reception of Th. See my paper in *JHS* 115 (1995), 48–68 (esp. 53 on the present passage), where I argue that it is too often supposed that Th. virtually disappeared from view after his own time, until he became fashionable again in intellectual Roman circles in the first century BC.

9. καὶ αὐτός τε ἀνὴρ ἀγαθὸς γίγνου, ὥσπερ σε εἰκὸς ὄντα Σπαρτιάτην: 'Be a brave man, and a true Spartiate'. On ὥσπερ εἰκός, lit. '*as we should expect* from a Spartiate', see 3 n. on τοὺς γὰρ ἐναντίους etc., discussing εἰκάζω. For the form of the exhortation (ἀνὴρ ἀγαθός, 'brave man') see Tyrtaeus 10W line 2.

καὶ ὑμεῖς, ὦ ἄνδρες ξύμμαχοι: 'you, allies'. For the separate address see introductory n.: we do not have to suppose that Brasidas actually moved to a different position.

ἢ ἀγαθοῖς γενομένοις ἐλευθερίαν τε ὑπάρχειν καὶ Λακεδαιμο-νίων ξυμμάχοις κεκλῆσθαι, ἢ Ἀθηναίων τε δούλοις: 'freedom and the name of Spartan allies if you are brave, or else slavery to Athens'. Luschnat (65-6) compares iv. 86. 1, the speech at Akanthos, for the references to freedom, allied status, and Athenian slavery. See nn. there, and above, introductory n. to v. 9.

τοῖς δε λοιποῖς ῞Ελλησι κωλυταῖς γενέσθαι ἐλευθερώσεως: 'if you stand in the way of the liberation of the rest of Greece'. Again (see previous n.) cp., with Luschnat and Gomme, Brasidas himself at Akanthos, iv. 87. 3, with n. there on οἱ δὲ ῞Ελληνες etc.

10. 1. ἐπὶ τὰς Θρᾳκίας καλουμένας τῶν πυλῶν: 'at the so-called Thracian Gates'. These gates are now normally and probably rightly identified with the gate excavated by Lazaridis at the north-east of the city site, see Lazaridis 1994, 28 (with photograph); Pritchett, *SAGT* iii (1980), 340 and fig. 14 at 306; for another photograph see Lazaridis 1986, plate 146; Lazaridis 1994 or N. Jones, plate 2.1 (full refs at iv. 102. 1 n.). For the location of the Thracian Gates see above, Fig. 2, Gate A. Jones (93-4) conjectures that the Thracian Gates were in the eastern sector of the wall, but though his reconstruction is not unattractive in itself, Pritchett (301, cp. 340) rules this location out because the area has been excavated to bedrock with no sign of any gate.

2. περὶ τὸ ἱερὸν τῆς Ἀθηνᾶς θυομένου: 'sacrificing at the temple of Athena'. Not yet located, but see Jones, 88 and 103 n. 73, for a possible architectural fragment shown to Leake (2. 2 n. on κατέπλευσεν etc.), 198, cp. 191. On this evidence Leake reckoned the temple must have been small.

Pritchett, *GSW* iii (1979), 157, notes that this sacrifice is not a battle sacrifice (σφάγια, for which term see iv. 92. 7 n.). See also Pritchett, *EGH* 61.

καὶ ὑπὸ τὰς πύλας ἵππων τε πόδες πολλοὶ καὶ ἀνθρώπων ὡς ἐξιόντων ὑποφαίνονται: 'and that the feet of numerous men and horses were visible under the gate, and that they were about to come out'. This vivid detail has played a part in modern discussions of Kleon's position (7. 4 n.), see Jones, 88, Pritchett, *SAGT* i (1965), 42. The passage makes it clear that the gate was single, not double, see F. Winter, *Greek Fortifications* (Toronto, 1971), 213 n. 17: 'Kleon and his scouts could surely not have seen the feet . . . if there had been both inner and outer gates.' It is rather surprising that feet could be seen at all, without binoculars or telescope; more than a small gap would be a security risk because a child or small-statured person could be inserted under the gap so as to lift the bar from the inside.

3. σημαίνειν τε ἅμα ἐκέλευεν ἀναχώρησιν καὶ παρήγγειλε τοῖς ἀπιοῦσιν ἐπὶ τὸ εὐώνυμον κέρας, ὥσπερ μόνον οἷόν τ᾽ ἦν, ὑπάγειν ἐπὶ τῆς Ἠιόνος: 'So he gave the signal for retreat, telling the troops retiring on the left wing to do so in the direction of Eion, as that alone was practicable'. On this, Kleon's 'fatal order to retreat from before Amphipolis', see J. K. Anderson, *JHS* 85 (1965), 1–4 (above, introductory n. to 6–13). Anderson thinks that Kleon's signal was given by trumpet and meant 'Retire!'; some of the troops obeyed at once, but others hesitated: see next n. See also P. Krentz, in Hanson (ed.), *Hoplites*, 116–17: Kleon's order or signal was not enough without detailed instructions as to how it was to be carried out. The general interpretation and trans. of the passage given here follows Pritchett, *SAGT* iii (1980), 335.

4. ὡς δ᾽ αὐτῷ ἐδόκει σχολὴ γίγνεσθαι, αὐτὸς ἐπιστρέψας τὸ δεξιὸν καὶ τὰ γυμνὰ πρὸς τοὺς πολεμίους δοὺς ἀπῆγε τὴν στρατιάν: 'He thought he had plenty of time; so he completed a quarter-turn, thereby exposing his right or unshielded side to the enemy, and started to lead his army away'. Again (see previous n.) Pritchett's reconstruction and interpretation (see *SAGT* i (1965), 44, and iii (1980), 333–5) is here followed, as the only one which makes sense both of the Greek and of the manœuvre; Pritchett's view requires us to take ἐπιστρέψας intransitively, he 'turned' i.e. he executed a turning movement, cp. for the intransitive Asclepiodotus, *Tactica* xii. 11 (ἐπίστρεφε, 'turn!', as a command; Pritchett, *SAGT* i. 44, has '1. 211' by a typographical error); see also x. 5. On this view there is a pause in sense before τὸ δεξιόν, which (on this view) is not the object of a transitively used ἐπιστρέψας ('he turned his right wing'), but goes closely with τὰ γυμνά, 'he exposed [δούς, lit. 'he gave'] his right and unshielded side' [cp. v. 71. 1] to the enemy'. We might even insert a comma after ἐπιστρέψας. An awkwardness of this interpretation is that in paras. 8 and 9 below, Th. certainly uses τὸ δεξιόν to mean 'the right wing'. But it is not as if we were positing different *senses* for the adjective, which means 'right' both times; it is merely that different nouns must be supplied.

One advantage of this is that it involves no emendation of the OCT and Budé texts. Steup, Gomme, and Anderson, 4 n. 4 (see previous n.), emend σχολή to σχολῇ, 'at leisure' (i.e. he thought his men were moving off 'in too leisurely a fashion' instead of 'he thought there was leisure' i.e. 'he thought he had plenty of time in hand' as the Penguin trans. has it). B. Mitchell, *Historia* 1991, 185, is the best attempt to explain the text on the orthodox view that the right wing only was made to do a quarter-turn to the left and so somehow expose its shieldless side, but it is not clear to me how carrying out this order 'would have ensured a more orderly retreat', or what would be the supposed advantage of a march in the direction she suggests.

5. λέγει τοῖς μεθ᾽ ἑαυτοῦ καὶ τοῖς ἄλλοις ὅτι 'οἱ ἄνδρες ἡμᾶς οὐ μενοῦσιν. δῆλοι δὲ τῶν τε δοράτων τῇ κινήσει καὶ τῶν κεφαλῶν ...': 'He said to his companions and his troops: "These men are not going to face us: look at the way their spears and heads are shaking"'. This supremely confident remark is Brasidas' absolutely final speech. Pritchett, *GSW* i (1971), 107, notes that 'the rhythm-conscious Spartan, Brasidas, inferred from the gait of the Athenians that they would not await an attack'. Lazenby, in Hanson (ed.), *Hoplites*, 89, suggests that it is unlikely that every man in a hoplite army had a fixed position, and invokes this scornful remark of Brasidas to show that there may have been 'a certain amount of jostling as men found themselves a place'. See also Hanson, *Western Way*, 100, 145.

ἀλλὰ τάς τε πύλας τις ἀνοιγέτω ἐμοὶ ἃς εἴρηται: 'Open the gates for me as I ordered'. Luschnat, 68 (cp. also Steup), notes that this does not correspond exactly to anything in the speech at ch. 9.

6. καὶ ὁ μὲν κατὰ τὰς ἐπὶ τὸ σταύρωμα πύλας καὶ τὰς πρώτας τοῦ μακροῦ τείχους τότε ὄντος ἐξελθών: 'He himself then went out by the gate leading to the palisade—the first gate of the long wall as it now was'. This palisade, σταύρωμα, has not been mentioned so far (nor has Th. used the word before, though it will recur in the Sicilian expedition. The failure to introduce the palisade is, for Andrewes, *HCT* v. 364, one of the 'indications of incompleteness' in Th.'s Ten Years War narrative, but it is not abnormal for Th. to introduce items in this casual way). Any attempt to locate such an obviously temporary structure can only be guesswork; Pritchett, *SAGT* iii (1980), 335, suggests that it extended from the wall to the bridge, for which see iv. 103. 4 n. on ἐπὶ τὴν γέφυραν etc.: it was to the north of the town. On this view it makes sense to put the 'first gate of the long wall' near the bridge (above p. 321, fig. 2, Gate C; cf. Pritchett 336), and to identify the 'gate leading to the palisade' with this 'first gate', i.e. καί (represented by a dash in the English trans.) is here explanatory, it does not mean 'and'. For a different view, see N. Jones, 91, for whom there are three distinct gates (the third, he thinks, is the Thracian, for which see 1 n. above).

On τότε in the sense 'as it was now' see Pritchett, 336 f.: the reference must be to construction by Brasidas since 422, contrast iv. 103. 5 (the walls did not yet extend down to the river).

ἔθει δρόμῳ τὴν ὁδὸν ταύτην εὐθεῖαν: 'and charged up the main road'. There has been modern discussion of εὐθεῖαν. N. Jones (93) wants to interpret it 'taking it straight', and thinks ταύτην means 'the one under consideration', i.e. the road from the first gate. This does not translate easily, and there is another and better possibility. Pritchett (who seems to have Jones in mind when he refers at 337 to a recent 'effort to find a short straight segment of a road', cp. Jones's map at his p. 78) takes it to mean 'highway', 'road connecting cities'. (He adduces e.g. Paus. viii. 54. 5 and Th.'s own description of Archelaos' road-building at ii. 100. 2, he 'cut straight roads', ὁδοὺς εὐθείας ἔτεμε.) In the present passage Th. is perhaps referring (Pritchett, 338) to a road which went north of Pangaion 'like the later *via Egnatia*'; see Pritchett's map at 306.

ἧπερ νῦν κατὰ τὸ καρτερώτατον τοῦ χωρίου ἰόντι τροπαῖον ἕστηκε: 'where a trophy now stands on the steepest part of the hill'. The 'hill' is Amphipolis itself. Th. knew the city well, and not just in the period before his exile; cp. iv. 103. 5 and v. 11. 1 'what is now the Agora' and n. on καὶ τὸ λοιπόν etc. (section on ἐντέμνουσι). See p. 23.

καὶ προσβαλὼν τοῖς Ἀθηναίοις ... κατὰ μέσον τὸ στράτευμα τρέπει: 'He then attacked the Athenian centre and routed them'. As planned, 9. 6 and n.

πεφοβημένοις τε ἅμα τῇ σφετέρᾳ ἀταξίᾳ καὶ τὴν τόλμαν αὐτοῦ ἐκπεπληγμένοις: 'they were in a state of panic because of the audacity of his attack and their own disorder'. [Strictly there are two participles here, 'they were in fear because of their own disorder and they were panic-struck/thrown into confusion/thrown off balance (Warner) by his audacity'.] Just as Brasidas predicted at 9. 7, see Hunter, 37. On the Athenian 'disorder', ἀταξία, see Brasidas' remarks at para. 5, cp. B. Mitchell, *Historia* 1991, 184.

7. καὶ ὁ Κλεαρίδας, ὥσπερ εἴρητο: 'Klearidas carried out his orders'. See 9. 7.

ξυνέβη τε τῷ ἀδοκήτῳ καὶ ἐξαπίνης ἀμφοτέρωθεν τοὺς Ἀθηναίους θορυβηθῆναι: 'The unexpected and sudden attack at both points produced confusion in the Athenian army'. For ἀδόκητος, 'unexpected', see iv. 36. 2 n.

8. εὐθὺς ἀπορραγὲν ἔφευγεν: 'broke away and continued its retreat'. Or (reading ἔφυγεν, with Gomme) 'was cut off and fled'.

9. καὶ ὁ μὲν Κλέων, ὡς τὸ πρῶτον οὐ διενοεῖτο μένειν, εὐθὺς φεύγων καὶ καταληφθεὶς ὑπὸ Μυρκινίου πελταστοῦ ἀποθνῄσκει: 'Kleon himself had never intended to stand his ground, but fled at once, and was overtaken and killed by a Myrkinian peltast'. The most famous and extreme instance of a discreditable motive attributed on the evidence of overt action. The death at the hand of a peltast (not a hoplite) is an important touch: the *manner* of death is crucial in Greek thinking, cp. vii. 86. 5, where part of Nikias' misfortune is to

have died in that particular way (not in battle but in captivity at the hands of people who hated him). For the prejudice—as old as Homer— against light-armed, archers, etc. see iv. 40. 2 nn. Any attempt to use Diod. xii. 74. 2, to give Kleon a heroic end is misguided. What Diod. says is that Brasidas died heroically, ἡρωικῶς, and Kleon died similarly, ὁμοίως. But the similarity may in Diod.'s view have lain in the fact not the manner of the death. On Myrkinos see iv. 107. 3, first n., cf. v. 6. 4.

That the two opposing commanders should both have died in the same battle (see 11 below for Brasidas) is remarkable even in Greek hoplite warfare, with its high mortality rate among generals, see Lazenby, in Hanson (ed.), *Hoplites*, 98, and above, iv. 101. 2 n.

11. καὶ ᾔσθετο μὲν ὅτι νικῶσιν οἱ μεθ᾽ αὑτοῦ, οὐ πολὺ δὲ διαλιπὼν ἐτελεύτησεν: '[Brasidas] knew that his army was victorious, but soon afterwards he died'. So ends the *aristeia* of Brasidas, see Introduction, p. 41. But ch. 11 is a kind of funeral games, an *Iliad* xxiii.

Homeric wounds are described in appalling detail, but not the wounds in the classical Greek historians, for whom, as a rule, 'the details are unimportant': J. K. Anderson, in Hanson (ed.), *Hoplites*, 32–3, discussing the present passage (also E. Wheeler at 168 n. 42 in the same vol.).

11. 1. μετὰ δὲ ταῦτα τὸν Βρασίδαν οἱ ξύμμαχοι πάντες ξὺν ὅπλοις ἐπισπόμενοι δημοσίᾳ ἔθαψαν ἐν τῇ πόλει πρὸ τῆς νῦν ἀγορᾶς οὔσης: 'Brasidas was buried in the city with public honours in front of what is now the Agora. The whole body of the allies in full armour escorted him to the grave'. Brasidas dominates the narrative, in Homeric style (see previous n.), even after his death; contrast the contemptuous brevity with which Kleon was dispatched, 10. 9.

This (see p. 50) is the third and most splendid of the three 'Brasidas' passages in which Th., uncharacteristically, expatiates on religion: cf. iv. 116. 2 and 121. 1 (the Torone 'epiphany', and the semi-religious *adventus* at Skione). But the interest of the Brasidan aspect should not be allowed to obscure the innovative cultic importance of what, on the evidence of this ch. of Th., had been done to the *living* Athenian Hagnon back in 437, see below on καταβαλόντες etc. The treatment of Brasidas is after all posthumous and to that extent not out of line with traditional Greek religious treatment of human beings (though, as we saw at end of n. on iv. 121. 1, citing Habicht, *Gottmenschentum*[2], the behaviour of the enthusiastic Skionaians towards the living Brasidas has a religious tinge).

The best discussion of this whole long para. is now that of I. Malkin, *Religion and Colonization in Ancient Greece* (Leiden, 1987), 228–32.

It is unusual for Th. to dwell on the burial and funerary rites of any of his *individual* characters; the closest parallels to the material about

Brasidas in the present ch. are i. 134. 4 (Pausanias the Regent), 138. 5–6 (Themistokles), and viii. 84. 5 (Lichas the Spartan). Contrast Xenophon on Agesipolis, *Hell.* v. 3. 19, or Ephorus on Agesilaos (Diod. xv. 93. 6). As these passages show, Spartan kings were given more than human honours, though we should be cautious about speaking of outright heroization (for which term see next n.): R. Parker, 'Were Spartan Kings Heroized?', *LCM* 13 (1988), 9–10 (P. A. Cartledge disagrees, see his 'Yes, Spartan Kings Were Heroized', *LCM* 13 (1988), 43–4).

In the previous para. I emphasized 'individual', because Th. gives very full coverage to a famous burial at ii. 34. 1—that of the Athenian war dead, see n. there. But that was group burial. Note, however, that it resembles the present passage in its use of the word 'public', δημοσίᾳ, for the ceremony.

For the significance of burial of heroes in the agora (no pollution was feared from such special people), see Parker, *Miasma*, 42 (but see also 70–3 for doubts about the view that extramural burial generally was intended to stave off pollution); cf. also Habicht, *Gottmenschentum*[2], 205; E. Kearns (next n.), 72; S. Hornblower, *Mausolus* (Oxford, 1982), 255 f.; cp. ML 3 (Glaukos the friend of Archilochos). Th. actually has 'in front of' the agora, which may be slightly less grand. Note the ref. to 'what is now the agora', implying some change in topography, and personal knowledge and inspection (see above, p. 23); cp. 10. 6 n. on ἥπερ νῦν etc. Malkin, *Religion and Colonization*, 229, notes that the *agora* may not have been the *agora* in 422, but accepts that the location of the tomb was a prominent one. The rough location of the agora is not in doubt; it was surely (cf. Lazaridis 1994, 52) in the enclosed inner area south of the modern museum, and west of Gate E; see fig. 2 at p. 321 above, and Lazaridis 1994, fig. 5. (If we could be sure that the tomb found in the 1980s under the present museum was Brasidas', that would solve the matter. In that case the tomb would be just *outside* the enclosed area, which would be compatible with Th.'s 'in front of' as opp. 'in', see above.)

καὶ τὸ λοιπὸν οἱ Ἀμφιπολῖται, περιείρξαντες αὐτοῦ τὸ μνημεῖον, ὡς ἥρωί τε ἐντέμνουσι καὶ τιμὰς δεδώκασιν ἀγῶνας καὶ ἐτησίους θυσίας, καὶ τὴν ἀποικίαν ὡς οἰκιστῇ προσέθεσαν: 'The Amphipolitans fenced off his tomb, and to this day they cut the throats of victims to him as a hero, and have also instituted games and yearly sacrifices in his honour. They also made him their founder, and dedicated their colony to him'. The 'fencing off' made the area into a *temenos* or sacred precinct, see Habicht, *Gottmenschentum*[2], 140 and n. 11; for *temene* cp. iv. 116. 2 n. on νομίσας etc. For hero-cult generally see E. Kearns, 'Between God and Man: Status and Function of Heroes and their Sanctuaries', in A. Schachter (ed.), *Le sanctuaire grec* (*Fondation*

Hardt Entretiens xxxvii: Vandoeuvres, 1992), 65–107, and for heroic honours to founders or oikists see i. 4 n. on οἰκιστής, and modern literature there cited, esp. Leschhorn, and Malkin, *Religion and Colonization*. For heroic cults awarded to an outstanding benefactor, who is treated as a secondary founder, compare Xen. *Hell.* vii. 3. 12 (Euphron at Sikyon); and for changes of oikist see Malkin, *Religion and Colonization*, 230. How distinctive was this hero-cult awarded to the Spartan Brasidas in a colonial context? Here I wish to draw attention to an epigraphic item which has had practically no attention since its publication in the 1960s. It seems to attest a hero-cult at Thurii of the Spartan Kleandridas, father of Gylippos (for the filiation see Th. vi. 93). Now from Th. vi. 104. 2 we learn that Gylippos 'revived his father's citizenship at Thurii', an interesting statement which reminds us how little we know about citizenship rules outside Athens; such double citizenship looks Hellenistic, not classical. The inscription is on a tile, and is in Latin, which is perhaps why it eluded *SEG*. The excavators and Zuntz (see below) make the attractive suggestion that this marks a heroon to Kleandridas which must have continued in use for centuries. For our purposes the item's importance is as a colonial parallel to Brasidas' cult. See P. Zancani Montuori, *Atti e Mem. della Soc. Magna Grecia (1961)* NS iv (1962), 36–40; G. Zuntz, *Persephone* (Oxford, 1971), 287 and n. 2 (where for Th. vi. 63 read 93).

For archaeological remains under the Amphipolis museum which have been conjecturally or fancifully identified with Brasidas' tomb, see Lazaridis 1994, 24 and the magnificent plate 49 (for the original announcement see *Arch. Reps.* 1984/5, 47, derived from *ADelt.* 31 (1984) Chr. 307). The remains, which are striking even without the Brasidas connection, include a metal larnax or rectangular box for the bones, and a magnificent gold crown.

The verb ἐντέμνουσι [lit., 'they cut'] refers to the cutting of the throat of the sacrificial victim, see J. Rudhardt, *Notions fondamentales de la pensée religieuse et actes constitutifs du culte dans la Grèce classique: Étude préliminaire pour aider à la compréhension de la piété athénienne au iv-me siècle* (Geneva, 1958), 285–6, and J. Casabona, *Recherches sur le vocabulaire des sacrifices en grec des origines à la fin de l'époque classique* (Aix-en-Provence, 1966), 226, describing the present passage of Th. as 'le texte fondamentale'. The word, which Rudhardt says is peculiarly appropriate to sacrifice to heroes (see further below), is found only here in Th., and in religious as opp. botanical or medical contexts is (on the evidence of the computerized TLG) not a common one on its own anywhere; but cp. Plut. *Mor.* 290d (puppies sacrificed to Enyalios) and Lucian, *Scyth.* 1 (see also Plut. *Sol.* 9. 1, where it is combined with σφάγια or blood-sacrifices). See

Malkin, *Religion and Colonization*, 229–30. Cp., for Th.'s religious vocabulary, iv. 121. 1 n. on καὶ τὸν Βρασίδαν etc.

Gomme may be right to take the present tense, 'they cut the throats' (esp. so vivid a word), as indicating the eye-witness, presumably Th. himself. Malkin (229–30) insists on the difference between the present tense of this verb ('they cut') and the perfect ('they *have instituted* games and yearly sacrifices', δεδώκασιν ἀγῶνας καὶ ἐτησίους θυσίας). He conjectures that this difference expresses that between the on-going throat-cutting at the level of 'a continuing popular worship', and the decision to institute an 'annual event with state sacrifices on a grand scale'. This is much preferable to Gomme's odd view that Brasidas was getting cultic sacrifice both as a god (or else getting festivals at which sacrifice to the gods was performed), and as a hero, and that Th. expresses this distinction by θυσίαι (sacrifice to gods) and ἐντέμνουσι (sacrifice to heroes). As Malkin rightly says in rejection of Gomme, Th. is explicit that Brasidas was worshipped *as a hero*, ὡς ἥρωι. On Malkin's view θυσίαι is used, not because it is inapplicable to a hero, but because it is the more general word—the word, in fact, that that famous 'northern expert' Aristotle used (*NE* 1134b23) about the sacrifices to, precisely, Brasidas.

καταβαλόντες τὰ Ἀγνώνεια οἰκοδομήματα καὶ ἀφανίσαντες εἴ τι μνημόσυνόν που ἔμελλεν αὐτοῦ τῆς οἰκίσεως περιέσεσθαι: 'pulling down the cult buildings of Hagnon, and obliterating any other solid memorials of Hagnon's foundation'. See above, p. 63. For Amphipolis as 'Hagnon's foundation' see iv. 102. 4 (102. 3 in the OCT). Th.'s Amphipolis material is widely distributed, see i. 100. 3, iv. 102 and 108.

The present sentence, on the view to be followed here, has interesting and important implications for Greek cult of individuals, because (to sum up the following discussion) it attests cult of Hagnon *in his lifetime*. This, always assuming the interpretation here followed is correct, entitles it to close attention (which it rarely receives) in studies of Greek ruler-cult, the deification of Alexander the Great, and so forth. (NB: the outstanding modern discussion of this aspect of Alexander, namely E. Badian's 'The Deification of Alexander the Great', in H. J. Dell (ed.), *Macedonian Studies pres. C. Edson* (Athens, 1982), 27–66, should now be supplemented by *JRA* Supp. 17 (1996) 14 n. 21.) Thus S. Price, *Rituals and Power* (Cambridge, 1985), 74, discussing the Greek and Hellenistic beginnings of what eventually became Roman imperial cult, begins with Lysander, mentioning neither the dead Brasidas nor the living and therefore more remarkable Hagnon. In another sense it is true that Brasidas' treatment is epoch-making and forward-looking, because, as we have seen, he was not the actual but a kind of secondary founder—in fact a benefactor. Hagnon, by contrast, is a hero of an established type, an actual oikist. But oikists did not usually get cult until they were dead, and this brings us to the 'Hagnonian buildings'.

The expression τὰ Ἁγνώνεια οἰκοδομήματα is translated by Jowett in his main text 'the buildings which Hagnon had erected' (similarly Warner in the Penguin); Jowett gives the trans. 'shrine of Hagnon', adopted above, in a footnote and as an alternative. Everything turns on the word Ἁγνώνεια. If Th. meant 'the buildings which Hagnon had erected' there were straightforward ways of saying just that. But Th. has chosen instead to use an adjective of a distinctive type, the 'Hagnoneian buildings'. This general type of formation (to which the noun 'Mausoleum', Μαυσσώλλειον, also belongs) is called a *temenikon* (τεμενικόν), a word deriving from *temenos* or sacred precinct: see Chandler, *A Practical Introduction to Greek Accentuation²* (Oxford, 1881), para. 362. (The accentuation -εῖον is also possible.) Ἁγνώνεια is a word with undoubtedly religious implications.

For a different view see K/A *PCG* iv (1983), in their apparatus criticus on Cratinus F171 line 71, from the *Ploutoi* of c.430 BC. One restoration of the line is ἐξ [οἰκ]ιῶν ('from the buildings'), and K/A think there may here be a possible reference to the οἰκοδομήματα mentioned by Th. On this view the buildings are a source or manifestation of the wealth of Hagnon which is Cratinus' theme. K/A note that Hagnon in Thrace had the opportunity to enrich himself. But the restoration is very conjectural and others are possible e.g. Kuiper's [ὠν]ίων. Th.'s expression may itself have exerted a pull towards the reading ἐξ [οἰκ]ιῶν. In any case Cratinus seems to be saying that Hagnon was rich 'from the beginning', ἐξ ἀρχῆς, with which K/A compare Lys. xix. 58. If so it is hard to see how Amphipolis and the buildings there (very recent in 430) can be relevant. So I prefer the view that cult buildings are meant.

However Malkin, *Religion and Colonization* (iv. 102. 3 n.), 231, is right to stress that an actual hero-shrine to Hagnon would be called (not *Hagnoneia* in the plural but) a *Hagnoneion* in the singular, cp. the *Arateion* or hero-shrine of Aratos, Plut. *Arat.* 53, the *Sarpedoneion* at Lycian Xanthos (App. *BC* iv. 78, with R. Syme (iv. 103. 1 n. on καὶ ἀφικόμενος etc.), 283, or the famous *Theseion* at Athens; see also Kearns (as above), 66, and Habicht, *Gottmenschentum²*, 140 n. 12. Nevertheless Malkin believes that the word *Hagnoneion* in the plural has a religious meaning, the 'cult buildings' of Hagnon, and adduces the *Kimoneia* of Plut. *Kim.* 19. 5 (on which see A. Blamire's n.). 'It may seem bold to suggest that Hagnon enjoyed a cult while still alive, but in this respect he may have foreshadowed Lysander and Agesilaos' (Malkin, 231; but note that Badian, above, has queried whether even Lysander received cult in his lifetime. In other words Hagnon is even more remarkable.) Malkin

believes that Hagnon received the cult appropriate to an oikist, i.e.
heroic honours. Habicht, *Gottmenschentum*², 186 n. 11, believed that
Hagnon received oikist honours but not cultic ones, because he still
lived. But the distinction oikist/cultic honours is not easily established
from the ancient sources, and I believe Malkin is right against Habicht
that we cannot rule out, *a priori*, cult for a living oikist. Habicht himself
cites para. 3 of the anonymous *Life* of Th., which says that the Amphipolitans pulled down the Ἀγνώνεια οἰκοδομήματα and renamed them
Brasideia, Βρασίδεια ἐκάλεσαν. This has of course no independent value
as evidence for what actually happened, but it shows that one ancient
reader took Th. to be saying that the buildings for Brasidas (which were
uncontroversially part of a hero cult) were of essentially the same type as
the buildings for Hagnon.

Classen/Steup's view is rather different; they suppose that the 'Hagnoneian buildings' are the (secular) buildings put up by Hagnon; but
then they take the second part of the sentence ('any other solid
memorial', μνημόσυνον) to refer, by contrast, to cult buildings put in
honour of Hagnon after his death. This view, if right, would eliminate
the most singular feature of the present passage by making Hagnon's
cult posthumous. It therefore becomes crucial to determine whether
Hagnon was or was not living in 422. Classen/Steup, who thought that
Hagnon the oikist of Amphipolis was dead by 422, do not mention Lys.
xii. 65, which shows Hagnon to have been one of the *probouloi* appointed
in 413, cp. viii. 1. 3 n. Lysias actually refers to him not by name, but as
Theramenes' father. But Hagnon was the patronymic of the Theramenes
who was so active in 411, see viii. 68. 4, and it is usually thought that the
oikist of Amphipolis and the father of Theramenes are the same man.
Classen/Steup presumably believed they were different people. It is true
that no ancient source explicitly identifies Hagnon the oikist of Amphipolis and Hagnon the father of Theramenes; it is also true that there are
27 people called Hagnon in *LGPN* ii; but there is only one from Steiria.
That Steiria, the deme of Theramenes, was also the deme of Hagnon is
now known from Cratinus F171, mentioned above, line 67 (unknown to
Classen/Steup); and from the ostrakon at F. Willemsen and S. Brunn,
'Verzeichnis der Kerameikos-Ostraka', *AM* 106 (1991), 147–56, at 148,
which has 'Hagnon son of Nikias of Steiria'. And see below, 19. 2 n. on
Ἄγνων, for the likelihood that Hagnon belonged to the tribe Pandionis,
which includes the deme Steiria. (As will be seen in the nn. to that ch.,
Andrewes and Lewis, *JHS* 1957, made it very likely that the group of
Athenian names in which Hagnon features are in official Athenian tribal
order.) All this makes it very likely indeed that oikist and father of
Theramenes were the same. It therefore follows that Hagnon, the oikist

of Amphipolis, was alive in the period 437–422 (including 424–422 when, as Gomme says, Amphipolis and Athens were actively hostile), during the whole of which period cult buildings in his honour stood at Amphipolis until dismantled (the present passage). In other words a citizen of democratic Athens, pursuing a normal career (see ii. 58. 1 n. on Ἄγνων), was at the same time getting cult honours at a mainly non-Athenian (iv. 106. 1 n.) city of the north Aegean. As Lewis puts it, *CAH* v². 430 n. 154, 'the real founder, Hagnon, was still alive and well in Athens'. So too Habicht, 186 n. 11, and Malkin, *Religion and Colonization*, 230.

But Classen/Steup's objections do not exhaust the difficulties which have been felt about taking Th. to say that Hagnon was given cult, and here I acknowledge a helpful correspondence with George Cawkwell in 1992. He commented that the Amphipolitans could hardly have demolished a heroon without the consent of Delphi, though he went on immediately to answer his own point by saying 'not that Th. would have felt it necessary to record such consultation'. Cawkwell's second point is more general, there was nothing 'heroic' about merely founding a colony; Brasidas had by contrast saved the city, on which more in a moment; he was *soter* indeed. But the essential point, as Cawkwell acknowledged in 1992, is τιμάς at line 13, used of Hagnon. It is natural to take this to refer to the sort of τιμάς mentioned at line 5, where the reference is to Brasidas' honours, and in that sentence the word is surely predicative, as Classen/Steup saw. That is, the honours are the contests and yearly festivals which follow. We must, I think, take this to mean that Brasidas had got the same annual sacrifices as Hagnon had received.

For the trans. of ἀφανίσαντες I have followed Jowett. Malkin (232) ingeniously notes the use of the word at vi. 54. 7, which he takes to mean that the Athenians *erased* an inscription bearing the name of the tyrant Hippias, and suggests that the Amphipolitans may not have torn down buildings but erased inscriptions recording Hagnon's act of foundation. But vi. 54. 7 does not quite refer to deliberate *erasure* of inscriptions (for which activity Th.'s word is ἐκκολάπτω, see i. 132. 3) but to the obliterating effect of further building work.

νομίσαντες τὸν μὲν Βρασίδαν σωτῆρά τε σφῶν γεγενῆσθαι καὶ ἐν τῷ παρόντι ἅμα τὴν τῶν Λακεδαιμονίων ξυμμαχίαν φόβῳ τῶν Ἀθηναίων θεραπεύοντες, τὸν δὲ Ἅγνωνα κατὰ τὸ πολέμιον τῶν Ἀθηναίων οὐκ ἂν ὁμοίως σφίσι ξυμφόρως οὐδ' ἂν ἡδέως τὰς τιμὰς ἔχειν: 'For they thought Brasidas was their saviour, and in the present circumstances fear of Athens made them flatter their Spartan allies. The idea that Hagnon should retain the honours of a founder, now that they were enemies of the Athenians, seemed to them against their interests, and uncongenial'. The word 'saviour', σωτήρ, is familiar, as a cult title, from Hellenistic and Roman history (Habicht, *Gottmenschentum*², 158, citing e.g. *OGIS* 219 line 37 (Antiochus I); F. W. Walbank, *CAH* vii². 1 (1984), 91 and 93); but at the same time it is perfectly regular Thucydidean Greek, cp. iii. 59. 4, where the Plataians ask the Spartans to be their 'saviours', σωτῆρας. Cp. also Hdt. vii. 139. 5, the Athenians the saviours of Greece, Ar. *Knights* 149, and *Birds* 545, with N. Dunbar's commentary (Oxford, 1995): 'being hailed as saviour(s) seems to have been confined in 5th c. BC to a man or men who had saved a country or city from its enemies in war'. On Brasidas in particular as a 'saviour of the city' see the excellent remarks of Emily Kearns, in Murray and Price (eds.), *The Greek City* (iv. 93. 4 n. on εἶχον δὲ δεξιόν etc.), 328 and n. 9: Th. (as she points out) says that the Amphipolitans considered Brasidas not just founder but also saviour, and then he characteristically adds a more cynical motive as well (see next para.). She suggests that νομίσαντες ('they thought ...', but the Greek word can mean to 'believe in' a divinity) here carries the implication of a customary cult title, and comments that 'the pattern [i.e. treating a hero as saviour] becomes more satisfactory if the death can actually occur as part of the saving action, as Brasidas died in Thrace'. On the exceptional treatment of Brasidas see also R. Seaford, *Reciprocity and Ritual* (Oxford, 1994), 121.

The last few words of Greek have been taken (e.g. by Classen/Steup) to mean that the honours would no longer be congenial to Hagnon, rather than no longer congenial to the Amphipolitans themselves. But the scholiast is surely right to take it to refer to the Amphipolitans; so too Krüger in his edn., and Habicht, 186. Why should the Amphipolitans be so exquisitely sensitive to Hagnon's diminished pleasure in his oikist honours? Malkin (229 and 231) seems to allow both possibilities but slightly to prefer the scholiast's view.

For a story of a consolatory visit by the Amphipolitans to Brasidas' mother Amphileonis see Plut. *Mor.* 240 c.

2. ἀπέθανον δὲ Ἀθηναίων μὲν περὶ ἑξακοσίους, τῶν δ' ἐναντίων ἑπτά: 'There were about six hundred Athenian casualties, but only seven were killed on the other side'. Suddenly, after the Amphipolitan focalization of 11. 1, the focalization switches to Athens (or Th.), note τῶν δ' ἐναντίων, 'the other side', i.e. Sparta. The Spartan casualties are light, but not incredibly so for what was not a regular battle (see next n.), see Krentz, *GRBS* 1985 (iv. 44. 6 n. on ἀπέθανον etc.), 19–20, comparing Plataia, Marathon, and Th. iv. 38. 5, see n. there on ἡ γὰρ μάχη etc.

See Paus. i. 29. 13 for the monument at Athens.

διὰ τὸ μὴ ἐκ παρατάξεως: 'there was no regular battle' [lit. 'not in formation']. The noun means 'line of battle' (not 'phalanx', see E. Wheeler, in Hanson (ed.), *Hoplites*, 163 n. 72). See previous n.

3. **οἱ δὲ μετὰ τοῦ Κλεαρίδου τὰ περὶ τὴν Ἀμφίπολιν καθί-σταντο:** 'Klearidas and his companions remained and settled the affairs of Amphipolis'. See 12. 1 n. on καὶ ἀφικόμενοι etc.

12. 1. Ῥαμφίας καὶ Αὐτοχαρίδας καὶ Ἐπικυδίδας Λακεδαιμό-νιοι: 'the Spartans Rhamphias, Autocharidas, and Epikydidas'. For ham-phias see i. 139. 3; Poralla, *Prosopographie der Lakedaimonier*, identifies him with the father of Klearchos of viii. 8. 2 etc., and this may well be right, although the OCT name index distinguishes the two men. Auto-charidas and Epikydidas are mentioned here only.

καὶ ἀφικόμενοι ἐς Ἡράκλειαν τὴν ἐν Τραχῖνι καθίσταντο ὅτι αὐτοῖς ἐδόκει μὴ καλῶς ἔχειν: 'They went first to Herakleia in Trachis, and put right various things which seemed to them to be wrong'. For Herakleia see iii. 92–3 and nn.; on the present passage see Malkin, *Myth and Territory*, 224–5, who is surely right that the troubles are not just external. He comments: 'one suspects that a major re-ordering of the citizenry of Herakleia Trachinia was under way, probably involving an increase in the authority of the Spartan governor.' Malkin notes in this connection that the verb here used, καθίσταντο, is the same as that used at iii. 92. 1 of the original foundation. This is true, but the correspondence would be more striking if Th. had not just used the verb at the end of v. 11. 3 about Amphipolis, see n. there on οἱ δέ etc.

Note μὴ καλῶς, 'wrong' [lit. 'not well']. Th. uses it (or the closely similar οὐ καλῶς) repeatedly about, precisely, Spartan running of Herakleia. See iii. 93. 2, v. 52. 1. It is almost a *leitmotif*, a reiterated comment on the unsatisfactory nature of Spartan imperialism; see *JHS* 1995, 67.

13. 1. οἱ περὶ τὸν Ῥαμφίαν: 'Rhamphias and his army' [lit. 'those around Rhamphias']. But the expression means perhaps 'Rhamphias and his colleagues', cp. Xen. *Hell.* v. 4. 2. In Hellenistic Greek, 'οἱ περί so-and-so' comes to mean simply 'so-and-so' alone.

κωλυόντων δὲ τῶν Θεσσαλῶν: 'but as the Thessalians were unwilling to let them go further'. Cp. iv. 78. 4 and 132. 2. Gomme notes, against Steup, that the present participle means 'were for preventing them', *not that they actually stopped them*. For the significance of this see next n. at end and above, Introduction, p. 54.

νομίσαντες οὐδένα καιρὸν ἔτι εἶναι τῶν τε Ἀθηναίων ἥσσῃ ἀπεληλυθότων καὶ οὐκ ἀξιόχρεων αὐτῶν ὄντων δρᾶν τι ὧν κἀκεῖνος ἐπενόει: 'They felt that they were not competent to carry out the plans of Brasidas, and in any case the Athenians had been defeated and had left the country'. [In the Greek the Athenian defeat comes first and Brasidas' plans second, but Jowett has reversed the order to make the English flow better. There is no doubt that both parts—Athenian defeat and Brasidas' plans—represent the thinking of Rhamphias and his companions; they are not factual statements by Th.] I have changed Jowett's 'great designs of Brasidas' as being too favourable (or too sarcastic?); the Greek just means 'what he had intended'. See Introduction, p. 53, for the bearing of this on Brasidas' relations with the Spartans at home: despite the jealousy recorded at iv. 108. 7 the present passage surely implies some admiration, always assuming that Th. had good grounds for this ascription of motive. Note also that on the one hand the plans are here implied to be those of Brasidas alone (ἐπενόει is a singular verb, lit. 'he had in mind'), but that on the other hand they are not implied to be at variance with domestic Spartan wishes but merely to be thought to be impracticable in the new situation created by Brasidas' death.

The motive is, however, a double one; the other motive is the feeling that the danger from Athens had passed, and as Gomme notes this is superficially inconsistent with the first motive, which implied that the situation called for the superhuman Brasidas. Gomme suggests that Th. may mean 'as reinforcement against Kleon's attack we are unnecessary', which would be compatible with feeling that they were insufficient for anything more ambitious. Steup (with whom Gomme sympathized) wanted to read οὐδὲ καιρόν, 'that there was no occasion either'; this was part of his view that Thessalian opposition was the main reason why Rhamphias turned back; but see previous n.

2. μάλιστα δὲ ἀπῆλθον εἰδότες τοὺς Λακεδαιμονίους, ὅτε ἐξῆσαν, πρὸς τὴν εἰρήνην μᾶλλον τὴν γνώμην ἔχοντας: 'But their chief reason for turning back was that they knew that at that time when they left Sparta the Spartans were inclined towards peace'. Steup objected to this, partly because Sparta had wanted peace for some while already (contrary to the implication of 'at the time when they left', ὅτε ἐξῆσαν), partly because the last seven words of Greek (corresponding to the last six in the trans.) are more or less repeated at 14. 1 lines 5-6 (OCT), where they apply to both sides. (See Steup, Anhang, 248; this is the surviving part of a more comprehensive effort by Steup in *Rh. Mus.* 1870 (see introductory n. to 14-17) to damn ch. 13 from νομίσαντες on. Steup later relented about the earlier part of ch. 13, preferring the emendation mentioned at the end of the previous n.) The repetition is certainly clumsy, but not impossible. As for the content, Steup's point is strictly valid, but Th. is using Rhamphias' return as a link to the elaborate and symmetrical long section about Spartan and Athenian motives for wanting peace. The motive here given may be right, but the fact is, the reinforcements were sent in the first place. (ᾧπερ ἦγον, para. 1).

14-17. PEACE MOVES

On this whole section, see J. Steup, 'Der Abschluss des 50jährigen Friedens bei Thukydides', *Rh. Mus.* 25 (1870), 273–305 (with second thoughts in the 1912 Abhang to Classen/Steup, 247–53). Even in 1912, Steup wanted to delete large parts of 13–17. 2 as the work of an interpolator (for 13. 2 see previous n.). Though some of his reasons were hypercritical, and later editors have not followed him, his 1870 article contains many still valuable remarks on the content of these chapters.

This is the last of the six reviews of morale which punctuate iv–v. 24 at intervals, see Introduction, above, p. 109. As the last and longest of the six, the present section (which, like iv. 117, discusses both sides) is in a way cumulative, and picks up themes and phrases from the earlier excursuses. Cp. H.-P. Stahl, *Thukydides*, 155.

14. 1. πληγέντες ἐπί τε τῷ Δηλίῳ: 'The Athenians had been beaten at Delion'. See iv. 133. 1 n.; Th. does not always refer to the battle by this name. See also Introductory n. to iv. 89–101, citing iv. 108. 5.
2. καὶ τοὺς ξυμμάχους ἅμα ἐδέδισαν σφῶν μὴ διὰ τὰ σφάλματα ἐπαιρόμενοι ἐπὶ πλέον ἀποστῶσι: 'They were afraid too that their allies would be elated at their disasters, and that more of them would revolt'. But Th. has just said that the Athenians had lost confidence in their own strength (14. 1, οὐκ ἔχοντες τὴν ἐλπίδα τῆς ῥώμης πιστὴν ἔτι), and Steup (1870, 277–8, and in Classen/Steup, 248) objected to the illogicality: allied disaffection would in fact itself cause Athenian loss of confidence, but Th. presents allied disaffection as a new and separate factor. In any case (Steup at Classen/Steup, 248) the situation had, through Kleon's successes and Perdikkas' change of side, changed to Athens' advantage since the loss of Amphipolis. Steup therefore concluded that the present sentence could not have been written by Th. All this is too severe; the great northern prize was Amphipolis, which still eluded Athens. Th. is right to stress it.

For ἐδέδισαν ('they were afraid') see iv. 117. 1 and Introduction, above, p. 109.

For the fear of allied revolt cp. the verbally similar iv. 108. 1, καὶ τοὺς ξυμμάχους . . . μὴ ἀποστῶσιν. But now they are afraid of *further* revolt, ἐπὶ πλέον.

μετεμέλοντό τε ὅτι μετὰ τὰ ἐν Πύλῳ καλῶς παρασχὸν οὐ ξυνέβησαν: 'they regretted that they had not come to terms after the affair at Pylos, when they could have done so with honour'. As Lewis says, *CAH* v². 430–1, 'there had been something to be said for the warning that the Spartan ambassadors had given them' (iv. 17–20).

3. ἐν ᾧ ᾤοντο ὀλίγων ἐτῶν καθαιρήσειν τὴν τῶν Ἀθηναίων δύναμιν, εἰ τὴν γῆν τέμνοιεν: 'There was a time when they thought that, if they only ravaged Attica, they would crush Athens' power within a few years'. With this thought cp. i. 81. 6, iv. 85. 2 (Brasidas at Akanthos, also using the word καθαιρήσειν), and vii. 28. 3.

περιπεσόντες δὲ τῇ ἐν τῇ νήσῳ ξυμφορᾷ, οἷα οὔπω ἐγεγένητο τῇ Σπάρτῃ, καὶ λῃστευομένης τῆς χώρας ἐκ τῆς Πύλου καὶ Κυθήρων, αὐτομολούντων τε τῶν Εἱλώτων καὶ αἰεὶ προσδοκίας οὔσης μή τι καὶ οἱ ὑπομένοντες τοῖς ἔξω πίσυνοι πρὸς τὰ παρόντα σφίσιν ὥσπερ καὶ πρότερον νεωτερίσωσιν: 'but the disaster at Sphakteria was unlike anything Sparta had experienced before. In addition, their country was continually being ravaged from Pylos and Kythera, the helots were deserting, and they were constantly worried that the helots who had not yet deserted would rely on the help of those who had, seize their chance, and revolt, as they had done once before'. Much of this is recapitulatory in thought and expression; in particular there are echoes of the other chs. (see introductory n. to book iv) in which Th. stands back to examine morale at Athens or Sparta or both, see esp. (for the ravaging, λῃστευομένης) iv. 41. 2 ἐλήζοντο and 3 λῃστείας, and for fear of helot desertions iv. 41. 3 and 80. 2; cp. too iv. 55. 1 with Babut, 420 and n. 1. But as Lewis says, *CAH* v². 430 n. 155, 'we are not dependent on Thucydides' judgement, since the alliance with Athens of 421 contained a specific clause (v. 23. 3) by which Athens would help if the helots did revolt'. For the disaster at Sphakteria [lit. 'the island'] see iv. 29–41; for Kythera see iv. 53–7. The allusive 'as they had done once before' looks back to the helot revolt of the 460s, see i. 101. 2.

4. ξυνέβαινε δὲ καὶ πρὸς τοὺς Ἀργείους αὐτοῖς τὰς τριακοντούτεις σπονδὰς ἐπ᾽ ἐξόδῳ εἶναι, καὶ ἄλλας οὐκ ἤθελον σπένδεσθαι οἱ Ἀργεῖοι εἰ μή τις αὐτοῖς τὴν Κυνουρίαν γῆν ἀποδώσει: 'Moreover the Thirty Years Peace with Argos was on the point of expiring, and the Argives were unwilling to renew it unless they got back Kynouria'. So far there has been nothing new, but with para. 4 Th. looks forward, giving us the middle of book v in a nutshell. For this Thirty Years Peace (unexplained by Th.) see i. 115. 1 n. and iv. 133. 2 n. For Kynouria see iv. 56. 2 n. on ἥ ἐστι etc. The Spartans had installed the Aiginetans there.

ὥστ᾽ ἀδύνατα εἶναι ἐφαίνετο Ἀργείοις καὶ Ἀθηναίοις ἅμα πολεμεῖν: 'the Spartans thought it would be impossible to fight against the Argives and Athenians combined'. The literal meaning is 'so that it seemed impossible', etc. Steup thought this literal meaning absurd (the impossibility of fighting against both Argos and Athens is not actually a *consequence* of the difficult diplomatic situation with Argos), and in 1870

(281) suggested ἄφυκτα, 'so that it would be unavoidable that they should have to fight', etc., but in 1912, partly because this adjective is not found in Th., he preferred simply ὥστε δύνατα, 'so that it would be possible that they would have to fight': see Classen/Steup, Anhang, 249. But emendation is not necessary: the expression is condensed, but it surely means that the Spartans thought they would have to fight against Argos and Athens combined and that that would be too much ('imposs-ible') for them. Gomme quotes with approval Mervyn Jones's suggestion εἶτα for ὥστε, 'and then, it seemed impossible', etc.

Kleon negotiated with Argos in 425/4: Ar. *Knights* 465, with *CAH* v² 387.

τῶν τε ἐν Πελοποννήσῳ πόλεων ὑπώπτευόν τινας ἀποστήσε-σθαι πρὸς τοὺς Ἀργείους· ὅπερ καὶ ἐγένετο: 'They also suspected that some of the Peloponnesian cities would secede and join the Argives, as indeed they did'. Probably Mantinea and Elis are meant, see 29. 1 and 31. 5. This sentence thus prepares us for the period that followed the Peace of Nikias.

15. 1. ἦσαν γὰρ οἱ Σπαρτιᾶται αὐτῶν πρῶτοί τε καὶ †ὁμοίως† σφίσι ξυγγενεῖς: 'for the Spartiates among them were of high rank, and had influential relations'. The text is corrupt, but the rough meaning seems clear (and see the scholiast and Plut. *Nik.* 10. 8). It is tempting to think that ὁμοίως conceals a textually corrupted reference to 'peers', i.e. Spartiates, a special Spartan sense of ὅμοιοι known from e.g. Xen. *Hell.* iii. 3. 5; but Th. does not elsewhere use the word in this sense. (On iv. 40. 2 see n. there on ἀπιστοῦντες etc.) For the captured Spartiates (120 of them) see iv. 38. 5, and on Spartan anxieties see Lewis, *Sparta and Persia*, 31. See further below, 18. 7 n. on ἀποδόντων δὲ καὶ Ἀθηναῖοι etc.

2. ἀλλ' οἱ Ἀθηναῖοι οὔπω ἤθελον, εὖ φερόμενοι, ἐπὶ τῇ ἴσῃ καταλύεσθαι: 'but the Athenians were elated by their success and would not yet agree to reasonable terms'. For the phrase ἐπὶ τῇ ἴσῃ (lit. 'on equal terms') see i. 27. 1 and n. Steup notes the occurrence of ἀπὸ τοῦ ἴσου in the speech of the Spartans at Athens on the relevant occasion in 425 (iv. 19. 2, referring to the forcing of unequal oaths); the focalization in the present passage appears to be Spartan, or else Th. is criticizing Athenian behaviour, cp. iv. 23. 1 nn.

I have changed the OCT οὔπως ('not at all', 'no-how') to οὔπω, 'not yet', in view of Dover, *CQ* 1954, 81. The Budé also prefers οὔπω.

ποιοῦνται τὴν ἐνιαύσιον ἐκεχειρίαν, ἐν ᾗ ἔδει ξυνιόντας καὶ περὶ τοῦ πλέονος χρόνου βουλεύεσθαι: 'which is why they had immediately made a truce for a year, during which the envoys of the two states were to meet and consult about a lasting peace'. See iv. 118. 6 and 13–14; 119. 3 and n.

16. 1. ὁ μὲν διὰ τὸ εὐτυχεῖν: 'Brasidas because the war brought him success'. The reference to Brasidas' success picks up ηὐτύχει (same verb) at iv. 117. 2, from the fifth of the six excursuses on morale in iv–v. 24, cp. Introduction, above, p. 109 for the frequency of such echoes in the six passages, and iv. 117. 2 n. (Note, however, that the related word εὐτυχία is used about *Nikias*, below, line 17, see n. on διασώσασθαι etc.)

The μέν ('on the one hand' as it can clumsily be translated) is answered in the next line by a δέ referring to Kleon, but that is only the first such pair in this monstrously long (20-line) sentence, see lines 16 for Nikias and 22 for Pleistoanax.

It has often been noted, see e.g. de Ste. Croix, *OPW* 153, and Kallet-Marx, 179–80, that the motives given by Th. in this para. are purely personal. Kallet-Marx, as part of her general thesis that Athens was not broke, notes that 'significant depletion of the essential requirement for making war is not brought up as one of the compelling reasons for making peace'. She cites D. Kagan, *The Archidamian War* (Ithaca, NY, 1974), 336.

ὁ δὲ γενομένης ἡσυχίας καταφανέστερος νομίζων ἂν εἶναι κακουργῶν καὶ ἀπιστότερος διαβάλλων: 'he thought that in peace-time his criminality would be more transparent and his slanders less easily believed'. Notoriously, not the most objective-sounding sentence in all Th. Cp. Lang, *Mnemosyne* 1995 (iv. 9. 1 n. on Δημοσθένης δὲ ὁρῶν). See Ar. *Knights* (of 424) 801 ff. for very similar sentiments, with Sommerstein's n. (It is not clear why Lewis, *CR* 1983, 176, criticizes Sommerstein for not being alert to the Thucydidean aspect of those lines.)

τότε δὴ ἑκατέρᾳ τῇ πόλει σπεύδοντες τὰ μάλιστα τὴν ἡγεμο-νίαν Πλειστοάναξ τε ὁ Παυσανίου βασιλεὺς Λακεδαιμονίων καὶ Νικίας ὁ Νικηράτου, πλεῖστα τῶν τότε εὖ φερόμενος ἐν στρατηγίαις, πολλῷ δὴ μᾶλλον προυθυμοῦντο: 'In this new situation [lit. 'then'] the main claimants to political power at Athens and Sparta [lit. 'each city'] were Pleistoanax son of Pausanias, king of Sparta, and the Athenian Nikias son of Nikeratos, and so far the most successful general of his day. These two were both keener than ever to end the war'. This is roughly the meaning of the text as it stands, though with Jowett and Gomme we should add ἐν or οἱ ἐν before ἑκατέρᾳ, so as to get the meaning '*in* each city'. Stahl, followed by Steup, thought that ἡγεμονίαν should be deleted altogether, and that what Th. wrote was σπεύδοντες μάλιστ᾽ αὐτήν, where αὐτήν ('it') would refer to 'peace', εἰρήνην, i.e. the whole expression would mean 'those in each city who were most energetically pursuing peace'. This is ingenious but so radical a deletion is hard to justify; for ἡγεμονία in the sense of 'leadership in the state' see *Ath. Pol.* xxiii. 1 and Ar. *Pol.* 1296a39. It is a little odd, but not impossible, to speak of a Spartan king vying for leadership in the state: Th. is referring not to position but to influence. Drastic emendations which would make Brasidas and Kleon do the vying are superficially attractive but not necessary. Gomme considers and suggests other far-reaching emendations and attempts to re-order this long paragraph, but none seem absolutely compelling, though the Greek as it stands is difficult and perhaps impossible, i.e. corrupt at more than one point. The words πολλῷ δὴ μᾶλλον προυθυμοῦντο should mean 'Nikias and Pleistoanax were keener than ever [to make peace]'. It is not easy to give much meaning to this unless we have been told already that Nikias and Pleistoanax were eager for peace, and Stahl's emendation has the merit of supplying that idea. To make sense of the text as it is, we have to suppose Th.'s expression πολλῷ etc. to be highly elliptical, 'they were [keen before and they were] even keener now'. This would be hard to justify in itself, but 17. 1 does indeed imply that Pleistoanax, at least, had been anxious for peace since *before* 422 and the deaths of Brasidas and Kleon.

The casual introduction of Pleistoanax is remarkable; except as patronymic (iii. 26. 2) he has not been heard of since ii. 21. 1, and that was itself a back-reference to the events of 446 (see i. 114. 2), to which Th. alludes below at para. 3. The 'correct' place for a mention of his recall (for which see 3n. on ἔτει etc.) was perhaps iii. 89. 1, see n. there (summer 426). This is an extreme case of Th. waiting until an event is relevant before telling us about it. The oracle story in paras. 2–3, and the iterative material about Pleistoanax's enemies at lines 22 ff., is a large external analepsis or retrospective coverage of events not so far related.

βουλόμενος . . . διασώσασθαι τὴν εὐτυχίαν: 'wanted . . . to preserve his good fortune'. See above n. on ὁ μὲν διὰ τὸ εὐτυχεῖν, and for Nikias as εὐτυχής, 'successful', 'fortunate', cp. vi. 17. 1 with Dover's n. in *HCT*, and vii. 77. 2. As Dover says on vi. 17, the argument there only makes sense if εὐτυχία 'is treated as an abiding characteristic, and that is logically incompatible with its treatment as pure chance'. In view of what happens to Nikias, the use of the word here is ironic. On the participially expressed motivation see iv. 9. 1 n. on Δημοσθένης δὲ ὁρῶν, with iv. 28. 1 n.

πόνων πεπαῦσθαι: 'rest from exertions'. On this phrase see A. Boegehold, 'A Dissent at Athens, *ca* 424–421 BC', *GRBS* 23 (1982), 147–56, noting that it occurs in a number of literary works of more or less this time, as a way of saying 'let's stop the war'. The present passage of Th. is the main text, but see also Ar. *Knights* 579–80 and *Peace* (of 421) 918–21, and Eur. *Suppliants* 951–2 (see iv. 97. 2 n. on ἐκ δέ etc.). Boegehold also points to a number of instances of πόνοι, 'toil', in Pericles' last speech at Th. ii. 60–4 and suggests that these appeals to toil were a reply to critics dissatisfied with the war.

καταλιπεῖν ὄνομα ὡς οὐδὲν σφήλας τὴν πόλιν: 'to be remembered by posterity as a man who had never brought disaster on the city' [lit. 'to leave a name as having never . . .']. Not only is there irony of a general sort here, in view of Nikias' role in the Sicilian Disaster, but there is a notable set of verbal chimes with Hermokrates at vi. 33. 5 about foreign invaders, ἤν τε . . . ἐν ἀλλοτρίᾳ γῇ σφαλῶσι, τοῖς ἐπιβουλευθεῖσιν ὄνομα . . . ὅμως καταλείπουσιν, if they fail *disastrously* in a foreign country, they *leave a name*, i.e. glory, for those they had plotted against, i.e. the people whose land they had invaded. This idea (glory in the end redounded to the Syracusans) is itself resumed at vii. 87. 5, the end of the Sicilian Expedition; and Hermokrates' speech (vi. 33. 5) finds a further pre-echo in the present ch., see below n. on ὁπότε τι πταίσειαν etc.

Πλειστοάναξ δὲ ὑπὸ τῶν ἐχθρῶν διαβαλλόμενος περὶ τῆς καθόδου, καὶ ἐς ἐνθυμίαν τοῖς Λακεδαιμονίοις αἰεὶ προβαλλόμενος ὑπ' αὐτῶν: 'Pleistoanax wanted peace [these two words are supplied to make the sense run easier] because his enemies were making trouble about his return from exile; they constantly played on the religious scruples of the Spartans by bringing his name up' [lit. 'being accused by his enemies about his return, and being constantly brought up before the Spartans as a cause of misgiving'; that adopts the LSJ⁹ trans. of the noun, but the extra idea '*religious* misgiving' seems to be present, see below]. The feminine noun ἐνθυμία is here translated 'religious scruples' (Jowett had merely 'scruples', but this does at least suggest religion unlike other versions we shall consider). The word is found here only in Th. and is exceedingly rare anywhere. LSJ⁹ gives this as the only example. A search in TLG, the computerized thesaurus, produced just one more instance, namely Dio Cass. xxxix. 11. 1. But this is an obvious imitation of the present passage of Th.! It concerns the treatment of Cicero's house, a famous religious episode in the late Roman Republic: καὶ τοῦ Κλωδίου καὶ ἐπιθειάζοντος καὶ ἐς ἐνθυμίαν αὐτῷ προβάλλοντος, which the Loeb translates 'and though Clodius both called the gods to witness and placed religious scruples in his way'. Was Cassius Dio, discussing Cicero's house, reminded of the Th. passage by the mention of Pleistoanax's house at para. 3 below? Gomme does not discuss the word at all, but Steup renders ἐς ἐνθυμίαν προβάλλω in a secular and colourless way, 'to bring to their knowledge or consciousness', 'ins Gewissen rücken' (followed by Warner in the Penguin, 'in an attempt to convince the Spartans'). But at vii. 50. 4 we have the related but distinct adjectival expression ἐνθύμιον ποιούμενοι, used about the famous eclipse and about the Athenians' reaction to it (i.e. the context, which goes on to talk about Nikias' attitude to divination etc., is clearly religious), and this seems to mean 'they had scruples about it' (LSJ⁹); Dover regrettably does not discuss the word. Note that this passage, too, was imitated by Cassius Dio, see lviii. 6. 1, Sejanus and others 'took no notice of these portents', τούτων οὖν τῶν τεράτων οὔθ' ὁ Σειανὸς οὔτ' ἄλλος τις ἐνθύμιον ἐποιή-σατο. Bétant translates Th.'s two expressions by the Latin *religio*, giving *religio* for ἐνθυμία and *in religionem vertere* for ἐνθύμιον ποιεῖσθαι. To return to the feminine singular ἐνθυμία and to the present passage: if Bétant and Jowett are right, and I think they are (especially given that Cassius Dio understood the word religiously), the point is valuable for the understanding of the passage and of Spartan attitudes as Th. saw them. Cf. also E. Dodds, *The Greeks and the Irrational* (1951), 55 n. 146.

Note the iterative way Th. presents this material, Pleistoanax's enemies were constantly, αἰεί, stirring things up; this is Th.'s way of making up lost ground and covering a long period of trouble-making, see above n. on τότε δή etc. for the long period during which his narrative neglected Pleistoanax. Cf. ἐπὶ πολύ at 2 below, 'whenever' (Classen/ Steup).

ὁπότε τι πταίσειαν, ὡς διὰ τὴν ἐκείνου κάθοδον παρανομη-θεῖσαν ταῦτα ξυμβαίνοι: 'insisting that any misfortunate was to be put down to his illegal return from exile'. With πταίσειαν (lit. 'if there was any failure') cp. Hermokrates at vi. 33. 5, πταίσωσιν, with n. above on καταλιπεῖν etc. See Introduction, p. 120 n. 304.

Before we regard this as a typically Spartan piece of superstition, we should compare v. 32. 1, the Athenians replace the Delians on Delos, partly because of their recent defeats, partly because Apollo told them to. In any case see next n., citing Parker: religion is here being used to cope with special problems which could not be solved politically.

With παρανομηθεῖσαν, 'illegal', cp. the related noun παρανόμημα at vii. 18. 2 and 3, where again the context is Spartan retrospective religious scrupulosity.

2. τὴν γὰρ πρόμαντιν τὴν ἐν Δελφοῖς ἐπῃτιῶντο αὐτὸν πεῖσαι μετ' Ἀριστοκλέους τοῦ ἀδελφοῦ ὥστε χρῆσαι Λακεδαιμονίοις ἐπὶ πολὺ τάδε θεωροῖς ἀφικνουμένοις, Διὸς υἱοῦ ἡμιθέου τὸ σπέρμα ἐκ τῆς ἀλλοτρίας ἐς τὴν ἑαυτῶν ἀναφέρειν, εἰ δὲ μή, ἀργυρέᾳ εὐλάκᾳ εὐλαξεῖν: 'They alleged that he and Aristokles his brother had induced the priestess at Delphi to give the same answer whenever Spartan envoys came to consult the oracle. She would always tell them to "bring back to Sparta from abroad the seed of the Zeus-born hero; otherwise they would plough with a silver ploughshare"'. That is, their enterprises would be unprofitable. (The scholiast says, because starvation would mean food would be very expensive; alternatively, because ploughing the land would be as futile as it would be if silver ploughshares were used.) The best discussion of this para. is by R. Parker, 'Greek States and Greek Oracles', in *CRUX*, 318 and 324-5. At

318 he includes this response in the 'rare and spectacular category' of 'spontaneous' responses by which the Pythia issued an order unrelated to the question posed; for others see Hdt. v. 63 (late sixth cent.; the Alkmaionids allegedly persuaded the Pythia to tell any Spartan enquirer that Athens must be freed from the Pisistratids) and Paus. v. 21. 5 (Athenian enquirers told they must pay a sacred fine to Olympia). The present response also belongs (Parker, 319) to another and overlapping group of Pythian responses, those involving Spartan kings (others concern Demaratos, Agesilaos, and the kingship plans of Lysander), as if 'problems about the kingship could not be resolved by political means, because the kingship was the foundation of the political structure'. Note also Parker, 324 and n. 91, for the present passage as showing that 'most Greeks believed that the Pythia occasionally yielded to improper persuasion, whether by works or by gold'; he adduces Hdt. v. 63 again (see above for the Alkmaionids), also vi. 66. 2–3. 'By isolating this abnormal category of corrupted responses, they defended the purity of others.'

It will be noticed that a number of Herodotean passages have so far featured in this n. The present passage is certainly more in Hdt.'s normal manner than that of Th., see my *Thucydides*, 82; Connor, *Thucydides*, 145, as part of an argument against any assumption of Thucydidean homogeneity of manner (see above, introductory n. to iv. 117–19), nicely remarks that Th. here 'delights in the idiom of oracular discourse'. Note however that, though Th. is occasionally willing, as here, to allow the Delphic oracle some influence on political events, he gives no coverage whatsoever to the Delphic Amphiktiony, though that surely exerted influence (and could have influence exerted over it): see *HSCP* 94 (1992), 169–97, and John Davies in *Greek Historiography*, 201.

On the Heraklid line of the Spartan kings as 'Zeus-born heroes' see I. Malkin, *Myth and Territory*, 15 and n. 4, discussing the present passage: the myth helped to legitimate the status of the Spartan kings and provided a link between present and past.

3. ἐς Λύκαιον: 'at Lykaion'. A mountain in western Arkadia, between Bassai and the future Megalopolis, near the border with Sparta (actually with Messenia, but Messenia was under Spartan control). **διὰ τὴν ἐκ τῆς Ἀττικῆς ποτὲ μετὰ δώρων δοκήσεως ἀναχώρησιν:** 'On account of his retreat from Attica, when he was supposed to have been bribed'. See i. 114. 2 and ii. 21. 1. Each time Pleistoanax's 446 invasion and its domestic consequences are mentioned we are told a little more about them, by the Homeric technique of increasing precision (for which see iv. 66. 1 n. on αἰεί etc.). **καὶ ἥμισυ τῆς οἰκίας τοῦ ἱεροῦ τότε τοῦ Διὸς οἰκοῦντα φόβῳ**

τῷ Λακεδαιμονίων: 'he had lived in a house half of which was inside the sacred precinct of Zeus; this was because he was afraid of the Spartans'. For this passage as an example of 'sanctuary' (in the modern or rather medieval sense, i.e. refuge) see U. Sinn, in N. Marinatos and R. Hägg (eds.), *Greek Sanctuaries* (iv. 97. 3 n. on ὕδωρ etc.), 106 and nn. 49–52, noting how many Spartan kings chose such distant sanctuaries as refuges: Leotychidas and (king) Pausanias in Tegea, Kleombrotos at Tainaron, and Pleistoanax at Lykaion. As Sinn points out, Agis in the third century behaved differently, ostentatiously staying in the sanctuary of Athena in the town and courting his own death, Plut. *Agis* 16–21.

D. M. MacDowell, *Spartan Law* (Edinburgh, 1986), 147–8, discusses the house half-way inside the sanctuary, and comments that the apparent implication, that Pleistoanax feared death at Spartan hands, is odd because he had been condemned not to death but to a fine (*FGrHist* 70 Ephorus F 193; Plut. *Per.* 22. 3). MacDowell conjectures that the death penalty may have attached to failure to pay a fine. But Pleistoanax may more vaguely have feared the Trotsky treatment.

ἔτει ἑνὸς δέοντι εἰκοστῷ: 'after nineteen years of exile'. His return was perhaps at some time between late summer 427 (no earlier, because his (under-age) son Pausanias was on the throne earlier that summer, iii. 26. 2) and summer 426; see iii. 89. 1 n. His invasion of Attica was in late summer or autumn 446, but we cannot be sure if he was exiled straight away rather than in summer 445.

τοῖς ὁμοίοις χοροῖς καὶ θυσίαις καταγαγεῖν ὥσπερ ὅτε τὸ πρῶτον Λακεδαίμονα κτίζοντες τοὺς βασιλέας καθίσταντο: 'to bring him home again with the same dances and sacrifices as when they first enthroned their kings when Sparta was founded'. We should be grateful that Th. gives us this much, but we should like more, given that so much of our evidence about early Sparta is 'invented tradition'. (Even the "Great Rhetra" of Plut. *Lyk.* 6 does not pretend to cover anything so hazily distant as the beginnings of the kingship.) But how authentic were the traditions about the dances and sacrifices, and how were the traditions preserved? Presumably Delphi would be consulted on the details.

17. 1. ἀχθόμενος οὖν τῇ διαβολῇ ταύτῃ … προυθυμήθη τὴν ξύμβασιν: 'He was annoyed by these accusations … so he was very anxious for peace'. The implication of this whole sentence is surely that Pleistoanax had wanted peace for some time; this has a bearing on the problems of 16. 1, see n. there on τότε δή etc.
2. καὶ πρὸς τὸ ἔαρ ἤδη: 'Towards spring'. Gomme suggested that these words should be taken with what goes before, i.e. with the statement that they began negotiations, rather than with what follows, the

announcement of intention to build a fort; and he punctuated accordingly, with a pause after ἤδη. See, however, the objections of Andrewes, *HCT* iv. 21: the pause is not natural and there is no reason why the announcement or threat of a fort should not have been made at the last moment; 'the order to the allies would naturally come at the beginning of spring'.

ὡς ⟨ἐς⟩ ἐπιτειχισμόν: 'to build a fort'. See H. D. Westlake, 'The Progress of Epiteichismos', *Studies*, 34–47, reprinted from *CQ* 33 (1983).

ἐπειδὴ ἐκ τῶν ξυνόδων ἅμα πολλὰς δικαιώσεις προενεγκόντων ἀλλήλοις: 'After many conferences and mutual demands'. For the possibility that Th.'s brief account here masks a stage at which ten-man commissions of Athenians and Spartans conducted preliminary negotiations, see Andrewes and Lewis, *JHS* 1957, 177 (19. 1 n. on ὤμνυον etc.). They base themselves on Diod. xii. 75. 4. If they are right, this is a small example of Thucydidean selectivity. (The less attractive, biographical, alternative is to say that in his exile he was at a fact-gathering disadvantage.)

ξυνεχωρεῖτο ὥστε ἃ ἑκάτεροι πολέμῳ ἔσχον ἀποδόντας τὴν εἰρήνην ποιεῖσθαι: 'it was finally agreed that peace should be made on the understanding that both sides should give up what they had won by war'. The Peace of Nikias in a nutshell, except that the status of some glaringly problematic places remained unsolved. On this sentence see Kirchhoff, 33, and C. Meyer, *Urkunden*, 27, arguing that it was information which reached Th. independently of the treaty. This is not necessarily true, though it may be. As Lewis puts it, *CAH* v². 431, 'the framework selected was that each side should return its gains in the war'; he adds that iii. 52. 2 shows that this had long been in Spartan minds as a possible formula (for this passage, which concerns Plataia, see next n.).

Note, with Lewis, that Potidaia and Aigina ('intimately associated with the causes of the war', and now Athenian settlements) were tacitly forgotten, as were the changes in the region of Akarnania.

ἀνταπαιτούντων γὰρ Πλάταιαν οἱ Θηβαῖοι ἔφασαν οὐ βίᾳ, ἀλλ' ὁμολογίᾳ αὐτῶν προσχωρησάντων καὶ οὐ προδόντων ἔχειν τὸ χωρίον, καὶ οἱ Ἀθηναῖοι τῷ αὐτῷ τρόπῳ τὴν Νίσαιαν: 'This was because when they demanded back Plataia the Thebans protested that they had not acquired it by force or treachery, but by agreement; to which the Athenians replied that they had acquired Nisaia in the same way'. For the point about Plataia see iii. 52. 2 n. on βίᾳ etc. and for Nisaia see iv. 69. 4 n. on καὶ τὴν Νίσαιαν etc. and (for the 422 situation) iv. 118. 4 n. on τοὺς δ' ἐν Νισαίᾳ etc. As Gomme remarks, the Athenian point was specious because the place was surrendered by the Peloponnesian garrison, not by the Megarians.

πλὴν Βοιωτῶν καὶ Κορινθίων καὶ Ἠλείων καὶ Μεγαρέων ... (τούτοις δὲ οὐκ ἤρεσκε τὰ πρασσόμενα): 'except for the Boiotians, Corinthians, Eleans, and Megarians, all of whom were dissatisfied'. We shall hear more about all this later in book v; Th. understandably declines to say more for the moment, merely signalling in brief and general terms a dissatisfaction which will cause great trouble later. The Boiotians got away with keeping Plataia, but were aggrieved by the stipulations about Panakton, 18. 7 with 39. 2-3. Megara, associated with Boiotia at 31. 6 and later (cp. iv. 72. 1 n.), has grounds for dissatisfaction over Nisaia, see previous n. The motives of Corinth, so crucial in the first stage of the unravelling of the peace, are given at 30; and the Elean at 31, though Andrewes, *HCT* v. 376 (discussing the puzzling relation of the present passage to 22. 2, see n. there below), points out that the Elean grievances at 31 are given as the reason why they joined the Argive alliance, not as the reason why they rejected the peace.

The present passage surely means that the Boiotians formally voted against the Peace, i.e. they were members of the Peloponnesian League; so de Ste. Croix, *OPW* 336, and Andrewes, *HCT* on v. 32. 6.

De Ste. Croix, *OPW* 115 and n. 70, is probably right to interpret the reference to 'allies', τῶν ξυμμάχων, at v. 30. 2 (where he is speaking of allies who did not accept the peace) to refer to Spartan allies additional to Corinth, rather than allies *of* Corinth. Otherwise, as he says, 17. 2—the present passage—is misleading (by not specifying those Corinthian allies).

18-19. THE PEACE OF NIKIAS

For modern bibliography see, apart from Gomme's commentary in *HCT*, the works of Kirchhoff, Steup (*Thukydideische Studien*, 1, 29-71), and C. Meyer cited in the introductory n. to iv. 117-19; add Wilamowitz, 'Das Bündnis zwischen Sparta und Athen (Thukydides V)', *Kl. Schr.* iii (Berlin, 1969), 380-405 (originally *SBer. Berlin* 1919, 934-57); Gomme ignores this as completely as he did Wilamowitz's study of the 423 truce. Wilamowitz (389 n. 2, cp. 371 n. 2) was interested, as other scholars have tended not to be, in the personal names of the swearers. On the names of the Athenians who swore to the peace, A. Andrewes and D. M. Lewis made an important contribution in the *JHS* for 1957, the year after the appearance of the relevant vol. of Gomme's *HCT*; see 19. 2 n. on Ἀθηναίων δὲ οἵδε· But we shall see that on one point to do with

Isthmionikos (his possible identity with the Isthmonikos of *IG* i³. 84) Wilamowitz anticipated Andrewes and Lewis.

On the content of the peace see the excellent brief summary and comments of Lewis, *CAH* v². 431–2, already drawn on above at 17. 2 n. on ξυνεχωρεῖτο etc. The fullest analysis is now E. Baltrusch, *Symmachie und Spondai: Untersuchungen zum griechischen Völkerrecht der archaischen und klassischen Zeit (8–5 Jahrhundert v. Chr.)* (Berlin and N.Y., 1994), 169–85, valuable for its discussion of traditional and novel features of the peace, which (like the Thirty Years Peace between Athens and Sparta of 446) was an attempt, and indeed the last attempt (Baltrusch, 176), to regulate the affairs of all Greece by an essentially bilateral instrument. The limitation to 50 years was new (177). The basis of the treaty was the *status quo ante* rather than, as was more usual, the *status quo* (179 and n. 460).

To be more specific: each side is to return its wartime gains, with some notable exceptions and silences; Sparta abandons all pretence of interest in the north; Athens gives back Pylos, Kythera, Methana, Atalante, and the (for Sparta) all-important prisoners. As Lewis puts it: 'after ten years of war, Sparta had abandoned, not only all attempt to destroy the Athenian empire, but also some cherished interests of major allies, bargaining the liberation of Greece for the security of her own system. Athens had won the war.' (For a different view on this last point see D. Kagan, *The Archidamian War* (Ithaca, NY, 1974), 346.)

On the main compositional problem raised by Th.'s account of the treaty, see esp. Gomme, 680–2. He was surely right to reject the position of Kirchhoff, who once again (see on the 423 truce) argued that Th. did not see the document until after, and perhaps long after, he had written the preceding narrative. But Kirchhoff's position about the Peace of Nikias was different from his position over the 423 truce because (whereas he thought that the narrative before *and after* iv. 118–19 was written earlier than the truce treaty) he thought that v. 21 onwards (not just 25 onwards) were written after 404 and in knowledge of the detail of the treaty. Some of the same kind of counter-considerations apply to the Peace of Nikias as to the 423 truce, see introductory n. to iv. 117–19. Particular points are discussed in the commentary which follows. We shall see that at a number of points there is detailed correspondence between pre-treaty narrative and treaty text. Gomme, however, agreed with Kirchhoff to the extent that he was troubled by the inconsistency of the date at 20. 1 (from Th.'s narrative) on the one hand with that in 19 (from the treaty) on the other; on this see 20. 1 n.

For discussion of the general question why Th. included the verbatim texts of the peace (and of the alliance, ch. 23) see introductory n. to iv. 117–19, and Introduction, pp. 113–19.

The treaty is in four parts: (i) access to 'the common temples' (18. 2); (ii) general statement about duration and terms (18. 3–4); (iii) detailed undertakings, claims, and concessions (18. 5–8); (iv) provisions about oath-taking, publication, amendments, and date at which treaty comes into effect (18. 9–19. 1).

18. 1. Ἀθηναῖοι καὶ Λακεδαιμόνιοι καὶ οἱ ξύμμαχοι: 'the Athenians, and the Spartans and their allies'. As the Greek stands, the words 'and their allies' refer to Sparta's allies only, cp. Classen/Steup. I have therefore changed Jowett's 'and their respective allies'. Gomme, however, thought it possible that the word ἑκατέρων, 'of both sides', has dropped out, which would indeed give the sense 'respective'. This is by no means inevitable, though it is possible in view of e.g. para. 3 below; see n. there. But there is no sign of any Delian League consultation, i.e. Athens speaks for its allies as well as itself, whether or not we emend the text of the present opening sentence so as to produce a specific reference.

2. περὶ μὲν τῶν ἱερῶν τῶν κοινῶν, θύειν καὶ ἰέναι καὶ μαντεύεσθαι καὶ θεωρεῖν κατὰ τὰ πάτρια τὸν βουλόμενον καὶ κατὰ γῆν καὶ κατὰ θάλασσαν ἀδεῶς: 'As for the common temples, any one who pleases may sacrifice in them and travel to them and consult the oracles in them and visit them as sacred delegates, according to ancestral custom, both by land and sea, without fear'. Cp. iv. 118. 1, the opening clause of the 423 truce. (Gomme's reference to iv. 118. 2 is presumably a typographical error.) But the religious provisions of 423 (which concerned access to Delphi and recovery of sacred money) were specifically confined to Delphi. In the present treaty Delphi is *both* included in the 'access' provisions (but as one of several Panhellenic shrines) *and* dealt with separately (see next n.) and from an altogether different point of view: that of the independence of, as opposed to access to, Delphi. In the present clause, καὶ ἰέναι ('and travel to them') has been variously emended; it is odd to find it in second place after the infinitive verb meaning 'to sacrifice' which logically presupposes the travel in question. Some have simply deleted the two words; Kirchhoff suggested θύειν ἐξεῖναι, 'it is to be allowed to sacrifice', but as Steup says the extra word 'to be allowed to' is unnecessary, cp. the simple infinitive at iv. 118. 1 describing the activity to be permitted (χρῆσθαι, 'use'). Steup, followed by de Romilly in the Budé, transferred the words to a later point in the sentence, before καὶ κατὰ γῆν, i.e. 'to travel to them both by land ...'. Wilamowitz, 385 n. 1 (whose idea is not mentioned by editors or commentators) wanted to delete the first καί only, producing θύειν ἰέναι καὶ μαντεύεσθαι. He reckoned that the crucial idea was the travelling, and apparently wanted to take θύειν, μαντεύεσθαι and θεωρεῖν as infinitives of purpose (cp. Kühner–Gerth, ii. 2. 27, para. 473, who give as an example Th. i. 128, ἀφικνεῖται . . . πράσσειν, 'he sailed there . . . to carry on an intrigue'), with all these infinitives dependent on ἰέναι: 'people are to be free to travel so as to sacrifice, to consult the oracles' etc. This sort of double infinitive construction is not very easy.

The great common, i.e. Panhellenic, sanctuaries were Delphi, Olympia, Nemea, Isthmia; see N. J. Richardson in *CAH* v², ch. 8d; also *OCD*³ under the relevant entries. They were mostly in Peloponnesian territory, or for other reasons (see iv. 118. 1-2 for Delphi) difficult of access for Athenians. Hence it has usually and probably rightly been assumed that Athenian pressure was behind the access clause, now as in the more limited iv. 118. 1 about Delphi alone. But (see iv. 118. 1 n.) there had been no actual exclusion of Athenians or their allies.

Parker, *CRUX*, 298–326, at 325–6, cited this passage, as well as the 423 guarantee of access, as evidence of general belief in Apollo's fairness.

Baltrusch (178) puts the Delphi clause among the novelties of the Peace of Nikias. He is right that the Delphi provisions are more specific than those of 423, but we know too little about treaties (e.g. the detail of the 446 peace) to be confident about just how much of an innovation the 421 provisions represent.

τὸ δ' ἱερὸν καὶ τὸν νεὼν τὸν ἐν Δελφοῖς τοῦ Ἀπόλλωνος καὶ Δελφοὺς αὐτονόμους εἶναι καὶ αὐτοτελεῖς καὶ αὐτοδίκους καὶ αὐτῶν καὶ τῆς γῆς τῆς ἑαυτῶν κατὰ τὰ πάτρια: 'The sanctuary and the temple at Delphi, and the Delphian people, shall be autonomous and shall have control of their own revenues and shall have their own courts of justice, both for themselves and for their territory, according to their ancestral customs'. The word αὐτοτελεῖς is used in the sense 'having full judicial powers' at *Ath. Pol.* iii. 5, see Rhodes's n. on the passage; but in the present context (esp. with αὐτοδίκους immediately following, a word with an obvious legal sense) LSJ⁹ is surely right to take it as referring to revenues or taxation, cp. (with Gomme) ὑποτελεῖς, paying tax as a subject, or ξυντελεῖς, paying tax as a member of a federation, cp. iv. 76. 3 n. on Χαιρώνειαν δέ etc. Ostwald, *Autonomia*, takes the word to refer to taxation, and regards 'autonomy' here as meaning freedom to make political decisions without external interference. For the combination αὐτόνομοι . . . καὶ αὐτόδικοι Raaflaub, *Freiheit*, 187 n. 176, compares *Inscriptiones Creticae* iv. 80 line 1 (relations between Gortyn and Rhizon).

Unlike the earlier clause about access, which seems to have been inserted more for the benefit of Athens, the present clause is more directed *against* Athens, which had repeatedly tried to put Delphi under Phokian control, cp. i. 112. 5 n. on Λακεδαιμόνιοι etc. and iii. 95. 1 n. on ἐς Φωκέας etc. (the Phokians said to be friendly to Athens, despite ii. 9. 3 where they are listed as Peloponnesian allies). But the present clause may not be wholly one-sided in intention: recent Spartan efforts to maximize their influence in the Delphic amphiktiony, by the foundation in 426 of Herakleia in Trachis (see iii. 92. 1 n. on Ἡράκλειαν etc., and *HSCP* 1992, 190) may have worried the Athenians. Nevertheless there is no explicit mention of the amphiktiony here, and in a documentary context this cannot be put down to Th.'s own personal lack of interest in the amphiktiony (for this lack of interest see *HSCP* 1992, 176). The explanation may be that, whereas it was acceptable to demand the autonomy of the sanctuary and community of Delphi, it would be hard to devise a formula designed to protect the amphiktiony from manipulation. You could hardly stipulate 'the amphiktiony shall be autonomous' because such a term would hardly be appropriate to a multi-state entity, and because the acquisition of leverage in the amphiktiony was not so palpably outrageous as physical take-over or coercion of the sanctuary. Nevertheless I suggest that (despite Zeilhofer (iv. 118. 1 n.) 72 f.) it is reasonable to see the undertakings in the present clause as directed against the activities of Sparta as well as those of Athens. In this connection, note that at v. 32. 2 (421) we shall be told that the Phokians and Lokrians fought a war. Was this a sacred war like that at i. 112? It shows, at any rate, that the Phokians and Lokrians, bracketed together as Peloponnesian allies at ii. 9. 3 (the beginning of the war), and again at v. 64. 4 (418), came to blows soon after the Peace of Nikias was sworn to. (See Andrewes, *HCT* n. on v. 32. 2, for the possibility that the Phokian victory over Lokris, mentioned by Diod. xii. 80. 4 under 418/17, may refer to the war of 421.) If it was a sacred war, it shows that the issue of control of Delphi was a live one, and that the present clause was not a pious triviality. But we lack the evidence to say whether or how any of all this was related to the Delphic ambitions of either Sparta or Athens. See Zeilhofer generally for these ambitions.

For 'ancestral customs', τὰ πάτρια, see Ostwald, *Autonomia*, 3 and 44, regarding them as enforceable at law. Presumably the only possible tribunal was, precisely, the amphiktiony.

Gomme, discussing the mention of 'Delphians', Δελφούς, remarks that 'the shrine and the community of Delphians are almost one, at least so bound with one another that one could not be free without the other'. This is true, but there was a distinct community of the Delphians, see *Syll*.² 434 (not in edn. 3), most recent text Rougemont, *CID* i. 9, ordinances of the Labyadai, a phratry of Delphi.

3. ἔτη δὲ εἶναι τὰς σπονδὰς πεντήκοντα Ἀθηναίοις καὶ τοῖς ξυμμάχοις τοῖς Ἀθηναίων καὶ Λακεδαιμονίοις καὶ τοῖς ξυμμάχοις

τοῖς Λακεδαιμονίων: 'The peace between the Athenians and their allies and the Spartans and their allies shall last for fifty years'. Not for ever, like the alliance between the Serdaioi and Sybaris (ML 10) nor for a century like that between the Eleans and Heraians (ML 17, see comm. there for a century's alliance as 'practically unlimited'). Both these date to the late archaic period. On the other hand it was not made for thirty years like the Argive–Spartan treaty of 14. 4: just now, Sparta must have felt that thirty years was all too finite a period. The fifty years would have expired in 371, the year of the battle of Leuktra! For the 50-year term as an innovation see Baltrusch, 177.

Th.'s narrative at v. 27. 1 and 32. 5 shows knowledge that the treaty was for fifty years, cp. Kirchhoff, 66, and C. Meyer, *Urkunden*, 24; on Kirchhoff's view this was because he wrote everything from ch. 21 onwards after 404. But see Gomme, *HCT* iii. 680–1.

Note that here (and in paras. 4 and 5) Athens' allies are mentioned. Gomme says this is merely to 'show the area over which peace was to extend, rather than to give them any choice in the matter'. The second half of this is surely true, the first half less obviously so. The clauses surely refer to undertakings binding on the allies, not to a geographical area (or a political 'area' in a more metaphorical sense of 'area').

καὶ κατὰ γῆν καὶ κατὰ θάλασσαν: 'both by land and sea'. Steup, followed by C. Meyer, *Urkunden*, 25, took v. 56. 3 (Alcibiades persuaded the Athenians to write 'the Spartans have not kept their oaths') to be an implied reference to this passage, because of Agesippidas' journey to Epidauros κατὰ θάλασσαν, 'by sea', i.e. through Athenian waters (v. 56. 1); Meyer regarded this as an allusion to a detail of the treaty. If so this would be a further count against Kirchhoff, see introductory n. But see Andrewes on 56. 3: the reference is more general, to the kind of grievances enumerated at 46. 2, concerning Panakton, Amphipolis, and so on.

4. μήτε Ἀθηναίους καὶ τοὺς ξυμμάχους: 'nor the Athenians and their allies'. See 3 n. on ἔτη δέ etc.

δικαίῳ χρήσθων καὶ ὅρκοις, καθ' ὅτι ἂν ξυνθῶνται: 'by legal means and oaths, in ways to be agreed'. C. Meyer, *Urkunden*, 25, thinks that the reference at vii. 18. 3 to Athenian refusal of arbitration pre-supposes the present clause, and this is possible (though the language of arbitration is more obviously used at iv. 118. 8 than in the present passage, where δικαίῳ, 'legal means', is vaguer; but it is hard to imagine any other sort of tribunal). Dover in *HCT* on vii. 18. 3 notes that we do not hear of refusals of arbitration in the book v narrative, and suggests that 'the Spartan "summons" [to arbitration] is perhaps to be dated later than the events of vi. 104' (414; but for vi. 104 surely read vi. 105).

Ostwald, *Autonomia*, 4, notes that the reference to 'ancestral custom', κατὰ τὰ πάτρια, in the 423 truce (iv. 118. 8) has been quietly dropped in favour of a more realistic reference to mutual agreement.

5. ἀποδόντων δὲ Ἀθηναίοις Λακεδαιμόνιοι καὶ οἱ ξύμμαχοι Ἀμφίπολιν: 'The Spartans and their allies shall restore Amphipolis to the Athenians'. Section (iii) of the treaty (see introductory n.) begins with the demand which Athens cared most about (see iv. 108. 1 and n. for the value of Amphipolis), and which was never to be granted. The word 'restore', ἀποδοῦναι, is distinct from παραδοῦναι, 'hand over', used in the next clause. But at 21. 1-3 and 35. 5 (contrast 35. 3) 'hand over', παραδοῦναι, is used of Amphipolis. The narrative presupposes this (surely well-known) stipulation at 21. 1.

ὅσας δὲ πόλεις παρέδοσαν Λακεδαιμόνιοι Ἀθηναίοις, ἐξέστω ἀπιέναι ὅποι ἂν βούλωνται αὐτοὺς καὶ τὰ ἑαυτῶν ἔχοντας: 'The inhabitants of any cities which the Spartans have handed over to the Athenians may go where they please and take their property with them'. The best view of the contents of para. 5 is that it concerns three separate categories: (*a*) Amphipolis, so important that it is treated separately; (*b*) the cities in the present sentence: (*c*) the six cities (Argilos, etc.) covered by τάσδε δὲ πόλεις . . . to the end of the para.; that is, with the emendation τάσδε δὲ πόλεις for τὰς δὲ πόλεις (see next n.), and a full stop at the end of the present sentence.

As for (*b*), the cities probably include places like (Oi)syme (iv. 107. 3) and the cities in the Akte peninsula, Thyssos, Kleonai, Akrothooi, and Olophyxos, see iv. 109. 3. This is pure conjecture, but Thyssos, at any rate, is described at v. 35. 1 as an Athenian ally. Gomme conjectures that Galepsos (iv. 107. 3; v. 6. 1) and Mende (iv. 123. 1; 129-30) might also have been meant, although we know for sure that they had been taken by force rather than 'handed over' (which on this view would have to count as a diplomatic euphemism. But for all we know the same is true of Athenian acquisition of the Akte places).

Gomme, followed by Kagan, *Archidamian War* (introd. n. to 18-19), 342, explains the provisions about going where they want and taking their property with them, as designed for the avoidance of civil strife.

The subsequent narrative contains a definite reference to the content of the whole of paras. 5-8 of the treaty: see 21. 1, about the Chalkidian cities, which are τὰς σπονδάς, ὡς εἴρητο ἑκάστοις, δέχεσθαι [lit. 'to accept the treaty, as was said for each of them'], 'to accept the articles of the treaty which concerned them', see n. there. See Wilamowitz, *Kl. Schr.* iii. 392 n. 1; C. Meyer, *Urkunden*, 24-5.

τὰς δὲ πόλεις φερούσας τὸν φόρον τὸν ἐπ' Ἀριστείδου αὐτονόμους εἶναι· ὅπλα δὲ μὴ ἐξέστω ἐπιφέρειν Ἀθηναίους μηδὲ τοὺς ξυμμάχους ἐπὶ κακῷ, ἀποδιδόντων τὸν φόρον, ἐπειδὴ αἱ σπονδαὶ ἐγένοντο. εἰσὶ δὲ Ἄργιλος, Στάγιρος, Ἄκανθος, Σκῶλος, Ὄλυνθος, Σπάρτωλος. ξυμμάχους δ' εἶναι μηδετέρων, μήτε Λακεδαιμονίων μήτε Ἀθηναίων· ἢν δὲ Ἀθηναῖοι πείθωσι τὰς πόλεις, βουλομένας ταύτας ἐξέστω ξυμμάχους ποιεῖσθαι αὐτοὺς Ἀθηναίους: 'The following cities shall be autonomous, but shall pay the tribute which was fixed at the time of Aristides, and the Athenians and their allies shall not be allowed to do them wrong by making war on them, but they must pay the tribute, now that the treaty has been agreed. The cities are these: Argilos, Stagiros, Akanthos, Skolos, Olynthos, Spartolos; these cities shall be allies neither of the Spartans nor of the Athenians, but if the Athenians succeed in persuading them, they may make them allies of the cities' own free will'. The best view (see also previous n.) is that which emends τὰς δὲ πόλεις, 'and the cities', to τάσδε δὲ πόλεις, 'and the following cities'. That is, the reference is forward, to the cities shortly to be named, not back to the 'cities which had been handed over'. This view also requires that we punctuate with a colon after εἶναι. Definite choices must be made; it is unsatisfactory to say, with Bauslaugh, *Concept of Neutrality* (78. 2 n. on τὴν γὰρ Θεσσαλίαν etc.), 138, that the para. is 'surprisingly vague'; the issues must have been hammered out at the time and the frustrating character of the text as we have it is surely the fault of textual transmission not original fuzziness. Bauslaugh prints the unemended text but his comments are appropriate to a text emended as above. Zahrnt (68, 70) accepts the need to emend.

For Argilos see iv. 103. 3–4 and nn. (It is not mentioned at v. 6. 1–3 as having been recovered by Kleon.)

For Stagiros see iv. 88. 2 and n.; v. 6. 1 is explicit that Kleon was unable to capture it. (Lewis, *Towards a Historian's Text*, 140, noted that the manuscripts have the spelling Στάγειρος, Stageiros.)

For Akanthos, whose abandonment by Sparta now was the most shocking case of the six in view of Brasidas' fine words at iv. 85–7, see iv. 88. 1 and 124. 1 (Akanthian help to Brasidas for his Lynkestian campaign), also *Syll*³ 79, discussed at iv. 88. 1 n. on ἔγνωσαν etc. but nowhere mentioned by Gomme. (Skione's abandonment was even worse, see 7 below.)

Skolos, somewhere east of Olynthos, has not been mentioned by Th. before nor is it mentioned again. For Stolos (as it is spelt in inscriptions, not just the Athenian tribute lists but the Epidaurian list of thearodokoi *IG* iv². 1, 94 1 b line 23, and by Pliny, *NH* iv. 37) see Zahrnt, 244–6 (245 for a possible identification at a so far unexcavated site). It paid between 4000 drachmai and one talent tribute, a large amount in this region. Kirchhoff (37) and others actually wished to emend to Στῶλος, and

Lewis, *Towards a Historian's Text*, 140 and 153, cleverly adduced *Iliad* ii. 497 to explain why Stolos was displaced by Skolos: 'the name was altered to this Homeric form consciously or unconsciously'. Contrast below, 6 n.

For Olynthos and Spartolos see i. 58. 2 and ii. 79. 2 and nn. Olynthos, under the name 'the Chalkidians', had asked for Brasidas to be sent north in the first place (iv. 79. 2 and 81. 1) and had sent him help after that (iv. 84. 1; 123. 4; 124. 1; v. 6. 4). Spartolos did not join (some of) the other Bottiaian cities who allied themselves to Athens, Tod 68 (not in ML). See iv. 132. 1 n.

One would like the last words ἐπειδὴ αἱ σπονδαὶ ἐγένοντο to mean 'after the conclusion of the treaty' (Jowett) or 'once the treaty has been made' (Warner). But this cannot be extracted from the Greek, which means literally 'since the treaty has been made' or 'after/from the time when it had been agreed'. This may conceal a reference to the 423 truce, but emendation would be necessary.

The stipulation about tribute levels at the time of Aristides is a reference to the levels prevalent in 478, although Th. did not mention Aristides in this connection in book i but only at i. 91. 3 in connection with Themistokles' ruse about the walls. It is usually thought that 'Aristidean levels' are supposed to be generous or moderate, but note the doubts of Kallet-Marx, 180–1. The present stipulation surely affected only the six places named. *ATL* iii. 347–53 hankered for the view that tribute levels generally, with some admitted exceptions, were dropped to 'Aristidean' levels in the aftermath of the Peace of Nikias. See, however, Meiggs, *AE* 340–3, and Kallet-Marx, 180–1: the epigraphic evidence does not obviously support the *ATL* view (though the islands may have paid rather less after 421). In particular, the assessment list *IG* i³. 77 may date to 422 not 421 (see introductory n. to 2–3) and thus 'not reflect the Peace of Nikias at all' (Kallet-Marx, 181 n. 75).

The implication that tribute-paying status and autonomy were compatible is not new, indeed the combination 'autonomous and tribute-paying' was a feature of the Delian League from the outset, and probably characterized Aigina after its reduction in the 450s; see Ostwald, *Autonomia*, 9 and 28 (though Ostwald notes that forcing a state to pay tribute would naturally be seen as an infringement of autonomy); Raaflaub, *Freiheit*, 187; Bauslaugh, *Concept of Neutrality*, 137–40; Kallet-Marx, 181–2, arguing that what is new in 421 is the combination of tribute payment with non-allied status (unless the six places chose to be allied with Athens), and detecting a new pattern in which revenue was more important to Athens that the acquisition of allies. (She compares iv. 57, Kythera tributary but not brought into the league as a compulsory ally; see above, iv. 57. 4 n.) This is a valuable point, but the position of the six places was most unusual, and the decisions about them surely reflect Spartan wishes as much as independent Athenian thinking. It is relevant to Spartan insistence on autonomy for these places that Brasidas had at the outset made the Spartan authorities swear to respect their autonomy, see iv. 88. 1 n. on καὶ πιστώσαντες etc.

For the plausible suggestion that the 'autonomous-but-tribute-paying' status of the Thracian cities in the Peace of Nikias influenced the shape of the 'Treaty of Boiotios' (Xen. *Hell.* i. 4. 2) in 407, see Lewis, *Sparta and Persia*, 125. On Lewis's theory the 407 arrangement between Sparta and Persia settled that the cities of Asia were to be autonomous but to pay tribute to Persia, cp. Xen. *Hell.* iii. 4. 25.

As Bauslaugh and Kallet-Marx note, the permission to the six places to stay neutral (a dangerous status) was evidently not regarded as advantageous by the states themselves; they refuse to accept the treaty at 21. 2, and the Olynthians showed what they thought of Athens when they seized Mekyberna from an Athenian garrison at 39. 1. The present passage, together with para. 8 below, marks the dishonourable abandonment by Sparta of the liberation promises of Brasidas. The 'concession' about 'being allies of neither side' was worthless, its primary object being to save Sparta's face; nor was there any value to the six cities in the clause about Athens merely applying 'persuasion' to win them back. They were being handed over to Athens, bound hand and foot.

6. **Μηκυβερναίους δὲ καὶ Σαναίους καὶ Σιγγαίους οἰκεῖν τὰς πόλεις τὰς ἑαυτῶν, καθάπερ Ὀλύνθιοι καὶ Ἀκάνθιοι:** 'The Mekybernaians, Sanaians, and Singaians shall occupy their own cities on the same terms as the Olynthians and Akanthians'. For Mekyberna, which Th. has not mentioned before, see above, p. 94 and n. 218 (tribute), also M. H. McAllister, *Princeton Encyclopaedia*, 566, and Zahrnt, in Lauffer (ed.), *Griechenland*, 416. It was 4 km. south-east of Olynthos, on the coast (near modern Poliyiros) and is called the harbour of Olynthos by Strabo vii fr. 29. It was captured by the Olynthians (who evidently held the view of its status implied by Strabo) shortly after the Peace, see 39. 1 and above, previous n. For Singos on the north-east coast of the Sithonia peninsula, and (like Mekyberna) mentioned only here in Th., see Zahrnt, 226–9. It paid between 1 and 4 (usually 2) talents tribute, but only a nominal 10 drachmai in the assessment of 422 or 421 (*IG* i³. 77), see Pritchett, *Mnemosyne* 1973 (introductory n. to 2–3), 379. For Sane see iv. 109. 3 and 5 n. The name has, with no ms. authority, been violently emended to Gale (Γαλαίους) i.e. *Sithonian* Galepsos (see iv. 107. 3 n. on καὶ Γαληψός etc.) by *ATL* iii. 90 (following A. B. West, 'Thucydides v. 18. 6', *AJP* 58 (1937), 157–73), and this has been accepted by e.g. Zahrnt, 69, 71, 179, 220, and B. M. Mitchell, *Historia* 1991, 192.

Gomme is surely right that the change is not justified. Merely because the three places Mekyberna, Singos, and Gale are found together on the assessment lists of 425 and 422 or 421, paying the same nominal tribute of 10 drachmai, is insufficient grounds for emendation. We should not (see above, p. 6) try to make Th. and the tribute lists correspond at every turn. Gomme says 'we do not know enough of the history of these small places to justify West's alteration'. Zahrnt (220) says 'our information about the history of Sane, as well as the geographical order in this paragraph, are in favour of the emendation'. Of these two approaches, Gomme's is preferable. Meiggs, *AE* 211, actually prints 'Gale' in his text as if it were uncontroversial, though he gives the unemended text in a footnote, with a reference to Gomme (who rejected the emendation). Mitchell says that geographically and historically Sane is out of place, but since Mekyberna and Singos are here mentioned by Th. for the first time, our knowledge of their 'history' is slight. For once I cannot agree with Lewis, *Towards a Historian's Text*, 141, who referred to West's 'crushing arguments' and said (143) that West 'demonstrated' that Sane was a mistake for Gale. Lewis offered, on this occasion, no new arguments, and admitted that he could see no way of answering the question who made the mistake, the copyist, Th., or the drafters of the treaty.

Inscriptions would lead us to expect Σιγγίους rather than Th.'s Σιγγαίους; Kirchhoff (38) therefore emended (cp. 5 n.: Skolos). This 'suggests careless copying' acc. to West, 137, who used it as part of his argument for changing Sane to Gale. Such reasoning should be rejected. The tiny discrepancy between the transmitted forms of the name Singaians does not justify changing the Sanaians so as to make them come from somewhere else together. Lewis, *Towards a Historian's Text*, 149, thought the scribe might have been influenced by the preceding -αιοι forms, but added that we should be cautious about assuming that Th. always conformed to Attic epigraphic usage. Thus (as Lewis 150 put it), just because we have Κόρκυρα in ML 61, that does not mean we should go through Th. emending every occurrence of Κέρκυρα. Cf. p. 105 above.

On the tribute of Singos and Mekyberna (also Gale, though see above), Pritchett, *Mnemosyne* 1973, 379, notes as part of his rejection of Woodhead that they were assessed at 'only *ten drachmai*' (his italics). 'Villages of such extremely low assessment, reflecting presumably a very small population, could hardly have been of any military importance.' This (see p. 94 above) is misleading; Singos' tribute, as we have seen above, had normally been 2 talents. The 10 drachmai assessment was abnormal.

Gomme thought Mekyberna and the other places were being given security against Olynthos and Akanthos, rather than security against Athens of the sort enjoyed by Olynthos and Akanthos. Despite the doubts of Kagan, *Archidamian War* (introd. n. to 18–19), 344 n. 143, Gomme's view is attractive.

7. ἀποδόντων δὲ Ἀθηναίοις Λακεδαιμόνιοι καὶ οἱ ξύμμαχοι Πάνακτον: 'The Spartans and their allies shall restore Panakton to the Athenians'. For Panakton see 3. 5 n.; it was in Boiotian control, not Spartan, and though the Spartans tried to persuade the Boiotians to hand it over (35. 5 and 39. 2), the Boiotians demolished it (39. 3). The Spartans tried to brazen this out by saying it could no longer harm Athens (42. 1), but the Athenians took this badly (42. 2).

ἀποδόντων δὲ καὶ Ἀθηναῖοι Λακεδαιμονίοις Κορυφάσιον καὶ Κύθηρα καὶ Μέθανα καὶ Πτέλεον καὶ Ἀταλάντην καὶ τοὺς ἄνδρας ὅσοι εἰσὶ Λακεδαιμονίων ἐν τῷ δημοσίῳ τῷ Ἀθηναίων ἢ ἄλλοθί που ὅσης Ἀθηναῖοι ἄρχουσιν ἐν δημοσίῳ: 'The Athenians shall restore Koryphasion, Kythera, Methana, Pteleon, Atalante to the Spartans. The Athenians shall also hand over the Spartan prisoners whom they have in their public prison, or who are in the public prison of any place in the Athenian empire'. For Koryphasion (Pylos) see iv. 3. 2 n. and iv. 188. 4 n. (Th.'s preparatory explanation in the narrative at iv. 3 tells against Kirchhoff's idea that the documents were later insertions.)

For Kythera see iv. 53–7 and 118. 4.

For Methana see iv. 45. 2; against Gomme's idea that 'the island' of iv. 118. 4 was Methana see n. there on καὶ τὴν νῆσον etc.

Pteleon is obscure; one candidate is in Phthiotic Achaia. Steup preferred to think of an unknown place near Methana.

For Atalante (island off Lokris) see ii. 32 and iii. 89. 3.

For the prisoners see 15. 1 n. For Sparta this clause was crucial, almost the main reason for wanting the peace. Diodorus' two-line summary of the peace (xii. 75.2) says the terms were release of prisoners and return of wartime gains, in that order.

For τὸ δημόσιον (lit. 'the public thing') as the state prison see Lewis, 'Public Property in the City', in Murray and Price, *The Greek City* (iv. 93. 4 n. on εἶχον δὲ δεξιόν etc.), 245–63, at 255; but for 'the *demosion* was the goal' read 'the *demosion* was the gaol'.

καὶ τοὺς ἐν Σκιώνῃ πολιορκουμένους Πελοποννησίων ἀφεῖναι: 'and they shall allow the Peloponnesians who are besieged in Skione to leave'. See iv. 121. 2 and 131. 3. The reference here seems to be to those Peloponnesians whom Brasidas originally brought with him to the north; see next n. for other distinct groups currently in Skione. At iv. 122 Brasidas had maintained that Skione had joined Sparta before the truce of 423 came into effect, but the Spartans presumably did not urge this, or else they urged it unsuccessfully, in the negotiations leading up to the 421 peace. That Athens was (on Th.'s view, see iv. 122. 6) in the right on

the timing of Skione's adhesion does not extenuate Sparta's abandonment of Skione now. See 8 below, and 34. 1, with C. Meyer, *Urkunden*,
27–8: the troops brought south by Klearidas may have included the
Peloponnesian garrison from Skione.

**καὶ τοὺς ἄλλους ὅσοι Λακεδαιμονίων ξύμμαχοι ἐν Σκιώνῃ εἰσὶ
καὶ ὅσους Βρασίδας ἐσέπεμψε:** 'and any other Spartan allies who
are in Skione, and all whom Brasidas introduced into the place'. The
'other Spartan allies', who are apparently distinct from the Peloponnesians of the previous lemma, are either northern allies won over by
Brasidas and sent to Skione at iv. 123. 4; or else non-Peloponnesian allies
of Sparta, such as Boiotians and Megarians. The whole reference to the
non-Skionaians in Skione (see also previous n.) is cumbersome, and *ATL*
iii. 97 n. 11 may be right that there had been some argument about who
in the place was to count as a Spartan ally, given that the Spartans had
now abandoned their attempt to expand their sphere of influence, and
league membership, into the north. Gone is the time (see iv. 126. 1 n. on
ἄνδρες Πελοποννήσιοι) when Brasidas could encouragingly extend
'Peloponnesians' so as to include northern allies as well.

**καὶ εἴ τις τῶν ξυμμάχων τῶν Λακεδαιμονίων ἐν Ἀθήναις ἐστὶν
ἐν τῷ δημοσίῳ:** 'and they shall release any Spartan allies who are in the
public prison at Athens'. This probably includes e.g. the Torone garrison,
see 3. 4 n. on καὶ τῶν Τορωναίων etc. But the Toronaians themselves,
i.e. the male citizens, are dealt with separately below, para. 8.

**8. Σκιωναίων δὲ καὶ Τορωναίων καὶ Σερμυλιῶν καὶ εἴ τινα
ἄλλην πόλιν ἔχουσιν Ἀθηναῖοι, Ἀθηναίους βουλεύεσθαι περὶ
αὐτῶν καὶ τῶν ἄλλων πόλεων ὅτι ἂν δοκῇ αὐτοῖς:** 'As for Skione,
Torone, and Sermylia, or any other city now held by the Athenians, the
Athenians shall do with the inhabitants of the said cities, or of any other
cities, as they think fit'. Sparta can have been in no doubt what would
happen to Skione, which (we are meant to recall) had received Brasidas
so ecstatically at iv. 121. 1: the Athenian decision to execute the
Skionaians had already been taken (iv. 122. 5) and was carried out at v.
32. 1. Good discussion by Bosworth, *JHS* 113 (1993), 37, concluding 'the
fine promises of Brasidas had brought utter ruin in two short years'.

For Torone see 3. 4 n. on καὶ τῶν Τορωναίων etc.

Sermylia east of Mekyberna (Zahrnt, 225–6) has not featured in the
iv–v. 24 narrative until now (it was mentioned at i. 65. 2). It must on the
evidence of the present passage have been recently recovered by Athens.

'Any other city now held . . .' may include Mende and Galepsos, and
perhaps the other places in category (*b*) at 5 n. on ὅσας δέ etc.

If the text is sound, the words καὶ τῶν ἄλλων πόλεων 'any other cities'
(I have changed Jowett's loose 'any cities which are held by them') seem

to widen the scope considerably; in fact they have been supposed to refer to the whole Athenian empire, so Gomme; also Wilamowitz, *Kl. Schr.* iii. 387, citing e.g. Ar. *Ach.* 506, 642 and *Old Oligarch* i. 14 for the empire as 'the cities' (though surely an ampler expression might be looked for in this more than parochially Athenian context). But Kirchhoff (56) and Steup wished to delete αὐτῶν καὶ τῶν ἄλλων πόλεων as a marginal gloss, and this or some such remedy is surely preferable. Gomme resisted the deletion, but his view that the recognition of the maritime empire 'is as certain, though not as clearly expressed, as in the peace of 446-445' is wrong about 446-445 (see i. 140. 2 n.), and perhaps about 421 as well. If Gomme were right about the present passage, it would be an astonishingly perfunctory way of making so important a concession. Wilamowitz makes the best of this when he observes 'these few words sound harmless, but they have great importance, because in them is contained the recognition of the Athenian empire' ('die wenige Worte klingen harmlos, haben aber große Bedeutung, denn es liegt in ihnen die Anerkennung des attischen Reiches'). This is at least better (in that it recognizes the singularity of what is supposed to be happening), than Gomme's 'not as clearly expressed'. Historically, there is no doubt that the empire *was* recognized by the Peace of Nikias, but the recognition remained implicit, as it did in 446.

9. ὅρκους δὲ ποιήσασθαι Ἀθηναίους: 'the Athenians shall bind themselves by oath'. See Steiner, *The Tyrant's Writ* (introductory n. to iv. 117-19), 66.

ἑπτὰ καὶ δέκα ἑκάστης πόλεως: 'seventeen representatives from each city'. [On the emendation see App. to my vol. 3.] For the number seventeen see 19. 1 n. on ὤμνυον etc. It is remarkable, as Andrewes and Lewis observe (*JHS* 1957, 177), that the Peace of Nikias does *not* specify the authorities who were to swear. In this it is unlike fourth-century Athenian treaties like Tod 103 or 147, cp. 122; see also Th. v. 47. 9, with Andrewes's nn. in *HCT*; also two other treaties from the second half of the 420s, *IG* i³. 75 (Halieis) lines 27 ff. and 76 (Bottiaians) lines 7 ff. (but note 'five men' at line 32). See also D. J. Mosley, 'Who "Signed" Treaties in Ancient Greece?', *PCPhS* 187 (1961), 59-63.

The oaths are taken by the Athenians to Sparta, and then to Sparta's allies individually, i.e. the Athenians swear on behalf of their allies, who have no choice, but the Spartans do not swear on behalf of theirs, some of whom are reluctant. (Gomme may be right that the asymmetry arose because Athens knew of this reluctance and wanted to take no chances. But there may be religious reasons too. The Peloponnesian League was ancient, and there were perhaps stringent requirements about oaths.)

10. στήλας δὲ στῆσαι Ὀλυμπίασι καὶ Πυθοῖ καὶ Ἰσθμοῖ καὶ

Ἀθήνησιν ἐν πόλει καὶ ἐν Λακεδαίμονι ἐν Ἀμυκλαίῳ: 'and they shall erect pillars at Olympia, Delphi, and the Isthmus, at Athens on the Acropolis, at Sparta in the temple of Apollo at Amyklai'. Of the four Panhellenic sanctuaries, Nemea is the only absentee; it is also the only one never mentioned by Th., though Nemea features at v. 58 ff. as a place. Nemea was the least prestigious of the four; it was the only one to receive no victory dedication after the Persian Wars (Lewis, *CAH* v². 107). Of the other three, Olympia and Isthmus were, as Gomme noted (drawing on Kirchhoff, 65), 'controlled by states which refused to take the oath, Elis and Corinth' (Kirchhoff speaks of the 'Prostasie'–'stewardship', 'superintendence'—of Elis and Corinth rather than 'control'). For this reason Kirchhoff thought that the pillars (*stelai*) were not put up at Olympia or the Isthmus. We cannot be quite sure of this. Gomme's word 'control' is too strong and Kirchhoff's is better; on the other hand, Gomme was perhaps right against Kirchhoff that the *stelai* were nevertheless put up. For the Athenian Acropolis, and Amyklai, see 23. 5 n.

For the importance of such inscription of treaties and of the oaths they contained see Steiner, *The Tyrant's Writ*, 66, discussing the present passage.

11. εἰ δέ τι ἀμνημονοῦσιν ὁποτεροιοῦν καὶ ὅτου πέρι, λόγοις δικαίοις χρωμένοις εὔορκον εἶναι ἀμφοτέροις ταύτῃ μεταθεῖναι ὅπῃ ἂν δοκῇ ἀμφοτέροις, Ἀθηναίοις καὶ Λακεδαιμονίοις: 'If either side finds that it has forgotten something, it may, after proper consultation and with the full agreement of both sides, Athenians and Spartans, make any alteration on any topic without violation of oaths on either side'. This, the amendment clause, caused enormous offence subsequently because it high-handedly ignored Sparta's allies: see 29. 2 with *HCT* there, and cp. above, iv. 20. 4 n. By a slip, Th. at v. 29. 2 represents Sparta's allies as angry because the Spartans had arrogated to themselves in the peace-treaty the power to add or delete anything. Actually that slightly more extensive power was contained not in the peace-treaty but in the alliance, 23. 6, and this was strictly no concern of Sparta's allies because the alliance was made bilaterally, between Sparta and Athens. Gomme in his n. on the present passage noted that it did not give Athens and Sparta a general power of alteration but merely allowed them to 'change the wording' if something had been overlooked. But μεταθεῖναι means 'change' without qualification or restriction of scope (see Gomme's n. on 29. 2, which seems to be a change of mind since 18. 11, in that by 29. 2 he thought that 'changing' and 'adding and subtracting' came to the same thing), and one can see why the word should have been felt to be provocative.

C. Meyer, *Urkunden*, 24, is less than adequate on the relation between

v. 18. 11 (the present passage) and 29. 2, which he says 'presupposes' v. 18. 11 ('setzt 5, 18, 11 voraus'). In a sense it does, but because of the confusion between peace and alliance, 29. 2 cannot be straightforwardly cited (as by Meyer) as proof that Th. knew the contents of the treaty when he wrote the relevant piece of narrative. See rather Gomme, *HCT* iii. 695: Th. had perhaps been informed in some detail of the contents of both treatises when he wrote 29. 2 but had not got the texts 'in front of him' (whatever exactly that modern-sounding expression means). The alternative remains that 29. 2 is a simple slip by Th.

M. L. West (see below , 23. 6 n. on ὅτι ἄν etc.) suggests that the first ἀμφοτέροις should be deleted 'as an accidental anticipation of the second'. This would mean that in the English, where the order of words is different, we should discard 'on either side'. This may well be right, but West's 'reinforcing' argument from 29. 2 (where there is only one ἀμφοῖν, the equivalent of ἀμφοτέροις, and which purports to be a quotation from the Peace of Nikias) does not quite work because there Th. has in mind the wording of 23. 6, not 18. 11, i.e. it is not a quotation from the Peace of Nikias but from the alliance (see above for this curious slip), and at 23. 6 there is only one ἀμφοτέροις, see n. there. So 29. 2 is not evidence for the original reading at 18. 11.

19. 1. ἔφορος Πλειστόλας: 'in the ephorate of Pleistolas'. He is more than a date: he swears to the treaty on behalf of Sparta, see 2 below, where he is named first after the kings. The ephors were pro-peace: v. 32. 1.

Ἐλαφηβολιῶνος μηνὸς ἕκτῃ φθίνοντος: 'on the twenty-fifth day of the month Elaphebolion'. That is, at the beginning of spring (see 20. 1 n. for the problems raised by the relation between 19. 1 and 20. 1). But it is not until 24. 2 that Th. formally tells us that the eleventh year of the war began. As Gomme says, comparing iii. 116 (where Etna erupts in early spring in para. 1, but the 'end-of-year' formula is delayed until para. 3), Th. is not 'pedantically accurate in his narration of summers and winters'.

ὤμνυον δὲ οἵδε καὶ ἐσπένδοντο: 'The following persons took the oaths and poured the libations' [for the second expression I have changed Jowett's 'and ratified the treaty', giving instead the literal trans.]. The numbers on each side are seventeen, as stipulated at 18. 9. For the number seventeen see now Andrewes and Lewis, *JHS* 1957, 177–80, at 177, an improvement on Gomme's *HCT* n. on 18. 9 of a year earlier (1956). Kirchhoff (63–4) saw that the Spartan seventeen are probably the two kings, the five ephors, and a board of ten others, i.e. the initiative for seventeen came from the Spartan side. (On the board of ten, see further below.) However Gomme cited, as a possible alternative explanation, the suggestion of J. H. Oliver, 'Athenian Commissions of Seven-teen', *Class. Weekly*, 44 (1951), 203, that seventeen was a traditional number at *Athens*. Oliver adduced (as well as Th. v. 18. 9) *IG* ii². 40 and Plato, *Laws* 761e, and noted that seventeen is close to being a third of fifty (which is the number of members supplied annually, to the Council of Five Hundred, by each of the ten tribes or sub-divisions of the Athe-nian citizen body. These tribal groups of fifty presided as *prytaneis*, see iii. 36. 5 n., over the Council and Assembly for a month, i.e. one tenth of the Athenian year). But Lewis and Andrewes showed that the Plato example was not specially significant. Plato 'shows no general fondness for seven-teen'; as for *IG* ii². 40, it may not have been a treaty at all (Lewis and Andrewes, 177 n. 2). We should thus return to Kirchhoff's 'Spartan' explanation, and assume that the Spartans asked for parity with a (tribally-based) Athenian ten, hence the seventeen on both sides.

Andrewes and Lewis make the further suggestion, basing themselves on Diod. xii. 75. 4 with its mention of a ten-man commission, that Athens and Sparta had each appointed a ten-man board to conduct pre-liminary negotiations, a stage Th. must on this hypothesis have omitted to describe in detail, though see 17. 2 n. on ἐπειδή etc. This ingeniously explains why the number ten features in a Spartan context (see above); as Andrewes and Lewis say (177 n. 4), boards of three are more common at Sparta, though they note the ten advisers appointed to supervise Agis at Th. v. 63. 4. It seems from Diodorus' account that Sparta's allies com-plained that they were not represented on this board (cp. their later complaints at 29. 2, see 18. 11 n. above). The suggestion of Andrewes and Lewis is extremely neat, and almost certainly right. (But Diod.'s ten-man commission as it stands looks suspiciously like the Roman diplo-matic use of *decem legati*, cp. xxix. 11 for the Peace of Apamea, and one might wonder whether Diod. has not creatively reworked what he found in Ephorus. By 'as it stands' I mean that Diodorus actually says the ten-man boards were appointed *after* the peace, and Andrewes and Lewis have to suppose that this is a confusion by Diod. or his source with events *before* the peace.) See Introduction, pp. 106 f.

Would Th. have kept these names in a hypothetical final version? And even if we think he would, can we accept that he would virtually repeat two lists of seventeen names at ch. 24? See Introduction, pp. 107, 118 f.

2. Λακεδαιμονίων μὲν ⟨Πλειστοάναξ, Ἆγις,⟩ Πλειστόλας: 'On behalf of the Spartans Pleistoanax, Agis, Pleistolas'. I have added Pleistoanax and Agis, the two Spartan kings, to Jowett's trans. The emendation (Arnold's) is certain, in view of v. 24 and the stipulation at 18. 9 about numbers; the error is easily explained: the copyist's eye jumped from one name beginning Pleist- to the next. [See next lemma.]

Πλειστόλας: 'Pleistolas'. The ephor, see 1 n. The next four names are presumably the other ephors, and the remaining ten (Daithos or Daiochos to Laphilos) the board of ten identified by Andrewes and Lewis, see 1 n. on ὤμνυον etc. [This and the preceding lemma overlap.]

Δάιθος: 'Daithos'. Wilamowitz, unlike most scholars who have discussed the 423 truce and the Peace of Nikias, was interested, from an onomastic point of view, in the names listed at iv. 119 and v. 19 and 24, and he is right that they are a rich harvest. See *Kl. Schr.* iii. 372 n. 2, cp. 389 n. 2, for his suggestion that we should read 'the good Lakonian' name Δαίοχος, 'Daiochos' (cp. *IG* v. 1. 1228) here instead of Daithos which (he said) 'I cannot believe in'. But he seems to have thought Δαίαιθος possible (I assume the accent on his Δάιαιθος is a typographical error).

Ἰσχαγόρας: 'Ischagoras'. See iv. 132. 2–3, where he is one of the three who bring reinforcements to Brasidas, and young Spartan governors up to the north. At v. 21. 1 he will go to the Thraceward region with Menas and Philocharidas to announce the peace.

Φιλοχαρίδας: 'Philocharidas'. Son of Eryxilaidas, see iv. 119. 2, where he ratifies the 423 truce. See also v. 21. 1 and previous n. for the Thracian role which he shares with Ischagoras and Menas and v. 44. 3 for his mission to Athens with Leon and Endios. Th. there says that all three were expected to be acceptable, ἐπιτήδειοι, at Athens.

Τέλλις: 'Tellis'. Is this Brasidas' father? (So, cautiously, Lewis, *Sparta and Persia*, 42 n. 105.) See ii. 25. 2 and other passages. For Tellis as Peleus to Brasidas' Achilles see Introduction, p. 43. But it could equally be Brasidas' *son*. For Brasidas' mother Amphileonis see Plut. *Mor.* 240 c.

Ἀλκινάδας: 'Alkinadas'. Wilamowitz, *Kl. Schr.* iii. 372 n. 2, cp. 389 n. 2, thought this possible but preferred to emend to Ἀλκιβιάδας, the Spartan form of Alcibiades' name, cp. viii. 6. 3 for the name at Sparta. But the emendation is to be rejected: see *SEG* xxxii. 399 for an Alkinadas from Sparta (*c*.550–25 BC, cf. *LSAG*² p. 447 no. C).

Μηνᾶς: 'Menas'. Wilamowitz, 372 n. 1, preferred Μίνας, 'Minas', partly because he refused to believe in a fifth-cent. Greek name derived from the Asiatic god Μήν. (The premise may be right as regards *Sparta*; for Athens see Parker, *ARH* 193 n. 146.) But see Masson 1483–6 [325–8]: there is nothing basically wrong with the name as transmitted, but it comes from μήν, a month, and should probably be written Μένας or Μήνας.

See also v. 21. 1: like Ischagoras and Philocharidas he went to Thrace.

Ἀθηναίων δὲ οἵδε: 'on behalf of the Athenians'. The Athenian names have, inevitably given the state of our knowledge, been much more studied than the Spartan. Identification of individuals was placed on a much more secure basis by the acute observation of D. M. Lewis, see *JHS* 1957, 177 n. 7, that names six to fifteen are in official Athenian tribal order; for the resulting identifications see the full prosopographical study of Andrewes and Lewis, ibid. 177–80, cited at 1 n. on ὤμνυον etc. They suggest that the first two names are religious experts (Lampon, Isthmionikos), then follow three probable generals (Nikias, Laches, Euthydemos), then the ten-man board (see 1 n. on ὤμνυον etc.), then Lamachos and Demosthenes, who are separated from the generals and are therefore perhaps not generals themselves this year (though this cannot be ruled out); they were perhaps added when 'the presiding officer called for two more names' and someone suggested this well-known pair. This convincing analysis is accepted by Develin, *AO* 138–9. Of the ten-man board as a whole Andrewes and Lewis (180) say 'it seems to be composed of sound and trustworthy men, not specially committed to war or peace, and not the leading politicians of the time. The active work was no doubt done elsewhere, and mainly by Nikias and Laches (Thuc. v. 43. 2)'; they note in particular that Pythodoros, Hagnon, and Aristokrates were men of property (for *APF* refs. see below under the individual names).

It is curious that Wilamowitz, who (wrongly) believed the three Athenians at iv. 119. 1 (see n. there) were in tribal order, should apparently not have looked for tribal order at v. 19. 2.

Λάμπων: 'Lampon'. The well-known seer, see ML 73 (*IG* i³. 78), lines 47 and 60, the inscription about first-fruits for Eleusis; also Plut. *Per.* 6.

Ἰσθμιόνικος: 'Isthmionikos'. His father was presumably a victor in the Isthmian games; as Lewis and Andrewes (180) say, he 'evidently comes from an athletic family'. Wilamowitz, *Kl. Schr.* iii. 369 n. 1, already noted that he might be identical with the builder of the 'bath/bathroom of Isthmonikos', Ἰσθμονίκου (without the extra iota) βαλανεῖον at *IG* i³. 84, inscription about sanctuary of Neleus, line 37; this suggestion is made independently by Lewis and Andrewes, 180. M. Osborne and S. Byrne, *LGPN* ii, entry under Ἰσθμόνικος no. (1), identify the two men without discussion, and without noting that the form of the name in Th. has the extra iota. In *AM* 1991, 151 there are two ostraka against men called Isthmonikos, one from the deme Skambonidai, one from Kothokidai (*LGPN* ii, entry under Ἰσθμόνικος nos. (2) and (3)).

Νικίας: 'Nikias'. His appearance in this list and at this point is the main reason for supposing he was a general this year, see Andrewes and Lewis, 180, followed by Develin. For his role in promoting the peace later named after him see 16. 1 and 43. 2 (where he is coupled with Laches); and for gratitude felt towards him afterwards see Plut. *Nik.* 9. 7–9.

Λάχης: 'Laches'. For this famous figure see iv. 118. 11 n. on Λάχης εἶπε.

Again (see previous n.) he may well have been a general this year. For his role at v. 43. 2 see previous n.

Εὐθύδημος: 'Euthydemos'. Like Nikias and Laches (see two previous nn.), he is thought likely to have been a general this year, and may also be identical with the Euthydemos son of Eudemos who was general in 418/17 (*IG* i³. 370, ML 77 line 9) and also with the general appointed against Syracuse in 414/13, see Th. vii. 16. 1, with Dover's n. in *HCT*. M. Osborne and S. Byrne, *LGPN* ii, Εὐθύδημος no. 6, confidently identify all three.

Προκλῆς: 'Prokles'. The first name in the ten-man board detected by Andrewes and Lewis, see above 1 n. on ὤμνυον etc. He is plausibly identified by Andrewes and Lewis, 178, with Prokles of Euonymon, secretary of the Council of Five Hundred in 421/0: *IG* i³. 80 line 5 and 82 line 4 (restored). See *LGPN* ii, entry under Προκλῆς nos. (4) and (26), tentatively identifying the secretary and Th.'s swearer. For an ostrakon wth the name Prokles of Euonymon see *AM* 1991, 155 (*LGPN*, no. 25); perhaps the same as swearer/secretary?

If all this is right he is from tribe I, Erechtheis, to which the deme Euonymon belonged.

Πυθόδωρος: 'Pythodoros'. Probably son of Epizelos from Halai (*LGPN* ii, entry under Πυθόδωρος no. (57)) and general in 414, see vi. 105. 2 and Dover's n. in *HCT*. He was rich, see *APF* 481 (no. 12402). Hipparch (*IG* i³. 999) and choregos for his tribe Aigeis, *IG* i³. 960 line 2. Aegeis was tribe II.

Ἅγνων: 'Hagnon'. The famous Hagnon, oikist of Amphipolis, for whom see ii. 58. 1 n. (also iv. 102. 4 and v. 11. 1 nn.). He was wealthy; for his property see *APF* 227–8, entry no. 7234 under Θηραμένης. His deme was Steiria (see v. 11. 1 n. on καταβαλόντες) which is in tribe III, Pandionis. See *LGPN* ii, entry under Ἅγνων no. (22).

Μυρτίλος: 'Myrtilos'. In *JHS* 1957, Andrewes and Lewis (178) said 'only two are recorded' (in addition to Th.'s man) but in 1994 *LGPN* ii list a total of five and a possible sixth. Th.'s man needs to be from tribe IV, Leontis, for the Andrewes–Lewis theory to work. The two certain Athenian Myrtiloi unknown to Andrewes and Lewis are both from Steiria and are from the fourth century; if Th.'s Myrtilos was an ancestor of one of these, that would tell against the 'tribal order' theory. But there is no reason to suppose any connection with the Steirians, or indeed (as Andrewes and Lewis say at 178, cp. 180) with the Myrtilos from Prasiai, *LGPN* ii. no. (3). (M. Osborne and S. Byrne do not register the possibility aired by Andrewes and Lewis, that no. (3) is from Prasiai in Lakonia, not from the Attic deme of that name.) To conclude: the hypothesis of an unknown Myrtilos from tribe IV remains perfectly plausible.

Θρασυκλῆς: 'Thrasykles'. Surely the general of viii. 15 and the mover of *IG* i³. 80; *LGPN* ii, no. (5). Demotic unknown, i.e. there is nothing *against* the hypothesis that he is from tribe V, Akamantis.

Θεογένης: 'Theogenes'. Again, I have changed the OCT Θεαγένους, see iv. 27. 3 n. on μετὰ Θεογένους. If as Andrewes and Lewis (179) conclude, he was from Acharnai, he is from tribe VI, Oineis. The Andrewes–Lewis position is basically accepted at *LGPN* ii, entry under Θεογένης no. (15); that is, the man mentioned at Th. iv. 27. 3 is identified with the oath-taker of the present passage, and with the Theogenes of Ar. *Ach.* 63.

Ἀριστοκράτης: 'Aristokrates'. Probably to be identified as a well-known figure, son of Skellias: *LGPN* ii, entry under Ἀριστοκράτης no. (3); *APF* 56–9, no. 1904. See also Th. viii. 9. 2, with Andrewes's n. in *HCT*, for his generalship in 413/12, and N. Dunbar, *Aristophanes: Birds* comm. on line 126. He was *choregos* for his tribe Kekropis (tribe VII): *IG* i³. 964.

Ἰώλκιος: 'Iolkios'. Otherwise unknown. *LGPN* ii lists Th.'s man only. On the 'tribal order' theory he needs to be from tribe VIII, Hippothontis. The name is intriguing; is there some Thessalian connection (cp. Hdt. v. 94)?

Τιμοκράτης: 'Timokrates'. *LGPN* ii, entry under Τιμοκράτης no. (3). He needs on the 'tribal order' theory to be from tribe IX, Aiantis. But as Andrewes and Lewis (179) say, the name is common and attempts at identification are futile on present evidence.

Λέων: 'Leon'. There are a number of possible Leons. But Andrewes and Lewis (179) suggest that Th.'s man was from tribe X, Antiochis, because the general from that tribe in ML 56 (the Samian settlement of 439) line 32, cp. comm. at 153–4, has a four-letter name, and such names are not common at Athens. See *LGPN* ii, entry under Λέων no. (4), registering Andrewes and Lewis's discussion, and following them in distinguishing the Leon of the present passage from the general at Th. viii. 23. 1, on whom see Andrewes's n. in *HCT*.

Λάμαχος: 'Lamachos'. For this famous figure see iv. 75. 1 n. on ὁ γὰρ τρίτος etc. and Andrewes and Lewis, 180: he and Demosthenes seem to have been added at the last moment, and were probably not generals, see 1 n. on ὤμνυον etc.

Δημοσθένης: 'Demosthenes'. Again, surely the famous man, see previous n., and iv. 101. 3 n. Except for his appearance at ch. 24 below, he is not heard of again in Th. until the Epidauros episode at ch. 80 (winter 418/17). See, however, *IG* i³. 170, ML 77, payments to trierarchs 'with Demosthenes' in some connection with Argos (beginning of Attic year 418/17), with Andrewes's nn. in *HCT* on v. 75. 5 and 80. 3.

20. DATING OF THE TEN YEARS WAR

The key to the understanding of this chapter is to be found in
Andrewes's conclusion at *HCT* iv. 21, an improvement on Gomme in
HCT iii (including the appendix at 699–715). Andrewes makes a sharp
disjunction between para. 1, which he says 'gives us, in imprecise terms,
the result of an exact calculation made for this occasion only', and paras.
2–3, on the other hand, which 'invite the reader to verify, from the dis-
position of the narrative he has read, that the calculation is approximately correct, ten years and not eleven. The large controversy over this
passage has arisen from not keeping these two points distinct.'

**20. 1. αὗται αἱ σπονδαὶ ἐγένοντο τελευτῶντος τοῦ χειμῶνος
ἅμα ἦρι, ἐκ Διονυσίων εὐθὺς τῶν ἀστικῶν:** 'This treaty was concluded at the end of winter, just at the beginning of spring, immediately
after the City Dionysia'. The last day of the Dionysia was 13 Elaphebolion, see iv. 118. 12 n., though this is not quite as certain as Gomme
thought. But at 19. 1 Th. said that the treaty was to begin on 25 Elaphebolion. Perhaps, as Gomme suggests, some time was allowed for communication. The actual dates, then, can be reconciled, but the form in
which they are given is different: the dating in the present passage conforms to Th.'s normal method of dating by summers and winters.
Gomme agreed with Kirchhoff to the extent of supposing that Th. did
not see a verbatim copy of the treaty text until later. But surely Th. could,
from the outset, have juxtaposed two kinds of dating, given that one is in
a document, the other in his own narrative.

Andrewes, *HCT* iv. 22, discussing the present passage, suggested that
'if a reason is needed for Th.'s mention of the Dionysia, a possible answer
is that Spartan envoys came to Athens at that time to swear to the
treaty'.

**αὐτόδεκα ἐτῶν διελθόντων καὶ ἡμερῶν ὀλίγων παρενεγκουσῶν
ἢ ὡς τὸ πρῶτον ἡ ἐσβολὴ ἡ ἐς τὴν Ἀττικὴν καὶ ἡ ἀρχὴ τοῦ
πολέμου τοῦδε ἐγένετο:** 'Ten years, with the addition of a few days,
had passed since the invasion of Attica and the beginning of the war'. A
much discussed and disputed sentence; in addition to Gomme, see
Andrewes, *HCT* iv. 17–21, commenting on v. 27. 1; de Ste. Croix, *OPW*,
app. xii at 323–8; and J. D. Smart, 'Thucydides and Hellanicus' (iv. 133.
3 n. on οἱ δὲ ἄλλην etc.), 19–35. For the general problem of Th.'s date for
the beginning of the war see introductory n. to ii. 2–6. In the present
passage, the words ἡ ἐσβολὴ . . . καί should certainly be deleted, i.e. the
reference to the invasion of Attica should be removed. The period from
the invasion of Attica to the treaty of 421 was not ten years plus (or

minus) a few days, but ten years less two and a half months (ii. 19. 1). In recent years the deletion has been accepted by most scholars, but see H. R. Rawlings, 'The *arche* of Thucydides' War', in G. Bowersock, W. Burkert, and M. C. J. Putnam (eds.), *Arktouros: Hellenic Studies pres. B. M. W. Knox* (Berlin and New York, 1979), 272–9, who retains the reference to the invasion, but only at the cost of further alteration of the text. (See also Rawlings, *The Structure of Thucydides' History* (Princeton, 1981), 36.) H. Konishi, 'Ten Years and a Few Days', *LCM* 8 (1983), 69–70, tries to retain the text without emendation.

The words ἡμερῶν ὀλίγων παρενεγκουσῶν probably mean 'with the addition of a few days' (Steup, Gomme, Andrewes; Rawlings, *Structure*) rather than 'minus a few days' (Stahl, Smart 20 n. 5; 23). Note, however, that W. K. Pritchett, 'Thucydides' Statement on his Chronology', *ZPE* 62 (1986), 205–11, insists that Th. means no more than 'just ten years with the difference of a few days'.

By 'the beginning of the war' Th. is surely here referring to the attack on Plataia: ii. 2. 1.

The problem is to know what kind of year Th. was using. In addition to Gomme's main discussion in *HCT* iii, see his appendix at 699–715, a masterly exposition, although Andrewes in vol. iv is, I believe, to be preferred on the main point. Andrewes is followed in the main by de Ste. Croix (see esp. *OPW* 324); but see below.

The years cannot be the years of Th.'s own system of reckoning by campaigning seasons, for the reason given by Andrewes at 18: the attack on Plataia was *after* the beginning of spring 431 (ii. 2. 1) and the peace came into force *before* the beginning of summer 421 (v. 24. 2), and this is slightly less rather than slightly more than ten years (in this connection it should be noted that for Th. summer includes spring, see Gomme, *HCT* 703).

What kind of year then did Th. have in mind in para. 1? Gomme and Pritchett (see 'Thucydides v. 20', *Historia*, 13 (1964), 21–36, and now *Thucydides' Pentekontaetia and Other Essays* (Amsterdam, 1995), ch. 4, esp. 195) thought that Th. calculated with an astronomically fixed solar year, and that Th.'s seasons were tied to fixed points in this precisely calculable solar year. Andrewes (19) accepted that 'a man of Thucydides' calibre would be interested' in the calculation by a solar year, 'and, if he was, the required calculation was possible'; he cited W. K. Pritchett and B. L. van der Weerden, 'Thucydidean Time-reckoning and Euctemon's Seasonal Calendar', *BCH* 85 (1961), 17–52. (De Ste. Croix (324) disagreed on this point; he thought it unlikely that Th. made so abstruse a calculation or that it was at all easy to do so.) Andrewes therefore accepted that in the present passage Th. had in mind a solar year

(Andrewes (18–19) briefly and rightly dismisses the third theoretical possibility in addition to (*a*) Th.'s own seasonal year and (*c*) a solar year, namely (*b*), a *lunar* year). However, Andrewes parted company with Gomme on whether Th. tied the seasons of his own seasonal year (campaigning seasons, separated by summers and winters) to astronomical events like the rising of Arktouros, e.g. was spring fixed by the evening rising of Arktouros? For Andrewes, Th.'s summers and winters are not so fixed; see also Andrewes, *HCT* v. 148 f. As we have seen (see introductory n.) Andrewes perceived that the claim in paras. 2–3 is not directly connected to that in para. 1. The claim in paras. 2–3 is aimed at systems of dating by magistracies, because such systems would result in a false conclusion that there were eleven years, not ten, see below. That explains why the extra few days disappear from view in para. 3, where Th. is no longer concerned with precise or near-precise accuracy but with the general preferability of one system over another system which resulted in an error in the number of *years*.

2. σκοπείτω δέ τις κατὰ τοὺς χρόνους καὶ μὴ τῶν ἑκασταχοῦ ἢ ἀρχόντων ἢ ἀπὸ τιμῆς τινὸς ἐς τὰ προγεγενημένα σημαινόντων τὴν ἀπαρίθμησιν τῶν ὀνομάτων πιστεύσας μᾶλλον. οὐ γὰρ ἀκριβές ἐστιν, οἷς καὶ ἀρχομένοις καὶ μεσοῦσι καὶ ὅπως ἔτυχέ τῳ ἐπεγένετό τι: 'People should calculate the actual periods of time; they should not rely on lists of archons or other officials whose names may be used in different cities to mark the dates of past events. For such methods of calculation are inaccurate in that they leave it unclear whether an event occurred in the beginning, the middle or at some other point, of a magistrate's term of office' [the words 'in that they leave it unclear whether' are added to make the sense clear]. I have changed Jowett's 'I would have a person reckon ...' because, although Jowett is right that there is an implied dialogue here between Th. and the reader or hearer, i.e. Th. is saying 'I would like you to do this ... not that', he nevertheless avoids the first and second persons singular, achieving a greater impression of authority and detachment by confining himself to the third person. See *Greek Historiography*, 149.

The text as transmitted is disordered; the OCT, Steup, and Gomme follow Arnold who transposed τὴν ἀπαρίθμησιν τῶν ὀνομάτων from its ms. position after τινός. It is also probable that we should read τῇ ἀπαριθμήσει for τὴν ἀπαρίθμησιν, dative (as would be expected after πιστεύω) rather than accusative, i.e. the literal meaning of the emended text is 'believing in the calculation'.

Th.'s methodology here sounds polemical, and if so an obvious target is Hellanicus, for whose system of dating by priestesses of Argos see iv. 133. 3 n. on ἔτη δέ etc. and Smart there cited, who makes the case in detail. On Smart's view Th. emerges as ferociously hostile to Hellanicus. But Th. *may* also have in mind Hdt. who had also used some eponymous magistracies, see iii. 59. 4 ('when Amphikrates was *basileus* [presumably a religious magistrate] at Samos', a particularly unhelpful 'date') and viii. 51. 1, Kalliades the archon at Athens is used as a date.

Pritchett, *Historia* 1964 (above, 1 n. on αὐτόδεκα etc.), 25–6, rightly noted that Th.'s objection to eponymous systems is not just that they are local, i.e. parochial, but that they are inaccurate. Scholars have been puzzled by this objection; could not Th. have said e.g. 'on the thirteenth of Elaphebolion in the archonship of x'? Pritchett points out that this would still not be satisfactory because of the widespread habit of intercalating months.

In the Hellenistic period, people like Timaeus and Polybius used Olympiads; Th.'s own references to Olympic victors at iii. 8. 1 and v. 49. 1 are an anticipation of such systems. Lists of Olympic victors were compiled by Th.'s contemporary Hippias the sophist.

3. ἐξ ἡμισείας ἑκατέρου τοῦ ἐνιαυτοῦ τὴν δύναμιν ἔχοντος: 'and counts each summer and winter as a half year'. In fact, see Gomme, *HCT* iii. 710 and n. 1, Th. does not here mean anything like exactly half; winter was about a third and summer two-thirds of the year. What Th. means is that a summer and a winter, of the kind which punctuate his narrative, together make up a whole year.

δέκα μὲν θέρη, ἴσους δὲ χειμῶνας: 'ten summers and ten winters'. It is important that the 'few days' of para. 1 have dropped from view. See introductory n.: Andrewes (20) is surely right that Th. is here simply saying that 'counting of e.g. Athenian archons or Spartan ephors would give eleven names, whereas the seasonally organized narrative shows that there were only ten summers and ten winters'.

21. PROBLEMS ABOUT IMPLEMENTING THE PEACE

21. 1. Λακεδαιμόνιοι δέ (ἔλαχον γὰρ πρότεροι ἀποδιδόναι ἃ εἶχον): 'They drew lots to decide which side should be the first to restore what it held, and it fell to the Spartans'. Theophrastus, quoted by Plut. *Nik.* 10. 1, says that Nikias manipulated the lot by bribery.

The general decision to use the lot was presumably made in the preliminary negotiations of 17. 2, see n. there on ἐπειδή etc.

πρέσβεις Ἰσχαγόραν καὶ Μηνᾶν καὶ Φιλοχαρίδαν: 'three envoys, Ischagoras, Menas, and Philocharidas'. For these men see nn. on 19. 2.

ἐκέλευον τὸν Κλεαρίδαν τὴν Ἀμφίπολιν παραδιδόναι τοῖς

Ἀθηναίοις καὶ τοὺς ἄλλους τὰς σπονδάς, ὡς εἴρητο ἑκάστοις, δέχεσθαι: 'ordered Klearidas to hand over Amphipolis to the Athenians, and told the other cities to accept the articles of the treaty which concerned them'. For Amphipolis see 18. 5, and for the other cities see 18. 5–8. For the specific narrative reference to the treaty see 18. 5 n. on ὅσας δέ etc.

2. οἱ δ᾽ οὐκ ἤθελον, νομίζοντες οὐκ ἐπιτηδείας εἶναι: 'But they did not approve of the terms, and refused'. For the refusal, which shows what the northern cities thought of the peace and of Sparta's treatment of them, see 18. 5 n. on τὰς δὲ πόλεις etc., citing Bauslaugh and Kallet-Marx. It is equally true that their behaviour shows what they thought about Athens, see D. Bradeen, 'The Popularity of the Athenian Empire', *Historia*, 9 (1960), 257–69, at 268, who says that these actions of the Chalkidians and the Amphipolitans are 'the best evidence for the feeling towards Athens of the peoples in subject and allied states, and for their desire for freedom above all else.'

οὐδὲ ὁ Κλεαρίδας παρέδωκε τὴν πόλιν, χαριζόμενος τοῖς Χαλκιδεῦσι, λέγων ὡς οὐ δυνατὸς εἴη βίᾳ ἐκείνων παραδιδόναι: 'while Klearidas, acting in the interest of the Chalkidians, would not surrender the place, and said it was not in his power to do so against their will'. For Klearidas see iv. 132. 3 n. on καὶ Κλεαρίδαν etc., and for his behaviour on the present occasion see Westlake, *Studies*, 81.

3. μάλιστα μὲν καὶ τὸ χωρίον παραδοῦναι, εἰ δὲ μή, ὁπόσοι Πελοποννησίων ἔνεισιν ἐξαγαγεῖν: 'to give up Amphipolis, or if that was impossible, to pull out all the Peloponnesian forces there'. What was Klearidas' game? Westlake (see previous n.), thinks he was modelling himself on Brasidas, or at least that Th. has represented him in that light. He notes that Klearidas cannot have been prosecuted for his disobedience because he is sent back to Amphipolis after he learns that no modification of the treaty is possible; and he is used later, 34. 1. Westlake, as we saw at iv. 132. 3 n., thinks Klearidas was a possible informant of Th.

The Spartans' behaviour is also odd. Whatever their motives, the instructions to Klearidas are as Gomme says 'in direct violation of the treaty', which explicitly stipulated that the Spartans hand over Amphipolis to Athens. See Andrewes, *CAH* v². 433, singling this incident out in his account of the trouble the Peace of Nikias soon ran into: 'the home government allowed him instead merely to withdraw his troops.'

22-23. ATHENS AND SPARTA DECIDE ON AN ALLIANCE. THE ALLIANCE

For modern discussions see the works cited at introductory n. to 18-19, and add Steup, *Thukydideische Studien*, I, 72-89; Kirchhoff's section 'Bemerkungen zu Thucydides 5, 21-24' at 155-79; Schwartz (iv. 67. 3 n. on ὅπως τοῖς etc.), 48-56; Andrewes, *HCT* iv. 21 and v. 375-9; Dover, *HCT* v. 428-31. It has been thought (Kirchhoff, followed by Andrewes) that the alliance, and the subsequent allusions to it, were later additions to a narrative which contains only crudely inserted references to it. Schwartz went further: he believed that no such alliance was or could have been made; this extreme form of the interpolation theory is refuted by Dover, who adduces the bait—precisely a Spartan-Athenian alliance—offered by the Spartan speakers at iv. 19. 1, see n. there. The fact of the alliance should thus be accepted (Dover, 430), but it is a separate question whether the oddities of the narrative after ch. 24 (particularly the discrepancy between 22. 1, see n. there, and 27. 1) are such as to require us to suppose that the alliance was a later addition. Against such a supposition, Dover (see also Andrewes, 376, conceding the force of this point) cited 27. 2. There the Corinthians complain that the Spartans have made a treaty and alliance with the Athenians, *their old enemies*, τοὺς πρὶν ἐχθίστους. Here, as Dover insists, it is 'alliance', not 'peace treaty', which gives point to the words 'old enemies'. Dover prefers a less drastic view than Kirchhoff-Andrewes (and certainly less drastic than Schwartz): Th. composed or revised v. 1-24 later than 27 ff., and failed to note the contradiction between 22 and 27. The problems posed in detail by the narrative from 27 onwards will be dealt with in the next vol. of this commentary. For the moment, the position here taken is that the alliance was certainly historical; that the idea of wholesale interpolation is not acceptable; but that some definite narrative awkwardnesses should be explained by the assumption that Th. did not acquire his detailed knowledge of the diplomatic events of 421 all at once. (This is very similar to the Dover position.)

22. 1. οἱ δὲ ξύμμαχοι ἐν τῇ Λακεδαίμονι αὐτοὶ ἔτυχον ὄντες, καὶ αὐτῶν τοὺς μὴ δεξαμένους τὰς σπονδὰς ἐκέλευον οἱ Λακεδαιμόνιοι ποιεῖσθαι: 'The representatives of the allies were present at Sparta, and the Spartans urged the reluctant states to accept the treaty'. A much emended sentence. The best guide is Andrewes, *HCT* iv. 21-2, an improvement on Gomme; see also Andrewes, *HCT* v. 375-6. Gomme evidently took the 'allies' to be the delegates at 17. 2, and emended αὐτοί to ἔτι, 'still', i.e. they were still there. But, as Andrewes says, it is unlikely that they were still there. Far better to suppose that the delegates have now returned after going back to their home cities to report, in which case we should adopt H. Lloyd-Jones's elegant and convincing emendation αὖθις, 'again', suggested to Andrewes and Dover (see *HCT* iv, acknowledgements). This makes it easier to understand the reference in the next sentence to 'the same reasons as before', τῇ αὐτῇ προφάσει ᾗπερ καὶ τὸ πρῶτον, see next n.

  There is a problem about the relation of the present passage to 27. 1. There Th. refers to the 'fifty years peace and the alliance', and goes on to describe the departure from Sparta of the 'ambassadors who had been invited to the negotiations', αὐτά, lit. 'them', neuter plural. If we do not emend αὐτά, it ought to refer to both peace and alliance (see Andrewes, *HCT* iv. 18, and Dover, *HCT* v. 429 n. 1), and this would suggest there was what Andrewes (*HCT* iv. 18) calls 'one continuous conference of Sparta's allies lasting down to this point' (as Gomme thought, see his nn. on 22. 1 and 2). We have seen above that this is not probable, and that the adoption of αὖθις avoids the need to suppose that the conference first referred to at 17. 2 was not brought to an end until 27. 1. But the words ἔτυχον ὄντες ('were present') in the present passage, which precedes the Spartan alliance with Athens (para. 2), imply that 'their presence at Sparta between the journey of Klearidas and the negotiation of the alliance was not demanded by the Spartans in connection with that impending negotiation' (Dover, *HCT* v. 429); and indeed they are about to be dismissed, see below, 2 n. on ἐκείνους μὲν ἀπέπεμψαν. It therefore follows that 27. 1, which implies that the allies, who are about to depart, had originally been summoned in connection with 'the peace and the alliance', is not consistent with 22. 1. Cp. Andrewes, *HCT* iv. 21: the reference to the alliance at 27. 1 suggests 'that Sparta's allies were somehow concerned in the Athenian alliance, although we have just been told [this is an evident reference to 22. 2] that they were dismissed before the Spartans turned to Athens'. One solution to this difficulty is (with Kirchhoff, 156) to remove the reference to 'alliance' at 27. 1, by bracketing καὶ ὕστερον ἡ ξυμμαχία. Less drastically (cp. above), Dover concluded that when Th. wrote 27 ff. 'he regarded the alliance as tied very closely to the peace-treaty, in effect as following from it, and believed (mistakenly) that it was negotiated and made public while Peloponnesian representatives were still at Sparta'.

οἱ δὲ τῇ αὐτῇ προφάσει ᾗπερ καὶ τὸ πρῶτον ἀπεώσαντο οὐκ ἔφασαν δέξεσθαι: 'But they refused for the same reasons as before'. This makes much better sense on the view that the preceding sentence (see preceding n.) is talking about a fresh visit by allied delegates, i.e. on the view that we should read αὖθις.

2. ἐκείνους μὲν ἀπέπεμψαν: 'the Spartans dismissed them'. This is the natural way of taking the Greek. Gomme, for whom there was one long continuous conference of allies (see above, 1 n. on οἱ δὲ ξύμμαχοι etc.) had to take this to mean, not that the delegates left Sparta, but that 'the conference of Sparta with her allies was closed by Sparta, who at once turned to Athens'. But see Andrewes, *HCT* iv. 22, rightly calling this a 'minor but troublesome consequence of Gomme's view'; the Greek should be given its natural meaning, i.e. the delegates went away. But that brings us back to the relation between chs. 22 and 27. 1, see 1 n. on οἱ δὲ ξύμμαχοι etc. Dover, *HCT* v. 429, calls it a 'blatant contradiction' that at 22. 2 (the present passage) the Spartans are made to 'send away (ἀπέ-πεμψαν) *before* the making of the alliance those Peloponnesian representatives who objected to the peace-treaty', whereas 27. 1 keeps those representatives at Sparta 'until *after* the alliance'. We have seen that Dover's solution is that Th. originally believed, wrongly, that the alliance was negotiated while the representatives were still at Sparta. That is, the present passage, translated in the natural non-Gomme way, is factually correct and 27. 1 is wrong. I shall return to this in my n. on 27. 1.

αὐτοὶ δὲ πρὸς τοὺς Ἀθηναίους ξυμμαχίαν ἐποιοῦντο, νομίζον-τες ἥκιστα ἂν σφίσι τούς τε Ἀργείους ⟨ἐπιέναι⟩, ἐπειδὴ οὐκ ἤθελον Ἀμπελίδου καὶ Λίχου ἐλθόντων ἐπισπένδεσθαι, ⟨καὶ⟩ νομίσαντες αὐτοὺς ἄνευ Ἀθηναίων οὐ δεινοὺς εἶναι, καὶ τὴν ἄλλην Πελοπόννησον μάλιστ' ἂν ἡσυχάζειν· πρὸς γὰρ ἂν τοὺς Ἀθηναίους, εἰ ἐξῆν, χωρεῖν: '... and made a bilateral alliance with the Athenians. They thought that in that way the Argives, who were clearly hostile, because they had refused to renew the peace at the request of the Spartan envoys Ampelidas and Lichas, would be deterred from attacking them, and would pose no threat without the support of the Athenians, to whose alliances they would naturally turn if they could; and they thought that this would ensure that there was no trouble from the rest of the Peloponnese either'. ['were clearly hostile, because they' is added for clarity.]

Most editors and commentators believe that the sentence is corrupt, partly because of the repetition νομίζοντες followed by νομίσαντες, but partly because of the sheer difficulty of making sense of the Greek. The repetition is not fatal. But the more general difficulty of understanding the Greek as transmitted seems insuperable, and the text above adopts (see angled brackets) the two insertions suggested by Gomme, them-selves a refinement of a conjecture by Madvig. It is also possible that the final sentence (πρὸς γάρ ...) should be repositioned after δεινοὺς εἶναι.

For the problem (a textual and a focalization problem) see now the excellent discussion by Maurer, *Interpolation*, 80–5; does the second participle from νομίζω, 'I think', i.e. 'they thought', refer to the Spartans or the Argives? Maurer follows those who think the Argives are meant.

Maurer supports Madvig's conjecture (the insertion of some such infinitive as ἐπιέναι, 'from attacking them') by adducing an overlooked scholion.

The mission of Ampelidas and Lichas has not been referred to in the preceding narrative; this is a small internal analepsis or backward-looking reference to an event in the past. Lichas, if he is the son of Arkesilas at 50. 4 (see n. there), is prominent later in book v and in book viii. Ampelidas is not mentioned again, and as Dover observes, *HCT* v. 429, this circumstantial detail tells against attempts to argue that ch. 22 is an editor's interpolation, along with other passages which refer to the alliance.

23. 1. ἢν [δέ] τινες ἴωσιν ἐς τὴν γῆν πολέμιοι τὴν Λακεδαιμονίων: 'if any enemy invades Spartan territory'. The alliance is an *epimachia* or defensive alliance, see i. 44. 1 n. on μετέγνωσαν etc.

3. ἢν δὲ ἡ δουλεία ἐπανιστῆται, ἐπικουρεῖν Ἀθηναίους Λακεδαιμονίοις παντὶ σθένει κατὰ τὸ δυνατόν: 'If the slaves rebel, the Athenians shall help the Spartans with all their might and to the utmost extent of their power'. From Kirchhoff (82) to Lewis (*Sparta and Persia*, 28; *CAH* v². 430 n. 155, cited above 14. 3 n. on περιπεσόντες etc.) and beyond, it has been remarked that this undertaking is not symmetrical—nothing is said about Athenian slave-risings—and the asymmetry has been explained by the different social systems: 'a slave revolt at no time belonged to the eventualities with which Athenian policy had to deal' (Kirchhoff); similarly P. Cartledge, *Historia*, 40 (1991), 380. Spartan 'slaves' here referred to are helots, see iv. 80 and nn. Athens had nothing comparable to this numerous and discontented Greek-speaking population.

De Ste. Croix, *OPW* 97, conjectures that treaties between the Spartans and their allies usually contained such a clause as is here reported.

For the expression παντὶ σθένει κατὰ τὸ δυνατόν, 'with all their might and to the utmost extent of their power', cp. *SEG* xxvi. 461 = ML 67 *bis*, the Spartan/Aitolian alliance, lines 19 and 23.

4. ἐς Ἀθήνας πρὸς τὰ Διονύσια: 'to Athens at the Dionysia'. W. Burkert, 'Ein Datum für Euripides' Elektra: Dionysia 420 v. Chr.', *Mus. Helv.* 47 (1990), 65–9, at 67–8, suggests that Euripides' *Elektra*, with its 'marked sympathy for Sparta' and prominence accorded to Tyndareos, Helen, and the Dioskouroi, was first performed at the Dionysia of 420, the occasion of the first renewal of the oaths, when Spartans would be present. Against such political interpretations of Euripides' plays, and attempts to link them to precise moments, see G. Zuntz, *The Political Plays of Euripides* (iv. 97. 2 n.).

πρὸς τὰ Ὑακίνθια: 'at the Hyakinthia'. For the cult of Hyakinthos at Spartan Amyklai, linked to that of Apollo (see next n.) see S. Wide (iv. 119. 1 n. on μηνός etc.), 285–93; M. Petterson, *Cults of Apollo at Sparta: The Hyakinthia, the Gymnopaidiai and the Karneia* (Stockholm, 1992), 1–41, discussing the present passage of Th. at 11.

5. ἐν Λακεδαίμονι παρ' Ἀπόλλωνι ἐν Ἀμυκλαίῳ, τὴν δὲ ἐν Ἀθήναις ἐν πόλει παρ' Ἀθηνᾷ: 'one in Sparta at the temple of Apollo in Amyklai, the other at Athens in the Acropolis at the temple of Athena'. Cf. 18. 10. On this provision for the housing of the treaty in the temples, see Steiner, *The Tyrant's Writ* (introductory n. to iv. 117–19), 66. For Amyklai (one of the Spartan obes or villages, 5 km. south of Sparta) and its important cult and temple of Apollo, linked to that of Hyakinthos, see Paus. iii. 18. 6 ff. and Cartledge, *Sparta and Lakonia*, 79–80, 106–8, and in *Princeton Encyclopaedia*, 52–3. For the lodging of Athenian treaties in the Acropolis see introductory n. to iv. 117–19.

6. προσθεῖναι καὶ ἀφελεῖν: 'added to or deleted'. See 18. 11 n. and *HCT* on 29. 2: the complaint at 29. 2 is actually directed at the clause at the end of the Peace of Nikias, but the words there quoted appear only here, in the alliance.

ὅτι ἂν δοκῇ ἀμφοτέροις, εὔορκον εἶναι: 'if the Spartans and Athenians both agree ... this may be done without violation of their oaths'. The OCT prints the transmitted text ὅτι ἂν δοκῇ, εὔορκον ἀμφοτέροις εἶναι, which would mean that the word 'both' referred to the non-violation of oaths, i.e. 'without violation of oaths on either side'. This was emended by Herwerden, whose emendation was rejected by Classen/Steup on the grounds that the word 'both', ἀμφοτέροις, is superfluous in the provision about the Athenians and Spartans agreeing. But I follow M. L. West, 'Thuc. v. 23, 6', *Eikasmos: Quaderni Bolognesi di Filologia Classica*, 5 (1994), 137–8, who reasserts Herwerden's emendation, adducing the following parallels: *IG* i³. 89 line 24, προσθένaι] καὶ ἀφελὲν hότι ἂν ἀμφοτ[έροις δοκεῖ; Th. v. 18. 11 (see n. there), 29. 2, 47. 12, viii. 18. 2, and Pol. vii. 19. 7. I have therefore changed OCT.

24. THE SWEARERS TO THE ALLIANCE. END OF THE TEN YEARS WAR

1. Πλειστοάναξ ...: 'Pleistoanax'. The names which follow are the same as those at 19. 2, except that in the Spartan list, Alkinadas precedes Tellis and in the Athenian list Laches precedes Nikias. For commentary on the names see 19. 1 n. on ὤμνυον δὲ οἵδε etc. and 2 nn.

For the question whether Th. would have left such a list in a hypothetical final version, see Introduction, p. 107, 118 f. The problem is more acute even than that raised by ch. 19, given that the names in the present para. virtually repeat those given only five chapters earlier.

2. καὶ τοὺς ἄνδρας τοὺς ἐκ τῆς νήσου ἀπέδοσαν οἱ Ἀθηναῖοι τοῖς Λακεδαιμονίοις: 'the Athenians gave the Spartans back the prisoners taken at Sphakteria' [lit.'those from the island']. The Athenians soon regretted having done so, see 35. 4. For the prisoners see 15. 1 and n., also 18. 7 n. on ἀποδόντων etc.

καὶ τὸ θέρος ἦρχε τοῦ ἑνδεκάτου ἔτους: 'The summer of the eleventh year then began'. See 19. 1 n. on Ἐλαφηβολιῶνος etc.

INDEX

Note: I have, where the name or person is too familiar to be hellenized without a wrench, preferred Latin spellings to Greek, thus Pericles not Perikles; similarly with literary figures, thus Aeschylus, Callimachus, Ephorus, Hecataeus, Hieronymus, and indeed Thucydides. Otherwise I have generally preferred 'k' to 'c', 'ai' to 'ae', and '-os' to '-us'.

Index

Index

Isthmus of Corinth 201, 229, 364
Istone 204
Italy 5, 45, 75, 77 n. 179, 181, 429–35 cf. 120 n. 304
iterative presentation 230, 463, 465
Ithome 134, 165

jackets 190
Jason of Pherai 261
javelins 190
jealousy 386
see also *phthonos*
John, St 385
jokes, in Th. 155, 196
judges 274
jury pay 96
justice 54 ff., 270
Justin 5, 246

Kalamata 154
Kalchedon 246 ff.
Kales or Kalex (river) 247
Kalliades 493
Kallias (4th-cent. Athenian) 65 & n. 151, 66, 175
Kallias, Peace of 133, 209, 247
Kallikratidas (Spartan, in Hdt.) 136
Kallistratos 65 & n. 151, 175
kaloi kagathoi 195 f.
Kalymnos 372
Kamarina 96, 132, 144, 183, 221, 227, 274, 302, 429, 433
Kamikos 144
Kanastraion 351
Karkinos 97
Karia:
in Asia Minor, *see* Caria
river in Pylos region 365
Katana 183, 431
Kekalos 373
Kekropis (Athenian tribe) 489
Kelainai 181
Kenchreai 199
Kephissos 251
Kerdylion 437
Kerkyra 74
see also Corcyra
kerugma 336 f., 354, 356
Kimon 136, 319, 325, 372, 453
Kimoneia 453
Kinadon 214, 265
kings:
Epirote, *see* Pyrrhus
Macedonian 142; *see also* Alexander I and III; Amyntas III; Archelaos; Philip II and V; Perdikkas; Antigonos Doson

Persian 206–9; *see also* Artaxerxes; Darius; Xerxes
Spartan 126, 139, 143, 158, 169 f.; *see also* Agesilaos; Agesipolis; Agis; Archidamos; Pleistoanax; Kleombrotos; Kleomenes; Pausanias (king not regent)
Syracusan, *see* Agathokles
Thracian, *see* Demetrios; Oloros; Pittakos; Polles; Sitalkes
see also Antiochus; Ptolemy
kinship 1, 13, 61–80, 93, 175, 196, 240 cf. 220
see also *xyngeneia*
Klaros 247
Kleandridas 451
Klearchos 457
Klearidas 58 f., 409 f., 442, 444, 457, 481, 493 f., 496
Kleemporos 102
Kleinias 144
Kleombrotos 467
Kleomenes I of Sparta 30, 58, 63, 131, 406
Kleon 39 n. 99, 45, 48, 50, 77, 80, 94, 96, 109, 161 f., 170, 177–80, 185–9, 198, 204, 222, 224, 269, 319, 345, 379, 388, 424–7, 435–49 *passim*, 459, 461 f., 476
Kleonai (in Chalkidike) 35, 346 f., 475
Knemos 41, 164, 399
koinon 222, 260
Kolophon 380, cf. 425
komai 393
Komon 191
Konon:
Athenian commander 214
mythographer 77, 377
Kopai 251
Kopais, Lake 298
Kophos Limen (near Torone) 425 f.
Kore 65, 175
Koroneia, and battle of 84, 86, 132 f., 252, 291, 295 f., 298 f., 303, 317
Koryphasion 114, 119, 154 f., 365, 480
kotylai 114, 169
Kotyrta 219
Kratesikles 164
Krestonians 36, 348
Krommyon 201
Kroton 435
Kylon 31, 128 f., 140, 313, 422
Kynouria 219, 460
Kyparissia 158
Kytenion, *see* Kytinion
Kythera 44, 72 f., 108 f., 114, 145, 214–9, 264, 341, 358, 365 f., 460, 470, 477, 480
Kytherodikes 215 f.
Kytinion 61, 71 f., 79 and n. 184, 80, 93

510

Index

'Priestesses of Argos' (work by Hellanicus) 111 f.
prison 480 f.
prisoners 193, 361 f., 427 f., 461, 470, 480, 500
privateers 161, 236
    see also piracy
probouloi 232
processions 267
Prokles 488
prolepsis (anticipation) 101, 428
promethia 143
propaganda 47, 69, 27, 277, 285
    see also liberation
property 487
    see also wealth
prophasis 205, 400
prosarchomai 9, 376, 380–5
prose-writers 20
proserchomai 9, 376, 380–5
prosopography 94 & n. 219, 102–7, 118, 136, 487
    see also names, personal
Prote 167
Protesilaos 77, 145, 377
proto-harmosts 52
proverbs 143, 425 f.
proxenoi, proxeny 102, 103 n. 259, 133, 136, 137 & n. 33, 184, 249 f., 252 f., 257
prytany 368, 485
Psaumis 183
Pteleon 480
Ptoiodora 250
Ptoiodoros (of Thespiai) 103, 119, 249 f., 253
Ptolemy V 79 n. 185
'publication', publication dates 26 ff., 29, 37
puns 134 & n. 24
puppies, sacrifice of 451
purification (of Delos) 62, 122, 124, 143, 422 f.
Pydna 404
Pylos 16, 39 n. 99, 41, 43 f., 80 n. 188, 99 and n. 244, 108 ff., 113 f., 120 n. 304, 149–80 (esp. 150, 154), 184–98, 218, 238, 262, 341, 351, 358, 365, 459 f., 470
    narrative parallels with Pylos episode, *see* Chalkidike; Sicily; Syracuse
Pyrrhus 433
Pythangelos 136
Pythia 466
    see also Delphi
Pythian games, victors 306, 421
Pythodoros 106, 151, 487 f.

Quadruple alliance between Athens, Argos, Mantinea and Elis 99, 117
quietism 295

race, racial factors 71, 220 f., 224f 227, 283
rams, battering- 167, 439
ransom, of prisoners 427 f.
rations 169 f., 194
'reader-response' views of Th. 224 f., 332, cf. 120 n. 304, 263
reality 396, 400
    see also *erga*
reassessment(s) of tribute 7, 93–8, 198, 206, 210, 245 ff.
reception of Th. 21, 83, 181, 379, 444, 442
reciprocity 63
recitation 20, 26 ff., 119, 122
reconnaissance 439
redistribution of land 430 f.
refugees 211, 246
    see also exiles
regional experts 324, 332, 339, 452
religion 4, 9 ff., 37, 49 ff., 62, 80, 90, 123, 134, 136, 175, 281, 356, 381, 449
    see also amphiktiony; colonial relationships; cult of human beings; Delphi; Delos; festivals; Gerastios; gods; hero-cult; oaths; oikists; oracles; precincts, sacred; purification; Sacred Wars; sacrilege; sanctuaries; temples; *xyngeneia*; and *individual gods*
reminiscences in Th. 315
    see also Chalkidike/Pylos parallels; repetition; responsions; Sicily/Pylos parallels
rents, sacred 97 & n. 237
repetition in Th. 74, 80, 107, 118 f., 155, 499 f.
    in speeches 43, 47, 277, 281
responsions between Th.'s speeches 82, 85, 290, 303, 441, 445
revenge 221
revenue 52, 96 f., 320, 341 f., 472
    see also finance; tribute; wealth
reversal 166 f., 173
    see also inversion
revolts, from Athens 209 f., 341, 406, 459
revolution 244, 287
    see also *stasis*
rewards for valour, financial 49, 355
Rhamphias 53 f., 269, 457 f.
Rhegines, Rhegion 72, 118, 150, 180, 182, 184, 369, 433
Rheitos 199
Rheneia 97 n. 237, 124, 139
Rhesus 323 f.
rhetoric 18, 60, 83 f., 89, 97, 131, 172, 194, 225, 261, 392, 400, 443 f.
    see also narrative (for narratology i.e. study of rhetorical features of narrative); rhetorical handbooks; speeches
Rhetoric to Alexander 83 f., 171, 174
rhetorical handbooks 81, 83 f., 171

516